PSYCHIATRY
IN A TROUBLED WORLD

THE MACMILLAN COMPANY
NEW YORK · BOSTON · CHICAGO
DALLAS · ATLANTA · SAN FRANCISCO

MACMILLAN AND CO., LIMITED
LONDON · BOMBAY · CALCUTTA
MADRAS · MELBOURNE

THE MACMILLAN COMPANY
OF CANADA, LIMITED
TORONTO

PSYCHIATRY
IN A TROUBLED WORLD

YESTERDAY'S WAR AND TODAY'S CHALLENGE

BY WILLIAM C. MENNINGER, M.D.

General Secretary, The Menninger Foundation, Topeka, Kansas;

Chief Consultant in Neuropsychiatry to the Surgeon General

of the Army, 1943–1946.

NEW YORK   *THE MACMILLAN COMPANY*   *1948*

DEDICATION

This book is dedicated to three groups of people: to the many million GI's from whom we learned the lessons I have attempted to present; to my many colleagues in the field of psychiatry, both in and out of the Army, who carried on the work; and to those understanding military officers in every Division and Section of the War Department who helped those of us in psychiatry towards the accomplishment of our mission.

FOREWORD

THE SHOOTING WAR is over. Why should I write a book about it at this late date? First, I could not have written it before the facts were available and could be released; second, although the shooting is over, the chief implications of war-time psychiatric experience have to do with the postwar life; and third, the public interest in the problems of mental health and ill health and the challenge of that interest to professional psychiatry is at an all-time high, as a result of the war.

Or perhaps you might ask why I wrote a book at all. Anyone who attempts so colossal a job as writing a book must have a very strong urge. He is probably impelled to write for the purpose of satisfying an unrecognized inner need. The conscious motive undoubtedly varies widely with each author. He may want to create. He may want to save souls. He may want to vent his spleen. He may be a professional writer who has chosen that extremely difficult method of making a living. He may be one of the few who write for the love of it, if there are such people.

For the reader who is curious, my conscious purpose in writing this book was to record the evolution of psychiatric practice in the Army. Psychiatry struggled from the rear seat in the third balcony to finally arrive in the front row at the show. My responsibility to the Army, to psychiatry, and to the public who paid and suffered would be unfulfilled if I did not report that struggle. I also regard as an obligation the setting down of our experiences for whatever help this information might be in the event of another emergency. The first part of the book was, therefore, written chiefly for the record. It undoubtedly contains too many technical words, but probably the only person who will make psychiatry light reading will be a layman. In any case, an attempt has been made to make this book intelligible to any interested reader, lay or professional.

The second part of the book was written with the hope that it might be helpful to any person who has to get along with other people. For those who wish to use them, there were many lessons, learned painfully and at great cost, which can be applied in a postwar peaceful world. This part of the book is my view of the possible contributions of psychiatry to social experience. Or should I say my vision of the field that is open to research in applied and preventive psychiatry?

At the time of completion of the early drafts of each chapter, I was still in the Army. Each was submitted to the Bureau of Technical Information of the War Department, and, despite severe criticism of some Army methods, they were cleared for publication. The revisions since that time have not materially altered the original content. But this is not an official release; it presents my point of view and not that of the War Department.

Without the help of many friends and professional associates, this would never have seen the light of day, certainly not in its present form. I profited from the suggestions of at least twenty-five of my confreres, each of whom read two or three chapters in an early draft. Several were burdened with several chapters and responded with very helpful criticisms—my brother Karl, Dr. Eli Ginzberg, Mr. Tracy Voorhees, Dr. John Appel, Dr. Manfred Guttmacher. I "tried out" several of the chapters on my sons Roy, Phil, and Walt. Two of my friends have read the entire manuscript—Drs. Norman Brill and Margaret Craighill. To them I am especially grateful for many corrections and additional ideas.

Nor can I fail to acknowledge the immense investment of several stenographic assistants and librarians. I found this type of opus requires a near-endless amount of mechanical effort. Specially do I want to thank Aurelie Adams, Hazel Bruce, Leroy Bowen, Vesta Walker, and my personal secretary in the Surgeon General's Office, Mary Frances Mills, and my two in the Menninger Foundation, Loraine Nuzman and Lena Forbes.

Finally, and most important, I want to express and acknowledge my gratitude to my wife, Cay. So far as time invested and effort expended are concerned, she is a coauthor. She has edited every paragraph in the book. She has checked references, looked up and reviewed articles, compiled the index. In addition she "protected" my evenings from social engagements, excused me to my friends, and forwent pleasures and entertainment throughout the eighteen months we worked together on the writing. It was she who really made the book a reality. Had it not been for her constant stimulus and encouragement, I would often have stopped. Had it not been for her help, it would be a far more imperfect result.

WCM

CONTENTS

Introduction

Part I. IN WAR

Section I. BACKGROUND

Section II. THE SOLDIER

Section III. CLINICAL OBSERVATIONS

ix

INTRODUCTION

"OH, MY ACHING BACK"—GI JOE

NO OTHER PHRASE in all Army lingo was better understood, more frequently spoken with feeling and reason, and so tersely symbolic of the soldier's job. It typified his burden, his stresses, and his inevitable reaction to them. Not only was it symbolic of his role in the service, but it is symbolic of the world at the present time—perhaps for some time to come in the future. The world—people —is evidencing in a thousand ways, in feeling, thought, and action, the "aching back" the war has given it.

What did the war do to people? To you and to me? To our communities and our families? To our nation? To the international situation? One book can't answer all of these questions. One person couldn't answer all of these questions. But all the books and all the people who talk around the subject at all would include in their discussions the load we must carry, the ache in the heart, the fear of uncertainty, the terrific waste, the unlimited destruction. The lives and fortunes of most of the individuals on this globe have been more or less drastically affected. Of much greater significance is the fact that they will be further influenced—their backs will continue to ache.

The cost of World War II in money is a figure which is incomprehensible to most of us who think in terms of our annual incomes or the cost of our homes. The fact that the United States spent six and a half million dollars every hour, or more than one hundred and fifty-seven million dollars per day between July 1, 1940, and September 30, 1945, leaves us indifferent and uncomprehending. Yet the total sum, amounting to three hundred and thirty-five billion dollars [1] is more than twice the assessed value of all property in the United States.[2] It is more than twice the amount of all the life insurance in force in 1944 in this country.[3] Some other comparisons are equally startling. These amounts which

---

[1] Figures and dates provided by Martin L. Moore, U.S. Treasury Department. By permission of *The Evening Standard* (London), we reproduce from that paper of June 5, 1947, the following facts: "Lest we forget: Britain paid £34,423,000,000 [$138,724,690,000] to win the war. That is £765 [$3,083] a head for every person in Britain. The United States paid £82,500,000,-000 [$332,475,000,000] or £580 [$2,337] a head. Canada paid £5,063,966,499 [$20,407,-784,991] or £422 [$1,700] a head. Cash outlay is only a part of the British burden, for this country alone among the Western Allies suffered devastation. Three out of every ten houses were destroyed." (Computation of conversion to dollars made by the author on the basis of $4.05 per pound, quotation as of August 12, 1947.)

[2] *World Almanac, 1946, New York World Telegram*, New York, p. 35.

[3] *Ibid.*, p. 666.

were spent in constructive and cultural pursuits seem like pin money when contrasted with the huge expenditures for the destruction of war.

	Amount	Would Pay Cost of War for
Local and national budgets of the Boy Scouts of America in 1944	$ 11,119,920 [4]	1½ hours
Estimated minimum expenditure for medical research in 1944	54,650,000 [5]	8½ hours
Total disbursements for soldier and dependent pensions in 1945	739,581,651 [6]	4½ days
Endowments of public trusts and foundation	750,685,559 [7]	5 days
Expenditures for public schools in 1943	2,308,098,338 [8]	15 days
Total amount of permanent endowment funds held by 1,440 institutions of higher learning in 1940, plus the property of all sorts held by these same institutions in 1940	1,686,282,767 [9] } 4,518,383,918 }	5 weeks

Figures of money spent on the war effort do not include the concomitant emotional and economic costs which cannot be computed. The individual families paid dearly for dislocation, higher prices, and fewer satisfactions; business and industry faced a legion of economic and human problems in readjustment; international affairs were and are full of touchy relationships.

Millions of people endured separation, deprivation, loss, pain, sorrow. Millions were left maimed. Millions more were killed. The physical separation of us in America from personal contact with those who were greatest hurt allowed us to be preoccupied with our individual interests. It is impossible for us to realize the awful tragedy of the lives of more than sixty million persons [10] who were cruelly displaced as a result of this conflict. No one can fully grasp the extent of the emotional cost of the war, nor can anyone conceive of the

---

[4] Information received from F. S. Pease, Boy Scouts of America.

[5] Information received from Dr. Lewis H. Weed, National Research Council.

[5] *World Almanac, 1946, New York World Telegram*, New York, p. 291.

[7] *Ibid.*, p. 526.

[8] *Ibid.*, p. 580.

[9] *Biennial Surveys of Education in the United States: Statistics of Higher Education 1939–40 and 1941–42, Vol. II*, Federal Security Agency, U.S. Office of Education, Washington, D. C., 1944, Chap. IV, p. 31.

[10] Hoehler, F. K., *Europe's Homeless Millions*, Headline Series No. 54, Nov.–Dec., 1945, Foreign Policy Association, New York, p. 9.

possibilities if the same man power which was invested in destruction had been utilized for construction.

Can anything good come out of such war, other than the temporary destruction of some of the Nazi-Fascist governments and Japanese domination? Terrible as the war was, it directly initiated some constructive activities and hastened the development of others. Great advances were made in many fields of human activity. Conspicuous were the gains in physics and chemistry, in communication and transportation, in business and industry. Dramatic were the achievements in medical treatment with such therapeutic agents as plasma, penicillin, and the sulfonamides. Notable were malaria control and the use of DDT in the prevention of disease. Surgical procedures were perfected beyond prewar practice.

Great, though not as spectacular, strides were made in the prevention and cure of mental illness. Basic to these were the wider acceptance and better understanding of psychiatry. Millions of people became really aware, for the first time, of the effect of environmental stresses on the personality. They learned that such stresses could interfere with or partially wreck an individual's efficiency and his satisfaction with life. The universality of neurotic reactions became evident to the layman. Many discovered that failure in adjustment was not a disgrace and often could be avoided when an individual, finding himself in a blind alley, sought well-qualified help.

But psychiatry is a young and undeveloped science, with much yet to be learned. The war increased our understanding of ways in which its present body of knowledge can be helpfully applied to most, if not all, human activities. The war also emphasized the fact that its potentialities for usefulness cannot be fully realized until three further steps are taken: Research activities in the field of psychiatry must be increased and intensified many times over those now being carried on; the present desperate need for psychiatrists must be filled; psychiatry must gain for itself an even wider acceptance and a more intelligent understanding by the public.

While World War II served to decrease public prejudice against psychiatry, it has also placed psychiatry at a crossroad. One road leads to a continuation of its preoccupation with the end results of mental disease, i.e., concern about patients committed to state hospitals. The other road, however, invites psychiatry to discover how it can contribute to the problems of the average man and to the large social issues in which he is involved. Which road will psychiatry follow?

During the War, under the pressure of the job,[11] I often needed professional support, sometimes reassurance as to directions—"priorities," as we referred to them. At one of those moments I wrote to Dr. Alan Gregg, Director,

---

[11] Chief Consultant in Neuropsychiatry to the Surgeon General and Director of the Neuropsychiatry Consultants Division.

Division of Medical Services of the Rockefeller Foundation and an official consultant in neuropsychiatry to the Surgeon General. I asked: "What are the most important benefits psychiatry has to give?" His superb answer could well be a credo for every psychiatrist; certainly it describes the goals to which psychiatrists aspire.

First, psychiatry along with the other natural sciences leads to a life of reason. It explains what must otherwise excite fear, disgust, superstition, anxiety, or frustration. It breaks the clinches we otherwise get into with life and all the unnecessary, blind, infighting.

In the second place, by showing us the common rules, the uniform limitations, and liberties all human beings live under because they are human, psychiatry gives us a sort of oneness-with-others, a kind of exquisite communion with all humanity, past, present, and future. It is a kind of scientific humanism that frees us from dogma and the tyranny of the mind, a relief from the inhuman strait-jacket of rigid finality of thought.

Third, psychiatry makes possible a kind of sincere humility and naturalness I've never received from any other study or experience. Perhaps suffering accomplishes a similar miracle but too often suffering lessens one's delighted conviction in the liveableness of life—I don't know for I've not known much suffering yet. But I know that psychiatry provides the material for a quiet but extraordinarily tenacious kind of humility and a sympathy that is honest and eager.

And lastly, psychiatry makes it possible *to bring to others* these things I've mentioned: the light of reason, the oneness-with-others and an attitude of sympathetic humility, and understanding. Also it makes one able to receive these same gifts—and I would count him a poor physician who cannot receive as wisely and thankfully as he gives. So, in short, psychiatry makes possible by teaching and example the exchange of these things so desperately wanted by human beings and they are so healthy and happy when they get them and give them!

I am almost sure you will say 'But I don't mean that sort of thing! What specifically has psychiatry in the way of benefits?'

I didn't mention the rewards research offers to human curiosity. Nor the satisfaction of being of help to poor, battered, dependent, frightened people and the justice of giving them the breaks just for once. Nor the immense economy of patching lives to a point of meeting life's demands. Nor the hope that we may understand what disease connotes as well as what it denotes. Nor the possibility that through psychiatric understanding our successors may be able to govern human politics and relationships more sagely.

Part I

IN WAR

1

PSYCHIATRY PRIOR TO WORLD WAR II

AN ACQUAINTANCE with certain developments in the long history of psychiatry is particularly pertinent as background for a better understanding of the psychiatric experience in World War II. A little over 100 years ago 13 superintendents of mental hospitals organized what proved to be the forerunner of the American Psychiatric Association, now the official professional organization of psychiatrists. Some 16 years after this, the Civil War focused attention on certain psychiatric problems. To these the neurologists [1] seemed the most alert: nostalgia, malingering, return of the psychotic soldiers to their homes, and the problems arising from the teen-age draft.[2]

During the succeeding 50 years only a handful of physicians manifested interest in learning how and why the minds of people became sick. Nearly all of these men worked in those isolated institutions that were looked upon as necessary evils—the insane asylums. By the early twentieth century a few leaders—Adolph Meyer, August Hoch, Elmer Southard, Charles Burr, George Kirby, Albert Barrett—had emerged to achieve recognition on the faculties of some medical schools. The early studies of Sigmund Freud were being championed in this country by A. A. Brill, James J. Putnam, William A. White, and Smith Ely Jelliffe.

Then came World War I. Fortune smiled upon the Army and upon psychiatry when Pearce Bailey was chosen to serve as a consultant in the Office of the Surgeon General and Thomas W. Salmon as the chief consultant in

---

[1] Neurology is the special field of medicine which is concerned with organic diseases and disorders of the nervous system, such as tumors, infections, injuries, degenerative processes. Neurology as a profession developed rapidly after the Civil War, chiefly among physicians in universities and those in private practice. By contrast, the psychiatrists in 1860-70 were limited in their practice almost completely to the mental institutions and were often referred to as "alienists." As time has passed, the two groups have become more and more distinct in their interests—neurologists in the organic disorders, psychiatrists in the functional disorders. In practice the two fields can never be entirely separate; many physicians carry on a practice in both specialties, though having a major interest and usually being more proficient in one. In the Army in World War II they were assigned to the same service, which was labeled with the hybrid term, "neuropsychiatry."

[2] Deutsch, Albert, "Military Psychiatry: The Civil War 1861-1865," in *One Hundred Years of American Psychiatry*, ed. by Gregory Zilboorg, Columbia University Press, New York, 1944, pp. 374-377.

psychiatry with the American Expeditionary Forces. Before our entrance into
the war, Salmon was taken from the National Committee for Mental Hygiene
and sent to Europe by the Rockefeller Foundation to learn of the British experience with psychiatry in the war. His observations seem to have played a
major role in the shaping of American Army psychiatric policy. His keen, far-
sighted vision and his thoughtfulness, coupled with an unusual force and
ability, were the factors that guided military psychiatrists so wisely at that
time.

Very aptly, Salmon later portrayed psychiatry in World War I [3] as the
Cinderella of medicine, in that she had been ignored or unnoticed for so long
by her sister specialties. The acute mental health problems of the war demanded
that a search be made for the wearer of the slipper of healing for mental illness.
Psychiatry came forward to fit the slipper and so to take her rightful place
with the other specialties in the Army Medical Corps. Volume X of the history
of the Medical Department in World War I was devoted to neuropsychiatry.
To it Drs. Bailey, Salmon, and many others contributed freely from their experiences, reporting both mistakes and successes.

To read the papers of Col. Salmon, written shortly after the war, is to realize
the extent to which both civilian and Army psychiatry failed to profit from the
lessons learned in military experience. For example, the psychiatrists in World
War I, as we did also in World War II, found a minimal number of psychotic
patients in the Army, however psychiatric wards were arranged primarily for
their care. What Dr. Salmon wrote in 1919 he could as well have written in
1939. "For many years, indeed ever since the insane came into the hands of the
physicians from those of demon exorcisers, jailkeepers and poormasters, psychiatry has concerned itself almost exclusively with insanity. Today that term
is properly applied to only a relatively small proportion of all the persons in
whom psychiatrists are interested." Salmon lamented the inadequate number
of trained personnel and pointed out that "the demand for psychiatrists for
positions in juvenile and domestic relations courts and correctional institutions
would exhaust the annual out-put of men trained in the few existing psychiatric clinics." He deplored the separation of psychiatry from medicine thus:
"No one knows better than I do how much we have suffered and still suffer
from the unfortunate isolation from the rest of medicine which our early work
with the insane entailed. The fact that this isolation is breaking down, that the
familiar medical joke about all psychiatrists being a little crazy, is not nearly as
dependable a laugh raiser as it used to be, and the slow realization on the part
of our colleagues in other work that a psychiatrist may be a clinician working in

---

[3] A search of Salmon's writings has failed to locate this analogy. White mentioned it but gave
no reference for it. White, W. A., *Twentieth Century Psychiatry*, W. W. Norton & Company,
Inc., New York, 1936, p. 25.

a special field and not necessarily one part dreamer and one part humbug—all indicate that the future of psychiatry will be more closely linked with medicine than its past had been." He indicated that "every medical officer should know something of the nature of the disorders that, on the one hand make for the development and, on the other hand, for the control of personality disorders." He pointed out then that "distinguishing between mental deficiency and the mental reactions determined by deprivation of educational and social advantages, is one of the problems of the Army. It must be solved in the Army by the joint work of the psychiatrists and the psychologists, and will never be solved by either working alone." [4]

Psychiatry made progress, remarkable progress, between 1918 and 1941, but it did not reach the heights that Dr. Salmon envisioned and hoped for as a result of the impetus of the World War I experience. By 1941 the application of psychiatric principles had been proved valuable in the field of penology and in court work: a few courts had routine psychiatric counsel; the federal penitentiaries all maintained full-time psychiatrists. There were perhaps 10 psychiatrists who were devoting full time to personnel and counseling work in industry and business. The utilization of psychiatry in diagnosing and treating had extended beyond the confines of institutions in the form of outpatient clinics, child-guidance clinics, and counseling service for students in a few of our colleges and universities. In medical education psychiatry had been given a few more hours in the curriculum, and the number of residencies for specialist training had gradually increased. The fund of experience and new knowledge about the personality and how that personality functioned had grown tremendously, chiefly through the impetus of the discoveries of Freud.

The disproportionate concern with caring for the psychoses [5] decreased

---

[4] Salmon, Thomas W., "Future of Psychiatry in the Army," *Mil. Surgeon,* 47:200-207, Aug., 1920; "War Neuroses and Their Lesson," *New York State J. Med.,* 109:993-994, June, 1919.

[5] An interesting report is that of Maj. Leo Alexander on the development of psychiatry in Germany since the last war. This report is based upon his contact with Dr. Richard E. Siebeck, Professor of Internal Medicine, University of Heidelberg. All of the psychosomatic problems and many of the psychiatric disorders in the German army were treated by the internists. When Alexander asked the reason for this Siebeck replied: "Our psychiatrists were averse to psychotherapy and did not concern themselves with these problems. Psychotherapy is a curious development of medicine and although in other countries it sprang from psychiatry, in this country it somehow did not fit into the pattern of German classical psychiatry. Our psychiatry essentially originated from an interest in the knowledge of the organic diseases of the brain and that was not helpful in developing an active psychotherapeutic interest. The same happened to our psychopathology which remained essentially hidebound in the concept of constitution in a fixed and static way, as for instance in Jaspers. Therefore, even our psychopathology never progressed beyond schizophrenia, or rather did not concern itself with changes more subtle than schizophrenia. Thus our psychiatrists were all negativistic to therapy until the advent of the shock therapy with insulin, metrazol and electric shock, and that made them still less susceptible to an interest in psychotherapy. They did think in terms of occupational therapy, work therapy, farm therapy, but on the whole one must say that the attitude of psychiatry during the past few years became one of increasing therapeutic nihilism. Therefore, the psychotherapists belonged

somewhat as more psychiatrists shifted from institutional to private or out-patient-clinic practice. In 1920 over three-quarters of the members of the American Psychiatric Association were engaged in institutional work with 24 per cent in private practice. In 1930 this had shifted to 71 per cent in institutional work and 29 per cent in private practice. In 1946 (omitting the nearly 1,000 members in military service), only 62 per cent of the membership were practicing in institutions and 38 per cent were practicing privately.[6] Even with this high proportion of psychiatrists our state hospitals were grossly undermanned. Very few of them had sufficient staff to undertake research, few offered teaching programs,[7] and their medical men worked under the greatest handicaps, largely because of political control. In the eyes of the public and in the thinking of many medical educators and practitioners, psychiatry seemed only vaguely related to medicine because it was primarily preoccupied with the custodial care of the "insane."

The National Committee for Mental Hygiene, conceived by a layman, Clifford Beers, in 1909, was created in order to stimulate a closer application of psychiatric knowledge to the public need. Doctor Salmon (1915-21), Dr. Frankwood Williams (1921-31), and currently Dr. George Stevenson have served as one-man dynamos of the committee. Its functions have always been handicapped by lack of funds and man power. The committee has sponsored research and published material relating to ways of maintaining mental health; it has made surveys of mental hospitals in order to recommend standards; it has worked to improve commitment legislation; it has standardized psychiatric nomenclature and statistical methods in state hospitals. This is only a partial list of its achievements.

Psychoanalysis developed extensively between 1918 and 1941. Its discoveries are probably the most important contributions to our technical knowledge in the history of psychiatry. By virtue of its technique and the relative isolation caused by the limited sphere of activity of many of the analysts, it has not been widely understood and used. Medical schools have been slow to include it in their curricula as a means of indoctrinating medical students with some concept of the dynamics of personality development and function. Zilboorg pertinently pointed out: "Our experience to date in psychoanalytic work gave us no basis for meeting the challenge of the psychiatric needs of

---

more and more to internal medicine. We wanted them." Alexander, Leo, *German Military Neuropsychiatry and Neurosurgery*, CIOS Item 24 Medical File XXVIII-49, Combined Intelligence Objectives Subcommittee G-2, SHAEF (Rear) 1945, p. 80.

[6] Figures supplied through the courtesy of Austin M. Davies, Executive Assistant, American Psychiatric Association, February 27, 1946.

[7] Brilliant exceptions were the Psychopathic Hospitals in Boston, Mass., and Denver, Colo., the Psychiatric Institute in New York, and a few state hospitals, notably in Worcester, Mass., and the federal St. Elizabeth's in Washington, D.C.

masses of people and, therefore, had little application to the problems confronting military psychiatry." [8]

To some extent this isolated state is typical of *all* phases of psychiatry. Psychiatrists have not been sufficiently critical of their own field; their recruiting of students to enter the field has been inadequate; they have been conspicuously inarticulate to nonpsychiatric medical men and the public. Criticisms on all these scores were presented in a logical and forceful way by Alan Gregg [9] at the One Hundredth Annual Meeting of the American Psychiatric Association in 1944.

While psychiatrists have been diagnosing and treating patients, they have largely neglected the field of prevention of mental illness. Sometimes it has been argued that they were too few in number, and that there was hardly a sufficient body of knowledge to be certain about what constituted effective preventive efforts. For whatever reasons, the application of psychiatric principles to the solution of social problems has been minimal and has been the exception rather than the rule. There has been almost no organized or planned education in psychiatric principles for the public, despite its avid interest and desire. The misconceptions about mental health and about psychiatric patients seemed nearly as widespread in 1941 as in 1920. Despite remarkable progress in the fields of health and preventive medicine, only one university in the country had a psychiatrist in its school of public health.[10] Only seven states in the Union had a psychiatrist connected with their departments of public health.[11]

In summary, we find that at the outset of World War II, the status of psychiatry limited the immediate contribution that it could make. The rich knowledge gained from the experience of World War I had either been forgotten or neglected. The various medical specialties still held their traditional antagonistic or indifferent attitude toward psychiatry, which was colored by a mixture of prejudice and ignorance. Often when this newer science was accepted, it was with a kind of tolerance born of necessity, not with intelligent interest or warm welcome. The average man, both in and out of the Army, was afraid of or suspicious of psychiatry because of his inaccurate information about it or prejudice against it. The psychiatric patient was all too apt to be regarded as a total loss or was judged in terms of failure, sin, cowardice, or

---

[8] Zilboorg, G., "Present Trends in Psychoanalytic Theory and Practice," *Bull. Menninger Clinic,* 8:3-8, Jan., 1944.
[9] Gregg, Alan, "A Critique of Psychiatry," *Am. J. Psychiat.,* 101:285-291, Nov., 1944.
[10] Like other medical specialties, a physician going into public health work is required to have additional training. Several universities have established schools of public health in connection with their medical schools.
[11] A good many states had a mental hygiene commission, with a psychiatrist as a member who could act as a consultant, but his primary function was to supervise the state hospitals and institutions for the feeble-minded in that state and in some cases to organize outpatient clinics. He was not a member of the board of health.

perversity. Of perhaps more serious import was the lack of a wider experience of psychiatrists in the field of prevention of mental ill health. Psychiatrists also lacked information which could guide selection methods. There was not sufficient understanding of either the dynamics of or effective methods of dealing with the everyday problems of man in his attempt to adjust to life's demands.

It was with psychiatry in such a state of development that the United States entered World War II.

2

THE INITIAL HANDICAPS CONFRONTING ARMY PSYCHIATRY IN WORLD WAR II

THE INAUGURATION of a program of psychiatry for the Army took place against heavy odds. Psychiatry had neither the man power nor the knowledge to deal with the mental health problems presented by such large groups of people. Nor were the war agencies prepared to utilize psychiatry.

Some of the difficulties experienced by psychiatry, with all the attendant frustrations and disappointments, were due to the rapid expansion of the Army. From the skeletal organization that had been allowed by national and international policy, it grew rapidly into a complex machine. This huge machine, which functioned over a vast area under terrific pressure, did so because of the thousands of wheels within it that worked to solve almost countless problems. No one should underestimate the intensity of the drive that turned these wheels during the first years of the war by the effort of thousands of officers, enlisted men, and responsible civilians. To most of those men, whose energy and interest were absorbed in their work, psychiatry and its role in the organization were new and strange. The obstacles which delayed effective functioning were in part the result of problems inherent in Army organization and policy, in part the result of prejudice against psychiatry, and in part the result of the prewar status of psychiatry.

HANDICAPS DUE TO ARMY ORGANIZATION AND POLICY

Lack of plans. Early in 1917, before the United States had declared war, Col. Salmon selected a group of six psychiatrists to be sent overseas to observe what the British had done for neuroses and psychoses in their hospitals. As soon as the American Army arrived in Europe in force, these men were assigned as division psychiatrists. Base Hospital No. 117 was established at Lafoche, France, for the treatment of the neuroses. Later Base Hospital No. 214 was set up at Savenay, France, for the care of the psychoses. Following the armistice the latter became the clearing station for the evacuation of all the cases of psychoses then hospitalized in Europe.[1]

---

[1] Information furnished by Dr. Arthur H. Ruggles in a personal communication, August 6, 1946.

Despite the fact that the lessons learned in World War I were plainly and clearly recorded, there was in 1941 no effective preparation or plan for the use of psychiatry by the Army in World War II. After World War I considerable thought, time, and effort went into the preparation of the definitive history, *The Medical Department of the United States Army in the World War*.[2] Volume X was devoted to the history of military neuropsychiatry in the United States and in the American Expeditionary Forces. Into this monumental volume went the records of experience and statistical material which should have served as a basis for making detailed plans in World War II. Judging from the lack of effect of the psychiatric experience of World War I, the history volume seems to have rested quietly on the shelf between 1929 and 1941. There is little evidence that it influenced any planning for military neuropsychiatry between the two wars. Paradoxically enough, it was used as a guide by the British Army.[3]

The American Psychiatric Association had made some plans for the emergency. A committee headed by Col. Harry A. Steckel (Medical Research, U.S. Army) was appointed in May, 1939. It met with the Surgeons General of the Army and Navy on October 16, 1939. This committee surveyed psychiatric personnel and made a file of available men; it conducted a round-table discussion at the annual meeting of the association in May, 1940; it made an inspection trip of the Canadian Army; it participated in the early conferences with Selective Service.[4] Its members worked hard but met with lukewarm interest on the part of Army authorities.

In 1941 the subcommittee on clinical psychiatry of the National Research Council prepared an excellent statement on psychiatric problems of soldiers.[5] In 1942 the American Psychiatric Association appointed a special war committee of Drs. Arthur Ruggles, Edward Strecker, and Frederick Parsons. Not until 1944 did the Neuropsychiatry Consultants Division of the Surgeon General's Office request consultation with these men regularly.

Selection was one problem to which previous experience could have contributed. In spite of that experience the Army had not developed any tested procedure or criteria for choosing a fighting army. In 1929 it was written:

---

[2] *The Medical Department of the United States Army in the World War,* War Department, U.S. Government Printing Office, Washington, D.C., 1929.

[3] Rees, J. R., *The Shaping of Psychiatry by War,* W. W. Norton & Company, Inc., New York, 1945, p. 9.

[4] Steckel, H. A., "Psychiatric Aspects of the National Defense Program," *Ment. Hyg.,* 25:13-18, Jan., 1941; Report of the Committee on Military Mobilization, presented at Am. Psychiat. Assn. Meeting, Richmond, Va., May 5-9, 1941; see also a series of articles by Dr. Steckel in *Ment. Hygiene News* (New York State Dept. Mental Hygiene), Vol. 11, Mar. through June, 1941.

[5] Billings, E. G., "The Recognition, Prevention and Treatment of Personality Disorders in Soldiers," *Bull. U.S. Army M. Dept.,* No. 58, Oct., 1941, pp. 1-37.

Many of the purely physical disabilities which were noted and waived by mustering officers, or which disqualified recruits from service, were susceptible of improvement or cure by treatment, or got well of themselves under the favorable conditions of military training. This was rarely the case for any nervous or mental disease. On the contrary, the longer the training period was prolonged, the more pronounced these conditions became; the soldier was more and more constantly reported at sick call, or was suddenly seized with a nervous or mental collapse, or got into trouble by reason of repeated, and often unnecessary, military delinquencies. The strain of actual warfare, particularly of expeditionary warfare, with the unavoidable homesickness, loneliness, and depression—to say nothing of its actual physical dangers and hardships—brought first to the breaking point those whose morale, by reason of a general instability of the nervous system, could not be maintained. While such men were ultimately detected and discharged, it was not until after a considerable period of training during which they received pay, maintenance and equipment, wasted the time of those endeavoring to instruct them, interfered with the training of their brighter or better-adjusted comrades, and occupied hospital beds which often were urgently needed for others. Another unfortunate feature of the acceptance of such men for military service was that many of them, while unable to adjust themselves to the military environment, might be useful citizens if permitted to remain in their accustomed surroundings.[6]

In war the combat casualty, in particular, should be anticipated, and plans should be made to care for him. Out of an army of 3,500,000 men, 224,000 were wounded in World War I. It was a likely probability that many more would be wounded in this war. On this assumption, the Medical Department made elaborate plans to care for these men, and experience showed that the plans worked out very efficiently. Mobile field hospitals could be moved far forward to reach the men who needed immediate surgical treatment. The staffs of these hospitals covered themselves with glory by their spectacular work. Mobile auxiliary surgical teams, groups of two and four men, were especially trained to augment the services of the field hospitals.

The experience of the last war also taught us that for every four men wounded, there would be one psychiatric battle casualty. Yet no preparation was made to care for this fifth man, the psychiatric casualty. Until 1940, as a result of the very profitable experience of the last war, a psychiatrist had been retained in the personnel organization of each combat division. But a reorganization of 1941, in a move toward economy of personnel, dropped the psychiatrist from the combat divisions.[7] This omission was agreed to by those medical officers in charge of plans and training in the Surgeon General's Office at that time. Even the chief psychiatric consultant agreed to it. Later, theater surgeons begged that the psychiatrists be replaced, but their requests were

---

[6] Bailey, Pearce, "Detection and Elimination of Individuals with Nervous or Mental Diseases," *The Medical Department of the United States Army in the World War,* Vol. X, War Department, U.S. Government Printing Office, Washington, D.C., 1929, p. 57.
[7] For further details, see section on division psychiatrists in Chap. 17.

turned down in the Surgeon General's Office. It was not until nearly 2 years after war was declared (November, 1943) that the division psychiatrist was again included in the Table of Organization, and then only because the new Surgeon General Kirk personally insisted on them at War Department level, against determined opposition by the Army Ground Forces.

In the meantime, in the initial battles in Africa, psychiatric casualties were sent back to base hospitals, often hundreds of miles from the front. Only 5 per cent of these were able to return to duty. Later, because of the ingenuity of the Fifth Army consultant and the division psychiatrists, with the help of the theater surgeon, makeshift arrangements permitted treating these men in forward areas. From 50 to 70 per cent of those psychiatric casualties were able to return to duty. Other armies later adopted the same plan, but always with improvised arrangements.

This lack of preparedness was described by Dr. Eli Ginzberg, Chief of the Resources and Analysis Division of the Surgeon General's Office. He gave some startling figures from the experience of the First Army, which represented most of the American fighting strength during the first 2 months after D-day in France.

During these two months, eight divisions can be considered to have been actively engaged. The records of these divisions reveal that there was one neuropsychiatric admission out of every two medical admissions. In certain divisions, the admissions for neuropsychiatric causes swamped all other medical admissions. This can be illustrated by pointing to one division which had a per annum rate of 944 psychiatric admissions out of 1100 total medical admissions. In nonstatistical terms, this means that the entire strength of the division would have been dissipated within a year as a result of psychiatric casualties if men had not been treated and returned to duty.

In these eight divisions, neuropsychiatric admissions amounted to 200 per annum out of a total of 482 medical admissions per annum or approximately 40%. If these psychiatric casualties had not been effectively treated, one-fifth of the entire divisional strength would have been lost during the course of the year.

Shifting from rates to absolute figures, the First Army reported during June and July, 11,000 neuropsychiatric admissions, 16,000 admissions for disease and 60,000 battle casualties, half of which were classified as serious . . . of the 11,000 admissions, only 4000 were lost (to service). This means that approximately 65% of the men admitted for neuropsychiatric disorders were treated and returned to duty within the Army area. . . . In contrast, medicine was able to salvage about 60% of its admissions while surgery succeeded in returning within the Army area only 5000 of the 60,000 wounded or 9%.

In the light of this experience, it should prove profitable to review the War Department planning for the distribution of medical means. Based upon current tables of organization, a field army composed of three corps with supporting troops is assigned approximately 1500 Medical Corps officers. Of this number, the tables provide for 62 specialists in medicine. Experience indicated that approximately three "general duty" officers were assigned to medical work for each specialist or a total of 250 doctors in an Army area. In the First Army this group had to care for 16,000 disease admissions. The surgical staff amounted to 370 surgical specialists and 600 "general duty" officers. The surgical load totaled 60,000 patients. The remaining medical officers in the Army area were assigned to evacuation planning and other operational work.

These same tables of organization provided for 26 neuropsychiatrists. In the First Army, their work load amounted to 11,000 admissions. Theater surgeons recognizing on the basis of past experience the gross discrepancy between means and requirements, rose to the challenge as best they could by training battalion surgeons and by scraping together psychiatrists who could be spared from duties in the Communication Zone and bringing them forward to the Army area where the challenge was greatest.[8, 9]

Unexpected size of the psychiatric problem. A very real difficulty was the inability to forecast accurately the size of the task which would face this medical specialty. Many problems that arose were similar to those of the other branches of Army medicine. The peacetime Army had been only a token one, with inadequate plans for its expansion from 180,000 to 8,000,000 men. The necessity for building an enormous fighting force in so short a time produced bottlenecks everywhere, which necessitated numerous short cuts and expediencies. The psychiatric task was unexpectedly large, however, because not only were the Army psychiatrists to have a big job in terms of numbers of patients to be cared for, but their recommendations of measures to maintain mental health applied in areas new to psychiatric influence. Morale, job classification and placement, officer–enlisted-man relationships, and many other aspects of Army life became the concern of preventive psychiatry.

Absence of representation in the planning center. The Office of the Surgeon General made the plans for the medical services of the Army. Although a psychiatrist [10] functioned there before 1942, his chief responsibility was to review the papers of officers who were to be retired from the Army for any type of physical or mental condition. He had little or no responsibility for developing plans and recruiting personnel for the tremendous task ahead. Not until 7 months after Pearl Harbor was a psychiatrist appointed from civilian

---

[8] Ginzberg, Eli, "Logistics of the Neuropsychiatric Problem in the Army," *Am. J. Psychiat.*, 102: 728-731, May, 1946.

[9] Another evidence of this lack of planning for the heavy psychiatric load is found in some figures supplied by Dr. Perrin H. Long, Medical Consultant in the North-Africa–Mediterranean Theater. A general hospital overseas had two neuropsychiatrists. Long gives the breakdown of 70,365 patients admitted to the medical service of a general hospital in North Africa during a 25-month period: Malignant disease accounted for 0.07 per cent of patients; blood dyscrasias 0.08 per cent; metabolic disease 0.2 per cent; gastrointestinal disease 1.7 per cent; cardiovascular disease 3.1 per cent; arthritic conditions 3.7; dermatoses 10 per cent; "miscellaneous" 10.5 per cent; infectious disease 26 per cent; and *neuropsychiatric disturbances* 45 per cent! He commented that "medical officers became alert and at times one might say, almost allergic to the possibility that psychogenic disturbances might be the basis for the patient's complaint." Long, P. H., "Medical Progress and Medical Education during the War," *J.A.M.A.*, 130:983-990, Apr. 13, 1946.

[10] Colonel Patrick Madigan from August 1, 1940, to August 15, 1942.

life to serve as the chief consultant in neuropsychiatry to the Surgeon General.[11]

For the first 8 months he served in that capacity, he had only one assistant.[12] These two officers determined Army psychiatric policy and then had to "sell" such policy to those whose responsibility it was to implement it. In addition to his psychiatric work, this assistant was also assigned many administrative responsibilities in the Surgeon General's Office which were not related to the development of psychiatry.

Few specialists in the regular Army. In 1940 there were 35 medical officers in the regular Army who were assigned to psychiatric practice in hospitals. Of this number only four were qualified professionally as diplomates of the American Board of Psychiatry and Neurology. A great majority of the others had had no formal specialized psychiatric training. The medical officer in the small peacetime Army often had to serve as a Jack-of-all-trades. Assigned to an isolated post or a small camp, he had to carry on the duties of preventive medicine, act as the camp inspector, serve on numerous boards of officers, and administer his hospital. All branches of the regular Army Medical Corps had a dearth of qualified specialists. A medical officer might receive formal training in some specialty; however, it was quite possible that he would later have to accept an assignment in some other area of interest or even be assigned to field duty. Because of this system and through no fault or lack of ability in the men, there were no psychiatrists of outstanding national reputation in the Army. Therefore, to direct its wartime psychiatric program the Army had to recruit specialists from an already insufficient number of civilian psychiatrists.

Line of authority. Every organization can operate only as well as its line of communications functions. The Army had a remarkable system of command channels which were essential but which, at times, caused difficulties for every corps and every service. To send a message or directive "through channels" meant that the message must pass upward to a level of command where it could be transferred to the chief of a different service and then downward to the subordinate division or individual in that service for which it was intended. Potentially it could be disapproved at any one of these points and returned to the sender. Many short cuts in channels were authorized during the war, but always there were delays.

The geographical expanse of the Army greatly delayed other than emergency directives and undoubtedly many information bulletins never reached the field. This was a major handicap to psychiatry; almost no helpful informa-

---

[11] Doctor Roy D. Halloran, appointed August 17, 1942, with the rank of colonel; died November 10, 1943.
[12] Major (later Col.) Malcolm J. Farrell, assigned to the Office of the Surgeon General from April 10, 1942, until June 15, 1945.

tion or guiding directives were in print prior to 1941 and 1942. Numerous directives and technical bulletins were issued later, but delivery to the field was extremely unsatisfactory. Bulletins, once printed, had to be sent from an Adjutant General's depot to a command headquarters, to the surgeon of the headquarters, to the command of a post, to the surgeon of the post, to the commanding officer of the medical installation, to the chief of medicine, to the chief of neuropsychiatry, to the ward psychiatrist. They often were not received even in hospitals in this country. But when this routing was used for bulletins to be sent to a hospital in New Caledonia (or to any overseas unit) the chance of the psychiatrist receiving them was about 1 in 100. If and when they were received, they might be outdated!

Attitude toward psychiatric disability. To complicate matters further, an attitude seemed to prevail among many of those in authority that psychiatry was a sort of necessary evil. Very often all psychiatric patients except for the psychotic were suspected of being malingerers. When soldiers developed neurotic symptoms, misbehaved, or otherewise became mental casualties, something had to be done with them. It was generally assumed that a good officer or noncommissioned officer could force them to become good soldiers were it not for their intentional unwillingness, for which punishment was the best corrective. When men were obviously ill, the neuropsychiatrists in hospitals were told, by means of a directive, to make a diagnosis and discharge them home or to a state hospital. Give them a name and get rid of them! There seemed to be no recognition of the tremendous loss of partially trained man power occasioned by such a method. Such waste could have been reduced by adopting constructive policies, by supplying additional psychiatric personnel, and by obtaining adequate official support.

Disposition of psychiatric patients. During at least the first 2 years of the war an overwhelming majority of the patients admitted to the psychiatric wards of Army hospitals had to be discharged. This had been the peacetime practice, and it was carried over into wartime. Treatment was not approved. The patient remained in the hospital long enough to receive a diagnosis and then wait for his disposition. Two-thirds of the time of the psychiatrist was spent in disposing of patients by transfer or discharge. The psychiatrist became a mere name-labeler because the disposition of a patient either by discharge or by return to duty depended largely upon his particular clinical label, i.e., the diagnosis given him. Doctors developed a reluctance to call clinical entities by the correct designation while regulations necessitated discharge for certain diagnoses even though the man had recovered. Unfortunately, for some time the diagnosis of psychoneurosis was one of those which was tantamount to discharge.

After diagnosis had been made and the necessary time-consuming "boards" had been held, it required still more time of the psychiatrist to transfer discharged patients to state hospitals. Most states did not want to accept them, and a few would not. Their hospitals were full and also were understaffed; they believed that the Army or the Veterans Administration (which at that time had no beds available) should care for them. Individual arrangements had to be made for each patient.

Difficulty in reassigning men. The medical officer in a hospital had little voice in recommending the reassignment of a patient to a different type of job. He could make such recommendations, but in the early part of the war he was, in most instances, very much like a coyote howling at the moon—those in authority did not seem to hear. Consequently, there was a long interval of time during which patients became footballs. They were kicked into the hospital, then sent back to malassignments, shoved back into the hospital, returned to their assignments, and so on, until someone weakened. Usually it was the hospital which would then give such a patient a medical discharge.

Ineffective officers. A curious situation existed with regard to the assignment or reassignment of ineffective officers. This often became a concern of psychiatry and vitally affected its function. Although under the existing procedure an officer might be "reclassified" (i.e., demoted, separated, or permitted to resign from the service), to accomplish this consumed three or four months' time. It required the presentation of numerous supporting documents and affidavits of condemnatory nature, and finally a hearing before a board of senior officers. It was almost impossible to obtain such documents or evidence sufficiently strong to prove charges against an officer. As a consequence, the reclassification procedure was used rarely.[13] The result was that many totally inefficient officers remained in the Army. Such men would be assigned and reassigned and passed from one unit to another until eventually they found niches in which they were less troublesome or where they had a more tolerant commanding officer. Throughout the war, this system, inconceivable in any business enterprise, prevailed. There was no simple and effective method of "firing" or demoting a worthless officer.

This situation concerned psychiatry the more significantly because of the near-disastrous effect of such officers on the morale of a unit. They could cause much unhappiness and distress for all those serving under them. Occasionally they were subjects for examination by the psychiatrist, but most often the problem was not a medical one. Consequently, the psychiatrist could not recommend

---

[13] With a total of 872,000 commissioned officers in the Army, between September 16, 1940, and April 15, 1946, 6,700 or 0.77 per cent of officers appeared before reclassification boards. Of this number 327 were demoted, 2,593 honorably separated, 1,500 separated other than honorably, and 2,250 were reassigned to different jobs. In addition, reassignment was effected without board action on 1,887 officers as a result of their having been recommended for reclassification. Figures from Office of the Adjutant General.

them for retirement. When the officer in question was a psychiatrist himself —and that happened—he was sent to as "safe" an assignment as possible.

HANDICAPS DUE TO PREJUDICES AGAINST PSYCHIATRY

In addition to problems arising because of Army organization and policy, a second set of factors handicapping the function of psychiatry was the extent of prejudice against it and misconceptions about it. The lay attitudes of fear and skepticism, based on ignorance, were carried over by that portion of the public which came into the Army. These were operative from the first in making the effective practice of Army psychiatry more difficult. The average man has only a vague conception of what psychiatry is or what psychiatrists do. In spite of the fact that the number of psychiatric casualties created a problem of such size that it could not be ignored,[14] in too many instances psychiatrists were only tolerated very reluctantly; often they were resisted.

Psychiatry is that specialty in the field of medicine which concerns itself with the functioning of the personality in health and in ill health. More specifically, it deals with the prevention, diagnosis, and treatment of mental ill health. But such an abbreviated definition fails to indicate the psychiatric concept that any disease or illness affects the total person; there are unhealthy reactions to bosses and parents, to the stresses of military or civilian life, as well as to bullets and bacteria. If this concept were better known, psychiatry would be freed of much of the prejudice against it. If the average individual considers psychiatry at all, it is likely to be in terms of state hospitals, all too recently evolved from "insane asylums"! He thinks of it in terms of queer or crazy people, insanity, bars, padded cells. The more sophisticated may talk of complexes or inferiorities, usually without any real understanding of their words. It is the familiar experience of every psychiatrist to have some friend facetiously remark, "If this pressure does not let up, I will soon be under your care," as if to imply that "I'll soon be crazy and will then see you professionally." In the Army, prior to the war, the traditional name for the psychiatrist was "the nut-picker," a combination jibe and uncultured colloquialism.

---

[14] As evidence of this fact, the following quotation is taken from the factual account by Brig. Gen. Elliot D. Cooke. General Cooke, a line officer associated with the Inspector General's Office, was appointed by the Chief of Staff to investigate the problem of psychiatric casualties. "Secret weapons did not cause the only surprises in World War II. London's bewilderment over the first buzz-bomb was no greater than the consternation of our own General Staff in the spring of 1943 when the news suddenly burst upon it that nearly as many men were being discharged from the Army as were entering through induction stations. The number of these discharges was enough to alarm even the most complacent because it was well up into six figures. In fact, over a given period of time, more men were getting out of the Army than were being sent across the Pacific to fight the Japs. It is small wonder then that the Chief of Staff wanted to be informed immediately how such a thing could come about." Cooke, E. D., *All But Me and Thee. Psychiatry at the Foxhole Level*, Infantry Journal Press, Washington, D.C., 1946, p. 11.

The psychiatrist is considered by many people to be a mysterious person, surrounded with an occult aura. For some reason or other he is often regarded as related to and sharing the symptoms of his patients.[15] He is pictured popularly as wearing a long beard and being hermitlike; he is believed to be endowed with some magic power of perhaps being able to read minds and tell fortunes. Many people seem surprised to meet a psychiatrist who seems "normal." We have sometimes received the dubious compliment that "you have your feet on the ground," intended, no doubt, to convey the point that our explanations are grasped or that our suggestions seem sensible. Some well-meaning friends include in an introduction the explanation that "he is a psychiatrist, but, he *is* a good fellow," to indicate, presumably, a lack of eccentricity or queerness.

Fundamentally, everyone wants to consider himself as "normal" and to believe that therefore he has no need for psychiatric help. As a defense against the recognition of eccentricities in himself he uses a common mental mechanism called "projection," whereby he credits to another that which he cannot or will not face in himself. This is typified clearly in the well-worn story of the old Quaker. On his return from prayer meeting, where obviously he had been meditating on his friends sitting around him, he remarked to his wife, "Everyone is queer but thee and me, and even thee is queer at times." A fear of psychiatry and of the psychiatrist may be based on the need to protect one's own sense of personal integrity. No anxiety is more painful, as we see it clinically in patients, than the fear of losing one's mind. Even to have doubt expressed about it causes real concern. There is the lurking suspicion that consulting a psychiatrist will mean a confirmation of the fear. No doubt the historic era in which men were infested and infected with witches and incubi, werewolves and devils has some symbolic vestiges remaining today, for we still talk of imps and gremlins.

Throughout the war there remained a continuously obvious suspicion of psychiatry and prejudice against psychiatric patients among many nonmedical officers. Their comments implied: "What is the new-fangled stuff called psychiatry? The bird is yellow, that's all." The bullying techniques and "hard-

---

15 Psychiatrists have been and are aware of this attitude on the part of some medical colleagues: "The psychiatrist must always muster a certain temerity in his approaches to the busy halls and wards of a large general hospital. His entry is frequently eyed with suspicion. He is viewed as one who has the potentialities of peculiar and eccentric behavior. The keen, energetic surgeon becomes impatient or amusedly awaits the apparently theoretical formulations of the psychiatrist. The alert, discerning internist becomes reserved. The atmosphere is frequently chilly.

"The psychiatrist is often identified with his patients. Is he really safe? Is it alright for him to be outside his mysterious and cloistered walls? We do not identify the surgeon's assurance and impatience with his patient's gastric ulcer. The gynecologist is not thought to be effeminate because he treats women, nor the dermatologist angioneurotic or wayward because of the character of his practice. The medical man is not thought to be apoplectic or splenic because of his patient's disposition. And certainly, the atmosphere of affluence and euphoria which radiates from the obstetrician is not to be identified with that pride of possession which only pregnancy bestows. Why, then, should the psychiatrist be regarded as dangerous and peculiar?" Appel, K. E., "Psychiatry Today," *North Carolina M. J.*, 5:265-273, July, 1944.

boiled" tactics which they used indicated a total lack of comprehension of the problems of maladjusted soldiers. Almost invariably the line officer with combat experience was far more understanding than the infantry and service officers in the rear echelon. In fact, there were instances when the combat officer was far more open and receptive to psychiatric indoctrination than some medical officers.[16] However, where there was a total of only 47,000 medical officers to "educate," there were 872,000 other officers whose orientation to the problem was proportionately a larger and more difficult task. Most psychiatrists had to battle constantly against many odds in order to be given a fair hearing by line and medical officers.

Prejudices within Army medicine. The uninformed person expects psychiatric patients to be wild and dangerous, even homicidal. This naïve attitude is held by otherwise intelligent people. This is more evidence of the extent of the misconception that psychiatry is concerned only with severe psychotic reactions. It was perhaps in part because of this fact that the psychiatric sections of Army hospitals were usually placed on the distal end of the farthest ramp to the rear. The original plans called for these wards to be surrounded by high wire fence, in which, occasionally, barbwire was used. It was the exceptional visitor, or even inspector, who reached that far corner of the hospital.

As the psychiatrist was usually subordinate to the chief of the medical service, he first had to seek the approval of this nonpsychiatrist in order to make any change in his policy or practice. The chief of the medical service might be entirely uninformed or even antagonistic to psychiatry. In many of our large hospitals the broad discipline of psychiatry, with its social as well as clinical implications, was unwisely retained as a section under the chief of medicine. Probably such a procedure was warranted in a small hospital which had few patients, but it was not desirable in the larger hospitals.[17]

---

[16] Soon after reporting to the Office of the Surgeon General, I sought some advice from one of the regular Army medical officers in a position of much authority. He was cordial, though a little condescending. Before learning of my mission, he told me his ideas of psychiatry and how well he had handled psychiatric problems when he was a company commander. With an apparent sense of pride he described how he used an illiterate sergeant, who was a former boxing champion, to help him. He explained that he had posted prominently on all company bulletin boards a notice that under no circumstances was a noncommissioned officer ever to touch a private soldier. On one occasion a complaintive "neurotic" soldier came in to object to remaining on the latrine detail. As the commanding officer, he called for the sergeant to "give the soldier some help." Shortly the soldier returned with a blackened eye and started to report that the sergeant had beaten him. The officer stopped him, pointing to the sign on the bulletin board, and insisted that the sergeant certainly would not be disobeying his order. He equally proudly continued to explain how he had made the soldier "admit" that perhaps he had run into a door. This story was to prove how well HE could manage the psychiatric problems! Fortunately he was illustrative of only a small group.

[17] Not until February, 1945, did the official *War Department Technical Manual TM 8-262* specifically authorize that neuropsychiatry should be a service in named general hospitals. Even then, the resistance to change was so strong that it was not until December, 1946, that all hospitals conformed to this.

Though the study and "work-up" of the psychiatric patient required at least three or four times as long as that for the average physically ill patient, it was often only with the greatest difficulty that the psychiatric service or section could obtain additional help, either medical or clerical. Ward attendants were rarely available in sufficient numbers to provide the best patient care. Promotions for the chiefs of psychiatric services lagged conspicuously behind those for the chiefs of services in medicine and surgery; this was true also for the consultants in neuropsychiatry as compared with consultants in medicine and surgery. One can state bluntly that with all this prejudice and discrimination against him, the psychiatrist quite literally had to "win his spurs." If he won them, and thereby won a better chance to help his patients and have them better understood, in every instance it was because he worked very intensively and faithfully to do so. It is to the credit of general medical men and of the Army that, before the war ended, there was abundant evidence that many of the earlier prejudices and misconceptions had been overcome.

Stigmatization of patients. There was a tendency to stigmatize the neuropsychiatric patient as being a failure. In one sense such an individual was a failure if he became maladjusted early in his Army experience. But so also was the diabetic or the tuberculous patient. Certainly they could not be classed as successful in so far as their contribution to the Army was concerned. However, some persons presumed that individuals with psychiatric illnesses failed deliberately. They suspected or believed that such soldiers did not try. A sufficient number of soldiers had both defective attitudes and personality disorders to befog the layman's evaluation of the problem. It was easier to understand that a man could be noneffective because he wanted to get out of the Army by any means at all than that he was sick.

This stigmatization of psychiatric patients was probably carried over from civilian life. However, it was emphasized by the social situation of the Army in which the effort of everyone was evaluated in terms of the degree of achievement toward a common goal. In civilian life one could change the goal, but within the Army any deviation from maximum effort toward the common objective, regardless of cause, was likely to be looked upon as failure. When the cause was not physical, then the individual was variously regarded as perverse, subversive, unwilling, weak, dumb. He was likely to be labeled as a "quitter," "an eight-ball," "gold brick," or any of numerous other vernacular disparaging terms. The fact that many such individuals had a valid personality sickness often went entirely unrecognized.

In explaining this, one might be charitable and indicate that in part it was due to ignorance—ignorance of psychodynamics, of personality structure and function. The psychiatric battle casualty was a particular enigma to many combat officers. If a man "blew his top" it was quite possible, despite the validity of his illness, that he would be regarded as a coward or "yellow." Undoubtedly, the pressure of group opinion based on group ignorance, in some instances, emphasized and condoned such lack of understanding and consequent stigmatization of battle casualties by officers. Nearly every patient discharged from an Army hospital with a psychiatric diagnosis was himself greatly concerned about the possibility that his relatives or his friends might be afraid of his behavior or look upon him as a crazy man or as a failure.

Misbehavior in soldiers. Civilians also lack an understanding of the misbehavior of soldiers. There is no doubt that many misfits were, by mistake, taken into the Army. The Army could not use them once their pattern of behavior became apparent, and they had to be discharged, usually on an administrative rather than a medical basis. These soldiers had displayed antisocial behavior before they came into the Army, and the chances were that they would continue to do so upon their return to civil life. There were many appeals from communities about this type of individual, blaming the Army for having discharged them, sometimes even insinuating that the Army had made them what they were. Unless during his service the man had committed some offense with which he could be charged, the Army had no jurisdiction and no authority to confine him. When his tendency to misbehave made him an unsafe risk in the Army, he had to be returned to civilian life. Certainly it was not the mission of the Army in time of war to retain these men merely in order to protect the community. They had come from a particular town, and, if they returned there, they again became its problem.

Directly related to the matter of releasing this group from the Army was the problem of what type of discharge to give. Many of these men who displayed their maladjustment by going AWOL, by refusing responsibility, by disobeying orders, by chronic alcoholism, or by seductive homosexual behavior were given a type of discharge which, while not designated as "honorable," was also not designated as dishonorable. Because it was printed on blue paper, it became known as a "blue" discharge. Since the discharge was not specified as "honorable," it unquestionably carried a kind of stigma.

It is probable that in a small percentage of cases an injustice was done to certain soldiers.[18] On the other hand, from a psychological point of view, it was absolutely essential that most of these men should be given a type of discharge which indicated their failure to do their share. There had to be a differentiation between such individuals and the men who had carried their load and so contributed successfully and conscientiously to the mission of the Army. To discharge an undependable, lazy, disobedient soldier or an individual with chronic

---

[18] Army Regulations 615–360, 14 May 1947, changed discharges to: honorable (service excellent), general (under honorable conditions—service satisfactory), undesirable (under conditions other than honorable), dishonorable (sentence of general court martial).

alcoholism with the same honorable distinction which was accorded a veteran of five campaigns, or a wounded man, would have been a distinct injustice. The problem occasionally arose of a veteran of several campaigns who, upon being returned to this country, while still in the Army decided he could disregard all the rules of camp life. Such self-destructive, antisocial behavior would in a rare instance necessitate giving him a blue discharge.

The medical aspect of this type of person has been misunderstood occasionally. A good psychiatrist would certainly consider such maladjusted men as having serious character defects. If, as civilians, they sought or were brought to a psychiatrist, they would probably receive intensive study and be given the benefit of whatever treatment the physician deemed advisable. However, in the Army, problems that resulted from deep-seated, chronic character disorders which were not "service connected," could receive little treatment. There were neither adequate personnel nor facilities to undertake long-term treatment of a pre-service maladjustment with such a dubious outlook for recovery. The needs of the individual had to be considered as secondary to the needs of the group. In the social situation created by the Army, this was a necessity, so that whatever method of handling a particular individual was used, medical or otherwise, it had to be determined by its effect on the group. Were the kleptomaniac or the soldier with alcohol addiction permitted to be excused for his personality difficulties on the basis of being sick, and therefore permitted to hide behind the skirts of psychiatry, the devastating effect on the morale of his unit would have been incalculable.

An even more spectacular example of the necessity of demanding certain standards of behavior was concerned with the management of psychiatric casualties in combat. If the standards for evacuating casualties were lax, the wish to be evacuated was irresistible. Combat was literally hell, and no one wanted to be in it. If a soldier made a pretense of being ill and got away with it, every soldier in his platoon knew it, and the morale of each suffered accordingly. Many would have been prone to follow suit, which is quite understandable. If a soldier about to embark for overseas skipped his boat "because he forgot the time it left," the morale of the other 249 in his company could be maintained only by a knowledge of the fact that he would be punished. Most of those who shipped out on time did not want to go any more than the soldier who went AWOL. The fact that he might have been nervous or fearful or a misfit, and that his unconscious mental machinery was working overtime, was not a basis upon which the psychiatrist could excuse him and therefore condone his behavior.[19]

---

[19] There were many grossly distorted personalities in the group of ship jumpers. It was an extremely unwise policy for the Army to send them overseas, although this was the usual disposition for most of them. Brigadier General Cooke described from his personal investigation the

HANDICAPS PRESENTED BY THE STATUS OF PSYCHIATRY

In addition to whatever obstacles were placed in the path of the smooth functioning and progress of psychiatry in the Army by the inherent structure of the War Department and the prejudices which prevailed against it, some important difficulties were related to the status of psychiatry in the medical field and to the need for further development of its body of knowledge.

Position of psychiatry in medicine. The first of these difficulties was concerned with the relative position of psychiatry in medicine. The prevailing attitude and understanding of the many practitioners of medicine everywhere is that psychiatry is a specialty which is preoccupied with the care of "insane" people. The minor personality deviations, whether they occur in dispensaries or law courts, in a schoolroom or in a training camp, usually are not considered medical problems. It was not and still is not generally appreciated that these minor personality disturbances—the psychopathology of everyday life—are matters of psychiatric interest and concern and are, therefore, medical. Such problems need not always be handled by a psychiatrist. Most of us steadfastly believe that 90 per cent of them should be treated by the general practitioner or by the specialist of other medical fields. Our distress arises over the failure of medical men to generally recognize these conditions and apply scientific understanding and appropriate treatment to them.

Some of this lack of understanding is the fault of the psychiatrists themselves. As long as their practice is chiefly identified with state hospitals, it is understandable that not only laymen but also physicians may have the attitude that psychiatry and state-hospital practice are synonymous. This is related to the broader criticism of the status of psychiatry (referred to in the previous chapter) which Alan Gregg summarized in his critique: "You [psychiatrists] are badly recruited, you are isolated from medicine, you are over-burdened, and you are too inarticulate and long-suffering to secure redress from the public of some of the handicaps from which you and your patients suffer." [20] Much that Dr. Gregg criticized affected the function of Army psychiatry.

The inadequacy of some of our psychiatrists frequently became apparent. Some physicians were classified as psychiatrists because they presumably had practiced the specialty, though perhaps only for a year in a state hospital many years previously. Of those who were classified correctly, many had to learn how to function in a military setting and with the medical officers of other specialties. Only later was it possible, through careful selection and assignment

---

unfortunate and extremely costly results when 2,000 were sent in one consignment as infantry replacements to the North African Theater. Cooke, E. D., *All But Me and Thee. Psychiatry at the Foxhole Level*, Infantry Journal Press, Washington, D.C., 1946, Chap. 6, pp. 89-106.

[20] Gregg, Alan, "A Critique of Psychiatry," *Am. J. Psychiat.*, 101:285-291, Nov., 1944.

of the available men, to place superior individuals in strategic positions as consultants, as division psychiatrists, and as chiefs of services in hospitals.

It was the scientific ability, the sincerity, and the very strenuous effort displayed by these men in military psychiatric practice which won the wholehearted support and co-operation of the medical officers in other specialties and which in turn made psychiatry a truly integrated part of Army medicine.

3

THE PROBLEMS ARISING IN THE FURTHER DEVELOPMENT OF ARMY PSYCHIATRY

IN ADDITION to the obstacles facing Army psychiatry initially, many complications developed during the war. Perhaps this was inevitable. Surely some of them could have been avoided if sufficient attention had been given to the published record [1] of the neuropsychiatric practices of World War I. Others were unavoidably met in the search for improved methods. A few might possibly have been forecast and thus minimized with careful planning before, or immediately after, Pearl Harbor.

The causes of these complications were many. Personnel was inadequate. Army procedures for the selection and training of inductees and for the disposition of noneffective soldiers were inconsistent. The management of patients necessitated a reorientation of civilian-become-military doctors. They had to accept the fact that top priority for medical service in the Army belonged to the maintenance of the effectiveness of a military unit—the platoon, company, or division. This meant that all able men had to be kept in action. The treatment of psychiatric patients was handicapped by physical facilities which were planned for the care of disturbed patients. Releases of any news to the public about military neuropsychiatry was blocked "for security reasons." Psychiatrists blundered often in their trial-and-error development of a program.

Personnel inadequacies. From the beginning to the end of the war there were never enough qualified neurologists or psychiatrists. Nor were their important "right hands" sufficiently numerous to offset that lack. Well-trained clinical psychologists, psychiatric social workers, and psychiatric nurses and ward attendants could multiply one doctor's effectiveness many times. Instead, a constant undertone to the straining effort of professional workers on psychiatric services, was a desperate appeal for more, and still more, trained workers.

Although the war forced a spotlight of public interest onto the gap between the supply of and demand for psychiatrists, it did not create the problem. In

---

[1] *The Medical Department of the United States Army in the World War,* Vol. X, War Department, U.S. Government Printing Office, Washington, D.C., 1929.

the peacetime Army of 180,000 men, 37 of the 1,200 regular Army doctors were classified as psychiatrists. Only a small percentage of them had any formal psychiatric training or experience. The Army Medical Corps required such varied tours of duty that specialization was practically out of the question.

Furthermore, for at least 10 years there had been a relative shortage of psychiatrists in civilian life. The total membership of the American Psychiatric Association [2] at the beginning of the war was less than 3,000. This number represented only approximately 2 per cent of the estimated 180,000 doctors in the country. Consequently, despite the fact that over one-third of them volunteered for military service, the total number of Army psychiatrists at no time represented more than 3 per cent of the doctors in the military forces.

On the basis of their assignment the personnel division listed 2,404 physicians as neuropsychiatrists. However, numerical strength did not tell the entire story. Many of these doctors lacked the training and experience which would qualify them professionally. Some of them were so assigned because of early training in psychiatry. For example, an obstetrician of many years' experience was classified for a psychiatric assignment because part of his medical training was a residency in a mental hospital 20 years previously. There were also doctors who requested service on psychiatric wards because of their own unrecognized need for psychiatric help. If that need was too great, such motivation made it difficult for them to work satisfactorily either as physicians or as a part of the Army.

Although the ratio of psychiatrists to all the doctors in the Army was somewhat greater than that in civilian medicine, the nature and demands of Army psychiatric practice made this number still insufficient. The responsibility of and opportunities for psychiatry in the Army were far, far more inclusive than in civilian life. Also the social situation created by the Army showed up individuals in need of psychiatric help who would have never seen a doctor as civilians. Psychiatrists were needed for so many different kinds of military installations—induction centers, hospitals, rehabilitation centers, disciplinary barracks, consultation services, divisions, separation centers, redistribution centers, and hospital ships. The patients on the average psychiatric service constituted about 10 per cent of the total number of patients in a medical installation, but rarely did that service have more than 3 or 4 per cent of the medical staff.

Paper work diluted professional services still further. In addition to his heavy clinical load, the Army psychiatrist was burdened with numerous administrative procedures. One who is not familiar with it cannot appreciate the amount of recording that is required for the care and disposition of just one psychiatric patient.

---

2 Professional organization of psychiatrists.

Because of its nature the medical record of a psychiatric case is long and detailed. The conversation, behavior, and attitudes of the patient all have meaning to the psychiatrist. Since doctors, like their patients, were subject to sudden and unexpected transfer, they recorded in the case history all pertinent information. Only thus could treatment proceed with some degree of consistency.

Several senior officers met as a board to determine the disposition of patients who were ready for discharge or transfer. Different boards passed on different types of problems. There were the "disposition board," the "discharge board," the "section eight board," and the "retirement board." Although the practice was not prescribed by regulation, a psychiatrist was almost always assigned to the most active board—the discharge or CDD Board—because psychiatric patients constituted 40 per cent of their work. In many hospitals this required three afternoons a week. Every board made its decisions on the basis of a summary of the medical history and findings of each case presented to it. The summary was part of the essential paper work. Only the doctor could sift the more vital material for such a report. To complicate life further, many posts were located in geographical areas where civilian stenographic help was almost impossible to obtain. Although dictaphones were installed in many hospitals, the lack of clerical help made an acute bottleneck. The frequent result was that the doctor himself had to write lengthy reports and records by hand.

The long-delayed emphasis on treatment required drastic changes in order to permit more effective use of the comparatively small number of experienced psychiatrists. Patients were moved to neuropsychiatric treatment centers. Personnel in related fields were increased. In-service training was established.

Despite the earlier recognition of the necessity for such a step, it was nearly 2 years after the war began before there was a concentration of the psychiatric patients in specialized hospitals. These were located at such places as would enable patients to be in the same geographical area as their homes. Such concentration made possible a much more effective use of auxiliary personnel. Civilian experience discovered that adequate psychiatric treatment required the assistance of the clinical psychologist and the psychiatric social worker. Against many odds, Army policy and practice were revised to include the services of both of these specialists in so far as they were available. These ancillary personnel, of whom also there were never enough, partially compensated for the shortage of psychiatrists.

The development—again through necessity—of the School of Military Neuropsychiatry offered the opportunity for some training and experience in this specialty. Through 1943 the school gave 1-month courses on the specific problems and methods of military psychiatry to orient the doctors newly commissioned from civilian life who were assigned to neuropsychiatric services.

As the acute shortage of psychiatrists persisted, the school was enlarged. Newly recruited medical officers went from civilian internships to the Medical Field Service School at Carlisle Barracks, Pennsylvania, for basic training. Then, those who desired were sent to a 3-month course at the School of Military Neuropsychiatry from December, 1943, until December, 1945, at Mason General Hospital under the able leadership of Col. W. C. Porter. During this period the amazing total of 1,000 medical officers attended as students and were subsequently classified on their personnel records as neuropsychiatrists.

Various other schools were conducted. The psychiatric and neurological faculties of Columbia and New York Universities taught three sessions each for medical officers. A total of 260 men were sent to these 3-month courses. Extensive and intensive training in the psychiatric treatment of battle casualties was provided for 758 general medical officers in the European Theater. Courses were given for division medical officers in the South Pacific. Graduation from any of the overseas courses did not qualify men as psychiatrists, but it did enable many physicians to serve more usefully in an understaffed field.

Certain special instruction was given. With the assistance of the Adjutant General, a training school was established in clinical psychology which was attended by approximately 250 students. Unfortunately no school for psychiatric social workers was ever organized. However, outlines of lectures were distributed to the hospitals, some of which gave courses in social work to enlisted personnel. Three-month courses in psychiatric nursing were offered in eight of the nine Service Commands. These schools graduated nearly 700 nurses.

There was extreme difficulty in obtaining and retaining an adequate number of enlisted men to serve as ward attendants. Because of this, such personnel remained on duty 12 hours a day in many hospitals. Almost every general hospital and many of the small hospitals conducted training courses for their attendants. However, no one could be kept on a specialized assignment without an "MOS number" on his record, in spite of particular qualifications. In the Army, a man was assigned by his military occupational specialty (MOS) number. If he did not have one, he was sent to any "unskilled" job which, of course, was most often combat training. Despite repeated efforts, no MOS number was obtained during the war for ward attendants. The assumption apparently was that anyone could take care of psychiatric patients. A compromise was finally reached when permission was granted to add the letters NP to the MOS number of the "Medical Technician MOS 409." [3] There is no doubt that in the

---

[3] In July, 1946, the psychiatric ward attendant was finally given a new title, "psychiatric technician," and a separate MOS, 1409. Another postwar gain! War Department Circular 209, 13 July 1946.

meantime many of these greatly needed attendants were lost to the NP service after having received considerable training and experience.

The American Red Cross was a very great source of help in all the hospitals. They supplied psychiatric social workers when they had them. They also furnished one or more full-time recreational workers to neuropsychiatric sections.

As a result of great effort on the part of many people, by the end of the war psychiatric personnel was nearly sufficient in quantity to meet the needs of the psychiatric patient load. It still was far from adequate in quality of training and experience.

COMPLICATIONS RELATED TO ARMY METHODS

At least three major complications for wartime psychiatry resulted from military procedures—selection of men at induction centers, the program for their mass training, and the method of disposing of noneffective soldiers.

Selection. At the induction centers psychiatrists (and often nonpsychiatrically oriented physicians assigned to that work) were included in the examining line. However, they too often were not used very effectively. In a 2- or 3-minute examination the psychiatrist was expected to evaluate the draftee. Would he or would he not make a good soldier? The generally accepted assumption was that the misfits and the obviously potential psychiatric casualties would not. Therefore, it was further assumed, if these were eliminated at induction, there would be essentially no psychiatric problem in the Army. Time and early experience proved how erroneous this thinking was. The inclusion of the psychiatrist on the draft examination team was an extremely important, practical, and worth-while effort. Nevertheless, it is to be regretted that everyone concerned did not recognize the limitations of his mission. The provision of more time, resources, and personnel would have made the selection more effective.[4]

Training methods. The soldier, shortly after his induction, landed in a basic-training course in some camp—Air Forces, Ground Forces, or Service Forces. He found this a very strenuous life both physically and emotionally. At the same time he met acute problems of adjustment to military life as a whole. A good many psychiatric casualties consequently developed in these training camps.

The charge has been made, and with some validity, that the training methods themselves produced psychoneuroses. There were some obvious defects in the program which did seem definitely to contribute to the evolution of neurotic responses. A questionnaire was used to solicit the opinions of the psychiatrists

---

4 See Chap. 19.

in the basic-training camps regarding the psychiatric implications in the training procedures.

Universally criticized was the assumption behind the training program that all inductees were of equal caliber, physically and mentally. Regardless of any difference, even of age, they were all given the same course at the same speed. The result was that individuals with superior qualifications were held back, and those of inferior ability were pushed too fast. In addition the status of some of the older men was such as to be a heavy handicap in the enforced, rapid physical-conditioning program. Their lesser ability contributed to the production of psychological reactions.

There were other adverse criticisms. Fear was too often used as a major incentive for learning. The destructive risks rather than the constructive opportunities were emphasized. More than once I heard the tough, hard-boiled instructor shout in the vernacular to a group of recruits, "Keep your ass down or you will be a dead duck." Perhaps it is unfair to be critical of this point of view; at least the instructor was realistic. Nevertheless the unfortunate result, in too many instances, was the inculcation of fear beyond the capacity of some recruits to manage.

Psychiatrists, at least, were impressed with the result of the lack of mental hygiene orientation of both commissioned and noncommissioned officers who failed to recognize neurotic tendencies in the trainees early enough for them to be relieved or corrected.

Finally, there was no flexibility which would permit the soldier of limited capacity to be assigned to training of a different type. In most camps if he couldn't keep up with the training program he had to be discharged. In a few of the posts with unusually enlightened commanding officers, a special training unit for handicapped or maladjusted men was established. This occurred before the "special training unit" was universally prescribed for the training of illiterates. In the training camps where this local arrangement did not exist, the psychiatrist had no choice; he had to discharge the men who could not make the grade.

On visits to the basic-training camps, as neuropsychiatric consultants, we were impressed with the very great loss of man power because certain individuals could not match the tempo of training. We recommended the establishment of labor battalions for men of low and marginal intelligence. We never knew why no action was taken on the matter. During a discussion with an officer in G-1 of the War Department (personnel), a rumor was reported that the White House would not approve of such a plan. Presumably, approval was withheld because of possible accusations of racial discrimination. Any plan for a labor unit would have affected a higher proportion of negroes. Numerically, it would have included far more white soldiers.

The high incidence of psychoneuroses in training camps led to the establishment of Mental Hygiene Consultation Services to which the men could be referred instead of being sent to the hospital. In this way they could receive outpatient treatment while remaining on duty. The psychiatrists in these installations gained a great measure of understanding of the failures and successes of training methods. To them the symptoms of patients often appeared to result from poor teaching procedures. They also saw the relationship of the action of commanding officers to the mental health of the soldiers. In fact, their efforts to orient line and medical officers psychiatrically frequently resulted in changes of procedure. Reduced attendance at sick call and improved morale of a unit then followed inevitably.

Late in the war the ideal relationship between commanding officers and psychiatrists was defined officially:

The majority of the factors which determine the mental health of the military personnel are functions of command. In other words, the main job of preventive psychiatry must be done by commanding officers of the line. It is a responsibility of command to obtain maximum utilization of manpower by providing proper incentive and motivation, and such reclassification, reassignment, rest, relaxation, and recreation as exigencies of the military service permit. The psychiatrist acts as adviser to the command. In training centers or Army divisions as a member of the division surgeon's staff, he is to be regarded as having a staff function in advising the command on policies and procedures which affect mental health and morale.[5]

Disposition of the noneffective soldier. In so huge an army, the induction of a certain percentage of ineffective soldiers could not have been avoided. In other words, regardless of the care used in screening, there were many individuals whose handicaps escaped detection in the course of induction. Ineffectiveness became apparent only when, because of minor physical handicaps, faulty attitudes, or poor motivation, they could not withstand the strenuous demands of Army life. Such men became acute problems for the psychiatrist, for it was usually he who was forced into the position of having to decide what to do with them. The criteria for their disposition changed frequently during the war. Variations in man-power needs, poor planning for the assignment of partially effective personnel, and the lack of understanding of the psychiatric problems involved dictated the changes in these policies. Nearly all of them were made without psychiatric advice.

Servicemen with minor physical disorders or defects were subject to varying directives from the War Department. At one time their assignment for "limited service" was mandatory. Later, orders stated that there would be no soldiers so classified. When that order [6] was issued, several hundred thousand limited-

---

[5] War Department Circular 81, 31 March 1945.
[6] War Department Circular 161, 14 July 1943.

service men with actual and demonstrated capacity to serve were discharged from the Army.

So many men were lost by this policy that it was abruptly canceled in November, 1943, as was the term "limited service." Discharges were then sharply reduced and "limited-assignment" jobs were filled. As opportunities for this type of placement diminished, a backlog of this category of soldiers accumulated. Then another circular [7] momentarily reopened the floodgates of discharge. Four months later this had to be rescinded by telegraphic instructions.

Such changes were of particular concern to the psychiatrists whose clinical experience gave them an understanding of the effect of this variable policy on the motivation of many soldiers. When the standards were lowered, the unconscious urge to escape the unpleasantness of military service gained support. The soldier was constantly confronted with the possibility of returning to civilian life and home and job if he became ill, or of having to remain in the Army with all its stresses and demands, including combat, if he stayed well. When the discharge floodgates were opened to those with minor physical defects, thousands of soldiers with marginal adjustment suddenly developed an intensification of previously minor symptoms. Many officers, including some in the Medical Corps, had difficulty accepting the fact that this was not an intentional, conscious falsification. Very few appreciated the power of the unconscious personality factors which came into play with the changes of policy. If a soldier knew that laxity existed in the standards of discharge, only strong motivation toward staying in the Army could counteract unconscious desires to get out. On the other hand, if standards could have been maintained constant, i.e., had not varied with man-power needs, thousands of men who would have rendered valuable service could have been kept in the Army. Great moral support would have come from the realization that everyone, even those with restricted ability, who could serve would have to do so. Instead, as the standards were relaxed, the incidence of psychiatric casualties increased.

In the usual course of events, when a company commander found a non-effective or ineffectual soldier, if company manipulation or punishment failed to effect his improvement, the officer referred the soldier to the Medical Department. Unless there was some physical cause for his hospitalization, the soldier invariably ended up on the psychiatric service or section of the hospital. There, the psychiatrist who examined him would find that his attitude was faulty, or that he was inclined to magnify some insignificant physical complaint. In such a case, the difficulty was not due to a psychiatric illness but to a defective attitude; the soldier was resentful of being in the Army and was unwilling to do

[7] War Department Circular 370, 12 September 1944.

his job. Since it was not a medical problem, he was referred back to his company. There again, the company commander either tried to utilize him or transfer him to another unit. Almost always he was given a "satisfactory" indorsement. If a man was rated less than "satisfactory" he could not be transferred.[8] If the CO did not succeed in finding a place where the soldier could be effective, the man was sent back to the hospital. There again, the psychiatrist would probably find that, except for being more complaintive, crying louder about his vague symptoms, the "patient" was not incapacitated for duty. So, the doctor would return him to his company. This process could go on for a long time and sometimes did. The man was certainly not to be regarded as sick. To do so was an abuse of the standards of medical practice.

When units were preparing to move, particularly when the prospect of going overseas was imminent, the effort to clean out the noneffectives was much greater. At such times large numbers of them were sent to the hospital. Then not infrequently those in command exerted influence on medical officers to facilitate the disposition of these noneffectives clear out of the Army. This pressure was sometimes practically mandatory.

As a result, the medical channels for discharge became abused.[9] They were used as an exit from the Army for men who incapacitated themselves by their defective attitudes. "Psychoneurosis" became the diagnosis commonly used for that purpose. It was undoubtedly not warranted when applied to many such cases, as first seen. However, after the soldier had been used as a football between the company and hospital, he might readily develop a neurotic reaction.

The situation became sufficiently grave so that, at the request of the Chief of Staff, the Inspector General made an extensive survey late in 1944. His conclusions completely supported and verified the claims of the psychiatrists regarding the misuse of certain diagnoses. This inspection resulted in what was

---

[8] This point is also brought out clearly by a line officer, Brig. Gen. Cooke. He reported his experiences in looking into the psychoneurotic problem at the request of the Chief of Staff in a somewhat humorous though nonetheless factual style. He quotes from an interview with a post commander who had been complaining that a departing Ground Forces division had sloughed off 824 noneffective men into his post complement.

"'Personally, I don't think he [director of personnel] could find anything worthwhile [about a soldier's record] if he went through all the records in the Army. I've never seen anything about psychoneurotics on any of the service records I ever looked at, nor any other kind of a remark that would prevent or hinder a man's transfer out of a unit.'

"'You mean that company commanders are giving satisfactory ratings to men who are not adaptable to the service?'

"'Sure, they mark men satisfactory who aren't adaptable to anything. Otherwise the company commanders would have to put their undesirables up before a Section Eight Board and the number they get rid of that way you could put in your eye.'"

Cooke, E. D., *All But Me and Thee. Psychiatry at the Foxhole Level,* Infantry Journal Press, Washington, D.C., 1946, p. 42.

[9] This abuse was emphasized by Maj. Gen. Howard McC. Snyder in "Observations of Psychiatry in World War II," *Am. J. Psychiat.,* 104:221-225, Oct., 1947.

probably the most significant single directive to affect military psychiatry. To quote briefly from this:

The diagnosis of any type of psychoneurosis implies sickness and disability of some duration. It is not to be applied for reasons of expediency in order to effect disposition. It will be applied only when its use is justified by the existence of a clinical picture which satisfies the criteria for psychoneurosis as established by good medical practice. The mere presence of psychoneurotic symptoms which do not significantly impair the individual's efficiency or the presence of a predisposition to psychoneurosis does not warrant a diagnosis of any type of psychoneurosis. Such individuals if otherwise sound will be considered as having no disease. . . . In determining dispositions of cases, it must be clearly understood that there are many causes for noneffectiveness other than sickness. Among these are ineptness, inadaptability due to emotional instability, lack of physical stamina, misassignment, defective attitude and unwillingness to expend effort. Those who are ineffective by reason of any of these causes will be disposed of administratively.[10]

Other problems of disposition. Related to the abuse of diagnosis was the prevalent policy of presuming that because a soldier received a diagnosis of psychoneurosis he had fallen below the standards of admission and therefore was no longer qualified for military service. Therefore he was to be discharged. The same circular endeavored to change that practice also.

It should be clearly recognized that the presence of any type of psychoneurosis should not lead automatically to separation from the service. Many individuals with psychoneurosis recover and even if not fully recovered are capable of performing full duty. The disposition should depend solely upon the degree of incapacity after adequate treatment. In itself a mild psychoneurosis of any type will not be considered adequate cause for disability discharge. When an individual is suffering from a psychoneurosis which is not incapacitating, he will be returned to duty.[10]

While the psychiatrist was sometimes pushed into giving medical discharges to men who were ineffective for nonmedical reasons, he also had trouble, on some posts and in some hospitals, in procuring certificates of disability for bona fide medical cases. When the company commander or the dispensary physician thought the neurotic complaints were merely goldbricking, the soldier was usually not able to gain permission to see the psychiatrist. If the chairman of the discharge board was unsympathetic or ignorant or stupid, he could and often did refuse to discharge the man. The commanding officer of the hospital had to give final approval and could, if he wished, disapprove the discharge. Because there was so much criticism of the number of discharges for psychoneuroses, one large Service Command headquarters for a period of some months reviewed every case before giving permission for such a discharge. This ruling had some merit but many disadvantages. It made most of the psychiatrists

---

[10] War Department Circular 81, 31 March 1945.

angry because it was a slap at their professional judgment. It resulted in the subterfuge of using other diagnoses which did not require approval. It added several days of hospitalization for every such case while the record was being shipped to headquarters and returned. Most serious, it allowed the accumulation of a tremendous backlog of noneffective men whose discharges were disapproved at the headquarters. We in Washington learned of 5,000 such at one post; we could do nothing but protest.

These obstacles to obtaining a discharge for bona fide medical cases were minor compared to those met on some posts when trying to secure approval for administrative discharges (Sec. VIII for mental deficiencies, sexual deviates, alcoholism, psychopathic personalities). Actually, such a discharge was not the responsibility of the psychiatrist. He saw the case for professional evaluation; then he usually made a recommendation to the soldier's company commander, who could bring the case before the proper board. After the board decided the case, the report usually had to be sent on to a higher headquarters for final approval. Certain of these headquarters were famous for disapproving the discharge. Thus the soldier was left on duty to disrupt his company or remain in the hospital or, if possible, be sloughed off to an unsuspecting unit. Again, a subterfuge was the only course left for the hospital staff—to give the man a medical diagnosis and then discharge him with a certificate of disability!

Another factor which contributed to the ineffectiveness of some men was the great difficulty, or usually the impossibility, of procuring a transfer to a different assignment. Often special training and aptitudes were ignored for some reason in making a man's initial assignment. That reason was usually that, while the inductee was awaiting assignment, no request had come in for personnel with his special ability. Therefore he was sent out on an order for so many men whose qualifications were more general. If a man was an expert photographer and the particular reception center where he was had no call for a photographer but an urgent demand for 200 infantrymen, it was, "to hell with his photographic ability!" He became and he stayed—an infantryman!

COMPLICATIONS IN THE MANAGEMENT OF PSYCHIATRIC PATIENTS

There were three complications arising from the methods of management of the psychiatric patients. Two of these concerned the necessary reorientation of the attitude of the psychiatrist. The psychiatrist had to learn to regard the need of his patient as secondary to the need of that patient's military unit. This meant that the psychiatrist had to return the patient to duty if he was able to render further service, whether or not he was completely recovered from his illness. The third complication arose from the fact that the tremendous case load of nonpsychotic patients had to be treated by psychiatrists who had had experience only in the care of psychotic illness.

Importance of the group vs. the individual. The practice of civilian medicine is based entirely on the tradition of the pre-eminent importance of the individual. When a patient goes to a doctor he expects that doctor to treat *him* without particular concern for other people in his environment. The civilian doctor plans treatment, rightfully, for its effect upon the patient. If the practices or relationships of social or business associates, or even the family, interfere with proper treatment, the patient is removed to a place where his care can be of prime concern, probably in a hospital.

By contrast, the chief interest of the Army medical officer had to be centered on the welfare of the military unit. His principal aim was to maintain that unit at its effective strength by keeping its men well enough to remain on duty. When a patient came to him complaining of some vague symptoms, the psychiatrist determined his recommendations by the manner in which they would affect the group from which the patient had been referred as well as for their effect on the patient himself. Were he to honor a thinly disguised desire to get out of the Army with a medical diagnosis, when this fact became known to the other soldiers in the unit their morale would suffer seriously.

The psychiatrist was thus continuously confronted with the necessity of making a distinction between the patient with a true and valid neurotic reaction and the man with a social maladjustment. In the first instance, the soldier was incapacitated by an illness just as if he had pneumonia or a broken leg. In the latter instance, whether he was a chronically unreliable, antisocial person or a consistently deceptive exhibitionist, he was incapacitated by a defect in his personality. In the Army he could not be dealt with in the same manner as if he were ill, because of the apparent volitional component in his misbehavior. A related aspect of this problem had even more cogent significance in the combat situation. There the work of the psychiatrist was often defined as the separation of the "I won'ts" from the "I can'ts"—making the decision as to whether a faulty attitude or a psychoneurotic illness led to the noneffectiveness. In some cases, they might both be present. But, before giving a medical diagnosis, the psychiatrist had to be very sure that he was not excusing from military service an individual with defective attitudes; [11] that he was not rewarding him with an escape from duty.

Defective attitudes in combat troops were rarely verbalized directly. A soldier didn't say that he wouldn't fight; he indicated it by a poor imitation of his more sick comrade, or he exaggerated some physical difficulty or found some excuse to report to the doctor. By contrast, every Army psychiatrist in any post

---

[11] See Chap. 13.

in the United States had many examples of individuals who frankly said they did not want to be in the Army. Sometimes they cloaked it in superficial complaints; sometimes they said it politely by indicating how valuable they could be in civilian life; not a few expressed directly their resentment of the Army, and, sometimes perhaps justified, of their mismanagement or misassignment. Every psychiatrist, in fact every physician, saw a disconcertingly large number of men who wanted to pick up their marbles and leave the game. Despite physical complaints they were not really sick medically; they had defective attitudes, and many of us in psychiatry didn't feel they should hide behind us in the guise of being our patients. Some of them could be spotted readily, but unfortunately many of them could not be. To do so required a psychiatrist with considerable clinical experience, and these were too rare in the Army.

Misbehavior as most often encountered in camp differed from neurotic illness in that it was not greatly influenced by external stresses, nor did it result from them. An individual with a long history of misbehavior could not have developed his maladjustment as the result of military experience (although it may have intensified it). Even had the Army been able to attempt treatment, morale would have been severely jeopardized had men been routinely pardoned and discharged for their misconduct. For example, in civilian life if an individual with chronic alcoholism comes to him as a patient, the psychiatrist is correct in regarding him as a fit subject for psychiatric treatment. Experience has indicated that such difficulties have their origin in deep-seated character defects. Even though the outlook may be dubious, treatment is often justified. But in the Army, for many reasons it was impossible to provide adequate treatment for this type of psychological defect, as well as for many others—neurotic characters, chronic disciplinary problems, or drug addiction. Certainly in war there was no reason to invest the time and effort of experienced psychiatrists in treating pre-service disabilities with gloomy prognoses.

Returning men to combat. War was a dirty job, and one of the very important functions of the psychiatrist was therefore also a dirty job. The existence of the Army depended on the principle that every man *must* do his duty and contribute his share. The daily responsibility of every psychiatrist who worked with troops in action was to aid the psychiatric casualty sufficiently to justify sending him back into the line. In other words, the medical officer treated the casual soldier only until he was able to return to combat, even though after so doing he would probably again become worse. A psychiatric casualty was no more and no less expendable than a physical casualty. If a man could give 2, 5, or 10 days more of fighting service, then it was up to the psychiatrist to send him back to that duty. There is no comparable problem which confronts the psychiatrist in civilian life. Ideal psychiatry was impossible to practice under conditions of combat; combat psychiatry consisted of makeshift applications of some of the principles and techniques learned in civilian practice.

The psychotic-nonpsychotic ratio. In the early stages of the war it was apparently assumed that psychotic patients would comprise the major portion of the psychiatric case load. It was expected that men with serious tendencies to neurotic illness would be rejected at the induction centers. Consequently it came as a great surprise that over 90 per cent of the psychiatric cases in Army hospitals were suffering from psychoneuroses or other types of personality disturbances. Only 7 per cent had psychoses. This unanticipated state of affairs created many problems and demanded a marked change in strategy.

A really big problem lay in the physical arrangement of Army hospitals, whose neuropsychiatric sections had been built on unrevised blue prints of 1918. Their "closed wards" with locked doors, barred windows, and high fences were designed to be used for the actively disturbed psychotic patients. Such places were not suitable for housing psychoneurotic patients. However, very often they were so used, without alterations. In very few hospitals were there enough open wards to accommodate the number of mildly ill mental patients, while there were often more closed wards than necessary for the number of disturbed patients. Sometimes the commanding officers insisted that all the available closed-ward beds be used before additional open-ward beds would be allotted. Periodic shortages of bed space also made it necessary to use these wards for the less ill patients. Barred wards undoubtedly aggravated the illness of the neurotic individual.

To make matters worse, general prisoner patients (with their guards) were often housed in the closed psychiatric wards while awaiting transfer or examination. Another unwise practice, still in vogue in some Army hospitals, was the use of the closed-ward section as a detention ward. When a surgical patient or an attendant got drunk, he was "punished" for a day or two by being placed on this ward, too often along with psychiatric patients. An unhappy identification for the patients!

Because there was an early referral to the hospital of soldiers who were only mildly incapacitated, the inadvisability of placing them in a hospital environment, even on open wards, presented a problem. Once they were subjected to the long, tedious examination and the calm hospital routine, they had a tendency to settle down and enjoy their symptoms and the respite from arduous training or combat. Too often their symptoms became fixed, and they were thereafter a liability to a fighting Army. This was one reason why in the early stages of the war a very small percentage of men were ever returned to duty from the neuropsychiatric wards. It was apparent that strenuous efforts were necessary to keep many of these men out of the hospital if at all possible. This led to the development of the outpatient clinics, the Mental Hygiene Consultation Services, in the basic-training camps. Later, similar outpatient clinics became a part of the routine service of the neuropsychiatric section of every hospital. It was here that further screening and simple treatment could be given while a man continued with his training and duties.

In the summer of 1944 the return of patients from overseas caused an acute shortage of hospital beds for medical and surgical cases. This lack of space happened to coincide with the clearer recognition that the sending of neurotic patients to general hospitals was deleterious to their welfare. These patients did not get along well lounging around in bathrobes on a hospital ward, usually with no opportunity to participate in any activity. Most of them were not incapacitated physically. Although some efforts had been made toward organizing a program of treatment through activities in the neuropsychiatric section of general hospitals, physical facilities and personnel were too insufficient to accomplish much. Many such patients became worse. In fact, some men with neurotic symptoms were hospitalized into real neuroses.

The necessity for providing more general hospital beds for surgical and medical patients forced the establishment of convalescent hospitals. In these a major portion of the organization—always at least one-third of it—was devoted to the treatment of psychoneurotic patients. When they were in full operation, the 12 convalescent hospitals provided treatment for nearly 50 per cent of all the current psychiatric cases. The men lived in barracks under military discipline. In addition to receiving supervision and treatment by a physician, they participated in an unusually varied occupational, educational, and recreational program.

PUBLIC EDUCATION AND THE MISTAKES OF PSYCHIATRY

Finally, two unrelated complications are worthy of report: the difficulties in procuring the release of information about Army psychiatric experience, and psychiatrists' own blunders which complicated their function.

Public education. One of the special complications in the functioning of psychiatry throughout much of the war was the public-relations policy of the Joint Chiefs of Staff as placed in effect by the Joint Security Board. Throughout the war, any release, either to the lay public or the medical profession, had to be reviewed. If deemed necessary, it was censored before it could be sent out of the War Department.

In the initial phases of the war a reasonably free discussion of psychiatric problems was permitted. However, no statistics were released. When the psychiatric casualty rate became so heavy, in the fall of 1943, the Joint Security Board clamped down on the publication of all psychiatric articles, both lay and scientific. Despite this, two significant articles appeared. One was published in

Fortune Magazine.[12] One was released shortly thereafter by the Office of War Information.[13] Both contained inaccurate statistics of psychiatric casualties. Presumably because of these particular articles and the increasing number of neuropsychiatric casualties, a complete black-out was enforced. No information about our losses in man power from psychiatric casualties could be published lest it "give comfort to the enemy."

As an immediate result of this black-out, newspaper reporters and magazine editors sent a barrage of requests for information to the Office of the Surgeon General. When that information was not forthcoming, reporters became suspicious and even more insistent. At the same time medical groups could not discuss any phase of the subject among themselves or present papers dealing with it. By the spring of 1943 nearly 150,000 soldiers had been discharged for psychiatric causes. Yet their communities, which sought information and assistance in planning for their rehabilitation, could not be helped; nor could their families be told (by those of us in the service) how to help.

This black-out was finally lightened late in April, 1944. The subject of psychiatry and the experiences in this field of Army medicine could be discussed. Since no statistics could be released, there was still no way to assist communities in planning intelligently. They could not be told the size of their problem. We in the War Department were suspected of hiding a much bigger problem; we were called on to answer specific incidents; the policy forced us always to be on the defensive.

From the Neuropsychiatry Consultants Division's point of view, subscribed to by the Surgeon General, it seemed desirable that a public education program should be launched. The large number of veterans returning to civilian life with psychiatric diagnoses made the nation more conscious of the field of psychiatry than at any previous time in our history. It seemed to be an appropriate and most propitious time to educate the public in regard to mental health and mental hygiene precepts. Unfortunately, the War Department never undertook this task, nor could the American Psychiatric Association be persuaded to accept the responsibility. The lack of lay understanding was one of the most pressing problems confronting every psychiatrist. The period from 1944 to 1946 still appears to have been the golden opportunity for a well-planned, extensive program of news releases, articles in papers and magazines, and features over the radio and on the screen. What publicity was given was, however, lamentably unplanned and undirected and was often quite erroneous.

Mistakes of military psychiatrists. In listing all these obstacles it is most important to point out those which we in military psychiatry placed in our own

---

12 "The Psychiatric Toll of Warfare," *Fortune,* 28:141, Dec., 1943.
13 Reported in *Sunday Star,* Washington, D.C., Jan. 9, 1944.

path by our own mistakes and shortcomings. First among these was the slowness in indoctrinating psychiatrists with the governing principles of military psychiatry. Only with reluctance did we shift our primary interest from the needs of the individual patient to those of his group. Delay in doing so undoubtedly contributed to the loss of man power and must have aggravated the problems of the line officers.

We expected too much from the induction-center screening and fell in with the overselling of what psychiatry could accomplish at this level. We too often confused laymen and nonpsychiatric medical men by our lingo, by making meaningless diagnoses. We even tried to give a diagnosis as justification for each rejection, after a cursory examination,[14] because regulations said we should.

Initially we were blind to the needs and ignorant of the methods of preventive psychiatry. In this field the problems were hardly touched in comparison with what could and should have been done about them. Before the war few psychiatrists had thought in terms of active measures to prevent mental ill health; almost none had devoted full time and efforts in this direction. Regardless of this, we should have seen that morale factors were mental health factors; that policies controlling mass activities and behavior were all-important in determining individual men's feelings and satisfactions.

Until the war was half over, we, as psychiatrists, failed grossly in not appreciating the tremendous importance of distinguishing between emotional illness and faulty attitudes.[15] As a result, we undoubtedly discharged too many soldiers who should have been handled administratively. We also neglected educating many persons, particularly medical officers, as to this distinction until it was too late to change the accepted practices of disposition. We did not, until late, adequately grasp the relationship of mental health to group attitudes and pressure, nor did we understand how these could be molded, supported, and changed through leadership, orientation, and information. Many of us did not realize the remarkable readjustment capacity and adaptability of the personality under favorable leadership and environment. Too often did we discharge soldiers solely on the basis of the symptoms they presented, rather than consider how environmental support could counteract the cause of these symptoms.

Finally, individual personalities of psychiatrists made some problems. The misplacement of a few undiplomatic or eccentric psychiatrists (even though competent) did much to interfere with the acceptance of our specialty. Also,

---

14 This was changed by *War Department Technical Bulletin, Medical 33,* 21 April 1944.
15 Captain Francis Braceland, Chief of Psychiatry, Bureau of Medicine and Surgery in the Navy, made the indictment that "most psychiatrists entered the military service with insufficient knowledge of the normal reactions to the vicissitudes of everyday life and the slight deviations of young adults under stress, and thus were unprepared for most of the situations which they were to encounter." Braceland, F. J., "Psychiatric Lessons from World War II," *Am. J. Psychiat.,* 103:587-593, Mar., 1947. With this statement, the author was in full agreement.

on more than one occasion a hard-boiled or "organically minded" or narrow-thinking psychiatrist who gained a position of some authority or influence did great damage to the practice of the specialty through his bad or opinionated advice to those in charge. Such people, when able to determine policy, made the practice of much more capable psychiatrists relatively ineffective. Psychiatry has no monopoly on "unusual" characters, but the placement of the wrong men in strategic positions could and did prejudice many individuals against the acceptance of all psychiatrists. For better or worse, in many places this specialty had to be "sold." Unfortunately, success often depended initially on the personality and only secondarily on the professional ability of the medical officer. Given time, a capable man could "deliver the goods," but to be granted even a fair chance to function required great patience, perseverence, and persuasion. Sometimes all efforts were to no avail when the superiors were misguided or too stubborn to be influenced.

All of us engaged in the practice of military psychiatry are well aware of the wide gap between what we should have done and what we did, what we wanted to do and what we were allowed to do. We were never in a position to do much more than attempt to meet belatedly the most pressing needs. What we achieved was the result of the professional ability of many individuals and the devoted application of that ability to intensive hard work with unfailing persistence and determination.

4

THE PERSONALITY OF THE SOLDIER

IN HIS MEDICAL education the doctor-to-be learns about the human body in anatomy. He discovers how the organs work in physiology; how disease is manifest in pathology. In addition, the psychiatrist, in his training, learns how the personality is formed and develops, how it functions, and what its manifestations are in disease. To him such words as "ego," "id," "neurosis," "psychosis," "mental deficiency," and "behavior disorders" become meaningful.

However, as a result of the war some technical psychiatric terms have become part of the everyday vocabulary of the soldier and his civilian relatives. Many people who use them do not know their meaning or comprehend their medical significance. This incomplete understanding has led to confused thinking about emotional reactions. It has also stimulated the popular use of inaccurately descriptive labels for psychiatric patients and illnesses—"psychos," "combat nerves," and many others. A discussion of the many types of maladjustment reactions seen in the Army [1] must therefore be prefaced by some correct though sketchy information about the structure, development, and function of the personality as the psychiatrist understands them.

The psychiatrist conceives of personality as the product of growth and accumulated experience, habits, and memories. Therefore he is interested in the background, the "history" of his patient. Of special interest to the Army psychiatrist were the many statistical studies of the age grouping, marital status, and other characteristics of the American soldier. All of these varied according to the standards of admission in force at different times. Similarly, the psychiatrist is interested in what his patient thinks and how he feels about many problems, both those specific to himself and those related to his environment. Surveys of the attitudes of soldiers, and other reports, were extremely helpful in giving psychiatrists and other Army officers greater understanding for their better dealing with those soldiers. Such surveys, some of which have been

---

[1] Brosin, Henry; Grinker, Roy; and Menninger, William, "Wartime Lessons for Peacetime Psychiatry," *University of Chicago Round Table,* No. 445, Sept. 29, 1946, p. 4.

abstracted,[2] present a background against which to view the "normal" and "abnormal" reactions of men in the Army.

The elementary principles of personality structure, development, and function which are presented on the following pages apply equally to the soldier in the Army and to the man in civilian life. Their external expressions differ only because of a difference in the milieu in which the individual lives.

PERSONALITY STRUCTURE AND FUNCTION

Personality structure. To the psychiatrist the term "personality" means the sum total of the characteristics and reactions, both physiological and psychological, of an individual. "Personality" is not synonymous with "mind" but is inclusive of it. "Personality" encompasses the intellectual and emotional make-up, the physical structure, and the responses of every part of the body. So used, it refers to the individual as a whole. "Personality" might be defined as all that a person has been, all that he is, and all that he hopes to be. Consequently, when we consider the "parts" of the personality, they should be regarded as interrelated functions rather than as anatomical or physical units. They are forces rather than matter.

One approach to the understanding of the personality structure is through consideration of the layers of consciousness. For purely descriptive purposes the personality can be divided into three levels: consciousness, preconsciousness, and unconsciousness. These may be thought of as zones, perhaps comparable to daylight, twilight, and darkness. Consciousness is closest to the surface, adjacent to the external world. Below the conscious zone is the preconscious zone; there is no sharp boundary between these. Names, events, and ideas fade from consciousness through the transition zone of preconsciousness to the deeper level of unconsciousness. Sometimes recall of ideas, events, or memories from the preconscious is easy; sometimes difficult. We are all familiar with the experience of knowing a name well but being unable to remember it, even with effort. The unconscious is beyond the reach of the conscious part of the personality by any ordinary means of contact.

In order to explain human emotions and thought and behavior the psychoanalytic school ascribes to the personality three interrelated systems, each of which has certain functions and characteristics. They are each to some degree dependent upon the others. They are the id, the ego, and the superego. The id, the infantile part of the person, can be described by saying "it wants." The phrase is in the third person because the id includes that part of all of us which often we would rather not claim—our most primitive self. It is in the

---

[2] Appendix C.

unconscious. In the commonly expressed phrase, "something within me made me do it," the "something" refers to the id. The id "wants" because it represents that part of every person that is selfish, that makes unreasonable demands, that gives rise to spontaneous, uncontrolled, and primitive behavior and wishes. In response to the id's request (whatever it may be) the conscious part of the personality—the ego—answers "I will" or "I will not." The ego thus represents rationality, the judgment and the will power that decides whether or not to accede to the demands of the id. The third part of the personality, the superego, speaks up as the conscience or the referee to say, "You must not." The superego is the doubter, the skeptic, the critic; it denies, forbids, or disapproves.

Such a concept as this three-part system must be recognized as a formula— a formula which gives meaning and significance to the internal struggles and consequently the behavior of the individual. It is not an anatomic differentiation. To date these functions have not been localized in any specific part of the brain or body.

At birth the personality is dominated by the id—primitive, asocial, and completely selfish—and is endowed with the two basic energy drives of aggressiveness and erotism. These drives are more broadly described as destructive and constructive impulses and more often expressed as hostility and love. As the ego develops with growth and experience, the child learns to curb his instinctive infantile behavior through the restraint and supervision of parental training. When he controls his aggression he is rewarded with love and gradually learns to return that love. Beginning in his early childhood, he incorporates the parental control function within himself where it becomes the basis of his superego, his conscience. This conscience was of special significance to the soldier in that his own critical standards regarding some kinds of behavior had to be relaxed. His ideals or code, his conscience, had to be displaced to some degree by the conscience of the whole group of individuals of which he was one.

The conscious ego has the continuous function of maintaining contact with the external world and of attempting to help the personality adjust itself to the demands placed upon it by the environment. Simultaneously it must control the superior strength of the id and guide and appropriately modify its expressions of hate and love. When the ego momentarily fails in its function, it is subject to criticism by the superego. This criticism creates anxiety within the personality.

Anxiety thus becomes the signal of distress in personality adjustment. It is indicative of inability to adapt or accept an uncontrolled or inappropriate or threatening impulse. Unless equilibrium and harmony are again established by some solution of the conflict between the ego and the impulse, the individual develops a neurotic symptom. The symptom represents an attempt on the part of the personality to divert the impulse that gives rise to the anxiety. Thus the anxiety may be relieved through forgetting (amnesia), through conversion into a physical complaint or disturbed function, through projecting blame on some outside person or force, through atonement, or through any of many other means.

Anxiety resulting from an internal threat to personality function may or may not be easily differentiated from the apprehension or fear of an external threat in the form of danger. These may resemble each other closely and under prolonged stress may be combined.

The development of the personality. The process of development of the personality is subject to many variations caused by numerous potent factors. The early relationship of the son to his father greatly influences his later acceptance of maturity. During childhood an important struggle takes place in the process of orientation to authority. In the normal development of a boy, competition with and unconscious resentment of parental control are succeeded by the abandonment of these in favor of identification with his parent. The son becomes his father's ally instead of his rival. When he can do so he is able to accept the role of submission to the authority of his father. The soldier developed a relationship and attitudes toward his commanding officer which were patterned after those established previously toward his father. A deviation from this ideal pattern is seen in the son who made no identification with his father and so continued to resent him and his authority. In all subsequent situations where he has to be subservient to a father (authoritarian) figure, he will have difficulty. This was frequently the reason for the maladjustment of a soldier to his leader. The man who defied authority, even as an eccentric daredevil, was a liability, especially in combat. The rash, death-flirting individual was more than likely to threaten the security of his associates unless he was carrying out a solo act.

Relationships between brothers and sisters establish unrecognized patterns of reaction which continue into maturity. Both the positive feeling of affection and the negative one of hostility operate in fraternal contacts, in both children and adults. Attitudes toward friends and associates are influenced by these same patterns. A friend may unconsciously represent a particular sibling (brother or sister), and reactions toward that friend are predetermined by previous relations to that sibling. Since at times brothers and sisters are the real or suspected cause of each others' deprivation, there are times when siblings hate each other regardless of how much they may also love each other. Beloved persons can provoke hatred under certain conditions. They can also have hatred "projected" upon them, i.e., they may be the recipient of hate "displaced" from someone else or carried over from a previous situation.

Army life was conducive to the formation of brotherlike ties between men.

They shared training, experiences, and dangers in 24-hour-day association, week in and week out. This welded together emotionally the members of a squad or crew. In the psychological breakdown of a patient, which was apparently caused by the death of a close pal, the psychiatrist often discovered that a previous sibling relationship was a factor in the emotional upset.

A person "loves" those who contribute to his comfort—physical or psychological. He "hates" those who interfere with or destroy his real or imagined well-being. Because our culture disapproves of hatred, it is usually denied by the ego and repressed to the unconscious. However, what is repressed may have such a strong urge for recognition that it may gain release in disguised form or provoke conflict within the personality.

Personality–environmental struggle. The personality and the environment both subject each other to change. That interaction can be referred to as the "personality-environmental struggle." This is clearly described in my brother's book, *The Human Mind.*[3] As the personality and situation meet, each is affected by the other. As the situation develops, sometimes from minute to minute, the individual has to adapt his conduct to the new demands which are made upon him both externally and internally. If such adaptation provokes a psychological conflict, the outcome can be successful or unsuccessful. Successful adjustment may be dependent upon changes made in the personality or in the situation or in both. In either event success depends upon removing the cause of the conflict or modifying its effect. Maladjustment indicates either a failure of the personality to change its behavior and attitudes sufficiently, or a situation which demands too much. The conflict therefore continues.

The citizen-soldier came from a life in which he faced the day-by-day emergencies with minimal conflict, as the result of an established pattern of living. Also, he was free to choose a different environment if his situation became too uncomfortable. His life in the Army, however, presented many unfamiliar situations which provoked emotional resistance. He had no chance to change his assignment or location. Because regimentation was imposed upon him, any conflict over its acceptance could be resolved only by a change in his own attitude. The situation could not be modified in order to make his adjustment to it less difficult. Therefore, extra adaptability was demanded of the personality. For the soldier's personality not only had to resolve conflicts between new and lifelong tenets of behavior and thought, but also it had to accept an unchangeable environment which continuously threatened its very existence.

Psychological changes required in the soldier. Dynamic alterations in the

[3] Menninger, K. A., *The Human Mind,* 3rd ed., Alfred A. Knopf, New York, 1945, pp. 29-34. A diagrammatic concept was modified and utilized in "Lecture Outline for Officers on Personnel Adjustment Problems," *War Department Technical Bulletin, Medical 12,* 22 February 1944.

personality of the soldier were necessary in order to effect the adjustment from civilian to military life. In the majority of instances these were largely unconscious. Therefore they were automatic. They had to occur if the individual was to meet effectively the demands made upon him.

Of great importance to the new soldier was the necessity to shift part of his investment of affection from familiar individuals to a strange group. Throughout his life he had had a fixed and more or less constant association with certain people—mother, father, siblings, wife, children, and lifelong friends—whose love and interest he shared. These had quite literally made up his personal world. He tried to maintain these ties with his past, but for the major portion of his investment and source of affection while in the military service he had to turn this previously specific love to a diffuse group love. Certain members of his unit gradually became his inner circle and perhaps his chief psychological support. But the greater affection was spent on the group as a whole, into which the emotional life of its individual members was fused. Pride and belief in the platoon or company or Army gave evidence of satisfaction from this emotional investment.

Another essential change was the shift from civilian independence with an opportunity for initiative and self-expression to a dependence upon and submission to orders. Only rarely and to a very limited degree could the soldier act as an individual. The winning of a battle demanded that he be trained to rely on his superior officers and comrades automatically. At times he had to depend upon them for his very life. If separated from them, as in a replacement depot, he felt lost and orphaned. His was a predominately dependent emotional role. While it was difficult for some, this dependence was welcomed by others to whom it brought unconscious satisfaction. It required a man to shed responsibility, to live by the decisions of others, to wait until told what to do, to be the passive recipient of food, clothing, and shelter, such as they were. This entailed a regression to an earlier stage in psychological development. However, it did not require an intellectual regression nor did it lessen the need for a soldier to protect himself. Nor need it be permanent.

This passive relationship grew rapidly. It became acceptable when the soldier felt secure through his confidence in the symbolically all-knowing, all-powerful father, his commanding officer. Subservience to this officer helped him modify previous control of his behavior in order to permit the release of his primitive drive to kill. Only with help from authoritarian figures could the average man accept the shift from a constructive civilian life to a potentially destructive military life. Simmel [4] pointed out that the soldier, even

4 Simmel, E., "War Neuroses," from *Psychoanalysis Today,* ed. by Sandor Lorand, International Universities Press, New York, 1945, pp. 227-248.

before he went into combat, was in the predicament of being threatened both internally and externally. He faced an extremely dangerous external threat of injury or death. Also, there was the internal threat from the anxiety created by the psychological conflict between the necessity to kill and the lifelong training not to. By emotional regression he was able to release the aggressive drive which is latent in everyone but must become active and be directed effectively by the fighting man. The full approval of the father-leader and the sanction of associates helped the soldier to ignore his personal conscience. Where hand-to-hand combat took place, the imminent external threat of being killed was sufficient to overcome the disapproval of the conscience, even in those individuals who, under less threatening circumstances, found difficulty in killing.

There were, of course, many soldiers with combat duties who never had to make the psychological adjustment to the process of actual killing and seeing the effect of their aggression. The bombardiers and the artillerymen rarely, if ever, saw the consequence of their work at close hand. In contrast, the infantry soldier often, if not regularly, was in a position to observe the results of his destructiveness. Consequently there were infantrymen who either could not allow themselves to kill or were unable to continue killing, even under the threat of loss of favor from their leaders and comrades. A commission of civilian psychiatrists, which was sent to the European Theater in 1945, reported briefly the story of a soldier who had been a Y.M.C.A. athletic director and scoutmaster. He had seen extensive combat and had won numerous citations. He had reached such a saturation point: "I never killed anything— never believed in it—couldn't kill a cat. When I first had to kill a German I dreamed about it and worried about it for a week. Now I try not to think about it—I have had to kill so many. But now I can't do it any more." [5]

It is paradoxical that one in our culture should be expected to maim, kill, and destroy, yet that was the required assignment of every fighting soldier. Since psychiatrists had to help soldiers perform the distressful service demanded, they were forced to shift their orientation, as pointed out by Farrell and Appel.[6] As civilian doctors they had to understand and correct abnormal reactions to normal situations. As medical officers they had to help normal personalities maintain their integration under horribly abnormal conditions. The Army psychiatrists saw war as a pathological activity which tended to force the development of psychopathology in its participants.

---

[5] *Medical Reports on Morale and Psychiatry,* No. 17, Office of the Surgeon General, 25 August 1945, p. 24. Reprinted: Bartemeier, L. H.; Kubie, L. S.; Menninger, K. A.; Romano, J.; and Whitehorn, J. C., "Combat Exhaustion," *J. Nerv. & Ment. Dis.,* 104:358-389, Oct., 1946; 489-525, Nov., 1946.

[6] Farrell, M. J., and Appel, J. W., "Current Trends in Military Psychiatry," *Am. J. Psychiat.,* 101:12-19, July, 1944.

The environment of the basic-training camp was not without its grossly abnormal features, as judged by civilian standards. The neuroses developing as a result of training were the same in their psychological dynamics as those developing in combat. There was no difference between a conversion reaction developing in a Georgia training camp from one in the combat zone or on an airfield in Italy. Typical neurotic reactions sometimes developed, as the result of experiences in training as well as in combat, in soldiers who showed little or no predisposition to mental illness. Anderson [7] has given some excellent histories of several fliers in this category. Combat was, of course, even more abnormal; the most stable individual could not face death for days and weeks on end and remain "normal."

Personality disintegration. The personality maintains its integration as long as the conflict between its various components can be resolved. The individual can "adjust" his personality to the demands of the environment or he can "adjust" the environment to satisfy the demands of his personality. When the struggle within the personality or between the personality and the environment cannot be allayed, maladjustment results.

The maladjustment may appear as irritability or as any other emotional response for which there seems to be insufficient reason. The response may last for a few minutes or hours or days. When severe or prolonged or frequent, it can be regarded as a symptom of mental illness. Symptoms may become so numerous or distressing that they are incapacitating. Such a state of affairs has received the popular diagnosis of "mental breakdown." This is a graphic term but is an inaccurate one which is therefore subject to misinterpretation. There are far more instances of individuals who "bend" than of those who "break." Loss in effectiveness and personality integration may be only partial. The change in psychological status usually develops slowly. In a perusal of the personal history of the patient the sudden "break," upon close scrutiny, can nearly always be discovered to have been preceded by indications and earlier signs. However, Army psychiatrists frequently applied the term "breakdown" in the same sense as in its colloquial use in civilian life.

Early in the war there were repeated forecasts that the neurotic or unstable personality would have a lowered resistance to psychological pressure. It was also believed that the adjusted, stable individual could survive military experience because of greater tolerance for strain. However, many psychiatrists who were directly concerned with the problem were forced to a broader point of view. Many studies [8] in the literature have dealt with the so-called "breaking

---

[7] Anderson, R. C., "Neuroses of Peace and War," *Occup. Med.,* 1:121-144, Feb., 1946.

[8] Many psychiatrists have indicated their belief that any soldier, if subjected to sufficient stress over a prolonged period, may reach a "breaking point." E. Wittkower and J. P. Spillane, in *The Neuroses in War,* ed. by E. Miller, The Macmillan Company, New York, 1944, on p. 10

point" of an individual. It often appeared that when stress increased or continued too long, it exceeded the ability of ebbing energy to cope with it. Many psychiatrists believe that some men, regardless of earlier effectiveness, were forced to a point of noneffectiveness which was sometimes brief and sometimes prolonged. In such cases, ego strength was worn down until the cumulative effect of stress reached a place where a minor emergency was the end point of the capacity to adjust. Often such a soldier placed much importance on that final event as the "cause" of his illness. However, the history obtained both from himself and from his associates usually indicated a gradual lessening of his efficiency under a long period of stress. The precipitating incident was like the straw that broke the camel's back. It was not a sudden emotional blow of great specificity for the particular personality but just too much stress for that soldier to manage. These breakdowns were chiefly the result of the environmental stress and not inherent in personality weakness.

The commission of civilian psychiatrists reported:

It is difficult for us to formulate clearly any or all of the determinants of the relative vulnerability of combat soldiers conducive to these developments. We heard from many that "constitutional differences" were significant determinants. We know of no body of data nor any method which allows one to distinguish behavior alleged to be due to certain inherited predispositions from behavior said to result from the effects of certain early life experiences. Theoretically, one would assume that the ostensibly normal person who is able to make and maintain friendly relationships, one who has good home ties, one who is able to tolerate a reasonable amount of pain, danger and deprivation, and one who is able to adjust equally to roles of dependence and responsibility, would have a more or less normal degree of vulnerability—assuming few, if any to be completely invulnerable.[9]

indicated that. G. Roussy (1918), D. Forsyth (1915), R. Dupony (1915), and H. Campbell (1916) expressed their belief on this point on the basis of experience in World War I. It was anticipated in the prewar paper of R. P. Knight and D. W. Orr, "Psychiatric Problems of the Armed Forces in Training and in Combat," *Bull. Menninger Clinic*, 5:176-180, Sept., 1941. It has been expressed by psychiatrists during World War II as follows: Rees, J. R., *The Shaping of Psychiatry by War*, W. W. Norton & Company, Inc., New York, 1945, p. 111; Halloran, R. D., and Farrell, M. J., "Function of Neuropsychiatry in the Army," *Am. J. Psychiat.*, 100:14-20, July, 1943; Murray, J. M., "Psychiatry in the Army Air Forces," *Am. J. Psychiat.*, 100:21-24, July, 1943; Grinker, R. R., and Spiegel, J. P., "Brief Psychotherapy in War Neuroses," *Psychosom. Med.*, 6:123-131, Apr., 1944; Kennedy, F., "Functional Nervous Disorders in Last War, Spanish War and Now," *Trans. Am. Neurol. Assoc.*, 69:79-83, 1943; Farrell, M. J., "Developments in Military Neuropsychiatry," *J. Iowa M. Soc.*, 34:387-391, Sept., 1944; Hanson, F. R., in the introduction to *Combat Psychiatry Among American Ground Forces in the Mediterranean Area.* (To be published.) Many statistical studies have indicated a considerable number of psychiatric casualties who gave little evidence of predisposition: Weinberg's study of 276 battle casualties returned to the United States for treatment showed 40 per cent relatively nondisposed to neuroses before induction: Weinberg, S. K., "The Combat Neuroses," *Am. J. Sociology*, 51:465-467, Mar., 1946. The statistics cited earlier in the chapter from Grinker, *et al.*, indicated that between 50 and 66 per cent gave little evidence of precombat neurotic tendencies.
9 *Medical Reports on Morale and Psychiatry*, No. 17, Office of the Surgeon General, 25 August 1945, p. 18. Reprinted: Bartemeier, L. H.; Kubie, L. S.; Menninger, K. A.; Romano, J.; Whitehorn, J. C., "Combat Exhaustion," *J. Nerv. & Ment. Dis.*, 104:358-389, Oct., 1946; 489-525, Nov., 1946.

Chisholm [10] never agreed entirely with the theory of a "breaking point" for everyone. He felt that it was such a variable, even in the same individual, that the concept was not only useless and generally misleading but, if widely known among soldiers, might be a threat to the integrity of a fighting unit. This last point was refuted by the fact that many combat soldiers were reassured by a belief in the existence of variable vulnerability to combat strain.

Meager statistics suggest that some soldiers continued to stand stress indefinitely. There is the saying that "old soldiers never die." This may have a grain of truth in it. Experienced fighters have learned how to protect themselves better. In addition they have developed a tolerance to combat and established a tempo of life under fire which is not known to the nonprofessional, newly conscripted soldier. However, even some of these men, after long periods of service, break down emotionally.

The psychiatrist saw soldiers who had developed protective mechanisms which had enabled them to carry on for a long time. Then some apparently minor episode precipitated a pathological state which rendered the soldier ineffective. The real basis of the illness was to be found in the specificity of that episode to cause hurt to that personality; it hit the Achilles heel.

The training, experiences, and relationships—in other words, the total environment of infancy, childhood, and adolescence—mold the reaction patterns of each personality. In the process of growing up no one escapes having at least minor psychological wounds or injuries. Some such experiences may have been severe enough to leave deep imprints on the personality; some, though apparently minor in their effect, can be the basis of later neurotic behavior. Most, if not all, persons have an unrecognized, vulnerable facet to their personalities which is related to such a psychologically difficult or traumatic experience in early life. Under most circumstances they are reasonably successful in isolating and completely forgetting (repressing) the experience. Thus, it causes neither awareness nor difficulty in adjustment.

However, when a painful emotional experience occurs in later life which closely parallels the earlier one, the reaction to the new stress is similar to that of the initial one. For example: Toward his younger brother, a small boy

---

[10] Chisholm, Maj. Gen. G. Brock, Director General, Royal Canadian Army Medical Corps; Statement at Meeting of Association for Research in Nervous and Mental Diseases, New York, Dec., 1944. J. B. Dynes, in "Mental Breaking Point," *New England J. Med.,* 234:42-45, Jan. 10, 1946, was even more positive in stating that experience at the naval receiving station does not support the widely accepted theory that all men have mental breaking points. His experience did not include the toughest job in war—the combat infantryman. Anderson regarded as trite the saying that "every man has his breaking point." For every individual there could probably be an intolerable situation which would vary greatly as to type and quantity, depending on past experiences. This does not mean that all persons in any group exposed to maximum quantitative external stress would develop neuroses. Anderson, R. C., "Neuroses of Peace and War," *Occup. Med.,* 1:121-144, Feb., 1946.

felt not only affection but also great hostility because of jealousy. Then in early childhood that little brother died. Part of the bereavement of the survivor was related to his sense of guilt about his occasional wishes that he did not have a brother to rival him in winning his parents' affection. In time this was forgotten. When, as a combat soldier, a brotherlike comrade was killed, the long repressed sense of guilt was activated. The traumatic event in adult life was so like that of childhood that it touched the vulnerable spot in his personality [11] and precipitated a psychological crisis.

Predisposition to mental illness. At the present time there is no certain way to anticipate which personalities can or cannot adjust themselves to particular situations. By questioning an individual, his relatives, and his associates, the psychiatrist or psychiatric social worker can procure a detailed record of remembered events and thoughts which is called a "case history." This history can give clues to the influence of his inheritance and environment upon that person. It can reveal obvious personality weaknesses. Certain psychological tests present a cross section of a personality for psychiatric evaluation. But both of these processes, which are most properly used together, are time consuming and not always too revealing even when well done.

Even with sufficient time allowed at the induction examination to permit the gathering of pertinent information, only those persons could be eliminated who were grossly maladjusted. Too often the psychiatrists employed in the selection process were inexperienced. But, regardless of time or experience, no positive criteria for evaluation for combat service have yet been determined. It is certainly true that many men were accepted for service whose predisposition to mental disorder should have been discernible. Some psychiatrists in military hospitals felt strongly that many of their patients should have been rejected at the induction center. However, in view of the fact that everyone has neurotic tendencies, a more serious mistake of psychiatrists was their failure to recognize the remarkable capacity of soldiers to adjust themselves, even those with life-long histories of neurotic responses. Highly neurotic individuals achieved outstanding success for a prolonged period when able to serve under strong leadership and with strong conviction as to the importance of their service. On the other hand, men, who presumably had led well-adjusted lives previously, developed neurotic illness after short exposure to combat.

Many of the soldiers who broke down in training would have been ac-

---

[11] This was the point of view of some psychiatrists in World War I. "It is evident that we must look within the individual for the most important factors in the etiology of a war neurosis but heredity and environment may not be excluded." Zabriski, E. G., and Brush, A. L., "Psychoneuroses in War Time," *Psychosom. Med.*, 3:295-329, July, 1941.

ceptable for Army service on the basis of a study of their life histories. Most of the men who developed psychiatric disorders in combat would have been regarded as "normal" at any previous time. They displayed no conspicuous neurotic behavior and gave no history of serious maladjustment. Even if they could have been "spotted" and screened out with sufficient psychiatric study, men who were able to give excellent service for long periods before breaking should not have been eliminated. However, many susceptible persons could not have been detected prior to their illness because their survival or the development of mental ill health depended upon many factors besides that of personality structure.

Efforts were made to study samples of combat casualties to determine the possible predictability of breakdown.[12] The research section of the Information and Education Division compared 400 psychiatric casualties with 1,750 infantry soldiers who did not break down in combat. Its findings indicated only minor differences and furnished no real criteria for guidance.

Of some significance is the fact that statistical comparisons invariably showed a history of neurotic adjustment or illness prior to Army service in a higher percentage of the psychiatric patients than of normal soldiers. Fisher,[13] in an evacuation hospital in the South Pacific, judged that 79 per cent of 500 patients admitted to the neuropsychiatric section had been neurotic before entering the service. Henderson and Moore went so far as to state that "war neuroses are 'made in America' and only come to light or are labeled in combat."[14] Grinker[15] and his associates made a questionnaire survey of fliers with "combat fatigue" and of a control group of normals. Of the psychiatric casualties, one-third to one-half admitted significant degrees of precombat anxiety and neurotic trends as compared with only 11 per cent of the control group.

However, the conclusion reached by many military psychiatrists was that, regardless of the strength or weakness of the personality, there was a point at which a man decompensated. This point varied greatly depending upon many factors both within the personality and in the environment. Also, the effect of a specific trauma upon the personality which otherwise seemed

12 *Report on an I and E Study in the Mediterranean Theater*. Subject: Report 114-M4, The Prediction of Neuropsychiatric Breakdown in Combat, 13 September 1945. Reference No. A9 330.11-488, I&E-O.
13 Fisher, E. D., "Psychoneurosis as Observed in the Armed Forces," *Bull. U.S. Army Med. Dept.* 7:939-947, Nov., 1947.
14 Henderson, J. L., and Moore, M., "The Psychoneuroses of War," *New England J. Med.*, 230:273-278, Mar. 9, 1944.
15 Grinker, R. R.; Willerman, B.; Bradley, A. D.; and Fasotvsky, A., "A Study of Psychological Predisposition to the Development of Operational Fatigue," *Am. J. Orthopsychiat.*, 16:191-214, Apr., 1946.

resistant to stress could indicate a vulnerable point. It became obvious that the question was not *who* would break down, but *when*.

This is a brief and simplified version of how the personality functions and of the psychological problems inherent in becoming an American soldier in wartime. It is presented so that his response to the stresses and strains to which he was subjected can be better understood.

5

THE ENVIRONMENT OF THE SOLDIER: ITS STRESSES AND STRAINS

He [the soldier] knows the real story [of what war is]: he feels it sharply, but he couldn't tell it to you, himself. If I plucked one from his foxhole now and put this microphone before him, he would only stammer and say something like this: "Well, uh, I was lying there, and, uh, I saw this Jerry coming at me with a bayonet, and. uh, well. . . ." That's how most of them would talk. I know because I have tried them. If the soldier can't tell you what happened to his stomach at that moment, what went on in his beating heart, why the German's belt buckle looked as big as a shining shield —if he can't tell you, no onlooker ever can.

The army treats all men alike, but the war does not. Not this war. It's too big and far flung. It has a thousand faces and a hundred climates. It has a fantastic variety of devilish means for testing a boy's brain, for stretching his nerves, for making him ashamed or making him proud, for exposing his heart or for burying his heart. It treats no two exactly alike: and so even two soldiers from the same front sometimes don't understand each what the other is talking about.

Generals—and journalists—use big, standard words like "teamwork" or "soldierly behavior," which are like interchangeable parts and can be fitted into the machine without thinking. But the soldier's handbook gives little guidance on such matters as how to learn the patience of a saint, how to quench bitterness when his officers make a costly mistake, or how to master the homesickness that comes at sunset.

Who is to relate these things, which make up the real but secret story of the war? Who is to reconstruct, in scenes and acts, the drama of that American on the desolate airfield in the Gulf of Aden? The one who sat for three hours, unmindful of the crushing heat, his eyes fixed upon a stone. He had been there eighteen months, and he didn't talk to his comrades any more.

What about the soldier with the child's face, who stumbled from the exploding field near Anzio with not a mark on his body, but with his eyes too big, his hands senselessly twisting a towel, and his tongue darting in and out between his teeth?

What was it that had expanded in the soul of a young man I first knew when he was a press-agent lieutenant three years ago? Then, he was rather silly and talked too much, and his men smiled behind his back: I met him next in a French forest. He had learned control and dignity. He was a major commanding a fighting battalion, and the general was quiet when he spoke.

There was a regimental colonel at Anzio who received notices one night that he could leave next day for Des Moines, where his business was prosperous and his family large. His division had been decimated, but this man's life was now assured. Why, at dawn, at his regular hour, did he risk the mortar shells and crawl on hands and knees from foxhole to foxhole, not missing one, just to speak a confident word to his men?

Who could really explain about that young corporal with the radio post deep in the Burma jungle? The one who rose suddenly from his bunk in the night and walked straight into the woods, walking westward.

Only the soldier really lives the war. The journalist does not. He may share the soldier's outward life and dangers, but he cannot share his inner life because the same moral compulsion does not bear upon him. The observer knows he has alternatives of action: the soldier knows he has none. It is the mere knowing which makes the difference. Their worlds are very far apart, for one is free, the other a slave.

This war must be seen to be believed, but it must be lived to be understood. We can tell you only of events, of what men do. We cannot really tell you how or why they do it. We can see, and tell you, that this war is brutalizing some among your sons and yet ennobling others. We can tell you very little more.

War happens inside a man. It happens to one man alone. It can never be communicated. That is the tragedy—and perhaps the blessing. A thousand ghastly wounds are really only one. A million martyred lives leave an empty place at only one table. That is why, at bottom, people can let wars happen, and that is why nations survive them and carry on. And, I am sorry to say, that is also why in a certain sense you and your sons from the war will be forever strangers.

If, by the miracles of art and genius, in later years two or three among them can open their hearts and the right words come, then perhaps we shall all know a little of what it was like. And we shall know, then, that all the present speakers and writers hardly touched the story.[1]

When a professional writer who has spent many months with troops in combat cannot "describe" war, it seems futile for the rest of us to try. It is, however, possible to pick out of the total experience of war certain specific experiences for detailed consideration. There were big problems and little problems that with some unrecognized or unanalyzable ones added up to the stress of the hell and horror and "glory" of battle.

Because of the emphasis on the study of personality structure and function during recent years, the most frequent approach to the interpretation of behavior has been in terms of changes within the personality. On the basis of Army experience, it would seem that insufficient attention has been given to the evaluation of current environmental stresses. War altered somewhat this focus of emphasis for some of us. This came about because there was little time to study the psychodynamics in each individual case. Also, the psychiatrist himself was exposed to the same stresses as his patients, in greater or lesser degree. Therefore, he was more keenly aware of these and of the varying abilities of individuals to withstand them. Furthermore, the role of adjustment demands as the cause of psychiatric illness in a soldier was more

---

[1] A broadcast Eric Sevareid made from London before the final decision in the European Theater of War. Reprinted from *Not So Wild a Dream* by Eric Sevareid, by permission of Alfred A. Knopf, Inc. Copyright 1946 by Eric Sevareid, pp. 493-495.

grossly apparent to the psychiatrist than it is in the study of the average neurotic patient in civilian life. For instance, in a combat situation of even brief exposure, it was obvious that emotional feelings would be seriously affected. Comparable external threat is rare in civilian life. When present, it never demands more than momentary adjustment and is rarely shared by many people. Only in modern war do many hear and see and wait for death for hours and days and weeks on end.

The following discussion is limited to environmental stress. It is not intended thus to minimize the importance of the internal stress, the psychological forces, the power of the id, the authority of the conscience. Rather it is to emphasize those factors which seemed very important and were so conspicuous in the special environments provided by military life.

It is not possible to localize sharply the stresses which were most productive of symptoms at a specific time or situation in the total experience of the soldier. Many were operative from induction to discharge. There were a few, however, which, either because of the timing or because of a particular assignment, occurred in different phases of Army experience. For convenience in discussion, the various types of stress are classified by the period and type of service in which their occurrence was predominant: those seen in the basic-training camp in this country; [2] those seen on the trip overseas and in non-combat activities prior to combat; [3] those seen in combat; [4] those seen in the period of redeployment from one theater to another,[5] and finally those specific to officers.

STRESSES DURING TRAINING PERIOD

The number-one factor which affected the adjustment of the new soldier was the loss of the emotional support in his previous environmental situation. The efficiency and happiness of the normal individual are dependent upon the emotional support which is given him by the people and events in his environment. Thus, the incentive of the average man to work is to provide well for his family and his home; his job is made satisfying by the mutual

---

[2] The soldier went from the induction center, to the reception center, to camp where he received 17 weeks of training in basic military subjects. He was then assigned to a unit for special training for a varying period of time. One of the best descriptions of the changes from civilian to soldier was given by M. H. Maskin and L. L. Altman in "Military Psychodynamics, Psychological Factors in Transition from Civilian to Soldier," *Psychiatry*, 6:263-269, Aug., 1943.

[3] Most units had a further period of training overseas. All had periods of waiting.

[4] Never more than 7 per cent of the Army was engaged in front-line combat at any one time. During the war, it is estimated that between 2,000,000 and 3,000,000 men had some combat experience.

[5] From VE-day, May 8, 1945, until VJ-day, September 2, 1945, "redeployment" was a major activity of the Army.

confidence felt between himself and his associates, his employer, or employees; life becomes more satisfying and rich through his friends; upon these relationships he becomes emotionally dependent. The man who went into the wartime Army left all of these abruptly. This loss was perhaps more significant for the relatively immature young man, whose dependence on his original home was still great, and on the husband-father of a closely knit family unit.

There are only suggestive figures available,[6] but thousands and thousands of men left their homes for the first time when they were inducted into the Army. For many additional men it was the first time to leave home for any extended period. The sudden and complete loss of established emotional supports, which are so important to everyone, made the soldier particularly vulnerable to the stresses that confronted him upon his entrance into military life.

The social organization of the Army was very different from that of our civilian society. It was characterized by a hierarchy of rank and authority which controlled every member through a "chain of command." An order or directive issued from the highest headquarters had to be transmitted through the headquarters of the corps, the division, the regiment, the battalion, and the company, and was finally issued to the soldier. In reverse, any special request from the soldier (such as for a transfer) had to be transmitted upward through the same channels to the headquarters having jurisdiction to act on the request. No soldier or officer could circumvent his superior. The society was rigidly stratified into officers and enlisted men who had no off-duty contacts or social relations.

The recruit was thrust unprepared into this social structure to begin a new life. The customs and rules were such as to make the average soldier feel that his civilian life had become foreign and almost alien to him. It was a self-contained society,[7] so that, regardless of his background, a man might be given any type of job that needed to be done in order to feed, house, maintain, and care for the group. After only a few days in the Army he became aware that being a soldier isolated him from a civilian status and gave significance

---

[6] "A Study of Psychoneurotics in the Army," made by the Morale Services Division Report B-107, Headquarters Army Service Forces, Washington, D.C., 23 May 1944. Among other questions was one relative to the emancipation from parents. In this study, 40 per cent of the cross section of normals and 37 per cent of the neurotic patients never had lived away from their parents.

A second question was asked as to the longest time that the individual had been away from his family or anybody related to him, and the cross section indicated that 7 per cent of the normals and 10 per cent of the neurotic patients had never been away; 12 per cent of the cross section of normals and 15 per cent of the neurotic patients had been away less than 1 week; and an additional 21 per cent of the cross section and 19 per cent of the neurotic patients had been away between 1 week and 1 month.

[7] The social structure of the Army was well discussed, making the above points, by H. Brotz and E. Wilson in "Characteristics of Military Society," *Am. J. Sociology*, 51:371-373, Mar., 1946.

to "You're in the Army now." [8] He was later to learn that he and his associates were likely to be referred to as so many "bodies," as if they were cattle or trucks or rounds of ammunition. Unfortunately, high-ranking officers in positions of planning operations tended to look on man power as they did upon matériel. The enlisted soldier became acutely aware of this.

The demands of the new life. One of the first new experiences of a recruit was the regimentation [9] of Army life. He found himself herded into an induction center. He was lost in a crowd in which he rarely knew any other person. He lined up nude with 100, or often more, other men, like so much livestock. He exchanged his name for a number; he became a cog in a huge, impersonal machine, the Army, in order to do a job in an impersonal, machine-age war. He immediately had to become sheeplike and be led or "follow the line" from one examination to another. He was given various tests. He was provided with clothing which might or might not fit. He learned quickly to cue up for all formations. He was introduced to a system in which he got up and went to bed by the bugle, and in which every other movement and activity was rigidly scheduled. Regardless of his feelings or habits, he was forced to be prompt, to be exact, to be neat. Regardless of his background he was given assignments which one day might be scrubbing pans and another day picking up cigarette butts. Always he functioned with a group that was just one small unit within a larger one.

Discipline. Though essential, discipline was a stress factor of considerable importance in the first days of Army life. For the submissive, insecure person, it may have been a support. Later it became such for most soldiers. However, in the average American it stimulated resentment initially. A man was "ordered" around by his noncommissioned officer. He was introduced to "military courtesies" and had to salute his officers. Occasionally there was a man who, as a result of tactless handling, harbored the feeling that the salute was a forced admission of his inferiority to his officers, instead of a courteous greeting. Along with his individualism he lost his freedom of action, of choice. Never before had he lived in an environment in which every move was dictated by orders as to what he must do and when and how he must do it.

Strenuous physical demands. It was a universal experience that during the first weeks of basic training a soldier went to bed so tired that his muscles ached. The daily program was full, and it was the same, regardless of variation of age or previous physical condition. The required early rising, followed

---

[8] Hollingshead, A. B., "Adjustment to Military Life," *Am. J. Sociology,* 51:439-447, Mar., 1946.
[9] The lectures given to new recruits by psychiatrists in basic-training camps outlined in *War Department Technical Bulletin, Medical 21,* 15 March 1944, included a discussion of regimentation. An illustration of what the psychiatrist said on this subject is given by R. R. Cohen, "Factors in Adjustment to Army Life; Plan for Prevention by Mass Psychotherapy," *War Med.,* 5:83-91, Feb., 1944.

by a long day of strenuous physical activity often ending with a study period in the evening, was a stress of major proportions. It was not surprising that the orthopedic clinic was continuously filled with trainees who complained about their backs and knees and feet.

Lack of privacy. Another major stress for some individuals, unusually sensitive men, was the presence of someone else 24 hours a day. Most soldiers accepted it quickly, but for others to do so was a big hurdle. The soldier had no choice of his bunk or platoon mates. He had little choice as to the time for taking a shower, or making his personal toilet. To many men, it was a distinct shock to go into a large latrine and see a dozen bare porcelain toilets lined up in a totally exposed row. One never had a chance to be alone. He lived 24 hours of the day in a group. His only home base to which he could go when not on duty was his bunk. But usually his free time was that of the other men in his unit, and thus the barracks were likely to be filled. This close and continuous proximity to other men was a special stress for the latent homosexual.

Frustrations. These began the first day of Army life and continued until the last day of service. They were more acute at first because a man had to make a conscious effort to accept the fact that his individual and personal wishes did not count for much. He could not ask "how" or "why"; an order was an order. Any ideas a soldier, or even an officer, might have about his orders did not matter.[10] Obedience had to be prompt and without question. Army life has been described as made up of being "in a great hurry only to wait." The waiting, with its inactivity, was an intense frustration for most men. When that waiting was coupled with uncertainty about what would follow, the stress was greatly increased.

There were many personal frustrations. A man had no choice about his food; he either took it or left it. He could not take time out when he wanted to; if he asked for leave in time of war, unless for an emergency, he might not get it. An extremely important frustration which was imposed by Army life and was a cause of special stress, had to do with the modification in the sexual life of the civilian soldier.[11]

A complicated type of frustration was woven into the structure of the Army. Nearly every soldier and officer gained an impression of excessive buck passing, red tape, formality, endless paper work, confusion, and rigid regulation. From the private to the general, one was handicapped by the requirement of authorization for nearly everything he wanted to accomplish. Often he could not get to tell his story, or if he could, it was not to the right

---

[10] Sevareid, Eric, *Not So Wild a Dream,* Alfred A. Knopf, New York, 1946, p. 366. He reported very vividly a general's protest against an order in the Italian Campaign. The protest did no good.
[11] See Chap. 16.

man. Many must be the tales of such experiences. The axiom of obey first and question afterward fell short because too often there was not a chance to question. This state of affairs was the result of the combination of the dictatorial nature of the Army and human frailty. During the war it was aggravated because of the huge size of the machine, the speed with which it had to function, the necessary ignoring of personal wishes and needs, and the mediocrity of some individuals in positions of authority.

One generally assumed, often correctly, that he was stymied by ignorance, stupidity, or prejudice concerning his project in all those who obstructed his progress by differing in the interpretation of regulations. One of the best humorous stories of the war was so widely acclaimed because it was illustrative of the dilemma of many. A psychiatrist at Walter Reed received an emergency call from the director of a division in the Pentagon. Upon his arrival, the general explained to the doctor that he had recently acquired an officer in his division who during his first day of service had moved his desk from one room to another. During the second day he had moved into still another room, and the third day he moved into the lavatory. The general felt that the new man must be mentally unwell and asked the psychiatrist to examine him. The psychiatrist went to the men's room and found the man working away at his desk and quite open to conversation. The psychiatrist tactfully led up to the question of why he had moved his desk there, of all places; the prompt response of the officer was that it was the only place where people seemed to know why they were there and what they were doing.

The Pentagon was not the only place where confusion seemed to reign, and with it insecurity and uncertainty. This was not as important, however, as the hopelessness that a man felt when confronted with a bad situation which he could not correct, because of lack of understanding, unfairness, or just plain delay. Between an enlisted man and an officer, between one officer and another, a request or recommendation could be stopped by 10 people; between Guadalcanal and Washington, it could be stopped by 50 people! One truly wonders how the Army accomplished so much with so many cooks stirring the broth, so many "channels," with so many way stations, so many immature power-bent officers, from lieutenants to generals! But the Army's accomplishments were not sufficient comfort or satisfaction to ease the stress of the frustrations to the individual.

Assignment. There were two features in the assignment of an officer or soldier in the Army which were always potential, and in many instances real factors of major stress. Throughout an Army career, there was always uncertainty, first, as to whether or not a man would be assigned to a job that he could do, and, second, if so, how long he would be permitted to remain there. The man with special talents who came into the Army looked forward hopefully to the utilization of those talents.

Every enlisted man, regardless of his ability, went through the same basic training. After that it was never possible to anticipate with assurance what his assignment might be except in those comparatively rare special services such as medicine. Even in this field there were misassignments.[12] Therefore, a soldier was concerned as to just how he would be allowed to serve. Despite a very elaborate system of classification of various types of special jobs, it was impossible to employ correctly the special talents of every member of the Army. In the first place there were only 800 different jobs in the Army, in contrast to 8,000 in civilian life.[13] There was no civilian counterpart of the infantry "doughfoot" or the artilleryman, or the bombardier. In reality, every man, other than the professional soldier who was trained to kill the enemy, was misassigned. Yet the chief function of the Army was to fight. While it needed a large supporting organization, it could use only a limited number of specialists. The highest priority for man power was for combat soldiers, regardless of the previous civilian experience.

Where weeks of uncertainty, and perhaps hoping against hope as to the type of assignment, were followed by misassignment, an individual sometimes became a psychiatric casualty. The illness resulted from a combination of lack of understanding on the part of the patient, frustration of his personal wishes, and, no doubt in some cases, error on the part of the Army. However good the reason, many officers and soldiers felt so strongly that they were being inappropriately or inadequately utilized that it seriously affected their ability to function. Their complaint that the Army was unappreciative of their potential contribution and was "wasting them" was often justified; [14] probably no human activity is so wasteful as war, in man power as well as in matériel.

Another common complaint, unfortunately also sometimes justifiable, came

---

[12] An internist might be assigned to surgery, or vice versa. As far as psychiatry was concerned, such misassignment was rare, and through the presence of consultants in all Service Commands and theaters, such individuals were usually quickly reassigned. Following the loss of the consultants by demobilization, such slips occurred more frequently.

[13] "The Evaluation, Classification and Assignment of Military Personnel in the United States Army," *War Department Pamphlet* 12-8, 28 July 1944.

[14] One of the loud and frequently reiterated complaints concerned the wastage of doctors. Particularly in 1942 and 1943, because many had little or no clinical work, doctors were wasted like every other group of specialists. Many individuals (doctors included) failed to accept one fundamental necessity for a successful prosecution of war—preparation. The War Department could not wait until D-day and then recruit the doctors. In 1942 no one could foresee the date or location of D-day. Everyone knew it was coming and all had to be in readiness. This preparation and training did keep many physicians relatively or completely idle in so far as doing medical work. But among the complainers I rarely encountered any with a practical solution. Certainly, once the fighting began, there were few doctors in medical installations who had enough time. Most of them were greatly overworked. More of the terrible waste of war!

from the soldier who was "kicked around," i.e., shifted from one place to another, from one job to another. This did occur sometimes in error. In other instances it happened because a man who may have far overrated himself was ineffective and so was moved about in an effort to find the place for his best service.

Danger, without doubt, was the most important stress to which a soldier was subject. As a cause of fear it produced more psychiatric casualties than any other single factor.[15] It was, of course, greatest in combat. However, the soldier became aware of it even in basic training. A man came into the Army knowing full well that in the normal course of events his chief job was likely to be killing and trying to avoid being killed.[16] He was made aware promptly of the power of lethal weapons. A major emphasis was placed on how to protect himself from the enemy. For better or for worse, one of the common incentives in training was to arouse fear as a protective device. Many instructors tried to stimulate soldiers to learn self-protection by bluntly telling them that unless they did so they would "all be dead ducks." The trainee soon learned the statistical chances of his survival on the basis of his specific assignment. Pilots and bombardiers had a fairly accurate estimate of the life expectancy of their jobs. Because of the significance of fear in combat, it was deemed advisable to discuss the subject freely and frankly even with the trainees in their basic-training courses. Consequently it was included as the main subject in one of the three lectures on personal adjustment which were given by the psychiatrist.[17]

There were three other fears of which the beginning soldier became conscious. One of these was the fear of punishment. Every soldier knew that the infraction of even the simplest order, such as being late for formation or the

---

[15] Some figures suggestive of the element of danger even in basic training were given by Bick. In an outpatient psychiatric clinic in a basic-training camp, a comparison was made between the diagnostic categories of patients seen in January, 1944, and January, 1946. In approximately an equal number of patients seen, there were 51 per cent of the patients diagnosed as anxiety reaction in 1944 as compared with only 8 per cent of the patients seen in the same month in 1946. This difference is interpreted by Bick as related to the fear of the danger of combat which was felt by the soldiers during their training in wartime. Because the selection methods at induction after VJ-day were not as effective in eliminating mental deficiency and character disorders (psychopathic states), these occurred in a larger percentage, and other diagnostic groups were proportionally lower. Bick, J. W., Jr., "Observations on Current Army Psychiatric Problems. Comparison of Outpatient Records of January 1944 and January 1946," *J. Nerv. & Ment. Dis.,* 105:73-76, Jan., 1947.

[16] Chisholm suggested an interesting cultural aspect of this problem. He called attention to the emphasis in English-speaking countries on "safety first," with the inculcation in the child's conscience of the moral principle that he must take no chances of getting hurt. Children are taught to abhor their aggressive urges, to be ashamed of and repress their desires to hurt or kill. Fear has been made taboo after childhood. All of these Chisholm regards as factors decreasing the soldier's capacity to face danger, thus increasing the number of neuropsychiatric casualties. Chisholm, G. B., "Some Factors in the High Rate of Neuropsychiatric Casualties," *Bull. Menninger Clinic,* 8:36-38, Mar., 1944.

[17] *War Department Technical Bulletin, Medical 21,* 15 March 1944.

failure to carry out a duty, was not only punishable but usually resulted in punishment. This discipline was very necessary, particularly as support for the laggard, the careless, and the thoughtless individual. Nonetheless it was an added stress for those who feared authority and for those who had difficulty in accepting discipline. Perhaps most conspicuous in officers' training camps was the fear of failure. This was certainly no different from its analogue in any civilian situation. However, it was the cause of the constant concern of many men and undoubtedly produced extreme anxiety in some.

A third type of fear in some individuals was of their own aggressions. This is seen commonly in psychiatric patients. In the course of treatment, the psychiatrist discovers that a powerful force in the patient's personality is a desire to harm others—friend, employer, mate, or even a small child. Often the person has no conscious awareness of this aggressive tendency. When he does recognize the presence of such a desire, he is terrified by it.

In the Army, training to kill often activated such an anxiety. To some recruits, the rifle [18] unconsciously represented a means of expressing his aggressions. His introduction to it and its use precipitated acute emotional distress. The great majority of men had never handled a gun before, and for many their attitude was colored by their respect for a lethal weapon and the memory of parental admonitions about the danger of firearms. For a few, it stimulated a fear of their own aggressions. There were those who were afraid to shoot it; some who could not permit themselves to handle it; some who, despite intellectual capacity, could not learn its parts. Such anxiety led to the referral of many soldiers to the mental hygiene unit in the basic-training camp.

Competition. In basic-training camp a difficult stress for many soldiers was the constant competition. All soldiers, regardless of physical, intellectual, or emotional endowment and development, were assigned to the same course of training. In the Army, the dullard, the man with a slight physical or emotional handicap, all had to try to make the grade of the group. Minor impairments or handicaps of many men might not have interfered with their civilian lives because of their adjustment to them. However, there was no way to tailor-make military training to the individual. There is no doubt that in some instances the speed, the strenuous physical exertion, and the element of competition intensified the neurotic tendencies of many men. There were special features in the training which were particularly difficult. In rifle practice, for example, there was often tremendous pressure placed on individuals to "qualify."

---

[18] This subject, with these and many other illustrations, was discussed in detail in an excellent study titled "Fear of the Rifle Among Trainees," by one of our more experienced mental hygiene unit psychiatrists, Dr. Harry E. August. This manuscript is on file in the Historical Division of the Office of the Surgeon General and will probably be included in one of the clinical historical volumes from this office.

The stresses in basic-training camps were felt the more keenly because of the necessary organization of these units. They were essentially temporary assignments where the soldier went for a relatively short period of time. While there he knew that he would be assigned to a permanent unit at the end of the period. His officers knew also that they were only momentarily in this unit. Consequently, it was the unusual officer who would or could develop a close personal interest in each trainee under his jurisdiction. The trainees, knowing that they would be separated, made few close friends within the group. This temporary organization, therefore, furnished little opportunity for the formation of new emotional ties to compensate for those the soldier had lost in joining the Army.

Personal problems. Comparatively few men came into the Army or remained there any length of time without being troubled by personal problems. These were concerned with the soldier's immediate environment or, more often, with the situation at home.[19] There was no one [20] with whom to talk about his problems except his associates, and in some instances his problems concerned his adjustment to these—his bunkmate or corporal or sergeant. Personal problems at home became precipitating factors in emotional disturbances. Sometimes these were social, sometimes familial, sometimes economic. A special stress which affected the soldier, many times at a particularly vulnerable period, were doubts about the faithfulness of his fiancée or his wife.

It might have been wise to have had a nation-wide educational course in letter writing to soldiers. There were literally thousands of instances in which families who either knew no better, or perhaps saw no other course, reported to the soldier in a far-off post or in an overseas area about the troubles at home: the family was hard-pressed economically; someone was critically ill; or the family was going to have to move out of the house. Mail was irregular and uncertain; any change for the better, even though dispatched promptly, might take weeks to reach its addressee. The officer or the soldier could never do anything about such problems except worry. He had not really relinquished his dependence on the support from home, and so such news turned out to be an additional stress.

In addition, there were the minor foci of irritation from home about which most soldiers knew and felt strongly. They were, therefore, important factors in lowering morale.[21] Overseas soldiers could not understand or sympathize with the strikes that occurred in this country. Resentment was invariably stirred

---

19 "Mental Reconditioning," *What the Soldier Thinks,* No. 8:3, Aug., 1944.
20 The chaplain, personal-affairs officer, and Red Cross workers were frequently the outlet and a source of help, but they were not always handy and in some cases were not the desired choice.
21 This subject has been outlined and documented in detail by Maj. Stephen W. Ranson, "Psychiatric Effects on the Troops of Defective Civilian Attitudes and Behavior," on file in Historical Division, Office of the Surgeon General.

up by news of men who had stayed at home and were reported to be making lots of money in defense industries. Soldiers were angered by news that "business was going on as usual." Their intelligence told them that it should go on. But since their own lives had been upset and they had to pay so dearly, it usually created a feeling of envy in them when someone else was apparently not only having no difficulty but profiting. News that we here in America were having a hard time because of rationed gasoline or the lack of butter or steaks always served as a red flag to arouse the ire of the soldier, especially the combat soldier. When a national magazine came forth with a full-page picture of the vacationists in Florida, a wave of anger swept through the overseas Army. All of these annoyances added together left few soldiers who were not affected by at least some of them, in addition to their personal problems.

Stress [22] resulted also when unit censors deleted material from the letters written by soldiers on purely moral grounds—because of arguments with the girl friend or the telling of a dirty story. Where the mail was read by a base instead of a unit censor and where scrupulous secrecy was maintained, complaints were fewer.

Promotions. The system of rank and promotion, while probably a necessity, was the source of countless disappointments and frustrations. It is difficult for one living outside that type of organization to appreciate fully the meaning of promotion to the soldier and the officer in the Army. Rank is of almost irrational importance. In the case of noncommissioned officers there was undoubtedly much favoritism in the matters of selection and promotion. Despite the Army's effort to establish an impartial system, one doubts its effectiveness, either in the selection of noncommissioned officers or in their regular promotion.

With promotions for commissioned officers, there were various difficulties: the personal equation in selecting and rating, chance, existing vacancies, or waiting for (and often not receiving) "approval from higher headquarters." The British had a partial solution in giving rank to a particular job rather than to a particular person. In the American Army promotion was often handicapped by regulations: An officer was moved from one post to another just at a time when he would have been eligible for promotion, perhaps even after having been recommended; but the promotion could not follow him. The fact that he was moved would then require a three months' duty in the new post before he would again become eligible for recommendation. Periodically, because of an excess number of officers, all promotions would be "frozen"; if and when "unfrozen," a new recommendation would have to be submitted. The criteria for eligibility in terms of length of service were changed several times. Every unit had what was known as a Table of Organization which permitted only so many officers

---

[22] "Censorship," *What the Soldier Thinks,* No. 6:2, 25 May 1944.

of each rank. Too often the quota in the higher grades remained full, allowing no vacancies for promotion.

Commissioned rank was given usually more often on the basis of length of service [23] than on ability. In some degree this was also true of noncommissioned officers. Consequently, there were many, many instances of inequality—of teachers whose students had a higher rank; of relatively incompetent individuals who supervised men with intellectul or professional capacities far exceeding their own. That such a situation should be a stress of great magnitude against effective personality function of their subordinates in rank is obvious.

STRESSES MOST FREQUENTLY ENCOUNTERED IN OVERSEAS NONCOMBAT DUTIES

This category includes those units which were in further combat training overseas, or in rest periods following combat, as well as all the noncombatant supporting personnel.

Uncertainty, as to where and when and what, filled the mind of the average soldier after his unit received orders to move. It went with him through the staging area, onto the ship, during landing in some foreign country, and while awaiting the assignment to action. Rumors in the Army were always rife, but the impending departure from the United States speeded and multiplied these a hundredfold. One can imagine the intense emotional feelings of the soldier at the time he was leaving his country, going to a place about which he could guess only perhaps from the nature of the clothing issued to him, facing the prospect of thousands of miles separating him from home for a long time, knowing that he would cross water, every mile of which might be infested with potential threats to life. All of these were stresses of no small moment. Stress was particularly conspicuous on a ship which was assumed to be heading for an amphibious landing. No one knew whether the "show" would start that day or the next or the next week. Of necessity, the men were cooped up in a small area with little or nothing to do but sit and think and wonder.[24] Uncertainty became nigh unbearable through such waiting periods. Those necessary transitions sometimes lasted days and sometimes dragged into months during which

---

[23] There was much feeling on the part of many reserve officers and AUS (Army of the United States—the volunteers) that the Regular Army officers were "well taken care of" with regard to rank. There were, for instance, 1,249 Regular medical officers on December 26, 1941; the corps was expanded by reserves and AUS officers to a maximum of 47,000. At this peak, there were 71 generals in the Medical Corps; 65 were Regulars; 6 were reserve or AUS (Bayne-Jones, Cutler, Menninger, Morgan, Rankin, and Ravdin). Several other Reserve or AUS officers were recommended by the Surgeon General but were not approved by "higher authority."

[24] An attempt was made, where possible, to continue training aboard ship. For amphibious landings, men were briefed on their jobs.

no one seemed to know the why of the waiting, whether or not it was necessary, or what was to come after the wait.

Along with the uncertainty regarding the landing or possibility of combat was the uncertainty about other lurking dangers, particularly for soldiers in the Pacific. A specific fear was of the unhealthy climate which carried with it strange tropical diseases. Every soldier became somewhat educated about malaria. He had to take atabrine as a preventive or suppressive measure. Even so, rumors developed that made this requirement more difficult to carry out. There was a widespread, groundless belief that the drug made one sexually impotent. Another rumor was that the drug made one crazy. There was suggestive but rare evidence that some psychotic reactions were related to taking atabrine. However, because of the rumor, at least two papers [25] on the subject were not printed for many months after they were submitted. Soldiers would hear of other new or strange diseases—hepatitis, filariasis, kala-azar, scrub typhus. Each would produce mild concern in the susceptible personality. At one of the general hospitals,[26] the reactions of men with schistosomiasis called for special psychiatric help; their recovery was impeded by their anxiety.

Separation from the familiar was an important cause of emotional distress for many of our soldiers who had never been out of the county in which they were born and then found themselves going thousands of miles to foreign lands. It is not surprising that many showed excitement, tenseness, anxiety. There was uncertainty not only as to where they were going but also as to when they would be coming back. Certainly there was the fleeting thought of "Will I be coming back?" There was the nostalgic reviewing of things that had happened at home, the farewells, the last time they saw their wives or families. These memories became treasures, magnified in emotional importance as the distance increased and as time passed. One could not minimize this as a stress factor, even though the thrill of adventure compensated somewhat, and even though it was accepted and adjusted to by the great majority.

Privations are an expected part of the difficult life of a soldier. However, when continued for a long time, they became severe stress for many men. When camp was established it was a luxury to find even as much as a box for a washstand. It was a special privilege to have soap, clean clothes, a comfortable chair, a china plate, a warm shower (or a cold one, as the climate might require).

---

25 Mergener, J. C., "Psychosis Following Administration of Quinacrine Hydrochloride for Malaria," *War Med.,* 8:250-252, Oct., 1945; Gaskill, H. S., and Fitz-Hugh, T., Jr., "Toxic Psychoses Following Atabrine," *Bull. U.S. Army M. Dept.,* No. 86, Mar., 1945, pp. 63-69.

For a vivid description of the soldier's fears of the drug, see the excellent narrative by Michener, J. A.: *Tales of the South Pacific,* The Macmillan Company, *New York,* 1947, p. 121.

26 Frank, J. D., "Emotional Reactions of American Soldiers to an Unfamiliar Disease," *Am. J. Psychiat.,* 102:631-640, Mar., 1946.

These little advantages were rare, so rare that many GI's did not have them in many months of overseas service. Perhaps the privation which was felt most keenly was the lack of variety in food. Food became charged with an increased emotional value for a soldier. The monotony of the mess in most overseas units was nigh intolerable. The soldier had to live chiefly on food from cans; in all of the South Pacific and Orient, all food had to be boiled. Fresh milk was never available, and rarely were fresh vegetables or salads to be found in most overseas posts.

In a fighting unit food was devastatingly monotonous. It was unusual for a combat soldier to have any hot food in cold weather. The "K" and the "C" rations were sufficient in caloric value. They provided a reasonably good variety when one had to eat them for only a few days. However, when they were the sole diet for weeks on end, just as any food, they became almost nauseating. It probably could not have happened in wartime, but it is heartening to see the Army is sufficiently human to take a nationally known chef to Europe to consult about the menus of our occupation troops. A news release from Frankfurt on January 11, 1947, reported George Mardikian, famed San Francisco restaurateur, as pepping up the morale of mess sergeants, telling them that soldiers like mother's cooking so they have to be mothers. Through the kindness of Chaplain Tom McKenna of Letterman General Hospital, I was George Mardikian's guest at his Omar Khayyam restaurant. Not only was his food something to remember, but I found that as evidence of his gratitude to America, GI's were regularly guests of the house.

Bombing in noncombat areas added to the stress, when men had to live and work under its constant threat. This was the situation in many of the Pacific Islands, where, as has been described so often, the Japs seemed to take particular delight in bombing at night.[27] A somewhat similar situation existed in England, as also in much of Belgium, where buzz bombs and the other types of rocket bombs were ever-present. My personal observation impressed me with the fatalistic attitude that one adopts in such a situation. One evening in London, as Col. Lloyd Thompson [28] and I were leaving the hotel for an engagement, the sirens began to blow. Not knowing the ground rules, I asked him if we were not expected to stay under cover. His answer was that no one paid any attention to the bombs! [29] We had walked down the street a bit farther when the sky became brilliantly red. In amazement I exclaimed to him about it. In a very nonchalant manner his answer was, "If you see them, you don't need to

---

[27] Smith, E. R., "Neuroses Resulting from Combat," *Am. J. Psychiat.*, 100:94-97, July, 1943.
[28] Consultant in Neuropsychiatry to the European Theater. This incident took place en route to the home of Brig. J. R. Rees, October 6, 1944.
[29] The "buzz" bombs, although less devastating than the V-bombs, caused more fear and tension because they could be heard a comparatively long time going overhead. The V-bombs gave no warning until the explosion, which if you heard, you had survived.

worry!" Such an attitude seemed to be adopted universally by the British, as well as by the Americans who were stationed in that area. Both the GI's and the people assumed that "It either had your number or it didn't." An intellectual acceptance did not, however, erase the emotional distress over the risk.

Isolation was another of the special stresses for many troops.[30] The constricted nature of the living area often imposed a further stress. There were literally hundreds of installations in which the soldier was limited to a small section even though on a large land area. This was also a problem when men were stationed at little outposts or on tiny islands. Leaves could not be granted for there was nowhere to go; there were minimal facilities for recreation; often there were no other white people. The effect of continued monotony, often coupled with terrific extremes of climate, uncertainty, separation from familiar surroundings and activities, and too much time for thinking, was always disastrous in its effect on morale. There were situations in which men were isolated for months at a time in small groups, such as in Greenland. An extremely interesting though unpublished document was once sent to our division. It was entitled "Isolationitis" and was written by a staff sergeant in a weather observation area in Greenland. In a very clear fashion, he had pointed out with much feeling not only the monotony but the complications of life in intimate living conditions. A small group of persons learned to know each other far too well, yet had to exist for months on end, otherwise separated from the world. We understood that the writer became a psychiatric casualty.

Climate.[31] The fact that World War II truly involved the whole world necessitated the subjection of many American soldiers to extremes of climate for long periods of time. The effect of extreme cold or heat, humidity or drought cannot be measured, but many men have attested to the influence of such factors on the mental health of both combat and rear-echelon troops. The temperature in many places in India would remain above 110 degrees for months, and it would often go as high as 120 degrees. In the Lido area the rainfall was as much as 240 inches a year in contrast to the average of 30 or 40 in much of the United States. On the Burma border, during the monsoon period, between 120 and 160 inches of rain fell each year, accompanied by a temperature of 90 to 110 degrees throughout the 24 hours. In October, 1943, there were 36 inches of rainfall in 24 hours on Goodenough Island. In April, 1944, when we had a large number of troops in Milne Bay, New Caledonia, there were 44 inches of rain in 48 hours. In Greenland, the temperature from Christ-

---

[30] This is well described by M. A. Zeligs in "War Neuroses: Psychiatric Experiences and Management on a Pacific Island," *War Med.*, 6:166-172, Sept., 1944.

[31] This subject was studied and reported on in great detail by Maj. Stephen W. Ranson, "Psychiatric Aspects of Climate in World War II," on file in the Historical Section, Office of the Surgeon General.

mas till April was below zero, often ranging as low as —40 degrees. More than once many of our Alaskan troops withstood a temperature of 60 degrees below zero. The fog and cold and wind and snow in the Aleutians was specially described as a causative factor in psychiatric problems.[32] The dry heat in parts of the Near East was equally insufferable.

Life for weeks and months in such areas meant submission to extremely severe physiological and consequently psychological stress. Fear of both the heat and, in India, the monsoon was an important factor. Once a person survived a season, that fear was lessened. One of the psychiatrists in the Persian Gulf Command, where the temperature is the highest of any place in the world, did much to reduce heat exhaustion through a program planned to reduce fear of heat. Troops going to this area were oriented to that fear even before landing. They were given a booklet entitled "How to Keep Alive in Persia!"

STRESSES MOST COMMONLY ENCOUNTERED IN COMBAT

Danger made all other stresses pale into relative insignificance. Baptism by fire and enforced continued exposure to it in combat was so charged with emotion that it cannot be described. It was an experience that no one can really know or fully appreciate without living through it. The sense of personal danger was enhanced by various circumstances which were characteristic of life in combat.

The terrific noise of bombardment made the oncoming shells seem very personally significant; it kept the soldier from minimizing his danger. The sounds of certain weapons were particularly terrifying (as intended by psychological warfare on both sides). The average soldier soon learned to know the difference between them—the bark of the bazooka, the rattle of a machine gun, the crack of a German 88. One of the more terrifying situations, and most conducive to psychiatric casualties, was the predicament in which a soldier was tied down or hemmed in by enemy shellfire, helpless in a foxhole not nearly so deep as he wished. It occasionally happened that although a man was under fire he could not return fire. There were also times when he dared not move from his shallow foxhole because it would reveal his location and make him, or others near by, a target for the hidden enemy. As a rule, only one person could occupy a foxhole. Thus one man, unable to share his fears, lacked the reassurance of companionship as might have been the case in the trench warfare of World War I.[33]

---

[32] Burns, G. C., "Neuropsychiatric Problems at an Aleutian Post," *Am. J. Psychiat.*, 102:205-213, Sept., 1945.
[33] Porter, W. C., Discussion of paper by Foster Kennedy in *Trans. Am. Neurol. Assoc.*, 69:83, 1943.

Soldiers who had not been in combat dreaded the experience partly because they feared they would be afraid and might misbehave under its stress. This has been described as "fear of fear." To help them, there was a concerted effort made to educate the soldiers to accept fear of the dangers of combat as a normal reaction and to find ways in which it could be reduced to a minimum in order to enable the personality to handle it. The mental hygiene lectures for enlisted men included a discussion of it.[34] The widely read little book, *Psychology for the Fighting Man,* presented the subject at length.[35]

Several scientific studies have been made of the occurrence of fear in battle. The most widely circulated of these was *Fear of German Weapons,*[36] a report made by Maj. John W. Appel and Dr. Sam Stauffer. They found that among American soldiers, the German 88-millimeter gun was considered the most frightening and most dangerous weapon; the dive bomber was the second most frightening. Excellent observations were made by John Dollard [37] and by Mira [38] in the Spanish War. In their training, American soldiers were exposed to battle noises and gunfire, and were given infiltration courses for the purpose of accustoming them to combat environment.

Certain frequently recurring hazards increased the danger to the individual soldier and therefore fed his fear.[39] He was aware of these possibilities and extremely sensitive to them. Were they to occur following any prolonged period of combat, at a time when he was functioning on a marginal reserve, they often served as precipitating factors in a breakdown. A soldier in such a situation is not capable of standing a sudden increase in stress. The most important of these hazards, as pointed out by the commission of civilian psychiatrists,[40] was the pattern of the soldier's group relationship. If the composition of a group was disturbed, if its pattern of relationships was shattered, the individual soldier who was left alone was easily overwhelmed. If anything happened to his leader, he was particularly vulnerable to a psychological break. Troops were supposed

[34] *War Department Technical Bulletin, Medical 21,* 15 March 1944.
[35] *Psychology for the Fighting Man,* prepared by the Committee of the National Research Council with the collaboration of Science Service, Infantry Journal Press, Washington, D.C., 1943, pp. 296-306.
[36] *Fear of German Weapons,* Report No. B-66, 1 October 1943. Joint study by Neuropsychiatry Branch, Surgeon General's Office and Research Branch, Special Service Division, ASF, War Department.
[37] Dollard, John, *Fear in Battle,* Institute in Human Relations, Yale University Press, New Haven, 1943.
[38] Mira, E., *Psychiatry and War,* W. W. Norton & Company, Inc., New York, 1943, pp. 26-41.
[39] "A state of tension and anxiety is so prevalent in the front lines that it must be regarded as a normal reaction in this grossly abnormal situation." Spiegel, H. X., "Psychiatric Observations in the Tunisian Campaign," *Am. J. Orthopsychiat.,* 14:381-385, July, 1943.
[40] *Medical Report on Morale and Psychiatry,* No. 17, Office of the Surgeon General, 25 August 1945. Reprinted: Bartemeier, L. H.; Kubie, L. S.; Menninger, K. A.; Romano, J.; and White-horn, J. C., "Combat Exhaustion," *J. Nerv. & Ment. Dis.,* 104:358-389, Oct., 1946; 489-525, Nov., 1946.

to be briefed as to the plan or aims of a mission. Sometimes they could not be. Then uncertainty intensified their emotional insecurity. The occurrence of heavy casualties was also a powerful personality stress,[41] not only because of the increased danger to every soldier, but also because of the loss of a special associate or associates, and the gruesome sights of disfigurement, dismemberment, and death. When casualties ran high, the soldier wondered if the "brass" knew what really was happening and doubted that they did. He questioned as to whether or not they were experimenting. When were they going to send relief? Was someone trying to get a promotion by the ground his men gained?

One of the problems in the recent warfare was the co-ordination of all forces in an attack. Tragedies resulted where that co-ordination did not or could not occur.[42] For instance, when the Infantry had pushed back the enemy and occupied its position sooner than scheduled, the Air Forces could not be informed in time. It was very difficult at night to distinguish our planes from those of the enemy, and the "trigger-happy soldier" did not always wait to verify a tentative identification. Consequently there were a few situations and times when fire from our own antiaircraft guns and planes caused as much or more anxiety than an enemy attack.

Fatigue, a result of stress, was both physical and mental and could not be separately identified. Unfortunately, there was a tendency on the part of some physicians to regard the physical factors as being all-important. This was rarely if ever the case.

Lack of sleep added to the strain of the excessive physical exertion and the emotional and mental tension. A man in combat had to sleep when and if he could, usually grabbing it in snatches. Most of the heavy attacking took place at night; much of the bombing was done at night. Words cannot adequately describe the experience of trying to sleep in a muddy or snow-filled foxhole, under constant bombardment and bombing. It is a wonder that anyone could sleep at all, and undoubtedly some men did not, for several days at a time. Many a soldier, as he approached the limits of his ability to withstand such stress, was afraid to go to sleep, despite the fact that he wanted and needed to so much. His dreams were often so terrible that he would wake up with a start, feeling more agitated than before.

The unlimited tour of duty was an administrative practice which acted as

---

[41] The infantry soldier was the recipient of 79.8 per cent of all the casualties; the Air Corps received 12.3 per cent and the Service Forces 7.9 per cent. These and other extremely interesting data are graphically portrayed in Gen. Jacob L. Devers' *Report of the Army Ground Forces Activity,* 319.1 (AGF) (10 January 1946) GNDCG (printed) to Chief of Staff.

[42] Ernie Pyle described in a vivid fashion his own experience on the day of the break-through in the Normandy campaign when our planes bombed in our own forward area. They missed Ernie but they did get Lt. Gen. McNair. Pyle, Ernie, *Brave Men,* Henry Holt and Company, Inc., New York, 1944, p. 438.

one of the more severe stresses of combat. The soldier felt hopeless of survival because of a failure to establish any definite end to active fighting. Day after day, the infantry soldier slogged ahead with nothing to look forward to except more fighting, more mud, more death, and no way to escape from it except by a wound, by going to pieces mentally, or by court martial (desertion), or death. In World War I, there was a rotation system and a plan of relief, but, presumably because of our man-power problems, this was never uniformly allowed in this war. Toward the end of the European combat there were some units which did provide rest periods.

The replacement system was another administrative practice which had a direct relationship to psychiatric casualties. The process of supplying new soldiers to fill in the gaps caused by loss of men in combat gave the War Department much concern. Initially, replacements for a particular unit were sent forward more often as individuals than in groups. In urgent or tense combat situations a man might come into the rear area one day and be sent up to the front to fight that night or the next day. In such cases he had no opportunity to learn to know his associates or his leaders. He also lost all emotional support from one of its strongest sources, namely a close emotional tie to his associates.[43] The casualty rate among individual replacements was definitely higher than among seasoned troops. Only toward the end of the war was it possible to integrate individual replacements into a unit before sending them forward to combat as a group.

Reassignment of battle casualties was an additional stress for many soldiers who could not do further combat duty. They were normally sent from a forward area hospital or exhaustion center to a replacement depot for reassignment to noncombat duty. Unfortunately, often a man would get "kicked around." On October 3, 1944, Col. Lloyd Thompson and I made a visit to the 107th Evacuation Hospital, north of Bastogne in Belgium, and encountered four patients in the psychiatric section of the hospital who told the following story: They had all been psychiatric casualties from combat with the Fifth Armored Division. From the division clearing station they were sent to the convalescent hospital. There they were given a transfer slip recommending that from the replacement depot they should be assigned to noncombat duty. On arrival at the replacement depot, the suggested disposition by the convalescent hospital was ignored. They remained for 8 days along with over 1,000 men in this installation that was supposed to have taken care of 250 men. While they were there they were with-

---

[43] The civilian psychiatric commission included this point in one of their recommendations, regarding it one of the major psychiatric stresses needing correction. *Medical Report on Morale and Psychiatry*, No. 17, Office of the Surgeon General, 25 August 1945, pp. 69, 77. Reprinted: Bartemeier, L. H.; Kubie, L. S.; Menninger, K. A.; Romano, J.; and Whitehorn, J. C., "Combat Exhaustion," *J. Nerv. & Ment. Dis.*, 104:358-389. Oct., 1946; 489-525, Nov., 1946.

out blankets or shelter halves, and each night went AWOL 2½ miles to sleep in a barn. They were sent from there to another replacement depot, then to a third, successively to a fourth. From a fifth replacement depot, despite their little notes recommending noncombat duty, they were sent back to the Fifth Armored Division. We saw them in the evacuation hospital. They claimed they had traveled 1,200 miles between August 12th and the 3rd of October. In every place they would beg to work and to help in some way, but they had been refused. Fortunately, this is a very extreme case. The fact that it could happen indicates the basis for what the commission of civilian psychiatrists described as "repple-depple exhaustion." [44]

Disparity of privilege was a source of stress for the combat soldier. It became a special problem on such leaves as he could occasionally take. The feeling was widespread that the combat soldier did the dirty work in contrast to the men who worked in rear areas. Yet he could not even enjoy what he had fought for. His frequent gripe was, "We take a city and then they put it off limits." In many instances there were good reasons for so doing, yet nothing was so irritating to the combat soldier as to find a potential spot to enjoy himself and be greeted with the sign, "Off Limits to U.S. Personnel," or the much more disturbing, "Off Limits to Enlisted Men." He was convinced that the men in the rear areas were getting the "gravy." [45] Much more serious was the effect on combat troops, on their return from an operation, of seeing rear-echelon troops living in comparative luxury. Too often they were given a "break" by being sent to a "rest camp" which they had to build themselves, furnished with only limited recreational equipment. In the Pacific area there were frequent difficulties between combat troops and the military government officials. Because of the possibility of sabotage, the presence of enemy personnel or spies, it was the custom to segregate the natives. The soldiers specially resented this. The GI felt that since he had just conquered the territory and was interested in the people, he should be allowed to be friendly and to trade with them. But this was forbidden. The original ruling of no fraternization with the German women caused a special flurry of resentment. A solution on the part of unit commanders in some localities was to shut their eyes in so far as possible to such rulings and to the inevitable clashes resulting.

---

[44] *Medical Report on Morale and Psychiatry*, No. 17, Office of the Surgeon General, 25 August 1944, pp. 31, 69. Reprinted: Bartemeier, L. H.; Kubie, L. S.; Menninger, K. A.; Romano, J.; and Whitehorn, J. C., "Combat Exhaustion," *J. Nerv. & Ment. Dis.*, 104:358-389, Oct., 1946; 489-525, Nov., 1946.

[45] This theme was frequently portrayed in the cartoons of the remarkable GI, Bill Mauldin. See pp. 79 and 189 of *Up Front*, Henry Holt and Company, Inc., New York, 1945. Mauldin, with rare intuition and expressive ability, showed in his cartoons the soldier's feelings about many of these stresses—danger, interpersonal relations, officer-enlisted-man relationships, disappointments, frustrations. His book is one of the most important psychological contributions to understanding the GI "doggie" that has appeared.

Another aspect of the disparity of privilege which greatly affected morale, particularly in the Pacific area, was the inequality in the distribution of supplies. Most of the Army felt the Navy had much more comfortable quarters and many more luxuries. On my visit to Okinawa, the Navy enlisted personnel could each have a case of beer a week in contrast to a ration of two bottles a week for the soldier. The Navy officers' clubs always seemed to have plenty of hard liquor; the Army officers' clubs very rarely had any at all. The inequalities of food, vehicles, supplies, equipment led to the "rustling" and "promoting" of needed articles. This occurred of course "without the knowledge" of the unit commander but with his delighted approval, and no questions asked. It is understandable that many officers felt perfectly justified in their attitude when the needs of their men were acute. There was much unofficial exchange of services and supplies between unrelated units. This often increased morale and produced good working spirit between organizations in the Army, Navy, and Marine Corps.[46]

STRESSES RELATED TO REDEPLOYMENT

It was announced that when the war was over in Europe, military forces would be transported to the Pacific. A large percentage of the men in the European Theater thought they had done their share. Even the troops who had been in that theater only a relatively short time adopted that attitude. On the other hand, those who had to take a total point of view fully realized that the job might possibly be more difficult in the Pacific than it had been in Europe. If so, all available trained troops would be required. Nevertheless, it was early evident that there would be a terrific reaction on the part of soldiers against their redeployment from one theater to the other.

This stress was anticipated by the psychiatrists. A special bulletin,[47] published in June, 1945, pointed out that this necessary move would precipitate many psychiatric casualties. Therefore it would require the utmost in keen alertness and positive preventive measures to minimize the problem.

Before Japan capitulated on September 2, 1945, a sufficient number of soldiers had been returned to this country, following VE-day on May 8, 1945, en route to Japan to give some indication of the type of their reaction. These battlewise veterans could not fit into the retraining program. They felt they knew how to fight from experience, and they did not want any "desk com-

---

46 Numerous instances of such exchanges were related to me by my professional associate, Lt. Comdr. H. H. Crank, who had been stationed on Okinawa.

47 "Medical Problems of Redeployment," *War Department Technical Bulletin, Medical 170,* June, 1945.

mandos" giving them lessons out of a book.[48] They believed they had done their share, they were "browned off," "fed up." Even where this attitude could be modified somewhat, it was difficult for them to accept the fact that the type of fighting might be very different from what it had been in Europe. It was apparent that a major problem, in addition to neurotic reactions, would be faulty attitudes. For this reason it was strongly recommended that hospitalization of individuals with such faulty attitudes should be avoided unless there was definite need of hospital treatment or study. When they were hospitalized, experience taught us that they were usually lost to the service. Fortunately the necessity for redeployment, according to the extensive original plans, was averted by Japan's surrender. During its short life, the stress of anticipated transfer from Europe directly to Japan undoubtedly precipitated some psychiatric casualties.

SPECIAL STRESSES AFFECTING OFFICERS [49]

Some officers were subject to two additional psychological stresses. The first was the assumption of a role of authority, and the second the frustration resulting from the lack of opportunity for advancement.

There were men who, strange as it may appear, could not permit themselves to wear a commission's badge of authority. They developed a maladjustment after they had striven against odds to become officers, had managed to go through an officers' training course, and had been commissioned. In the great majority of these cases, one found dynamics that were related to a fear of excelling the father which was coupled with guilt for having tried. This dynamic is well accepted by and well known to civilian psychiatrists who see it in the man who appears to be about on the threshold of success, only to fail. The un-

---

[48] The jungle fighting in the Pacific was different from that in the European Theater. In so far as possible all retraining for deployment to the Pacific was to be conducted by battle-experienced veterans from that area, though this was not always known to these redeployed soldiers.

[49] Between December 7, 1941, and September 2, 1945, there was an aggregate of 872,000 male commissioned officers in the Army. Of these about 47,000 were medical officers and 27,000 were chaplains. Of the remaining 800,000 some 531,000, or 66.37 per cent, were commissioned after serving as enlisted men in this war. Most of these officers were former enlisted men who were graduates of Officer Candidate Schools. Others were commissioned after receiving Air Forces training, and some won battlefield promotions for conspicuous gallantry in action.

Nine thousand officers of the wartime Army were graduates of the United States Military Academy at West Point. An equal number came from Regular Army officers who were originally commissioned from sources other than West Point.

The Officers' Reserve Corps furnished 206,000 officers and the National Guard, 21,000. Of these many had previously served as enlisted men. Nearly all of the 72,000 doctors, dentists, veterinarians, pharmacists, and chaplains were commissioned directly from civilian life, as were 24,000 other officers, many of whom were specialists, such as lawyers, scientists, and industrialists. A half million enlisted men became officers. *Bull. U.S. Army M. Dept.*, 5:391, Apr., 1946.

conscious explanation for this failure is never apparent to the victim, nor to others without psychiatric experience. Fundamentally, such an individual is often emotionally very dependent on his father while feeling hostile toward him. If such a son exceeds his father's success or power, he develops an acute sense of guilt.

A second aspect of this reaction to authority was seen in those men who had been successful in civilian life but failed as officers in the Army. This can be explained on the basis that the civilian success was achieved as an exaggerated protest against early authority, but because in the Army the individual could not be the final authority, he therefore became a failure. Another phase of the same problem is seen in individuals who made a success in civilian life because behind the scenes they could be dependent on someone—a maternal wife, a protected position or profession. These two types are well described by Reider.[50]

Lack of promotion was a special stress for some officers who needed constant advancement or achievement [51] in order to maintain a sense of individual worth. Because rank was so important in military life, failure to increase it was almost always interpreted as an indication of being unappreciated. This provoked the fear that everyone, including an officer's subordinates, would assume that he was a failure. Many very capable men who did excellent jobs were not promoted. The lack of advancement was such a blow to the pride of these men that it sometimes led to a feeling of insecurity, of worthlessness, and, most important, to a loss or serious impairment of leadership ability. As Evans and Ziprich [52] pointed out in describing those who so reacted, they usually had endured excessive denials and deprivations in childhood and thus were never able to develop a tolerance to them. The current denials of needed compensatory outlets (promotions) could not be tolerated. These factors were among the many operative to produce psychiatric casualties among officers. The rate of incidence was always less than in enlisted men.[53]

A final word is in order regarding the stress of being a junior officer. The lowly lieutenants or captains too often were the commissioned "office boys." In combat, they were the expendables; the mortality rate of second lieutenants was higher than that of any other rank in the Army, from private to general. Even though it was unfair, the junior officer came last in every officers cue, waited on

---

[50] Reider, Norman, "Psychodynamics of Authority with Relation to Some Psychiatric Problems in Officers," *Bull. Menninger Clinic,* 8:55-58, Mar., 1944.

[51] No doubt this also applied to many noncommissioned officers but was more apparent in commissioned officers because their attitudes and effectiveness affected so many subordinates.

[52] Evans, H. S., and Ziprich, H. F., "Minor Psychiatric Reactions in Officers," *War Med.,* 8:137-142, Sept., 1945.

[53] Total psychiatric admissions and annual rate per 1,000 mean strength among officers in 1942 was 12.69 per 1,000, compared to a rate in enlisted men of 29.46 per 1,000, and enlisted women of 48.08 per 1,000; in 1943, the officer rate was 12.35 per 1,000, enlisted men 43.29, and all female personnel 39.61 per 1,000 per year.

all "superiors," and in other ways was confronted with the special emotional stresses of being a "shavetail." In addition, his youth and inexperience were so apparent to enlisted men that he became the immediate brunt of many of their jibes. The commission of civilian psychiatrists reported: "junior officers are keymen in military action. . . . 'The Lieutenant' is a well-nigh ubiquitous figure in our case notes [of enlisted men]. He is somehow concerned in nearly everything that goes well or goes badly with the troops. He is the focal point of leadership and command functions." [54]

Many of the long list of special psychological stresses which are so apparent in military life are not without analogues in civilian life. However, in the Army they were active with much greater intensity, on so many personalities, and they required adjustment with lightninglike rapidity. No doubt could remain in the minds of the psychiatric observers in the Army that they were as important for consideration as causative factors in mental illness as the personality make-up of a patient. Stress factors were so obvious, touched so many facets of past experience, were so ever present, so very real, and so irreducible that the average military psychiatrist in his hurried work was prone to see them as *the* causes of psychiatric casualties in war.

---

[54] *Medical Reports on Morale and Psychiatry,* No. 17, Office of the Surgeon General, 25 August 1945, p. 67. Reprinted: Bartemeier, L. H.; Kubie, L. S.; Menninger, K. A.; Romano, J.; and Whitehorn, J. C., "Combat Exhaustion," *J. Nerv. & Ment. Dis.,* 104:358-389, Oct., 1946; 489-525, Nov., 1946.

6

THE ENVIRONMENT OF THE SOLDIER: ITS EMOTIONAL SUPPORTS

DESPITE THE HELL of war, most men weathered their period of service quite successfully, were glad to have had the experience, and, undoubtedly, in many ways profited from it. Some found strength, comfort, and satisfactions in the relationships and duties of the war years which will continue to be significant in civilian life. Others, to whom postwar civilian work and contacts proved less satisfying emotionally, returned to military service. Certain factors evidently gave strong emotional support and great satisfaction to military personnel. The machinery and methods of waging war provided some of these, and others developed within the personality as a defense against stress.

One important factor colored the entire military picture, namely, the social milieu of the soldier. The study of an isolated individual soldier would never adequately explain behavior which was the result of his being knit closely into a new social unit. The mighty chaos in which the war engulfed the world might be described reasonably accurately as an international effort to control a few psychotic nations. America was forced to share it if the world were to survive and, more particularly, if its way of life were to continue. In order to exert sufficient force, 12,000,000 American men and women were mobilized into the tremendous organizations of the Army and the Navy which consisted of many small units, working as teams.

All of these teams shared a single common goal. Every plan and every policy of the War Department was aimed toward winning the war by the development of interrelated teams that could and would work together under a controlled dictatorship. For its best functioning, the Army had to create a system whereby it could not only train every man to be a fighting soldier but also could maintain him as an effective member of a unit in which the will of the group superseded that of the individual. The effort of every man, regardless of personal interest or wish, had to be directed to the completion of the Army's purpose. There were, of necessity, requirements of conformity, of regimentation, of discipline, of military law, from which there was no escape. Each person had to become a cog in the wheel which rolled toward the group goal, in spite of individual unhappiness, discomfort, or sacrifice. In the laboratory thus created, the psychiatrist could study the reactions and the interactions of individuals and groups.

The compensations and satisfactions which the soldier found in this new life served as individual and collective emotional supports. For convenience, and somewhat arbitrarily, these supports are divided into those which were dependent upon relationships with people, those which were derived from outlets and diversions, those which were related to physical well-being and security, and those which the soldier gained from the acquisition of new knowledge and experience. Certain essential adjustments had to be made within the personality in order to make it possible for the soldier to utilize these supports for his benefit.

SUPPORTS FROM INTERPERSONAL RELATIONSHIPS

Leadership. Familiar is the axiom that leadership can make or break its followers, but the psychological basis for the relationship of the leader to the mental health of the men led has only recently received scientific consideration. The effects of "good" or "bad" leadership were apparent so frequently in the Army as to drive home the simple fact that if a leader met the emotional needs of his men adequately they were greatly supported against personality disturbances.[1]

As discussed in an earlier chapter, the leader became the symbolical father of his group. He was expected, by its members, to supply their emotional needs that were like those for which every child seeks satisfaction from his father. By personal concern for his men a leader won their respect, co-operation, and affection.

The ideal company commander knew each of his men by name;[2] he knew

---

[1] So far as I know, there was not any contact between the groups responsible for planning courses in leadership for the officers of World War II and the Neuropsychiatry Consultants Division of the Office of the Surgeon General. They perhaps did not expect psychiatry to have anything to offer them, and the psychiatrists in the Division were so pressed for man power and time that they had no chance to do missionary work in this field. Just how much was taught officer candidates about the unconscious factors in the leader and the follower is not known. Recently, certain courses were initiated at 12 Army schools for officers in which the advanced curriculum devotes 4 hours to "Psychiatry" and several hours to "The Psychology of Leadership." File No. WDGOT 352 (18 July 1946), Subject: Course Outlines, Common Subjects, Advanced Course (Regular).

[2] The German Army gave very specific directions to its officers in regard to their relations with their soldiers, stressing the personal touch. "He must act as a teacher rather than as a superior. . . . He must give sufficient time to acquaint himself individually with every one of his soldiers. . . . The officer must inspect his company or regiment every day. . . . A casual atmosphere should prevail during these inspections, the officer looking into the eyes of his men to detect personal problems in their looks. . . . The officer must never expose his soldiers to ridicule. . . . He is expected to congratulate his soldiers on their birthdays." From *German Psychological Warfare: Survey and Bibliography,* ed. by Ladislas Farago, Committee for National Morale, New York, 1941, pp. 40-42.

something about their home situations and problems; he took into account their individual strengths and weaknesses and was on the alert for those who needed special support; he was responsible for seeing that his men were well fed, that they had the right clothes, and that they were allowed rest and had blankets to keep them warm. The men were dependent on the commanding officers for providing them special considerations of passes, furloughs, beer, candy, cigarettes, shows. These, as will be indicated later, were far more important as a source of satisfaction in the Army than similar privileges or opportunities in civilian life. The wise commanding officer assumed certain responsibilities pertaining to personal needs of the soldier. Through his first sergeant he checked on whether or not shoes and socks fitted properly, whether or not each had a fair share of the chores, and received enough rest or the proper medical care.

In addition to the supplying of physical needs there was the problem of assisting the men in retaining their individual dignity as human beings in the midst of nameless numbers. The soldiers wanted to be treated like men, not like so many cattle. Some of them were asked: "What would you do if you were company commander in combat and had been given the authority to do anything you felt would make your company better in working together and doing its job?" [3] Their answers made suggestions such as: "I'd treat all my enlisted men alike and not show partiality"; "I'd recognize and reward men's abilities"; "I'd improve job assignments in the company; right man for the right job"; "I'd go to bat for my men"; "I wouldn't be too GI."

Judicious provision for the basic needs of the soldier for food, clothing, shelter, safety, equipment, and approval supplied an important emotional support against stress. When the officer with the authority to do so provided for the soldier's wants, that soldier gained a feeling of confidence in his leader. This confidence simplified the problem of adjustment to the regimentation of his behavior. The closer the relationship of the leader [4] to his men, the more reassuring and thus the more helpful he could be in their acceptance of new and trying situations. As he could gain satisfaction in a passive dependence upon his leader, the new soldier was able to give up his personal initiative, wishes, preferences, and liberty, to become submissive and obedient.

---

[3] "If I Were the C.O.," *What the Soldier Thinks*, No. 7:1-4, 25 July 1944.

[4] The psychological value to the American people of President Roosevelt's fireside talks was well appreciated. Mackintosh described Churchill's speeches to the British people as of great reassuring value, particularly early in the war. (Mackintosh, J. M., *The War and Mental Health in England*, Commonwealth Fund, New York, 1944, p. 34.) The radio served to permit such leaders to reach their followers, to give reassurance, to express personal concern. For unknown reasons, very few of our top military leaders used this method to encourage the troops during the war. We in the Neuropsychiatry Consultants Division strongly recommended that they should do so because of potentially beneficial effect on morale. It is doubtful if our recommendation was ever sent beyond some intermediate office en route to the persons concerned. We never heard from it.

For some time, responsibility for the maintenance of the physical health of a unit has been recognized as a function of the officers. If the commanding officers had not insisted that every man take his atabrine, all the doctors in the world could not have prevented malaria in certain areas. During the recent war psychiatrists discovered the extent to which the mental health of the Army was also dependent upon its commanding officers. The incidence of ill health could have been, as it actually was in a few cases, used as an index of leadership ability. Where the commanding officer applied the principles of mental hygiene by setting an example, by establishing definite standards and policies, by creating healthy attitudes and confidence, by interest in the personal affairs of his men, the incidence of mental illness decreased in that outfit. By such means the successful leader-officer, noncommissioned or commissioned, welded his men into a psychological whole. Then all the men functioned as one, each identifying himself with the others and with the whole and gathering strength in the process. This identification enabled the soldier to accept the aim of the group and the orders of its leader, for they became his aim and orders. There were countless recorded instances where the efficiency of a particular group was increased or decreased out of all proportion to its numerical strength by an unusually able or poor leader.

Motivation. The Army used the term "motivation" to describe the conscious attitude of the soldier toward his assignment. An intelligent determination to accomplish a job often assists an individual in overcoming both personality handicaps and external obstacles. Therefore, positive motivation, to do or die in the attempt, was regarded as "good" and an important factor in maintaining mental health, particularly when the assignment was an extremely difficult one or was made difficult by the environmental situation.

Only a small proportion of the entire armed force was capable of feeling an emotional urge toward the real purpose of American participation in World War II. Consequently, against great odds,[5] the Army was forced to assume the responsibility of harnessing unconscious emotional pressure to the performance of the routine necessary to being a soldier. Only so could the nation move nearer to its ultimate goal. Although few, if any, of the morale builders knew the psy-

---

[5] These odds were understandingly and sympathetically presented by David L. Cohn in *This Is The Story*, Houghton Mifflin Company, Boston, 1947, p. 359. He compared the Army's task at orientation to the dilemma confronting American universities, in that many men are incapable of learning, others have been inadequately prepared, and then there is the group who go for many ulterior motives other than actually learning. When the man came into the Army he didn't know why he was coming except in a very vague way. "The Army had to attempt to give the soldier a rudimentary political education and do for him what his civilization had not done for him. His political perspectives, like those of the nation, were not broad but narrow. He was ill informed about international affairs. He was a citizen of a country which had never made up its mind about its relationship to other people, but had merely essayed the impossible feat of being in the world but not of it."

chological dynamics of their activity, nevertheless their information, education, and leadership did stimulate action toward *secondary* aims. These aims were to be a "good" soldier or officer, to do one's duty, to refuse to be a quitter, and to make one's unit the best. When these pseudo goals brought behavior and performance into line with action necessary for winning the war, the motivation was labeled as "good."

A survey of the motives which men thought helped them in combat when life was hard and the struggle intense showed the role of the secondary aims. In the Pacific area hatred of the enemy was a more powerful incentive than in some other theaters. An even more potent motive was the belief that getting home depended on finishing the job. Still more effective was the desire "not to let the other men down." In an opinion survey [6] in the South Pacific area, 94 per cent of the officers and 78 per cent of the enlisted men reported that concern about doing their part to support their comrades helped them overcome their fear in battle. The strength of the emotional attachment to other men with whom they lived a 24-hour day for months at a time has no parallel in any civilian relationship. Thinking of what they were fighting for "helped" 46 per cent of officers and 58 per cent of enlisted men "when the going was tough."

Whatever could calm anxiety, modify fear, renew a will to keep going made a difficult and unwanted job somewhat easier to do. There were many variations in the kind of motivation operative in the course of a soldier's experience; it was modified by the period and the area in which he served; it varied widely in different individuals.

Some of our Army leaders held the belief that hatred of the enemy should be mobilized in our soldiers to serve as a motive to kill.[7] In some units an effort

---

[6] "When the Going Gets Tough," *What the Soldier Thinks,* No. 5, 25 April 1944, p. 3.

[7] In the attempts to motivate the soldier, special consideration was given to whether they should be taught or encouraged to hate the enemy. The observations were that this was not necessary in the Pacific; no particular stimulus was required. On the contrary, it was not effective in the European Theater. Whatever attitude one had toward the Germans, for the most part they were clean fighters. Again and again our soldiers saw specific instances where wounded were exchanged at night or where a German tank would stop and a soldier would dismount and remove a wounded man from the road before the tank went on. Such instances became such common knowledge that it was not possible to inculcate hate widely. Against the opinion of several high-ranking officers, in the outline of the fourth lecture to be given to all officers, the following statement was made: "The indoctrination of hate is not desirable. Resentment against the enemy is important, but love for home, leader and buddies is a much more powerful stimulus for fighting. It is the skillful, cool boxer who wins his bout, not the 'mad man.' Hate is essentially self-destructive in that it prevents the objective utilization of available skills and weapons." This attitude regarding the value of this motivating ideology was strongly supported by the great majority of objective observers. "Lecture Outlines for Officers on Personnel Adjustment Problems," *War Department Technical Bulletin, Medical 12,* 22 February 1944. The same experiences and conclusions were reported by Rees of the British Army: Rees, J. R., *The Shaping of Psychiatry by War,* W. W. Norton & Company, Inc., New York, 1945, pp. 80-82. A survey of combat soldiers fighting in Germany showed that only 27 per cent of them were helped by thoughts of hatred of the enemy (38 per cent in the Pacific); 18 per cent were helped some (23 per cent of Pacific soldiers); 23 per cent helped little or none (18 per cent

was made to do so. On superficial thought such a motive might seem desirable, assuming it *could* be mobilized. It is doubtful, however, if psychiatric advice was sought in such a program since, essentially, the plan is unsound. One cannot stimulate an emotion intellectually. Moreover, the aggressive element varies widely in different personalities. Some individuals have an abundance of hostility that can be released with slight provocation. More mature individuals with healthier developmental backgrounds have a minimal amount of the hate component in their make-ups.

Hate can be mobilized in varying degrees by fear or threat or frustration. Once aroused, it can be fanned to some degree by intellectual rationalizations—injustice, cruelty, torture, arrogance, and other reported or observed behavior of an enemy. But the fact remains that hate was never aroused in America as it was by the threat to life felt by the Russians or English or Chinese. Most Americans never felt really endangered. Consequently it was not possible to tell a bunch of American soldiers to "hate" and expect them to turn on the emotional spigot of aggression. In addition, training to kill went against all the "higher" ideals which had been instilled in Americans from childhood.[8] To hate required a regression to a more primitive level of personality function or an arrest at an early stage of immaturity, when hate and destruction and emotional shows were much less well controlled.

There were many other reasons why hate could not be effectively mobilized. However, even if one could, there would be questionable value in doing so. The wrought-up individual is least competent to manage himself. The emotionally laden individual cannot be a calm, cool fighter and have objective judgment. Is the naughty child best managed if the parent becomes hostile toward it? Regardless of the pros and cons, the attempts to instill hatred of the enemy in our soldiers was never successful in the European Theater. It was somewhat more effective in the Pacific areas, probably because the Japs were more ruthless, less considerate, more feared, and (an important psychological fact) were of a different race.

When war was declared and certain men from the citizenry were selected to go forth to fight, few really wanted to go. Many chosen thought war was necessary, but many others were not so sure; still others questioned why they should have been involved. Thus there was a varying degree of initial conviction among

in the Pacific); 25 per cent had no such thoughts (18 per cent in the Pacific); 7 per cent no answer given. "Hatred of the Enemy," *What the Soldier Thinks,* No. 7, 25 July 1944, p. 8.
[8] The effect of our cultural background on the release of aggressions was discussed in connection with several points in a book by one of our leading anthropologists: Margaret Mead, *And Keep Your Powder Dry,* William Morrow and Company, Inc., New York, 1943. An interesting study of soldiers with widely different motivations was reported by R. A. Clark in "Aggressiveness and Military Training," *Am. J. Sociology,* 51:423-432, Mar., 1946.

draftees as to the importance of their assignment to military service; most accepted military service as a necessary chore.

Many men could be informed sufficiently to realize that even though their own lot was poor or their job undesirable and difficult, neither could be improved if Hitler took over. Moreover, they would probably be made worse. From grim facts they could discover a personal stake in winning the war. The Information and Education Service [9] exerted great effort to provide such facts. This task undoubtedly was harder because of an all-too-prevalent attitude of unconcern in the nation at large. For a month or two after Pearl Harbor the country was aroused to the indignity, the inhumanity, and the unfairness of the Japanese attack. The nation put forth a united effort, but, as time wore on, this emotional reaction became less and less potent. Though many homes were affected by members going into the armed forces, there was an obvious drop in the national enthusiasm for the war effort.[10]

---

[9] The accomplishment of the Information and Education Service under Maj. Gen. F. H. Osborne was phenomenal. It was responsible for the publication of *Yank,* magazine for servicemen, which began June 17, 1942 with 175,000 copies and on August 1, 1945 had a circulation of 2,400,000 copies with 14 separate editions covering the globe. The Armed Forces Radio Service broadcast from 177 Army radio stations all over the world, plus 54 foreign-government and commercial stations and 113 sound systems in hospitals. Over 120,000 radio transcriptions were being distributed at the peak load in August, 1945, with an average of 86,000 monthly. There were 18 different editions of the daily newspaper, *Stars and Stripes,* the European Theater edition alone having a daily net circulation of 1,200,000. Large bulletin-sized news maps were issued weekly, beginning with 18,000 copies with the first issue April 27, 1942, and reaching a total distribution of 190,000 copies in August, 1945. Descriptive pocket guides were written for 26 foreign countries and 7 others for European cities for the special use of the soldiers. Informational films known as the "Why We Fight" series, seven in number, were shown to an estimated audience of over 45,000,000 persons in the United States alone, the first of which "Prelude to War," had an audience of 9,700,000 men. In addition there were special informational pictures on "The Negro Soldier," "Our Ally Britain," "Our Enemy German," "Enemy Japan," "Your Job in Germany," "The Army Navy Screen Magazine." Under the Armed Forces Institute with headquarters at Madison, Wisconsin, correspondence courses at grade-school, high-school and junior-college levels, as well as technical courses, were provided through 10 branches to a total student group of 874,515 up to August, 1945. On that date, 575,711 were actively enrolled. A total of 364 self-teaching educational manuals were published, covering different subjects in many different fields. For the purpose of round-table discussions, a large series of discussion pamphlets, prepared by the American Historical Association, were issued. Foreign-language guides were published covering 29 different languages. Five university schools were established in Europe, two in England, one each in France, Italy, and Hawaii, utilizing 300 civilian instructors with an average enrollment of approximately 13,000 men. This division prepared a series of orientation skits to be used by a leader in every unit for a 1-hour weekly "orientation" discussion of the war. Research of soldier attitudes was carried out continuously, the findings of many of which affected basic staff policies. They included the point score system, attitudes of infantrymen, fraternization, statistical studies of casualties, attitudes of soldiers towards deployment. These were published in a restricted monthly bulletin, *What the Soldier Thinks* and roughly 110,000 copies of each issue were distributed down to company officers.

[10] With biting sarcasm, Sevareid described the contrast between the situation at home and the crisis at the time the first American division landed in Great Britain:

"Rommel's Legions reappeared at Tobruk, and the whole middle East was again under mortal threat; enemy torpedoes sucked American ships below the surface of the crystal Caribbean, so close that a chorus girl in a Miami penthouse could see men die in flaming oil, and all the

Many observers have noted the evidences of a much higher emotional tone on the home front in World War I than in World War II. Whether the observations are valid or not, it is difficult to say. But the popular and widely known songs of World War I were not superseded by those of World War II which could not compare in emotion arousing to any of half a dozen written in 1917-18. There were fewer parades and patriotic gatherings in this last war. After the first few months most draftees reporting to camp went to the hometown railroad station and left—alone. Perhaps the disillusionment that followed the outbreak of another conflict after the "war to end wars" made patriotism baiting seem empty of meaning. Or perhaps we never doubted our victory.[11] In any event, as the war continued, there was less and less enthusiasm for its prosecution on the part of the average inductee and his family. It became proportionately more difficult to give an indifferent recruit such strong convictions regarding the importance of his task that he would be willing, if need be, to sacrifice his life in its accomplishment.

In an opinion survey [12] of a cross section of company officers and enlisted men in three infantry divisions, all but 7 per cent of the officers and 1 per cent

---

work to mobilize the southern continent faced humiliating failure; Englishmen, the Lords of the East, were stripped and beaten on the streets of Singapore; all of Australia lay exposed, and on a rock in Manila Bay exhausted, ragged men, suffered too deeply for tears, hoisted a white flag in the first real American surrender in more than a hundred years of secure existence.

"And in the crowded night clubs of New York men and women danced slowly to the saccharine melodies of a song called 'Remember-R-R Pearl Harbor-R-R,' and rapidly to the frenzied strains of the latest jive hit. There was money to burn, and it was burned in a bright gay flame. Fifth Avenue shops have sold handkerchiefs embroidered with patriotic monograms for $10.00 a piece, news reels pointed out the 'military motif' in the latest fashions, and the expanded society pages gave convincing proof that the Junior League had indeed gone into uniform. Resort hotels ran out of space, and gasoline and rubber bootleggers became our richest citizens. Six-column headlines blared the good news every time that three Jap planes went down; full page advertisements announced the inspiring news that Lucky Strikes had gone to War; street placards in three colors advised the nation that its war production would be increased if everyone masticated a few extra sticks of Wrigley's per day, and a hundred local radio stations offered the virtues of laxative and liver pills along with the news of humanity's crisis and in the same fulsome tones. The cuffs were eliminated from men's trousers, and it made front page news; coffee and sugar were rationed to the accompaniment of loud complaints, and neighbors were encouraged to spy upon one another's pantries." Reprinted from Not So Wild a Dream by Eric Sevareid, by permission of Alfred A. Knopf, Inc. Copyright 1946 by Eric Sevareid, pp. 213-214.

Maj. Stephen W. Ranson, a combat psychiatrist, prepared an analysis of the effects of civilian attitudes on the soldier, a paper titled "Psychiatric Effects on the Troops of Defective Civilian Attitudes and Behavior," on file in the Historical Division of the Office of the Surgeon General. Ranson pointed out the three things which appeared to be most resented; civilian indifference to the war and the soldier, the high prestige value granted by civilians to "homefront" activities as opposed to military service, and the apparent unwillingness of civilians to undergo any important degree of deprivation.

11 "Artificial mass enthusiasm for war is fear of death in disguise. A civilized nation has no enthusiasm for war; it suffers war as a duty and not as a frenzy." Meerloo, A. M., Aftermath of Peace, International University Press, New York, 1946, p. 85. This does not contradict a real "enthusiasm" if a real threat of death exists.

12 "What the Soldier Thinks About the Orientation Course," What the Soldier Thinks, No. 4:14, 15, 25 March 1944.

of the enlisted men felt that having a clear understanding of what they were fighting for was one important objective for the orientation program. All but 4 per cent of officers and 5 per cent of enlisted men agreed that another objective was the feeling that their outfit had a vital mission. Yet both personal experience and opinion surveys tell a tale of indifference on the part of administering officers toward the orientation program. It was rare that the material supplied to meet the avowedly important objectives was used effectively. A measure of the effect of knowledge of the events shaping the world around them demonstrated that those who gained the most information displayed the most improvement in attitude.[13] Again the test tube provided for psychiatry in this laboratory of war showed up the understanding and capable leader as the all-important implement for increasing the soldier's determination to stay in the fight. His was the task of interpreting to his men the information which special sections of the Army sent him; his was the most potent example of attitude and behavior; his approval was essential for the release of aggressive urges which had previously had to remain under tight control; his respect for and appreciation of his men built up their morale. Even the individual with obvious neurotic tendencies or a heavily laden disposition to mental illness derived strength from emotional dependence upon the leader who accepted the obligations of his role.

The priming of motivation was a continuing problem for the leader. At times of inactivity the men did not see any reason for not doing something worth while. So, in addition to keeping the soldiers posted on the progress of the total war effort, the commanding officer found it important to explain how the assignment of his particular unit fitted into the total plan. One enlisted man verbalized the problem: "Some of the guys griped a lot, because we wanted to be doing something important to get the war over and get home. Then we got a new CO. He told us about the war picture as a whole and showed us how necessary our job was. Now we all know our job is important." [14]

Positive or "good" motivation was significant to the psychiatrist because of its direct relationship to mental health.[15] Even in the most willing soldier there was some repressed resentment against the forces that had caused the upheaval in his life which had taken him away from his home, his work, his friends. This normal resentment, if coupled with a negative or weak motivation, weakened conscious control of powerful unconscious urges. Such urges were then able to

---

13 "Influencing Attitudes with Information," *What the Soldier Thinks*, No. 11:9, 20 January 1945.
14 "Morale Problems Emerging Where War Tensions Relax," *What the Soldier Thinks*, No. 10, 25 November 1944, p. 2.
15 A psychiatrist with combat experience reported that providing information—"the unvarnished truth"—was an important instrument in reducing the incidence of neurosis in combat soldiers. Stein, M., "Neurosis and Group Motivation," *Bull. U.S. Army M. Dept.*, 7:317-321, Mar., 1947.

gain indirect expression in illness. Many parents have seen a similar phenomenon in the child who became ill and so prevented them from leaving home or forbade his own attendance at school. Such behavior was the result of unconscious motivation and should not be confused with conscious intention. Psychiatrists saw similar unconscious dynamic forces function as determinants of behavior in soldiers. Unconsciously motivated purpose was apparent when there was a lack of a sense of personal obligation. This was more obvious when combined with either conscious or unadmitted fear of death or injury, or when related to other types of unhappiness from misassignment, lack of promotion, separation from home. In brief, wherever there was poor *conscious* motivation, individual or collective, there was also poor morale and poor mental health, individual or collective.

On the other hand "good" motivation strengthened conscious control and in varying degrees counteracted the pressure from unconscious motives. With deep conviction Army psychiatrists approved of any techniques which could channel both unconscious and conscious motivation toward the immediate goals which paralleled the more remote ones. Thus could men be supported against the emotional stress of their difficult lives.

Identification with a group. Because a soldier was an integral part of a very closely cemented functional unit—a platoon or a company, a bomber crew or a demolition squad—he was very greatly influenced by his membership in that group. Its attitudes and thinking in most instances were his attitudes and thinking. Its loyalties and gripes were his loyalties and gripes. If able to fit into a group which had good leadership, his membership on that team gave the soldier one of the strongest possible supports against stress.[16]

The commission of civilian psychiatrists, in their study of the European combat psychiatric problems, regarded the position of the soldier in his social group, the combat team, as the most significant factor in maintaining his integrity. "His assimilation into the group had been facilitated by various factors, including the over-evaluation of the group and the depreciation of other groups, the personal attachments to individuals of the group and to the leader, the security resulting from training for his specific job in the group, and the assurance obtained from adequate supplies brought to his group. Belonging to the group enabled him to share his successes, satisfactions, horrors, dangers, deprivations and discomforts and, in turn, to be protected by its strength and to be united with it in purpose."

The commission also reported: "The organized pattern of the unit and its emotional bonds constitute the dominant, constructive and integrative force for

---

[16] Thirty per cent of overseas veterans from various theaters and branches said that teamwork and pride in their outfit was the reason for the "high" morale of their outfits: "Things Which Tend to Make or Break Morale," *What the Soldier Thinks,* No. 15:3, 25 July 1945.

the individual soldier in his fighting function. This group life *is* his inner life. When an individual member of such a combat group has his emotional bonds of group integration seriously disrupted, then he, *as a person* is thereby disorganized. The disruption of group unit is, in the main, a primary causal factor, not a secondary effect of personality disorganization!" [17]

Another aspect of the supportive character of the group was pointed out by Grinker and Spiegel: "The American combat soldier is strongly attached and devoted to his group. The affection which he invests in this group is not lost and therefore his emotional economy is not disturbed for long periods of time because of several factors. For one thing, contact with a group is continuously maintained. Conversely, nothing is more painful than the necessity of leaving the group because of illness, detached service or transfer. In many instances, a man will refuse a transfer, although it involves a promotion or a better job, simply in order to stay with his group. Secondly, his super-ego is strongly identified with the group and, as he loves the group, he loves himself as a member of the group." [18] This last sentence might also be interpreted to mean that as a soldier respects the group, he respects himself as a member of the group.

Letters. A fourth emotional support dependent on relationships was the mail from home. As was indicated under the discussion of stress in the last chapter, the soldier reacted with surcharged emotional value to the news in letters. Consequently letters bearing unpleasant or disturbing news were a major stress, but "good" letters were of tremendous support. "Good" letters contained chatty news, details of family life which did not emphasize the unpleasant angles; they answered questions or remarks in the soldier's last letter; they sent a pat on the back in expressed affection, moral support, and pride in his service. As the commission of civilian psychiatrists pointed out, the nostalgic effect created by news from home need not be deplored, for it added to the emotional value of victory and maintained a sense of emotional solidarity with one's own people. It thereby helped to counteract the very real tendency for the soldier in the fighting zone to identify himself more closely with the enemy soldier, who is right there in the same section of hell and has to "take it, too," than with folks safely back home.

Discipline. The system in the Army which regulated the relationships between men, called discipline, was undoubtedly a powerful support to the individual. The War Department Army Regulations defined military discipline as "that mental attitude and state of training which render obedience and proper

---

[17] *Medical Report on Morale and Psychiatry,* No. 17, Office of the Surgeon General, 25 August 1945, pp. 14-15. Reprinted: Bartemeier, L. H.; Kubie, L. S.; Menninger, K. A.; Romano, J.; and Whitehorn, J. C., "Combat Exhaustion," *J. Nerv. & Ment. Dis.,* 104:358-389, Oct., 1946; 489-525, Nov., 1946.

[18] Grinker, R. R., and Spiegel, J. P., *Men Under Stress,* The Blakiston Company, Philadelphia, 1945, p. 122.

conduct instinctive under all conditions. It is founded upon respect for and loyalty to properly constituted authority. While it is developed primarily by military drill, every feature of military life has its effect on military discipline. It is generally indicated in an individual or unit by smartness of appearance and action; by cleanliness and neatness of dress, equipment, or quarters; by respect for seniors and by the prompt and cheerful execution by subordinates of both the letter and the spirit of the legal orders of their lawful superiors." [19]

From the psychiatric point of view the whole subject of discipline is a complicated one. There were many, many examples of the disastrous effect of the hard-boiled attitude of an officer; as also of weak, indecisive softness. Discipline amounts to far more than the neatness or snappiness of the unit or the uniform. From the psychological point of view, the unquestioned and positive orders of a superior officer could be a support to the soldier, just as in the family, the firmness and, if necessary, severity of the father maintains a standard of behavior. At the same time both officer and father can be affectionate and understanding. Undoubtedly the number of men referred to the psychiatrist in the training camp or in combat was in some degree dependent on the standards of discipline in the unit. In some instances it was too severe and in others too lax. The officer who was firm and yet understanding gave support and reinforcement to that individual who was on the border line of his ability to adjust to the stress of the moment. Even ideal discipline could not have prevented all psychiatric casualties.

The physician also had to use discipline in the battalion aid station and in the collecting station. The psychiatric casualties which appeared before him, almost without exception, hoped that their condition was a ticket out of combat. The psychiatrist was in the extremely difficult spot of deciding who was able to go back to combat and who was too sick. Personal and group discipline were therefore essential.

ENVIRONMENTAL SUPPORTS THROUGH RELIEF OR CHANGE

A fair percentage of our soldiers faced either combat on the one hand or monotony, inactivity, lonesomeness, and isolation on the other hand. In either case, it was obvious that relief, relaxation, or recreation would serve as a significant factor in combating stress. As indicated elsewhere, at least in the European Theater where fighting was continuous, there was little opportunity until nearly the end of the war for relief from combat, despite strong psychiatric recommendations regarding this point. Apparently the tactical situation did not permit it, because there were not sufficient replacements in reserve strength. Usually,

---

[19] Army Regulations 600-10, Subject: Personnel. Military Discipline, 8 July 1944.

after a severe campaign in the Pacific, the combat unit was given time for recuperation.

Leaves (for officers) and furloughs (for enlisted men) were recognized as important and desired features of military life, though actually during the war, except for emergencies, these were rarely given. The exception to this rule was to allow them the week following induction and 2 to 3 weeks just prior to overseas shipment if the time permitted. The latter was of special value in the maintenance of good morale. There were many complaints, however, that there was too little leave, but vacations can hardly be justified in time of war.

Programs to provide change, relaxation, and recreation were planned by the Army as well as by affiliated organizations, even though in many instances they were executed with difficulty. Great credit must go to the American Red Cross for the establishment of a recreational and diversional program on every post and in every hospital, including the provision of a special center as a place to loaf. Credit should also go to the chaplains, who acted as morale officers in every unit.

The efforts of the Army in this direction were extensive although not uniformly effective. The Special Services Division with its three sections of Army Exchange Service, Army Motion Picture Service, and Army Athletic and Recreation Service, was spread over the globe to provide relaxation for our troops.[20] The Army Exchange Service, which ran the post exchanges, did $134,000,000 worth of business with a turnover of inventory 13 times a year. The Army Motion Picture Service sent to all theaters of operation an average of three films a week including (according to the Special Services Division booklet) many world premiers. My own experience with movies in both camps in this country and units overseas left much to be desired, but they were well attended because of nothing else to do. Many of the films were wretched. The Army Athletic and Recreation Service supervised the recreational buildings in every post and camp; they arranged for the soldier shows; they provided the athletic equipment of all types. But 3 out of every 10 GI's included in an opinion survey indicated they did not have enough recreation equipment.[21] The Special Services screened and routed to all theaters the acting, singing, and dancing stars of radio, motion picture, and stage. They published handy pocket-size paper-bound books, and sent 62,000,000 of these popular editions overseas up to September 1, 1945. They published the overseas lightweight edition of 32 popular weeklies and monthlies with a total distribution of 120,000,000

---

[20] Facts and figures supplied by Col. William H. Quarterman, Chief, Army Athletic and Recreation Service, Special Services Division, 30 April 1946. Some of these achievements are described in a Special Services Division booklet entitled, "Special Service for Fighting Yanks," dated 15 February 1944. A detailed outline for the athletic and recreation officer is presented in *War Department Technical Manual TM 21-205,* July, 1945.

[21] *What the Soldier Thinks,* No. 2, August, 1943, p. 71.

magazines a year. Their personnel numbered thousands of officers, enlisted men, and civilians on full time, with hundreds of trained librarians and hostesses. The sum total of these efforts as supports against stress can hardly be estimated. They were often the main, sometimes the only, antidote for the idleness and lonesomeness of many soldiers.

PHYSICAL COMFORTS AS ENVIRONMENTAL SUPPORTS

No one who knew the Army expected too much in the way of physical comfort. Yet obviously, a minimum of necessities was required. The presence or absence of these constituted either a major support or a major stress. Lack of proper food or proper clothing weakened the men both physically and emotionally. On the contrary, good food and comfortable living conditions were important supportive factors against many types of stress. Even in the most impossible physical conditions of combat, there were sometimes small things which materially affected the life of the soldier and could be changed to his great advantage by observant and alert leaders. It is with special pride that I have often repeated the story of our neuropsychiatric consultant in the Mediterranean Theater, Col. Fred Hanson, who circulated in the front lines and carried the nickname of "phantom" because he turned up so unexpectedly. He found that in many places the soldiers had had wet feet for days at a time, without a change of socks. Through his suggestion an order was given to the theater quartermaster to provide a change of socks at definite intervals for the combat soldier. This example of a supportive physical comfort that could be provided even under the worst conditions was suggested by a psychiatrist!

Another of the physical needs of soldiers which had great psychological implications was prompt medical attention in case of illness or injury. The efficient and high-caliber professional medical service provided was an important support.[22] Comparative statistics could be presented to show the progress of medical science and its reflection in the care of our Army in World War I and World War II. For example, the mortality rate from wounds was reduced from the 8 per cent in World War I to slightly more than 4 per cent who died

---

[22] An exception, in varying degrees, was in camp dispensary care. For many reasons, the average dispensary in the average camp gave mediocre care. In many posts, the dispensary physician was an inexperienced young doctor with little authority and minimal supervision, who was rushed at sick call, with no chance to get back to hospital work. His morale was low. Too often he could give the patient only a fraction of a minute of time and the enlisted man felt he was getting the "brush-off." (See Goldman, G. S., "The Psychology of Sick Call," *Bull. U.S. Army M. Dept.*, 6:71-75, July, 1946.) On the basis that such management might produce or aggravate personality disorders, the Neuropsychiatry Consultants Division, through Maj. (later Lt. Col.) John W. Appel, initiated a survey, collected data, and stimulated the publication of War Department Circular 387, 29 December 1945, with its reorganization of the dispensary function.

in this war. The annual death rate from disease was lowered from 16.5 per 1,000 per annum to a rate of 0.6.[23] Of great significance is the fact that 360,000 of our 571,000 wounded were returned to duty. The annual death rate per 1,000 for all diseases (excluding surgical conditions) was reduced from 15.6 in World War I to 0.6 in World War II. The death rate in specific diseases was spectacularly reduced: [24]

	World War I	World War II
Meningitis fatality	38.0%	4.0%
Pneumonia fatality	28.0%	0.7%
Tuberculosis fatality	17.3%	1.8%
Dysentery fatality	1.6%	.05%

These remarkable results were reflected in the confidence which the soldiers expressed in the Medical Department, as indicated in a survey by the Research Branch of the Special Services Division. Of these soldiers, 80 per cent felt that good medical attention was being provided in the Army, 15 per cent were uncertain or did not know, and only 5 per cent felt that such was not provided.[25]

SUPPORTS PROVIDED BY EXPERIENCE

All the life experience of the soldier either aided or hindered his adjustment in the Army. His personality was largely the composite result of that experience. All of his childhood background added up to or against his credit in terms of character assets or defects. He brought into the Army with him a good or poor constitution, a strong or a weak back, a keen or perhaps a dull mind. Experience and training in the Army was marshaled to his advantage or disadvantage. Two potential supports, provided by experience, about which one can generalize are: one, ties to home, and the other, training to do the job provided for him in the Army.

Home. Nearly every soldier was a civilian at heart. Even though he came into the Army willingly, sometimes enthusiastically, he looked on it as a temporary experience. His behavior and his standards for decisions were largely dependent upon his emotional ties to home. Therefore, specific relationships, namely, to a particular house in a particular place, and to the people who lived in it, could be either a support to help him make a good adjustment or a factor mitigating against it. This paradox depended upon the previous relationships at home—the lifelong patterns of dependency that he had established. The attitude of the youngster of 18 years was very different from that

---

[23] Kirk, Norman T., *Army Day Review*, Army Day Committee, 1700 I Street N.W., Washington 6, D.C., 6 April 1946, p. 90.
[24] Morgan, H., "The Internist at War. A Glance at the Record," *Ann. Int. Med.*, 20:881-883, June, 1944.
[25] *What the Soldier Thinks*, No. 46, December 1942.

of an older married man with children. In all cases this influence on his behavior and feelings while in the Army depended on the stability of the home and his responsibility for it, his attachment to it.

The home was an extremely important support for many men who were emotionally tied to it but were not necessarily overdependent upon it. I recall my own feeling when my family toyed with the idea of joining me at my first post. Partly for selfish reasons I found myself not wanting them. The new life in the Army was strange, uncertain, insecure, subject to unexpected change. Far more important, however, was the fact that home had become something of a bulwark and anchor that tied me to a very real and secure past life. Most of us carried the illusion that somehow home represented real life instead of our unreal life in the Army.[26] Even though we knew that it was not so, we wanted to think that things were going on just as they had gone on; that home would remain just as we knew it when we were there. We treasured the idea, sometimes quite deeply under the surface and sometimes very superficially, that that was the place we were most anxious to get back to and as quickly as we could. It was "home" in a very sentimental sense. It symbolized our chief source of affection, regardless of the identification that we might be able to make with the military unit. The people back there were the ones to whom we wanted to tell our experiences. We knew that they would have a very personal interest in us as an individual at a time when we felt the impersonality of the huge machine of which we were an infinitesimally small part.

No doubt there were men for whom the home provided little if any support. Where there had been little or no attachment to it, no sentiment about it, home was of no emotional importance. Ties to the family also could be detrimental where previous relationships to it were pathological in nature. In many instances the dependence upon the mother or the wife had been too great; the soldier himself was immature. Consequently, the soldier's longing and homesickness were pathological. His real inability to carry his load or to fit into the Army was because of a too great dependence on the mother. This was a serious problem and, by some, was believed to be an indictment of American family life. Doctor Strecker has blamed the "moms" for much of the immaturity and maladjustment that we saw in the Army.[27]

---

[26] Benedek portrayed this struggle as a "double orientation" of the soldier's personality: with one part "he learns to be a part of a big organization and learns to function within it; and with the other part he struggles to preserve his past personality and strives away from his military existence." (Benedek, T., *Insight and Personality Adjustment,* New York, The Ronald Press Company, 1946, p. 47.) No one would disagree with her thesis that the soldier who had emotional ties to the past wanted to preserve these. There were few evidences that the adjusted man strove away from his military existence.

[27] Strecker, E. A., *Their Mothers' Sons,* J. B. Lippincott Company, Philadelphia, 1946; "Psychiatry Speaks to Democracy," *Ment. Hyg.,* 29:591-605, Oct., 1945.

The home was a disturbing factor in some degree in those cases where the wife, of necessity or by preference, went to work. The soldier was apt to be disturbed if the family had to move or if the home was sold. Many of the most distressing letters I received from soldiers were not about their tough life; they concerned the unhappiness of the family situation at home, of the man's uncertainty about that home.

There have been numerous expressions of opinion as to the importance of these home and family relationships, either as a support to the soldier's adjustment or as a handicap to such adjustment. In a veterans' clinic a study was made by Doctor Kasanin and his workers [28] of a group of men who had been psychiatric casualties, as compared to a control group of nonpsychiatric veterans. The control group showed strong family loyalties, a certain idealization of the father, and a strong affectionate relationship with the mother. The interests of the child had been respected and encouraged by the parents, and there had been a good deal of general family activity and contact with relatives. By contrast, the psychiatric veterans had been overly dependent. In spite of physical separation, they remained emotionally bound to members of the family. Grinker and Spiegel were impressed with the fact that soldiers who had had a previously happy, rich family and home life seemed to have a reserve to draw upon under stress that was not evident in men who had missed such a childhood home.[29]

The soldier who had some responsibility toward the home but no deep attachment found a kind of relief in the regression the Army permitted the individual. He could legitimately cast off civilian responsibilities. He escaped the cares and burdens of a family; decisions, if made, were strictly the responsibility of the folks back home. Dependents automatically (if so authorized by the soldier) received an allotment that was not an out-of-pocket contribution. He was doing his duty and simultaneously avoiding any responsibility to make ends meet or plan the future in terms of self-denial in the present. To be sure, one corollary of that state of mind was that when no one knows what tomorrow will bring, today can be lived to the hilt! Many soldiers did so!

Army Training. There is an old adage that experience is the best teacher. One reason that Army life was so difficult for most civilians was because nearly everything about it was to some degree new. Many of the more difficult stresses of military life could only be withstood at all because men were taught and trained to meet them by experience in living with them. The purpose in sending a recruit to a basic-training camp was not merely to give him physical

---

28 Kasanin, J.; Rhode, C.; and Wertheimer, E., "Observations from a Veteran's Clinic on Childhood Factors in Military Adjustment," *Am. J. Orthopsychiat.,* 16:640-659, Oct., 1946.
29 Grinker, R. R., and Spiegel, J. P., *Men Under Stress,* The Blakiston Company, Philadelphia, 1945, p. 248.

vigor and strength over his pre-Army status but chiefly to teach him what to expect, how to expect it, and what to do about it. Following this general basic training he was given specialized training for the particular job which he was expected to fill. The net result was to create in the soldier a sense of confidence in himself because he knew his job and knew he was able to function in it. Inseparable from this experience was the confidence that he developed in his weapons and in his equipment. He knew how they were made, what they would do, and how to handle them. "A soldier's best friend is his rifle." "A flier's best friend is his plane." These inanimate objects became surcharged with much emotional value to the soldier who depended upon them. The extent to which he learned the "how," the degree of his confidence in his own ability and in his own weapons, served as a very important environmental support in the accomplishment of his mission.

EGO BUILDERS

Finally, there were some supports to aid the soldier in his adjustment that were inherent in Army methods and in his own adaptations to Army life. These were intangible; they were psychological stimuli or reassurances that he, or the Army, used to aid him in coping with the situation. They made it easier for the individual personality to make adjustments to the abnormal situation of war and Army life.

The *uniform* became a badge of honor for most soldiers. It immediately identified the man with his mission. During the war this was particularly important as indicating his association with the biggest social movement of the day. Almost every soldier was proud of it; he got tired of it, and he was glad to take it off, but he was still proud of it. Directly related to the uniform was the badge of identification of the corps to which the man belonged. Depending on his pride in his corps, this little insigne took on special significance. The chevrons and the ranks of officers acquired an emotional value. At least to the individual, they signified his progress, his achievement, his position. The outstanding feature of his uniform to the soldier was his array of service ribbons. The more "salad" that a man could display over his left breast pocket, the prouder he was. They were the badges of his experience. Despite the fact that he knew and many other soldiers knew that many of them had comparatively little significance, they indicated where he had been; the soldier who did much traveling could acquire at least a half dozen ribbons. Most prized was the ribbon with battle stars or citations. The wearing of ribbons was one of the devices along with the regulation uniform and the insignia of unit and rank in which the soldier could take pride and by which he could indicate to the world his importance. Even if he did not wear them or had them under his pocket flap, the recognition of service rendered built up his self-esteem.

Closely allied to these outward evidences of membership and achievement were the numerous methods of showmanship by which the Army catered to the individual's love of self-aggrandizement and self-appreciation. There is reflected glory in the military ceremonies, the rituals, the parades, the inspections, the reviews. There were many individuals who obtained a great sense of personal satisfaction from these. In addition, they basked in the homage paid by civilians to the heroes of wartime. It seemed to increase their sense of virility and masculinity.

Every normal individual appreciates *recognition* of his services.[30] The Army tried to supply this, not only with chevrons for overseas duty but, much more important, with award of citations and medals for "gallantry" and "service beyond the call of duty." As of January 31, 1946, the Army had granted 1,736,549 such awards.[31] To Napoleon was ascribed the remark, "Give me enough ribbon to place on the tunics of my soldiers and I can conquer the world." Certainly the policy of decoration was followed in our Army. While there undoubtedly were many disappointments and miscarriages, the morale support and stimulus were very great.

At least initially, a support for many soldiers was the excitement and the thrill of *adventure* that an experience in the Army seemed to promise. This was usually most impressive as a recruit looked at the bulletin boards and saw the posters of "Join the Army and see the World"; the monotony, the lonesomeness, the bloodshed, the suffering, obviously were never shown. Nevertheless, most men on their entrance into the Army did feel a thrill of anticipation of the future experience. In this connection, the hunting for souvenirs or awards of enemy captured material satisfied some of the urge for adventure. In a personal communication to me, Lt. Col. Oscar Markey mentioned seeing evidence that souvenir collecting in the Ryukyus campaign was a positive emotional support even during battle, though it is true that great risks were taken and deaths occasionally ensued.

---

[30] Ernie Pyle sketched a brief scene of a presentation of awards in a combat area: "The moment the last man was congratulated, the general left and the whole group broke up in relief. As a spectacle it was sort of dull, but to each man it was one of those little pinnacles of triumph that will stand out until the day he dies. You often hear soldiers say, 'I don't want any medals. I just want to see the Statue of Liberty again.' But just the same you don't hear of anybody forgetting to come around, all nervous and shined up fit to kill, on the evening he is to be decorated." By Ernie Pyle. From *Brave Men,* copyright, 1944, by Henry Holt and Company, Inc., p. 82.

[31] The figures for several types of citations for all branches of service in the Army were 255 awards of the Medal of Honor; 69,504 of Silver Star; 347,301 of Bronze Star; 1,164,199 of Air Medal; 125,165 of Distinguished Flying Cross; 1,107 of Distinguished Service Medal; 10,408 to officers and 2,874 to enlisted men, of Legion of Merit. Decorations and Awards, prepared by Strength Accounting Branch, the Adjutant General's Office, 1 April 1946.

Interesting psychological devices used by most soldiers were various types of *totems, magic formulas, amulets*. These were described in part by the commission of civilian psychiatrists as "unrealistic motives and rationalizations which contributed to the soldier's defenses in mastering his fear . . . fantasies of invulnerability, 'they won't get me.' Many men actually wore amulets and many of the men who did not wear them fancied themselves invulnerable, either protected by God or by the goddess of luck. Some of the more realistic fantasies were of the nature of pure gambling; the chances were against it, 'I can outdraw fate.' Akin to this was the philosophy of fatalism, 'If my number comes up they will get me, whether I am here or somewhere else and if it isn't, I am as safe here as I would be somewhere else so what is there to worry about?' " [32]

This will to believe is reflected in the support from projection. The history of psychiatry is replete with demonology,[33] witches, incubi, and devils. Man has always sought support against his own frailties by placing the blame for them elsewhere. While usually referred to facetiously, "gremlins" operated in all theaters, or "Kilroy" [34] had already been on the job—and as always—had left.

Still another type of support was *prayer*. A survey [35] indicated that among combat officers and enlisted men:

Officers	Enlisted Men	
53%	63%	felt that prayer helped "a lot"
15%	13%	felt that prayer helped "some"
6%	6%	felt that prayer was "little or no help"
26%	18%	"did not think of it"

Surprisingly, there was no mention of prayer as a support in the report of a study [36] of American prisoners of war held by the Japanese.

Mention was made previously of the necessity for the soldier to accept a passive attitude. To do this a certain amount of psychological regression to an earlier developmental level was necessary. In the process he found certain compensations. These have been excellently presented by Janis.[37] He explained

---

[32] *Medical Report on Morale and Psychiatry*, No. 17, Office of the Surgeon General, 25 August 1945, p. 13. Reprinted: Bartemeier, L. H.; Kubie, L. S.; Menninger, K. A.; Romano, J.; and Whitehorn, J. C., "Combat Exhaustion," *J. Nerv. & Ment. Dis.*, 104:358-389, Oct., 1946; 489-525, Nov., 1946.
[33] Menninger, Roy W., "The History of Psychiatry," *Dis. Nerv. System*, 5:52-55, Feb., 1944.
[34] It is not surprising that in a situation of continued uncertainty where the average soldier would have wished for omnipotence, that the mythical GI Kilroy was developed. There are numerous stories of his origin—from the Air Forces, from the Infantry, but always he was a GI. See Davidson, B., "Kilroy Has Been Here," *Collier's Magazine*, Dec. 28, 1946; French, W. F., "Who is Kilroy?" *Saturday Evening Post*, Oct. 20, 1945.
[35] "When the Going Gets Tough," *What the Soldier Thinks*, No. 5, 25 April 1944, pp. 1-3.
[36] Brill, N. Q., "Neuropsychiatric Examination of Military Personnel Recovered from Japanese Prison Camps," *Bull. U.S. Army M. Dept.*, 5:429-438, Apr., 1946.
[37] Janis, I. L., "Psychodynamic Aspects of Adjustment to Army Life," *Psychiatry*, 8:159-176, May, 1945.

in a very rational fashion the significance of buffoonery and joking about menial jobs and sexual behavior; of profanity and the use of tabooed words; [38] of mimicry and derogatory gossip about superiors; of the importance and legitimacy of griping. All of these were techniques the personality used to support acceptance of the stresses imposed by Army life.

Summary. There were many positive factors which aided a soldier in his adjustment to the Army life and war experience. By all odds the most important sources of these were his leadership, his motivation, and his ability to identify with his unit. Other factors that aided directly in proportion to their quality were relief and recreation; the physical supports of food, clothing, and medical attention in at least a minimal form; training; prewar ties; and experience. Finally there were a number of psychological devices which the soldier adopted in a supportive fashion to protect himself against the emotional stress caused by the demands of his enforced military service.

---

[38] The language of the soldier was replete with words and phrases used in a strictly male society with its less strict social taboo. It served as one form of release of tension. An excellent review was given by F. Elkin in "The Soldier's Language," *Am. J. Sociology,* 51:414-422, Mar., 1946. An entertaining dictionary has been compiled by Elbridge Colby: *Army Talk, A Familiar Dictionary of Soldier Speech,* Princeton University Press, Princeton, 1942.

7

WOMEN IN THE ARMY

BEFORE THE WAR, approximately eleven million women worked outside the home; 2,500,000 more wanted or needed work. In March, 1944, there were over 16,000,000 at work away from home, 7,000,000 of whom were single, 7,000,000 were married, and 2,000,000 were widowed or divorced.[1] This trend in American life aided the Army in recruiting enough women to release more men for combat service. These women were needed in two distinct services: in the new experiment of the Army, the Women's Army Corps, and in the Medical Department as nurses, dietitians, physiotherapists, and doctors. These two services were very different in make-up and in some of the problems that confronted them.

THE WOMEN'S ARMY CORPS

The Women's Army Auxiliary Corps was created as a civilian organization in July, 1942. It became a military unit, the Women's Army Corp, in July, 1943. Between 1942 and 1945, 140,000 women served in these organizations. While this was not a large group numerically in proportion to the total size of the Army, it was an extremely important one which served its country well. Earlier, the British had developed such an organization which was regarded as being eminently successful. The utilization of women in the American Army seemed a practical method of increasing man power by releasing men from jobs that women could fill as well.

Although later the women in the Army "won their spurs" as evidenced by the enthusiastic comments of Lt. Gen. Ira C. Eaker,[2] the WAAC got off to a bad start. The Women's Army Auxiliary Corps, as a civilian organization, had

---

[1] *Women in the Post-War World*, Women's Advisory Committee of the War Manpower Commission, Washington, D.C., Apr., 1945.

[2] "They (women) keep more calm than men in emergencies. . . . They were intelligent and learned quicker. . . . They were the best foreign interpreters . . . keener, more intelligent than men in this line of work. . . . Another characteristic of women . . . is that they are more patriotic and less selfish." Lieutenant General Ira C. Eaker at the WAC officers graduation class, No. 60, Nov. 17, 1945.

none of the prestige, advantages, or privileges that the Army gave its personnel. Originally there were no definite plans for the placement of the women after their initial training. The result was that too many of them were doing nothing but administering their own organization. At first, many inappropriate assignments [3] were made. Unhappiness and dissatisfaction resulted. The WAAC's were not wanted by some sections of the Army. Nor was proper equipment available for their training. Women who were drilling in Des Moines, Iowa, in January, had only cotton fatigue clothes and GI overcoats.

The corps was made a part of the Army in the hope that some of these problems would be solved. The legislation to accomplish this was effected July 1, 1943. Of the original 61,000 women who went into the WAAC, nearly a fourth of them, 14,199, dropped out. In April, 1943, a Gallup poll of WAAC recruits gave an index of the acceptance of the idea of women in the military forces. Of the women interviewed about half had either a husband, brother, or boy friend in the service. By these men, about three-fourths of this group of recruits were advised not to join the WAAC; a year later (after incorporation into the Army) an even higher number (83 per cent) were so advised. The widespread resistance to the idea of women in military service was related fundamentally to the psychology of female development and the attitude of men toward women in our culture.[4] It was an uphill road to gain the approval of civilians and the respect of both the "brass hats" and the GI's in the Army.

PSYCHOLOGICAL ASPECTS

Development of femininity. No psychological problem is more complicated than the determination of what is meant by femininity, and how it develops. There is a fair degree of unanimity of opinion that it is related to a definite cultural pattern. Consequently, the theories of its development and the factors which influence it are very different in an American woman and in a Melanesian woman. In any case the process is one which is not entirely controlled consciously.

For the first months and perhaps for the first year or two of its life, a child is bisexual. The early training and attitudes of parents and society begin the sexual differentiation. As the child develops she learns to recognize the anatomical differences in sexes. Through her relationship to her parents she also discovers psychological differences. The baby develops the closest initial attach-

---

[3] Initially there were four types of jobs; later there were 250 different noncombatant jobs. Boyce, W. B., "All Good WAC's Have Straight Backs," *Army Day Review,* Washington, D.C., 6 April 1946, p. 112.

[4] This subject is discussed in a clear and helpful manner by Therese Benedek in *Insight and Personality Adjustment,* The Ronald Press Company, New York, 1946, pp. 269-282.

ment to the mother who feeds and cares for her. In the normal course of events the girl child becomes more devoted to the father and tends to regard the mother as a rival for his attention. The resulting emotional conflict resolves through the identification of the daughter with the mother in order to share the father. The mother then, as the pattern, becomes the model of female behavior.

This behavior is affected by the mores of each particular society. Each culture, through its social influences, forces a woman into a certain role. For many centuries she was practically the slave of man; in some cultures, even in our own time she still is. Our soldiers in Japan have seen women at hard physical labor in rice fields. Rees,[5] in discussing the women's service in the British Army, pointed out that the attitude toward women was one of the main differences between the Fascist and the democratic cultures.

Even in our own democracy the approved feminine role is a passive and dependent one. Only since 1920 have women had suffrage in this country, an event so recent as to have occurred since World War I. In some states women still have few legal rights. Before 1942 they were not supposed to fit into a fighting army except as nurses or Red Cross workers. The average man thought of women in an army as mythical Amazons, or the guerrilla fighters of revolutions, or camp followers with very specific business purposes. It took World War II with its great need for man power to open the doors of military service, as well as of industry, science and business, to women in any number. Those doors may be hard to close!

The increasing opportunity for American women to modify their traditional position complicates their acceptance of the feminine role. It allows women to choose their pattern of behavior. This is more difficult than it is for men to accept the unchanged concept of the masculine role. Furthermore, our educational philosophy differs from our current standards. The modern girl child in America is not taught to be the passive, dependent individual our culture has conceived of as the normal of adult femininity. So that when grown she is faced with some surprising facts: the "important" work of the world is supposed to be done by men; her early educational, social, and economic preparation for independence conflicts with the limitations of the accepted feminine role; the approved field of her interest seems unbalanced with too much routine for some years and too much leisure in later years. Furthermore, from childhood on, the girl, whether or not she wishes to do so, is expected to assume the role of a "weaker" sex, because of man's greater physical strength. It is reasonable to assume that a girl educated in the American way has to be "broken in" to being feminine. For she was born into what appears as a "man's world," in which she

---

[5] Rees, J. R., *Shaping of Psychiatry by War*, W. W. Norton & Company, Inc., New York, 1945, p. 93.

is supposed to "love, honor, and obey" and to make a home for some man.[6] It is not surprising, therefore, that in our culture women should acquire and retain strong masculine strivings.

Psychological significance of WAC for women. In evaluating the psychological significance of the military service for women, one must keep in mind that all WAC members were volunteers. What happened either in terms of success or failure or in terms of psychiatric problems would undoubtedly have been very different had it been a drafted Army. The appeal of an Army experience in time of war had a special attraction for some women, so that appeal was in itself part of the selective process. One must also recognize that conscious reasons for enlisting, while highly commendable (though possibly in some instances reprehensible), are not the total explanation of motivation.

Emancipation from psychological and environmental shackles certainly was a reason for enlistment in some instances. Here was an ideal opportunity to respond to a patriotic call and at the same time to escape the dependence on a home situation or subjection to its responsibilities. No doubt, it was sometimes an escape from what may be regarded as feminine duties. Many women joined against strong protest of their families—probably the most common problem which they had to solve (or ignore). Patriotism was an airtight rationalization for some women who left excellent jobs or apparently comfortable homes. The unconscious motive could have been a resentment toward their civilian (or feminine?) role or situation.

Identification with a specific male person in the Army, or an unconscious masculine identification, must have been the deciding psychological factor in many cases. War and an army always have been the epitome of a strictly masculine activity. This is as well known and accepted by women as by men. Almost every woman at some time in her life, and perhaps for a long period, has wished she were a boy or a man. Perhaps she was envious of the privileges and the opportunities of men, or irked by having to play the traditional role of a woman. Many women have very definite and strong masculine strivings. Often the motivation for joining an essentially male organization was probably stimulated by an unconscious competition with a consciously loved person—the hus-

---

6 "It is that many Americans overseas have come upon a woman whose kind they had apparently never met or perhaps had been unable to summon up even in their imagination, the woman who tries to please the man toward whom she stands in a relationship of mutual devotion whatever its actual or probable duration. The woman who places the man's career, desires, hopes and needs before her own; who is thoughtful of his comfort, watchful of his health, careful of his *amour propre,* zealous for his dignity, responsive to his moods. Such a woman is not dependent; not complete but complementary; and by turn incendiary and inflammable.

"She has filled many of our men with wild surmise and given them intense pleasure, not because she is per se extraordinary, but because she is the antithesis of the only kind of female— whether mother, sister, wife, or sweetheart—many of them had ever known: the spoiled American woman." Cohn, D. L., *This is the Story,* Houghton Mifflin Company, Boston, 1947, pp. 213-214.

band, the brother, or the boy friend. Such competition is often evident in sibling rivalry.

Closely allied to the mechanism of identification is the related motive of protest. This is a denial of the feminine role as if the unconscious were saying, "You see, I can even be a soldier, truly serve in a man's job." Undoubtedly, this sometimes took the form of aggressive behavior as if the unconscious were saying, "See here, husband, brother, father, I'll show you I'm as good as you are. I'll join the Army, too." One might well include in this constellation an aggressiveness against the mother who had different hopes and aspirations for her daughter.

Still another motive may have been the need to find a sense of security. This was sometimes fostered further by a sense of boredom or lonesomeness in the woman's civilian role. Joining the WAC was a way of helping the war effort in a commendable fashion which was reasonably safe. It would also give her something to do and provide her, as it does all soldiers, with the security and satisfaction of passively receiving food, a bed, a job, and clothing.

Some women joined the WAC merely as another escape from numerous previous unsuccessful attempts to adjust themselves in civilian life. These were maladjusted individuals who had never been able to fit into their environment and used the Army as an opportunity to make another trial. These were the problem personalities of the WAC.

Probably an unrecognized motive in a certain number of women was the desire to enlist in order to be with other women. Perhaps a very small number were overtly homosexual, though this problem was never a serious one in the WAC. It was anticipated that it would be more prevalent than it actually was. The reaction to homosexuality was interesting. Many women were ignorant of it prior to their coming into the WAC. Some were overconscious of it as a possibility. There was a strong tendency toward "witch-hunting" on the part of some prudish or sadistic officers, who suspected normal friendships of being tinged with homosexuality. On the other hand, it was a surprise to many persons, in and out of the WAC, to learn that some of the most efficient and admirable women had homosexual tendencies.

Finally, a motive in some cases was the search for an opportunity to express femininity. One must suspect, on the basis of psychological knowledge, however, that this was less frequently operative. Some women could have assumed, justifiably, that here was a chance to do an important job within a woman's capacity which would spare a man for a strictly masculine job. They must have hoped that, like Army nurses, they might play something of the mother or the sister role. Normal feminine urges to do secretarial and clerical work, housekeeping and cooking, could find expression in enlistment, regardless of what other desires might have been present. Another aspect of this same motive was seen in those who sought masculine company and felt that the Army was obviously the place to find it.

In considering these various conscious and unconscious motivations, one cannot and should not ignore the external pressure of the country being at war. It needed man power badly; women could replace men and thus free them for other duty. The fact that psychiatric experience gave an insight into unconscious motivation should not in any sense impugn the women who contributed so much to the success of the war effort. The unconscious motives, however, do throw light on some events that transpired in the Women's Army Corps during the war.

Psychological significance of WAC for men. The initial attitude of many of the male personnel in the Army toward the WAC was that the Army was very considerate in providing a female contingent! This psychological response was based in part on the narcissism of the male who too often assumes that women exist to serve him; in part on the automatic exaggeration of the sexual interest in women in an all-male society; and in part on the need for an antidote to the unconscious, vague fears of impotency that exist in a strictly one-sex group. Interestingly enough, Rees [7] called special attention to the presence of this same fear in the British Army. He mentioned the frequent recurrence of the unfounded rumor among soldiers that the use of atabrine caused impotency (also circulated in our Army). He also reported that among the women in the British Army who were working with radiolocation apparatus, there was a widespread rumor that the machinery would produce a sterilizing effect.

In spite of the general opinion that the WAC did a very capable job, its existence was accepted by the men with ambivalence; that is, while consciously recognizing its accomplishments, male officers and soldiers denied its value emotionally.

This was indicated by the Gallup poll figures cited above (see page 103). These men were willing only that women of whom they were not fond should come into the Army. In some way this attitude was less threatening to their supremacy or possibly to their concept of femininity. Undoubtedly it was an expression of their own unconscious simultaneous desires to possess and protect women. In essence it was an expression of their own struggle with the double standard for men and women.

Many men will of necessity be forced by the success of the experiment to make a readjustment in their concepts of the feminine role. Maskin and Altman,[8] who discussed this point, believed that this experience will ultimately beget a new, freer, collaborative and democratic relationship between men and

[7] Rees, J. R., *op. cit.,* pp. 93-96.
[8] Maskin, M. H., and Altman, L. L., "Military Psychodynamics. Psychological Factors in the Transition from Civilian to Soldier," *Psychiatry,* 6:263-269, Aug., 1943.

women. This sounds a little optimistic, but among those couples where wives were in the WAC, there is likely to be a new alignment. This will apply equally to families in which wives gained a wider horizon by experience in industry.

What types of women came into the WAC. Fortunately, an extremely interesting personality study was made by Maj. Albert Preston, M.C.[9] He served for almost 2 years as the psychiatrist in the Mental Hygiene Consultation Service at the Des Moines Training Camp. During that period he and his associates surveyed approximately 18,000 members of the Women's Army Corps, 10,000 of whom were referred to him for some type of psychological help and 8,000 of whom were "normals." Unfortunately, his figures are not broken down comparatively and for this reason lack the validity that a division into the two groups might have given. On the other hand, they do represent a cross section of WAC's. The great majority of the 10,000 seeking psychological help were upset by very minor disorders.

In general he found that 45 per cent had had "satisfactory" homes with both parents, 36 per cent had lost one or both parents, 19 per cent came from broken homes, and 2.2 per cent were raised in institutions. In his estimation, 35 per cent enlisted because of either conscious or unconscious urges to make a masculine identification, either with the intention to be like or to compete with husband, brother, father, or boy friend; 16 per cent enlisted for patriotic and service reasons. An additional 16 per cent enlisted on the basis that they felt compelled to help in the emergency at the sacrifice of themselves, manifesting some conscious or unconscious compulsive expression of guilt, and 13 per cent indicated their reason as a method of escape from the monotony of civilian life or any unpleasant home situation. The remaining 18 per cent presented various other types of motivation, some in combination.

The whole problem of motivation for enlistment into the WAC raises the question of the disadvantages of a voluntary enlistment for women. It suggests possible advantages of having them subject to Selective Service, not alone for military duty but for assignment to civilian work. The British had fewer problems when they ceased to have a volunteer organization. Many of the difficulties encountered in the WAC were due to the voluntary nature of enlistments. Specifically, many unsuitable individuals such as the maladjusted and those seeking glamour were attracted to the organization. Because they were volunteers, they felt they had more privileges and more inherent right to have some choice in their assignments, duties, and locations in contrast to men who *had* to be in the Army. They might as well be in the service as to be on some other job (although there was much dissatisfaction here too). Some women were

9 These data were furnished by Maj. Preston who plans to write them up in detail. Some of his experiences were reported in "The Mental Hygiene Unit in a W.A.C. Training Center," *Ment. Hyg.,* 30:368-380, July, 1946.

constantly comparing their WAC job with what they might be doing in civil
life, wondering if they were contributing enough to make their "sacrifice" worth
while. Such conflicts would have been eliminated in a group chosen arbitrarily.

The marital status of this group is of interest, although the available figures
are not adequately broken down for detailed information.

Marital Status of Female Personnel as of 30 June 1945

	WAC Officer	WAC Enlisted	Nurses
Married	28.80%	26.0%	14.70%
With children	3.09%	4.0%	.45%
Single	71.13%	74.0%	82.20%
With collateral dependents	4.12%	7.0%	7.70%

These figures, which were obtained from the Statistics Division of Army Service
Forces, included those individuals who had been divorced or separated from
their husbands under the heading of "single." Preston's survey of 18,000
WAC's indicated that approximately half had been or were married: 44 per
cent were married at the time of their enlistment, 26 per cent had been divorced,
and 2 per cent had been divorced twice or more; 8 per cent had been married
twice; 10 per cent had been separated, and 6 per cent were widowed.[10]

Of interest are some figures from the Medical Statistics Division, Surgeon
General's Office, with regard to the medical discharge rates in the different
marital states:

Marital Status	Medical Discharges per 1,000, October, 1943 to October, 1944	Enlisted (White) Less than 6 Months of Service
Single	27.9	16.2
Married	73.0	41.3
Other (widowed, divorced, separated)	68.7	36.1
Total	44.7	25.1

The Army gave what is known as the AGTC Test to all enlisted personnel
coming into the Army. This was not an intelligence test, and yet it gave a fair

---

[10] For comparison the percentage distribution of selected age groups of white females by marital
status, based on figures taken from 1940 U.S. census report were:

	Married (Including "Separated")	Divorced	Widowed	Total
20–24	97.06	2.24	0.70	100
25–29	95.91	2.91	1.18	100
30–34	93.95	3.70	2.35	100
35–39	91.48	4.08	4.44	100
40–44	88.66	3.83	7.51	100
45–49	84.97	3.35	11.68	100
Total 20–49	91.84	3.42	4.74	100

estimate of the knowledge and intellectual capacity and so was helpful in placing the individual in an appropriate assignment. It was of considerable significance that the scores of the WAC enlisted personnel were on the whole considerably higher than those of the male enlisted personnel, as shown in the following table as of March 31, 1944. (Grade 1 is the highest.)

	WAC	Enlisted Men
Grade 1	4.90%	6.34%
Grade 2	37.07%	31.00%
Grade 3	39.89%	30.68%
Grade 4	17.87%	25.12%
Grade 5	0.27%	6.86%

It will be noted that there are essentially no Grade-5 members among the WAC's, and that among enlisted men this grade makes up about 7 per cent. Undoubtedly, the fact that the WAC was a volunteer group accounts for their average higher mental capacity.

Even though the actual percentage of Group 5 was small, both Group 4 and Group 5 gave considerable trouble in the WAC. The special "opportunity" school at Des Moines trained these individuals as ward orderlies. All WAC assignments were made to special jobs, for which training, special aptitudes or qualifications were required. There were no all-drudgery jobs, such as continuous KP. This minority, then, was relatively more important than the mere figures indicate. Men in Groups 4 and 5 could be absorbed in the undifferentiated combat troops.

The educational achievement was higher in WAC officers than in male officers and in the WAC enlisted personnel than in the male enlisted personnel. The figures given here, as of June 30, 1944, were supplied by the Statistical Service of ASF.

	WAC Officer	Male Officer	Enlisted WAC	Enlisted Men
Grammar school	.26%	1.5%	8.99%	28.6%
1-2-3 years high school	4.01%	12.0%	28.62%	32.6%
High-school graduates	27.84%	22.2%	42.21%	27.6%
1-2-3 years college	26.98%	26.2%	13.76%	8.2%
College graduates	26.23%	21.7%	5.36%	2.1%
Postgraduate	14.68%	16.4%	1.06%	.9%

It is especially significant that the WAC enlisted personnel show slightly over 20 per cent with some college training in contrast to only 11 per cent of male enlisted personnel having such training. The high educational level of WAC officers was even more remarkable in that they were not chosen as specialists. The male officers included all the professional workers who came into the Army as specialists, such as physicians, engineers, lawyers, teachers, and chaplains.

Consequently, the figure of 14.68 per cent of all WAC officers who had had postgraduate work indicates their unusually high intellectual caliber. Many of the WAC officers had been specialists in civilian life, such as teachers, lawyers, physical educators, secretaries.

Finally, we can learn something about this branch of the service from the age distribution. The following table indicates the age distribution as it existed at two different dates. The second column shows an increase in the younger age group, which reflects the result of an intensive recruiting drive:

Age Distribution—WAC Enlisted Personnel

Age	June 30, 1944	Dec. 30, 1945
20-24	44.80%	48.65%
25-29	24.73%	26.47%
30-34	13.32%	12.02%
35-39	8.61%	6.43%
40-50	8.54%	6.43%
Total	71,287	80,787

Probably the most significant of these figures is the high percentage of women over 35 years of age. Despite the counteradvice from the Office of the Surgeon General, a woman up to the age of 50 could enlist in the WAC. Older women, because of menopausal difficulties and rigidity of personality, were much more likely to become psychiatric casualties. This recommendation was overruled, presumably because of the need for man power. In other words, it seems to have been assumed that the need for additional help warranted taking the chance that a fair percentage of these older women could be fitted into some sort of useful jobs.

The very high discharge rate of women over 40 years of age (104.4 per 1,000) supported the recommendation of the Office of the Surgeon General and should have been sufficient basis to reduce the age limit.

Medical Discharge Rate per 1,000 [11]*—Enlisted (White) Females*

Age	October, 1943 to October, 1944	Less than 6 Months of Service
20-24	30.6	18.0
25-29	42.8	22.7
30-34	45.6	25.1
35-39	60.7	30.6
40 and over	104.4	59.2
All ages	44.7	25.1

Psychiatric observations. A tremendous effort was expended on the enlistment program of the WAC. A large recruiting staff operated recruiting centers

---

[11] "Trend of Medical Rejections Nov. 1942—Dec. 1944 and Sample Study of Medical Defects (Oct. 1943—Mar. 1944)," Women's Army Corps, Medical Statistics Division, S.G.O., p. 100.

in between 200 and 300 communities. Because of the national advertising and the large staff, the effort and money spent made the members of this group the most expensively procured personnel in the Army. One of the specially planned features of the enlistment effort was to make entrance into the Army as easy and as fast as possible. Many of the recruiting centers were not close to an induction center or to an Army medical installation; therefore the volunteer was examined locally.

Women were accepted without even a semblance of a psychiatric examination. As a consequence, from August, 1943 to May, 1944, 53 per cent of the discharges were for psychiatric causes. The need for psychiatric examination was even more important than in the case of male inductees not only because of the variation in motivation for enlistment but because of the older age. Beginning in August, 1943, an intensive effort was made to provide an adequate neuropsychiatric examination as well as to develop the machinery to obtain an adequate social history. Lt. Col. Margaret Craighill, in charge of women's health in the Army under the Surgeon General, with the full support of the Neuropsychiatry Consultants Division, strongly recommended a reduction in the number of enlistment centers so that a better examination could be given. She also recommended a reduction in the age limit of from 50 to 35 years. In part, these aims were accomplished when the psychiatric examination became standard required procedure. A War Department technical bulletin [12] was prepared by the Medical Department to assist the examiners in understanding the stresses to which women in the WAC would be subjected. Unfortunately, by the time this bulletin was published and procedures were established, the main recruiting was over.

There were special stresses implicit in the organization of a feminine component in the Army. Many of these entailed the necessity for partial abnegation of typically feminine pursuits and interests, and of habitual responses developed by environment and training. Often, most distressing was the lack of privacy, which was necessary in a barrackslike living area. Girls are raised in a manner entirely different from boys in relation to the emphasis on modesty and privacy in dressing, bathing, and toilet. Regimentation and discipline were extremely difficult for some women, particularly when they had to be under the direction of other women. Women in a home are entirely independent, with no one to boss them.

They are also much more independent in dress than men. Initially the uniform was not attractive. According to the Gallup poll, it was regarded by prospective recruits as the least attractive of any of the service uniforms. Style is sub-

---

12 "WAC Recruiting Station Neuropsychiatric Examination," *War Department Technical Bulletin, Medical* 100, 4 October 1944.

ject to much more individual interpretation by women. Whereas men are uncomfortable if they dress differently from other men, women are unhappy if they dress like other women in civilian life. This attitude was carried over into the Army and was expressed in unofficial variations in uniform. Also the accessories of adornment were sorely missed. Overseas, many of the women wore hair ribbons and flowers with their uniform. This was especially apparent where they were forced to wear slacks (that is, men's clothes) all the time. Deprived of various means of expressing their femininity, they felt the lack more acutely when they could not even wear skirts.

Perhaps it was more difficult for women than for men to live and mix indiscriminately—dullards with college graduates, the poor with the rich, the gauche with the cultured. While the physical demands of training were severe, it is not believed that they were detrimental. In fact, they seemed to be of benefit to most, as revealed by a survey made by medical officers who investigated the problem at training centers. Life in the training camp was, however, more strenuous than the life of the average American woman.

The special difficulties in the relationships to men confronted not only the WAC but every female in the Army—nurses, dietitians, physical therapists, and to nearly the same degree, women Red Cross workers. Because of Army regulations, officer personnel, either male or female, were forbidden to associate socially with enlisted personnel.[13] Other problems arose from the unbelievable pressure that was placed on any women in a foreign Army post [14] where there were 500 to 1,000 American soldiers to each American girl. In the midst of loneliness, isolation, physical discomfort, lack of old friends and familiar activity, and in a position to be the object of both the platonic and sexual attention of hundreds of men, emotional conflicts arose within every woman in an overseas unit. The double standard and suspicion about sexual behavior in American culture added to the castigation heaped so unfairly upon the members of the WAC.

Colonel Craighill, in her report of a visit to the India-Burma Theater where marriage was forbidden among American personnel within the theater, wrote the following significant observation:

Women overseas, because of their scarcity, are subject to great emotional strain. Added to their own inner conflict is the outside pressure from a group of isolated and lonesome men. There tends to be a change in standards and sense of values in

---

[13] In their report of a round-the-world survey of the WAC, Col. W. B. Boyce, Director of WAC, and Dr. Marion E. Kenworthy (September-November, 1945) made the very practical recommendation that there should be a "publication of War Department policy asserting that laws of natural selection will govern off-duty associations between male and female personnel." [14] On VE-day, 16,873 WAC's were serving outside the continental limits of the United States— over 7,000 in the European Theater, 2,000 in the Mediterranean Theater, 5,600 on the islands of the Pacific. Boyce, W. B., *Army Day Review,* 6 April 1946, p. 114.

both sexes. Their previous and future lives become vague and unreal so that only the present is of importance. Time overseas is viewed as an interlude in life and whatever makes it more bearable seems justifiable. Men are apparently better able to partition off their lives adequately so that they do not as readily become deeply or permanently involved emotionally. They are, therefore, less liable to lasting psychic trauma from transient attachments.

Between June, 1943, and October, 1945, there were 9,193 discharges from the service for pregnancy among the enlisted group. Between January, 1944, and October, 1945, there were 310 separations among officer personnel for pregnancy. This amounted to 7.5 per cent of the total strength of the WAC between 1942 and 1945 and was only 250 less than the number of medical discharges for all other reasons.[15]

The actual number of marriages in the Army is not accurately known, but it is presumed to have been large. However, it is not related to the number of pregnancies. There were other psychological aspects of this problem.[16] The tendency toward increased fertility was apparent in women who had never been able to become pregnant. This was probably due to a routine, healthy life, plus the temporary separation from the husband. Many became pregnant during high emotional states while on leave. It is believed that there was an increase in the pregnancy rate as the war progressed, in part because of a desire to get out of the Army or to return from overseas from which there was no other means of escape. In other cases a family was desired before becoming too old. There was a willingness to forgo this responsibility during the early days of uncertainty, but, as the war dragged on indefinitely and again when the end was in sight, the pregnancy rate rose sharply.

The percentage of medical discharges for neuropsychiatric causes was approximately 10 per cent higher in the WAC than in the total Army. The number of psychoneuroses was 10 per cent higher in the WAC than in the Army as a whole, whereas the number of psychoses was 5 per cent less. Prior to 1944 the psychiatric causes for discharges amounted to more than half of all medical discharges. This was undoubtedly reduced by the better screening of recruits which became effective that year.

---

15 These figures are not so surprising if one is realistic and is familiar with current trends in the sexual life of Americans. Terman reported that of women married before 1912, 12 per cent were nonvirgins at marriage; between 1918 and 1922, 26 per cent were not virgins; between 1922 and 1931, 49 per cent were not virgins; between 1932 and 1937, 68 per cent were nonvirgins. Terman, L. M., *Psychological Factors in Marital Happiness,* McGraw-Hill Book Company, Inc., New York, 1938.

16 These points were suggested by Lt. Col. Margaret Craighill who was responsible for the supervision of women's health in the Army. Dr. Craighill has recorded some of these observations from her rich experience in "Psychiatric Aspects of Women Serving in the Army: The Motivation of Women Volunteers," presented at Am. Psychiat. Assn. Meeting, New York, May 22, 1947. *Am. J. Psychiat.* 104:226-230, Oct., 1947.

Medical Discharges

	Enlisted WAC 49.1%		All Enlisted Personnel 39.0%	
Percentage of All Medical Discharges as Neuropsychiatric	Percentage of NP Medical Discharges		Percentage of NP Medical Discharges	
Psychoneuroses	3,818	79.5%	224,000	70%
Psychoses	503	10.4%	48,000	15%
Neurological	314	6.5%	35,000	11%
Other psychiatric	163	3.6%	13,000	4%

In conclusion, there is no question whatever that the Women's Army Corps was an extremely valuable and effective segment of the Army. It must be recognized that it was, however, a pioneering effort somewhat contrary to the concept of femininity in American culture. From a psychiatric point of view the effort seems to represent a healthy trend, and its impact on society should benefit women [17] and help in the reorientation of men. The results will be evaluated by the oncoming generation.

We must accept the many psychological hazards that are connected with a Women's Corps in the Army. We should attempt to mold and modify the program to provide sufficient flexibility to allow for specificity in assignment and an opportunity for expression of feminine traits, characteristics, and ability. Most important would seem to be psychiatric screening at the time of enlistment, with special consideration of the emotional maturity and the motivation of the enlistee.

THE WOMEN IN THE MEDICAL DEPARTMENT

Women have been identified intimately with military medicine for a century, chiefly as nurses and dietitians. The great majority of the women in the Medical Department of the Army were in the Nurse Corps, although some 10,000 commissioned and enlisted members of the Women's Army Corps became attached to and a part of the Medical Department as technicians, social workers, stenographic and clerical assistants, and in other jobs.

Within the last 25 years an increasing number of women have become doctors. Prior to this war, there had been no women physicians in the Army. During World War II, 75 women physicians were commissioned—3 majors,

---

[17] Colonel Westray Battle Boyce summarized their gain: "Tolerance, confidence, self-respect, a heightened idealism, a fundamental knowledge of world politics and a sound respect for the Army of the United States, are by-products of the service they rendered. These women will carry into civilian life the fusion of these characteristics." *Army Day Review,* 6 Apr. 1946, p. 116. This same opinion has been expressed by Mildred McAfee Horton in "Women in the United States Navy," *Am. J. Sociology,* 51:448-450, Mar., 1946.

32 captains, and 40 lieutenants. Up to VJ-day only one-third had had any further promotions, of which only three were above the rank of captain.[18]

Physical therapists and dietitians were employed on a civilian status until Congressional action in December, 1942, when they were given officer status in the Army. At the peak of the strength of the military forces, there were 1,648 physical therapists [19] and 1,599 dietitians.[20] To this number of the female component should be added the 900 occupational therapists for whom commissions were never obtained and who were affiliated as civilian employees, as were the 450 civilian dental hygienists and 2,900 dental chair assistants. An important civilian group of women were the Red Cross workers of whom, at the peak, 1,722 serving overseas (21 May 1945) and 3,853 (31 October 1945) in the United States were affiliated with the Medical Department. Nearly 9,000 women were employed in the many other Red Cross activities [21] throughout the Army.

The nurses. The nurses were all commissioned as officers. Between July, 1940, and August, 1945, 65,371 [22] women had been connected with the Medical Corps as nurses. The maximum number on duty at any one time was 57,285 on VJ-day.

Prior to the Spanish-American War nurses had no official connection with the Army. In 1901 they were "militarized" but were not given either officer rank or enlisted status. In 1920 legislation was enacted which made them military officers and created a nursing corps within the Medical Department. A majority was the highest rank provided, and all nurses received pay on a lower scale than other officers, but their uniforms were provided. This status continued until December, 1942, when further legislation permitted them to be paid the same as other officers. This change gave the general impression to the public (and to some military personnel) that they were given officer status for the first time. This legislation only changed the pay scale. It was not until June, 1944, that further legislative enactment actually raised them to the full status of officers with privileges equal to those of male officers.

The Army Nurse Corps, like the other expanding divisions of the War Department, had many growing pains. For the first 2 years of the war the newly commissioned nurse was given no orientation to the Army or to her job in it except as some considerate chief nurse already on the job in a hospital might give it to her. She went directly to her first assignment in some medical unit and was supposed to function without any knowledge of military organization, cour-

18 Craighill, Margaret D., Presentation at the Medical School Convocation, University of Wisconsin, 14 February 1946.
19 Total number commissioned to 1 May 1946. Figure from Maj. E. E. Vogel, Director of Physical Therapists.
20 Number on duty 31 August 1945. Figure from Maj. Helen C. Burns, Director of Dietitians.
21 Figures supplied by Mrs. Imogene S. Young, American Red Cross, 27 May 1946.
22 Figures supplied by the Nursing Division, Surgeon General's Office, 1 May 1946.

tesies, or law. In July, 1943, however, a center was established in each Service Command where all nurses received 3 weeks of training and 1 week of processing. They were given a total of 176 hours of instruction as preparation for their first assignment. The initial lack of orientation was responsible for some subsequent psychological problems among nurses.

The psychological aspects of Army nursing. A great difference between the WAC and the Nurse Corps was the fact that a nurse was sure of continuing her chosen life work for which she had been specifically trained. Furthermore, nursing was universally regarded and accepted as a feminine function so there was no civilian or military resistance to its female contingent in the Army. On the other hand, the available handful of civilian male nurses was never commissioned in the Army, in spite of the need for them on psychiatric services where they have a very important function. The generally accepted concept of the nurse as a skilled maternal figure could not be changed.

Nurses came into the Army to work in the same type of environment in which they had previously existed, namely, the hospital. The care of the sick in the Army hospitals was essentially the same as the care of the sick in the civilian hospitals. The nurses could therefore proceed immediately to utilize their former training and experience. Many of them even came into the Army with the same doctors with whom they had worked in civil life. This was the case in most of the "affiliated" medical units that were organized in medical schools and metropolitan hospitals. Also, the life of a nurse, either civilian or Army, is controlled to a greater degree by discipline and orders than is that of most American women.

Nurses, like all Army women, had problems which were related to the scarcity of feminine companionship for American men in Army camps and in overseas posts. Unpleasant pressures were often put on them in these circumstances. It was not uncommon for the commanding officer of a post to request the release of a certain number of nurses to be present at social affairs so that there might be American women present. Sometimes the pressure went beyond merely requiring their presence at social functions. Unfortunately, many of the nurses had no clear idea of their own rights. They were new to the Army and had been impressed with the significance of discipline and "orders." Before taking the orientation courses, they had little opportunity to learn how much authority of "superior" officers was legitimate. If they were reluctant to accede to these "social" orders, all too frequently they were subject to vague threats relative to their promotion or their transfer or their living conditions. Few of them knew with whom they could counsel when official demands were excessive.

One of the special stresses was inactivity. There were several large "pools" where nurses were collected and held until conditions would permit their going forward to their hospital or their unit. As new areas were invaded, in the

Pacific campaign for instance, there were many times when living conditions and facilities were presumably too rugged or without accommodations for women. As a result, as many as several hundred would be held, sometimes for months, in the "pool" with nothing to do.

Another stress factor was the lack of administrative experience. Just prior to the war (September 1, 1940) there were only 957 nurses in the regular corps. Many of these had had no administrative assignment. There were not nearly enough nurses with previous service as a chief nurse to fill that position in the hundreds of hospitals. The result was considerable maladministration for which a high emotional price was paid by the junior nurses.

Malassignment was another cause of special stress for some nurses. Within the broad field of nursing many specialties have developed. Prior to the war, every Army nurse was a general nurse and was expected to do any type of nursing. Civilian practice had extended beyond this to recognize specialties in nursing which corresponded to the specialties of surgery, medicine, pediatrics, psychiatry, public health, and industrial medicine. However, the civilian nurse who came into the Army was assigned with minimal consideration for her previous specialized training. The result was, in many instances, misassignment, with concomitant psychological stress for the nurse concerned.

The handicaps in attending to their personal wants were stresses of no small importance for all women in the Army, especially when assigned to isolated outposts. The stories were legion of the difficulties encountered in so simple a procedure as laundering clothing. Similarly, in many places, it was impossible to obtain any sort of beauty-parlor equipment. The Army women overseas lived and worked in the mud and the sand, in the tundra of Alaska and the jungles of New Guinea. They had to be resourceful and adjustable, in some respects more so than the men. They often had to give up their female attire for the necessity of wearing slacks and dungarees. Many indicated that they missed most an opportunity to wear evening clothes! They "took it," however, with good grace, and the psychiatric breakdowns among nurses, at least those so labeled diagnostically, were low.

Vital statistics. In a sample [23] of 5,000 nurses, it was found that only 10 per cent had done any other type of work than nursing, 6 per cent had done stenographic work, 3 per cent had done some teaching, and 1 per cent had been in clerical work. All of the others had gone continuously through their education and directly into nursing.

The American Red Cross [24] made an extensive tabulation of the qualifica-

---

23 From the Nursing Division, Office of the Surgeon General.
24 Supplied by Gertrude S. Banfield, Director Nursing Enrollment of the American Red Cross, June 26, 1946. Furnished through courtesy of Col. Florence Blanchfield, Army Nurse Corps.

tions of the 75,029 nurses in the service—12,239 in the Navy and 62,790 in the Army. Many of these figures are of special interest in evaluating the make-up of this large feminine component of the services. For instance the Navy had a much larger number of younger nurses as shown by the following:

Age	Navy	Army	Total
21-25	34.6%	26.8%	28.1%
26-30	40.0%	34.6%	35.5%
31-35	15.6%	18.2%	17.8%
36-40	6.9%	11.4%	10.6%
41-45	1.8%	6.3%	5.5%
46 or over	1.1%	2.6%	2.4%
No record		0.1%	0.1%

In educational background, 97 per cent of the Navy nurses were graduates of high school, 94 per cent of the Army nurses. Of the 75,000 nurses, 20 per cent had had some college education, either before or after their nursing education (in some instances both). Almost 90 per cent had their nursing education after 1931. Nurses usually obtain a more rounded and better course in larger hospitals; 72 per cent of the nurses graduated from hospitals having a daily average of more than 100 patients. Of particular interest is the report that just 16 per cent of the total had had any undergraduate training in psychiatry either in their home school or through affiliation. Yet it rates high in comparison to postgraduate training. Only 0.7 per cent of the entire group had had any postgraduate work in psychiatry (compared to 1 per cent with postgraduate training in communicable diseases, 1.3 per cent in operating-room technique, 0.7 per cent in anesthesia, and 4.1 per cent in public health).

Figures about the type of nursing experienced prior to military service are not very satisfactory, since the nurse often changed her work; also she may have been classified by a temporary position which she held while awaiting orders into the service. According to these figures, of the total number 55.2 per cent were in institutional work, 14.9 per cent in private duty work, 4.2 per cent in public health, 3 per cent in industrial positions, 5.1 per cent on miscellaneous jobs, and 17.6 per cent did not report.

Certain recommendations are pertinent in looking toward the future of the women in the Medical Corps from the point of view of mental health. Plans should be made to give the nurse, dietitian, and physiotherapist an opportunity during peacetime to obtain further specialized training or academic education if it is wanted. These women should be encouraged to identify themselves with local, state, and national professional organizations. The privilege of wearing civilian clothes, especially evening dresses, is almost an essential to feminine morale. Proportionally, such personal privileges are far more important to women than to men. It is to be hoped that they, as well as WAC personnel, may be permitted to choose their own social contacts without regard to rank. In the event of another emergency more consideration should be given to the personal problems of the women in the Army—their protection from ruthless male officers in their environment, their personal needs for clothes, laundry, coiffure. Such steps would greatly improve their morale, i.e., their mental health.

8

PSYCHONEUROTIC DISORDERS

What are psychoneuroses? Why are there so many cases of them? What can be done to reduce their high incidence? These were the queries from the puzzled public, some members of whom were relatives of discharged neuropsychiatric veterans. Much of the energy of the Neuropsychiatry Consultants Division in the Office of the Surgeon General was directed toward formulating the answers to such questions. That information was then passed on, in so far as possible, to line officers, medical officers, enlisted men, and even the public. To verify these answers the Chief of Staff sent out nonpsychiatric, high-ranking investigators.

Definition of psychoneurosis. Psychiatrists were quite familiar with these illnesses. Most doctors knew something about them, but the public and military personnel did not. To the uninformed, psychoneuroses seemed to spring up suddenly. In their great numbers they became frightening as ruthless robbers of man power. The misconception prevailed that "it"—in general, all varieties of psychoneuroses were considered as one illness—was a hopeless and incurable scourge. When those of us responsible for interpreting psychiatric concepts tried to explain what the psychoneuroses were, we hit a snag. There is no simple, adequate, one-sentence or even five-sentence definition.

Most medical disorders can be described quite clearly by specifying the physical location and the cause of the trouble. Thus one can make an unfamiliar term like osteomyelitis readily understandable by indicating that it is an infection within a bone. One can describe pneumonia by saying that it is an infection in the lung with resultant secretion that fills up the air spaces. To indicate that a psychiatric illness is within the personality seems quite indefinite. The personality cannot be located in the mind or in the brain or even in the total nervous system. While most physical diseases have several causes, this is even more true of psychiatric illnesses. In mental illness the symptoms are variations from usual behavior which cannot be described briefly. So it is that the definition of a psychoneurosis is not possible in terms analogous to those which describe a physical illness. Neither the location nor the causative agent nor the pathology can be simply stated.

Psychoneurosis and neurosis now are both used to label the same group of disorders. Historically, psychoneurosis referred to the maladjustments that were presumed to be caused by purely psychic factors. The neuroses were assumed to have some physiological basis for the psychological symptoms. The two terms have become interchangeable and therefore synonymous for lack of scientific evidence that any differentiation is valid. The psychoneuroses (neuroses) are disorders in thinking and feeling, and therefore in ideation and emotion. By their varied symptoms, several types of psychoneurotic reactions are identified and given different diagnostic labels. The layman cannot be expected to understand such a definition until it is amplified further.

The major portion of the personality [1] is the "unconscious" which is not directly accessible to the "conscious." All psychological energy springs from the unconscious and seeks expression in primitive, tabooed outlets. In the processes of development, training, education, and acquisition of social behavior, the conscious portion of the personality tries to learn to control and modify these primitive expressions by directing them into socially acceptable responses. However, one's conscious ego cannot always do this. Sometimes it is caught off guard; sometimes it is under terrific external pressure; sometimes it is worn down and becomes "weak"; not infrequently its development is defective. Whatever the cause, when the conscious ego is threatened with being overpowered by unconscious impulses of which the ego does not approve, the individual is made aware of anxiety arising from this conflict within the personality. In the average person such anxiety may appear as inexplicable "nervousness" or tenseness or excitement. Sometimes its manifestations are disguised beyond recognition. They appear in exaggerated behavior: in the man who drives himself in overwork, or cannot sleep, or drinks too much, or develops a headache, or becomes irritable or, very commonly, worries. This behavior represents a compromise between the conscious ability to repress, because the ego is less powerful or weakened, and some powerful unconscious wish seeking expression. The result: a neurotic symptom.

But, the short-lived expression of one neurotic symptom is not a neurosis. All of us occasionally develop one, or even several neurotic symptoms under special duress: the headache when the going gets tough, the disappearance of appetite in fear, excessive concern over the minor ailment of a child. These and many similar responses are so common as to be regarded as "normal." The psychiatrist recognizes that everyone may, and does at times, exhibit a neurotic symptom.

One can correctly describe a transient symptom of the normal individual as an indication of a "neurotic reaction." Present-day psychiatry regards all behavior as reaction to forces. The process of adjustment is reaction to internal

---

[1] See Chap. 4 for a more detailed presentation.

and external pressure. Mental illness is not an end point or a clear-cut, circumscribed, localized disease such as one often sees in certain physical illnesses. It is rather the unhealthy reaction of a personality to situations and emotions. In itself the term "reaction" does not carry a quantitative value of intensity, duration, chronicity, or severity.

We see many individuals who continuously manifest neurotic symptoms, although these do not seriously incapacitate them in carrying on in their life situations. The psychiatrist describes these people as making a chronic neurotic adjustment. Very often such persons have no recognition of their behavior as neurotic, even though they may be aware of the fact that they worry too much or are too irritable or too tired. They may feel ill at ease in certain types of situations or afraid in others. Chronic or recurring mild physical difficulties may also be expressions of such an adjustment. Psychological immaturity is often the cause of a chronic neurotic adjustment. In that case a person is able to meet life's demands only when provided with some sort of extra support, some special indulgence, some particular type of relationship. There are many variations in such adjustments: the husband who lets his wife assume the masculine role, the wife who plays the role, the joiner and the hermit, the braggart, the gossiper, the exhibitionist, and the timid soul. Fortunately many of these individuals manage to get along reasonably well: they work, they play, they socialize. Rarely do they seek the advice of a doctor. Nor does their adjustment preclude productive life in the community. However, technically, they maintain a neurotic adjustment.

There is no sharp dividing line between a neurotic adjustment and a neurosis. In the former the individual "adjusts" to his neurosis or "lives with it." Perhaps he is even more productive because of it—for instance, as a temperamental but excellent artist or musician. If the symptomatic expressions become incapacitating, i.e., prevent him from working or getting along with people, even temporarily, the individual has a neurotic reaction that psychiatrists have labeled as a *neurosis* (psychoneurosis).

Because the type and the severity of a neurotic reaction varies so widely, merely naming it fails to give a helpful evaluation of a patient's condition. For this reason the revised Army nomenclature required additional information in a diagnosis. The label, i.e., specific kind of neurotic reaction, was modified as "mild, moderate or severe," and amplified to state (1) the predisposition to neurosis, (2) the nature and degree of the external stress factor, and (3) the degree of incapacity resulting.

Elsewhere attention has been called to the many instances in which the neurotic reaction takes the form of physical complaints.[2] Lay, and unfor-

---

[2] See Chap. 10.

tunately, some medical opinion place more validity on a physical symptom as a basis of incapacity than on a directly expressed emotional reaction. The awareness (unconscious and/or conscious) of this fact was an undoubted influence in converting a soldier's psychological maladjustment into a physical symptom. The subtle but powerful motive (to be considered unfit for required activity) in the development of neurotic illness is referred to by psychiatrists as a "secondary gain." The primary gain or purpose of the psychoneurotic illness is the relief of inner emotional tension. The secondary gain is the trade of a primary, difficult environment, such as an unwanted, dirty, strenuous or dangerous job, for the more comfortable, "safe" illness. Whatever the symptoms are—anxiety, stomach trouble, aches or pains—they become the means to an end. Although they may be painful and represent a symbolic (and often, real) punishment, they also provide distorted satisfaction in more attention, safety, comfort. The total symptom picture represents an unconscious aggressive demand. The awareness of every soldier, in fact of every individual, of the secondary gain in psychological illness must be reckoned with as one of the factors that brings about this form of retreat.

Unfortunately, even this oversimplified explanation of the tendency of all of us to react neurotically, of the neurotic adjustments by which many of us live, of the incapacitating psychoneurosis, was not familiar to most of the Army doctors. This lack of knowledge on the part of nonpsychiatric medical officers complicated the problem of correct diagnosis and treatment. No medical schools in years gone by (unfortunately, even some today) taught their students sufficient psychiatry. It is no wonder that the internist and the surgeon in the Army were ill-equipped to understand the emotional factors in the symptoms so commonly encountered in their patients. Furthermore, we must admit frankly that all of our Army psychiatrists did not have a common understanding about the classification of neurotic reactions.

Therefore, it is hardly to be expected that the line officers and the public could have understood. A most elementary task both within the War Department and with the civilian public was to try to explain that individuals with illnesses correctly diagnosed as psychoneurosis were not "crazy" or "insane"; that the prefix "psycho" did not mean "psychotic." In the neurosis the patient does not distort or misinterpret or falsify the external environment or life situation, whereas in psychoses [3] we commonly find fixed, mistaken ideas (delusions), or false perceptions (hallucinations), or misinterpretations of the external environment (illusions).

The long-standing and widespread ignorance of psychoneurotic illness has led to gross misconceptions and misinterpretations about it. The many thou-

---

[3] See Chap. 11.

sands of men displaying these reactions magnified the effect of such misunderstanding manifold. Part and parcel of this lack of knowledge were the inappropriate regulations concerning the handling of psychoneurotic patients in
the Army.

Regulations. War Department regulations directing the induction process
caused the initial difficulty. They required the psychiatrist to give a rejectee
a diagnosis which would indicate not merely maladjustment but a definite
illness.[4] The emotional pressure of being drafted was sufficient to bring to the
surface in some individuals the transient or quiescent neurotic symptoms which
are universal to us all. The ultraconservative attitude, based on good but mistaken intention, that prevailed in the early years of the war caused the rejection
of all questionable prospects, often with the diagnosis of psychoneurosis. In
many, many instances this diagnosis was unwarranted. Not only did we reject
many men from the Army who undoubtedly could have given good service,
but at the same time we did them a great injustice in labeling so many 4F's with
the diagnosis of a condition they did not have.[5]

Any individual in the Army who developed neurotic symptoms with sufficient intensity to place him in a hospital was subject to discharge. Because of
the very definite War Department rulings [6] on rejection at the induction center,
the development of similar reactions after entering the service was assumed
to disqualify a man. Such a policy totally ignored any potential restorability or
prompt recovery; it also ignored the contribution that even the partially handicapped individual could make to repay the expense of his training, at least in
part. In the initial years of the war, regulations did not prescribe or, in fact,
even permit treatment [7] of the patient who was hospitalized for a psychoneurosis. Nor was there any type or class of duty authorized for him. He had
to be discharged!

Many soldiers knew of these regulations. The lack of desire to be soldiers,
the many stresses and deprivations that the soldier had to accept, plus the
knowledge of a method of escape led to a result which should have been
anticipated. By its own policies the War Department created a system that
encouraged the development of a neurosis. Therefore, it was with very good
reason that the Chief of Staff of the Army became greatly concerned [8] when

---

[4] Mobilization Regulations 1-9, 19 April 1944, and all preceding issues of these standards.
[5] See Chap. 19.
[6] Army Regulations 615-360, November, 1944. Sec. I, paragraph 1c (1). Even after induction,
if a man fell below the requirements for admission to the Army, he was no longer considered
acceptable for military service.
[7] For reference see Appendix A, noting Adjutant General Memoranda W600-22-43, W600-30-43,
W600-39-43.
[8] Cooke, E. D., *All But Me and Thee. Psychiatry at the Foxhole Level.* Infantry Journal Press,
Washington, D.C., 1946, p. 11.

the losses of man power through rejection and discharge for psychoneurosis rose to unprecedented heights.

Disposition of ineffective soldiers added to the problem of the use of the diagnois of psychoneurosis. The lack of motivation toward fighting a war made many soldiers lackadaisical. Certain types of men wanted to "soldier" on the job, or gold-brick. Men who, because of their disinterest or in many instances because of their personality maladjustment, could not fit into a smooth-running organization, were "sore thumbs." In other words, there were soldiers with defective attitudes, psychological immaturity, or antisocial personalities whom no company commander wanted if he could get rid of them. They could have been removed through administrative discharge on the responsibility of the company commander. However, this was a complicated, difficult procedure. Consequently, the custom of referring such individuals to the hospitals became routine.[9] Either through a mistaken conception of co-operation or as the result of direct pressure on the medical officer and the psychiatrist, such individuals were often given a diagnosis of psychoneurosis in order to be discharged with a certificate of disability.

Initially, the whole subject of psychoneurotic reaction was so seriously misunderstood by the War Department that the individual with this difficulty was ruthlessly treated. He was excluded in the draft or discharged from the service on the assumption that he had a total and permanent disability. There is no evidence of any awareness of the elementary facts about the neurotic tendencies of all of us—that many of us have neurotic symptoms and yet carry on to do a productive, perhaps a superior job. Nor was there sufficient appreciation of the fact that under sufficiently prolonged stress anyone might develop neurotic behavior, quite possibly of sufficient degree to incapacitate him. In short, anyone can develop a neurosis.

One might justifiably ask why the psychiatrists, if they knew better, did not protest. They did—as soon as they obtained sufficient standing to be heard. Great credit should go to the War Department for its effort to alter the situation. The powers-that-be did listen, and radical changes were made—but very late. The making of a diagnosis at the induction level was discarded;[10] treatment for psychoneuroses was authorized and made mandatory;[11] the policy of discharging all soldiers given a diagnosis of psychoneurosis was reversed, and this condition was eliminated as a sole basis for discharge;[12] men with defective attitudes

---

9 This was partially stopped by a forceful directive, War Department Circular 81, 31 March 1945.
10 First outlined in *War Department Technical Bulletin, Medical 33,* 21 April 1944; re-enforced and made official by Mobilization Regulations 1-9, Change 3, 4 June 1945.
11 Set forth in *War Department Technical Bulletin, Medical 28,* 1 April 1944, although Army Regulations 615-360 were not changed till Change 2, 1 March 1945. War Department Circular 162, 2 June 1945.
12 War Department Circular 81, 31 March 1945; also Army Regulations 615-360, Change 2, 1 March 1945.

or ineptitude could be released through nonmedical channels by an administrative discharge; [13] we were even able to drop the abused and misused generic term "psychoneurosis" from the individual hospital record and substitute the term which identified the specific type of neurotic reaction.[14]

Regulations ruled military practice, yet psychiatry had no representation in the making of these regulations at the beginning of the war. Alas, in the Army the subordinate in rank, no matter what his ability or experience, does not "tell" his superior officer; he takes orders. The War Department directives and old Army policies were quite clear about the management and disposition of neuropsychiatric patients. Outworn practices were thus retained in spite of more recent thinking which came into the Army with civilian psychiatrists.

As discussed elsewhere, the psychiatrists were not without blame. They did have a hearing in the early innings of Selective Service, and somehow the ball was muffed. In the Army they were kept too busy "moving patients" and all too obediently discharging, "under orders," soldiers who should have been salvaged for further duty. We in the Office of the Surgeon General progressed too slowly in educating those who made the rules in the rapidly changing and growing Army.

Extent of the problem. The only available figures on the incidence of psychoneurotic reactions in the Army are those which can be culled from the records of hospital admissions. From January, 1942, to June 1945, there were about 15,000,000 admissions to Army hospitals all over the world for all types of medical problems. Of these, 6 per cent (918,961) were on neuropsychiatric services. Almost two-thirds of these psychiatric admissions (586,518) were listed as psychoneuroses.[15] During the same period there were 256,134 individuals discharged from the Army with a diagnosis of psychoneurosis. Roughly speaking, the number of cases of psychoneuroses in World War II was five times that of World War I.[16]

These statistics are not valid as a measure of the number of men and women in military service who were psychoneurotic patients at some time or other. As has been indicated, there was a great variability in the usage of diagnostic terms. In many cases so listed, psychoneurosis was an inaccurate diagnosis. Moreover, persons with neurotic reactions were sometimes labeled as suffering from "simple adult maladjustment" in order to permit the physician to return the man to duty. This was common practice during the period when

---

[13] War Department Circular 391, 21 December 1945.
[14] War Department Circular 81, 31 March 1945; War Department Circular 179, 16 June 1945.
[15] An analysis of the statistics shows a higher rate of admission in overseas hospitals (71.5 per cent) than in hospitals in the United States (51.9 per cent).
[16] Bailey, P., and Haber, R., *The Medical Department of the United States Army in the World War*, Vol. X, U.S. Government Printing Office, Washington, D.C., 1929, p. 157.

the diagnosis of psychoneurosis required discharge. Since some patients were admitted to the hospital more than once, the record of admissions does not show the number of different patients. In addition, many, many surgical and medical cases who remained on those wards or were discharged with medical diagnoses were essentially psychoneurotic patients. None of these figures include that even larger number of soldiers seen by psychiatrists in the outpatient clinics of our basic-training camps. Despite temporary or even chronic neurotic symptoms these men were able to carry on in their training or on duty. Nor do these figures include the many cases that were essentially neurotic reactions which were given other diagnostic labels, such as operational fatigue, combat fatigue, or combat exhaustion. These diagnoses were temporary, until a more careful study could be made [17] or the condition cleared up while the patient was still in a forward area.

Even though our statistics are inaccurate, neurotic reactions were *the* major psychiatric problem. Their full extent was indicated in many ways other than tabulations of hospital admissions. Morale problems, sick call, venereal disease rates, AWOL, alcoholism, frequency of company punishment, and disciplinary problems were supporting evidence of their prevalence. It would be grossly incorrect to assume that all maladjustment was neurotic in origin, but it is certainly safe to assume that much of it was.

Types of reactions. Many of the concepts [18] of psychiatric illnesses changed between World War I and World War II. The psychiatric literature and the reports to the Office of the Surgeon General impressed the Neuropsychiatry Consultants Division with the lack of uniformity in the present-day concepts of different psychiatric entities. Reports of neurotic reactions in the two wars could not be compared, nor could reports from different psychiatrists in this war be accurately compared.

Statements of observer-psychiatrists are the only sources for generalizations as to predominant responses. Thus Mira, in discussing the Spanish war, stated that "the core of the overwhelming majority of the war neuroses is constituted by conversion hysteria." [19] Grinker and Spiegel stated that, "In World War II conversion hysteria was rare." [20] Stimulated, at least in part, by this comment,

---

[17] See Chap. 18.

[18] Dunn, Wm. H., "War Neuroses," *Psychological Bull.* 38:497-504, June, 1941; Billings, E. G., "The Literature on Military Psychiatry Since 1938," *Am. J. M. Sc.,* 201:905-918, June, 1941; Maskin, Meyer, "Psychodynamic Aspects of the War Neuroses, Survey of the Literature," *Psychiatry,* 4:97-115, Feb., 1941; Zabriskie, E. G., and Brush, A. L., "Psychoneuroses in War Time," *Psychosom. Med.,* 3:295-329, July, 1941.

[19] Mira, E., *Psychiatry in War,* W. W. Norton & Company, Inc., New York, 1943, p. 83.

[20] Grinker, R. R., and Spiegel, J. P., "The Management of Neuropsychiatric Casualties in the Zone of Combat," *Manual of Military Neuropsychiatry,* W. B. Saunders Company, Philadelphia, 1944, p. 526.

Davis and Bick [21] reported that conversion hysteria had not been rare, and the various disorders described as "shell shock" in World War I were not infrequent in this war. Such differences of opinion are largely the result of different psychiatric orientation. These frequent divergencies and discrepancies gave strong confirmation of the need for a better standardized nomenclature of the psychoneuroses.

Eventually it may be possible to present some statistics which would indicate the frequency of occurrence of the different types of neurotic responses. It is to be hoped that those who compile or interpret or use them will recognize their extremely questionable reliability.

The anxiety reactions would seem to have predominated greatly. Figures taken from various theaters and types of installations at different times during the war indicated that 44 to 70 per cent of the neuropsychiatric cases were anxiety reactions.[22] Conversion reactions would appear to be the next most frequent type of neurotic response. Undoubtedly some psychiatrists included functional gastric disorders as conversion symptoms, while others restricted this designation to paralysis, stuttering, and the more classical types. From the meager statistics now available, conversion reactions constituted between 10 and 25 per cent of the total neurotic responses.

Amnesia was very common, particularly in combat. Often, however, it was only a part of a total clinical picture and did not remain as the outstanding symptom. It was observed repeatedly that once a man was out of the stress of combat his memory gradually returned. Furthermore, many men who claimed to have been knocked unconscious from a shell burst could recall most of their experiences under careful questioning.[23] In those cases where the traumatic experience had been so severe that there was repression of the episode, psychotherapy under sedation proved most useful in bringing about recovery. The same recall could be brought about in some instances through hypnosis.

Other types of neurotic reactions were much less frequent, few of them running more than 5 or 6 per cent in any of the reports. Hypochondriacal reactions were seen most commonly in the basic-training camps. The obsessive-compulsive reactions were nearly always of long duration, and only infrequently did they develop as a direct result of war experience. Fliers developed phobic

---

[21] Davis, D. B., and Bick, J. W., "Hysteria in Military Personnel," *Bull. U.S. Army M. Dept.*, 6:82-85, July, 1946. In the Air Forces Regional Hospital at Mitchell Field, they reported 220 conversion reactions among a total of 1,218 neurotic reactions.

[22] Burns, G. C., "Neuropsychiatric Problems at an Aleutian Post," *Am. J. Psychiat.*, 102:205-213, Sept., 1945; Brussel, J. A., and Wolpert, H. R., "The Psychoneuroses in Military Psychiatry," *War. Med.*, 3:139-154, Feb., 1943. Dillon, F., "Treatment of Neurosis in the Field, the Advanced Psychiatric Center," in *Neurosis in War*, ed. by Emanuel Miller, The Macmillan Company, New York, 1944, p. 120; Henderson, J. L., and Moore, M., "The Psychoneuroses of War," *New England J. Med.*, 230:273-278, Mar. 9, 1944.

[23] Brill, N. Q., "War Neuroses," *Mil. Surgeon,* 90:390-400, Apr., 1942.

reactions in connection with their planes, and in infantrymen similar reactions were noted toward bombing. A common phobic expression of the severe combat exhaustion case was the cowering and hiding in the event of even hearing an airplane motor.[24] Neurotic depressive reactions were relatively infrequent; when occurring they were associated often with a sense of guilt in relation to the death of an associate, or as an unconscious defensive (and aggressive) reaction to failure.

There has been much discussion as to whether any new type of neurotic reaction was seen in the war.[25] The report [26] of the commission of civilian psychiatrists suggested the differentiation of a type of reaction, appearing typically as an aftermath of combat exhaustion, for which they suggested the term "morbid resentment state."

The significance of the high incidence of neurotic reactions. Ignorance and misunderstanding caused a considerable part of the problem of psychoneurosis in the Army. However, the fact remains that neurotic reactions developed in a tremendous number of soldiers, aside from those cases which were due to the misuse of diagnoses, unsound policies of management, and inadequate treatment opportunities and facilities. It is true also that the incidence of psychiatric illness was higher in World War II than in World War I. This high incidence has been ascribed to decadence of the American people, to the extent of neurosis in American life, to overzealous psychiatrists, to the demands of the Army, to the tougher, harder war, and to various other causes. Occasionally, the lack of conviction on the part of the American public as to the necessity for the prosecution of the war as well as poor leadership in the military organization have been correctly indicated.

There is, of course, no one reason for this state of affairs. Numerous cases of psychoneurosis resulted from an intensification of prewar maladjustment and the effect of the stress of combat experience on "normal" persons.

Very certainly the American soldier was not decadent; after all, more than 90 per cent of them stood up against all of the stresses without psychiatric illnesses. One of the most disillusioning evenings that I spent during the war was in the European Theater as a dinner guest of one of our very high-ranking medical officers. Another guest was a high-ranking medical officer with a breast full of ribbons. I learned later that in spite of the ribbons he had made no mark

24 See Chap. 9.
25 Mira, E., "Psychiatric Experience in the Spanish War," *Brit. M. J.,* 1:1217-1220, June, 1939. Mira described "psychorhexis," a condition of malignant anxiety that developed in war-experienced civilians, as a new syndrome.
26 *Medical Report on Morale and Psychiatry,* No. 17, Officer of the Surgeon General, 25 August 1945. Reprinted: Bartemeier, L. H.; Kubie, L. S.; Menninger, K. A.; Romano, J.; and Whitehorn, J. C., "Combat Exhaustion," *J. Nerv. & Ment. Dis.,* 104:358-389, Oct., 1946; 489-525, Nov., 1946.

of distinction in medicine, and there were few indications of being highly regarded by his own regular Army medical confreres. However, he had an assignment of great responsibility. During much of the evening he decried the decadence of American youth; how the boys in 1917 were much "tougher" than
the present generation. He knew, for as a battalion surgeon he "did not have
any psychiatric casualties in World War I." His stupidity was only exceeded by
his ignorance both of medicine and history. Nevertheless, an officer of such a
high rank with such a point of view did a great injustice to the American soldier,
the greater because of his own medical training and experience.

There were some weak men, too many of them, in this war and in World
War I and in the Spanish-American War and the Civil War. But because of
a small number of them we cannot indict the Army or the nation. In the small
segment of American personnel confined in Japanese prison camps there was
a conspicuous absence of "weakness" or "decadence." [27] Some people seemed
to make an illogical connection between the idea expressed in the term "decadence" and the resistance to the change from the "softness" of American
civilian life to the "toughness" of military life. Old-time Army officers were
not prone to realize the amount of adjustment required to change from one
to the other. The relative automatism and regimentation of the Army had to
supersede civil individuality and freedom. Difficulty in making this shift
was a factor of major importance in the high rate of neurotic reactions. They
were the normal results of an enforced and sudden loss of a democratic way of
life rather than a sign of decadence.

Also contributing to the incidence of psychiatric illness was the fact that
although we excluded many men at the induction center who could have
rendered service, the converse was also true. We took in men with strong neurotic predisposition. They were placed in the Army where they did not want to
be; they were subjected to many stresses, both physical and psychological. With
both a weak motivation and a weak personality the Army did not have much
chance of making good soldiers out of such men.

Not infrequently some line officer, or even occasionally a medical officer,
would offer the opinion that the psychiatrists "caused" the high neuropsychiatric casualty rate. However, the laboratory man did not "cause" the high incidence of malaria because he was the zealous agent who located the parasite.
Nor did the psychiatrist "cause" an illness which he discovered in his role of
identifying, diagnosing, and treating the mentally ill and the misfits. He did
not go out and hunt up his patients; they were invariably brought to him, very
often through the direct effort of the same officer who wanted to play ostrich

---

[27] Brill, N. Q., "Neuropsychiatric Examination of Military Personnel Recovered from Japanese
Prison Camps," *Bull. U.S. Army M. Dept.*, 5:429-438, Apr., 1946.

and say that the problem did not exist. One could not dictate, adjudicate, or deny neurosis out of existence, although this inane step was considered by certain high-ranking nonmedical officers.

Demands of the Army, on the other hand, did produce neuroses both by aggravating existing tendencies that the individual had previously been able to handle and by imposing sufficient stress on "normal" men to provoke a neurotic reaction. From training camp to combat, military life presented new and tough assignments. Many of the stresses seemed unnecessary. One could list a host of such examples. Competition, as it was developed on the rifle range to force qualification, was extremely difficult for many men. Psychiatrists could see no sense in making every physician and every nurse go through the infiltration course with live ammunition overhead. Little or no cognizance was taken in modifying the physical demands on older men. Existence under the direction of a stupid or an incompetent officer sometimes became unbearable. Battle training in preparation for explosions, loud noises, and danger was very worth while when properly carried out. It did desensitize an individual to some degree; too often, however, it was improperly used so that it actually sensitized many soldiers to battle sounds. To sit in a replacement depot for weeks awaiting assignment created intense resentment. Certainly there were many other procedures that were routinely enforced in certain camps or certain areas which adversely affected mental health.

The Army figured the incidence of neurosis by counting the number of men who received that diagnosis in a hospital. Many soldiers with neurotic reactions would not have required hospitalization in civilian life [28] nor would even have sought a conference with a doctor, even though this would have been advisable. The great majority who would have asked for treatment would have received it on an outpatient basis in a doctor's office. Every man who could not go on duty, even temporarily, was sent to the hospital or the guardhouse. Therefore Army rates of incidence are higher than civilian rates would probably be, if they could be compiled similarly.

Probably most important in explaining the high incidence of neurotic reactions was the fact that World War II was a "tougher" one than World War I. It was nearly three times as long; it was fought on a rapidly moving and shifting basis instead of on fixed lines; it required many amphibious landings; it was fought in every extreme of climate; the lethal devices were far more devastating and nerve-racking than ever before; and more men were kept away from home for longer periods. All of these were sources of emotional stress. Along with the tougher war, many of us working in military psychiatry believed that the

---

[28] For a more full discussion see J. W. Appel, "Incidence of Neuropsychiatric Disorders in the United States Army in World War II," *Am. J. Psychiat.*, 102:433-436, Jan., 1946.

lack of positive motivation on the part of the soldier contributed to the production of psychoneurotic responses. Poor leadership often weakened the motivation [29] of enlisted men still further.

In general, the colossal odds of ignorance, surcharged with misconceptions, led to the mismanagement of psychiatric casualties and the continuance of psychiatrically unsound administrative and training policies. Added to that was the fact that the country went into the most pathological of all human activities —war—against its desire and without preparation. Men who had been ill-prepared for war by peaceful life in our democracy had to face a tough, hard, long, costly conflict. Thus, an incidence of psychoneurosis in only 6 per cent of the men selected for military service does not compare too unfavorably with the civilian rate. It is estimated that 50 per cent of all patients of civilian doctors [30] suffer from emotionally caused disorders.

---

[29] See Chap. 6 for further discussion of motivation.
[30] In a radio appeal for the sympathetic understanding of the psychoneurotic soldier, Maj. Gen. Norman T. Kirk, the Surgeon General, referred to this figure over "The March of Time" program, May 11, 1944. His remarks were published in *Bull. U.S. Army M. Dept.*, 78:40, July, 1944.

9

REACTIONS TO COMBAT[1]

How MANY soldiers took part in actual combat? This question can be answered only approximately and with qualifications. Participation in combat was very different from the "contact with the enemy" of many officers and soldiers. Men brought up ammunition and supplies to the fighting divisions; thousands of men came from rear areas into the combat zone periodically. The medics, the engineers, the Signal Corps, the Quartermaster Corps, and many others who were attached to the Army Ground Forces, though in close proximity to enemy soldiers, did not have to fight them. The Army Ground Forces organization included both the fighting men and a limited number of men who supplied and cared for them.

The Army ground soldier was the most elemental of modern warriors. He fought, not from battleships or airplanes, but hand to hand. Where he was, there was battle; and where he was there was modern battle. The ground soldier of this war needed not only personal courage, but also a high degree of skill to make him proficient in the use of complicated mechanisms and to fit himself into the interwoven ground-air-navy team. He took the ground and held it. He imposed his will upon the conquered. He was in the tradition of Bunker Hill and Yorktown, of the Alamo, of Shiloh and Gettysburg, of San Juan Hill, of Belleau Woods and the Argonne. Most of the sweat and blood were his. His family shed most of the tears.[2]

The number of men who had combat duty can be estimated roughly as between 2,000,000 and 3,000,000. There were 89 divisions, each with a strength of 15,000, all but 1 of which were engaged in combat. Many of these divisions required thousands of fresh soldiers to replace casualties.[3] As of July 31, 1945, the Ground Forces made up a third of the Army personnel in all theaters, but it had had four-fifths of the casualties.[4]

---

[1] Some of the points in this chapter were taken from the Ludwig Kast Lecture by the author, published in the *Bull. New York Acad. Med.,* 22:7-22, Jan., 1945, under the title "Modern Concepts of War Neuroses."

[2] Report of the Army Ground Forces Activities. Memorandum for Chief of Staff, U.S. Army, from Gen. J. L. Devers, 10 January 1946, Ref. 319.1 (AGF) (10 January 1946) GNDCG.

[3] By January 1945, 47 infantry regiments in 19 divisions had lost from 100 per cent to 200 per cent of their strength in battle casualties alone.

[4] Total casualties in combat divisions: 731,814. Killed in action, 144,160 men; wounded in action, 552,299 men; missing in action, 35,355 men.

Force	Army Strength	Army Casualties
Service	49.6%	7.9%
Air Corps	15.5%	12.3%
Ground arms	34.9%	79.8%

The fighting men in the Ground Forces—the infantry, airborne, armored, cavalry, and mountain divisions—had by far the toughest assignment [5] in the Army. They could remain effective as fighting men only as long as, in addition to staying alive and physically whole, they were able to control their emotions. It is safe to state that they *all* had strong emotional reactions. Most of them could and did successfully manage their emotional responses sufficiently to remain effective fighting men for long periods; others became psychiatric casualties early.

An Air Forces "fighting man" would likely contest the above statement that the infantryman had the toughest assignment. In making that statement, there is no intent to minimize the very tough job of the fliers who flew their fighters and bombers on daily sallies from which they never knew whether they would return. The emotional stress was somewhat different; there was much more element of suspense—of "sweating it out"; there was little or no physical action and therefore physical fatigue; but the essential effects on the emotions were the same. Every flier who participated in such combat missions, like the infantryman, had strong emotional reactions; many of them became psychiatric casualties, too.

The effective soldier. Most of the psychiatric literature dealing with the soldier has been understandably concerned with describing the causes, types, and treatment of noneffectiveness and illness. Circumstances forced military psychiatrists to devote most of their time to the treatment and disposition of the psychiatrically disabled. It was many months after the war began before they gave serious consideration to the use of measures which might prevent mental illness. At no time did the field of preventive activity contribute nearly as much as it might have if its prewar experience had been greater and if many psychiatrists could have devoted their full attention to it. The great need (and opportunity) was the institution of measures to aid the soldier in his adjustment, and thus maintain or increase his ability to function.

When one attempts to discuss the subject of the effective soldier he, of necessity, meets with semantic troubles. Words like "successful" or "effective" as applied to the combat soldier are relative. There are varying degrees of success or effectiveness. Undoubtedly many soldiers died in displaying their effectiveness. The best integrated personalities might be effective for a long period

---

[5] Within the Ground Forces 67.8 per cent of all casualties were in the infantry divisions. Within these divisions 94.25 per cent occurred in infantry soldiers.

of time, only to disintegrate as the accumulation of stress became too great.[6]

In one of several investigations of "successful" soldiers Sheps [7] made a study of enlisted men, half of whom were in various stages of training and half in the theater of action. He compared his findings with those of several men who had analyzed the histories of soldiers who had been discharged because of psychiatric disability. In this comparison he found that there was a much lower incidence of childhood neurotic traits, of unsatisfactory home situations, and of previous personality or mental disorder in his still-functioning subjects than in those with psychiatric disabilities. This study was apparently an attempt to justify the psychiatric screening standards of the Canadian Army. In his report the author concluded that soldiers who stood the stresses of army life without developing a psychiatric disability were differentiated from their neurotic fellows by being more stable and better adjusted, with fewer and milder significant psychiatric stigmas.

A study of two groups of 100 soldiers each was made by two other Canadians, McNeel and Dancey.[8] It also revealed a relatively low incidence of nervous difficulties, such as unstable parents and siblings and broken homes, in the families of the effective soldiers. One of the groups was composed of soldiers who had seen continuous combat; the other was a mixture of replacements and service troops, many of whom had seen combat. The investigators attempted to evaluate the subjective explanations given by the men as to why they were able to withstand the stress of battle and were impressed with the number who gave the chief credit to "how one was brought up." These workers concluded that, for the most part, the men who were good soldiers showed certain tendencies in common: ready adjustment to new situations, acceptance of responsibility and discipline.

David Wright [9] investigated in considerable detail the background and histories of 100 American fliers who had completed a tour of combat duty. His findings showed a rather high percentage of history of psychoses in the family (6 per cent), of alcoholism or nervousness in the family (35 per cent), of the early death of a parent (16 per cent), of divorced parents (11 per cent), and of an unhappy childhood home (15 per cent). These figures are in considerable contrast to those of Sheps and McNeel and Dancey. Yet these individuals, despite the high incidence of psychopathology in their backgrounds, were also successful soldiers.

---

6 The environmental stresses in the life of a soldier are discussed in Chap. 5.

7 Sheps, J. G., "Psychiatric Study of Successful Soldiers," *J.A.M.A.*, 126:271-273, Sept. 30, 1944.

8 McNeel, B. H., and Dancey, T. E., "Personality of the Successful Soldier," *Am. J. Psychiat.*, 102:337-342, Nov. 1945.

9 Hastings, D. W.; Wright, D. G.; and Glueck, B. C., *Psychiatric Experiences of the Eighth Air Force*, Josiah Macy, Jr., Foundation, New York, Aug. 1944, p. 113.

Another approach to the study of why a soldier is successful was used when a series of psychiatric casualties was contrasted with a control group of effective soldiers. Needles [10] submitted a list of 86 questions to 100 psychiatric combat casualties and to a control group of 100 noncasualties. The soldier filling out the questionnaire remained anonymous. The resultant information is summarized in the following chart.

Anonymous Questionnaire Answers Indicated That of

Educational Level Essentially the Same	100 Psychiatric Combat Casualties	100 Non- casualties
Had an unhappy childhood	22.8%	11.1%
Had some of 14 neurotic traits	5.9%	3.6%
Were treated for nervousness prior to induction	29.0%	7.2%
Were treated for nervousness in Army	23.1%	1.0%
Were discontented with Army	26.0%	22.0%
Were very or moderately religious	96.0%	89.0%

In a second study of 200 soldiers with combat-induced mental illness Needles [11] found that his original criteria of selection—the history of psychiatric treatment prior to combat and the occurrence of 8 or more neurotic traits out of a possible 14—were not valid. He found no essential difference in the occurrence of these criteria in soldiers with an early breakdown and in those with a relatively long survival period in combat. His detailed study of 17 highly neurotic soldiers with 60 or more days of combat indicated that the presence of powerful compensating mechanisms—determination, externally directed aggression, fear of disobedience, effort to live up to lifelong patterns of conscientiousness, attachment to buddies—operated to keep these men in combat, in spite of their neuroses.

It was revealed by the Research Branch of the Information and Education Division that in a group of men selected for study, the home had been broken by divorce or death before the age of 16 in 23 per cent of the families of successful soldiers and in 29 per cent of the families of psychiatric casualties (scarcely a statistical difference!).

Coleman [12] reported on a group of 46 infantry soldiers, every one of whom was considered unfit for combat duty at the time of a psychiatric examination just prior to movement overseas. At the end of 18 months of duty in the Pacific, 35 of the 46 men were still on duty with the division.

---

10 Needles, W. A., "A Statistical Study of 100 Neuropsychiatric Casualties from the Normandy Campaign," *Am. J. Psychiat.*, 102:214-221, Sept. 1945.
11 Needles, W. A., "The Successful Neurotic Soldier," *Bull. U.S. Army M. Dept.*, 4:673-682, Dec., 1945.
12 Coleman, J. B., "Prognostic Criteria in Soldiers with Psychiatric Problems," *J. Mil. Med. in the Pacific*, 1:32-35, Dec., 1945.

Review of Service of 46 Infantrymen After 18 Months' Pacific Duty

With the Division	Not in Division
Satisfactory in original assignments 27	Less than 12 months overseas 4
Unsatisfactory performance in assignments 4	Psychiatric disability .... 7 including psychiatric combat casualties 3
Reassigned to service units 4	

This division psychiatrist concluded that there was a tendency to underestimate the adaptive capacities of neurotic soldiers. In this he had the strong agreement of many other Army psychiatrists. The psychiatric evaluation apparently did not reveal the "group aspect" of a personality. It explored anxiety and neurotic tendencies but not the capacities which could be utilized as a result of group participation nor the extent to which identification with a group might help the personality master its anxiety.

Greater knowledge of these would have been of great help in the maintenance of an effective unit. Many soldiers with apparently healthy backgrounds often became noneffective on short exposure to the stress of combat, whereas highly unstable individuals who were neurotically constituted often made successful soldiers. In a review of the experience of World War I, it was pointed out that certain neurotic officers often displayed great courage, even though torn between fear and the showing of fear. Wittkower and Spillane [13] quoted German sources as stating that such officers, on the whole, received more decorations than nonneurotic officers.

The conclusions about the soldier who remained effective throughout his combat experience would seem to be these:

(1) A psychologically traumatic childhood and a neurotic or unstable adjustment in later life made successful adjustment in the Army more difficult and less probable.

(2) On the other hand, many unstable individuals successfully adjusted to the Army stresses, even of combat, and made effective soldiers.

(3) The failure or ability to remain effective apparently depended upon the absence or presence of potent psychological compensations—both internal and external.

(4) The effectiveness of performance had a variable time element: an individual might be highly successful for a given length of time, depending upon the accumulation of stress that was uncompensated.

Effectiveness in a soldier, like effectiveness in a civilian, depended upon native capacities which were either stimulated and supported or limited by an external situation. It might and often did not have any relation to obvious neu-

13 Wittkower, E., and Spillane, J. P., "A Survey of the Literature of Neuroses in War," in *War Neuroses,* ed. by Emanuel Miller, The Macmillan Company, New York, 1944, p. 17.

rotic traits. A stable, intelligent personality, strong motivation, and good leadership appear to have been the most important factors in success. Some of us in the Army were impressed with our prewar overevaluation of the role of defective personality structure and underevaluation of the external stresses in the development of a neurosis.

Physiological manifestations of emotion in combat. Evidences of the effect of emotional reactions were the "symptoms" combat soldiers developed. The interrelationships of the mind and body were most vividly demonstrated in the physiological responses under combat conditions. Merely a listing of these and their frequency is impressive.

Reactions Under Fire	Dollard [14]	Kaufman [15]	
		Occurred Often	Occurred Sometimes
Violent pounding of heart	69%	48%	39%
Sinking feeling in stomach	44%	30%	46%
Feeling of weakness	14%	19%	33%
Sick at stomach	14%	23%	37%
Cold sweat	18%	27%	33%
Vomiting		8%	20%
Shaking or trembling all over	25%	26%	32%
Involuntary urination	6%	5%	6%
Incontinence of bowels	5%	10%	13%
Feeling of stiffness		23%	29%

The above chart records information from the reports of "normal" men about their behavior in combat. It would hardly have been forecast that 5 to 13 per cent of all combat soldiers would have involuntary defecation.

These figures showing the high incidence of "symptoms" in combat soldiers indicate the problem of reorientation confronting the combat psychiatrist. In civilian life he would have regarded these symptoms as indicative of truly serious personality disturbance. In combat they were the "normal" reaction. Every infantry soldier who remained for any length of time in a combat job developed some or even many of these symptoms, and yet he was not incapacitated by them. By civilian standards he would have been evacuated to the rear, but, with experience, the combat psychiatrist recognized these physiological reactions to be normal responses to great stress. Some of the manifestations indicated a need for rest but did not merit a diagnosis of abnormality, either physical or psychiatric. If they were persistent or developed with inap-

---

[14] Dollard, John, *Fear in Battle,* Institute of Human Relations, Yale University, New Haven, Conn., 1943, p. 19.
[15] Kaufman, M. R., "Ill Health as an Expression of Anxiety in a Combat Unit," read at Am. Soc. for Research in Psychosomatic Problems, New York, May 11, 1946. *Psychosom. Med.,* 9:104-109, Mar.-Apr., 1947.

propriate stimuli, then and only then were they to be regarded as pathological. An excellent and detailed description of the many varieties of normal reactions to combat has been given by Ranson,[16] a psychiatrist of much combat experience.

The research group of the Information and Education Division compared a cross section of troops in the zone of the interior (United States) with a group of psychiatric patients. Combat reactions of a group of 1,754 "normal" soldiers and 400 psychiatric casualties from combat were also studied.

| | Zone of Interior | | | | Combat | | | |
| | "Normals" Occurred | | "NP" Occurred | | "Normals" Occurred | | "NP" Occurred | |
	Sometimes	Often	Sometimes	Often	Sometimes	Often	Sometimes	Often
Sick headaches	31%	12%	46%	40%				
Cold sweats	37%	5%	55%	25%				
Nightmares	32%	4%	50%	30%	39%	9%	47%	14%
Trembling	25%	7%	40%	40%	48%	16%	45%	31%
Biting fingernails	22%	10%	30%	23%				
Fainting spells	18%	4%	42%	20%	19%	6%	30%	8%
Upset stomach	15%	4%	38%	20%	38%	10%	39%	13%
Sweaty hands	43%	18%	33%	57%				
Nervousness	48%	17%	25%	70%	41%	19%	29%	42%
Heart pounding	41%	13%	41%	45%				

The high incidence of neurotic and psychosomatic reactions in the so-called "normal" is again striking—nearly half had sick headaches, over half were "nervous," and about a third had nightmares. Until such symptoms incapacitated a man they were not matters of serious concern.

COMBAT EXHAUSTION [17]

When, however, the combat situation with its physical fatigue, its continuous threat of death, its single or repeated psychological shocks demanded

---

[16] Ranson, Stephen W., "The Normal Battle Reaction and its Relation to the Pathological Battle Reaction," in Combat Psychiatry among American Ground Forces in the Mediterranean Area, ed. by Frederick R. Hanson. (To be published.)

[17] The subsequent discussion is concerned with the combat reactions of the infantry soldier. The reactions of combat fliers differed very little, if at all. For these differences, the reader is referred to any of several excellent studies by Air Forces psychiatrists. Grinker, R. R., and Spiegel, J. P., Men Under Stress, The Blakiston Company, Philadelphia, 1945; and by the same authors, War Neuroses, The Blakiston Company, Philadelphia, 1945; Levy, N. A., Personality Disturbances in Combat Fliers, Josiah Macy, Jr., Foundation, New York, Oct. 1945; Hastings, D. W.; Wright, D. G.; and Glueck, B. C., Psychiatric Experiences of the Eighth Air Force, First Year of Combat (July 4, 1942-July 4, 1943), Josiah Macy, Jr., Foundation, New York, Aug., 1944.

more than the capacity of the personality to give, a casualty resulted.[18] The common immediate reaction was one that did not, in its early symptomatology, fit into any of our known diagnostic categories.[19] For this reason the widely used terms of "combat exhaustion" and "operational fatigue" probably had a very practical, utilitarian aspect. They did, however, have the disadvantage of implying that physical exhaustion or fatigue played a more major role than it did. Fatigue undoubtedly decreased the individual's capacity to withstand emotional stress but did not itself often cause the neuroses which developed in combat.[20] Though the influence of fatigue varied in different situations, it was never possible to set up a series of physiologic experiments which would have given some index as to its actual effect. On the basis of broad experience it has been estimated that not more than 3 to 5 per cent of the reactions were due entirely to fatigue. The great majority of cases diagnosed as "combat exhaustion" were primarily due to personality disturbance and were so treated.

The term "combat exhaustion" applied to a temporary condition out of which various more definite and more familiar syndromes evolved. This diagnostic label did not apply beyond the initial state. It designated a transient psychiatric reaction to combat which might or might not progress to a more clearly

---

[18] All soldiers in combat were under sufficient emotional stress to have a keen awareness of the psychiatric casualties. An overwhelming proportion of soldiers believed that these casualties should be treated as sick men. Only a relative handful regarded them as cowards who should be punished. A survey showed:

Questions: "In your opinion what should be done with men who crack up in action, that is, men who get shell-shocked, blow their tops, go haywire? (Check the one answer that comes nearest to what you think should be done with them)."

	Mediterranean Division, Officers	Pacific Division, Officers	Pacific Division, Enlisted Men
Most of them should be treated as sick men	79%	68%	73%
Most of them should be treated as cowards and punished	6%	3%	2%
Most of them should be treated some other way	15%	29%	25%

"Attitudes Toward Men Who Crack in Battle," *What the Soldier Thinks*, No. 5, 25 April 1944, p 7.

[19] Capt. (Later Lt. Col.) John Appel has given thumbnail sketches of 14 patients picked as characteristic of cases seen in an exhaustion center and presented because the clinical features "were different from those customarily ascribed to psychoneurosis." Appel, J. W., "A Note on the Teleology of Combat Incurred Neurosis," *Military Neuropsychiatry*, Proc. Assn. for Research in Nerv. & Ment. Dis., 1944, The Williams & Wilkins Company, Baltimore, 1946, pp. 125-138.
[20] Hanson, F. R., "The Factor of Fatigue in the Neuroses of Combat"; also Weinstein, E. A., and Drayer, C. S., "A Dynamic Approach to the Problem of Combat Induced Anxiety." Both papers in *Combat Psychiatry Among American Ground Forces in the Mediterranean Area*. (To be published.)

defined clinical entity. It did not apply to the delayed symptoms, those typically
regressive phenomena so often seen in men who had completed their tour of
duty and became ill when removed from the support of the group and its
leader.

The clinical picture of the combat psychiatric casualty has been described
by several experienced psychiatrists.[21] One of the best descriptions was given
in a report which was made by the commission of civilian psychiatrists who
were sent to the European Theater of Operations especially to study this question.

There is almost unanimous agreement that the first symptoms of the failure to
maintain psychological equilibrium are increasing irritability and disturbances of
sleep.

The irritability is manifested externally by snappishness, over-reaction to minor
irritations, angry reactions to innocuous questions or incidents, flare-ups with profanity and even tears at relatively slight frustrations. The degree of these reactions
may vary from angry looks or a few sharp words to acts of violence.

Subjectively, the state of irritation is perceived by the soldier as an unpleasant
"hypersensitiveness" and he is made doubly uncomfortable by a concomitant awareness of his diminishing self-control. One patient put this very vividly by saying—
"The first thing that brought home to me the fact that I was slipping was this
incident: A fellow next to me took some cellophane off of a piece of hard candy
and crumpled it up, and that crackling noise sounded like a forest fire. It made me
so mad I wanted to hit him. Then I was ashamed of being so jumpy."

In association with this "hypersensitiveness" to minor external stimuli, the
"startle reaction" becomes manifest (increasingly so as time goes on). This is a
sudden leaping, jumping, cringing, jerking or other form of involuntary self-pro-
tective motor response to sudden, not necessarily very loud noises, and sometimes
also to sudden movement or sudden light.

The disturbances of sleep, which almost always accompany the symptom of
increased irritability, consist mainly in the frustrating experience of not being able
to fall asleep even upon those occasions when the military situation would permit.
Soldiers have to snatch their rest when they can. They expect a rude and sudden
awakening at any time. Opportunities for sleep become very precious and an inability to use them very distressing. Difficulties were experienced also in staying
asleep because of sudden involuntary starting or leaping up, or because of terror
dreams, battle dreams and nightmares of other kinds.

---

21 Some excellent descriptions, especially the papers by Hanson, Ranson, Glass, and Ludwig,
were given in *Combat Psychiatry Among American Ground Forces in the Mediterranean Area,*
ed. by F. R. Hanson. (To be published.) Brody, M. W., "The Battle Neurosis," *Bull. U.S. Army
M. Dept.,* 5:412-419, Apr., 1946; Ludwig, A. O., "Neurosis Occurring in Soldiers After Pro-
longed Combat Exposure," *Bull. Menninger Clinic,* 11:15-23, Jan., 1947; Grinker, R. R., and
Spiegel, J. P., *War Neuroses,* The Blakiston Company, Philadelphia, 1945, pp. 4-48; Levy, N. A.,
Personality Disturbances in Combat Fliers, Josiah Macy, Jr., Foundation, New York, 1945;
Hastings, D. W.; Wright, D. G.; and Glueck, B. C., *Psychiatric Experiences in the Eighth Air
Force,* Josiah Macy, Jr., Foundation, New York, Aug., 1944. One of the most comprehensive
reports of combat psychiatry has been made by P. S. Wagner, "Psychiatric Activities during the
Normandy Offensive, June 20-Aug. 20, 1944," *Psychiat.,* 9:341-364, Nov., 1946.

This triad of increased "sensitivity," irritable reactions and sleep disturbances represents the incipient stage of "combat exhaustion." It usually does not lead to referral. It may exist without much change for days, weeks or even months. Sooner or later, often upon the occasion of some incident of particularly traumatic significance to the soldier, the marginal and very unstable equilibrium is upset and the soldier becomes a casualty.[22]

There was a monotony in both the complaints and symptoms as seen by the physician in the aid station or by the psychiatrist at the clearing station. They differed only as they represented the stage of personality disorganization. In the majority of cases they followed a stereotyped pattern: "I just can't take it any more"; "I can't stand those shells"; "I just couldn't control myself." They varied little from patient to patient. Whether it was the soldier who had experienced his baptism of fire or the older veteran who had lost his comrades, the superficial result was very similar. Typically he appeared as a dejected, dirty, weary man. His facial expression was one of depression, sometimes of tearfulness. Frequently his hands were trembling or jerking. Occasionally he would display varying degrees of confusion, perhaps to the extent of being mute or staring into space. Very occasionally he might present classically hysterical symptoms. Some of the combat-exhaustion casualties knew that they were "combat saturated" and that they might be through so far as the fighting was concerned.

Grinker and Spiegel [23] very adequately described the various types of regressive behavior in the clinical pictures. These were classified by their chief symptomatic expressions as passive dependency, psychosomatic reactions, guilt and depressive reactions, aggressive and hostile reactions, and psychotic-like states. Sobel [24] and Ludwig [25] described a type of reaction that came to be known as "the old sergeant syndrome." It was seen in a large number of previously efficient soldiers of all ranks after an exposure to combat of 6 to 14 months, with little or no relief. It was characterized by a slow progression of anxiety over a long period of months, culminating in a break. The common symptoms were apathy, depression, and sense of emptiness, superimposed on the usual anxiety. Guilt feelings were prominent in all. These men were always

---

[22] *Medical report on Morale and Psychiatry*, No. 17, Office of the Surgeon General, 25 August 1945, pp. 19, 20. Reprinted: Bartemeier, L. H.; Kubie, L. S.; Menninger, K. A.; Romano, J.; and Whitehorn, J. C., "Combat Exhaustion," *J. Nerv. & Ment. Dis.*, 104:358-389, Oct., 1946; 489-525, Nov., 1946.

[23] Grinker, R. R., and Spiegel, J. P., *Men Under Stress*, The Blakiston Company, Philadelphia, 1945, p. 208; *War Neuroses*, The Blakiston Company, Philadelphia, 1945, p. 4.

[24] Sobel, Raymond, "The 'Old Sergeant' Syndrome," *Psychiat.* 10:315-321, Aug., 1947. (This paper was written in 1944 when the author was on duty in the Italian Campaign as Division Psychiatrist, 34th Infantry Division.)

[25] Ludwig, A. O., "Neurosis Occurring in Soldiers After Prolonged Combat Exposure," read at New York Acad. of Med., May 14, 1946. *Bull. Menninger Clinic*, 11:15-23, Jan., 1947.

willing to work and in Ludwig's series 94 per cent later performed satisfactorily in noncombat units.

In World War I, the explosion of a shell in the close proximity of a soldier was originally assumed to produce organic injury to the nervous system. This impression proved to be erroneous. However, the term "shell shock" remained in common usage. It was applied to a rather wide variety of psychiatric casualties. Again in this war about one out of every four or five psychiatric casualties would tell the story of having been in close proximity to an exploding shell which "knocked him out." There was discernible in a very small percentage of cases what became known as "blast concussion" in which the concussion caused some physical injury to the central nervous system. These cases usually also showed psychologic symptoms.[26] In the Fifth Army [27] less than 1 per cent of the admissions to the neuropsychiatric center were cases of true blast concussion as manifested by a history of disturbed consciousness, retrograde amnesia, perforated eardrums, and/or evidence of pulmonary injury. With one exception all of this group presented an anxiety neurosis. In the opinion of the commission of civilian psychiatrists,[28] the so-called "blast syndrome" seemed to bear a very close relationship to combat exhaustion.

Some special treatment measures were developed for these patients by Maj. Howard Fabing [29] in the 130th General Hospital in Belgium. The patient was given pentothal to permit psychotherapeutic recall of his amnesia and then suddenly returned to consciousness by the stimulant drug coramine. By this method Maj. Fabing returned nearly 90 per cent of his 80 cases to duty. This experience cast doubt on the presence of any organic damage.

Psychodynamics of combat exhaustion. Four significant features played their roles in combat exhaustion: mobilized aggression, depletion or loss of ego strength, loss of the ego supports in the form of leadership and group identification, and specific precipitating trauma.

To be able to fight, a soldier had to mobilize and release his primitive aggressive drive. It was this drive which he had spent his previous lifetime in learning to control and direct into useful or at least socially approved channels. By "sublimation" he had diverted this pressure into participation in or

---

26 Anderson, E. W., "Psychiatric Syndromes Following Blast," *J. Ment. Sc.,* **88**:328-340, Apr., 1942.

27 Weinstein, E. A., and Drayer, C. S., "A Dynamic Approach to the Problem of Combat Induced Anxiety," in *Combat Psychiatry Among American Forces in the Mediterranean Area,* ed. by F. R. Hanson. (To be published.)

28 *Medical Report on Morale and Psychiatry, No. 17,* Office of the Surgeon General, 25 August 1945, p. 31. Reprinted: Bartemeier, L. H.; Kubie, L. S.; Menninger, K. A.; Romano, J.; and Whitehorn, J. C., "Combat Exhaustion," *J. Nerv. & Ment. Dis.,* **104**:358-389, Oct., 1946; 489-525, Nov., 1946.

29 Fabing, H. D., "Cerebral Blast Syndrome in Combat Soldiers," presented at Am. Neurol. Assn., San Francisco, June, 1946. *Arch. Neurol. & Psychiat.,* **57**:14-57, Jan., 1947.

observation of a closely fought football game, a vituperous political campaign, a battle of wits in a sales-promotion program. As a soldier he had to be ready to kill in order to live. To do this meant that he had to arouse the very powerful latent emotion and then release it into previously taboo channels.

Most people are aware of the fact that to become extremely angry or emotionally worked up is a very fatiguing process. One may feel physically exhausted after such an episode. The combat soldier's emotional state was stimulated for days and weeks on end. Keeping himself alert against death and ready to kill meant a continuous and excessive drain on his emotional energy. Regardless of this exhaustion the ego had to try to balance and integrate the personality. In coping with the stress of the external environment and the pressure of turbulent emotions, even the "strong" ego of an individual might become "weak." The ability of the ego to maintain its control was fortified or depleted depending upon the balance between the drain to which it was subject and the supports of leadership, companions, and rest. When the soldier had to wrestle for long periods with his complex internal fears and anxieties in a situation where the external environment always threatened him, he could run out of the energy that was required to keep his emotions under control. Under such circumstances some men became "trigger happy"; sometimes they did not wait to distinguish between friend and foe.

The ego's capacity to control the forces within the personality was decreased in varying degrees by the cumulative effect of unrelieved emotional stresses. Certain types of personalities could withstand strain over a longer period of time than others. The breakdown of a soldier in combat, whether it was during his first week or his fifteenth month, was related to the ability of his personality to maintain further the balance between stress and compensating support. Support was derived from various sources. The external situation which presented the necessity of killing in order not to be killed was a stimulus to keep the aggression mobilized for action. Fear, if controlled, was a factor in maintaining tense muscles, faster circulation, increased alertness. Very significant aids in the control of this aggression were the approval and command of the leader and identification and close association with a group of men who shared the same plight.

The same psychological re-enforcements which made it possible for the soldier to fight were potential causes of the development of a psychiatric casualty, if they suddenly disappeared. Because of great dependence upon them, the ego was left without support in their absence. When his leader was killed or when he was lost from his unit, the combination of his helplessness and his frustrated impulse to fight back invariably created anxiety. The very occasional soldier might carry on alone; such as he were likely to win the

Congressional Medal of Honor. More often, as the tension increased, the personality tried to relieve its distress by transforming the anxiety into symptoms. In the acute situation some soldiers became suddenly panicky. More often the symptoms developed gradually. Sleeplessness, tenseness, jumpiness, irritability, depression, inability to concentrate or accomplish relatively small tasks, dreams —these made up the preclinical picture of the combat casualty. Sometimes the crisis was past before the symptoms became incapacitating.

A loss of an outlet for the discharge of a high degree of activated aggression also led to psychiatric disability. This happened in those situations when the soldier was pinned in a foxhole by enemy fire. Under such circumstances he could neither protect nor revenge himself. I recall numerous instances of men in the division clearing station telling me, between their sobs or their jerks, "Doc, there just wasn't anything to shoot at. I couldn't do a thing."

An event of some psychological specificity to the individual could overbalance his abiltiy to adjust to external demands. Obviously, the soldier was more vulnerable when his ego strength was at low ebb. The immediate cause of the breakdown might have appeared trivial or been undiscernible. The soldier might or might not have been able to describe as "the final straw" the death of a comrade, the hopelessness of a particular assignment, a broken promise. Nevertheless, just as in civilian psychiatry, during the treatment of many cases a precipitating factor is found to be related to a childhood psychological injury.[30]

In many medical conditions, the pathology presents an unhealthy effort to remove or alleviate the pressure causing the illness. This phenomenon also is common in psychiatry where the personality tries to use symptoms to resolve its inner conflict. The process is a conspicuous feature of "combat exhaustion." One of the best illustrations of this is the symptom of recurrence of the same dream.[31]

In general, the dynamic significance of dreams [32] is that they are an effort of the unconscious to find a solution to its conflict and thus relieve the anxiety created by that conflict. Since the dream process is unconscious, it does not solve anything. The conflict continues, and the unconscious continues to attempt to dream its way out of its difficulty. Recurrent dreams are an example of the

30 See Chap. 4.
31 Saul, Leon J., "Psychological Factors in Combat Fatigue," *Psychosom. Med.,* 7:257-272, Sept., 1945.
32 Lidz regarded the combat-provoked nightmares as expressing a conflict concerning interest in and resistance to suicidal thoughts provoked by extreme hopelessness, in men whose early life experiences made them incapable of withstanding the withdrawal of affection and security. He also suggested that they may represent a need for punishment for their extreme hostility. Lidz, T., "Nightmares and the Combat Neuroses," *Psychiatry,* 9:37-49, Feb., 1946. The same author has reported an excellent review of his experience and observations on Guadalcanal. Lidz, T., "Psychiatric Casualties on Guadalcanal," *Psychiatry,* 9:193-213, Aug., 1946.

use of the same mechanism again and again in the presence of neurotic conflicts. This was first observed and described by Freud as the "repetition compulsion." [33]

When a symptom, like a dream, does not bring about relief, it may increase
the individual's distress. This frequently occurred in "combat neurosis." The
repeated dreams might be so terrifying that the individual was afraid to go to
sleep. Unless aid was given to bring the conflict into consciousness and to
achieve a solution, the neurosis continued, often in a more aggravated form.[34]
The precipitating cause of the dream was the external threat of the combat
situation. Often, however, the symptoms continued even after the soldier was
out of danger. The personality had incorporated the threat. It had become
internalized. Without treatment a vicious circle developed: the unconscious
emotional pressure continued to produce anxiety in increasing amounts without conscious recognition of its cause; the pressure resulted in more dreams;
more dreams resulted in more anxiety. The neurosis then became acute.

Return to duty. Nervous reactions developing in combat either cleared
promptly under treatment in forward areas or developed into one of the familiar
mental illnesses. With intensive, efficient treatment [35] within 15 to 20 miles
of the front line, roughly 60 per cent [36] of the psychiatric combat casualties
were sent back to duty. There could be no accurate evaluation of this treatment
because of the difficulty in checking on relapses. Various division psychiatrists
attempted to keep track of the number of repeaters.[37] Thus in the Eightieth
Division it was recorded as 4 per cent; [38] in the Second Armored, it was 10

---

[33] Freud, Sigmund, *Beyond the Pleasure Principle,* International Psychoanalytic Press, London,
1922, pp. 17-25.

[34] Abram Kardiner described these pictures as "traumatic neuroses"—a true injury to the personality. He believed the soldier developed a type of adaptation in which no complete restitution
takes place, but in which the individual continues with a reduction of resources or a contraction
of the ego. This is a helpful concept in understanding what one finds on examination in some
cases. *Traumatic Neuroses of War,* Psychosomatic Medicine and Paul Hoeber, New York, 1941;
"Forensic Issues in the Neuroses of War," *Am. J. Psychiat.,* 99:654-661, Mar., 1943.

[35] Treatment of combat reactions is discussed in Chap. 20. Many of the references in this chapter
discuss treatment methods. An excellent summary, based on theoretical principles and World
War I experience was given by L. S. Kubie, "Manual of Emergency Treatment for Acute War
Neuroses," *War Med.,* 4:582-598, Dec., 1943. The organization of a treatment program was given
(as used in the Fifth Army) by C. S. Drayer and S. W. Ranson in "Combat Psychiatry," *Bull.
U.S. Army M. Dept.,* 4:91-96, July, 1945.

[36] This figure varied from 30 per cent to 80 per cent, depending on the length of combat exposure
of the parent unit. In the Seventh Army, the armored divisions with 1 to 2 months of combat
returned 80 to 90 per cent while the Third, Thirty-sixth, and Forty-fifth Divisions with 14
months of combat returned 30 to 35 per cent. Most of the psychiatric casualties from "old" divisions were "burned out" and could not be salvaged for further combat. Ludwig, A. O., and
Ranson, S. W., "A Statistical Follow-up of Effectiveness of Treatment of Combat-induced Psychiatric Casualties, I. Returns to Full Combat Duty," *Mil. Surgeon,* 100:51-62, Jan., 1947; "II.
Evacuations to the Base," *ibid.,* 100:169-175, Feb., 1947.

[37] The percentage of "repeaters" depended partly on prevailing policies in divisions and Armies.

[38] Data obtained on a personal visit to the combat area in October, 1944.

per cent; in the Thirtieth Division it was 7 per cent. The psychiatrist of the Seventh Army estimated [38] combat casualty repeaters as 15 per cent who served an average of 40 days before the second breakdown. They were not returned to combat duty for a third time.

A few follow-up studies are available. Maj. D. I. Weintrob,[38] the psychiatrist of the Twenty-ninth Division, checked the records of nearly 1,000 patients who had been returned to duty from 1 to 10 weeks previous to his study. Of these a little more than half had continued at combat duty.

On combat duty 52%
On noncombat duty 16%
In hospital, wounds or illness 29%
Killed or missing in action 3%

Ludwig and Ranson [36] investigated a group of men which was returned to full combat duty and another group which was assigned to limited service. The men who returned to full combat duty were rated as having been "useful" if they had remained on duty for 30 days; if not, they were rated as "poor." According to these criteria, 149 of 316 men, or 47.2 per cent, were considered "useful." The study of men who were returned to limited service was carried out 6 to 8 months after they had been evacuated from combat areas. Of the 358 men who were sent to the rear areas, 33, or 9.2 per cent, were further evacuated to the United States. Before reassignment could be consummated, 15 men had been rehospitalized. The remaining 310, or 86.6 per cent, casualties had been assigned within the theater.[39] Of these, 93 per cent had performed satisfactorily or better, according to the replies received from officers of their units.

Berger,[40] the Seventh Division psychiatrist, followed up 92 psychiatric casualties returned to combat duty in the 184th Infantry Regiment of the Seventh Infantry in the Okinawa campaign, of whom 62 were veterans of four previous campaigns (Attu, Kiska, Kwajalein, and Leyte). Of these men, 24 had one recurrence of "combat fatigue" and 5 had two recurrences; the remainder, 68.5 per cent, were able to remain on combat duty without relapse.

A small series of 146 Navy psychiatric combat casualties have been reported.[41] These came directly from land fighting on Saipan, Guam, and Peleliu

---

39 Of 100 psychiatric battle casualties, an average of 30 per cent were salvaged for noncombat duty. Often, though reassured about not again being eligible for combat duty, some of these were unable to continue in any military service. This was discussed by B. Cohen and R. L. Swank, in "Chronic Symptomatology of Combat Neuroses," *War Med.,* 8:143-145, Sept., 1945.

40 Berger, M. M., *Study of Combat Fatigue Cases Returned to Front-line Duty.* (To be published.)

41 Owen, J. W., "Prognosis in Combat Neuroses," *Bull. Menninger Clinic,* 11:24-32, Jan., 1947.

to a naval hospital in the Solomon Islands. The results are shown in the accompanying table.

	Saipan	Guam	Peleliu	Total
Psychiatric cases admitted	26	68	52	146
Returned to full duty	9	42	39	90
Adequate follow-up on cases returned to duty	8	41	27	76
Cases returned to duty who received a nonpsychiatric discharge after the War	3	22	25	50

All of these figures, while varying rather widely, would strongly support belief in the validity of returning all possible men to combat duty. However we should have no illusions about those casualties who were returned to combat. Many of them were not well when sent back; most of them needed more treatment than they received. Nevertheless, the function of the Army medical officer was to return the soldier to duty if his personality was sufficiently stabilized to enable him to serve further. Neuropsychiatric casualties, if adequately rehabilitated, were no less expendable than rehabilitated surgical casualties. If they were well enough to return to duty, that was their required assignment. Many were again able to carry on indefinitely. The permanent effect of their Army experience, and specifically that of combat, on their personalities will only be known with the passage of time.

Delayed reactions to combat. The ability to carry through a particular combat assignment with a reasonable degree of effectiveness may have cost that individual dearly for the effort expended. Many men developed their emotional symptoms after the combat was over, after the completion of their tour of duty. This was particularly true in air-combat crews.[42] Although the tour of duty was effective, the fact that a pilot or other crew member broke afterward makes questionable his classification as a successful soldier. It is somewhat analogous to the situation in which the operation was successful, but the patient died.

This is a familiar phenomenon in civilian life. A person holds up under acute stress, and then finds himself exhausted. In such a state, symptoms first appear—tears, nervousness, weakness, depression, irritability. When the individual can "let down," the ego no longer can or, often, even attempts to control the personality expressions. If the stress occurred over a long period, if the ego was greatly depleted, the aftermath is the more pronounced. In the

---

[42] Grinker, R. R., and Spiegel, J. P., *Men Under Stress,* The Blakiston Company, Philadelphia, 1945, p. 181.

case of combat soldiers we saw many instances where long-standing latent conflicts came to the surface after the tour of duty. Although they had been superficially well handled before the period of stress, afterward the ego could not successfully repress them. The result was symptoms.

A small minority of combat soldiers were unable immediately to rechannel their aggressive behavior into socially approved activity. Following VE- and VJ-days in the various theaters, although no figures are available, it was apparent that automotive and traffic accidents increased. On a personal visit I saw numerous (and presumably more so than before VJ-day) soldiers in the rehabilitation center outside Manila who had had good combat records but had committed acts of violence after the fighting had stopped. Such reactions must be regarded as pathological: The effectiveness of such men was high when the situation permitted direct outlet for their aggressiveness; when it did not, they became social offenders and noneffective soldiers.

The attitudes and reactions of soldiers who were about to return home have been the object of several studies. In one of these Corwin [43] found that the returning combat soldier was apparently free from disabling neuropsychiatric symptoms. However, a reservoir of anxiety-producing factors in his personality modified his outlook and provoked the resentment and hostility toward civilians and present social conditions which were so frequently expressed. Under certain circumstances the anxiety might become great enough to produce a neurosis. Sturdevant [44] reported on 23 patients whose symptoms were probably combat-induced but did not develop until weeks or months after removal from the battle situation. They seemed to be precipitated by problems in their readjustment on return from overseas.

Upon their return home a reactivation of old conflicts incapacitated some men without regard to any psychological effect of combat service. Two such cases are described by Eisendorfer and Lewis [45] which will serve as examples of a reasonably common observation. In both instances the men had withstood all the stress of combat experience and developed anxiety only after returning to this country. One soldier feared to come home because of an emotional conflict with his mother. The other feared to face a marriage which was consummated at the time he left for the Army. The Army had served as a means whereby both of these men avoided their neurotic anxiety. Their return from the external dangers of the war to the relatively greater internal dangers of their unresolved conflicts in family relationships resulted in the reappearance of

[43] Corwin, W., "Attitudes of Soldiers Returning from Overseas Service," *Am. J. Psychiat.*, 102:343-350, Nov., 1945.
[44] Sturdevant, C. O., "Residuals of Combat Induced Anxiety," *Am. J. Psychiat.*, 103:55-59, July, 1946.
[45] Eisendorfer, A., and Lewis, M. D., "Internal and External Causes of Anxiety in Returning Veterans," *J. Nerv. & Ment. Dis.*, 103:137-143, Feb., 1946.

anxiety. We must, therefore, as these authors concluded, expect certain veterans who consistently followed a successful and symptomless Army career, to show definite emotional disturbances on their return home. The inference might also be drawn that some men who were rejected because they were unable to adjust at home could have become good soldiers.

CONCLUSIONS ABOUT THE WAR NEUROSES

Men reacted to combat in many ways; 90 per cent of the men came through without serious impairment of their function and with no serious changes within their personalities. But every "normal" soldier developed fear; they all manifested some or many physiological "symptoms." Some remained effective despite a neurotic make-up; others failed who had had a "normal" background. In either case the men with "combat exhaustion" presented clinical pictures that were remarkably similar in their initial development and symptoms. The response to treatment varied widely.

The so-called "war neuroses" or "combat exhaustion" represented only a small percentage of the total psychiatric problem of the Army. It did not include the neurotic reactions which occurred in basic training or those which developed upon the boarding of a ship for overseas service or while sitting on a lonely South Sea island or weathering a monsoon season in India. Nor did it include the 25 per cent of all psychiatric discharges which were due to warped character development. All of these neurotic reactions were familiar to psychiatrists, and they differed in no way from the same pictures seen in civilian clinical work except for the environmental situation in which they developed or were discovered. Very often they were revealed only because of that situation; they might have gone completely unnoticed in civilian life.[46]

Because of the frequency of the reaction which has been described on the previous pages, it was practical to give it a label, even though only for temporary use. With relief from stress, symptoms either cleared or assumed the pattern of a classical neurosis. Undoubtedly the outcome of the illness depended in part on the degree of predisposition. Many "normal" soldiers must have had some predisposition, minor though it might have been. It is gratifying to know that the majority, probably the great majority, of combat psychiatric casualties responded sufficiently under appropriate treatment to permit them to carry on. That their experiences left scars there is no doubt, but certainly, in

---

[46] Rado, in discussing the "normal" person with minor (and undiscernible) predisposition, explained the symptomatology as having been built up as a result of fear of trauma. The stress of the fear caused the individual to lose his "emergency control." Rado, S., "Pathodynamics and Treatment of Traumatic War Neuroses (Traumatophobia)," *Psychosom. Med.*, 4:362-368, Oct., 1942.

many men, these scars are not sufficient to disable them seriously or permanently.

Only as we understand these dynamics can we understand the symptoms which we may see in the combat veteran patient. In his solution he regressed to a simpler functioning level. In some cases, instead of returning to his normal adjustment, he will remain in the regressed stage. There he can express his passive dependency, his depression, his hostile reactions, his somatic complaints. He will not be able to explain his symptoms—his feeling of helplessness, his stomach disorder, his irritability and impatience, his tendency to fly off the handle, his failure to find satisfaction, his resentfulness of all but his own group.

Some men will return to civilian life with a tendency to feel that no one understands them. Others will have latent, or expressed, paranoid attitudes. In a sense they have entered a temporarily strange atmosphere. However, their attitudes are not caused so much by this fact as by the fact that their personalities are heavily burdened with the trauma of and the conflicts arising from their battle experience.

Three hundred and eighty thousand soldiers were discharged from the Army for neuropsychiatric reasons. A fair percentage of them had combat experience. Some will present to civilian physicians the clinical picture, the dynamics of which are described in this chapter. Combat or even military experience is not essential or necessary to understand and help these men. It is to be hoped that all physicians will prepare themselves to accept and to treat what the Army medical officers discovered were among their biggest problems—the emotional factors in the production of illness.

10

THE PSYCHE AND THE SOMA[1]

PSYCHIATRISTS SEE physical symptoms resulting from emotional disturbances. Doctors in other specialties see emotional responses in physically ill patients. More and more, all physicians are becoming aware of the close relationship between the psyche (mind, emotions) and the soma (body). From this realization, psychosomatic medicine [2] has developed. Young though the usage of that descriptive term is, it has two somewhat incompatible connotations. By some people "psychosomatic medicine" is used to refer to a limited number of diseases.[3] By others, including the author, it is regarded as a guiding principle of medical practice which applies to all illness.

A psychosomatic [4] approach to the medical, surgical, or psychiatric case considers the sick person, not merely his disease. Thus, the reaction of a patient to bacteria or bullets is seen to be affected by the mental and emotional struggles of his everyday life. An increasing number of medical men join Weiss and English [5] in the belief that there should be a new emphasis on a method of case study in which there is no less consideration of the soma but much more consideration of the psyche.

---

[1] This chapter is a modification of a paper read at the Annual Meeting of the Am. Soc. for Research in Psychosomatic Problems, New York, May 11, 1946. *Psychosom. Med.*, 9:92-97, Mar.-Apr., 1947.

[2] In answer to a query about the origin of the term, Ruth Potter, formerly managing editor of the magazine *Psychosomatic Medicine*, wrote on March 7, 1946: "Dr. Dunbar first used this word, having translated it from German in a footnote in her book *Symbolism and Medieval Thought* published in 1929. This book was a thesis which she prepared in 1926. Dr. Felix Deutsch says that he is the first person to have used the word in German. [Deutsch, F., 'The Use of the Psychosomatic Concept in Medicine,' *Bull. Johns Hopkins Hosp.*, 80:71-85, Jan., 1947.] In 1932 Dr. Dunbar first defined this term in a paper 'Medicine, Religion and the Infirmities of Mankind,' which was published in 'Mental Relationships in Illness: Trends in Modern Medicine and Research as Related to Psychiatry,' published in the *American Journal of Psychiatry* in 1934; again described in *Emotions and Bodily Changes*, published in 1935."

[3] Rowntree, L. G., "Psychosomatic Disorders as Revealed by Thirteen Million Examinations of Selective Service Registrants," *Psychosom. Med.*, 7:27-30, Jan., 1945; Halliday, J. L., "Concept of a Psychosomatic Affection," *Lancet*, 2:692-696, Dec. 4, 1943.

[4] The introductory statement in the journal, *Psychosomatic Medicine* (1:3-5, Jan., 1939), gives the definition of the editors: "Psychosomatic medicine concerns itself with the psychological approach in general medicine."

[5] Weiss, E., and English, O. S., *Psychosomatic Medicine*, W. B. Saunders Company, Philadelphia, 1943.

The medical training of the average physician has been inadequate to teach him either to understand or to treat the psychological and emotional factor in illness. Consequently, there has been justifiable criticism by lay and medical people of the evaluation of an illness which is made solely on the basis of the organic pathology found.[6] On the other hand, there has been equal validity in criticism of the psychiatrist for his neglect of a consideration of the physical and chemical factors in the examination and treatment of his patient. Instead of the psychosomatic concept being regarded as a subtle effort on the part of the psychiatrist to widen his clinical field, it should be looked upon as an interpretation of illness which considers the contributory causes and symptoms of both the psyche and the soma.

The psychosomatic concept is not new. No doubt the historian could find evidences, at least as far back as Hippocrates, that emotions had a causal relationship to some physical diseases. Zilboorg[7] reported that the fight, led by Nasse and Jocobi, to emphasize the emotional factors was on 100 years ago. The observations of Beaumont, followed by those of Pavlov and later Cannon, Bard, Gantt, and a horde of others, laid the foundations. As pointed out in a squib in the *New England Journal of Medicine,* these workers built the groundwork "for a scientific approach for the study of mind and matter, and the influence of the former over the latter—a reality empirically accepted and never for an instant doubted by Bishop Berkeley, the homeopaths, the mesmerists, Elisha Perkins, and the followers of Mary Baker Eddy.

"Except for a few ardent and credulous cults, however, and a numerically less imposing group of psychologically and scientifically minded physicians, it has required for the population at large a second world war and a popular pictorial magazine[8] to acquaint the people with the actuality of psychosomatics."[9]

Certainly the war has given added emphasis to the psychosomatic point of view. Every Army physician was confronted with a far greater number of patients having physical complaints in which no organic pathology could be found than he saw in civilian life. Such a condition has sometimes been designated as "functional."[10] The stresses and strains of military life contributed to the high

---

[6] Galdston protested against the perpetuation of the dualistic nature of the term "psychosomatic." He set forth numerous arguments for a term suggesting the origin of all disease or dysfunction. His preference was for "biodynamic." Galdston, I., "Biodynamic Medicine versus Psychosomatic Medicine," *Bull. Menninger Clinic,* 8:116-121, July, 1944.

[7] Zilboorg, G., "Psychosomatic Medicine, A Historical Perspective," *Psychosom. Med.,* 6:3-6, Jan., 1944.

Wickware, F. S., "Psychosomatic Medicine: Upset Emotions Can Cause Illness, Obesity and ·idents," *Life,* 18:49, Feb. 19, 1945.

itorial, *New England J. Med.,* 232:545, May 10, 1945.

inctional" is not an entirely satisfactory term since all organ activity is "functional." When ᵔ apply to a disorder, it means a disturbance in operation of the organ for which there ᵔarent physical cause. "Psychogenic" is often used to denote the same concept.

incidence of such functional complaints as were seen in patients on both medical and psychiatric wards. A man with even a minor incapacity which kept him from going on duty was hospitalized, usually on the type of ward to which his complaint was referable—gastrointestinal, cardiac, orthopedic, etc. These illnesses in which the complaints were physical but not caused by any organic physical disease were variously called "neuroses," "organ neuroses," "psychosomatic illnesses." A more specific designation, "somatization reactions," was used for this type of neurotic reaction in the revised nomenclature.

The incidence of these physical complaints without organic basis was shown by various surveys. The internists of 11 Army general hospitals in the United States [11] found that about one-fourth of the patients on the cardiovascular wards and one-fifth of the cases on the gastrointestinal wards were suffering from disorders in the function of these organs, with no physical pathology. A survey made by or with a psychiatrist who would be more cognizant of psychological factors would have disclosed an even greater number of such cases.

On the other hand, an investigation of the incidence of physical complaints in psychoneurotic patients was reported by Brill.[12] In two-thirds of 600 unselected cases of psychoneuroses in six Army general hospitals, some organ dysfunction was a major symptom. Of the entire group, 29 per cent had gastrointestinal reactions, 14 per cent had cardiovascular reactions, and 9 per cent had rheumatic reactions.[13]

In a study made by Poliak [14] of neuropsychiatric patients in the Naval Hospital at Great Lakes, the findings were similar. About half of his patients had complaints which concerned only one body system, but 15 per cent had complaints which involved three or more body systems. Probably typical of all emotionally caused disorders, nearly three-fourths of those cases in which the symptoms were related to the gastrointestinal tract were admitted first to the medical or surgical wards.

One thousand admissions to the neuropsychiatric service in a general hospital in Italy during the Rome-Arno campaign were studied by Boshes and Kean.[15] Of the cases that were classified as psychoneuroses, 40 per cent were hospitalized primarily for psychosomatic complaints. The patients with cardiovascular symptoms had the shortest mean combat time. The accompanying charts

[11] Unpublished study by the author, made in 1944.

[12] Brill, N. Q., "Incidence of Somatization Reactions in Psychoneurotic Disorders," *Bull. U.S. Army M. Dept.*, 5:383-384, Apr., 1946.

[13] Psychogenic disorder characterized by joint or musculo-skeletal pain resembling myositis or fibrositis.

[14] Poliak, P., "Psychosomatic Observations on Five Hundred Neuropsychiatric Patients," *Dis. Nerv. System*, 6:301-306, Oct., 1945.

[15] Boshes, B., and Kean, J. E., "The Psychosomatic Patient in the Theater of Operations. A statistical profile at the Base Sector Level." In *Combat Psychiatry in American Ground Forces in the Mediterranean Area*, ed. by F. R. Hanson. (To be published.)

present the varying combat service periods and the differing incidence of symptoms in combat and noncombat troops.

Mean Period of Combat Duty

Patients with psychosomatic complaints	2.4 months
Patients with cardiovascular symptoms	1.8 months
Neuropsychiatric patients	4.6 months
Normal controls	5.8 months

Incidence of Psychosomatic Complaints

Complaint	Total Group	Combat Veterans	Noncombat Troops
Gastrointestinal	29.7%	85.4%	14.6%
Orthopedic	23.5%	88.5%	11.5%
Multiple symptoms	17.3%	84.3%	15.7%
Cardiovascular	15.9%	88.1%	11.9%
Headache	8.1%	86.6%	13.4%
Genitourinary	5.4%	80.0%	20.0%

Men who were referred to mental hygiene clinics [16] in basic-training camps presented a somewhat similar picture. One-third of 1,800 consecutive cases presented physical complaints.

Incidence of Physical Complaints which Occurred in 598 (33.2 per cent) of 1,800 Consecutive Cases Referred to Mental Hygiene Clinics in Basic-training Camps

Asthenic complaints [17]	24.9%
Gastrointestinal	22.6%
Rheumatic	19.9%
Cardiovascular	13.7%
Genitourinary	10.7%
Allergies and headache [18]	8.2%

The chief significance of these figures lies in their emphasis on the physical evidence of emotional illness and the emotional factors in physical illness. As the statistics indicate, organ dysfunction was frequently found on medical or surgical wards, and physical complaints were numerous in psychiatric patients. Medical personnel in every specialty were brought face to face with the need

---

[16] Menninger, W. C., "Somatization Reactions as Seen in Mental Hygiene Consultation Services," *Bull. U.S. Army M. Dept.,* 5:640-642, June, 1946.

[17] Asthenic complaints include weakness, with frequently changing and ill-defined physical complaints.

[18] Only two instances of psychogenic dermatoses (skin) reactions were reported. D. J. Sullivan and E. S. Bereston, in "Psychosomatic Dermatological Syndromes in Military Service," *Am. J. Psychiat.,* 103:42-49, July, 1946, reported 26 cases. D. B. Davis and J. W. Bick, Jr., reported three cases in the Army in "Skin Reactions Observed Under Wartime Stress," *J. Nerv. & Ment. Dis.,* 103:503-508, May, 1946.

for greater understanding of the physiology, anatomy, and pathology of the psyche.

It is intriguing to speculate as to why many physicians have been blind for so long to the emotional factors in disease. The swing to the study of the soma initiated by Virchow's [19] brilliant work in pathology is not a sufficient explanation. Nor should all blame be laid at the door of medical education, as much as that has been at fault. Regardless of the causes there was a paucity of physicians in the Army who possessed sufficient understanding of the psychosomatic concept adequately to diagnose or treat many illnesses.

TYPES OF SOMATIZATION REACTIONS

The types of organic complaints on an emotional basis seen in the Army were no different from those seen in civilian life. They ran the gamut of illnesses in which the organs of the body act as mirrors for the emotional maladjustments of the individual. It is not difficult to grasp the fact that blushing is a physiologic change which is due entirely to emotion. However, many physicians are entirely ignorant of the mechanism by which chronic emotional tension at an unconscious level may produce major physiologic changes which interfere with the normal function of body processes. Such changes are often revealed as "organ neuroses." As yet there is no complete explanation of the reasons for a choice of neurosis. In all cases it is automatic and unconscious. There is no doubt that a personality is subject to a particular neurosis as a result of its specific life experiences.

In revising the psychiatric nomenclature for Army use, much thought was given to a term for this group of neurotic illnesses. The term "psychosomatic" was considered but discarded, because it refers to a point of view toward all medicine rather than to a specific group of illnesses. Because the neurotic symptoms are manifested through physical organs, i.e., through the soma, it was felt advisable to term these the "somatization reactions." In these illnesses the impulses, which in other types of neuroses may give rise to anxiety, are channeled into organ symptoms and complaints through a special part of the nervous system, the autonomic portion. By such a device the patient usually feels much less conscious anxiety, for the physical symptoms absorb it. If the condition exists over long periods of time, it is believed that structural changes may take place, such as in the case of gastric ulcer.

In general, there are four body systems used most frequently for emotional expressions which repeatedly and continuously come under the scrutiny of every physician: the cardiovascular, the gastrointestinal, the allergies, and the great

19 Alexander, Franz, "Psychological Aspects of Medicine," *Psychosom. Med.*, 1:7-18, Jan., 1939.

group of aches and pains included in the cephalalgias, arthralgias, and myalgias.

Such emotional reactions as the anxiety after a heart attack and the delirium of fever are not included in this category of illnesses. They are psychosomatic reactions but are not neuroses. Nor are the psychological effects of any serious illness included, nor of an operation, amputation, facial disfigurement or paraplegia, or loss of sight or hearing. However, the emotional aspects of these also should be the object of special study and therapeutic effort by the physician in charge.

Cardiovascular disease has as its five most common signs or symptoms: pain, shortness of breath, palpitation, murmur, and fatigue. All of these may be the expression either of emotionally or organically caused heart disease. There are many heart disturbances which are purely functional, such as pounding of the heart, rapid heart rate, awareness of tightness over the heart area. A very common type of disorder so frequent in military experience that it became known as "soldier's heart" was included in the previous Army nomenclature under the neuroses. In civilian life the same disorder is referred to as "effort syndrome" or, more frequently, as "neurocirculatory asthenia." [20]

No other body system is used so frequently in a symbolic sense to refer to love and hate. This should point out at least one lead as to the emotional significance of disturbances involving the heart. The heart is used as a symbol of affection in the valentine, in the various expressions of "loving with all my heart," a "warm heart," "heart throbs," "heartfelt." Such terms as "fainthearted," "chickenhearted," "thin-blooded" are used to describe the individual whose capacity to pursue his purpose is questioned. The lack of love or the presence of hate is indicated in such words as "hardhearted," "cold-blooded," "heartless," "heart-rending." One may be "heartsick" or may cause "heartache."

These familiar references to the heart as a symbol of affection or hatred are not the only evidence of the emotional investment that the average individual makes in it. Usually it is regarded as the most vital organ in the body, despite the fact that other parts of the body are equally necessary. Many physicians have observed that an individual receives the news of a damaged kidney with much more equanimity than he does information about a heart which is not functioning properly. Consciousness of a rapid or slow or uneven heartbeat is usually distressing. Under the stress of physical exertion or excitement everyone be-

---

[20] William H. Dunn made one of the most complete studies of this subject in "Emotional Factors in Neurocirculatory Asthenia," *Psychosom. Med.,* 4:333-354, Oct., 1942.

Contrary to expressed opinions, neurocirculatory asthenia was more common in World War II than in World War I. According to the statistics furnished by the Medical Statistics Division of the Office of the Surgeon General, between April 1917 and December 1919, there were 4377 cases with this diagnosis, or an annual rate of 1.06 per 1000 men in the Army. Between January 1942 and December 1945, there were 35,763 cases reported, an annual rate of 1.40 per 1000. Furthermore, after the issuance of the new nomenclature in October 1945, the term was used as a type of psychogenic cardiovascular disease.

comes conscious of his heart action. It should not be surprising then that 50 to 70 per cent of the soldiers in combat were frequently aware of their hearts pounding. As was indicated above, an emotional maladjustment was the fundamental difficulty in a fairly consistent number, at least 25 per cent, of the soldiers admitted to general medical wards for cardiovascular disorders. The heart symptoms were merely part of the expression of this maladjustment. Careful investigation shows that this type of symptom is most commonly related to deep-seated and unrecognized resentments and hostilities which the person subject to them had not been able to express directly.

The gastrointestinal tract presents a wide variety of functional disturbances, and, in general, probably lends itself as a mirror to emotions better than any other body system. This may be because it is partially under voluntary control. Next to the skin, the gastrointestinal system has more contact with the external world than any other part of the body. It receives more direct demands for adjustment and accommodation, more insults and abuses, and has a greater variety of opportunities for gratification than any other set of organs. Emotional disturbances cause lack of appetite, nausea, indigestion, constipation, etc., in civilians. Similar physical manifestations of stress were frequently seen in soldiers.

The gastrointestinal system is particularly well adapted to expressing the individual's attitude toward taking in or receiving, holding onto or retaining, and finally eliminating or giving. One of the simple, now fairly well-accepted, illustrations of the use of this mechanism is the patient with a strong unconscious need for affection, a strong desire to be appreciated and taken care of, who translates these into a need for food. In a sense the gastrointestinal tract, and particularly the stomach, tries to serve a double function—that of receiving emotional as well as physical nourishment.

Perhaps because of their organic interest, their enthusiasm for pathology, too many physicians ignore these obvious and familiar facts. Crookshank expressed this paradox in medical attitude by stating:

It always seemed to me odd in the extreme that doctors, who, when students, suffered with frequency of micturition before an examination or when in France, had actual experiences of the bowel looseness that occurred before action, should persistently refuse to seek a psychological correlative—not to say an etiological factor—when confronted with a case of functional enuresis or mucous colitis. I often wonder that the hard-boiled and orthodox clinician does not describe emotional weeping as a new disease, calling it paroxysmal lacrimation and suggesting treatment by belladonna, astringent, local application, avoidance of sexual excess, tea, tobacco and alcohol, and a salt-free diet with restriction of fluid intake, proceeding, in the event of failure, to early removal of the tear glands. Of course, this sounds ludicrous, but a good deal of contemporary medicine and surgery seems to me to be on much the same level.[21]

[21] Crookshank, F. G., "Organ-Jargon," *Brit. J. Med. Psychology,* 10:295-311, Jan., 1931.

It is encouraging to see the increasing emphasis placed on the emotional factors in disease as exemplified by such gastroenterologists as Alvarez and Palmer. The latter described certain individuals as having a "barometric abdomen," which serves as an indicator of the total personality functioning.

The layman's language suggests an intuitive recognition of the psychological factors in gastrointestinal disease which exceeds that of the average physician. Many terms indicate a very definite relationship between personality traits and various parts of the gastrointestinal tract. A "sucker" is a man who "bites" and is fooled. Certain persons are "leeches" because of a propensity to hang on. One "sinks his teeth" into a job or is not able to "stomach" his work. "Guts," "intestinal fortitude," "having a bellyful," "not being able to swallow it," "biting off more than he can chew," are expressions in common use. A large number of vulgar words for feces are used colloquially to indicate depreciation or disparagement or hate.

As in the case of functional heart disorders, the soldier with the functional gastrointestinal disturbance was usually sent to the hospital and first studied on the general medical wards. All of the surveys referred to previously indicated that this group of disorders constituted the most frequent of the somatization reactions. Several special studies [22] of gastrointestinal disturbances have resulted from our wartime experiences. While the actual incidence in the military forces

---

[22] An excellent review of these disorders was made by W. H. Dunn in "Gastroduodenal Disorders, an Important Wartime Medical Problem," *War Med.*, 2:967-983, Nov., 1942. British experience was reported by W. Brockbank in "The Dyspeptic Soldier," *Lancet*, 1:39, Jan. 10, 1942. There are two excellent studies of gastrointestinal reactions in combat: E. A. Weinstein and M. H. Stein, in "Psychogenic Disorders of the Upper Gastrointestinal Tract in Combat Personnel," *War Med.*, 8:365-370, Nov.-Dec., 1945, described their findings and the treatment used, which was essentially the same as for other neuroses. The second study was also made in the Fifth Army by J. A. Halstead, I. R. Schwartz, S. R. Rosen, H. Weinberg, and S. M. Wyman, in "Correlated Gastroscopic and Psychiatric Studies of Soldiers with Chronic Non-ulcer Dyspepsia." *Gastroenterology*, 7:177-190, Aug. ,1946. They described their findings in 110 cases, 84.5 per cent being psychoneurotic and 15.5 per cent psychiatrically normal. The gastroscopic abnormalities noted represented functional circulatory changes which were a manifestation of emotional conflict rather than signs of organic disease.

There was a widespread impression that gastric disorders were by far the most common psychosomatic response in soldiers. Because of diagnostic terminology, no statistical comparison is possible. Nor is it even possible to compare all types of neurotic and physical disorders of the gastrointestinal tract in the two world wars. Tentative figures furnished by A. J. McDowell of the Statistical Division, Office of the Surgeon General, show that the incidence of duodenal ulcer was higher in World War II. Figures for World War II include estimated admission figures for the year 1943. Overseas admissions for that year are based on overseas experience for the first nine months of the year. Complete tabulations are not yet available.

	World War I Apr. 1917—Dec. 1919		World War II Jan. 1942—Dec. 1945	
	Number of Admissions	Annual rate per 1000	Number of Admissions	Annual rate per 1000
Peptic ulcer: stomach	1,755	0.43	6,259	0.25
Peptic ulcer: duodenum	1,164	0.28	63,096	2.50
Total peptic ulcers	2,919	0.71	69,355	2.75

is probably no greater than in civilian life, Army doctors were impressed with the frequency of its occurrence.

Psychogenic physical disorders occurred which were related to many other sets of bodily organs. Of special importance because of their frequency were the functional complaints seen by the orthopedists in the forms of low back pain, muscle pain, or joint pain.[23] Two of my former consultant associates, Col. I. M. Gage, a surgeon, and Col. Mather Cleveland, an orthopedist, inspected hospitals with me in the Fourth Service Command. In a somewhat facetious vein but with good reason, they used to say that about half of the patients on the orthopedic service should be moved to the neuropsychiatric service. Many of them were so transferred. Headaches, often associated with organic causes, were also frequently recognized to be the result of emotional stress. They were one of the more common types of somatization reaction seen by Army medical men.

There were psychological concomitants that were the mutual concern of the urologist and the psychiatrist. On August 28, 1946, the Associated Press carried a story from American Headquarters, Frankfurt, Germany, to the effect that "progressively larger" numbers of American soldiers were developing mental disturbances as a result of "sexual promiscuity." This undoubtedly was a news release of a survey made in a general hospital which sorted and returned patients to this country. The study conducted there by Wessel and Pinck [24] indicated that many of the soldiers had no concern about their sexual activities at the time they occurred, even though they may have acquired a venereal disease. But as the time for the return home approached, anxiety was awakened. On the other hand, there were many individuals who did have great concern at the time of the sexual indulgence because of having violated their previous code or standard of behavior. As a part of their guilt reaction they frequented dispensaries seeking blood examinations and smears, presumably for their reassurance. Psychologically such behavior is a kind of confession and atonement for guilt. Many other types of genitourinary responses of emotional origin were seen in the Army, including most commonly impotence, dysuria (painful urination), enuresis (bed wetting) and among women, menstrual disorders.

IMPLICATIONS FROM ARMY EXPERIENCE

An understanding of the somatization reactions, termed "psychosomatic" if one chooses, is probably of more importance to the general practitioner, the

---

[23] Two Army doctors, E. W. Boland and W. P. Corr, were sufficiently impressed with their experience to report on "Psychogenic Rheumatism," *J.A.M.A.*, 123:805-809, Nov. 27, 1943.
[24] Wessel, M. A., and Pinck, B. D., "Venereal Disease Anxiety," from the 121st General Hospital, A.P.O. 69. *Ment. Hygiene*, 31:636-646, Oct., 1947.

internist, the surgeon, and the specialists in other fields than is that of any other type of neurotic responses. They are believed to constitute 50 per cent of the daily practice of the average doctor. Experience in the Army indicated that in many if not most instances, the general medical officers were not sufficiently oriented and trained in this phase of medicine to provide the most effective treatment. Too often they did not even understand the mechanisms by which the incapacity was produced. Sometimes this resulted in mistreatment or over-examination, which aggravated the illness by magnifying the problem in the mind of the patient. On admission to the Army hospital, most of these patients were sent directly to the medical or surgical wards, many of whom never had a psychiatric evaluation.

In some Army hospitals it was the routine procedure to transfer patients with somatization reactions to the neuropsychiatric service, following a con-sultation with the psychiatrist. However, the psychiatric wards were often lamentably understaffed and crowded. If the physicians on the medical services were capable of giving appropriate treatment to these patients, it was far more practical to leave them on the medical wards. This saved time and the confusion of transfer; the patient remained under the same doctor; he was not identified as a psychiatric patient and so stigmatized. For these reasons tentative plans have been made for the uniform establishment of such a policy throughout the Army.

The too prevalent belief that the organic medical problem is the most in-teresting is due to medical training which has emphasized the organic and often failed to impress the student with the validity and importance of illness caused by emotional maladjustment. To offset this, a close liaison [25] was formed be-tween the Medical Consultants Division and the Neuropsychiatric Consultants Division in the Office of the Surgeon General. Jointly they planned an educa-tional program for Army doctors. This effort bore its first fruit in the publica-tion of a technical medical bulletin,[26] "Neuropsychiatry for the General Medical Officer," which was distributed to every medical officer in the Army. The War ended before all of the plans could be converted into action. The goals for this

---

[25] This formal statement of the liaison does not begin to tell the full story. Brigadier General Hugh Morgan, Chief Consultant in Medicine to the Surgeon General, is one of the very superior internists in this country. He has been president of the American Association of Phy-sicians and is now president of the American College of Physicians. We worked together closely on many problems. He spent many hours on the joint bulletin referred to in footnote 26. He wanted his medical consultants to consider the psychosomatic problems and asked me to present the subject to them. I recall that, when we were working on the revised psychiatric nomenclature, he gave us several suggestions regarding the section on "somatization reactions"; when I sent the final draft to him for his official "concurrence," he promptly sent it back with the informal note, "I'd concur in anything you developed." When I saw him shortly afterward and com-mented that this was a broad commitment, he remarked, "Well, don't kid yourself. I wouldn't have two years ago!" His greatly increased interest in the psychiatric aspects of disease was paralleled by that of many of the leading internists in the Army.

[26] *War Department Technical Bulletin, Medical 94,* 21 September 1944. Reproduced in part in Chap. 28.

program, however, would be equally valid for any physician or any group of physicians.

First should come a reorientation of the physician from a strictly physical viewpoint of illness to one which encompasses the role of emotional maladjustment. This would include the correction of mistaken attitudes and practices concerning psychosomatic illness. It would entail gaining more information about how to help a patient understand the functional aspects of his illness. Recognition of clinical entities requires clear definition of them. Brigadier General Hugh Morgan and his staff in the Medical Consultants Division gave helpful suggestions in the revision of the psychiatric nomenclature. The somatization reactions are so described that nonpsychiatric medical personnel can understand them.[27]

Essential to the management of somatization reactions is an acquaintance with the dynamics of personality and its defenses against anxiety which are represented by the various physical symptoms that physicians see. The knowledge of the machinery by which and through which the personality operates is fundamental in understanding the reaction. The physician must have some grasp of what is meant by, and what happens in, both the unconscious and the conscious parts of the personality.[28]

Finally, the physician must have a knowledge of treatment measures which should be more than an appreciation of the irrationality of therapy by platitudes and placebos. There are positive measures and steps a physician can and should take to help the patient with these types of problems. One of the conspicuous shortcomings in the management of such individuals on the medical wards of our Army hospitals was the absence of any program of psychiatrically oriented treatment.

One of the gratifying relationships in the war experience was the close unity of action and thought between the other professional Consultants Divisions and the Neuropsychiatry Consultants Division. Progress in the field of psychosomatic medicine was due to the working and counseling together not only in the Office of the Surgeon General but in many of the Service Commands, theaters, and hospitals. It is to be hoped that this mutual co-operation can be maintained and furthered through continued intimate co-operation between psychiatry and all the specialties of medicine. If medical practice is ever to progress to the ideal of psychosomatic medicine, it will require the reorientation of medical training and of all practitioners so that equal emphasis is placed upon the roles of the psyche and of the soma in all illness.

---

[27] Appendix B.
[28] Chap. 4.

11

THE PSYCHOSES

PSYCHOSES CONSTITUTED a small but troublesome percentage of the total neuro-psychiatric case load in Army hospitals. These are the illnesses whose varied symptoms represent a distortion of reality or the patient's relation to reality. The symptoms are easily diagnosed and often are manifested in bizarre behavior: delusions (of persecution, of misidentity, or wealth), hallucinations (hearing voices or seeing visions), illusions (false interpretations of perceptions that are not amenable to reason), confusion or disorientation.[1] It is to this group of illnesses that the legal term "insanity" refers.

Among psychiatrists there is little difference of opinion about the identification of the psychotic reactions. For this reason and because most psychotic patients require hospitalization, hospital admissions are an accurate measure of the incidence of the psychoses in the Army. Between January, 1942, and June, 1945, about 7 per cent of the neuropsychiatric admissions to Army hospitals all over the world were diagnosed as psychoses. The incidence in overseas hospitals was slightly higher (8.3 per cent) than in hospitals in the United States (5.8 per cent). The rate was lower for officers than for enlisted men. The highest rate was that of enlisted women, probably because no psychiatric examination was made at the time of their enlistment during 1942 and 1943.

Psychoses, Rate per 1,000 Mean Strength per Year

Year	Officers	Enlisted Men	Enlisted Women
1942	1.30	3.66	7.11
			All Female Personnel
1943	0.76	2.63	3.22

About 45 per cent of all the hospital beds in the United States are occupied by psychotic patients. This makes the percentage of the psychiatric hospital practice devoted to psychoses in the Army seem very small. Braceland [2] reported a rate of 1 per 1,000 in the Navy, with a total of only 13,778 patients admitted

---

[1] Delirium is a temporary type of psychotic reaction.
[2] Braceland, F. J., "Psychiatric Lessons from World War II," presented at the Am. Psychiat. Assn., Chicago, May, 1946. *Am. J. Psychiat.*, 103:587-593, Mar., 1947.

to naval hospitals under psychotic diagnoses. In speaking of the British Army, Rees wrote that "this [referring to the psychoses] is not at all a large or important group of disorders in the Army." [3] In their outpatient-department screening, the British found only 3½ per cent (of 130,312) to be psychotic.

Comparison of civilian and Army statistics to determine whether or not military life increased the incidence of psychoses is difficult. The few figures now available seem to indicate a surprising difference. There appears to be two to four or even five times greater incidence in the Army.

Age Group	Civilian [4] Male First Admission to State, Veterans', County, City Hospitals for U.S., 1940.		Army [5] Net Admissions for Psychoses Among Male Army Personnel, 1943	
	First Admission	First Admission per 100,000 Population	Rate per 100,000	Total Admission for Psychoses
Under 20			162	1,145
20–24	3,460	60.8	231	6,145
25–29	3,929	72.1	260	4,393
30–34	4,025	79.4	291	2,617
35–39	4,374	92.2	326	1,620
Over 40				
40–44	4,521	102.3	524	693
45–49	4,292	102.0		
50–54	4,015	107.0		
Total	28,616	85.8	254	16,613

These Army figures were further checked against the disability (medical) discharges for psychoses in the Army for the same year, 1943. There were 13,591 discharges for psychoses, a rate of 219 per 100,000.

Was the incidence of psychoses in the Army actually two to five times greater than in civilian life? The answer is probably "No." Part of the difference is to be explained by the fact that state-hospital admissions do not represent the actual rate of civilian incidence. They only represent those patients who become so sick they cannot be cared for at home or under other auspices. Second, the Army figures include a considerable number of men who had short-lived psychotic episodes. In civil life these men probably would not be regarded as sick enough for admission to a state hospital. There is, however, the probability that the true incidence of psychoses in the Army is higher than in the same age

---

[3] Reprinted from *The Shaping of Psychiatry by War* by John Rawlings Rees, M.D., by permission of W. W. Norton & Company, Inc. Copyright 1945 by the publishers, p. 37.
[4] Figures supplied by Bureau of Census, through J. C. Capt, Director, May 8, 1946.
[5] Office of the Surgeon General, Medical Statistics Division, 22 May 1946.

groups in civil life. A soldier in a fighting army is subject to much greater stress than is a man in civil life. It is therefore to be expected that this type of personality reaction would be more frequent in military life. Perhaps at some later date we may have the data on incidence in combat, probably a still higher rate.

Types of reactions. The types of psychotic reactions did not vary greatly, either in kind or in relative proportion, from those seen in civilian life. Unfortunately, no official statistics are available to show the relative frequency of each type of reaction. Numerous studies indicated that schizophrenia, a serious illness most frequent also in civilian life, was by far the most common psychotic response, constituting 60 to 70 per cent of all psychotic reactions. Depression probably occurred somewhat more often in officers than in enlisted men. In the studies of both Duval [6] and Lebensohn,[7] approximately one-third of each series of 100 cases in officers were manic-depressive in nature.

Depressions severe enough to be classified as psychotic reactions were relatively infrequent. No official figures are available as to their incidence in the Army, but a rough estimate would suggest that they constituted perhaps 1/10 of the psychoses. One type of symptomatic behavior associated with depressions, either neurotic or psychotic in type, is suicide. Between July, 1940, and June 1946, there were 2,214 suicides in the Army, 300 of which occurred among officers.[8] McDowell [9] showed that these figures represent a sharp drop during the war period from the peacetime suicide rate in the Army. There was also a sharp decrease in the number of suicides in the Army in World War I, although that of World War II was much more pronounced. Thus in World War I, the suicide frequency in the Army as a whole declined from a prewar rate of 53 per 100,000 mean strength per annum to an average war rate of 15. The rate increased between the wars to twice this level. During World War II the rate declined from a prewar level of around 30 per 100,000 mean strength to an average war rate of 9.

The suicide rate among officers has always run from two to three times the figure for enlisted men. This can be explained on the basis of the officers being an older aged group (suicide rate goes up with age), with greater responsibilities, less adaptability, and other personality factors. The civilian suicide rate was unusually high in 1941, averaging 19.3 per 100,000 per year, but fell to approximately the average civilian rate of 14.9 in 1944.

[6] Duval, A. M., "Psychoses in Officers in World War II," *War Med.,* 5:1-5, Jan., 1944.

[7] Lebensohn, Z. M., "Psychoses in Naval Officers, a Plea for Psychiatric Selection," *Am. J. Psychiat.,* 101:511-516, Jan., 1945.

[8] An Associated Press release of October 23, 1946, quoted a study from the Army Institute of Pathology by Capt. Norman Zamcheck and Dr. Murray A. Geisler on 1,179 suicides and 656 homicides in the Army. The release indicated that the number of doctors and nurses who killed themselves was far out of proportion to any other group.

[9] McDowell, A. J., "Suicides in the Army," *Health of the Army,* 1:2-3, Report 6, 31 December 1946.

Suicides have always been of special interest to psychiatrists because they represent a symptom of serious maladjustment. It is not surprising that the rate would fall in the Army during the war. There are the superficial though valid explanations that the individual makes a major change in his job and relationships, has a new outlook, enlists in a mission of great social importance and distinction, and becomes identified with a group of like-minded public servants. It is possible that better psychiatric screening and better psychiatric treatment facilities were responsible in some degree for the lowered rate. Probably more important, the war gave many opportunities for the direct expression of aggressive tendencies.[10] Suicide is always an aggressive act; it is the expression of a deep-seated, unconscious, destructive drive. When this impulse can be satisfied by direct expression into the environment instead of being distorted and directed onto the self, it could be anticipated that there would be far fewer suicides. This result is reflected in the recorded observations cited above.

Without a doubt, the most interesting type of reaction was a comparatively short psychotic episode lasting from a few days to 2 or 3 weeks, in which most of the symptoms presented were characteristic of schizophrenia.[11] The recovery was sudden and abrupt. The following case is illustrative:

The soldier was a private in a Technical Training School in his sixth week of an intensive twelve-week course. He was a healthy, social-minded twenty-year-old man without unusual features in his family history or in his previous personal history. He had completed high school and had worked at one job before coming into the Army. Because the school was crowded, he attended class on a night shift, going from four in the afternoon until midnight. Without previous conspicuous or unusual behavior, he returned from class one night and decided that he should study. His bunk mates tried to persuade him to go to bed but he steadfastly refused. He became argumentative and although he remained in the barracks, he sat up all night. The following morning he was brought to the hospital at which time he was confused, somewhat silly and unpredictable in behavior; said he did not know his name, and was mildly agitated. His stream of conversation had to do with momentary passing stimuli. He was kept in relative seclusion and given sedation for a period of forty-eight hours and within five days began to clear mentally and within a week again seemed perfectly readjusted. He was kept in the hospital for an additional ten days for observation, during which he was restless to return to classes but adjusted very well. He seemed entirely clear and at the end of that time was returned to duty. It is known that he successfully completed the training course, but there is no further information as to his subsequent course in the Army.

---

[10] In a detailed study of 30 psychotic soldier patients, Kupper concluded that there was no basis to assume that the war or redeployment were related to the suicidal wish. Kupper, W. H., "A Study of Suicidal Soldiers in the European Theater after VE-day," *J. Nerv. & Ment. Dis.,* 105:299-303, Mar., 1947.

[11] Somewhat similar, if not the same, observations were made in World War I and reported in *The Medical Department of the United States Army in the World War,* Vol. X, War Department, U.S. Government Printing Office, Washington, D.C., 1929.

This type of short-lived schizophrenic episode is referred to by Braceland and Rome as "three-day schizophrenia." [12] These workers suspect that it probably occurs in civilian life, but because of its brief duration and relative infrequency it rarely is observed by psychiatrists. Porter [13] also described this disturbance as a form of acute schizophrenia. He regarded it as being peculiar to the military service or to prison life. In his experience the recovery began to take place almost as soon as the individual was hospitalized, with no special therapy required. Some of the cases reported by the Malamuds [14] were characterized by an unusually short course. Klow [15] described what he called schizophreniform episodes. His cases cleared in from 2 to 10 weeks and constituted nearly one-fourth of 67 psychotic patients admitted to the Elgin, Ill., State Hospital directly from military camps. Parsons [16] reported 11 cases in a group of 37 psychotic patients, all of whom recovered on a regimen of protection, reassurance, and graduated activity.

Another type of reaction which also justifies special attention has been described under the term of "pseudo-psychosis" and refers specifically to a combat reaction. This was a temporary reaction which was precipitated by battle stress and differed from any clear-cut, accepted category of psychoses. It was characterized by a return to conscious control within a few hours or days, at which time the psychotic symptoms were displaced by a neurotic reaction. In most instances, this was regarded as a variety of "combat exhaustion."

Boshes and Erickson, on the basis of approximately 100 cases of "pseudo-psychoses," delineated six subgroups:

1. Acute delusional reaction in which the soldier had difficulty in recovering from a dissociated state.

2. Prolonged panic reaction, with violent overactivity with danger to self or others.

3. Epileptoid states, in which the battle situation released violent, unpredictable, explosive behavior resembling epileptic furor.

4. Depressed reaction, beyond the mild reactive depression often seen.

5. Acute regressive or catatonic reaction, the largest group, who were inaccessible, retarded, mute, withdrawn, confused, perplexed, and resistive.

---

12 Braceland, F. J., and Rome, H. P., "Problems of Naval Psychiatry," *War Med.*, 6:217-220, Oct., 1944. Braceland and Rome used this term in quotations for which no reference is given, but in a personal communication I was told they were quoting Col. Roy D. Halloran.

13 Porter, W. C., "Psychiatry in the Army," in *Psychiatry and the War*, ed. by F. J. Sladen, Charles C. Thomas, Publisher, Springfield, Ill., 1943, p. 245.

14 Malamud, Wm., and Malamud, I., "Socio-Psychiatric Investigation of Schizophrenia Occurring in the Armed Forces," *Psychosom. Med.*, 5:364-375, Oct., 1943.

15 Klow, S. D., "Acute Psychosis in Selectees," *Illinois M. J.*, 83:125, Feb., 1943.

16 Parsons, E. H., "Military Neuropsychiatry in the Present War," *Ann. Int. Med.*, 18:935-940, June, 1943.

6. Schizoid reaction, separated arbitrarily from the last because of the slower development.[17]

In all these types, the evolution to a neurotic reaction occurred with treatment.

The commission of civilian psychiatrists which visited the European Theater in 1945 also described the clinical picture of the "pseudo-psychotic" stage, in which there was a complete disorganization of the personality. They portrayed it as "the end result of a continued intensive stress from combat, in which a soldier may become unstable, erratic, obviously confused, savagely irritable, quite unreasonable and even defiant and recalcitrant. He may climb out of his foxhole in the face of danger or freeze to it when danger has passed or when it is safer to go elsewhere. He may run aimlessly about, exposing himself precariously. He may stand mute, staring into space; he may go to his commanding officer pleading that he is not fit to command his detachment. He may break into uncontrollable sobbing or screaming. His speech may become jerky and incoherent. He may babble like a baby or make smacking or sucking movements of the lips. There is apt to be some tremulousness, especially of the hands and head; physical movements become awkward and incoordinated." [18] This same picture is well described by Mulinder [19] on the basis of his experience in the British Army. He specially stressed the fact that if taken out of combat, the great majority of cases improved steadily and symptoms disappeared with striking suddenness at the end of 3 to 7 days. Very frequently it was followed by typically neurotic reactions.

The paranoid reactions, particularly those in which the symptoms were a chronic paranoid adjustment, caused special problems when occurring in officers. As long as such persons presented plausible rationalizations for their paranoid systems, they were not believed to be ill, so that they often remained on duty for long periods, invariably making life difficult for associates and unhappy for subordinates. Rosen and Kiene [20] described the picture of eight such officers seen in the 96th General Hospital in England. In civilian life such individuals can find a niche or be dropped from their job; in the Army such ready disposition is impossible.

Another type of psychotic reaction was associated with the drug atabrine

[17] Boshes, B., and Erickson, C. O., "Psychotic and 'Pseudo-Psychotic' States Arising in Combat," in *Combat Psychiatry among American Ground Forces in the Mediterranean Area,* ed. by F. R. Hanson. (To be published.)

[18] *Medical Report on Morale and Psychiatry,* No. 17, Office of the Surgeon General, 25 August 1945, pp. 21, 22. Reprinted: Bartemeier, L. H.; Kubie, L. S.; Menninger, K. A.; Romano, J.; and Whitehorn, J. C., "Combat Exhaustion," *J. Nerv. & Ment. Dis.,* 104:358-389, Oct., 1946; 104:489-525, Nov., 1946.

[19] Mulinder, E. K., "Psychotic Battle Casualties," *Brit. M. J.,* 1:733, May 26, 1945.

[20] Rosen, H., and Kiene, H. E., "Paranoia and Paranoiac Reaction Types," *Dis. Nerv. System,* 7:330-337, Nov., 1946; "Paranoiac Officer and the Officer Paranee," *Am. J. Psychiat.,* 103:614-621, Mar., 1947.

(widely used as a prophylaxis against malaria). This drug was occasionally toxic to the nervous system, even to the extent of causing convulsions.[21] In 35 cases in 7,604 atabrine-treated cases of malaria in the Gaskill-Fitz-Hugh series in India,[22] its administration produced, or at least was associated with, a toxic psychotic reaction. This fact gave rise to the widespread rumor in the Army in the Pacific that the drug made one crazy. This was a serious handicap to effective prophylactic administration. Actually, the incidence was very small even in the intensively treated cases of malaria. The great majority of these psychoses recovered with prompt treatment.

Special characteristics. As might be expected, the incidence of psychotic reactions was much higher in men with less than 1 year of military service than in those with 2 or 3 years. The relatively early breakdown of a strongly disposed man supports the assumption that the stress in his Army experience served merely as a precipitating factor. Unfortunately there are no studies of the rate of incidence of psychotic reactions following combat. However, there are several which point to the high incidence of psychotic illness in the first few months in the service.

Will [23] made a study of 100 Naval inductees who developed psychoses within 15 days of active duty. Hecker et al [24] reported on 48 soldiers, 31.6 per cent of whom became psychotic within the first month; this study was made prior to routine induction screening. Simon et al [25] found that 42 per cent of 183 officers who broke down did so in the first 6 months, but this study was made in 1941, also before there was any psychiatric screening; Duval [26] reported that 45 per cent of 100 officers who broke down developed their psychosis in the first year. Hitschmann and Yarrell [27] reported on 100 soldiers with psychoses, 70 per cent of whom developed their illness within the first 5 months; 23 of them became ill within 2 weeks.

In the studies cited above, as well as in many others,[28] the same point is strongly stressed—that if the preinduction screening had been adequate, it

---

21 Newell, H. W. and Lidz, T., "The Toxicity of Atabrine to the Central Nervous System," *Am. J. Psychiat.*, 102:805-818, May, 1946.

22 Gaskill, H. S., and Fitz-Hugh, T., Jr., "Toxic Psychoses Following Atabrine," *Bull. U.S. Army M. Dept.*, 86:63-69, Mar., 1945.

23 Will, O. A., Jr., "Psychoses in Naval Inductees with Less than 15 Days' Active Service: Need for Early Elimination of Potential Psychoses," *U.S. Naval M. Bull.*, 43:909-921, Nov., 1944.

24 Hecker, A. O.; Plesset, M. R.; and Grana, P. C., "Psychiatric Problems in Military Service During Training Period," *Am. J. Psychiat.*, 99:33-41, July, 1942.

25 Simon, A.; Hagan, M.; and Hall, R. W., "Study of Specific Data in the Lives of 183 Veterans Admitted to St. Elizabeth's Hospital," *War Med.*, 1:387-391, May, 1941.

26 Duval, *loc. cit.*

27 Hitschmann, M., and Yarrell, Z., "Psychoses Occurring in Soldiers During a Training Period," *Am. J. Psychiat.*, 100:301-305, Nov., 1943.

28 Gray, R. C., "Minnesota Soldiers Discharged for Mental Disability," *Minnesota Med.*, 26:791-795, Sept., 1943; Brown, W. T., and Moore, M., "Soldiers Who Break Down in Battle," *Mil. Surgeon*, 94:162-163, Mar., 1944; Malamud and Malamud, *loc. cit.*

would have eliminated many of these cases on the basis of previous social and medical history. Some of these writers gave the frequency with which they gleaned from the patient a pre-service psychiatric history. In 100 patients of various diagnostic categories, Billings et al [29] estimated that 88 presented evidence of maladjustment or illness that should have excluded them from induction. It has been assumed by many people, including psychiatrists, that any history of psychosis or even of psychiatric treatment should prevent acceptance by the Army. In fact, this was the intended policy at induction centers.

However, probably much reassurance as to the effectiveness of psychiatric treatment in bringing about permanent readjustment could be found in a study of previously psychotic individuals who served in the armed forces successfully. Kopetzky,[30] the medical officer in charge of the New York City induction center, made an extensive study of men inducted who had a history of previous mental illness or commitment. Of 128 men accepted for service, 75 per cent were still in the Army. One-third of those still on duty had a history of psychotic illness before induction.

An example of a successful tour of unusually stressful duty is illustrated in the following case from our clinic in Topeka:

The patient first came to us at the age of 14. He required treatment in the hospital for a period of three months because of pathological excitement and aggressive attitudes which were accompanied by paranoid delusions, chiefly involving his parents. This initial attack had been precipitated by a series of rather severe infections. He recovered on that occasion but two years later at the age of 16 he was brought back for a milder episode, at which time he was given insulin shock treatment with twenty shocks in all. He remained in the hospital on this occasion for nearly five months and again seemed to return to good health. He made a good adjustment for the next 18 months and at that time, 1939, at the age of 18, joined the Marines and went overseas. He put in a period of service in Shanghai and when the Japanese occupied Shanghai, his unit was sent to the Philippines. He went through the struggle of Bataan and Corregidor and was taken prisoner by the Japanese. He survived the March of Death and three years in a prison camp without any apparent disturbance of his mental equilibrium. He lost some 60 pounds in the course of those three years but on his return to this country after some months of rest, he seemed well and returned to school where he has adjusted himself excellently.

It would be very helpful if we could make a better evaluation of the precipitating factors in a psychotic break for the purpose of developing preventive measures. Homesickness was the initial symptom in a third of the cases studied by Will.[31] Many of the soldiers who were taken into the Army were away from

[29] Billings, E. G.; Ebaugh, F. G.; Morgan, D. W.; O'Kelly, L. I.; Short, G. B.; and Golding, F. C., "Comparison of One Hundred Army Psychiatric Patients and One Hundred Enlisted Men," *War Med.*, 4:283-298, Sept., 1943.
[30] Kopetzky, S. J., "Validity of Psychiatric Criteria for Rejection for Service with the Armed Forces," *War Med.*, 6:357-368, Dec., 1944.
[31] Will, *loc. cit.*

home for the first time. This was true of three-fourths of 100 cases at St. Elizabeth's Hospital in which the psychosis developed within 15 days after induction. Separation from home and homesickness are mentioned by other writers.[32]

The initial and early stresses in the experience of a soldier are not the only ones which precipitated a psychosis. Studies made in general hospitals overseas by Rothschild,[33] Fox and Schnaper,[34] and Brown and Moore,[35] cited instances in which the illness developed after the soldiers had been in the Army from 1 to over 2 years. One must conclude that, as in the case of neuroses, the capacity to adjust was decreased by vulnerability to special stresses. A man reacted to the total situation with whatever he had, and when the stresses were specific or too great, he was overwhelmed.

No one has given any clear or concise explanation as to why in some cases the response to a situation is neurotic and in other cases psychotic. The "pseudo-psychosis" of combat appeared to be a hybrid of the two.

Disposition. Once a man developed a psychosis in service, he was almost surely discharged from the Army. The only exceptions to this practice were made for some cases of the short-lived schizophrenia. In such instances it was necessary to give the sickness some label other than psychotic reaction in order to return him to duty. The regulation was quite clear that if a soldier developed a psychosis he was not to be returned. Yet every psychiatrist was confronted with the problem of the disposition of a few patients who had recovered and were keen and apparently able to return to duty. It did not seem proper to discharge for disability (in the case of enlisted men) or retire (in the case of officers) men who were no longer incapacitated. If a protected assignment could be given for a time, there was every reason to believe that these men could give further duty, probably both to the advantage of the man and the Army. The number so assigned, however, regardless of psychiatric judgment or wishes, was extremely small.

Through 1942 and into 1943, psychotic patients were discharged from the Army hospitals to state institutions. A few were sent to veterans' hospitals and a few to St. Elizabeth's Hospital. Many of the states were reluctant to accept these patients on the basis that they had become ill in the Army and therefore were the responsibility of the Army or at least of the national government. In

---

[32] Hitschmann, *loc. cit.;* Duval, *loc. cit.*

[33] Rothschild, D., "A Review of Neuropsychiatric Cases in the Southwest Pacific Area," *Am. J. Psychiat.,* 102:454-459, Jan., 1946. In a personal communication he explained that in 1,000 cases, 41.8 per cent were psychoses; 35.6 per cent were psychoneuroses; 6.0 per cent neurological cases and the balance minor conditions. Censorship prevented inclusion of these figures in his paper.

[34] Fox, H. M., and Schnaper, N., "Psychiatric Casualties in a General Hospital Overseas," *Am. J. Psychiat.,* 101:316-324, Nov., 1944.

[35] Brown, W. T., and Moore, M., *loc. cit.*

some instances, if they were accepted, they were given no treatment for months, pending transfer to a veterans' hospital. Late in 1943 the whole system was changed, and all psychotic patients were sent to veterans' hospitals, except those who were able to return to their homes.

In the original wording of AR 615-361, it was definitely stated that psychiatric patients were not to be retained for treatment except in those instances where immediate short-time help could return the man to duty. In the latter part of 1944, as the result of continuous efforts, permission was finally gained to treat some psychotic patients intensively while they were still in the Army. Approval for treatment of chronic psychotic patients was not requested, chiefly because of lack of facilities and personnel. Therapeutic efforts for the readily salvable portion of the psychotic group were increased. Shock therapy was approved in 1943 [36] in cases where disturbed or excited patients could be quieted with two or three treatments. However, it became obvious that many of the psychotic reactions could be greatly helped by intensive shock treatment, and equipment was distributed to every psychiatric center late in 1944. At this time these centers were instructed to provide all other forms of treatment which were necessary for the psychotic patients.

Results. Only later "follow-ups" will show whether or not the brief treatment of psychotic patients was successful. There is a wide agreement that the psychoses as seen in the Army were not as malignant as those customarily admitted to state mental institutions. There are several reasons for this phenomenon: the Army patients were seen at a much earlier stage of illness; the acute precipitating stresses were promptly alleviated; the illness often sent the patient back to the security of his home; in the latter part of the war he received intensive as well as early treatment which was probably much more adequate than that given in most of our state institutions. In addition, clinical observation indicates that the psychosis with a sudden acute onset clears much more quickly and completely than that which develops insidiously and slowly.

There was a comparatively high rate of recovery from psychoses in Army hospitals and in those patients who were sent to the veterans' hospitals. Brill and Walker [37] made a follow-up study of 183 soldiers 6 months or more after they were discharged from the military service because of psychoses. Of these, 62 were reported by their families as having completely recovered. Only 34 still required hospital care. In their report they cite observations of a similar high recovery rate as reported by Frankwood Williams as well as Brown and Thornton in the last war.

[36] Surgeon General's Letter 88, 23 April 1943.
[37] Brill, N. Q., and Walker, E. F., "Psychoses in the Army," *Bull. U.S. Army M. Dept.*, **79**:108-115, Aug., 1944.

Braceland [38] reported that of all Navy psychotic patients who were sent to St. Elizabeth's Hospital or the U.S. Public Health Hospital at Ft. Worth, 65 per cent were returned to their homes at the end of 3 months and that an additional 20 per cent were returned within the next 3 months. There were many informal reports from the Veterans Administration on the short period of residence which was required before they were able to discharge psychotic veterans of World War II. In fact, there were two official complaints from the Veterans Administration to the Army, 1945, to the effect that patients were being referred to them needlessly. The explanation for this was that a psychotic soldier whose recovery would be doubtful would be admitted to an Army hospital. While waiting for the approval of an application for admission to a veterans' hospital, which sometimes required weeks to obtain, the patient was treated. If the Army physician had any doubt about the state of health of the patient at the time the transfer was finally ready, he erred on the conservative side and sent him on to the veterans' hospital, where he often recovered more rapidly than anticipated.

The result of treatment is at least suggested by spot surveys from some of the psychiatric centers in Army general hospitals in this country. In 1942-1943, approximately 40 per cent of the psychotic patients were well enough to be sent directly home. After treatment had been authorized as judged in 1945, 60 to 85 per cent were well enough to be discharged to their homes. (See Appendix D.)

Summary. The psychoses in the Army numbered approximately 65,000 cases, which constituted 6.7 per cent of the admissions to the neuropsychiatric services and sections of our hospitals. The rate of incidence was higher than in civil life and greatest during the first 6 months of military service. With more adequate data available to the examining physician, many of these individuals could have been screened out at induction; on the other hand, there is evidence to believe that many men with a history of psychosis survived and served a period of duty very creditably. I know of at least six from our clinic in Topeka. Schizophrenic reactions predominated and many short, self-limited episodes of this reaction were observed. Psychotic reactions among Army personnel did not appear to be as malignant as those seen in civilians, but this may have been due to earlier recognition and treatment. Certainly the provision of prompt treatment, when this was finally permitted and provided, produced a gratifying recovery rate, an average of about 60 per cent of all psychotic patients recovered within a period of 2 to 3 months from the time of onset of the illness.

---

[38] Braceland, F. J., "Neuroses and the War." Reprinted from the 33rd Annual Meeting of the Medical Section of the American Life Convention, Chicago, Ill., June 22, 1944. These figures are also given in a report by this writer in the *U.S. Naval M. Bull.,* 43:621-627, Oct., 1944.

12

OTHER MALADJUSTMENTS

SOME OF US are "queer," some of us "strange." Many of us have reputations for always being on time or always late, for appearing meticulous or for being carelessly dressed. All of us are aware of having "off days," of sometimes being "nasty" to our family or friends, of having moments or hours or days of depression or irritation. In short, all of us, at times, show "psychopathological" traits and behavior, even though we may or may not recognize them as such. In one of his early books [1] Freud discussed these various quirks and eccentricities. The types of personality disorders which were most numerous in the Army can be regarded as exaggerations of the psychopathology of everyday life.

Personality characteristics which may be obnoxious to others, or which mildly incapacitate the individual, are handicaps. These handicaps are the result and symptoms of incomplete emotional or intellectual maturity. Under pressure or stress or unhappy circumstances these characteristics often are accentuated. In civilian life they are compensated for by various types of supports in the form of mothers and wives and fathers and husbands. Crutches to adjustment are found in tolerant employers. Long-suffering friends serve as leaning posts. Often the symptoms are relatively inconspicuous to others or even to the possessors themselves. With his supports, such an individual may have "gotten by" in civilian life. Nonetheless he is, in varying degrees, a handicapped or crippled personality.

When an immature personality entered the Army, "hidden" personality disorders often became not only inconvenient but incapacitating. Lack of freedom, separation from supports and crutches, strict discipline, and strenuous physical demands intensified them. Some of these defects caused their possessors to be nuisances who irritated and annoyed fellow soldiers and commanding officers by often expecting or demanding special favors or concessions. Because of their helpless, dependent make-up, some of them became stigmatized with nicknames such as "Sad Sack," "Softie," "Sister." The usual attempts to improve

---

[1] Freud, S., *The Psychopathology of Everyday Life,* Ernest Benn, Ltd., London, 1914. This was first published in 1904.

their status by change of assignment or medical or psychiatric help frequently failed to solve the problem.

As might have been expected, many men with these so-called "minor" disorders were referred to Army psychiatrists. Such disorders were "minor" only in so far as they were less incapacitating than the neurotic or psychotic reactions, but most of them represented gross personality defect. Also, because of their lesser seriousness, they received "minor" treatment consideration in the Army.

A heterogeneous assortment of reactions are included in the following discussion: nostalgia, gold-bricking, acute situational maladjustment, emotional instability, enuresis, somnambulism, nonmarital sexual activity, alcoholism, and accident proneness. Of the men who were referred to the outpatient and consultation services, 25 to 50 per cent were suffering from such disorders.

Many of these difficulties were manifested predominantly in the soldier's first 6 months in the Army; others, like nostalgia, gold-bricking, and acute situational maladjustment, were largely dependent upon environmental factors and occurred at any stage of Army experience. Some of them like enuresis, somnambulism, sexual promiscuity, alcoholism, and accident proneness were recognized as having deep-seated origins in the personality structure. In every case, the degree of pressure of external forces on the personality was an important causative or provocative factor.

Homesickness. Homesickness in one or another form was probably the commonest minor maladjustment. It was most frequent in the basic-training camp but also occurred upon going overseas. Its expression was varied in many ways. Most often it appeared as a mild depression with introspection, seclusiveness, sensitiveness, vague fears, or tenseness, which sometimes developed into physical symptoms of stomach trouble or heart complaints.

Any psychiatrist in a basic-training camp could cite many illustrative cases. I recall, especially, one that I saw in the little circular meetinghouse that had been converted into the hospital at Camp Toccoa in northeast Georgia. The lad, a youngster of 20, had become a sergeant. He had made a good record as a machine-gun instructor for some 6 months. Without apparent explanation he lost his appetite, had vague abdominal complaints, and began to lose weight. He was admitted to the medical ward in the hospital after losing 20 pounds. He had repeatedly negative physical and laboratory examinations. When given the opportunity he told me his story about his fear that his girl at home had been going around with another man. He had heard that she was promiscuous, and he didn't know what to do about it. He wanted to go home and get it straightened out, but he thought no one would understand and that perhaps a good soldier should not be troubled by such things. Consequently he told no one about it. He was greatly relieved by merely the opportunity to talk it over, even though it was a tearful session. Arrangements were made for a visit home. He began eating immediately and I heard later that he did "straighten it out." His general reaction was not at all atypical of those seen in many soldiers.

In the medical literature of World War II [2] homesickness was described several times. Nostalgia was also a major problem in previous wars.[3] According to Deutsch,[4] the official medical and surgical history of the Civil War, 1861-65, records a total of 5,213 cases of nostalgia among the white troops of the North during the first year of war, or 2.34 cases per 1,000 strength. In the second year, the rate rose to 3.3 per 1,000.

Very young soldiers seemed to be more subject to homesickness. It is interesting, in light of the experience during the recent war, to note the parallelism of the concern about drafting of the youth. There was much discussion during the Civil War about the immaturity of 18-year-olds. The Assistant Surgeon General, Dewitt C. Peters (cited by Deutsch), wrote a forceful paper on "The Evils of Youthful Enlistments and Nostalgia." In this war, when in the fall of 1942 the draft age was lowered to 18, there was much agitation by the "Committee on Drafting Youth" who protested strongly against lowering the age. Their chief objection was the immaturity of the younger men.

The treatment for homesickness in this war, if it came to the attention of a physician, was kindly consideration of the emotional needs of the soldier. Actually, this was provided more often by the good leader than through referral to a physician. Sometimes the alleviation of homesickness required modification of the external environmental stress, where this could be accomplished. Often the chaplain and the Red Cross workers were the most competent to help. Psychiatrists recognized well that if homesickness were unrelieved, it might develop into major maladjustment.

Gold-bricking. Gold-bricking was an Army slang term which was applied to a variety of reactions that were characterized chiefly by lack of motivation, laziness, shirking, alibiing, finding excuses, and in general dodging assignments or responsibilities. It seems to have been the World War II equivalent for the older, now nearly obsolete term of "soldiering," meaning to loaf on the job. It was used by some to apply to malingering.[5] Ordinarily, however, it had a

---

[2] Flicker, D. J., and Weiss, Paul, "Nostalgia and its Military Implications," *War Med.*, 4:380-387, Oct., 1943; Wittson, C. L.; Harris, H. I.; and Hunt, W. A., "Cryptic Nostalgia," *War Med.*, 3:57-59, Jan., 1943.

[3] "Nostalgie Militaire," *Lancet*, 2:1261, 1914.

[4] Deutsch, Albert, "Military Psychiatry: The Civil War 1861-1865," in *One Hundred Years of American Psychiatry*, ed. by Gregory Zilboorg, Columbia University Press, New York, 1944, p. 377.

[5] Kraines, S. H., "Malingering," in *Manual of Military Neuropsychiatry*, W. B. Saunders Company, Philadelphia, 1944, p. 482.

much wider application to soldiers who were never malicious malingerers but who carried into Army life the kind of gold-bricking which is a rather typical American characteristic: trying to get out of dirty jobs, unwanted invitations, or unpleasant chores. In the Army it was very often observed before hikes and other strenuous activity, most commonly in an exploitation of a pre-existing but not incapacitating ailment. Sometimes there was complaining about vague symptoms that could be interpreted as an initial symptom of serious illness. Gold-bricking became an acute problem in those soldiers who "rode the sick book" (reporting frequently to the dispensary) or who developed a headache or a toothache at the time of a hike, or trumped up an emergency requiring them to go home.

Keen understanding of gold-bricking was shown by Janis.[6] He believed that its essential feature was a mental dissociation of the soldier from the performance of his job by doing as little of it as he could "get away with." A large percentage of all recruits engaged in self-justified gold-bricking on a part-time basis when they were obliged to perform such menial labor as mopping floors, cleaning latrines, washing dishes, cleaning out greasy pots, picking up cigarette butts, and dumping garbage. Janis interpreted the thoughts of the soldier at such times as: "I am really not doing a lowly kind of work for which I might feel ashamed because I have decided just to play the game of appearing to do it." This attitude enabled the recruit to deny to himself that he was, at the moment, a garbage man, a street cleaner, or a janitor. By so doing, gold-bricking served as a defense against feelings of loss of self-esteem through showing the soldier's secret contempt for and defiance of the assignment. Simultaneously it enabled him to express his hostility in this subtle disguise.

The extent of gold-bricking was undoubtedly dependent upon the ability of a leader to harness the motivation of his men to the required work. Napoleon said that "there are no bad soldiers, only bad officers." The treatment or management of gold-bricking was almost entirely a function of command rather than of medicine. If and when a soldier did come to the dispensary or found his way into a hospital, it was the task of the psychiatrist to help his patient recognize the basis for his behavior and, with sufficient firmness and kind severity, send him back to his job.

Acute situational maladjustment. The diagnosis of "simple adult maladjustment" was used extensively to identify the reactions which resulted from the stress of the immediate, external environment rather than from any deep-seated personality conflict. It was more frequently evident in overseas troops. Challman described it well in a psychiatric nomenclature which was specially

---

[6] Janis, I. L., "Psychodynamic Aspects of Adjustment to Army Life," *Psychiatry*, 8:159-176, May, 1945.

prepared for use in the Southwest Pacific Theater.[7] He called attention to the frequent symptoms of disgruntlement and resentment. The commission of civilian psychiatrists [8] was especially impressed with certain patients in whom resentment seemed to be the outstanding characteristic of maladjustment. They suggested the term "morbid resentment state" for a "disgruntled, resentful, embittered, aggressive, unamiable state in which the patient is particularly resistant and irritable about what he calls 'being shoved around.' " The diagnosis of "simple adult maladjustment" was also given for physical complaints due to environmental stress and, less frequently, for purely psychological symptoms such as insomnia and difficulty in concentration.

Certain cultural patterns were often the basis for maladjustment which was sometimes labeled "simple adult maladjustment." The psychiatrist occasionally was asked to see the hillbilly or the illiterate soldier from a rural background who was trying to compete unsuccessfully with the more educated or sophisticated bunkmate. A homely illustration of this type of problem, which confronted thousands of our soldiers, was an experience on a Pullman train. As I sat in the men's smoking room, eight GI's, under the charge of a private first class, got on the train. They dumped all their big duffel bags on the limited floor space of the smoking room. The berths had been made up, and they cautiously investigated but did not know how to proceed. Seeing the three washbowls, one of them decided to wash. Like so many sheep they all followed suit and began digging in their duffel bags for their towels and soap. When I told the soldier in charge that towels and soap were furnished by the Pullman Company, a hurried whisper traveled through the group, whereupon all soap and towels went back into the duffel bags. A little later when the conductor took my Pullman reservation, one of the GI's overheard me say "lower No. 2." He hesitatingly came to me as soon as the conductor had left to tell me that he had No. 2. He was greatly reassured when he learned that there were two bunks in section No. 2.

Often in the barracks, the inexperienced, provincial type of soldier was the butt of joking by his more worldly-wise company mates, sometimes to an almost unbearable degree. Wide personality variations were found which were due to cultural and biological backgrounds: the slow-moving, unimaginative, illiterate soldier; the dull, phlegmatic, rural plow hand, the high-strung, restless, loquacious, highly temperamental city type, and a dozen others. For each of these there were the minor difficulties in adjustment connected with the leveling

[7] Technical Memorandum No. 5, Hdqts. the U.S. Army Forces in the Far East, Office of the Chief Surgeon, 11 May 1944. Written by Col. S. A. Challman.
[8] *Medical Report on Morale and Psychiatry,* No. 17, Office of the Surgeon General, 25 August 1945, p. 39. Reprinted: Bartemeier, L. H.; Kubie, L. S.; Menninger, K. A.; Romano, J.; and Whitehorn, J. C., "Combat Exhaustion," *J. Nerv. & Ment. Dis.,* 104:358-389, Oct., 1946; 489-525, Nov., 1946.

forces of the Army melting pot. The solution of these problems was chiefly a function of command.

Unfortunately, for a long period, the diagnosis of "simple adult maladjustment" became a wastebasket of identification for a wide variety of transient personality reactions. In addition to all the above conditions it often was applied to soldiers with any one of many types of neurotic reactions, if the medical officer wished to return them to duty. For some time the diagnosis of psychoneurosis was so used because it almost automatically meant discharge from the Army.

That label of simple adult maladjustment was definitely a misnomer. None of the reactions it was intended to identify could be regarded truly as "simple." The use of the adjective "adult" was obviously superfluous. So, eventually, the term was changed to "acute situational maladjustment." This reaction is defined in the new Army nomenclature as "transient personality reaction manifest variously by anxiety, alcoholism, asthenia, poor efficiency, low morale, unconventional behavior, etc. The clinical picture of this reaction is primarily one of superficial maladjustment to newly experienced environmental factors, to specially trying and difficult situations, with no evidence of any serious long standing or underlying personality defects or chronic neurotic patterns. If untreated or unrelieved, such reactions may progress, in some instances, into a typical psychoneurosis or psychopathic reaction." [9]

Emotional instability reaction. This rather loose designation, although a diagnostic category, was not used very widely. It covered the same type of response included under the older diagnosis of "psychopathologic personality, with emotional instability." Psychiatrists in the consultation services and in the hospitals would see individuals whose emotional temperament was so labile that they were incapacitated periodically as a result of minor stress.

I recall an illustrative case that I saw at Tyndall Field, on the gulf coast in Florida at one of the Air Corps gunnery schools. A soldier patient of about 20 years of age, reasonably intelligent, tried to explain to me his unhappy 4 months in the Army. Every time he was ordered to shoot he would get so jumpy and excited that he could not even hit the target. If he were bawled out he would become tearful. He embarrassedly tried to explain that when the sergeant would shout at him he could not tell right from left. He had been made the brunt of jokes and had gotten the nickname of "dumb cluck," despite the fact that he was not "dumb." He had been transferred three different times on one pretext or another but almost assuredly because of his emotional instability. Even a cursory review of his history before he came into the Army indicated that he

---

[9] *War Department Technical Med. Bull. 203,* 19 October 1945.

had always been this type of an individual, related to a neurotic, invalided mother and an overexacting, tyrannical father.

This type of personality defect was manifested by inability to handle aggression, by guilt, and by anxiety. The symptoms, induced very often by slight mental stress, were expressions of insecurity. Such individuals were frequently regarded as being totally unadaptable to the demands of military life. They were usually discharged through an administrative rather than a medical channel because they were "lacking in the required degree of adaptability." [10] It was correctly assumed that the basis for the condition had existed prior to enlistment or induction.

Enuresis (bed wetting). Military experience revealed a surprisingly high incidence of enuresis in adults. In civilian life it is very rarely that an individual with this difficulty seeks medical help, perhaps because of embarrassment, perhaps because treatment offers so little help. Persistent enuresis is most common in individuals with behavior problems for the solution of which a physician's help is not sought.[11] The enuretic makes his adjustment through the tolerance and sufferance of his family who often temporize with the assumption that "he'll outgrow it." In a communal life such as exists in the Army, the enuretic individual cannot be given the tolerance and indulgence of his home life. He becomes a problem because of his symptom.

At the time of induction, if it could be shown and definitely proved that the man was enuretic, he would not be acceptable. To rule out the possibility of deceitfulness [12] the regulations were that unless a man had documentary evidence of his handicap, he was to be placed under observation for a 1- to 3-day period at the induction center. Even then it was not at all difficult for an individual to appear to be an enuretic. However, any person who would go to this length in deceitfulness would probably make a poor soldier. In a more common type of deceitfulness individuals refused to admit or to report an enuretic condition so that they might be taken into the Army. The conscious motives for this are multiple: enuretics commonly believe the regularity of life and the probable improvement of their physical condition will "cure" their ailment. They are often supported in this erroneous belief by their family and even by some physicians. Others undoubtedly hoped for an escape into a new environment away from the criticism and condemnation at home. Still others believed, in their patriotic fervor, that their assets were greater than this liability.

---

[10] Army Regulations 615-369, 20 July 1944.

[11] Michaels has repeatedly stressed the differentiation of enuresis on the basis of its persistence. He regarded it as a reflection of an ill-balanced personality. Michaels, J. J., "Significance of Persistent Enuresis in the History of the Psychopathic Personality," *Mil. Surgeon,* 95:315-316, Oct., 1944. This article gave references to several pertinent articles on this subject.

[12] Not infrequently selectees would falsely claim persistent enuresis. Rottersman, W., "The Selectee and His Complaints," *Am. J. Psychiat.,* 103:79-86, July, 1946.

The extent of this problem [13] is suggested by some figures. In 1943, 230,770 psychiatric patients were admitted to all Army hospitals, and of this number 9,470, or 4 per cent, were enuretic. Also in that year, despite careful pre-embarkation screening, 1.1 per cent of all neuropsychiatric admissions to Army hospitals overseas (531 cases) were for enuresis.

Many causes have been given for enuresis. The Army Regulation 615-369 dated July 20, 1944, states that "underlying causes of enuresis may be organic disease, psychoneurosis, psychosis, mental deficiency, psychopathic personality and lack of proper juvenile training." This list presented some of the associated conditions but not the causes. As in many psychiatric conditions, the "cause" is often ascribed according to the personally prejudiced point of view of the examiner. As one example, Capt. Samuel Karlan at the Boca Raton Army Airfield Station Hospital suggested that a high percentage of cases of enuresis which he had investigated were due to a small bladder. This is not incompatible with the psychological immaturity and chronic muscular tension characteristic of these individuals. Other organic approaches to this study have been made. The great majority of psychiatrists, particularly those dynamically oriented, regard it as a defect in personality development. It is an aggressive, hostile response to a situation. It also provides a type of infantile physical gratification.

Several interesting studies were made of enuresis in the Army. One made by a psychiatric social worker, Benowitz,[14] at Sheppard Field, and one made by Shlionsky, Sarracino, and Bischof,[15] reported similar findings. Of 10,000 soldiers referred to the psychiatric clinic of the station hospital at Sheppard Field between June, 1943, and September, 1945, 325 cases of enuresis were admitted. Of these, 172 were studied sufficiently to permit tabulation of personality factors. Shlionsky et al studied 100 cases referred to an Army hospital. Benowitz reported that 76 per cent were 25 years of age or younger, and only 3 per cent were over 36 years of age. While the rural-urban ratio for the camp was unknown, 73 per cent of the enuretics were from rural areas. (Shlionsky found 61 per cent from rural areas.) A significant finding was that in 49 per cent of the cases, the parents of the soldiers had been either separated

---

[13] An amazing fact worthy of special psychological study is that enuresis is practically nonexistent in women. Major Albert Preston reported only four cases at the WAC Camp at Des Moines in 20,000 examinations! On the other hand, Stalker and Band, in a study of only 67 patients, included 16 females. Stalker, H., and Band, D., "Persistent Enuresis: a Psychosomatic Study," *J. Ment. Sc.,* 92:324-342, Apr., 1946.

[14] Benowitz, H. H., "The Enuretic Soldier in an AAF Basic Training Center," *J. Nerv. & Ment. Dis.,* 104:66-79, July, 1946.

[15] Shlionsky, H.; Sarracino, L. R.; and Bischof, L. J., "Functional Enuresis in the Army," *War Med.,* 7:297-303, May, 1945. An excellent study of 150 consecutive cases in a Naval Training Station was given by A. Levine, in "Enuresis in the Navy," *Am. J. Psychiat.,* 100:320-325, Nov., 1943.

or divorced. Equally significant was the fact that 60 per cent indicated that they had either been rejected by the father, had feelings of hostility toward him, or that he was absent from the family picture, while 50 per cent of them gave a history indicating extreme dependence on the mother. Of the total, 55 per cent were married and 39 per cent had children. This suggests that in many instances the wife served as an overprotective mother figure.

As a group, men with enuresis tend to have little or no conflict with authority in civilian life. Fifty-one per cent had gone no further than the eighth grade and 71 per cent were engaged in civilian life in farming, truck driving, or unskilled labor. Fifty-three per cent were presumed to show some disturbance in their psychosexual development, 10 per cent being actively homosexual. Approximately 88 per cent came to the attention of the psychiatrist during their first 6 months of service and only 4 per cent after 1 year of service (20 per cent of Shlionsky's series had been in service over a year). An estimate of their job performance in the Army indicated a poor adjustment. They were often the target for jibes, teasing, and name calling by their barracks mates. Of this group nearly 9 per cent were returned to full duty despite their enuresis, and an additional 20 per cent were given restricted duty.

Enuresis appeared occasionally during or following combat in persons who had had no previous difficulty, though such cases often gave a history of bed wetting until late childhood. It was also observed to develop in a few cases as a result of the stress of basic training (perhaps 5 to 10 per cent of all cases). In such instances, the outlook for treatment benefit was much better than in those whose problem had persisted since childhood.

When referred to the medical services, efforts were made to treat these individuals. Relatively few cases were proved to be due to physical or mental disease, and rarely was treatment effective.[16] More often, line officers assumed that these men could be "disciplined into overcoming the habit." Thus, instead of being referred to a doctor or given an administrative discharge, the individual might be turned over to the proverbial tough sergeant.[17] By such techniques as having the man awakened every hour through the night, or out of pitiless ridicule, he was expected to effect a cure. In one post considerable effort was made to persuade men with enuresis to purchase, with their own money, a specially designed rubber bag which was to be worn at night. None

---

[16] P. L. Backus and G. S. Mansell, in "Investigation and Treatment of Enuresis in the Army," *Brit. M. J.*, 2:462-465, Oct. 7, 1944, reported sending the surprising number of 113 of 277 cases treated back to duty, using training in sphincter control and bladder relaxation along with supportive psychotherapy. (No other reports indicated nearly this high return to duty.)
[17] Alexander reports the Germans as having an "electrical treatment center for bedwetters organized at Rodewisch in Saxony." This was a widely used sadistic method of "treatment" for many personality disorders, utilizing strong (and painful) galvanic current. Alexander, Leo, German Military Neuropsychiatry and Neurosurgery. CIOS Item 24, Med. File No. XXVIII-49 Intelligence Objectives Sub-Committee G2, SHAEF (REAR) (1945), p. 55.

of these treatments affected the real cause, and the sadistic methods often only increased the difficulty.

The disposition of enuretic patients was a cause of much confusion in the early years of the war. There was a lack of understanding of the problem in some cases. Even though this was the one and only significant incapacity, the soldier might in some camps receive a medical discharge; in other camps an administrative honorable discharge; and in still others an administrative (unspecified) blue discharge—which is neither honorable nor dishonorable. Individuals were sometimes given other diagnoses in order to circumvent a particular commander who insisted that all enuretics should be given blue discharges. A revised regulation [18] definitely prescribed administrative, honorable discharge.

Somnambulism (sleepwalking). Somnambulism was never specifically listed as a cause for rejection at the induction center. It was suggested as one of the "physical disorders which may furnish important clues . . . to psychoneurotic disabilities." [19] The reason for this omission, undoubtedly, was the incidence of somnambulism in many children and adolescents. A considerable number of adults give a vague history of having had nocturnal episodes of some type. Experience taught us that each case in the Army had to be investigated. Because of a lack of understanding of what was meant by sleepwalking, some men would describe a trip to the toilet in a half-awakened state as somnambulism. It was not the intention of the Army to accept those who currently or even recently had walked in their sleep. They were regarded as being too great a liability. On the other hand, in the induction examination a history of sleepwalking in childhood had little or no significance.

No figures are available as to the extensiveness of somnambulism since it is only a symptom and not a diagnosis in itself.[20] It usually existed in association with other symptoms which determined the particular type of neurotic reaction. Thus, in one case, it may have been part of a dissociative reaction; in another, of conversion reaction; in still another, of an anxiety reaction. There were also cases which could not be classified as neuroses. Sleepwalking was often a single symptom. There may have been no other significant evidence of maladjustment, either in ideation or behavior. However, persistent somnambulism made a soldier a poor risk.

---

18 Army Regulations 615-369, 20 July, 1944.

19 Mobilization Regulations 1-9, Change 3, 4 June 1945.

20 In Rottersman's survey of 1,300 men at induction, about 2 per cent complained of sleepwalking occurring at least once every 3 months, persisting to the time of examination. In a tabulation of 100 men giving a history of sleepwalking, 21 stopped the somnambulism before the age of 13 years; 25 stopped between 13 and 18 years; 26 stopped between 18 and 37 years; 28 professed to episodes at least once within 3 months prior to their examination. Rottersman, W., "The Selectee and his Complaints," *Am. J. Psychiat.*, 103:79-86, July, 1946.

Curiously, somnambulism has been given scant scientific attention in medical literature. Sandler [21] studied 22 cases in a mental hygiene unit in basic-training camp. His observations are interesting, but his conclusions seem to have been extracted rather forcibly. They were summarized in psychoanalytic jargon as a "furious conflict between the ego and the id."

Somnambulism was no serious problem when it was discovered. Often psychiatric help inhibited its expression sufficiently to permit the individual to continue on duty. Where this was not possible, the patient was given a medical discharge. Like many of these regressive expressions of personality, it was precipitated by stress, at times, in an individual in whom it had been absent or minimal for many years. It is possible that there is a common denominator in somnambulistic behavior and battle dreams, though the latter represents a more recent and superficial conflict.

Nonmarital sexual activity. The problems inherent in the sexual life of soldiers have been studied from many angles: the results of enforced abstinence, venereal-disease control, supervision of licensed prostitution, military brothels, etc.[22] They have been the focus of heated moralistic arguments, particularly on the part of those who believe that the soldier is, or should be, asexual.

On the contrary, the greater part of our wartime Army consisted of men who were psychologically and physiologically in their sexual prime. Yet being a soldier required separation from home and from normal feminine companionship, as well as adjustment to a strictly male culture. Such a very abnormal life and living arrangement was bound to produce stress in men who were at the most active stage of heterosexual interest. In addition, there was the subtle (and usually unconscious) masculine implication that being a soldier meant being a tough, crusty, "he man." This undoubtedly tended to stimulate some individuals to relieve their stress and to express their masculinity directly in sexual exploits. The long separation, often by great distance, from the normal love objects—the sweetheart or the wife—weakened resistance to the appeal of momentary satisfaction. Many a combat soldier rationalized his sexual indulgence by "tomorrow I may die." The fact that he was with others who shared his attitude supported his action.

To the Army, sexual excess was a problem of logistics rather than of morality. The continuing loss of man power through the contraction of venereal disease was a matter of special concern. It was important to find out the type of individual who would expose himself to infection. Psychiatrists became

---

[21] Sandler, S. A., "Somnambulism in the Army Forces," *Ment. Hyg.,* **29**:236-247, Apr., 1945.
[22] On 5 April 1946, Army Regulation 600-900 was issued on the repression of prostitution, for the purpose of "reducing venereal exposures and the incidence of venereal disease." "Houses of prostitution will be declared off limits, disciplinary measures will be taken against military personnel entering such, and full cooperation will be given other agencies in the repression of prostitution."

concerned with discovering those toward whom educational efforts should be directed. Certain men, because of personality factors, were thought to be the most likely to take sexual risks.

Few psychological studies have been made of those who indulge in sexual excesses. Wittkower and Cowan [23] made one of the best to date. These workers investigated 200 soldiers with veneral disease and controlled their study by a group of 80 patients with impetigo (a type of nonvenereal skin disease).

Psychological Aspects of Sexual Promiscuity

	Impetigo Patients (86 Men)	Venereal Disease Patients (200 Men)
Immature personality types	19%	59.0%
Borderline types	19%	30.0%
Mature personality types	62%	11.0%
Heavy drinker	2%	29.5%
Discontented in Army	29%	54.5%
Inadequate prophylaxis	3%	22.0%
No prophylaxis	8%	68.5%
Occasionally promiscuous	⅓±	⅔±

The conclusion was that sexual indulgence of the type which leads to venereal disease seldom resulted from mature sexual interest but mainly from attempts to relieve acute psychological stress. Consequently, neither punishment nor counsel with regard to the risk reduced such contacts to any marked degree. Promiscuous sexual activity, like drunkenness and absenteeism, was a matter of morale rather than morals. The most profitable attack on the problem was any approach which improved group morale, such as the provision of adequate recreational facilities and easily accessible counseling about personal difficulties.

Alcoholism. Military leaders have tended to regard alcoholism as a kind of perversity for somewhat different reasons than civilians do. Because it is so frequently associated with misbehavior, many soldiers with this affliction were handicaps to their units. In civil life no one but the individual and his family are much concerned about the problem. In so far as possible, individuals known to use alcohol intemperately were rejected at the induction center. It was always a difficult problem to evaluate the amount a man drank merely on the basis of his statement. As with enuresis and even with epilepsy, a good many individuals tried to hide their weakness in order to be admitted into the Army. Undoubtedly some who had never drunk excessively in civil life, under the stress of Army life manifested their personality instability by additional

23 Wittkower, E. D., and Cowan, J., "Some Psychological Aspects of Sexual Promiscuity," *Psychosom. Med.,* 6:287-294, Oct., 1944.

drinking. Along with promiscuity, certain immature personalities regarded their capacity to drink as a manifestation of their masculinity.

Psychologically,[24] such individuals are fundamentally passive, dependent persons in whom the alcoholism symbolically represents a craving for the original nursing bottle. Like many other symptomatic acts, alcoholism, viewed psychologically, is only one symptom of an often very complex clinical picture.

The actual incidence of alcoholism in the Army is not known. In many cases it was accurately classified as a severe neurotic reaction. Very often it was the symptomatic act of a depression. Only in those instances where it became a periodic administrative problem for a commanding officer, without evidence of other conspicuous maladjustment, was it likely to have been classified as "alcoholic addiction." In 1943, of the 230,770 psychiatric admissions to Army hospitals in the United States, 1 per cent (2,420) were diagnosed as alcoholism.

Alcoholism was regarded officially as being an administrative problem [25] rather than a medical illness. Even if, in keeping with modern psychiatric thought, it had been considered a neuropsychiatric illness, there were neither sufficient personnel nor facilities for adequate treatment. Mild cases could be and were helped. It is safe to say that it was the rare exception that the alcoholic individual did not receive two or more hospitalizations. When a man's proclivity in this direction was sufficiently severe, he was discharged on an administrative basis, usually with a blue discharge.

The question was often raised as to whether or not the man who had so behaved before entering the Army [26] should be regarded as a medical problem and given an honorable discharge. However, such individuals as got into the Army did so on false pretense, by hiding the severity or the extent of their affliction. In spite of the psychiatric opinion that alcoholism is a personality disorder, there were morale factors involved in the method of disposition.

Had the chronic alcoholic been routinely given an honorable discharge, he would have received the same type of recognition as the battle casualty and the man who had rendered honorable, prolonged, and effective service. Because there is a large element of volitional behavior in alcoholism, such recognition would have adversely affected the morale of his entire unit. The other men would have justifiably regarded it as unfair and grossly unjust to them. The psychiatrist was forced to reorient his point of view toward alco-

---

[24] Knight, R. P., "Psychodynamics of Chronic Alcoholism," *J. Nerv. & Ment. Dis.*, **86**:538-548, Nov., 1937.

[25] Challman, S. A., and Moore, M., "The Soldier Who Drinks Too Much," *Mil. Surgeon*, **91**:648-650, Dec., 1942.

[26] H. J. Lawn, in a survey of 623 Army prisoners, in a rehabilitation center, who drank in varying degree, found no evidence that the alcoholism originated in the Army. "The Study and Treatment of Alcoholism in the Fifth Service Command Rehabilitation Center," *Am. J. Psychiat.*, **102**:479-482, Jan., 1946.

holic patients in order to place the needs of the individual second to those of the morale and mental health of the military unit. Were he to permit misbehavior, in which there was a large conscious element, to hide under the guise of an illness, he would have jeopardized the mission of the Army. For these reasons, and despite his knowledge that alcoholism is a deep-seated personality disorder, he subscribed to the use of a discharge which, to some degree, stigmatized the individual.

Accident proneness. A relationship between personality make-up and the occurrence of accidents long has been recognized and described as accident proneness. Insurance companies have compiled statistics which show that only 10 to 20 per cent of all accidents can be ascribed to mechanical causes, and that 80 to 90 per cent are due to personality factors. The National Safety Council, in a recent and more detailed study of 1,000 accidents, announced that 18 per cent were due to mechanical causes, 22 per cent resulted wholly from personality causes, and in the remaining 60 per cent both causes were operative.[27] Furthermore, in industry it is known that only slightly more than one-fourth of the accidents to workers happen while the individual is on the job.[28] Many of the on-the-job accidents are caused by deliberate rule breaking. For some years, it has been known that a high percentage of the accidents in any concern were limited to a comparatively small number of individuals. Thus, in Bristol's study,[29] 10 per cent of a group were responsible for 75 per cent of the accidents, and Moorad estimated that 12 to 15 per cent were responsible for 100 per cent of accidents. Rawson [30] quoted two authorities to the effect that 15 to 33 per cent of truck drivers account for 100 per cent of the accidents.

There are three significant features of accident proneness in the Army. Although there is no possible way of ever estimating incidence, there is no doubt that many soldiers were wounded because of their emotional state. Observation has indicated that under the stress of battle most individuals, because of their tension and fear, use poorer judgment. The purpose of the intensive precombat training was to make a man's reactions as automatic as possible, knowing that at times his life would depend upon this. Regardless of training, in some cases, the emotional state of the man predisposed him to the accident or injury which incapacitated him. In other cases certain deepseated personality traits contributed to his receiving the wound. In a survey

27 "Proximate Causes of 1,000 Accidents," studied by Committee on Fundamental Causes of Accidents, Engineer. Sec. of National Safety Council, ESMWT-17, 25-10-200. Furnished through the courtesy of Gene Miller, Senior Statistician.
28 Dunbar, Flanders, "Medical Aspects of Accidents and Mistakes in the Industrial Army and the Armed Forces," *War Med.,* 4:161-175, Aug., 1943.
29 Bristol, L. D., "Medical Aspects of Accident Control," *J.A.M.A.,* 107:653-655, Aug. 29, 1936.
Moorad, P. J., "Human Factors in Accidental Liabilities," *Indust. Med.,* 16:494-498, Oct., 1947.
30 Rawson, A. J., "Accident Proneness," *Psychosom. Med.,* 6:88-94, Jan., 1944.

of successful soldiers, McNeel and Dancey [31] found a much higher incidence (40 per cent) of neurotic history in the group of men who had been evacuated for wounds than in any of several other groups of "successful" soldiers studied. This led them to the speculation that accident proneness might have been a factor in receiving those wounds.

A second interesting corollary to accident proneness was the number of patients whose psychological reaction to a wound was one of great satisfaction which was later superseded by anxiety about being returned to duty. A soldier was often heard to refer to his "million-dollar wound." This attitude, which was quite understandable, expressed appreciation for the potential saving of his life by removing him from danger.[32] The wound was a legitimate and honorable ticket out of battle. A personal observation made in several hospitals in the European Theater was the relatively high frequency of referrals from the surgical service to the neuropsychiatric service.[33] Many psychiatrists commented on these personalities who, only after their wounds healed, developed anxiety about returning to combat and as a result were referred to the psychiatric section of the hospital.

The Tenth Replacement Depot in England was where men were sent for reassignment, including those who had recovered in hospitals. At the time of my visit, September, 1944, approximately 1,200 men were going through this depot daily, each of them receiving a physical checkup. The three psychiatrists working there, who averaged 50 to 100 examinations a day, saw only those patients who were referred to them by the other examiners. A surprising number of those who were judged to need further hospitalization were previous surgical patients in whom the anxiety had not been recognized before their discharge from the hospital.[34] A physical wound became psycho-

---

[31] McNeel, B. H., and Dancey, T. E., "The Personality of the Successful Soldier," *Am. J. Psychiat.,* 102:337-342, Nov., 1945.

[32] R. B. McElroy reported that "it was not unusual for a soldier to say that he prayed to be hit or have something honorable happen to him to remove him from battle." "Psychoneuroses, Combat Anxiety Type," *Am. J. Psychiat.,* 101:517-520, Jan., 1945.

[33] Major Philip H. Gates, Chief of the Neuropsychiatric Service of the Seventh General Hospital, whom I visited in September, 1944 provided me with some corroborative figures from his hospital during July and August, 1944 (following the Normandy invasion in June). Of 91 consultations, 32 were requested by the surgical service on psychiatric problems in wounded men. Of 88 patients on the neuropsychiatric service, 30 had been transferred from the surgical service, and 18 of the 40 patients received from other hospitals were combination psychiatric and surgical patients. In a report to the staff of the Seventh General Hospital, he and Sidney Cohen reported Ernest Parsons (312th Station Hospital—the Neurosis Treatment Center) as stating that of patients referred from the replacement depot in need of treatment, 41 per cent were surgical cases never seen by a psychiatrist, and an additional 41 per cent were combination psychiatric and surgical patients either inadequately treated or improperly disposed of. Quoting Gates and Cohen, "to date [August, 1944] over a third of our battle cases have come from the Surgical Service."

[34] In World War I, Thom reported that "on the whole, one did not find neurotic soldiers among wounded." Thom, D. A., "War Neuroses: Experiences of 1914-18; Lessons for Current Emer-

logically crippling when it destroyed the belief of a soldier in his personal invulnerability, which may have been a previous strong support in combat.

A third point which suggests the factor of accident proneness in casualties was the relatively high incidence of wounds among psychiatric patients. There is no proof that there is necessarily any direct relationship between accident proneness and frank psychiatric difficulties, but at least the observation is interesting that in 6 weeks, in 1944, 38.5 per cent of the patients admitted to the 312th Station Hospital, the neuroses treatment center, had been awarded the Purple Heart or were entitled to it. An analysis of 469 patients received from the continent at the 98th General Hospital in England (a psychiatric hospital for the reception of psychotic patients) showed that 27 per cent had received the Purple Heart. The Information and Education Division Survey [35] of "normals" and psychiatric casualties with combat experience, showed that among those men with less than 3 months of combat, 49 per cent of the neuropsychiatric cases and only 20 per cent of the "normals" had been wounded. In this same group, 23 per cent of the neuropsychiatric cases and only 8 per cent of "normals" had received the Purple Heart award. Among all combat soldiers, without regard to the length of service, 50 per cent of the neuropsychiatric cases and 42 per cent of the "normals" had been wounded; 15 per cent of the neuropsychiatric cases and 17 per cent of the "normals" had received the Purple Heart. One can only speculate as to the significance of these figures, but they certainly would indicate that great profit might be derived from a systematic study of accident proneness as related to military service. If the features of the personality which mark accident proneness could be more clearly delineated, it might be possible to utilize these as criteria in selection and in more appropriate placement.

Summary. At least five of these types of adult maladjustment, which were all common in military psychiatry, ordinarily do not come under the observation of civilian psychiatrists—nostalgia, gold-bricking, enuresis, nonmarital sexual activity, and accident proneness. They certainly occur in civilian life and might well be the subjects of special investigation and research. They were sources of great loss of military man power and as such became the concern of Army psychiatrists. Steps toward prevention and correction of similar civilian maladjustments could be accomplished through greater psychiatric understanding and knowledge.

---

gency," *J. Lab. & Clin. Med.,* **28**:499-508, Jan., 1943. Observations in World War II were in marked contrast to this.

[35] *Report on an I and E Study in the Mediterranean Theater.* Subject: Report 114-M-4, The Prediction of Neuropsychiatric Breakdown in Combat, 13 September 1945. Reference No. A9 330. 11-488, I&E-0.

13

BEHAVIOR DISORDERS

IN THE ARMY, as well as in civilian life, there are those who have difficulty in playing the game according to the rules. They are the bluffers and pretenders who never seem to profit from their mistakes. They cannot develop a lasting sense of loyalty to any cause or to any person. Psychiatrically, such persons have often been described as "psychopathic personalities." For a long time there has been dissatisfaction with this diagnostic label, because it is too general and too inclusive. There has also been a wide variation in opinion among psychiatrists as to the meaning of the term "psychopath." [1]

Originally it was believed that some organic change caused this type of misbehavior. Psychiatrists thought (and some still believe) that a person so afflicted was "born that way." Therefore he was a "constitutional psychopathic inferior." Porter, for example, stated, "One must regard the psychopath as an individual who has anatomical or morphological deficiencies or stigmata with a resulting malfunctioning of his biological mechanism and peculiar emotional and intellectual variations from the average normal way of reacting to social demands." [2] Many would agree with Malamud [3] who suspects that in some instances there may be some inherited factor. As yet this cannot be measured or proved. Since the electroencephalograph has been used more widely, many persons with severe behavior disorders have been shown to exhibit abnormal brain waves. No one is too sure what the significance of these tracings may be. They can hardly be used to support, or on the other hand to deny, the existence

---

[1] Menninger, Karl A., "Recognizing and Renaming 'Psychopathic Personalities,'" *Bull. Menninger Clinic,* 5:150-156, Sept., 1941. My brother here presented a brief and one of the best reviews of the history of this term, with its many ramifications and its many proposed synonyms. He also attempted to delimit its diagnostic use to one specific reaction type which he described as follows: "(1) The patient who puts up a front or facade for the benefit of the person he desires to impress or exploit; usually he is a hyperagreeable, sometimes the reverse; (2) he irritates, disappoints and distresses the doctor (and everyone else); (3) he does this by dissembling, lying, play-acting, pretending to cover up all sorts of aggressive self-exploiting behavior—in short, fraudulency and insincerity; (4) he breaks the rules as if he had a presumed impunity from the consequences which effect other people; (5) he maintains no consistent fealty."
[2] Porter, William C., "The Military Psychiatrist at Work," *Am. J. Psychiat.,* 98:317-323, Nov., 1941.
[3] Malamud, W., "Psychopathic Personalities," in *Manual of Military Neuropsychiatry,* ed. by Solomon and Yakovlev, W. B. Saunders Company, Philadelphia, 1944, pp. 160-179.

of organic brain changes. Certainly, no pathologic studies have shown any change.

So, we must follow further our most helpful lead—that the behavior of these individuals is the result, possibly, of some defective germ plasm, but certainly of their early life environment and experiences.

Unfortunately, in the Army the widely used term "constitutional psychopath" was applied as a catchall description for misbehavior of numerous types with various causes.[4] Misbehavior varies in its psychological significance and occurs in different personality structures. By differentiating into more specific categories, the newer Army nomenclature avoids the popularized but nearly meaningless term, the "psychopath." To be sure, some individuals are psychopathic; literally everyone is during a period when he is behaving pathologically. However, this term is not specific enough for a scientific diagnosis.

Incidence in the Army. Unfortunately, the statistics of neuropsychiatric hospital admissions do not give any accurate data about the number of antisocial personalities in the Army. This is due to the fact that the personal opinion of the psychiatrist largely determined the diagnosis in many cases. Also, in the meager statistics which are available, all types of "psychopaths" are lumped in one general group, the only subcategories being homosexuality and emotional instability. From January, 1942, until June, 1945, there was a total of 36,308 persons admitted to the Army hospitals with the diagnosis of "psychopath," or 3.9 per cent of all neuropsychiatric admissions. The percentage was noticeably higher among those admitted in the United States (5.1 per cent in contrast to 1.7 per cent of all the neuropsychiatric admissions to hospitals overseas). Another very rough estimate can be gained from the fact that there were 168,000 soldiers discharged on an administrative basis between January, 1942, and December, 1946, 42,000 of whom received a not honorable, or blue, discharge.[5] But this figure of 168,000 included all individuals discharged for mental deficiency, as well as for behavior problems.[6] For reasons previously

---

[4] In the "standard" nomenclature, psychopathic personality was broken down into several subcategories, such as "inadequate personality," "emotional instability," "pathologic sexuality," "drug addiction," "pathological lying," etc. The revised Army nomenclature which was published in *War Department Technical Bulletin, Medical 203*, 9 October 1945, substitutes "personality and behavior disorders" for "psychopathic personality." Some of the old subcategories remain, such as "inadequate personality" and "emotional instability." Others, "antisocial personality," "asocial personality," and "sexual deviate," are new terms.

[5] These and many other statistics on this subject were given by Col. John M. Caldwell in his paper at the Am. Psychiat. Assn. meeting, New York, May 21, 1947, on "The Problem Soldier in the Army."

[6] Because this method of discharge (Sec. VIII) was so difficult to accomplish in some posts, many soldiers belonging in this category were discharged medically (Sec. II) with a diagnosis of "psychoneurosis." Many more were let out under Circular 161, 1943, and under Sec. X, both special regulations for discharge not intended for this type of individual. From January, 1942, through December, 1945, there were approximately 35,000 men discharged under Sec. VIII, 145,000 under Army Regulations 615-369, and 212,000 under "limited service" directives.

discussed, men who were misbehaving, and so were ineffective as soldiers, were sometimes discharged medically. Between November 1, 1940, and December 3, 1945, there were 22,535 dishonorable discharges,[7] all of which represented some form of misbehavior.

Course in the Army. Misbehaving individuals, because of the very nature of their problem, were a source of continual difficulty for commanding officers.[8] Their lack of social adaptation seemed to keep them always out of step. A large percentage of the administrative problems in running a company could be blamed on them. They were late or unexcused; they were troublemakers and shirkers. Most often they were unable to make a permanent identification with a unit, and thus be loyal to it and its leader. They accounted for much of the insubordination. They were the chief recipients of "company punishment." Even when they became heroes, as some of them did because of their daredevil or exhibitionistic natures, there was a good chance that they were disobeying orders when they did so. Invariably, in their blunt airing of grievances, they caused dissension through their belligerent attitudes and their open expression of resentment toward the Army regime. Undoubtedly, many of them were tolerated until some breach of behavior became sufficiently gross to vitally affect the morale of the unit.

As was customary in the Army, such men, when company punishment failed, were sent to the hospital, where there was ample opportunity for the psychiatrist to evaluate their behavior. Their traits were very well described by Casey [9] who had an extensive contact with such individuals in a psychiatric hospital in Europe. A sociological study by Lemkau and Kent [10] pointed out the frequency of the familiar family history of broken homes, and the factors of inadequate family incomes and disorganized work histories.

Flicker and Coleman,[11] at Camp Blanding, studied 182 so-called "psychopaths," including 67 cases of mental deficiency, whose stay in the hospital averaged 40.7 days. These patients represented 0.6 per cent of the camp population but accounted for 2.6 per cent of hospital days. A great majority were

---

[7] Figures obtained from Chief of Manpower Control Group, War Department, General Staff, 10 May 1946.

[8] The remarks and figures in this chapter refer only to enlisted men. The disposition of officers is handled differently. In 1942, the rate of "psychopathic personality" diagnoses in officers was 0.70 per 1,000 men strength per year compared to 2.67 per 1,000 enlisted men and 6.69 per 1,000 in enlisted women. In 1943, the officer rate was 0.76 per 1,000; enlisted men, 3.73 per 1,000; all female personnel 2.78 per 1,000.

[9] Casey, J. F., "Disciplinary Problems in a Military Hospital," *Mil. Surgeon,* **97**:312-317, Oct., 1945.

[10] Lemkau, P. B., and Kent, F. E., "Sociological Factors in Patients in Army Neurosis Center and Their Relation to Disciplinary Actions," *Am. J. Psychiat.,* **102**:231-236, Sept., 1945.

[11] Flicker, D. J., and Coleman, O. H., "Military Discharge for Inadequacy," *New England J. Med.,* **228**:48-52, Jan. 14, 1943.

admitted for general medical and surgical complaints and, when found to be psychiatric cases, were transferred to the neuropsychiatric service.

The European Theater headquarters established what was known as the Recovery Center in England, in May, 1944. In the Theater Circular No. 67, its mission was stated as follows: ". . . to give special training under strict military discipline to enlisted men, who, because of personality or intellectual deviations, have not fitted into the combat or service organization of this theater." It was an attempt to retrain in order to retain the "unwilling soldier," the great majority of whom came directly from hospitals. At the time of a personal visit in September, 1944, they had had 437 men, of whom 125 had been "returned to full duty" and 135 "returned to limited duty." Only 8 had been recommended for discharge and returned to the United States. During his stay of from 5 to 8 weeks, the soldier was given a modified course in military training, along with special orientation lectures to help him accept his military role.

The theater was confronted with a serious problem in the utilization of these men. This effort was an attempt to meet that problem. Despite the number of men who, the record showed, were returned to duty, the effectiveness of this effort is open to question. The soldiers had been sent there by the psychiatrists of the many general and station hospitals all over England, by theater orders, but there were no psychiatrists stationed at this center. While it was visited by the theater consultant in neuropsychiatry, it can hardly be said to have been psychiatrically oriented. Hard-boiled punitive attitudes and methods were in vogue, with approximately 10 per cent of the "inmates" continuously in the guardhouse.

Psychiatry in civilian life as well as in the Army has contributed to the improvement of the handling of antisocial personalities in penal institutions. This military program should have been psychiatrically oriented. As it was, there was no assurance that chronic neurotic patients were screened from the misbehaving soldiers. Except for some similar methods (unguided as far as psychiatrists were concerned) used at the East Coast Processing Center [12] in

---

[12] The point for the east coast where all soldiers who had gone AWOL at embarkation time were processed to be sent overseas. A fair number of these were antisocial personalities (psychopathic personalities), and an additional large percentage were mentally dull. From a psychiatric point of view, the management of this group was never satisfactory. For the sake of the morale of the units from which these soldiers had gone AWOL such men could not be excused or pardoned or permitted to escape shipment. On the other hand, many were such severe misfits that they should not have been sent to any overseas assignment. An interesting analysis of 800 such men studied at the West Coast Processing Center at Camp McQuaide, Calif., by Mitchell, showed that 65 per cent had been AWOL twice or more; 35 per cent had been AWOL 6 months or longer; and 30 per cent gave problems in Army training or policy as their excuse. Mitchell, J. D., "A Study of Absences Without Leave on 800 Casuals at W.C.P.C.," Apr., 1945. Prepared for the C.O., W.C.P.C.

Massachusetts, this was the only effort the Army made to "train" this type of soldier.

One of the more serious disciplinary problems in the Army was the man who went absent without leave. Between 25 and 50 per cent of the most frequent AWOL offenders would have been classified as men with disordered personalities. The War Department was sufficiently concerned to issue a special pamphlet.[13] It included the results of a survey of the types of individuals who went absent without leave, their adjustment to Army life, their intelligence scores, and the incidence of mental problems among them. Also, helpful studies were made by several psychiatrists. In a group of 100 men, Davis et al [14] found that 50 per cent who went AWOL were "psychopathic personalities"; an additional 25 per cent were mentally defective; only 8 per cent were above average in intelligence. Guttmacher and Stewart [15] compared a control group of trainees with 133 cases of AWOL. They found that about one-third of the offenders were "psychopathic personalities" and that an additional one-third had some other type of psychiatric disorder. In both of these investigations, the individual case histories showed a high incidence of broken homes and frequent truancy in civilian life. Nearly half of them had had civil court records. Between 80 and 90 per cent expressed dissatisfaction with the Army.

For those whose behavior made them misfits and yet who had not committed sufficient offenses to be sentenced by general court-martial, the only practical solution was to discharge them. Each man was first studied in the neuropsychiatric service of a hospital (or outpatient clinic) and then referred back to his company officers with the findings and a recommendation for an administrative discharge. (Sec. VIII, Army Regulations 615-368.) Their difficulty was not a medical sickness (it was a social sickness) and for this reason they were not given a medical discharge. When such persons became involved in offenses against military law, they were sentenced to the Army correction system by court-martial. Of 24,327 general prisoners in military correctional institutions in 1945, 23.3 per cent were classed as "psychopathic personalities."

Probationers and parolees from state and federal prisons. Since 1878, there had been a federal statute which barred any man convicted of a felony from admission to the services. As a result of the enlightened attitude toward restored prisoners, this prohibition was amended by congressional legislation

---

13 *Absence Without Leave,* War Department Pamphlet 20-5, 3 March 1944.
14 Davis, D. B.; Wolman, H. M.; Berman, R. E.; and Wright, J. E., "Absence Without Leave. Psychiatric Study of 100 A.W.O.L. Prisoners," *War Med.,* 7:147-151, Mar., 1945. Eighty-three per cent of the group had been AWOL more than once; the average attendance at sick call was 15.5 times; 64 were "chronic alcoholic."
15 Guttmacher, M. S., and Stewart, F. A., "A Psychiatric Study of Absence Without Leave," *Am. J. Psychiat.,* 102:74-81, July, 1945.

in 1941.[16] After that time probationers and parolees (as well as "graduates") from state and federal prisons could be accepted into the Army. This move was stimulated and fostered by the Bureau of Prisons of the Department of Justice.

This change in policy encountered many snags in practice. One of the chief of these was the induction board psychiatric (and medical) examination. Many psychiatrists (usually those with little or no penologic experience) were inclined to reject a man merely on the basis of a history of any prison sentence. Also, there was some ignoring of this regulation by local boards which did not give such individuals an opportunity to serve even though the revision had the endorsement of the National Selective Service Headquarters. On the other hand, eligibility for military service was abused by some judges and other authorities who would tell a man that he could either go to jail or into the Army!

According to Mr. James V. Bennett,[17] Director of the Bureau of Prisons, special panels of Selective Service Boards were set up in almost all of the federal and state prisons. They registered, classified, and arranged for the induction of those men who were considered fit for service in the armed forces, despite their prior record. Roughly, 100,000 men were drawn from among probationers, parolees of prisons, and men no longer under supervision for felonies committed before the passage of the Selective Service Act. It was Mr. Bennett's belief, on the basis of brief surveys, that men drawn from these sources made as good a record as the general run of inductees selected without regard to criminal record. Many made outstanding records in the Army.[18] McCallum [19] reported that 3 per cent of his company had been engaged in criminal behavior in civilian life and none had gotten into trouble in the Army, though he doubted if this situation was generally true throughout the Army. He pointed out that many widespread practices in the Army are regarded as illegitimate outside of the Army system: 80 per cent of his men gambled; 60 per cent

---

[16] The Thomas Bill, S.1110. Reported and discussed in *The Osborne Assoc. News Bull.*, 12:1-2, Aug., 1941. The status of eligibility was most recently amplified in War Department Circular 110, 17 April 1946: "Classes ineligible for enlistment. Men (applying for original enlistments) having frequent difficulty with law enforcement agencies, criminal tendencies, a long history of antisocial behavior, questionable moral character, or traits of character which render them unfit to associate with enlisted men, *unless* waived in each individual case by the commanding general of the service command (after complete investigation through local law enforcement agencies) whose decision in this regard will be final."

[17] Personal communication, July 1, 1946.

[18] The record of about 2,000 men from New Jersey institutions is given in the report of the Director of Selective Service, *Selective Service as the War Turns, 1943-1944*, U.S. Government Printing Office, Washington, D.C., 1945, pp. 230-231.

[19] McCallum, M. R., "The Study of the Delinquent in the Army," *Am. J. Sociology*, 51:479-482, Mar., 1946.

had relations with prostitutes; 80 per cent engaged in looting; a considerable number conducted their own black market with their own property.

Correction division and correctional institutions. The Army correctional system, according to MacCormick,[20] was the largest prison system under American jurisdiction. On June 30, 1945, the Federal Prison System had a population of 19,987, including 2,676 military prisoners. The Army's organization had 32,562 prisoners. Without question, the theory and plan [21] of the Army correctional system, composed of rehabilitation centers and disciplinary barracks, was a model in penology.[22] There were six rehabilitation centers to which were sent those soldiers who had committed less serious offenses and for whom there were definite hopes for rehabilitation. Initially, the only disciplinary barracks were at Fort Leavenworth. On VJ-day, August 14, 1945, there were eight in the United States and others overseas.

During the war, over 50,000 men passed through one or another of these installations. Of this number, 19,930 or 40 per cent, had been restored to duty as of March 1, 1946. One wonders how effective the rehabilitation really was. No accurate, detailed, follow-up study could be made since many of these soldiers were immediately sent overseas and regulations prohibited further check on them.

Study of 3,560 Rehabilitated
Soldiers Who Remained in This Country [23]

81.3% were still in active service and in good standing 6 months after their discharge from the correctional institution
7.9% were absent without leave
7.6% were again in confinement or awaiting trial
2.7% had been separated from the service

Study of Those Who Had Remained
in Active Service for 6 Months or More

79.6% were rated as average or above average in the performance of duty
77.8% were rated average or above average in personal conduct
11.9% had been promoted to private first class within 6 months following restoration
5.5% had achieved noncommissioned-officer ratings

---

[20] MacCormick, A. H., and Evjen, V. H., "The Army's Rehabilitation Program for Military Prisoners," in the *1945 Yearbook of the National Probation Association,* 1790 Broadway, New York.
[21] The wording, "theory and plan," is used above, since the practical applications of it not infrequently fell down because of incompetent and frequently changing personnel.
[22] The system is well described by its director and guiding light, Col. Marion Rushton, in "The Army's New Correction Division," *Prison World,* 6:4-6, Nov.-Dec., 1944.
[23] Figures obtained by Maj. Saul Steinberg, psychiatrist assigned to the Correction Division from Neuropsychiatry Consultants Division, Office of the Surgeon General, May, 1946.

In interpreting these figures, one must keep in mind that many of these men had been prisoners for some purely military offense (such as AWOL) and were not essentially grossly disordered personalities.

Of particular interest is the contribution of psychiatry to this program. Much credit should go to Herman M. Adler,[24] who was instrumental in having a psychiatrist included in the staff of the correctional institutions during World War I. There was a psychiatrist at the disciplinary barracks at Fort Leavenworth, the only correctional institution maintained between the two wars. When the rehabilitation centers were activated in 1942,[25] the initial table of organization included a psychiatrist. The regulation which outlined his functions in 1930 [26] remained in effect. He was required to keep a permanent psychiatric and sociological register of every general prisoner. This was interpreted to mean that he should work up a psychiatric study of each man admitted to the center. To enable him to do this he was given, in this war, the help of a clinical psychologist and one or more psychiatric social workers. Several of the institutions had two or even three psychiatrists. It was the responsibility of the psychiatrist to make recommendations to the commandant with reference to the screening of prisoners, assignment to disciplinary companies, restoration to duty, clemency, vocational training and guidance, schooling, home, and local parole. He sat as a member on the parole, clemency, and restoration boards. The nature of his work made him the one officer who probably learned most about the prisoners. At times, this gave those in charge some concern that perhaps he wielded too much influence; it was potentially dangerous when the psychiatrist was not too experienced. In some installations we found far too many patients being diagnosed as "psychopaths"; in others, the percentage of those who were diagnosed as having psychoses was far out of line with the group as a whole. Such matters were investigated by the Service Command consultants in neuropsychiatry who visited these installations along with all others in which a psychiatrist was on duty.

At the time of the maximum expansion of the correctional installations there were between 30 and 40 psychiatrists working in them. Most of their time was devoted to the personality study of individual prisoners. The turnover was great. The shipping of prisoners from one type of center to another

---

[24] Adler, H. M., "Disciplinary Problems in the Army," *Ment. Hyg.*, 3:594-602, Oct., 1919. T. W. Salmon, in "Future of Psychiatry in the Army," *Mil. Surgeon*, 47:200-207, Aug., 1920, paid special tribute to Maj. Edgar King at Fort Leavenworth for his work in this field. Frankwood Williams wrote a detailed account of psychiatry's part in handling delinquency in World War I in *The Medical Department of the United States Army in the World War*, Vol. X, War Department, U.S. Government Printing Office, Washington, D.C., 1929, pp. 131-138.
[25] Letter Order from Service of Supply, AG. 383.6 (10-17-42) OB-I-SP-M, dated 28 October 1942, Subject: General Prisoners—Increase in Installations.
[26] Army Regulations 600-395, 1 January 1930.

often necessitated an additional personality evaluation when records were not transferred.

The following table represents a composite of the psychiatric diagnoses which were given to 24,327 general prisoners who were in confinement during the year of 1945.

Psychiatric Diagnosis of 24,327 General Prisoners in Confinement at Rehabilitation Centers, Disciplinary Barracks, and Federal Institutions During the Year 1945

Psychiatric Diagnosis	Number	Per Cent
Prisoners confined	24,327	
Prisoners reported upon	23,143	100.0
No diagnosis made	6,104	26.4
Diagnosis deferred	783	3.4
No neuropsychiatric disorder	3,241	14.0
Psychopathic personality	5,652	24.4
Emotional instability	721	3.1
Inadequate personality	495	2.1
Schizoid personality	184	0.8
Alcoholism	1,517	6.6
Drug addiction	124	0.5
Psychoneurosis	449	2.0
Mental deficiency	821	3.6
Borderline mental deficiency	749	3.2
Simple adult maladjustment	701	3.0
Emotional immaturity	397	1.7
Epilepsy	21	0.1
Schizophrenia	81	0.3
Other psychoses	25	0.1
Other diagnoses	1,078	4.7

A close scrutiny of the diagnoses given to 24,000 general prisoners who were confined during 1945 shows a gross lack of conformity. One must assume an equally gross difference in understanding of the meaning of the terms as used by the different psychiatrists. At a Correction Division Conference at Fort Leavenworth, November 14-16, 1944, there was unanimous agreement on the part of the psychiatrists present that in so far as possible they would avoid applying diagnostic terms in lieu of describing a personality as these were so often misinterpreted by lay individuals. Therefore in this table the group with "no diagnosis made" may or may not have included "normal" personalities. One can only estimate that the "normal" individuals made up about 14 per cent of the total. If those with "no diagnosis made" are included, nearly 40 per cent were "normal," but this is probably too high a percentage. Similarly, those diagnosed as "psychopathic personality" approximated 24 per cent. Many of those diagnosed otherwise could have been classified as types of psychopathic personalities by many psychiatrists. The neuroses accounted for only 2 per cent. On the basis of experience, this figure seems much too low. Psychoses accounted for less than 1 per cent, statistically.[27]

Numerous studies have been made of the sociological factors in the early lives of prison patients. Those that have been made in the Army show some significant differences [28, 29, 30] from studies made in civilian institutions. Perhaps this was due to the fact that several of the military offenses have no counterpart in civilian life. Approximately one-third of the offenses are for absence without leave, and an additional 20 per cent are for desertion. Other much less frequent offenses which were without any civilian parallel are disobedience to an officer, insubordination, and misbehavior as a sentinel. Civil offenses accounted for about 25 to 30 per cent of cases.

It was found that nearly 60 per cent [31] of the prisoners had at least one civil arrest for either a felony or a misdemeanor prior to their Army experience. Of all prisoners, 30 per cent had at least one civilian commitment, and approximately 13 per cent had two or more. The prognosis for rehabilitation was particularly good for those who had no pre-Army conflict with law.

One of the specially gratifying contributions of psychiatry was the initiation of treatment [32] in almost every correctional installation. The recommendations of the psychiatrist for rehabilitation efforts were welcomed and seriously accepted. In several of the installations the psychiatrist arranged for frequent contact with the prisoners in order to determine their problems and to better advise with regard to an improved therapeutic program.[33] From personal knowledge there is no question that the efforts toward rehabilitation in terms of occupation, vocation, recreation, and education were the primary aim. There was only secondary, and fortunately minimal, interest in punitive treatment in the rehabilitation centers in this country.

One of the outstanding developments, probably one of the best examples of effective group psychotherapy, was carried on in the rehabilitation centers.

[27] The incidence of acute mental disorders among military prisoners admitted to federal prisons in 1944 and 1945 was approximately 50 per cent higher than among civilian prisoners. Lipton, H. R., "Notes on the Military Prisoner," *Mil. Surgeon,* 99:103-105, Aug., 1946.

[28] Blackman, N., "The Psychopathic Military Prisoner," *War Med.,* 4:508-513, Nov., 1943.

[29] Schneider, A. J. N., and LaGrone, C. W., "Delinquents in the Army. A Statistical Study of 500 Rehabilitation Center Prisoners," *Am. J. Psychiat.,* 102:82-91, July, 1945.

[30] Lawn, H. J., "The Study and Treatment of Alcoholism in the Fifth Service Command Rehabilitation Center," *Am. J. Psychiat.,* 102: 479-482, Jan., 1946.

[31] MacCormick, A. H., and Evjen, V. H., "Statistical Study of 24,000 Military Prisoners," *Federal Probation,* 10:6-11, Apr.-June, 1946.

[32] Wagley, P. V., "The Army Rehabilitates Military Offenders," *Federal Probation,* 8:14-19, Jan.-Mar., 1944; Weiss, I. I., "Rehabilitation of Military Offenders at the Ninth Service Command Rehabilitation Center," *Am. J. Psychiat.,* 103:172-178, Sept., 1946.

[33] Knapp, J. L., and Weitzen, F., "A Total Psychotherapeutic Push Method in Rehabilitation Center," *Am. J. Psychiat.,* 102:362-366, Nov., 1945.

This form of treatment owes its origin largely to the efforts of Alexander Wolf at Fort Knox, Ky. Later the program was carried on there by a psychologist. Since 1944, Abrahams and McCorkle [34] (a psychiatrist and a sociologist at Fort Knox) have contributed to the expansion of the program by visual aids. The program of group psychotherapy, with several sessions a week, in large heterogeneous and small homogeneous groups, had the enthusiastic support of the commandant.[35] This procedure was later used in some form and in varying degrees in all the rehabilitation centers [36] and in most of the disciplinary barracks.

One can summarize the experience of psychiatry with this large group of misbehaving individuals as both a failure and a success. The emergency of the war did not justify the investment of unlimited personnel in the gamble of attempting to "treat" or to retrain large numbers of these men in the Army. However, when some of them ran amuck with the law and reached the bottom of the ladder as prisoners, they were then given the benefit of supportive discipline and a graduated program which was well permeated with psychiatric understanding. Through the warm support of Mr. Austin MacCormick and Col. Marion Rushton, psychiatrists had a chance to make a contribution, and they did so with effectiveness. Under this system a large number of men were rehabilitated, apparently successfully so. In many cases, perhaps we only succeeded in making the men more amenable prisoners. It is not likely that we affected the basic personality of more than a few. No conclusive results can be known except through a long-time follow-up study. Our experience makes one wonder whether a much greater effort should not have been made for the greater numbers who were discharged before getting into more serious difficulties.

---

[34] Abrahams, J., and McCorkle, L. W., "Group Psychotherapy of Military Offenders," *Am. J. Sociology,* 51:455-464, Mar., 1946; "Group Psychotherapy at an Army Rehabilitation Center," *Dis. Nerv. System,* 7:50-62, Feb., 1947.

[35] Through this medium, all workers, including Abrahams and McCorkle, attempted to foster group and individual integration in an atmosphere of neutral give-and-take through the mechanisms of identification, catharsis, and abreaction. The psychopathic, immature, and mentally deficient were drawn into the social experience to maturate along with the group. The "course" was later modified by Lt. M. C. Bettis into a preparatory phase of "catharsis," a preliminary phase of "introspection," then an "analytic," and finally a "synthetic" phase. See Bettis, M. C.: "A Method of Group Therapy," *Dis. Nerv. System,* 8:1-12, Aug., 1947.

[36] Berlien, I. C., "Rehabilitation Center: Psychiatry and Group Therapy," *J. Crim. Law and Criminol.,* 36:249-255, Nov.-Dec., 1945.

14

THE LOWEST EIGHT PER CENT

Joe Doaks Brown grew up as one of a flock of children—he didn't know how many there were—in a share cropper's shanty. His whole family tried to raise cotton. In between working periods he did "nothin'." He had gone to a shanty schoolhouse for a couple of years and could, after a fashion, scrawl his name. He was a husky youth of 19, and somehow he had gotten into the Army. His assignment to a basic-training camp was as much of a mistake as his admission into the Army. He couldn't read his own orders. He might have worked in a warehouse or as a stevedore—but not in the infantry!

Some of the Joe Doaks' with a little better background—perhaps better germ plasm—could and did make good in simple labor jobs under good leaders. For example, there was Joe Doaks Domingo who came from a non-English-speaking home. He was one of several children whose father was a railroad laborer not far from the border. Joe had never learned to speak English and had never had a chance to learn to read his own language. He was a water boy at 10 years of age and graduated to odd jobs at a little higher wage. But he did not have a chance as a soldier without special help. And many Joe Doaks Domingos had no chance even then.

Joe Doaks McGinnis rolled off his parents' production line as number seven. There is reasonably good evidence that father and mother McGinnis were both borderline if not actually mentally deficient. Psychological tests showed good-natured Joe to have the mental capacity of an average child of about 7 years. He was a good boy but not soldier material.

Joe Doaks' with other family names either had not had a chance to learn or could not have used one if they had had it. They were handicapped by lack of culture, or by nature, or by foreign birth. Many such Joes were caught in the draft to be eliminated at the induction center. Some slipped by and, unless through rare fortune they found a very special niche, they had to be discharged as quite unable to contribute in the wartime Army.

A large percentage of the jobs in our culture require individuals who are content to perform routine physical labor. More than one writer has called attention to the fact that many intellectually dull people are needed to clean the streets, wash windows, scrub the floors, etc. However, while many "dullards" serve as functioning members of the citizenry, there are also many who are liabilities. "The personality handicapped by deficiency and capacity for thinking, learning, reacting to perceptions, making decisions—such a personality belongs in a group long designated by the term feeble-minded, but better called hypo-(insufficiency) phrenic (mind). Mental deficiency varies in degree, as well as in kind, from complete 'lack of brains' (idiocy) up through gradations called imbecility and moronity to sub-normality, the latter being just less than 'average intelligence.' " [1]

The extent of mental deficiency was revealed by the draft in which 676,300 men were rejected on this basis between January, 1942, and August, 1945. This was approximately 4.5 per cent of all the men examined. This figure probably included some men who were rejected because of educational deficiency.

Not only were there men who were mentally deficient but also those who were handicapped to some degree by deficient cultural background. Men who lacked the opportunity for educational training, as well as non-English-speaking individuals were at a particular disadvantage in the Army. The British Army used the term "dullard" to describe such persons. There were thousands of instances where illiteracy was not an indication of mental deficiency, and yet it prevented a man from effective functioning in the Army because of his inability to read.

Induction policy in regard to the educationally deficient varied as the manpower needs fluctuated. Initially, from May 15, 1941, to August 1, 1942, when a quality army was the goal, there were more rejections for, and less discrimination between, mental and educational deficiency. From August 1, 1942, until February, 1943, 10 per cent of the inductees could be illiterates. Only 5 per cent were allowed between February and June, 1943. Again the policy was changed, and from June, 1943, until September, 1945, all illiterates were inducted if they could pass certain tests. After September, 1945, only those illiterates then in process were to be inducted.

Selection methods. Although testing procedures also changed periodically in the induction stations, the general psychological approach was rather standard throughout the war. The procedures to be described are representative of one period but serve to illustrate the general approach.

When a man reported for induction, he was presumed to be literate if he could show evidence of having completed high school. Those who did not complete high school were required to take a group mental qualification test which measured general intellectual capacity as well as literate status. Inductees who passed this test were not referred for any other mental or reading examination. Those who failed, however, were given an opportunity to demonstrate

[1] Menninger, Karl A., *The Human Mind,* 3rd ed., Alfred A. Knopf, New York, 1945, p. 48.

their ability on a group visual classification test. This test was administered in pantomime and did not require any use or understanding of reading. It consisted of a series of sets of five pictures of objects—four of which were similar in some way and one of which was dissimilar. This visual classification test was not a psychometric examination but rather a means of selecting those illiterate and non-English-speaking men who demonstrated sufficient intellectual capacity to make satisfactory soldiers. Inductees who passed the visual classification test were considered to have met the minimum mental standards required for military duty.

Those who failed this test were given a further opportunity to qualify for service on the basis of performance tests given individually. The individual character of this examination permitted the inductee to make a maximum response and the psychologist to determine whether or not he was malingering or being nonco-operative in any other way. In a final check, as a part of the medical examination, the psychiatrist could ask for a recheck by the psychologist of a man's intelligence by means of any of the standard intelligence tests.

Those men who were accepted by virtue of their being high-school graduates or on the basis of their score in the mental qualification test were subsequently given the Army General Classification Test at the reception center. This was not an intelligence test, but it provided a helpful impression of mental equipment and mental functioning. The scoring of the test sorted all soldiers into five grades.

Ten million men tested were distributed as follows: [2]

Grades	Scores	Actual in Grade	Anticipated in Grade
I	130 and over	5.8%	7%
II	110–130	26.2%	24%
III	90–110	30.7%	38%
IV	70–90	28.5%	24%
V	Below 70	8.8%	7%

The dullards were in Grade V.

The initial standards for physical evaluation [3] specified a mental age below which a man was to be rejected. This was an unsatisfactory criterion and was eliminated in the revisions of these regulations in April, 1944. In later instructions, the examiners were told specifically not to use such terms as "imbecile" and "moron." Elaborate psychometric measurement was not considered neces-

[2] Bingham, W. V., "Inequalities in Adult Capacity—From Military Data," *Science*, 104:147-152, Aug. 16, 1946.
[3] Standards of Physical Examination during Mobilization, Mobilization Regulations 1-9, 15 October 1942.

sary because intelligence cannot be definitely determined. No test was an infallible measure. Test results were only approximations to be evaluated in conjunction with accompanying factors and circumstances. A diagnosis of mental deficiency was based upon the results of objective tests which were interpreted in the light of the above consideration. Illiteracy per se was not classified as mental deficiency.

Extent of problem. Despite all the effort which was made to screen out these men at the induction- and reception-center levels, a considerable number did gain admission to the Army. As an indication of this, between January, 1942, and December, 1945, 3.9 per cent (36,308) of the admissions to the psychiatric services of all Army hospitals were for mental deficiency. Of this total:

Hospital Admissions for Mental Deficiency

	Number	NP Admissions
In United States	30,970	5.1%
Overseas	5,338	1.7%

These figures are interesting to compare with the neuropsychiatric diagnoses in the home forces in World War I, where of 69,394 cases, 21,853 (31.5 per cent) were found to be mentally deficient (almost twice as many as for any other diagnosis).[4] One must assume that the screening out of mental deficiency by the draft board and at the induction center was far more effective in World War II than in World War I.

Special training units. With the acceptance of such a large number of men of illiterate status and of borderline mental ability, it was soon apparent that the Army had to attempt to teach the rudiments of reading, writing, and arithmetic. The initial effort in this direction was to create "special training units" in the replacement training centers to which men were sent after their admission to the Army.[5] In addition, however, there were similar special training units established by other branches of the Army. The job became so big that by June, 1943, there were approximately 250 different organizations providing special training.

This training was not uniform, so at that time the whole system was revamped. Co-ordinated special training units were organized at the reception center. At the peak of their usefulness, there were 24 large units functioning in various camps in this country.

All the illiterates, as well as the men who scored in Grade V on the Army

---

[4] Bailey, P., and Haber, R., in *The Medical Department of the U.S. Army in the World War*, Vol. X, U.S. Government Printing Office, Washington, D.C., 1929, p. 157.
[5] These are described by M. A. Seidenfeld in "The Special Training Units of the Army," *Psychological Bull.*, 40:279-281, Apr., 1943, and in the *J. Educational Psychol.*, 34:26-34, Jan., 1943.

General Classification Test, were sent to these special training units. These units were staffed [6] with enlisted-men teachers who were trained to teach arithmetic, reading, and writing. They were also prepared to teach English to the non-English-speaking group. Along with the academic work went graded military training. Every unit was carefully subdivided in order to meet varying needs. Some men received 6 hours of military training a day and only 2 hours of academic classes; others received 2 hours of military and 6 hours of academic training. The typical program for the majority of the men included a half day of military training and a half day of academic education. With its various intergradations, the program was sufficiently flexible so that modification could be made to provide for individual needs. One of the special features of particular interest to the psychiatrist was the counseling under the direction of a psychologist. A psychiatrist was available, at least part time in most of the units and full time in at least one. The mental hygiene lectures for enlisted men were also given in these special training units.

A total of 685,362 [6] men in Grade V (the lowest 8 per cent of the general classification test scores) were inducted between March, 1941, and June, 1943. A total of 107,075 illiterates were inducted between August, 1942, and May, 1943. There was probably overlap in these two figures, since some illiterates were tallied under Grade V. Prior to June, 1943, it was not mandatory for the illiterate and the Grade-V men to receive special training, so that no figures are available as to the exact number who did so. A conservative estimate is that at least 200,000 were given this benefit.

After June 1, 1943, it was mandatory that both illiterate and Grade-V men be sent to the special training units organized at the reception centers. There were some remarkable achievements [7] from this work, at least statistically. There were 302,838 men who entered such units between June, 1943, and December, 1945. Of this number, 254,756 successfully completed the training and were forwarded then to regular training programs, and 44,617 men were discharged from the Army.

Dullards in service. The life of the mentally deficient soldier in the Army was complicated, not only by his own handicap but also because of the rigid demands within the Army. After his special training (when he had it), he was sent to the basic-training camp. There, with all other inductees, he followed an intensive 17-week training course. It was not possible to make individual

---

[6] Witty, P. A., and Goldberg, S., "The Army's Training Program for Illiterate, Non-English Speaking and Educationally Retarded Men," *Elem. Eng. Rev.,* 20:36-311, Dec., 1943; Witty, P. A., "Teaching the Three R's in the Army," *English Journal,* 34:132-136, Mar., 1945.

[7] These figures were obtained through the kindness of Maj. Samuel Goldberg who in large measure was responsible for the program developed in the special training units. His description of these is undoubtedly the best. Goldberg, S., "Psychological Procedures Employed in the Army's Special Training Units," *J. Clin. Psychology,* 1:118-125, Apr., 1945.

allowances. Each man was expected to memorize general orders, to learn mapping, to absorb first-aid information, and fill all the other intellectual requirements with the same speed as everyone else. Many of these men just could not do it, and therefore, they often became major liabilities.[8] They not infrequently developed neurotic symptoms, most often in the form of physical complaints.

Had the Army classification system been sufficiently flexible to permit their immediate assignment to limited duty or unskilled tasks, undoubtedly many more of them could have been used effectively. Instead, they turned up at station hospitals. There, too, it was often an extremely difficult problem to decide upon their disposition, when they could not be reassigned to simple unskilled tasks. Merely an evaluation of mental age was not always a good criterion for decision. In at least one Service Command an order was issued that "all cases of mental deficiency in which the mental age is lower than eight years" should be discharged.[9] However, there were many under this age level who could have served. There were many with a higher mental age who did not have the capacity to be effective soldiers in any job. Nor was it always a simple matter to distinguish between organically determined mental deficiency and mental reactions which resulted from deprivation of educational and cultural advantages. Without careful psychological testing, it would have been impossible. The same problem occurred in World War I, leading Col. Salmon to comment that in the Army it needed "the joint work of psychiatrist and psychologists and will never be solved by either working alone." [10]

Only a careful survey could determine the effectiveness of mentally deficient individuals by investigating particularly how long they served, their efficiency, and their assignments. Illustrative of this is the investigation made by McKeon [11] of a group of mentally retarded individuals with I.Q.'s ranging from 52 to 83 who were trained in a special school prior to the war. Of the 207 mental deficients, 55 per cent were inducted into the Army. Only 19 per cent were rejected, of which number only 9 per cent because of mental or educational inadequacies. Of the rest, a number were waiting for the draft, some had been deferred on defense jobs, and still others were too young to be eligible for service. Only 1.5 per cent of those who had been accepted had been discharged from the Army.

The British Army had a far more practical approach to the problem of utilization of the dullard than did the American Army. Probably it was stimu-

[8] Lewinski, R. J., "Military Considerations of Mental Deficiency," *Mil. Surgeon,* **95**:385-390, Nov., 1944; Esher, F. J. S., "Military Service for Mental Defectives," *Mental Health* (London), **3**:14-18, 1942; Menninger, W. C., "The Problem of the Mentally Retarded and the Army," *Am. J. of Mental Deficiency,* **48**:55-61, July, 1943.
[9] Letter, Subject: Disability Discharges, Hq. Fourth Corps Area, 220.811-Gen. 28 February 1942.
[10] Salmon, T. W., "Future of Psychiatry in the Army," *Mil. Surgeon,* **47**:200-207, Aug., 1920.
[11] McKeon, R. M., "Mentally Retarded Boys in Wartime," *Ment. Hyg.,* **30**:47-55, Jan., 1946.

lated by the fact that the British man-power situation was far more acute than ours.

Brigadier Rees pointed out that "where dull men had been incorporated into units, either prewar in the regular Army, or in the early days of the war, they often turned out to be a problem. A static unit when in training can carry quite a number of dullards by increasing the number of its 'stooge' jobs. Only when it has to prepare for active service are these men extruded, either by off-loading them onto other units or by some other means equally undesirable and wasteful." [12] He reported vividly how the dullard develops anxiety in the face of competition; how he disobeys and ignores regulations; how he often becomes a disciplinary problem. The British solved this difficulty with the Pioneer Corps which was in part armed and in part unarmed. The less dull could bear arms for purposes of self-defense and could be used as guards. The more dull group, when living and working together, found friends among those of the same intellectual level. Rees indicated that this is not only a problem of the military, but that in peacetime such individuals are likely to be lonely and relatively friendless. In the British experiment there were very few behavior or disciplinary problems in the Pioneers; further, there were few sexual difficulties and very little crime among these men. Their jobs of "roadmaking, hut erection, humping shells were well within their competence."

Being aware of efforts in the American Army during the last war to set up labor battalions, and knowing of the British success, the Neuropsychiatry Division of the Office of the Surgeon General several times strongly recommended the formation of such groups.[13] In the summer of 1944, one of the theaters of war requested the permission of the War Department to set up a labor battalion. In the requesting cable [14] it was stated that the purpose was to provide a situation more strenuous than combat in which they could place psychiatric casualties. The inference of such a purpose was that the casualties would want to go back to combat rather than remain out of combat under such circumstances. Because casualties were recognized as being medical problems, G-1 of the War Department referred the matter to the Surgeon General for advice. During my discussion of the punitive nature of the proposal with General Kirk, he expressed the opinion that the cable indicated a disagreement between line and medical officers. He assumed that the medical officers had lost the argument.

---

12 Rees, J. R., *The Shaping of Psychiatry by War,* W. W. Norton & Company, Inc., New York, 1945, pp. 42-45.
13 Forwarded through ASF Training Div., to WDGS, G-1, 25 March 1944, ref. SPTRR 220.3 (21 March 44); again to Deputy Chief of Operations, SGO re CM-IN 21806, dated 26 July 1944, in memo form from SPMDU, 28 July 1944.
14 Memorandum to the Deputy Chief of Operations, SGO, 31 July 1944, re CM-IN 21806— Subject: The Assignment of Cases of Battle Exhaustion not ready to return to Combat Duty, dated 26 July 1944.

War Department G-1 accepted our strong opposition and so refused permission for the proposed organization.

In spite of the refusal, I found on a trip through the theater some months later that a "battalion" had been organized by medical, rather than line officers! But the abortive effort was unsuccessful. I spent a day and an evening with a group of 10 psychiatrists who had been concentrated at a hospital for the purpose of re-evaluating about 4,000 soldiers who had been assigned to labor groups from hospitals, 55 per cent of whom had to be rehospitalized!

No recommendations, however, for the establishment of units in the U.S. Army comparable to the British Pioneer Corps were ever accepted. Just how far forward in the War Department these recommendations of the Neuropsychiatry Division went was never known. None were ever returned with any comments, but it was obvious that some high authority, perhaps with good reasons, opposed such a program.

The problem of handling the mentally deficient in the Army was essentially the same as that in civilian life: their recognition, their special training, and their disposition. For some, the Army did an outstanding job in furthering their development by the educational program of the special training units. However, the great majority were never inducted. The Army, along with the nation, has failed to develop a practical system for the utilization of this handicapped group. The military organizations can be excused for their rejection of this man power on the basis of the emergency, but one can hardly excuse the lack of national effort toward more constructive action.

15

MALINGERING

In December, 1942, on a visit to the Fort Benning, Ga., induction station, I watched each medical examiner as he performed his assigned task. As I paused at the eye examination station a well-built, good-looking, serious-appearing, 35-year-old inductee, wearing glasses, stepped up for his examination. As he took his seat, he told the doctor his eyes were no good and even with his glasses he couldn't see well. Quick inspection of his ill-fitting dime-store specks showed them to be weak help for close vision. As customary, the examiner asked the man to read the chart of test letters without and then with his own glasses. In both cases, he protested he could not. Suspecting some volitional element in the visual difficulty, the doctor became sympathetic; he carefully inspected the eyes; he lamented the ineffectiveness of the man's glasses; he asked if he had ever seen a good eye doctor (which he had not). After this build-up, the doctor told the man, with great emphasis, he was sure that *he* could give him glasses with which he could see. He then proceeded to put in lenses of plain glass and the man could read the letters! The doctor switched from one to another lens for trial so that he might verify his impression—and maybe to impress me. Normal glass again gave the inductee the best vision. Once convinced, he suddenly asked the man the question, "Why don't you want to come into the Army?" The inductee was taken aback and off guard. He broke down and explained a difficult situation at home. Still he did not recognize that the doctor was aware of the pretense about his vision. When the physician confronted him with the fact that he had seen through his action, the man reported that someone had told him that was the best way to get rejected!

That is malingering. It goes hand in hand with war. In fact, Webster's primary definition implies that the term applies only to military persons. In the Civil War malingering was a major problem. With little difficulty, a man could conceal a minor but disqualifying ailment until he was actually in the Army and had received his $300 bounty for enlisting. Grossly exaggerating his symptoms would lead to a discharge. A subsequent re-enlistment under an alias and false address would enable him again to receive the bounty.[1] In the

---

[1] Mitchell, S. W.; Morehouse, G. R.; and Keen, W. W., "On Malingering, Especially in Regard to Simulation of Disease of the Nervous System," *Am. J. M. Sc.*, **48**:367-394, 1864.

tabulation of admissions to hospitals for neuropsychiatric diseases in World War I, there is included a listing of 746 cases of malingering. Apparently only two cases were discharged for this reason.[2]

What is malingering? The Neuropsychiatry Consultants Division defined it in a War Department circular as "the intentional, calculated attempt to produce or simulate illness or injury for the purpose of evading duty or responsibility." [3] But many individuals, medical and lay, military and civilian, extend its meaning beyond this definition, sometimes with scientific validity, sometimes entirely as an emotionally conceived epithet.

Bowers [4] described a positive malingerer as one who feigns his disability and a negative malingerer as one who attempts to cover up a disability which might deny him a desired end. Many physicians, particularly medical officers, are inclined to the view that *conscious* capitalization on an existing symptom or condition should be regarded as malingering. In the induction center, we were confronted frequently with stories which were obviously built up to achieve a goal (which often was to get into the Army!). In basic training we saw backs and feet or an operative scar that conveniently became unreasonably painful.

However, an emotionally colored concept of malingering was much more frequent. Certain line officers and tough first sergeants insisted that most individuals with functional disorders were fakers or cowards [5] and would handle them accordingly. Many others thought that way. Although they did not translate their thoughts into words or actions, their general attitude was prejudicial.

Medical officers often were not able to distinguish between malingering and valid psychiatric symptoms. This in part was due to ignorance and in part to prejudice against psychiatric problems. Often it could be blamed largely upon their conscious and unconscious protest against their own role in the Army. For most of us, military service was a necessity and duty; it was not a course of action chosen for pleasure. Doctors who resented being subject to that necessity expressed their feeling by an attitude of irritation toward and lack of understanding of functional disorders, which relieved a soldier from his duty. Their

---

[2] *The Medical Department of the United States Army in the World War,* Vol. X, War Department, U.S. Government Printing Office, Washington, D.C., 1929, pp. 153-155.

[3] War Department Circular 298, 29 September 1945, Sec. IX.

[4] Bowers, W. E., "Hysteria and Malingering on the Surgical Service," *Mil. Surgeon,* 92:506-511, May, 1943.

[5] The subject of cowardice was frequently debated among combat personnel, perhaps more frequently by those of us not in combat. Don Wolfe quoted one of his disabled veteran students, a marine: "Nor can I forget a bristling clash of minds one day on the definition of cowardice, especially Spencer's last words, 'I don't see how a man can know another man well enough to call him a coward.'" Such would be the psychiatrist's attitude toward the careless name-calling of some Army personnel. From *The Purple Testament,* edited by Don M. Wolfe, copyright, 1946 by Don M. Wolfe, reprinted by permission of Doubleday & Company, Inc., page xvii.

reaction toward patients with such difficulties might have been vocalized as: "The bastard can't get away with that!" His unconscious thinking might have been interpreted as: "If I can't get away with it, I certainly won't let him do so," and at a little deeper level, "The lucky devil! I wish I could."

Malingering in all its connotations is difficult to regard objectively. It is not a medical diagnosis; it is rather a social-legal status, an accusation and an epithet all in one. Norris [6] called it a species of fraud and stated that a medical man has no qualifications to decide whether or not his patient is guilty.

Assuming malingering to be what the War Department circular defined it —"the intentional, calculated attempt to produce or simulate illness or injury"—one might ask how much of a medical problem it was in World War II. Judged by the statistical reports, its incidence was relatively insignificant. At induction centers doctors saw evidence of it probably more frequently than at any other stage of Army life. Here it was probably more common for the inductee to attempt to deceive the examiner in order to be inducted than it was to obtain rejection! [7] Although suspected malingering was the reason for referring some men to hospitals, it was not recorded as a medical diagnosis.[8] Instead, if no illness was found, the diagnosis of "no disease" was entered on the clinical record, and the soldier returned to his unit. The preferring of charges became the responsibility of his commanding officer, and the ultimate decision concerning the existence of malingering was left to a court-martial.

Few statistics of incidence are available, and what there are probably have little significance. There are some partial figures for 1943. Among 286,571 admissions to psychiatric services or sections of hospitals, 680 were presumably for this cause. But as stated above, malingering is not a medical diagnosis and the term was dropped from the Army medical terminology late in 1943. How many of these may have been so judged by court-martial is unknown. We do know that for the 4 1/2 years from July, 1941, to January, 1946, in the whole Army, only 47 cases were tried for malingering and 39 were convicted (25 of these were between July, 1944, and July, 1945). Only one was tried between July, 1945, and January, 1946. The rather widely quoted statement of Brussel and Hitch [9] that 7 per cent of all cases sent to the Fort Dix Station Hospital for

---

[6] Norris, D. C., *Malingering in Rehabilitation of the War Injured,* ed. by Doherty and Runes, New York Philosophical Library, Inc., pp. 123-134.

[7] Leavitt, H. C., "Neuropsychiatric Appraisal in an Induction Center," *Bull. U.S. Army M. Dept.,* 7:125-143, Jan., 1947.

[8] This seems at variance with the attitude in World War I as expressed by Bailey who stated that "malingering remained a matter of medical opinion." Bailey, P., "Malingering in U.S. Troops —Home Forces, 1917," *Mil. Surgeon,* 42:261-275, 424-449, Mar., Apr., 1918.

[9] Brussel, J. A., and Hitch, K. S., "Military Malingerer," *Mil. Surgeon,* 93:33-44, July, 1943.

neuropsychiatric consultation were regarded as malingerers gives a far higher percentage than elsewhere. Certainly malingering must have occurred in combat, but the wide consensus of opinion is that it was rare. In October, 1944, in one of our Armies in combat, the staff judge advocate knew of no cases of malingering being tried in any of its divisions.

One field army used a very questionable system to distinguish between the officer who became a neurotic casualty from one who might be a malingerer. The Inspector General made an investigation of every officer who was reported as a psychiatric casualty. As of October 2, 1944, 339 officers had been investigated. In 219 cases the Inspector General concurred with recommendations for medical disposition. He recommended 111 officers for reclassification because of failure to demonstrate leadership. (Such a high percentage would appear to be an indictment of either our officer selection or training methods, or both!) Nine officers were placed under suspicion of malingering or improper conduct in the face of the enemy. In other words, in 120 cases the Inspector General, a layman, overruled medical disposition! The principle here would have been more valid if only questionable or doubtful cases had been referred for investigation instead of all cases. While someone may have seen some merit in such a system, it certainly placed all psychiatric casualties under the pale of suspicion, at least temporarily. It tended to stigmatize neurotic reactions by inferring that they were variants of malingering.

Detection of malingering. The falsification of disease, or at least some symptoms, may be difficult to discover. Its detection is largely dependent on the attitude and acuity of the physician. The medical officer in the Army had to be constantly alert in order to detect it. In civilian life its incidence, except in compensation cases, is rare. Because of the expectation of malingering in induction centers [10] the mobilization regulations [11] which were used as a guide by the induction board examiners outlined many types and methods for their discovery.

These regulations did not help very much in hospitalized cases. I recall two soldiers in a station hospital who were placed there because of extensive ulcerations of the gums. They were studied thoroughly, and no one could find the cause. They were transferred to a general hospital to be studied by experts. Their sores were unlike anything anyone had known. Someone had the bright idea of locking them up and depriving them of all property. Under such a regime their ulcers began to heal! They then confessed that they had been rub-

---

[10] Kahn, Samuel, "Malingering in the Army," *Medical Record,* 156:416-418, July, 1943; Flicker, David J., "Psychiatric Induction Examination," *War Med.,* 2:931-943, Nov., 1942; Gill, Merton M., "Malingering," *Bull. Menninger Clinic,* 5:157-160, Sept., 1941.

[11] Mobilization Regulations 1-9, 19 April 1944, Sec. XXIV, pp. 104-112.

bing the sulphur from book matches on their gums. When they were prevented from getting the matches their ulcers healed. No directions would have helped in this case.

In combat troops it is perhaps more difficult to differentiate without the use of barbiturates (sedatives).[12] Malingerers resist narcosis; they fail to show the co-operative attitude of the neurotic patient; they usually react to examination with intense negativism. It has also been suggested that difficult cases might be detected through the use of psychometric tests [13] and the Rorschach ink-blot test.[14]

Every Army psychiatrist, and in fact every Army hospital physician, was repeatedly confronted with patients who appeared to be consciously capitalizing on their ailments. In some cases without organic disability, and often even in its presence, it was extremely difficult to differentiate how much of the incapacity was due to conscious attitudes and how much of it was neurotic in its reaction. In the Army a man was expected to do his assigned job and "his duty" regardless of his personal wishes. Under such circumstances the individual could avoid that responsibility only if there were a legitimate excuse for his inability to perform. Illness was the only allowable excuse from participation in hikes or drill or combat. Therefore the unconscious or conscious desire to be ill was apparent in many soldier patients, although it was not always identified as such even by the physician.

A backache could be due to organic causes. It could be a neurotic symptom, entirely unconsciously motivated. Or, it could have a neurotic basis and be exaggerated consciously by the patient. It was malingering when it was entirely feigned. The degree of the unconscious (neurotic) component and the conscious exaggeration of a particular symptom or group of symptoms had many quantitative gradations. This subject was very helpfully discussed by Brill and Farrell [15] who pointed out that, while malingering and neurotic reactions of the conversion type (physical and bodily symptoms) were separate entities, the two could and did merge to a varying extent. In some cases the conscious exaggeration was so great that the patient might most properly be classified as a malin-

---

12 Ludwig, A. O., "Clinical Features and Diagnosis of Malingering in Military Personnel. The Use of Barbiturate Narcosis as an Aid in Detection," *War Med.*, 5:378-382, June, 1944. Morris, D. P., "Intravenous Barbiturates, an Aid in the Diagnosis and Treatment of Conversion Hysteria and Malingering," *Mil. Surgeon*, 96:509-513, June, 1945.
13 Hunt, W. A., and Older, H. J., "Detection of Malingering through Psychometric Tests," *U.S. Naval M. Bull.*, 41:1318-1322, Sept., 1943.
14 Rosenberg, S. J., and Feldberg, T. M., "Rorschach Characteristics of a Group of Malingerers," *Rorschach Res. Exch.*, 8:141-158, July, 1944.
15 Brill, N. Q., and Farrell, M. J., "Neurotic Reactions in Psychopaths or Hystero-malingering," *Military Neuropsychiatry*, Assn. for Research in Nerv. & Ment. Disease Proceedings, New York, Dec., 1944, The Williams & Wilkins Company, Baltimore, 1946, pp. 11-25.

gerer; in others the clinical picture was chiefly a neurotic reaction. In the cases cited, the authors called attention to the frequency with which symptoms cleared up once the soldier knew he was to be discharged. Such a course of events is not, however, infallible evidence of pure conscious exaggeration, since even the neurotic individual may be greatly relieved of his symptoms if a part of his conflict is resolved.

Most malingering, if not all, occurs in pathologic personalities. Certainly malingerers are socially even if not medically ill. Often they have been labeled "psychopaths." If the effect on the morale of many could be disregarded and if the man-power needs were not great at the time of selection, the man who malingered to avoid military service should not be taken into the armed forces. Anyone with such distorted social values and personality characteristics is likely to make a poor soldier unless radically reoriented.

Malingerers who feigned psychiatric illnesses were in the minority in World War II.[16] Sight and hearing difficulties were most commonly blamed for their disabilities, but almost every type of illness and injury was imitated.

Self-inflicted wounds. By directive, self-inflicted wounds, like malingering, were not medically diagnosed as self-inflicted, though they often were so described in the history. Many were incurred, most often of the left hand or left foot, usually involving only fingers or toes. Just how many of these wounds were intentionally inflicted could never be determined. Only rarely did a soldier admit his conscious intention. For a time, the Medical Statistics Division of the Office of the Surgeon General attempted to tabulate the occurrence of self-inflicted wounds. In the 6 months of July through December, 1944, there were 220 cases reported from camps and posts in the United States. It is not known how many of these may have been suicide attempts which were associated with severe depressions or anxiety. The motivation in this type of case was so uncertain, so lacking in proof, that further records were regarded as valueless.

Ludwig, as psychiatric consultant to the Seventh Army, analyzed the self-inflicted wounds reported between January and May, 1945.

In sixteen divisions, fifteen of whom apparently saw action, there were 22,429 wounded in action; and 793 self-inflicted wounds or an average of 3.6% of war wounded. It was not known what percentage of the wounds reported was deemed deliberate or accidental.

During the period from August 15 to November 18, 1944 a survey of self-inflicted wounds in the 7th Army was made among a group of Army evacuation hospitals.

---

16 Bowman, on the basis of his experience in World War I, called attention to the fact that malingering was common in psychotic reactions. Bowman, K. M., "The Relation of Defective Mental and Nervous States to Military Efficiency," *Mil. Surgeon,* **46**:651-669, 1920.

Cases Reported by Hospitals	366	
Occurring in Line of Duty	128	35%
So Determined by a Board of Investigation	48	37.5%
Without a Board of Investigation	80	62.5%
Occurring Not in Line of Duty	9	2.5%
Line of Duty Status Not Determined or Questionable	229	62.5%

It seems obvious that some better means of dealing with this troublesome problem must be devised.[17]

The psychology involved in the self-infliction of wounds is complicated. Sometimes it is definitely purposeful self-mutilation, and other times it is "accidental." [18] This matter has been discussed in detail by my brother.[19] The differentiation between a consciously and an unconsciously motivated "accident" is at times tenuous. In a situation like the Army, where the individual may be highly resentful or fearful, it should not be surprising that his unconscious personality might lead him to an "accident" just as well as it does to neurotic sickness. A man's unwilling presence in the Army, a hated service or assignment, could be an obvious clue to his unconscious motives. Self-injury was an example of his unconscious thinking—and acting—so plainly that his conscious rationalizations were nearly in vain.

Of special interest are some data furnished by the Military Justice Division of the Office of the Judge Advocate General on the trials of individuals accused of attempted self-injury and of successful "self-maiming" during the war.

	Self-Maiming			Attempt To Self-Maim			For Comparison Total Trials Received by TAGO
	Con-victed	Ac-quitted	Total	Con-victed	Ac-quitted	Total	
Dec. '41—June '42	3	1	4	0	0	0	4,174
July '42—June '43	15	10	25	1	0	1	18,118
July '43—June '44	39	13	52	5	2	7	21,819
July '44—June '45	53	15	68	4	3	7	13,480
July '45—Mar. '46	43	26	69	1	0	1	7,491
Totals	153	65	218	11	5	16	65,082

[17] Major Alfred O. Ludwig, Headquarters, 7th Army, Office of the Surgeon, APO 758, Subject: Final Summary and Critique of the 7th Army Psychiatric Service for Historical Report; To: The Surgeon, 7th Army, 7 July 1945, p. 13.
[18] See Chap. 12, section on accident proneness.
[19] Menninger, Karl A., *Man Against Himself,* Harcourt, Brace and Company, New York, 1938, "Self-Mutilations," p. 231, "Purposive Accidents," p. 318.

Significantly, 70.1 per cent of the self-maiming cases tried were convicted, about the same percentage of those tried for attempting self-injury. One wishes it were possible to know how many of these were in this country, how many in rear areas, and how many in combat. How many were studied psychiatrically? These 234 cases represented only ⅓ of 1 per cent of all types of trials reported to the Office of the Judge Advocate General. (Those convicted and serving sentence until restoration to duty in a theater are not included.) But certainly they also represent a very small percentage of the men with self-inflicted wounds.

In 1943 I visited one hospital in which there were 19 cases of "accidentally" self-inflicted wounds. In 11 instances these had occurred at home during the week of furlough between the induction examination and reporting for active duty. In no case was there at that time any admission of conscious intention. The men had come from the same, though large, geographic area. The situation was made the object of an investigation. The astute examiner found among other facts that this number of gunshot "accidents" was *under* the average occurrence for the same proportion of civilian population in the same geographic area.

The problem of self-inflicted wounds in the Army was important [20] because of the apparent transparency of the unconscious motive. When other soldiers— and officers—believed that the injury was consciously inflicted (as some probably were), even though this behavior was pathological, lack of punishment was regarded as a miscarriage of justice. Few appreciated, as Miller [21] pointed out, that the mistake was made in the failure to notice and treat the preliminary phase of the maladjustment. When these "accidents" occur in a nonmilitary setting, they carry no onus.

Few people, including physicians, recognize the extent of "purposive accidents." My brother, in his excellent analysis of this subject in *Man Against Himself*,[22] collected press reports of six instances within 1 year of individuals who were caught in their own burglar traps! These "accidents" and many, if not the majority of the self-inflicted wounds seen in the Army were, without a doubt, *unconsciously* motivated. Therefore they were not due to malingering. The soldier whose neurotic needs led to an unintentional but nonetheless purposive "accident" did not malinger. On the other hand, a certain number of soldiers consciously used this means for personal and selfish motives and thus were to be regarded as malingerers.

[20] Flicker, D. J., "The Self-Inflicted Injury," *Am. J. Psychiat.*, 99:168-173, Sept., 1942.
[21] Miller, E.; Wilson, A. T. M.; and Wittkower, E., "Clinical Case Studies and Their Relationships," in *Neuroses in War*, The Macmillan Company, New York, 1944, p. 80.
[22] Menninger, Karl A., *Man Against Himself*, Harcourt, Brace and Company, New York, 1938, pp. 319-336.

When American prisoners in certain Japanese prison camps broke their own arms to prevent being sent to slavery in a coal mine, the malingering seemed justifiable. The injury was a means of self-preservation. Unjustified was the action of the soldier in training or combat who disregarded the total social needs and malingered in order to satisfy his personal wishes.

Proof of malingering. As has been indicated above, the decision as to whether or not a soldier malingered rested finally not with a doctor but with a court, a company commander, or with an Inspector General. Except in the case of a confession, it was nearly impossible to prove. The distinction between such complicated psychological phenomena as a partial suicide on a neurotic basis and a self-inflicted wound during the stress of battle becomes extremely difficult to make and probably never could be "proven beyond the question of a doubt."

Management of malingering. Experience seemed to indicate that strong group disapproval, prompt punitive action, and above all, good leadership, were the most effective controls of the rate of self-inflicted wounds. In contrast, it was reported by the Inspector General, following a survey of psychoneurosis in the European Theater of Operations in the spring of 1945, that "the combined expressions of many combat experienced line officers reflects their belief that stronger disciplinary action against malingerers, deserters and individuals proved to be suffering from self-inflicted wounds would greatly decrease the number of psychiatric casualties." The recommendation was made to the Deputy Chief of Staff that disciplinary examples should be made and sentences enforced in proved cases.

The War Department agency in charge of personnel, G-1, which was responsible for implementing this recommendation, sent it to the Office of the Surgeon General for an opinion, and with it, instructions to prepare a War Department circular on the subject. The Neuropsychiatry Consultants Division concurred in the principle that support from command was imperative to reduce these types of misbehavior and agreed on the desirability of a War Department circular to the field. However, doubts were expressed as to whether psychiatrists knew enough to write it. The comments were promptly returned from G-1 with the direct order to "prepare such a circular."

With much care and a review by several psychiatrists, a statement was prepared by the Neuropsychiatry Consultants Division. It appeared without essential change although, as usual with all circulars, it had to be passed upon by several higher authorities for approval and changes they might wish to make. It read:

MALINGERING   1. The problem of malingering and of a high disability rate from psychiatric disorders is often considered to be of importance only during periods of active combat. This belief is entirely erroneous. The experience with armies of occupation after the last war clearly demonstrated that the rate of occurrence of psychiatric disorders was approximately 40 per cent higher 10 months after the armistice than it had been during the peak combat period. There is every reason to believe that this same difficulty may occur in the present widespread occupation forces, and for this reason it is imperative that every possible counter measure be taken by command to prevent the repetition of this experience. One of the major factors to be considered in this problem is the proper disposition of malingerers.

2. Prompt disciplinary measures are to be taken against proven malingerers, including those indivdiuals with intentionally self-inflicted wounds. It is necessary to prove "intent" rather than accident in order to substantiate a charge of malingering, and experience has shown that such charges are extremely difficult to prove. Unless there is reasonably certain evidence of malingering, disciplinary action should not be undertaken. On the other hand, when such evidence exists it is imperative that disciplinary action be initiated without delay. Because of the importance of this problem, and because of the frequent mishandling of it, the following information is published for the attention and action of all commanding officers.

3. Malingering, correctly defined, is the intentional, calculated attempt to produce or simulate illness or injury for the purpose of evading duty or responsibility. Therefore, in its true form, it is an act or behavior which is *entirely conscious and premeditated.* Numerous behavior disorders arise as the result of unconscious (nonvolitional) motivational factors, which cannot be controlled by the individual's conscious mind or will. The differentiation between normal socially acceptable behavior and abnormal behavior often is explainable only upon the basis of such unconscious motivation. Many lay observers have failed to differentiate properly between the conscious and unconscious factors involved in abnormal or asocial behavior and as a consequence they tend to consider all such behavior as conscious or "malingering." A better understanding of the complicated structure of the personality and the significance of unconscious motivation would lead such lay observers to agreement with the incontrovertible scientific evidence that true malingering, as defined above, was relatively rare even among combat troops. A very real danger exists in the failure to differentiate the mentally ill soldier from the deliberate malingerer. Not only may gross miscarriage of justice result but also unit morale may suffer serious damage from the subsequent loss of confidence in leaders who erroneously prosecute or label mentally ill soldiers as malingerers.

4. Most commonly, malingering is apt to be confused with the various types of psychoneuroses. These psychoneuroses are a definite type of mental illness, psychologically dependent upon unconscious factors and beyond the individual's voluntary control. Malingering, on the other hand, is a voluntary and conscious process which is neither a medical diagnosis nor an illness. Psychoneurosis is never a type of malingering, although it is quite possible that the psychoneurotic individual may over emphasize and consciously attempt to capitalize upon the symptoms resulting from his illness. In the Army, however, for the sake of justice and morale, sharp distinction must be made between those individuals whose socially abnormal ideas, emotions, and behavior are the result of illness and those individuals in whom such deviations are deliberate and voluntary. It is obvious that such distinction, involving as it does medical and psychiatric considerations, cannot be made adequately without proper professional advice.

5. The motivation in self-inflicted wounds is a complicated psychological phenomenon. A type of personality is recognized as "accident prone," as attested to by

long experience in industrial plants where 90 per cent of all accidents occur in 15 per cent of the workers. Most self-destructive attempts, both mutilation and suicide, are symptoms of grossly abnormal mental states, and many of these mental conditions are not classifiable as psychoses (insanity). Such "accidents" are recognized to occur in mentally dissociated states such as amnesia or fugues. Individuals with psychoneurosis of certain types are known to attempt self-destruction, either by incomplete or completely successful suicides. In all cases, therefore, not only is it essential to exclude the self-inflicted wound as a symptomatic expression of mental illness, but it is also necessary to prove intent to evade duty.

6. It is believed that a firm, just, and positive leadership is the most effective aid in the prevention of malingering, and even more important, in the prevention of psychiatric disabilities. It is well known that there is a large group of individuals whose ability to withstand unfavorable stress is strengthened or weakened by the prevailing attitudes of their associates. They are dependent upon the support afforded them by those people in their immediate environment and particularly by such authoritarian figures as their leaders. In all social units, including the Army, the individual is dependent to some degree upon group pressure for support, and his actions are largely determined by group standards of acceptable and unacceptable behavior. If deviations from the acceptable standards of behavior are allowed to go unchallenged by those in leadership roles, the individual may conclude that the standards are wrong or that higher authority condones or even approves of such deviations. The loss of this important support obtained from authority may further increase the individual's conflict between his wishes (to escape unfavorable stress) and his sense of duty. Consequently, when misbehavior such as malingering is not dealt with promptly, it is conceivable that the added conflictual, psychological burden placed upon any personality under stress may precipitate a psychoneurotic response.

7. The extent of malingering probably can be reduced if such behavior, particularly in the flagrant cases, is promptly apprehended and the individual punished. Often the best means of handling suspected malingerers is to return them promptly to full duty with a stern warning but without preferring charges against them. If the problem is not dealt with promptly, the morale of the unit may suffer.

8. On the basis of the above discussion, the following directions will be carried out:

a. On the authority set forth in the 96th Article of War, commanding generals of all major commands in occupied territories will issue, and periodically reissue an order, to be placed upon all bulletin boards, and to be read to all troops, reaffirming the policy that all instances of presumed malingering (including self-inflicted wounds) will be thoroughly investigated by the appropriate authorities, and, if it is indicated, promptly brought to trial, and the appropriate punishment promptly administered. Such announcements are to reach all soldiers, regardless of rank.

b. The services of an experienced psychiatrist, when available, will be utilized for a thorough examination of the suspected individual before charges are made against him. The psychiatrist will submit a written report of his findings to the referring authority. This report will include, in nontechnical terms, the social history, mental status, and the circumstances surrounding the charges, and it will state clearly the presence or absence of significant psychiatric disorders and their relation to the act for which the soldier is charged. The psychiatrist will maintain a scientific and not moralistic role and serve purely in advisory capacity. If the individual is brought to trial, the psychiatrist may serve as a neutral expert witness for the court.

c. The attention of all commanding officers is directed to the fact that the reduction of the malingering rate is a responsibility of command. Positive, strong leadership is the most effective method of reducing noneffectiveness from all psychiatric and psychologic causes. Fear of punishment is, in itself, totally inadequate as a means of preventing malingering.

d. The attention of all medical officers, particularly psychiatrists, is directed to their responsibility for the detection of malingering and for reporting suspected cases to command.

e. Prompt action will be taken by command in the investigation of all suspected cases of malingering. No individual or group of individuals will be needlessly detained for investigation unless there is reasonable supposition of guilt and charges will not be made unless evidence is reasonably certain. Great care must be exercised to prevent the miscarriage of justice or defamation of character through the filing of erroneous charges of malingering.

f. It will be mandatory to publish the findings of the court, in each case found guilty of malingering, in such a manner that these findings will be brought to the attention of each soldier within the command involved. (AG 710, 26 May 1945.) [23]

---

[23] War Department Circular 298, 29 September 1945, Sec. IX; reissued as War Department Memorandum 600-510-1, 18 February 1947.

16

HOMOSEXUALITY

THE VERY WORD "homosexuality" carries great emotional charge, either in civil life or in the Army. As with all sexuality, there is evasion, rejection, or suppression of its discussion. If mentioned at all, it is apt to be with a mixture of emotional moralization and deprecation. Although in many European countries there is much more tolerance and much less sexual taboo, in our particular culture homosexuality is considered a crime; the term itself is almost an anathema. The general attitude of condemnation and intolerance is shared even by many physicians.

In contrast to this restricted point of view, the psychiatrist most frequently uses the term to refer to one stage in the psychological and social growth of the child. At birth, a baby does not distinguish his environment as being apart from his own body. Not until he is several months old does he discover that his hands and his feet are a part of himself and are subject to his control, but the rattle and mother are not.

By the end of the first year of life the infant has become well aware of himself as a person. From then until he is 5 or 6 years old, his chief interest is invested in himself, although he gradually learns that if he is to receive love he must also give it. While the young child's chief emotional interest is directed in toward himself, i.e., he loves himself best, he is going through the phase which is referred to technically as the "narcissistic stage" of development. It is named for Narcissus, the Greek god who fell in love with himself.

At the age of 8 or 9 years the child begins to transfer much of his interest to others of his own sex, and thus he enters the "homosexual stage" of object interest. During this period, interests, play, and associations are largely concerned with those of his or her same sex.

During late adolescence, the developing youth normally shifts his interest and emotional investment to members of the opposite sex and thus enters the "heterosexual stage." Eventually he establishes a relationship with one of the opposite sex which is reciprocal in its emotional "give and take." At that time he is regarded as having reached psychological maturity. Even in maturity, all persons show residuals of each earlier stage; we continue loving our parents;

we have varying degrees of self-love; we enjoy emotional attachments to members of our own sex.

The transition from early self-love to the homosexual stage is a comparatively simple one, because in a sense the child becomes interested in his mirror image, i.e., in another person just like himself. The predominance of homosexual interests is quite normal for everyone at this stage and is expressed acceptably in the tendency to form gangs and to choose chums. It is the age of "crushes" and of hero worship. Youth organizations such as the Boy Scouts, the Girl Scouts, the Girl Reserves, the Hi-Y, and the Campfire Girls thrive because of this normal interest in persons of the same sex.

This interest in one of the same sex continues throughout life, though with much less intensity than between 8 and 15 years of age. The satisfaction derived from such associations is the basis of all social impulses. Close friendship, comradeship, and *esprit de corps* are the forerunners of the interest, devotion, and love of the individual for mankind in general. While the normal mature adult reaches a developmental level at which his sexual satisfactions are largely invested in one chosen individual of the opposite sex, he does not give up social enjoyment of individuals of the same sex. The participation of men and women in separated social groups, clubs, fraternal organizations, and religious societies contributes importantly to our culture. It is a form of sublimated homosexual gratification.

Certainly there is no better example than the wartime Army of an organization built on entirely masculine lines. Therefore, in a technical, psychiatric sense, it was fundamentally a homosexual society. Yet it was in no sense a pathological unit. Its success depended on the ability of men to get along with, live with, and work with other men, and to accept the almost total exclusion of women from their lives. The introduction of the Women's Army Corps did not change this situation to any great degree. Therefore, certain adjustments were required of the "normal" adult when he moved into a society made up so exclusively of members of his own sex, particularly if he was between the ages of 18 and 35.

Since all sexuality is so closely linked with morals in our culture, only occasionally does one find an objective attitude toward it. The fact that a subject may be taboo because it is unpleasant or "not nice" should not deter the thoughtful person from considering its problems. Those who manifest excessive emotional feeling about any particular subject often develop such an attitude as a protection against their own unconscious and unacknowledged interest in that subject. This is well illustrated by the minister in the play *Rain*. One can suspect that those who denounce adult homosexual individuals with feelings of great hostility may very possibly be overreacting to their own unconscious wishes in that direction.

Due to their emotional blind spot, some people assume that a man who goes into the Army must become asexual, certainly so if he is married. However, no amount of wishful thinking will change the fact that he does not. Human nature is not like that. When individuals are forced into a homosexual society, mature as well as immature personalities have to find outlets or sublimations for their normal sexual energies, drives, and interests. Many soldiers found direct outlets, whether autoerotic, homosexual, or heterosexual. This group probably included almost as many married as unmarried men, if they had been separated from home for a long period.[1] The armies of some other countries have a different attitude than does ours, and provide "comfort girls." In America, we placed from 50,000 to 100,000 healthy young men in a camp and in essence told them to forget the most powerful drive in their lives. They were supposed somehow to adjust to an exclusively male society and remain completely continent and abstinent. This did not happen. Some thought they had to have physical substitutes; others managed with psychological substitutes.

The physical substitutes were varied: many men discovered satisfaction in a physical interest in other men, which often surprised them; others resorted to masturbation; still others, including many married men, found "women" to satisfy their need.[1] The Army did not sit in moral judgment on the nonmarital sexual relations of the soldier as long as these were with women,[2] except when they interfered with his effectiveness. However, great efforts were made to control venereal diseases.

There were numerous psychological substitutes used: possession of "pin-up girl" photographs; an increased interest in "dirty" stories, in profanity, and in homosexual buffoonery. Another substitute was writing and receiving frequent letters to and from a wife or sweetheart (or often sweethearts). A most important substitute had to be the satisfaction the soldier derived from the comradeship and fellowship of his associates—his male friends—a disguised and sublimated homosexuality.

The gallery of pin-up girls had a double value. It gave evidence of its owner's virility to all those who viewed it, in addition to the individual's enjoyment, according to Elkin. "Similarly, a connection with a woman, however shabby and perfunctory, was recounted in an adventurous spirit and in terms that never failed to do credit to the subject's virile capacities."[3]

An interesting sublimation has been excellently described by Janis[4] as

---

[1] Confirmation of this statement is available from various sources. See the remarkable survey of the Information and Education Division on venereal disease among our troops in Italy.

[2] See Chap. 12, section on nonmarital sexuality.

[3] Elkin, H., "Aggressive and Erotic Tendencies in Army Life," *Am. J. Sociology,* 51:408-413, Mar., 1946, Univ. of Chicago Press.

[4] Janis, I. L., "Psychodynamic Aspects of Adjustment to Army Life," *Psychiatry,* 8:159-176, May, 1945.

"homosexual buffoonery," one of several common methods by which a soldier relieved his emotional tension. In the barracks, usually when the men were getting undressed, one frequently observed play-acting in which various persons "kiddingly" assumed the role of overt homosexuals. One soldier, returning from the shower room in the nude was greeted with catcalls, salacious whistling, and comments like, "Hey, Joe, you shouldn't go around like that—you don't know what that does to me." Joe responded by coyly draping a towel around himself and wriggling his hips in feminine fashion. Some of the men joined in the buffoonery by playing the role of the appreciative spectator: "Ain't he hot stuff though!" "C'mon, take it off." Others acted the part of active solicitors for sexual favors: "How much do you want for sleeping with me tonight?"; "Come into my bed and I'll give you the time of your life."

As Janis pointed out, the spirit in which the homosexual role was acted was unquestionably that of "kidding around." The buffoonery was carried to such extremes that no one participating in it ever considered in his own mind the disturbing possibility of any seriousness in it. It was as if the individual thought, "I really have no inclinations of this sort at all; otherwise I would never be so free about kidding around in this way." Janis further made the point that when the entire group participated in the acting out of homosexual play it served to eliminate individual feelings of guilt.

Sometimes, however, there is homosexuality which represents an arrest in psychosexual development. Instead of the normal progress from one stage to another, a personality may stop at the homosexual level or regress back to it so that a preference for members of the same sex to the exclusion of interest in the opposite sex persists into adult life. When the ultimate in gratification in sexual relations is found with one of the same sex it is regarded as pathological.[5]

The "problem" of homosexuality in the Army, as it referred to the overt sexual relationships between men, was not nearly so large as one might have judged from the emotional discussions of the subject by some officers. Some figures for 1943 showed that 20,620 men in the Army were diagnosed as "constitutional psychopaths." Of these 1,625 were presumably of the "homosexual type." In the same year among 3,175 patients diagnosed as "constitutional psychopaths" in overseas theaters, 237 were designated as being homo-

[5] The amazing findings of a very large survey of cross sections as to the sex life of American men, by A. C. Kinsey and his associates of Indiana University, indicates that from 10 to 45 per cent of all individuals have overt homosexual contacts during their life. An incomplete report is given in "Criteria for a Hormonal Explanation of the Homosexual," *J. Clin. Endocrinol.*, 1:424-428, May, 1941. A more complete report is a remarkable and revolutionary document: 37 per cent of the total male population has at least some overt homosexual experience to the point of orgasm between adolescence and old age. Kinsey, A. C.; Pomeroy, W. B.; and Martin, C. E., *Sexual Behavior in the Human Male*, W. B. Saunders Company, Philadelphia, 1948, p. 650.

sexual. These figures, however, are probably of little if any importance as an indication of either the true incidence or significance of the problem.

Among Americans in Japanese prison camps, food and not sex was the one great motivating factor in the prisoners' lives. Thoughts and dreams of women disappeared. Homosexuality became a negligible factor. The few examples of it were to be found among kitchen and hospital help, who were able to receive slightly better nourishment.[6]

In general, there were four types of homosexuality that came to the attention of the psychiatrist. One of these is described as latent homosexuality. There were men in the Army who had never had any consciousness of particular interest in men or knowledge of this twist in their personality who, when placed in a strictly male communal life, became disturbed and anxious. Many of them were embarrassed while in the toilet or when undressing in front of other men; they found themselves unnaturally interested in the physical build of other men. Some of them became acutely distressed and tense as a result.[7]

The second type was the homosexual individual who, prior to his Army experience, had accepted his make-up and had satisfying contacts and sexual relationships with other men. He was able to do this without any distress or emotional concern to himself. Usually he remained discreet about it and very often got along well socially. Undoubtedly there were many such men in the Army. Only a few of them were detected by accident and thus brought to the attention of the psychiatrists.

There was a third group of men who revealed no homosexual interest or proclivities except in certain very special situations, usually when under the influence of excess alcohol. Often these men were unable to remember their homosexual behavior which had occurred while they were drunk. This was a particularly unfortunate type of problem in the social milieu and organization of the Army. Alcohol often reduces inhibitions. The *Gemütlichkeit,* the "fraternal spirit," the warm good will characteristic of a "wet" stag party with its flow of salacious stories is a more socially acceptable release of emotional tension than the play of buffoonery. The arm-in-arm affection of drinking companions and the arm-around-shoulder stance of the barbershop quartette are commonly accepted practice. Such activity creates no hazard for the mature man, but an immature person who drinks too much may go further to indulge in undisguised sexual activities. In civilian life this may put the man on a social black list; in the Army it may be the end of his military career. The

---

[6] Morgan, H. J.; Wright, I. S.; and Ravenswaay, A. V., "Health of Repatriated Prisoners of War from the Far East," *J.A.M.A.,* **130**:995-999, Apr. 13, 1946.
[7] This reaction is well described by M. H. Maskin and L. L. Altman in "Military Psychodynamics: Psychological Factors in the Transition from Civilian to Soldier," *Psychiatry,* **6**:263-269, Aug., 1943.

same immature behavior toward a woman produces a less emotional condemnation.

Last, there was that comparatively small group of individuals who were a social menace in the use of their deliberately seductive tactics. Their judgment was so badly warped that they made open propositions or gave exhibitions of their interests and desires.

Probably for every homosexual who was referred or came to the Medical Department, there were 5 or 10 who never were detected. Those men must have performed their duty satisfactorily, whether assigned to combat or to some other type of service. This is always surprising to those who so heatedly condemn the homosexual. Such critics also assume that feigning homosexuality to escape service is a very common procedure. They fail to see that if a man does wish to malinger he has a far easier time of it if he chooses a simple expedient like a backache or headache. No doubt there were some warped personalities who hoped to avoid service by claiming to be overt homosexuals, but this surely was a very small number of the antisocial personalities, who would have been poor military material in any event.

Fry and Rostow [8] made a detailed, confidential survey of 183 men whom he knew from prewar studies to be homosexual, either as active participants, as probable active participants, or as having a latent interest in homosexuality. All of them were examined for induction. Of the 183, 51 were rejected at the induction center, but, interestingly enough, only 29 for neuropsychiatric reasons. Of the remainder, only 14 were discharged from the service. That meant that 118 served from 1 to 5 years. This psychiatrist had regarded only 31 per cent of the group as acceptable for service, though 72 per cent were admitted. Of those admitted, 58 per cent were officers in the Army, Air Force, and Navy. The amazing fact is that they concealed their homosexuality effectively and, at the same time, made creditable records for themselves in the service.

An extensive descriptive study by Loeser [9] of 270 patients who were admitted to the 312th Station Hospital in England for problems of homosexuality disclosed that 78 per cent (210 individuals) were overt homosexuals; 63 per cent had entered the hospital involuntarily because they had been reported or apprehended, and 37 per cent came of their own volition. This number, according to Loeser, represented the only cases of homosexuality hospitalized in the entire theater over an 18-month period between February, 1943, and August, 1944.

In a survey of this group, Loeser noted no difference in the incidence between Negro and white soldiers. The majority came from urban areas; 41

[8] Fry, C. C. and Rostow, E. G., National Research Council, interim report OEM cmr. 337, Apr. 1, 1945.
[9] Loeser, L. H., "Sexual Psychopath in the Military Services, A study of 270 Cases," *Am. J. Psychiat.*, 102:92-101, July, 1945.

per cent gave a history of broken homes. Two special features of these men are well known to be characteristic of adjusted homosexuals: the predominance of skilled over semiskilled workers (less than 2 per cent were unskilled), and an average mental age well above that for the Army as a whole (79 per cent being average or higher). There were no illiterates in the entire group; 86 per cent had finished the eighth grade and 54 per cent had graduated from high school. In this survey Loeser reported that in general they were law-abiding; arrests were very infrequent. Their record of good health was impressive, with accidents and illness at a very low rate. Among these men were 10 master sergeants, 6 technical sergeants, 19 staff sergeants. Many others had ratings of considerable talent in clerical, musical, and dramatic ability. He commented further that the temperament and skills necessary for the combat soldier were infrequently seen. He believed that homosexuality should not be a punishable offense; that discharge from the Army is not necessary for most cases, and deferment in the draft is not advisable in all known cases. A large percentage possess sufficient restraint and insight and have sufficient talent to justify individual evaluation.

The standards for admission to the Army as outlined in Mobilization Regulations 1-9, dated April 19, 1944, specifically state that "persons habitually or occasionally engaged in homosexual or other perverse sexual practices are unsuitable for military service and will be excluded. Feminine bodily character-istics, effeminacy in dress or manner, or a patulous rectum are not consistently found in such persons but where present should lead to careful psychiatric examination. If the individual admits or claims homosexuality, or other sexual perversion, he will be referred to his local board for further psychiatric and social investigation. If an individual has a record as a pervert, he will be re-jected." Obviously only the very pathological would admit their homosexuality, with the possible exception of those who felt sufficient concern and anxiety about their inability to resist overt activity in the Army. It was extremely diffi-cult for the examiner, however, to judge this adequately and the inductee was usually accepted for service unless he expressed anxiety.

Disposition of the homosexual. The problem of what to do with the homo-sexual individual in the armed services when he was having or causing diffi-culty was, is, and probably always will be a difficult one for solution. As Dr. Edward A. Strecker commented to me, "In both the Army and Navy we failed to solve the important matter of how these chaps should be discharged. I think it was not for want of trying, because in both services we tried very hard. The difficulty was that there was a good deal of real objection, *in some instances,*[10] to a straight medical discharge. On the other hand, a blue discharge hardly

---

[10] Italics inserted by author.

seemed fair since it penalized a man occupationally and socially in a certain degree, and furthermore, since many of these fellows made an earnest effort of service; others simply evaded induction on the grounds of homosexuality." [11]

The policies for the management of homosexuals in the Army were revised only after a long, difficult period of education. Initially all cases who were not tried by court-martial (where offenses were involved) [12] were given blue discharges. A man on his own initiative, or because of noticeable difficulty in adjusting himself, might visit or be sent to a psychiatrist for consultation. When it was found that the basis of the difficulty was homosexuality, if this was reported to his commanding officer, the man probably received a blue discharge, or perhaps would be tried. Objections to this were raised by many homosexual individuals, whose request for help from a medical officer ended up in a discharge "without honor." This action undermined confidence in medical officers. Furthermore, the Army required that doctors report even those statements given in confidence in a consultation room. The homosexual was no more responsible for his personality difficulty than a mental defective was for his. Even so, the old procedure, based on prejudice, singled him out for punishment. This resulted in many instances of careful avoidance in the case records of the word "homosexuality."

Some progress in the handling of the problem came with the publication of War Department Circular 3, dated January 3, 1944. This directive applied only to those who were discovered or reported to have performed homosexual acts. It did not apply to the soldiers who sought advice from a physician because of their fear of committing such acts. It provided for hospitalization of those who were deemed reclaimable. It permitted the giving of a blue discharge to an offender who was deemed not reclaimable, in lieu of court-martial. Included in the category of "reclaimable" were those who were guilty of first offenses, those who acted as the result of intoxication or curiosity, or "those who acted under undue influence, especially when such influence was exercised by a person of greater years or superior grade."

For this particular disability the commanding officer of the hospital was required to transmit to the Adjutant General (and to the theater headquarters, if overseas) a full report of the diagnosis, treatment, results of treatment, and the recommendation as to the disposition of every homosexual patient. This information was to be kept on file. Depending upon the results of treatment, the individual was returned to duty, separated from the service, or tried

[11] Personal communication, June 26, 1946.
[12] Weiss has made a strong and logical argument that the War Department should send many of the homosexuals confined as military prisoners home; the present policy tends to fix and confirm their sexual abnormality, and many other men are introduced to it. Weiss, I. I., "Homosexuality with Special Reference to Military Prisoners," *Psychiat. Quart.*, 20:485-523, July, 1946.

by court-martial. When returned to duty, he was assigned to a different organization so that he could start anew.

Actually there was little in the way of intensive treatment that could be given to such men. Adequate evaluation was possible, however. It is not known how many homosexual offenders were salvaged for further duty under this system, but probably not a significant number. Certainly many who were fundamentally homosexual were returned to duty with no mention or indication to commanding officers of the root of their difficulty. The fact that any were salvaged seems surprising in the light of the prevalence of such strong prejudices.

Neither Army regulations nor the above War Department circular specified the method of disposition of the homosexual who was not guilty of any offense. It was common practice, however, to give "discharges without honor" to any homosexual, on the premise that homosexuality constituted an undesirable trait of character.

To correct this action the Office of the Surgeon General desired to state in Army regulations [13] that those who were not guilty of any offense and who had had a good record should not be given a blue discharge. Concurrence in this could not be obtained. It was apparently feared that many homosexuals who were well adjusted would seek to be discharged, and that others might claim to be homosexual for the purpose of getting out of the Army with honorable discharges.

Without the prior knowledge of the Office of the Surgeon General, Army Regulations 615-368 was revised 1 month later, to the effect that "the mere confession by an individual to the psychiatrist that he possesses homosexual tendencies will not in itself constitute sufficient cause for discharge. . . ." Provision was made for hospitalization upon the recommendation of the psychiatrist for the purpose of determining if the individual should be restored to duty or separated from the service. However, the implication was that, if separated, it would be with a blue discharge.

After a series of conferences with the representatives of the major forces of the Army, a special memorandum was forwarded in July, 1945, by the Surgeon General to the Assistant Chief of Staff, G-1. It expressed the opinion that "personnel who were inadaptable for service by reason of homosexuality were entitled to honorable discharges, providing they were guilty of no offense and that their service had been honorable and faithful." It also pointed out that when an individual voluntarily sought medical assistance which led to a blue discharge, faith in medical officers was lost; furthermore, when such individuals received a blue discharge they were given the same treatment as those

---

[13] Army Regulations 615-368, 7 March 1945.

who had committed homosexual offenses and as those whose services had been unsatisfactory. It was suggested that a person with homosexual tendencies, as also the mental defective, is not responsible for his condition. Men in the latter category are given honorable discharges when released because of ineptness.

This memorandum resulted in a very progressive step, namely a special order that was sent out on October 31, 1945.[14] In that order it was made clear that enlisted personnel who were inadaptable because of homosexual tendencies, who had not committed any sexual offense while in the service, whose record of service was honorable, would be discharged honorably. This did not permit discharge merely on the basis of a confession of homosexuality. It required adequate evidence of an existing psychological maladjustment which rendered the individual inadaptable for service for this reason. The order further indicated that those relatively rare cases whose homosexual tendencies constituted symptoms of a psychiatric condition, such as psychoneurosis or psychosis, should be discharged on a medical basis.

Throughout the war, and increasingly in late 1945 and 1946, reports came to me of individual soldiers who had given months or even years of good service and had then received a blue discharge because of homosexuality. Many soldiers wrote me; many physicians wrote me. It was apparent that the blue discharge had sometimes been punitive and unfair, certainly nonmedical. An appeal for a reconsideration of their discharge can be addressed to the Secretary of War Review Board. It may be well for these men to recognize, however, that the odds are against them; the prejudice still exists!

Neither the Army nor the psychiatrists condoned overt homosexual activity. But the Army regulations based on old prejudices were modified in favor of a more objective appraisal of the problem. Homosexuals, in the opinion of the psychiatrist, have immature personalities which make them and their lives and some of their personal relations grossly pathological. Like any sick person, they deserve understanding instead of condemnation. At the same time it is necessary to realize that as citizens they vary in their usefulness. Some have unusual talent and may make important contributions to society. At the other end of the scale is the homosexual who is a menace, and society has a right to be protected from him. Persons afflicted with a homosexual make-up should not be condemned wholesale but instead should be considered individually.

---

[14] This came out 23 March 1946, as War Department Circular 85.

17

THE PEOPLE WHO DID THE JOB

THE BEST thought-out policies, the most carefully worded regulations, or the wisest of orders could be negated completely by the men who were in a position to implement them. The ill-informed or stubborn or stupid officer could block intelligently directed action. From general to corporal, one or several people sometimes interpreted rulings so as to cause unbelievable (to the civilian) harm. Just as true is the reverse. An intelligent officer often minimized the mistakes in ill-conceived regulations. When given the double favor of "good" officers and "good" rules, the benefit to the enlisted men was very great.

In a review of the personnel who contributed to the mental health of the soldier, first mention and credit should go to many of the Army leaders. Some of them aided by design; some did so by intuition. Morale experts, appreciating the magic influence of the personal word, urged that the top military leaders speak to the troops over the radio. For undivulged reasons, their voices were not heard. However, their activities and some of their thoughts were fully reported. Those reports were often of tremendous morale value. For instance when one great officer, on a visit to the States after VE-day, was asked if he were going to take his wife back to the theater with him, he promptly replied, "Not until the GI can do it too." Such passing, off-hand remarks created more confidence and better morale among troops than hundreds of "orientation" lectures could.

Personal affairs and line officers, chaplains and many others all played important roles in the maintenance of the mental health of the Army. The Special Services and Information and Education Divisions were created quite specifically to combat tendencies and forces which were antagonistic to good morale, i.e., good mental health. Red Cross workers gave invaluable assistance.

But the real responsibility for the prevention and cure of mental illness belonged to the Medical Department. Psychiatry is more than a particular specialty of medicine. It encompasses a code of dynamics which is or can be the tool of all medical practitioners. Just as in civil life, every doctor in the Army had to practice some psychiatry; probably more than did his civilian counterpart. Many soldiers were sent to the internist for stomach upsets and heart complaints and to the orthopedist for backaches that were in large part emotional in origin. Consequently, in enumerating those who practiced psychiatry in the Army, one cannot forget the major contributions made by medical men other than the specialists in this field.

Within the Medical Department was the division of neuropsychiatry. To the neuropsychiatrists fell the task of curing and preventing mental illness. The specialized field of neurology concerns itself with the organic disorders of the nerves, brain, and spinal cord. The specialty of psychiatry concerns itself with disorders of emotion, thinking, and behavior. Traditionally these specialties have been inseparably linked. This linkage continued in the Army where the proportion of neurological cases was about 1 in 10 neuropsychiatric cases. In many places the psychiatrist did what neurological practice there was.[1] Likewise, if only a neurologist were present, he cared for the psychiatric cases. How wise this may have been is a debatable question; very few psychiatrists know much about neurology and few neurologists are really interested in, or know, dynamic psychiatry. But there was not time for argument about it during the war.

Organization of the Medical Department. In order to understand why some things were allowed or just happened, and why other things were not permitted or forbidden, a brief description of the organization of the Medical Department and its relationships to other parts of the Army seems important.

The commander in chief of the Army is the President of the United States. His representative, the Secretary of War, administers the Army and issues orders and sets forth regulations in line with Congressional action and military necessity. His military adviser also serves as the senior officer of the Army— the Chief of Staff. Assistants to the Chief of Staff serve both as members of the General Staff and as heads of divisions: G-1, Personnel; G-2, Military Intelligence; G-3, Operations and Service; G-4, Supply.

It might be helpful to the uninformed to have some general conception of the organization of the Army. To present this accurately either in narrative or chart form would be beyond the ability of but very few people in the War Department. The Army grew so fast and became so large and so complicated that one of the practical, everyday problems of any officer in the War Department was how to find out whom he should see about a particular matter.

---

[1] This was true from the Surgeon General's Office throughout the field. Major (later Lt. Col.) William H. Everts was brought into the Neuropsychiatry Consultants Division to direct neurology. There were many times, however, when, because of personnel shortage, Col. Everts devoted much of his time to psychiatric problems. He was responsible, however, for all policies and directives regarding neurology. See Everts, W. H., "Neurology in the Army," *Bull. Menninger Clinic,* 8:136-137, Sept., 1944.

Many of us who were there even 2 or 3 years continued to have difficulty in discovering what persons we should see for consultations or to obtain concurrence or authority for an action. Relationships were very involved and changed frequently.

Generally speaking, the man power of the Army was divided into three major groups. The Army Ground Forces included the Infantry and the Artillery and all the fighting soldiers. The Army Air Forces included not only the bomber and fighter crews but also the Transport and Evacuation, Troop-carrier, and other Commands. The Army Service Forces included all the technical services of Finance, Ordnance, Quartermaster, Engineers, Chemical Warfare, Transportation, Military Police, Signal Corps, and Medical Corps. The Adjutant General's and the Judge Advocate General's Departments were also in the Service Forces. Each of the three major forces had a commanding general who was responsible to the Chief of Staff, but all of their work had to be coordinated through the "G's" described above. Each major subdivision of the Army, such as the Third Army or the Fifth Air Force, had staff organizations whose functions were similar and parallel to the "G's" of the War Department. It also had its own finance, quartermaster, engineer, medical, and so on, officer or department.

The Medical Department was one of the technical services in the Army Service Forces. This location in the Army organization was a great handicap. Although the Surgeon General was theoretically responsible for medical service to the entire Army, he was never in a position to supervise such service. He was not a member of the General Staff.[2] Because of the hierarchical system, he had to refer matters concerning the Air or Ground Forces to his own chief, the commanding general of the Service Forces, who, in turn, would pass it to the commanding general of the other force for eventual referral to the surgeon concerned. There was a considerable medical establishment responsible to the Air Forces Surgeon and many physicians served under the direction of the Ground Forces Surgeon. Over neither of these groups of medical personnel did he have any jurisdiction. The Surgeon General of the Army was sometimes ironically referred to as being merely the Surgeon General of the Army Service Forces.

As might be expected, there was some undercover rivalry between the three major forces for man power, authority, and credit for accomplishments. For instance, the Air Forces Surgeon, paid much more attention to the directions from the commanding general of the Air Forces than he did to the Surgeon General. For to him the Surgeon General was only the chief of a subsection of

---

[2] Civilian medical organizations strongly advocated having the Surgeon General put on the General Staff. E. A. Strecker, when president of the American Psychiatric Association, spoke out definitely about it. "Presidential Address," *Am. J. Psychiat.*, 101:1-8, July, 1944.

a parallel sister organization—the Army Service Forces. It was obvious to those who worked in the Office of the Surgeon General that neither the Air Forces Surgeon nor the Ground Forces Surgeon appeared to feel any responsibility to the Surgeon General. These surgeons were invited to and were wanted at the biweekly staff meetings of the Surgeon General. However, during much of the war the Air Forces Surgeon only occasionally sent a representative; during all of the period that I attended, I never saw the Air Forces Surgeon himself at a single meeting. The Ground Forces usually sent a representative when the Surgeon himself did not attend.

Although the Surgeon General nominally had the responsibility for the health of the Army, his authority and function were greatly limited even though in case of a major calamity he certainly would have been blamed for any failure. All general and regional and station hospitals in the United States were under the Army Service Forces, and consequently were under his jurisdiction. However, he had little or no authority in the many Air Forces hospitals in this country. He was able to prevent the Air Forces from operating separate hospitals overseas. He also had the responsibility for preventive medicine and sanitation throughout the whole Army, except that these particular features, like the practice of medicine, were taken over in the theaters of operation by the theater surgeons who actually ran their own shows. Because all of the fighting Armies were under the Ground Forces, all of their medical personnel were responsible to the Ground Forces Surgeon. Therefore, the theater surgeon, who was the nominal representative of the Surgeon General, had no direction over the surgeons of the various field Armies.

Any medical policy that affected the entire Army, i.e., Ground Forces, Air Forces, and Service Forces, had to have concurrence from the separate forces before it could be approved as an Army-wide, War Department circular. This put the chief medical officer in the Army, namely the Surgeon General, in the ridiculous position of having to obtain concurrences from those who were theoretically his subordinates, the Air Forces Surgeon and the Ground Forces Surgeon.

Lack of authority over personnel was another great handicap to the Surgeon General in carrying out his mission. The medical personnel of the Air Forces were under the sole jurisdiction and control of the Air Forces Surgeon. This was a very sore point, for at times the Service Forces installations needed more doctors who might have been available from the Air Forces, for, in proportion to the number of patients, the Air Forces had a much higher percentage of doctors than did the Service Forces. Yet all Air Forces patients in overseas theaters were sent to Service Forces Hospitals.

The Ground Forces supplied medical attention only in combat areas. Therefore, except for patients in the field and evacuation hospitals in the combat

zone, all Ground Forces soldiers, both overseas and in the United States, were
also sent to Service Forces Hospitals. Yet Ground Forces medical personnel,
too, were beyond the power of the Surgeon General to control, either by assignment or policy. Ginzberg painted the picture graphically: "There were at least
four War Department agencies controlling medical personnel: (1) the General Staff; (2) Headquarters, Army Service Forces; (3) Headquarters, Army
Air Forces; and (4) the Service Commands. Each had authority over medical
personnel. Only the Surgeon did not!" [2a]

In the planning of some major campaigns he had no voice as to the medical
personnel or equipment or supplies to be used. Neither he nor his representatives were permitted, except by invitation, to visit field installations in certain
areas that were under the jurisdiction of the other two major forces. Such an
arrangement seriously interfered with the efficient functioning of the medical
services.

The situation was somewhat improved by the important War Department
circular in 1945 which said, in effect, that the Surgeon General was THE
Surgeon General.[3] However, this was never effectively implemented. It was
indeed lamentable that the Surgeon General, himself, was not permitted to
inspect certain overseas areas. Nor were his consultants in medicine, surgery,
and neuropsychiatry wanted in Air Forces hospitals in some areas in this country.

Of specific significance is the fact that the neuropsychiatry consultant to
the Surgeon General had no official relationship to, or responsibility for, psychiatry in either the Air or Ground Forces. The Ground Forces Surgeon did
not even have a psychiatrist in his office until the last 6 months of 1945.[4]
The Air Forces Surgeon, however, had a neuropsychiatric consultant during
most of the war.[5] Nevertheless, the very creditable work of the Air Forces consultant and psychiatrists was often carried on with the serious impediment of
active animosity toward psychiatry on the part of certain individuals in the
Office of the Air Forces Surgeon.[6]

The directives and publications [7] dealing with neuropsychiatry which were

---

[2a] Ginzberg, E., "Army Hospitalization, Retrospect and Prospect," *Bull. U. S. Army Med.
Dept.*, 8:38-47, Jan., 1948.
[3] "The Surgeon General—Functions," War Department Circular 120, 18 April 1945.
[4] Lieutenant Colonel Alfred O. Ludwig, previously Consultant in Neuropsychiatry, Seventh
Army.
[5] Successively, Lt. Col. John M. Murray, Lt. Col. Donald Hastings, and Maj. Douglas Bond.
[6] Murray, J. M., "Accomplishments of Psychiatry in the Army Air Forces," *Am. J. Psychiat.*,
103:594-599, Mar., 1947.
[7] These included such publications as *Outline of Neuropsychiatry in Aviation Medicine.* This
was a 100-page booklet written by Lt. Col. R. C. Anderson for the School of Aviation Medicine
at Randolph Field, where Anderson was the instructor in psychiatry. This outline was a complete
revision of Training Manuel 8-325 with the same title, which was written largely by Col. Walter
Jenson.

issued by the Air Forces Surgeon were never sent to the Neuropsychiatry Consultants Division of the Office of the Surgeon General. Nor were many of those from the Office of the Surgeon General welcomed by the Air Forces Surgeon. Although personal relationships between the psychiatrists of the different services were close and contacts frequent, there was never any official sanction for them. Therefore, psychiatric practice of the Air and Ground Forces is not reported in any detail here because of the lack of direct and intimate knowledge of it.[8]

Location of neuropsychiatrists by the type of installation in which they worked and by their geographic locations. Neuropsychiatrists were placed in all of the 108 induction centers; they served in all of the 65 general and the 57 regional and most of the 306 station hospitals in the United States, and in the 217 general, 196 station, and 91 evacuation hospitals overseas. There were 10 specialized hospitals devoted entirely to neuropsychiatry, 8 overseas and 2 in this country, 5 of which were primarily for neurotic patients and 3 for psychotic patients. Psychiatrists were placed in the outpatient units, the Mental Hygiene Consultation Services, in 36 basic-training camps. They were assigned to all large transports and to hospital ships which carried psychiatric patients. They were stationed in disciplinary barracks and in the centers for the rehabilitation of military prisoners. They were assigned to 91 combat divisions; they were included in the examining teams of the 8 redistribution centers and the 27 separation centers; they served as consultants in 7 theaters, 9 Service Commands, and 10 Armies, and to some Air Forces as well as in the Office of the Surgeon General and the Office of the Air Forces Surgeon. The staffs of the 13 convalescent hospitals operated by the Service Forces (and the 10 by the Air Forces) included many psychiatrists.

Psychiatrists were widely distributed geographically; as of VE-day (May 2, 1945) 2,402 were scattered in every theater: European Theater, 488; Mediterranean Theater, 66; Southwest Pacific, 98; Pacific Ocean area, 39; China-Burma-India Theater, 43; other smaller theaters (Alaska, Caribbean), 28. There were 125 carried as attached to the War Department, 90 per cent of whom were assigned to Veterans Administration hospitals. In the United States 1,012 neuropsychiatrists served with the Army Services Forces (42 with the Army Ground Forces; 200 with the Air Forces). There were 43 en route overseas; 26 were with numbered hospitals preparing to go overseas; 129 were in War Department replacement pools awaiting assignment; 44 had just returned from overseas and 19 were patients in hospitals. The total number of neuro-

---

[8] In two different papers, Murray described the psychiatric program in the Air Force. Murray, J. M., "Psychiatry in the Army Air Forces," *A. J. Psychiat.*, 100:21-24, July, 1943; "Psychiatric Aspects of Aviation Medicine," *Psychiatry*, 7:1-7, Feb., 1944.

psychiatrists included 16 of the 75 women physicians who entered the military service. Also included were 7 Negro psychiatrists, all of whom were used in their specialty.

In peacetime the assignment of all medical personnel was made through the Office of the Surgeon General. In wartime this became far too great an undertaking. Just as in all other arms and services, the process of placement was decentralized by moving it to the nine Service Command headquarters for medical installations in the United States, and to the various theater head-quarters for overseas assignments.[9] When physicians came into the Army they were allotted by the War Department to the various Service Commands and assigned from those headquarters to specific units or posts or camps. By this means each Service Command headquarters was made responsible for the proper placement of men in its area. When units moved overseas, theater headquarters took over that responsibility. As replacements were needed in the theater, it requisitioned the War Department for so many doctors. The War Department then called for a quota from each Service Command. Except under very special conditions it was not possible to shift specific individuals through the headquarters in Washington or to transfer them from one Service Command to another.

Since it was essential that the best-qualified psychiatrists be given the most responsible positions, all of them had to be evaluated. There were two methods of rating. At first a classification by the National Research Council was used. However, this did not prove to be practical. Later, the physicians were graded professionally as A, B, C, or D, according to their experience and qualifications. Grade-A men were of "professorial" rank, i.e., they had had long experience, their ability was widely recognized, and they stood high in their profession. At the peak neuropsychiatric strength of 2,402, only 21 men were so classified. At the same time 401 men were classified as B. These neuropsychiatrists were either "diplomates" of the specialty board or qualified for it, and were capable of running a large hospital service or of being a consultant. There were 729 men classified as C who were reasonably well trained, with 3 to 5 years of experience, and were capable of running a psychiatric section in a station hospital, serving as a division psychiatrist, or working elsewhere without supervision. Finally there were 1,251 men in the D category whose neuropsychiatric training consisted of only the specialized 3-month course provided by the Army or whose training or experience was insufficient to qualify them as C. The intent was to assign these men to work only where there was supervision. In addition

---

[9] Except Air Forces medical personnel who remained under the Office of the Air Forces Surgeon and his field representatives (Air Forces, Training Command, Transport Command, etc.).

to a professional rating, an officer also was supposed to have an administrative rating.

There are two significant facts to note about the figures just cited. First, a very small number of Grade-A neuropsychiatrists came into the Army. All of them were given positions of high responsibility as Service Command and theater consultants. Conservatively, at least 200 or more neuropsychiatrists who remained civilians would have been so graded. Many of these, however, were ineligible for the Army because of their age; many others were unavailable because they had been designated by medical schools or hospitals as "essential" to the maintenance of the civilian unit with which they were connected. Nevertheless, the Army undoubtedly suffered for lack of more older, experienced, outstanding neurologists and psychiatrists.

The second point of interest is the very high number of Grade-D neuropsychiatrists. This was due to the system of classification and assignment of medical officers. The large number of doctors entering the Army from general practice received no specialty designation. Unless a man had such a rating and was given a military occupational specialty number, he was subject to assignment to any type of medical work. Therefore, it was necessary to give even inadequately qualified men specialty ratings in order to retain their greatly needed services in a neuropsychiatric position.

Many untrained men thus fell heir to great responsibility. In one particular hospital, the chief of the NP Service was a youngster who had had 1 year in a southern state hospital prior to entering the Army. Under him was a physician, who, following his graduation from medical school in 1922, had taken a state-hospital job for 1 year because of economic difficulties. He had then gone into surgery which he practiced until the beginning of the war. On joining the Army, because of the great need for psychiatrists and his history of 1 year in a state hospital, he was assigned to the psychiatric service. A second assistant was a well-qualified obstetrician. Since such a specialty was less needed and neuropsychiatrists were too few, he also was assigned to the psychiatric service. Two other assistants were recent medical students who, after finishing their civilian internships, had taken the Army's 3-month course in neuropsychiatry. These five men constituted the psychiatric service of a rather large and important station hospital. Some of our very good division psychiatrists were internists as civilians; three of our Mental Hygiene Consultation Services psychiatrists had been pediatricians.

The national examining boards of each medical specialty have developed yardsticks of qualification for their practitioners. The requirements for admission to examination by these boards are very high, usually including 5, 6, or 7 years of training and experience. There is a combined board of neurology and psychiatry. Unfortunately, complete figures which would show how many of the Medical Corps had passed the examinations of this board have not yet been compiled. In July, 1944, when there were about 1,490 neuropsychiatrists in the Army, 136 of them had qualified in psychiatry, 14 of them in neurology, and 121 in both neurology and psychiatry, making a total of 271 men so qualified (18 per cent) of the men practicing Army psychiatry.

With the war over, some other interesting facts about this group are available. Thirteen [10] medical officers of the Army of the United States (commissioned from civilian life) became full colonels in professional work and 18 additional [11] received a "terminal" promotion to this rank at the time of their separation from the Army. One became a brigadier general. Two medical reserve colonels were in administrative work.[12] One Regular Army psychiatrist was a brigadier general and 14 were full colonels, 10 [13] of whom had general administrative and 4 [14] had psychiatric clinical assignments. There were 21 physicians in psychiatry in the Veterans Administration who ranked as full colonels.

An incomplete list shows that 101 citations or awards were made to neuropsychiatrists; one received the Distinguished Service Medal, 31 received the Legion of Merit, 28 received the Bronze Star, 23 received the Army Commendation Ribbon, 6 received the Selective Service Medal, 2 received the Purple Heart, 2 received the Certificate of Merit.[15]

While 2,402 has been given as the number of neuropsychiatrists, this figure represented the maximum personnel at one time and not the total of all those who served during the war. This total, unfortunately, is not known. Never were there sufficient men to begin to handle the job. Some co-operation was gained in meeting this shortage when in May, 1945, a special circular [16] was published directing commanding officers of hospitals to utilize any excess medical officers on the neuropsychiatric service until such time as they were needed elsewhere.

---

[10] W. J. Bleckwenn, W. Bloomberg, H. W. Brosin, S. A. Challman, O. Chamberlain, F. G. Ebaugh, T. C. Fong, R. D. Halloran, M. J. Musser, P. L. Schroeder, L. H. Smith, D. A. Thom, and L. J. Thompson.
[11] R. C. Anderson, Clarke Barnacle, Martin Berezin, E. G. Billings, Roscoe W. Cavell, Henry Cotton, John E. Davis, Jr., Albert M. DeArmond, Malcolm J. Farrell, George Frumkes, John H. Griest, Roy R. Grinker, M. R. Kaufman, Merrill Moore, Samuel Paster, F. F. Senerchia, Joseph Skobba, and W. A. Srodes.
[12] John I. Marker and F. Garm Norbury.
[13] Brigadier General: Eugene G. Reinartz; colonels: J. M. Caldwell, W. A. Carlson, R. E. Chambers, Sidney Chappel, F. H. Dixon, George Hesner, W. S. Jenson, E. J. Kendricks, E. B. Littoral, and S. C. Sitter.
[14] E. H. Parsons, W. C. Porter, C. C. Odom, and F. E. Weatherby.
[15] Many of these citations were published in the *Am. J. Psychiat.,* 102:411-413, Nov., 1945; 102:830-833, May, 1946.
[16] Army Service Forces Circular 189, 26 May 1945.

NEUROPSYCHIATRY IN THE OFFICE OF
THE SURGEON GENERAL

Professional Services,[17] in the Office of the Surgeon General, prior to the war, had two full-time and one half-time officers on the staff. By 1944, 65 officers were devoting full time to professional problems in the medical department. The psychiatrist who came into this office in February, 1942, had as his function the review of the retiring board [18] proceedings and the reports of line of duty boards.[19] With the progress of induction and the growth of the Army, the psychiatric branch [20] of the Professional Services received an additional officer. It was not, however, until August, 1942, that an outstanding psychiatrist came from civil life to serve as consultant to the Surgeon General and to head the neuropsychiatry branch. In March, 1943, another officer was added to advise about and to supervise mental hygiene efforts. A neurologist was assigned in October, 1943.

The neuropsychiatry branch became a division under the chief of the Professional Services as of January 1, 1944. The reorganization of October, 1944, abolished the Professional Services as such and made the Consultants Divisions for surgery, medicine, neuropsychiatry, and reconditioning responsible directly to the Surgeon General.

From 2 men in April, 1942, the neuropsychiatric staff in the Office of the Surgeon General grew to a maximum strength of 11 men in 1945, who were organized into the following branches: [21] psychiatry, neurology, mental hygiene, clinical psychology, and psychiatric social work.

The Neuropsychiatry Consultants Division of the Office of the Surgeon General had to be the heartbeat for neuropsychiatry in the Army. The autonomy of the Service Command and theater consultants was limited, but there was no limit set for their initiative except the necessity for procuring the backing and authority of Washington headquarters. The NP Consultants Division established policies, composed directives implementing those policies, and then

[17] Other Services were Operations, Preventive Medicine, Supply, Administrative.

[18] The medical records of all retiring officers are reviewed in the Office of the Surgeon General.

[19] Medical records are reviewed to confirm or revise the decision as to whether or not illness or injury came in line of duty.

[20] As a "branch" in the organization structure, neuropsychiatry was subservient to the Medical Division which in turn was a part of the Professional Services.

[21] Director, Col. (later Brig. Gen.) William C. Menninger; Deputy Director, Lt. Col. (later Col.) Malcolm J. Farrell; Chief of Psychiatry Branch, Lt. Col. Norman Q. Brill; Personnel, Maj. (later Lt. Col.) Ivan C. Berlien; Mental Hygiene Consultation Services, Maj. (later Lt. Col.) Manfred Guttmacher; Chief of Neurology Branch, Lt. Col. William H. Everts; Chief of Mental Hygiene Branch, Maj. (later Lt. Col.) John W. Appel; Assistant, Maj. David W. Hilger; Chief of Psychological Branch, Lt. Col. (later Col.) Morton A. Seidenfeld; Assistant, Capt. (later Maj.) Lawrence O'Kelly; Chief of Psychiatric Social Work Branch, Maj. (later Lt. Col.) Daniel E. O'Keefe.

worked toward having them published. Only so could the men in the field derive the authority to develop and practice the highest caliber of psychiatry and neurology, clinical psychology, and psychiatric social work.

In peacetime the Army issues the majority of its instructions as to methods and procedures in the form of Army regulations, field manuals, and technical manuals. In time of war, rapid and numerous changes and temporary expedients necessitated the use of "letters," "memoranda," and "circulars," issued by the War Department, the Air Forces, the Ground Forces, the Service Forces, and the Field Services. These served as vehicles for new information, and for changes in or supplements to previously established practices.

Every officer and every soldier had to have authority under which he could act. For procedures as well as for leaves and furloughs, such authority came from written "orders" which had to pass through certain "channels" of command. Only after the receipt of copies of the orders or circular or regulation could an officer or soldier proceed.

A "circular" which implemented new rulings first had to be prepared; then concurrence had to be procured from all concerned parties (often those without any real interest in the matter); finally approval of numerous higher authorities was necessary for an order to appear in print for distribution to the field. The most difficult portion of this task was the gaining of "concurrence." Too many of those who had to agree were unfavorably prejudiced; some were ignorant; some knew the answer before they knew the question; too rare were those who were helpful and understanding. Nevertheless, without their permission, except in great emergencies, even the most minor changes could not be instituted.

Before the war there were almost no instructions relative to psychiatry in any military publication. The only exceptions were regulations dealing with the management and discharge of psychotic patients and those that were concerned with the physical standards of induction. Presumably the only function of the psychiatrist was to make diagnoses and dispose of patients as rapidly as possible. As a result, even after the war began, the neuropsychiatrist in the hospital was not allowed to treat patients until the War Department policy was changed and orders to do so were written and circulated. Nor could the nonspecialist doctor in the field learn the best way in which to manage psychiatric patients without specially prepared circulars or bulletins. However, each enabling "piece of paper" required an educational campaign by the personnel of the Neuropsychiatry Consultants Division concerning each point, often necessitating personal contact with every individual who had to concur or approve.

Beside the formulation and publication of policies,[22] a second function of

22 See Appendix A.

the Division was to maintain close contact with the field. Only in this way could it learn of the problems. Service Command consultants were the chief source of this information. In addition, three different members of the staff made trips to the European and four made trips to the Pacific Theaters of War. There were many inspections of installations in the United States.

From a very weak start, the Neuropsychiatry Consultants Division grew to a reasonably strong unit. Throughout the war, Maj. Gen. Norman T. Kirk, the Surgeon General, gave excellent leadership and support. His confidence in the Division never failed. Brig. Gen. Raymond Bliss, the Deputy Surgeon General, gave the same type of backing. Other strong supporters in the Office of the Surgeon General, in addition to the other professional consultants, were Brig. Gen. C. C. Hillman, the Chief of Professional Services, Col. Tracy Voorhees, a lawyer who was Chief of the Control Division,[23] and Dr. Eli Ginzberg, an economist with excellent psychiatric orientation who was Chief of Resources and Analysis Division. To the understanding and support of these men, wartime Army psychiatry owes much of its progress.

The civilian consultants to the Secretary of War, who were appointed in January, 1944, gave additional support to the Neuropsychiatry Consultants Division. Both as a group and as individuals they periodically gave advice on neuropsychiatric policies and practice. Three of these men represented the American Psychiatric Association: Dr. Edward A. Strecker of Philadelphia, Dr. Frederick Parsons of New York, and Dr. Arthur Ruggles of Providence. The other men were: Dr. Edwin G. Zabriskie, then president of the American Neurological Association, and Dr. Alan Gregg, Director of the Division of Medical Services of the Rockefeller Foundation. Their unfailing backing and assistance were of immense value. Other civilian consultants were appointed later. Mrs. Elizabeth H. Ross advised the Division with regard to psychiatric social work. When the clinical psychologists were moved from the jurisdiction of the Adjutant General, his group of psychiatric and psychologic advisers [24] became advisers to the Office of the Surgeon General.

Clinical psychologists. In World War I psychologists assisted with the examination [25] of the draftees. In some camps they also contributed toward

---

[23] The function of the Control Division was to increase the efficiency of the Medical Department and co-ordinate medical services with other sections of the War Department.

[24] The Adjutant General appointed a board of civilian consultants to serve in an advisory capacity. When the psychologists were transferred to the Medical Department, this board was continued as advisers to the Surgeon General. The chairman, Dr. Walter V. Bingham, was always very helpful. The other members of the board were Drs. Frank Fremont-Smith, Lawrence Kubie, Walter R. Miles, Miles Murphy, David Rapaport, Arthur H. Ruggles, Robert R. Sears, and F. L. Wells.

[25] *Memoirs of the National Academy of Science,* Vol. 15, ed. by Robert M. Yerkes, U.S. Government Printing Office, Washington, D.C., 1921, pp. 30-40. In the annual report of the Surgeon General, 1919, Vol. 2, p. 1075, there is a statement dated 9 November 1918 that "examining

the maintenance of morale.[26] A total personnel of 118 officers and approximately 250 enlisted men served as psychologists in the Sanitary Corps under the administration of the Surgeon General. Many of these worked with psychiatrists. After World War I the psychologists were transferred to the Office of the Adjutant General.

There was sufficient precedent, however, at the beginning of World War II to permit the commissioning of six clinical psychologists in the Sanitary Corps. They were assigned to psychiatric services in general hospitals. The plan was not developed further because of a lack of vacancies in this corps and the absence of authority to appoint them elsewhere. In the meantime the psychologists in induction-center examining teams remained under the jurisdiction of the Adjutant General. Although in civilian life experience had shown the importance of the clinical psychologist and his contribution to psychiatric practice, it was not until 1944 that further effort was made at War Department level toward increasing his service to Army psychiatry. In some hospitals enlisted men had worked as psychologists, although, except for the allocation of a military occupational specialty number (289) for them, there had been no official approval of their assignment.

Both the skill of the clinical psychologist and the shortage of neuropsychiatrists strengthened the effort to obtain this ancillary worker in all medical installations. In the spring of 1944, Dr. Walter Bingham helped establish a liaison between the Neuropsychiatry Consultants Division of the Office of the Surgeon General and the Office of the Adjutant General for the purpose of developing a plan to utilize the clinical psychologists in psychiatric work. Lieutenant Colonel (later Col.) Morton A. Seidenfeld,[27] the initial liaison officer, presented a plan to screen from the list of psychologists all those who were competent to serve as clinical psychologists. Only 130 such men were found among those who had been working under the Adjutant General. Consequently an allotment was requested from the War Department. Permission was granted for the commissioning as second lieutenants those enlisted men, who had previously been serving in many localities, who could qualify as clinical psychologists in hospitals.[28] A total of 244 such officers was located and commissioned.

Subsequently a 4-week course for training this group of workers was established in the Adjutant General's School. The school graduated enough officers

---

staffs had been organized in 33 stations. The total personnel included 97 officers and 424 enlisted men."

26 Copeland, Norman, *Psychology and the Soldier,* Military Service Publishing Company, Harrisburg, Pa., 1942, p. 2.

27 Seidenfeld, M. A., "The Clinical Psychological Program in the Army," *Bull. Menninger Clinic,* 8:145, Sept., 1944.

28 War Department Circular 270, 1 July 1944.

to assign one each not only to the general and regional hospitals to assist in the psychiatric program, but also to 5 of the consultation services in basic-training camps and to 29 correctional institutions.[29] The program was further implemented by the War Department technical bulletin [30] which described in detail the relationships and functions of the clinical psychologists.

A total of approximately 450 officers was assigned to clinical psychology, including those originally commissioned in the Sanitary Corps, those commissioned as a result of the special allotment and the training course, and certain others. Nearly 100 of these were assigned to hospitals overseas, and over 200 were assigned to general, station, and convalescent hospitals in this country. In September, 1945, the clinical psychologists were transferred from the Adjutant General's Department to the Medical Administrative Corps and became a branch of the Neuropsychiatry Consultants Division of the Office of the Surgeon General.[31]

The clinical psychologists proved their value to Army psychiatry. There were a few difficulties however: [32] some psychiatrists did not know how to use or to help them; occasionally the psychologist was a better trained man than his ranking psychiatrist; their commission in the Adjutant General's Department was a handicap because it did not identify them with medicine. Even after their transfer to the Medical Administrative Corps, they occasionally were assigned to nonpsychologic duties by pressed (or stupid) commanding officers. Unfortunately, many of them, like our young psychiatrists, were inadequately trained or inexperienced. But the net result was very much on the credit side; their contribution was great. It is to be hoped that the War Department does not discard the system as it did after World War I.[33]

Psychiatric social workers. It was far more difficult to procure and assign psychiatric social workers than psychologists who, from the first, had a military

---

[29] The status at the time of this assignment is well described by M. A. Seidenfeld, in "Clinical Psychology in Army Hospitals," *Psychological Bull.* 41:510-514, Oct., 1944.

[30] "Clinical Psychological Service in Army Hospitals," *War Department Technical Bulletin, Medical 115,* 15 November 1944; revised 21 November 1946.

[31] War Department Circular 264, 1 September 1945.

[32] One of our technical problems in the utilization of the clinical psychologists was the difficulty in the use of psychological tests. They were hard to acquire; they lacked standardization in application; many of our psychiatrists had no understanding of them; some of our psychologists attempted more than their qualifications warranted. Through the generosity of the Josiah Macy, Jr., Foundation and its medical director, Frank Fremont-Smith, a *Manual of Diagnostic Psychological Testing,* prepared by David Rapaport with the collaboration of Roy Schafer and Merton Gill, was printed and distributed to all clinical psychologists in the Army. It was available to all psychiatrists as well.

[33] The post-World War II cut in personnel, as it affected the Neuropsychiatry Consultants Division, did not permit the retention of officer psychologist personnel, but my successor, Col. John M. Caldwell, did obtain approval to have a psychologist in the office on a civilian status. In 1947, he was successful in obtaining four officers, including one in clinical psychology and one in psychiatric social work.

occupational specialty number which usually facilitated finding them.[34] Before the lamentably late establishment of a classification number for social workers, psychiatry lost such greatly needed personnel to other types of assignment within the Army. Finally, in October, 1943, all enlisted men with sufficient qualifications, who could be located, were given MOS 263 and assigned to social work. In 1944, the Women's Army Corps conducted a campaign to recruit social workers; those who were interested but lacked training were accepted as "psychiatric assistants."

In spite of these two actions, there were still not enough social workers. A War Department circular issued in July, 1944, called special attention to the great need for them.[35] For the remainder of the war, they appeared on the list of "critically needed specialists" which was published periodically. When finished with basic training or when declared "surplus" at a particular station, men qualified as such specialists were to be reported for assignment rather than given some other type of job.

Detailed plans were developed for in-service training courses in psychiatric social work for those who, in spite of only minimal training or experience, were pressed into service. Unfortunately, the course was not ready before the war ended, although informal training on the job was given in some 20 hospitals.

Equally critical was the inability to secure commissions for social workers; not until months after VJ-day was an occupational number for officers assigned to this specialty.[36] In the meantime, approximately 50 graduate psychiatric social workers were commissioned as clinical psychologists, chiefly because they were able to meet the requirements of personality-testing experience and in this way could obtain a commission. About 200 others received commissions in other corps after attendance at Officer Candidate School but were not assigned as social workers.

By August, 1945, there were 711 individuals with a military occupational specialty designation of psychiatric social worker; there were requisitions on hand at that time for an additional 201 persons who were not then available.[37]

---

[34] The early status is well described by Malcolm J. Farrell and E. H. Ross, in "Military Psychiatric Social Work," *Bull. Menninger Clinic,* 8:153-155, Sept., 1944. The nearest job classification to social work was "sociologist." The Army apparently did not know how to use social work except when provided by the American Red Cross. The first official recognition of this speciality in Army directives was AG 201.6, dated 18 Oct. 1943 (C-A-EZ-MB-A, 1 Nov. 1943).

[35] War Department Circular 295, 13 July 1944, described the importance and the method of assignment of such personnel. This and all other plans for psychiatric social work were made in consultation with Mrs. Elizabeth H. Ross, the official consultant from 1944 until 1946.

[36] *War Department Technical Manual, Officers' Classification, Commissioned and Warrant, TM 12-406,* February, 1946, p. 117, in which psychiatric social work (MAC) (3605) is defined and qualifications of the worker are described.

[37] Among the best descriptive papers on the psychiatric social work were: Lehman, A., "Case Work Goals in Military Social Work," *The Family,* 25:169-173, July, 1944; Greving, F. T., and

A War Department technical bulletin [38] outlined their functions in detail. They worked in hospitals, consultation services, disciplinary barracks, rehabilitation centers, redistribution centers. A request for their assignment to induction centers could not be filled because of the lack of sufficient personnel. During demobilization, social workers acted as personnel counselors in separation centers.

The American Red Cross recruited and supplied psychiatric social workers to hospitals and consultation services. They did extremely valuable work. Approximately 100 of these worked in medical installations. Their chief responsibility was to establish contacts outside the Army, usually for the purpose of obtaining from the people in his home community the social history of a soldier, which was necessary under certain circumstances.

Psychiatric nurses and psychiatric attendants. In many ways the problems concerned with the personnel of these two groups were similar. Despite the continued wartime efforts of the Nursing and Neuropsychiatry Consultants Divisions there was no way found to designate or mark the records of those nurses who had had special psychiatric training. Postgraduate courses in psychiatric nursing were given in every Service Command; nearly 600 women were so trained, but there was no way in which to show that training on the individual record card of those nurses. This was because of the inability to win other than Service Command recognition of the courses. In practice, this resulted in failure to secure the services of many of these nurses with such special training for the neuropsychiatric section of the hospital. They were often assigned to some other field of nursing.

The same situation prevailed for ward attendants. No organized or recognized educational work was ever instituted by the Army for these people. In almost every general hospital there were courses given continuously by a psychiatrist for the enlisted men who were assigned to psychiatric wards. Usually there was no opportunity to select these men; then, unfortunately, after they were trained, they were often lost to other assignments. After much persuasion a directive [39] was published in September, 1944, which allowed the modification of the specialty number of "medical technician" by placing NP after the number 409, on the records of attendants with psychiatric training and experience. After that, except under unusual circumstances, these persons could not be taken out of the type of work [40] for which they had qualified.

Rockmore, M. J., "Psychiatric Case Work as a Military Service," *Ment. Hyg.*, **29**:435-506, July, 1945; Segal, C., "Functional Aspects of Military Case Work," *Am. J. Orthopsychiat.*, **15**:597-606, Oct., 1945.

[38] *War Department Technical Bulletin, Medical 154*, June, 1945; revised and reprinted 4 December 1946.

[39] Army Service Forces Circular 310, 16 September 1944.

[40] War Department Circular 209, 13 July 1946, finally established the military occupational

Consultant system. For the medical organization of the American Expeditionary Forces of World War I, well-known specialists were chosen from civil life to serve as consultants in medicine, surgery, and neuropsychiatry. They proved of such value that there seems to have been no question as to their use in this war. Thus, early in 1942, specialty consultants were appointed to the European and the Southwest Pacific Theaters. However, the utilization of professional consultants for the vast Army in training in the United States had apparently received no consideration until suggested by Col. (later Brig. Gen.) Hugh Morgan. In the spring of 1942 he pointed out the desirability of a consultant plan for the zone of the interior. Colonel (later Brig. Gen.) Fred Rankin heartily indorsed this proposal. These two civilian physicians had been appointed as consultants to the Surgeon General, one in medicine and the other in surgery. Some 6 months after their appointment in July, 1942, Col. Roy D. Halloran became the Consultant in Neuropsychiatry to the Surgeon General. In spite of the formidable obstacles, Col. Morgan's initial suggestion resulted in the appointment of prominent civilians as consultants in internal medicine, surgery, and neuropsychiatry for assignment to the staffs of each of the nine Service Command surgeons. The first consultant was Lt. Col. (later Col.) Henry M. Thomas, an internist, who was appointed in July, 1942, and assigned to the Fourth Service Command.

Even though approved in Washington, the consultant plan was accepted reluctantly by medical personnel in some of the Service Commands.[41] A few saw no need for additional professional men. Some Service Command surgeons regarded the consultants as intruders. Initially, in the field (and always by Maj. Gen. David Grant, the Air Forces Surgeon), we consultants were classed as "inspectors," who in the Army rate dubious welcomes and often are feared.

Most of us civilians knew of this feeling in the field and on the part of the chief surgeons in the Service Commands. Colonel Bill Hart, surgeon in the Eighth Service Command had accepted his three consultants (Walter Bower in medicine, Brad Coley in surgery, and Frank Ebaugh in neuropsychiatry) with pleasure and, much to the envy of some of the rest of us, promoted them to the rank of full colonel in 6 months.

Before reporting for duty in the Fourth Service Command (Atlanta) in December, 1942 (as the second neuropsychiatric consultant to be appointed), I tried to find out about my boss, the Service Command Surgeon, Col. Sandford French. Each regular Army officer I would ask seemed noncommittal. One told

---

specialty "neuropsychiatric technician (SSN 1409)" pending revision of TM 12-427, 12 July 1944.

[41] It is of interest that no War Department directive appeared on the subject of the consultants until War Department Circular 140, 12 May 1945, which merely gave the Surgeon General authority to appoint consultants. Their functions were never outlined until plans were made for their postwar use as civilians in War Department Circular 101, 4 April 1946.

me briefly that he was "tough." This silence gave me some qualms. I knew psychiatry was going to have an uphill road at best. But from the hour of my arrival throughout the year that I remained, I was wholeheartedly accepted. I found that Sandy French was "tough" and plain spoken, but with no reservations apparent in his acceptance of me and my specialty. Perhaps it was because on my first official call to his home, we found a mutual interest in our stamp-collecting hobby. Instead of leaving at the end of the prescribed 15-minute call, I stayed 4 hours going over his philatelic "treasures." We started our association with much in common, even if it wasn't psychiatry. For the duration of that assignment, he backed me up in psychiatry. With his authority I mimeographed a bulletin on treatment (the first, I believe, in the Army) to send to each of the psychiatrists in the Service Command; a bulletin on journal clubs; a bulletin on in-service training in psychiatry. He gave me a free hand and supported my decisions about methods, reports, personnel. Never in that year, on those days when we were both in the office, did Sandy fail to come in to say hello each morning. His "three musketeers" (Hal Thomas in medicine, Arnold Griswold in surgery, and myself) became his close professional advisers.

The consultant system became probably the most potent force in the Medical Department in developing and maintaining the high standard of professional medicine. Policies and directives issuing from the consultants in the Office of the Surgeon General were thus implemented in the field. They were interpreted and their use was checked by the respective consultants in the Service Commands and the theaters. These men traveled almost continuously from one camp to the next, throughout their areas, for the purpose of consulting, counseling, teaching, and making recommendations with regard to the professional work in every type of medical installation. The Service Command consultants [42] in turn served the consultants to the Surgeon General by sending in, through

---

[42] Neuropsychiatric Service Command Consultants:

I	Maj. (later Col.) Wilfred Bloomberg	29 June 43	21 August 45
	Col. Lloyd J. Thompson	4 September 45	21 December 45
	Col. Wilfred Bloomberg	17 December 45	30 April 46
II	Lt. Col. (later Col.) Douglas A. Thom	25 March 43	31 January 46
III	Lt. Col. (later Col.) Henry W. Brosin	15 April 44	21 December 45
IV	Lt. Col. W. C. Menninger	25 November 42	10 December 43
	Lt. Col. (later Col.) Paul Schroeder	7 February 44	1 November 45
V	Maj. (later Lt. Col.) William H. Dunn	22 August 44	15 February 46
VI	Col. William J. Bleckwenn	5 August 44	12 December 45
VII	Maj. Garland C. Pace	1 January 43	25 September 43
	Lt. Col. (later Col.) Clarke Barnacle	10 June 43	10 August 45
	Lt. Col. (later Col.) John Greist	12 June 45	15 February 46
VIII	Lt. Col. (later Col.) Franklin G. Ebaugh	27 August 42	28 May 45
	Lt. Col. Perry Talkington	20 July 45	20 September 45
IX	Lt. Col. (later Col.) Lauren H. Smith	16 October 43	15 December 45

official channels as well as by informal reports, their findings and recommendations from the field.[43] Of particular help were the conferences of all the Service Command consultants held in the Office of the Surgeon General.

When difficulties occurred requiring a change in current policy or adoption of a new policy, it was the consultants in the field who provided the Surgeon General's consultants with the data and the evidence to show this need. They visited not only hospitals but induction centers, rehabilitation centers, redistribution centers, ports of debarkation and embarkation, separation centers, and disciplinary barracks—in short, every installation in which psychiatry functioned.

The consultants [44] in the theaters had a similar relation to the theater surgeon as did the Service Command consultants to the Surgeon General.[45] They, too, visited hospitals and counseled with the psychiatrists. In addition they had considerable staff work, i.e., the adaptation and dissemination of policy within their area of jurisdiction. It was they who established the psychiatric hospitals, stimulated and planned on-the-job psychiatric education, determined the local evacuation policy, supervised and helped develop the front-line treatment methods, and backed up the Army [46] and division psychiatrists.

Most of this group of consultants were eminently successful; they func-

---

[43] Excellent descriptions of the neuropsychiatric consultant's job were given by F. G. Ebaugh, in "Major Psychiatric Considerations in the Service Command," *Am. J. Psychiat.*, 100:28-33, July, 1943, and by L. H. Smith, in "Treatment Activities in War Psychiatry," *Am. J. Psychiat.*, 101:303-309, Nov., 1944.

[44] Consultants:

Southwest Pacific	Lt. Col. (later Col.) S. Alan Challman	25 May	42	12 June	45
	Col. Franklin G. Ebaugh	12 June	45	1 December	45
	Lt. Col. Clarke Barnacle	10 October	45	23 January	46
	Maj. (later Lt. Col.) Ivan C. Berlien	26 September	45	19 January	46
European Theater	Lt. Col. (later Col.) Lloyd J. Thompson	12 August	42	12 August	45
	Lt. Col. (later Col.) Joseph Skobba	14 August	45	22 December	45
Mediterranean	Maj. (later Lt. Col.) Frederick Hanson	June	43	July	45
South Pacific	Lt. Col. (later Col.) M. Ralph Kaufman	26 October	43	20 August	44
	Lt. Col. (later Col.) Edward G. Billings	2 November	43	7 June	45
Pacific Ocean Area	Lt. Col. (later Col.) M. Ralph Kaufman	20 August	44	1 June	45
China-India	Maj. (later Lt. Col.) R. S. Mays	26 January	45	31 October	45
Middle East	Maj. John M. Flumerfelt	29 December	44	11 July	45

[45] Colonel L. J. Thompson described the organization of neuropsychiatry which he supervised in the European Theater. See "Neuropsychiatry in the European Theater of Operations," *New England J. Med.*, 235:7-11, July 4, 1946.

[46] Each combat Army had a neuropsychiatric consultant, shown in the table of organization as "assistant medical consultant," who was limited in rank to a lieutenant colonel, although the medical and surgical consultants could be—and generally were—colonels. The consultants and their period of assignment were:

First Army—Lt. Col. (later Col.) William Srodes	27 December	43	14 December	45
Third Army—Lt. Col. Perry C. Talkington	23 January	44	1 July	45
Fourth Army—Lt. Col. (later Col.) Joseph Skobba	20 August	44	28 September	44
Maj. (later Lt. Col.) Manfred Guttmacher	6 August	45	2 November	45

tioned as a superior team, carrying high standards of psychiatric practice to every Army installation in the United States and in every theater.

Division psychiatrists. In World War I, each combat division was provided with a division psychiatrist.[47] The table of organization of a division remained the same from 1918 until 1940.[48] Consequently, until just prior to World War II, psychiatrists were a part of each division medical staff, at least on paper. In 1940, the entire division organization was revamped and the psychiatrist was dropped "on the grounds that the consultants (referring to all medical specialists) should initially be held under Army control in order that they may be employed most economically." [49] It was not until the early fall of 1943 that sufficient pressure was brought to bear to again include the psychiatrist in the medical staff of each combat division.[50] There were 91 divisions, and, with one exception, a psychiatrist was assigned to each. Shortly after the appointment of the first group, they were brought to Walter Reed Hospital for an initial orientation conference in December, 1943.

While the division was in training, it was the function of the psychiatrist to screen out the men who were psychological misfits and to concern himself with the psychiatric aspects of training methods and morale. Many of these psychiatrists developed ingenious methods of evaluating the mental health and the leadership of each organization within the division. They used indices based on the rate of AWOL, of company punishment, of sick call, of NP hospital admissions. Another of their responsibilities was the indoctrination of all the medical officers with first-aid psychiatry. In combat, they directed the treat-

---

Fifth Army—Maj. Calvin Drayer	21 July	44	27 August	45
Sixth Army—Lt. Col. (later Col.) M. Ralph Kaufman	1 June	45	28 September	45
Seventh Army—Maj. (later Lt. Col.) Alfred O. Ludwig	21 July	44	10 July	45
Eighth Army—Maj. (later Lt. Col.) Josiah T. Showalter	17 June	44	1 October	45
Ninth Army—Lt. Col. (later Col.) Roscoe Cavell	20 May	44	18 September	45
Tenth Army—Lt. Col. Oscar Markey	10 August	44	15 October	45
Fifteenth Army—Lt. Col. (later Col.) Joseph Skobba	28 September 44		12 August	45

The job of the Army psychiatrist was well described by A. O. Ludwig, "Psychiatry at Army Level," in *Combat Psychiatry Among American Ground Forces in the Mediterranean Area,* ed. by F. R. Hanson. (To be published.)

[47] "Division, Corps, and Army Neuropsychiatric Consultants," in *The Medical Department of the United States Army in the World War,* Vol. X, War Department, U.S. Government Printing Office, Washington, D. C., 1929, pp. 303-324.

[48] The psychiatrist was included in *T/O 8-11 Medical Regiment* on 4 January 1939; it was omitted in the next edition containing the Division Surgeon's Office, *T/O 8-21, Medical Regiment,* dated 1 November 1940.

[49] Letter from Office of the Surgeon General dated 3 October 1940 to the Adjutant General, subject, "Medical Section, Headquarters, Field Army (T/O 200-1)."

[50] War Department Circular 290, 9 November 1943. One of our gratifying postwar accomplishments was the outline of the functions of the division psychiatrists in the *Medical Field Manual, FM 8-10,* Change 1, 28 June 1946.

ment of psychiatric casualties, working tirelessly in the clearing company of the division; they supervised psychotherapy under sedation, and the screening for the return to duty or evacuation to the rear of psychiatric casualties. These psychiatrists, assisted only by the few other psychiatrists in each Army, namely, those from evacuation hospitals, made the remarkable record of returning to combat between 55 and 65 per cent of the psychiatric casualties. Rarely did any of them have a chance to do much real psychotherapy, for they had either too many patients (in heavy fighting) or essentially none.

The division psychiatrist had certain handicaps. At the time his job was created, he was not given any means of transportation and so was often unable to visit all areas within his division. He was not provided with any official table of equipment so that he was without specified tentage or professional material. In most cases all these were acquired, in only a limited amount, by various methods: persuasion, pleading, inveigling, finagling. Special credit should go to most division surgeons for the aid they gave to the psychiatrist in the performance of his duties under such circumstances. In a few cases an unsympathetic division surgeon prevented the psychiatrist from passing on his needs, findings, and recommendations to headquarters. Despite all these difficulties, the average division psychiatrist became a key man.[51] His appointment was unquestionably one of psychiatry's most strategic and profitable moves.[52]

He was frequently called upon to advise or assist the battalion surgeon. A discussion of psychiatry in the combat division would be incomplete without paying full credit to the man who was in the most dangerous job in the medical department—the battalion surgeon. As Sobel described him, he had to be "a combination of automechanic, chaplain, platoon leader, engineer, military police and doctor." [53] In combat he was under fire continuously, and it was his function to treat and if necessary evacuate the casualties occurring in his battalion. Of necessity, although not a psychiatrist, he had a large psychiatric practice. In rest periods and in combat, 40 to 75 per cent of his patients presented themselves for psychological problems of one kind or another. His evacuation policy varied with many factors: the urgency of the military needs

[51] Recently two division commanders of World War II have paid high tribute to their psychiatrists: Maj. Gen. Louis A. Craig in an address to the Association of Military Surgeons in Detroit, October 9, 1946, and Maj. Gen. W. S. Paul in a presentation to the meeting of the Medical Consultants in World War II, in Washington, D.C., October 18, 1946. An excellent description of the experience of a division psychiatrist is that of Maj. Albert J. Glass, 85th Infantry Division, "Psychiatry at the Division Level," in Combat Psychiatry Among American Ground Forces in the Mediterranean Area, ed. by F. R. Hanson. (To be published.)

[52] Several divisions of Marines followed the Army procedure and appointed division psychiatrists. An excellent description of a Marine psychiatrist and his experiences in the campaign in Okinawa was given by P. Solomon, in "Incidence of Combat Fatigue," Arch. Neurol. & Psychiat., 57:332-341, Mar., 1947.

[53] Sobel, R., "The Battalion Surgeon as Psychiatrist," in Combat Psychiatry Among American Ground Forces in the Mediterranean Area, ed. by F. R. Hanson. (To be published.)

at the moment, the bias which he brought to the problem, the pressure under which he worked, the criticisms or pressures to which he was subjected from his superiors, and his own experience with the problem.[54] For better or for worse he was the most important medical officer in the prevention and treatment of psychiatric disorders occurring in combat.

Mental Hygiene Consultation Services. Reference has previously been made to the high incidence of psychiatric casualties in the basic-training camps. This stimulated the inauguration of outpatient psychiatric clinics, officially known as the consultation services.[55] Every basic-training camp of both the Army Ground Forces and the Army Service Forces had one,[56] making a total, at one time of 36 units.

They were also organized, late in 1943, in some of the larger Army Air Forces Training centers. Nearly all of these in the Air Forces were disbanded after a few months on the erroneous assumption that they were of little value and possibly called the attention of the trainees to mental ill health. Their elimination was decried by all military psychiatrists, including the consultant in the Air Forces Surgeon's Office.[57]

The consultation services were established primarily to counsel with the individual soldiers while they remained on duty, and to provide therapy for minor maladjustments. Statistics indicate that, at one time or another, between 3 and 7 per cent of all trainees were referred to the consultation service, from the dispensaries, the Provost Marshal, the Judge Advocate, and in many, many instances directly from the company commander. Of all the patients seen, approximately only 7 per cent were sent on to the hospital; about 15 to 25 per cent were recommended for discharge. The consultation service was thus capable of providing the needed psychiatric help in from 60 to 75 per cent of the cases.[58] These units did one of the best, if not the best, job of individual

---

54 From *Medical Report on Morale and Psychiatry,* No. 17, Office of the Surgeon General, 25 August 1945, pp. 39-40. Reprinted: Bartemeier, L. H.; Kubie, L. S.; Menninger, K. A.; Romano, J.; and Whitehorn, J. C., "Combat Exhaustion," *J. Nerv. & Ment. Dis.,* 104:358-389, Oct., 1946; 489-525, Nov., 1946.
55 Several papers have appeared which describe these installations. Among the most detailed are those by H. L. Freedman, "The Unique Structure and Function of the Mental Hygiene Unit in the Army," *Ment. Hyg.,* 27:608-653, Oct., 1943; "The Mental Hygiene Unit Approach to Reconditioning Neuropsychiatric Casualties," *Men. Hyg.,* 29:269-302, Apr., 1945.
56 The history of these units, prepared for the official Medical Department historical files, has been published. Guttmacher, M. S., "Army Consultation Services (Mental Hygiene Services)," *Am. J. Psychiat.,* 102:735-748, May, 1946.
57 Colonel John Murray stated that the units were rendered useless by the surgeon of the Air Forces Training Command who never accepted the adjustment difficulties of the trainee as medical problems. "Accomplishments of Psychiatry in the Army Air Forces," *Am. J. Psychiat.,* 103:594-599, Mar., 1947.
58 An analysis of the disposition of 12,000 cases seen in one center showed about 4,800 with minor disorders and 2,000 with difficulties that indicated duty should be limited to the United States. Nine hundred were sent to the hospital; 3,200 were recommended for discharge because of "inaptness or lack of adaptability." Roback, H. N., "The Emotionally Unfit Soldier. Psychiatric

psychotherapy of any psychiatric group in the Army,[59] and were an important dike against the loss of man power.

Before long, however, experience broadened the scope of the consultation service to include responsibility for the mental health of the entire training center.[60] Part of the work of its psychiatrist included indoctrination of the dispensary surgeons with knowledge of the psychological factors in illness. On matters which concerned the mental health of individuals or units, the psychiatrist contacted, individually and collectively, company commanders and instructors in visits to company areas, training maneuvers, bivouacs, rifle ranges. He presented the series of three mental hygiene lectures prescribed by the War Department [61] to each new class of trainees. He was called repeatedly in court-martial cases. A War Department directive [62] instructed the commanding generals to seek his advice on all matters pertaining to the mental health of the troops in training.[63] Fortunately the Mental Hygiene Consultation Service has been continued in the postwar Army.[64]

A concluding word about the people who did the job. Psychiatrists have the reputation of disagreeing, sometimes rather widely, among themselves. In civilian life they have tended to be medical isolationists who sometimes have been looked upon with skepticism. In the prewar Army, they were known as "nutcrackers" or "nutpickers." However, toward those in wartime service these attitudes and tendencies were changed. Among them there was a remarkable spirit of unity, regardless of their differing "schools of thought." Psychiatrists became an integral part of the medical service to the Army. They merited and usually received the confidence of their associates, whether medical or line officers. The ubiquitous nicknames disappeared.

Study of 12,000 Soldiers in an Infantry Replacement Training Center," *J. Nerv. & Ment. Dis.*, 104:526-532, Nov., 1946.

[59] The treatment program in the unit at Drew Field, Fla., is well described in much detail by B. M. Beck, in collaboration with L. L. Robbins, "Short Term Therapy in an Authoritative Setting," Family Service Assn. of America, New York. See also the description of L. L. Robbins, "The Mental Hygiene Unit: A Practical Approach to the Utilization of the Mild Psychoneurotic in the Armed Forces," *Military Neuropsychiatry,* Proceedings of Assn. for Research in Nerv. and Ment. Dis., New York, 1944, The Williams & Wilkins Company, Baltimore, 1946, pp. 78-86. Cruvant described his experience with psychotherapy in two mental hygiene units. Cruvant, B. A., "Pragmatic Psychotherapy in Military Training Centers, *Am. J. Psychiat.*, 103:622-629, Mar., 1947.

[60] *War Department Technical Bulletin, Medical 156,* June, 1945, on Consultation Service; revised and reissued 4 December 1946.

[61] War Department Circular 48, 3 February 1944.

[62] War Department Circular 81, 13 March 1945.

[63] There were many extremely interesting aspects developed in this assignment: Lt. Col. R. R. Cohen's locally printed "Mack and Mike," a booklet for the new recruit; Maj. Sam H. Kraines' "Advisor System" (*Ment. Hyg.*, 27:592-607, Oct., 1943) using trained noncommissioned officers in each training company; Maj. Bernard Cruvant's group training; Maj. Julius Schreiber's camp newspaper column, and many other "specialties."

[64] It is described and prescribed in War Department Circular 250, 1 August 1946, for all training centers.

Along with their associates—the psychologists, social workers, psychiatric nurses, technicians—they developed a remarkable team. Their service was characterized by devotion, hard work, and good judgment. Psychiatric personnel working in hospitals, clearing companies, induction centers, or disciplinary barracks were outspoken in their confidence in and appreciation of the counsel and support of the theater and Service Command neuropsychiatric consultants and their representatives in higher headquarters. This same confidence was also manifested by those in the field toward the Neuropsychiatry Division in the Office of the Surgeon General. The frequent circulars and bulletins dealing with the subject were tangible evidence to them that the Surgeon General was supporting them and their efforts. The entire group became a superb team in which the great majority were keen to practice the best possible type of psychiatry, neurology, social work, and psychology.

In my personal reminiscences three special points will stand out: first, the phenomenal harmony and intense industry of my associates in the Division in the Office of the Surgeon General; second, the earnest thought, unswerving loyalty, and devotion of the consultants; and third, the many very warm and almost eager receptions given me by psychiatrists and neurologists in their workshops—whether a clearing company on the European front, a station hospital in Saipan, a general hospital in Walla Walla, an airfield in Alabama, or an induction center in Mississippi—wherever I went.

18

DIAGNOSTIC LABELS

MANY PHYSICIANS and laymen have considered as both strange and confusing the terms of description and diagnosis which psychiatrists use.[1] The unfamiliarity of the psychiatric vocabulary has been to blame for some of the misunderstanding about mental illness. The technical language is probably no more complicated than that of any other medical specialty such as orthopedics or dermatology. Few people know that metatarsalgia is a callus on the ball of the foot; nor do they know that angioneurotic edema is a special variation of hives. However, in psychiatry even the common disorders do not have a layman's term unless one uses such vagaries as "nervous breakdown" or "nervous" or "crazy." At the same time, a greater interest in and the extensive applicability of psychiatric principles have exposed more people to its terminology. "Paranoia," "rationalization," "complex," "neurotic" have become a part of the everyday language of many laymen. Unfortunately, these terms are too often used without a realization of their scientific significance.

The current science of psychiatry differs somewhat from that of other medical specialties. In the practice of medicine, the patient and the doctor look for some physical or toxic or infectious or mechanical cause for the ailment, and often they find it. In psychiatry, on the other hand, the great majority of personality disorders are not due to some variation in the body structure or bacterial invasion or chemical alteration. A lack of agreement as to causes has resulted in a confusion in diagnostic terms.

There are some psychiatrists, described as "organically minded," who believe that many types of mental illness do have a physical or chemical cause. There are others who are willing to admit that we do not know those physical or chemical causes, but that some time our techniques will be sufficiently refined to demonstrate them. A minority of psychiatrists of an older vintage believe that heredity is the major causative factor in mental illness. There has always

---

[1] Strecker and Appel were very outspoken: "Our psychiatric terminology is anachronistic, esoteric, difficult, irrational and forbidding. It confuses our medical confreres, creates resistance and isolates our understanding and help which should be available to medical colleagues." Strecker, E. A., and Appel, K. E., *Psychiatry in Modern Warfare,* The Macmillan Company, New York, 1945, p. 51.

been a majority who regard mental disease in purely a descriptive light; they accept the clinical picture as they see it and describe it in terms of the symptoms. In contrast to these, there is an increasing number of psychiatrists, described as "dynamically oriented," who analyze the case on the basis of defective or misdirected psychological forces within the personality. This latter group includes, in general, the psychoanalytic school but also many others, and constitutes a large number of the leaders in the profession.

The psychodynamic point of view does not deny physical or chemical changes. Many mental illnesses are caused by such physical changes as syphilis, thickening of the blood vessels, and infections. On the other hand, for the large number of neuroses and many psychoses in which there are no physical changes, a dynamic analysis has proved to be far more helpful in understanding and therefore treating the patient than any other approach.

The inevitable result of the basic differences in these various "schools" over the last 30 years has been the description, and consequently the labeling of, mental illnesses according to their orientation. For this reason, it has been very difficult to establish a generally accepted and "standard" nomenclature of diagnosis for many types of personality disorders.

One can start a lively argument among a group of experienced psychiatrists by asking for a differentiation and definition of "mental disorders," "mental disease," "mental illness," "mental defects," "character disorders," and "personality disorders." No point better illustrates the lack of precision in psychiatric concepts than the usage of the dual set of terms "psychoneurosis" and "neurosis" to refer to the same group of reactions. Except for their original historical differentiation in meaning, there is no legitimate basis for the continued use of both of these terms. The term "psychoneurosis" is more widely used professionally and became better known because it was the word prescribed in the standard nomenclature. The term "neurosis," probably because it has the convenience of being shorter and much easier to pronounce, is more frequently used in colloquial discussions.

As psychiatric knowledge has increased, its terminology has been changed many times in the last 5 decades. Some of the terms commonly used at the beginning of this century, such as "puerperal insanity," "cyclic insanity," and others, have entirely disappeared. Thoughtful committees have worked on the problem from time to time. Nevertheless, it would be the unusual psychiatrist who would express complete satisfaction with any current nomenclature.

The major portion of psychiatric interest for many years was invested in the psychotic patient, the severity of whose illness demanded attention. Therefore, the diagnostic terms for the various psychoses are subject to less controversy. Fewer doctors and facilities were available either for the treatment or study of the many less severe types of mental illness, including a host which disguise themselves in physical symptoms. Only comparatively recently have certain responses become identified as specific neuroses. So that, in the most widely accepted *Standard Classified Nomenclature of Disease,* 1942 edition, which was compiled by a joint committee of the American Psychiatric Association and the American Neurological Association, there are 66 different categories defined as psychoses and only 22 as nonpsychotic disorders.

This recently revised nomenclature was most unsatisfactory: it was a conglomerate of terms based on a mixture of anatomical, psychological, historical, and pathological concepts; it confused, was misunderstood, and often was misused by the medical profession; it continued the lack of unity in psychiatric thought; it gave meager opportunity to "label" the many types of minor personality disorders; it carried on the psychiatry of the "custodial care" era of psychiatric treatment.

For some time the deficiencies in the terminology of psychiatric illness have been felt, particularly in the noninstitutional practice of psychiatry. Many of the progressive civilian clinics and hospitals treating nonpsychotic patients use their own modifications of the standard nomenclature, often adding diagnostic terms of their own choice. This has resulted in a still wider variation in the designations for various types of neuroses and behavior disorders.

Because of special problems encountered in the practice of psychiatry in the military setting, the *Standard Classified Nomenclature* proved to be totally inadequate. Doctors taken into the Army from every part of the country, representing various schools of thought, brought with them greatly differing concepts of psychiatric syndromes. The patient who was diagnosed in one way at one installation might be differently classified when transferred to another hospital. There were occasions when a patient would have oriented himself to one psychiatrist's interpretation of his diagnosis only to be given a new and perhaps conflicting explanation by the next physician to whom he was referred. Statistics concerning the incidence of the different types of mental disorders seen in the various Army installations—induction centers, outpatient clinics, hospitals—had little value because the use of the terms was not sufficiently standardized. This invalidated an important measuring stick of effectiveness or harmfulness of policies and practices. The lack of certain accurate statistical information was a serious handicap to an organization which had to use training methods and policies not previously tested in such large and frequently changing groups.

Especially serious were the differing, and often mistaken, interpretations of the term "psychoneurosis." The physical standards for admission to the Army (MR 1-9) initially stated that an inductee with a psychoneurosis of any degree was not to be accepted. This led to the erroneous deduction that if a soldier developed an incapacity which received this diagnosis, he was therefore not suitable to remain in the Army. Consequently, during at least the first 2 years of the war, it was customary to discharge most individuals so diagnosed. Unfortunately, Army directives [2] aided and abetted this state of affairs. In the minds of the writers of those directives, "psychoneurosis" was apparently confused with "psychosis," for all psychiatric illnesses were to be treated as if alike in degree of incapacitation. Thus one directive read, "There is no . . . classification (for assignment) for patients with psychiatric disorders." Another sounded ominous in the statement that, "Greater care will be taken . . . to prevent all individuals predisposed to or suffering from psychoneurosis . . . or having a proven history of such from entering military service."

The attitude, both official and unofficial, toward this medical diagnosis resulted in general confusion and the use of subtleties. If a psychiatrist felt that a patient, even though he might have a neurotic reaction, was capable of returning to duty, he used the more benign diagnosis of "simple adult maladjustment." Only thus could the discharge of a neurotic, though still potentially effective, soldier be avoided. Even a letter from the Office of the Surgeon General which specifically stated that, "A man will not be separated from the service merely because he has or has had a psychoneurosis or similar psychiatric disorder," [3] did not change the established procedure. Only after continuing effort on the part of the Neuropsychiatry Consultants Division was this unfortunate situation changed officially by a War Department circular [4] in which it was stated that a diagnosis of "psychoneurosis" was not necessarily a basis for discharge.

Early in the war misuse as well as misunderstanding of psychiatric diagnoses was a problem of considerable magnitude. After a man entered the service he could be discharged only by means of a medical diagnosis except in those comparatively few cases of misbehavior where an administrative discharge could be given. Men who were "temperamentally unqualified for service" were referred to the medical officer for disposition. The diagnosis commonly given to such patients was "psychoneurosis." Because of Army rulings their discharge then became automatic.

The Army system of disposition also placed various types and severities of disorder in a single category. There was no way to distinguish the mild from the severe or the truly justified from the propitious use of the diagnosis. When a variation was specified it was ignored by commanding officers, the public, even by the soldier himself. "Psychoneurosis" was attached to anything from a transient emotional upset to a severe hysterical paralysis.

Men discharged for this type of psychiatric disability became so numerous

---

[2] See also Chap. 8, and section on disposition of the noneffective soldier in Chap. 3.
[3] Surgeon General's Letter 194, 3 December 1943.
[4] War Department Circular 81, 13 March 1945.

that "psychoneurosis" became a household word. Familiarity did not, however, destigmatize its application. Its confusion with psychosis led to its slang designation of "psycho." As a result, individuals thus diagnosed were looked upon with suspicion by their associates in the Army and by their friends in civilian life.

The matter became so serious that in September, 1944, the Deputy Chief of Staff requested the Assistant Chief of Staff, G-1, to study the entire problem of "psychoneurosis." The resulting report stated:

If the War Department builds up a clinical record and a diagnosis that a soldier is a psychoneurotic it will probably impair the individual's future civilian usefulness and may greatly increase the number of men dependent upon government disability allowance. In many of these cases the individual became a psychoneurotic because he was unable to adjust himself to his position in the Army. Many of these individuals will have no difficulty in returning to their former civilian environment and will be normal in every respect in continuing a way of life to which they were accustomed and adjusted prior to their induction in the Army. If they are labeled as psychoneurotic their former employers will become convinced that they cannot readjust themselves to their previous civilian environment. It is understood that the Navy is now diagnosing these cases as "No Disease. Temperamentally unqualified for Naval service." It is suggested that the Army may well use a similar diagnosis.[5, 6]

The implication in this memorandum was that the Army should do away with the term "psychoneurosis." It almost implied doing away with the entity of neurotic illness, a suggestion that had been made verbally on several occasions by individuals high in the War Department. The Surgeon General answered the memorandum very boldly with the pertinent remarks that any stigma attached to this diagnosis would carry over to any other word used in its place and that the solution should be through education rather than through evasive terminology.

When *do* neurotic symptoms justify a diagnosis of psychoneurosis? This question recurred many times while we were working on our nomenclature. The answer we finally gave to this question was in terms of incapacity: When the symptoms prevented the individual from functioning in his niche, then he received such a diagnosis. This was technically accurate but not satisfactory, because it could never take into account the amount of precipitating stress nor the individual's attitude toward his symptoms. These two factors largely determined whether or not he was able to carry on in spite of neurotic symptoms. Thus, one person would present a resigned, defeatist attitude and give up; an-

---

[5] WDGAP (11 October 1944) Memorandum for the Deputy Chief of Staff. Subject: "Psychoneurotics."

[6] The Navy had a very practical method of discharge. It gave a man a period of trial of 4 to 6 weeks in a boot camp. If he was unable to adjust he could be discharged administratively: "No disease. Temperamentally unqualified for Naval service."

other, with the same clinical picture, would keep plugging. The real answer to the question will evolve only as a result of further psychiatric knowledge and experience.

Even at present there is a strong belief that we should forego any attempt to consider behavior in terms of a clearly defined end point—as a sharply delimited and, therefore, circumscribed entity—health or disease. Rather, it is the growing practice to regard all qualitative and quantitative deviations from "normal" behavior as "reactions" [7]—responses of the total personality to psychological, chemical, and physical forces within and without that personality. This point of view was reflected in the revision of the Army nomenclature. The terms "psychoneurosis" or "psychosis" were dropped; all of the types of psychiatric illness were described as "reactions," except pronounced personality types (schizoid, antisocial, paranoid, etc.). This nomenclature, however, did not and does not yet solve the problem of what to label the minor transient reactions of "normal" persons, including some of those we now regard as neurotic.

Aside from the lack of definition of specific neuroses and the lack of standardization in the use of psychiatric diagnoses, another deficiency in the *Standard Classified Nomenclature* was the lack of a successor to the misnomer "shell shock." The term was coined originally on the assumption that the shell concussion produced changes in the nervous system which resulted in more or less permanent psychologic symptoms. Although during World War I there had been ample evidence to question the presence of any physiological injury, the term remained in occasional use in the early part of World War II. Another diagnosis had to be found to apply to the psychiatric casualty in the front lines.

Everyone in the Army was aware of the effect of stress on the individual, which became evident in various neurotic responses. Many colloquial labels were coined to describe them: "gangplank fever," "shipboard jitters," "flak happy," "reple-deple exhaustion," "war weary." Similar but more severe neurotic responses developed in combat. Combat casualties who received immediate treatment either recovered or developed into the classical neuroses. The need arose for a label which could be used to identify that temporary state. In October, 1943, a Surgeon General's letter [8] directed the employment of the nonspecific diagnosis of "exhaustion" on the emergency medical tag worn by the patient en route from the clearing station to the hospital. There the case would be rediagnosed and the proper term recorded on the field medical record. Later

---

[7] This idea is not new. Doctor Adolf Meyer proposed all disorders should be regarded as reactions many years ago, but his terminology of the "ergasias" was never widely understood or accepted.

[8] Surgeon General's Letter 176, October, 1943.

in the war the Army officially adopted the term "combat exhaustion" for temporary diagnostic purposes.

In the Navy [9] the official diagnoses of "combat fatigue" [10] or "operational fatigue" were mandatory for neurotic illness which developed on duty overseas. By the time the patient was returned to the United States, the illness usually developed into one of the typical neurotic entities and then was so diagnosed. The Air Forces used the diagnosis "operational fatigue" [11] similarly.

There were many advantages as well as disadvantages in the use of such temporary diagnoses. They were convenient and reasonably appropriate descriptions of the short-lived emotional upheavals for which no term, needed in civilian as well as in military life, had been chosen. Their use was a theoretical protection of a man's self-respect by inferring that his problem was one primarily of fatigue. In the same way they saved the patient from varying degrees of stigmatization in the eyes of his associates. Probably the public had more sympathy for the man whose ailment was believed to have been incurred in combat, as specified by such a diagnosis. The provisional identification of the illness prevented a possibly erroneous permanent record; it also connoted a temporary and potentially reversible condition.

Among the disadvantages of such unscientific diagnoses was the fact that they represented euphemisms which, if so intended, fooled few people. Combat psychiatrists uniformly testified to the fact that their patients knew what the problem was, regardless of what it was called. There was a regrettable tendency for nonpsychiatric physicians to use these terms loosely and widely. Such diagnoses placed emphasis on the fatigue factor, which good authorities stated existed in unadulterated form in not more than 3 per cent of the cases. In the overwhelming majority the fundamental difficulty was psychological. This led to a misinterpretation of the real cause of the illness and gave the uninformed or nonpsychiatric physician the impression that rest was sufficient treatment.

Moreover, the use of the diagnosis "operational fatigue" led to official difficulties in the Air Forces. According to an Air Forces ruling, personnel suf-

---

[9] BuMed News Letter, Navy Department, 4:1-2, Aug. 18, 1944. See also the discussion of the differential criteria, as given by G. N. Raines and L. C. Kolb, in "Combat Fatigue and War Neurosis," *U.S. Naval M. Bull.*, 41:923-936, 1299-1309, July and Sept., 1943.

[10] In the Navy "war neurosis" was first used; this was changed to "combat fatigue." When the patient recovered he was discharged, "No disease." "Though the labels changed, the problems remained the same." Owen, J. W.; Hughes, J.; Saul, L. J.; and Bailey, P., "Neuropsychiatric Rehabilitation," *U.S. Naval M. Bull.*, supplement to Mar., 1946, pp. 322-331.

[11] The Air Forces psychiatrists held several conferences to determine and define this term, choosing it chiefly to indicate the initial ego (conscious) factors involved rather than unconscious conflicts. The subject has been thoughtfully presented by Lt. Col. John M. Murray, Consultant in Neuropsychiatry in the Office of the Air Forces Surgeon, in "Psychiatric Evaluation of Those Returning from Combat," *J.A.M.A..* 125:148-150. Sept. 16, 1944.

fering from "operational fatigue" could receive flight pay while hospitalized, in the same way as personnel who were physically injured during flight operations. If, however, the diagnosis was "psychoneurosis," they were not eligible to receive flight pay on the assumption that this illness was not the result of accident in the line of flight duty.

In the identification of mental disorders, numerous other problems developed. The terms "constitutional psychopathic inferior" and "psychopathic personality" had become general wastebaskets for every type of misbehavior. The term "simple adult maladjustment" had been used similarly to apply to any illness of a soldier, who, in the opinion of the psychiatrist, should return to duty without the risk of being prematurely discharged. The officers on the medical and surgical wards were perplexed as to what they should call the large number of disorders without physical abnormalities among their patients. For instance, should a functional stomach difficulty be labeled "gastric neurosis," "neurasthenia gastrica," "anxiety state," "conversion hysteria," "gastritis," or "no disease?" For these and other reasons, great need was felt for a revision of the terms used for psychiatric diagnoses.

The whole problem of nomenclature had become sufficiently muddled so that the Neuropsychiatry Consultants Division requested the help of the Neuropsychiatry Committee of the National Research Council on February 25, 1944. No action was taken. The problem was again clearly pointed out at the Centenary Meeting of the American Psychiatric Association in Philadelphia in May, 1944.[12] Again no action resulted.

After much investigation and preparation a conference was called by the Surgeon General on January 25, 1945. This meeting was attended by the civilian consultants in neuropsychiatry to the Secretary of War and representatives from the Veterans Administration, the Office of the Air Forces Surgeon, the Bureau of Medicine and Surgery of the United States Navy, and the United States Public Health Service. These conferees made two major decisions. First, the term "psychoneurosis" should be regarded as inclusive of various more specific types of reactions. On the patient's clinical record the type of reaction alone was to be recorded, rather than with the prefix "psychoneurosis." Second, the psychiatric diagnosis when recorded should include four parts: (1) the type of disturbance or disorder, (2) the external precipitating stress which caused the disorder, (3) the extent of the predisposition, and (4) the degree of impairment of functional capacity resulting from the disorder.

Prior to this conference opinions regarding these changes had been solicited from many American psychiatrists by means of a memorandum prepared by the

---

[12] Farrell, M. J., and Appel, J. W., "Current Trends in Military Neuropsychiatry," *Am. J. Psychiat.*, 102:12-19, July, 1944.

Neuropsychiatry Consultants Division. Following this conference these same and other psychiatrists were consulted. Throughout 1945 this project became one of the major undertakings of the Neuropsychiatry Consultants Division. Some 15 different drafts of the nomenclature were submitted to psychiatrists both in and out of the Army, in the United States and abroad. Numerous conferences were held.

With the unqualified approval of the five civilian consultants in psychiatry to the Secretary of War the final result was published, along with a revision of all medical nomenclature, in a War Department bulletin.[13]

The new nomenclature [14] greatly enlarged the categories of the neurotic syndromes. This entire section, in so far as possible, was based upon, and each category defined in terms of, psychodynamics. All the psychiatric syndromes were designated as "reactions," and their previous prefixes of psychoneurosis and psychosis were dropped. Several new categories were introduced, one of which was "combat exhaustion." The "somatization reactions" [15] included what previously had been loosely classed as "organ neuroses." A new section on personality types was added and also a series of immaturity reactions. The long list of psychoses due to, or associated with, infections, trauma, circulation, metabolism, and new growth was deleted. Instead, instructions were given to diagnose these as specific organic conditions to be qualified by "psychotic reaction" of a specific type. Finally, a detailed explanation was given regarding the method of recording the diagnosis with particular emphasis on the four-part elaboration.

This nomenclature, which arose from necessity, was regarded by all of those concerned in its formulation as merely another evolutionary step in clarifying and standardizing psychiatric diagnostic terminology. Of over 100 psychiatrists consulted, only 4 felt it inadvisable to make such efforts at revision. Among the reasons for the objections of 2 of them was the fact that all the statistics on the incidence of mental illness in the past would be interrupted!

---

13 "Nomenclature and the Method of Recording Diagnoses," *War Department Technical Bulletin, Medical 203*, 19 October 1945.

14 Reprinted in Appendix B. It was favorably commented upon in *Arch. Neurol. & Psychiat.*, 55:139, Feb., 1946; and in the *Psychoanalyt. Quart.*, 15:274-275, Apr., 1946. It was reprinted in full in *Ment. Hyg.*, 30:456-476, July, 1946; in *J. Nerv. & Ment. Dis.*, 104:180-199, Aug., 1946; in *J. Ment. Sc.*, 92:425-441, Apr., 1946; and in *J. Clin. Psychology*, 2:289-296, 1946.

15 It is of interest that the Germans also developed a nomenclature including the concept of "psychogenic" physical disorders. Alexander's report refers to Item 232 of a German Army directive issued 30 September 1944 relative to terminology for psychogenic functional disorders: "The terms 'neurosis,' 'war neuroses' and 'war hysteria' are no longer to be used. They are to be replaced by the term 'psychogenic functional disorder,' with the addition of the kind of disorder, such as "psychogenic speech disorder,' 'psychogenic gait disorder' or 'psychogenically fixed radial palsy' respectively. These diagnostic terms should be supplemented by a description of the personality of the patient and of the development of the disturbance." Alexander, Leo, "German Military Neuropsychiatry and Neurosurgery," *Combined Intelligence Objectives Item 24*, File No. XXVIII-49, 1945, pp. 17 and 38.

My own reaction to such an objection was that we should have started our collection of statistics with William Cullen's classification in 1760 or Wilhelm Griesenger in 1845. If statistics were the aim of a nomenclature, we would have lots of them!

Several large civilian clinics and hospitals adopted the Army nomenclature immediately. The Veterans Administration used it experimentally in several large psychiatric centers. On the basis of uniform approval from these centers, the advisory committee recommended its adoption in September, 1946.[16]

The search for a still more clear and concise designation of the various clinical syndromes remains one of the urgent fields for psychiatric research. Usage of the Army revision will be another trial-and-error study. The American Psychiatric Association was stimulated into appointing a new nomenclature committee in 1946, which has a great challenge and responsibility.

---

[16] With slight revision, the Veterans Administration published the Army nomenclature as *Technical Bulletin, TB 10A-78*, "Nomenclature of Psychiatric Disorders and Reactions," Oct. 1, 1947.

19

CHOOSING THE SOLDIER

SELECTING and screening men for a fighting Army proved to be a very complex process, particularly from a psychiatric point of view. In the first place the original physical standards, in so far as they attempted to evaluate personality, were inadequate, vague, and subject to loose interpretation. Furthermore, the psychiatric examination technique varied widely in spite of numerous efforts to standardize and supplement it with screening tests. From the beginning of the Selective Service program the psychiatrist was not provided with adequate information about the draftee. Nor did the great effort to develop the Medical Survey Program in order to supply him with essential data achieve its purpose in most areas. A serious complication arose when the civilian community was confronted with the special psychiatric problem of the men who became distressed over their rejection. In addition to assisting in the original process of selection at induction, psychiatrists were concerned with the "physical" standards of the men who were to be sent overseas. Relatively late in the war the additional screening-sorting procedure known as the "physical profile" definitely involved psychiatric participation.

INDUCTION SELECTION

Initially, some of us in psychiatry had some very definite opinions about the criteria for selection. Also, some of the line officers were equally sure about who could be made into good soldiers. But, by the standards of either group, some of the best prospects turned out to be poor fighting men and some of the poorest became heroes. Even though experience yielded new information about how to correct the defects of the selective procedures, the size and complexity of the military organization made revision of regulations slow and difficult.

In retrospect, it is doubtful that any of us—psychiatrists or others—knew enough about the hell of the war as it was to be fought to be very definite or specific about standards for the selection of the fighting men of 1942-45. Certainly, it also became apparent that we did not know enough about the "normal" personality or its resiliency of reaction in the face of stress. We ought to have learned a lot more than we did from the experience of the last war; we could have learned much more between wars. Instead, as psychiatrists, we struggled along against our own preconceived notions, our own inadequate body of knowledge, and the thousand and one obstacles placed in the way of carrying out plans. On the pages of this book is a record of our trials and errors and conclusions.

The importance of early elimination of potential psychiatric casualties was one of the lessons learned in World War I. A famous telegram [1] from General Pershing to the Chief of Staff on July 15, 1918, stated that the prevalence of mental disorders in replacement troops recently arrived in the theater suggested the need for intensive efforts to eliminate the mentally unfit before departure from the United States.

The desirability of screening was also emphasized by the tremendous cost of the psychiatric casualties of World War I. During that war the screening process was not consistently careful. A psychiatric examination was given, when possible, either at the time the recruit arrived at a camp or post or after his assignment to a new unit. Psychiatrists at the military installations in the United States made approximately 3,500,000 examinations which eliminated 69,395 men [2] for neuropsychiatric reasons. Only 40 per cent of these men (27,386) were rejected at the time of their entrance into the Army. Twenty-four years after that war, the government had spent well over $1,000,000,000 for disability, compensation, and hospital treatment of the neuropsychiatric casualties. This one clinical group made up more than one-half of the patients being treated by the Veterans Administration.[3]

---

[1] *The Medical Department of the United States Army in the World War,* Vol. X, War Department, U.S. Government Printing Office, Washington, D.C., 1929, p. 58.

[2] *Op. cit.* p. 85.

[3] Rowntree, L. G., Chief, Medical Division, National Headquarters Bureau of Selective Service of War Manpower Commission, Washington, D.C., Abstract of remarks made at the Public Service Meeting dedicated to the Local Selective Service Boards of the Michigan Society of Neurology and Psychiatry on "The Importance of Neuropsychiatry in the Selection of Men for the Armed Forces," Mar. 25, 1943, p. 6. He gives the cost as $30,000 per NP patient from World War I, a figure rather widely quoted in the literature.

Information on the reputed cost of $30,000 per World War NP veteran is furnished by Mary A. Coyne, Director, Claims Statistics Service, Veterans Administration, on November 29, 1946. "The figures of $30,000, $33,000 or $35,000 which have been quoted as the cost to the government of the neuropsychiatric World War I veteran in 1941 or 1942 are incorrect and have never been used by the Veterans Administration. In April 1941 the V.A. Budget Officer and Chief of Statistics studied a small group of neuropsychiatric cases where the veterans came on the compensation rolls immediately after discharge in 1917 or 1918 and were continuously on the rolls to 1941. The average cost to the government of this small group was approximately $30,500, and this included total amounts paid for disability compensation, vocational training, insurance, adjusted compensation and hospitalization. In other words, this was the maximum and not the average cost.

"There are no figures available as to the average cost of all benefits paid to neuropsychiatric World War I veterans. However, between 1919 and 1941 the total cost of hospitalization for veterans suffering from neuropsychiatric disabilities was approximately $332,000,000. During

Consequently the psychiatric selection methods of World War II received earnest and serious consideration. When war became imminent, Dr. Winfred Overholser addressed a letter to President Roosevelt, August 19, 1940, setting forth the imperative need for psychiatric screening of recruits. This letter was referred to Mr. Frederick Osborne, Chairman of the National Advisory Committee on Selective Service, who in turn passed it on to the Medical Division [4] of the National Headquarters of the Selective Service System. As a result, from the beginning of the draft, the process of induction included a psychiatric as well as a physical examination. However, the National Guard [5] units that were called to duty in 1940, the early volunteers [6] and the men who entered the Army as commissioned officers received only physical examinations.

When the draft began in November, 1940, the plans of the Selective Service organization called for the examination of all candidates by physicians in their own communities. They were then sent to the induction center where they received a second examination. The local medical examiners had the authority to reject men who were not qualified to meet the standards set forth in mobilization regulations. Specialists in the various fields of medicine served on Medical Advisory Boards to whom the local examiners sent selectees whose qualifications were questioned.

On October 24, 1940, the Director of Selective Service, Dr. Clarence Dykstra, representatives from various divisions of the War Department, and Drs. Overholser, Harry A. Steckel, and Harry Stack Sullivan conferred at the Selective Service National Headquarters. They made tentative plans for placing a psychiatrist on each of the 660 Medical Advisory Boards. Because there were, at the very most, only 4,000 psychiatrists in the United States, there were

---

this period there were 375,728 admissions and the average cost per admission was $883.62. However, this cannot be considered the average cost per veteran as many veterans had more than one admission and it is impossible, from the reports now available, to ascertain the number of individual neuropsychiatric veterans receiving hospital treatment during this period.

"The approximate cost of compensation to World War I veterans suffering from service connected neuropsychiatric disorders was $728,400,000 from 1918 to 1941, and for non-service connected pensions $92,900,000. For these benefits, it is impossible to obtain an average for individual veterans."

[4] *Ibid.*, p. 35.

[5] An unpublished study of J. W. Appel and G. W. Beebe of the Office of the Surgeon General is a comparison of the psychiatric discharge rates of early inductees and National Guardsmen which showed a consistently lower rate in the National Guard (5.2 discharges per 1,000 strength per year compared to 8.1 per 1,000 per year for inductees). This may be related to the fact that they were volunteers and therefore had stronger positive motivation. They also had had the test of experience in repeated summer camps. Furthermore, they belonged to an established unit made up of old friends, and with familiar leadership.

[6] One study of 669 psychiatric patients showed that alcoholism, epilepsy, psychogenic gastrointestinal disorders, and schizophrenia were more common in volunteers than in draftees. Mental deficiency and psychopathic personalities were common in draftees. Lemere, F., and Greenwood, E. D., "Ratio of Voluntary Enlistment to Induction in Various Types of Neuropsychiatric Disorders," *Am. J. Psychiat.*, 100:312-313, Nov., 1943.

not enough to have one on each of the 6,403 local boards. They also decided that 15 minutes should be the shortest time that should be used for the psychiatric examination. This plan was announced to the field through a letter from the Adjutant General to all corps areas, September 30, 1940.

In order to implement the programs, Dr. Harry Stack Sullivan was appointed as psychiatric consultant [7] to Selective Service. Under the auspices of the William Alanson White Foundation, he initiated and conducted 2-day seminars in nine of the large cities of the country for the Medical Advisory Board and Army Induction Board psychiatrists. The first meeting was held January 2 and 3, 1941, in Washington and the last one July 21 and 22 in Buffalo. A total of 312 of the 584 physicians serving as psychiatrists for the Selective Service System participated in at least one of the seminars.

Col. Rowntree, Chief of the Medical Division of National Headquarters, Bureau of Selective Service, reported that,

In these seminars an attempt was made to cover all psychiatric material pertaining to selection in a uniform manner to the end that all psychiatrists assisting in such examinations would follow the same system. These psychiatric seminars, like psychiatry in general, were planned and operated by psychiatrists, and were morally and financially supported by Selective Service. Despite their merits, they engendered much criticism. This criticism came to Selective Service Headquarters from outstanding leaders of medicine, from military authorities, but above all from other psychiatrists. After a trial test, extending well over six months, the Director was disappointed in the results. He was quite uncertain as to whether all rejections were justified and somewhat discouraged to learn that despite this psychiatric screening, considerable numbers of men were subsequently being discharged from the Army because of mental derangement.

After attempting to weigh the results against the time, effort and cost involved, it was considered wise to seek new advice, follow new lines and redirect psychiatric effort. As stated, it is not the purpose of Selective Service to criticize the program or the work of the psychiatrists. I think it is only fair to say, however, that the question arose in the minds of some of our medical men as to whether in the program followed, sufficient emphasis was being laid upon the study of the needs of the Army and of the local board examiners. Perhaps it would have been wiser to approach the subject more in the spirit of investigation. Because the plan did not appear to meet the expectations of National Headquarters, an appeal was made to the National Research Council for advice, and a committee of two was appointed by this Council to investigate and report. This committee consisted of Doctor Arthur Ruggles, President of the American Psychiatric Association, and Professor of Clinical Psychiatry and Mental Hygiene, Yale University School of Medicine, and Doctor Frederick L. Wells, Ph.D., Professor of Psychology, Harvard University. These gentlemen submitted two thoughtful and valuable reports, the preliminary one dated March 27, 1942, and

---

[7] In June, 1941, he was assigned a psychiatrist from the Army, Capt. Philip S. Wagner, who ran the psychiatric section of the Medical Division of the National Headquarters of the Selective Service System.

a supplemental one July 31, 1942, on the "Effective Use of Psychiatry and Psychological Knowledge Applicable in the Selection of Men for Military Service." [8]

Doctor Overholser described the differences in the opinions of Dr. Sullivan and the new Director of Selective Service, Maj. Gen. Lewis B. Hershey, as follows: "Unfortunately inertia and opposition have caused setbacks in the program with the result that any serious examinations at the local board level seemed to be threatened and that Dr. Sullivan has resigned as a consultant." [9]

According to Dr. Sullivan a single psychiatric examination at the induction center would be properly selective only

. . . if there are reasonably good results from Selective Service efforts to sensitize the non-medical members of Local Boards to the significance of mental and personality factors; if data of registrant's personal history are assembled on the initiative of Local Boards and supplied to the Army Examining Boards; if the psychiatrist or psychiatrists on these (Army Examining) Boards have opportunity to study each registrant for an average of fifteen minutes; and if the psychiatric work is both supervised and adequately utilized in the final classification of selectees.[10]

In February, 1942, the local medical examination was eliminated except for a very casual physical inspection. The questionable cases picked up in this inspection were referred to the specialists who constituted the Medical Advisory Board. One routine and complete examination was then given at the induction center. This change, to which many of the civilian examining doctors objected,[11] was made for several reasons: the local rejection rates were high, perhaps too high; men passed by local medical examiners who were later rejected by the induction board caused ill will between offended local physicians and induction-center draft physicians; there was complaint that the local board examiners received no compensation while civilian examiners serving at induction centers received $15 a day; there was some feeling on the part of the medical personnel in the induction center that their job was complicated by unstandardized local examinations; fewer doctors could handle more examinations at the induction centers.[12]

---

[8] Rowntree, L. G., "Eliminating Registrants Mentally Unfit for Service. The Importance of Neuropsychiatry in the Selection of Men for the Armed Forces," *Michigan Society of Neurology and Psychiatry,* Mar. 25, 1943.

[9] Overholser, W., "A Review of Psychiatric Progress in 1941," *Am. J. Psychiat.,* 98:581-583, Jan., 1942.

[10] Sullivan, H. S., "Editorial, Selective Service Psychiatry," *Psychiatry,* 4:442-444, Aug., 1943. Certainly the second and third qualifications were never carried out. Sullivan was so blocked in his efforts that he gave up. Great credit goes to him for the initial work accomplished.

[11] Overholser, W., "Some Possible Contributions of Psychiatry to the National Defense," *Danville (Penna.) State Hospital Mental Health Bulletin 20:* No. 1. Presented Feb. 10, 1942, at the Pennsylvania Psychiatric Society.

[12] In Illinois, 165 doctors performed the work which had been done previously by 2,000 doctors.

THE PROBLEM OF "PHYSICAL" [13] STANDARDS

The aim of the War Department initially was presumably to create a quality Army. This was perhaps more implicit than explicit, expressed more by word of mouth than by official directives. It was certainly the understanding of most of the medical officers. Consequently, there was a generally accepted impression that the Army wanted only the "best," the healthiest, the "supermen." It became the rule that if there were any doubt at all as to whether or not a draftee would stand the pace, he should be rejected. If the candidate gave any suggestive evidence of emotional instability, such as nervousness at the time of the examination, sweaty hands, transient anxiety, nail biting,[14,15] expressed fears, usually he was rejected. Even a history with a record of previous nervous disorders, or something suggestive of nervousness, like stomach trouble, could be the basis for rejection.

The original instructions to psychiatric examiners was conservative. A letter from the director of Selective Service to the State Directors stated:

Not only are the feebleminded and the "insane" unsuitable, but so also are certain of those handicapped people who are now doing well in civilian life only because they have found ways of protecting themselves from undue stress, by seclusiveness or by peculiar performances and odd habits of life. Military life requires that the soldier shall be able to live comfortably in continued close contact with a variegated group of other men. He cannot depend on any self-evolved protective mechanism that sets him apart from his fellows. Military and naval experience is in favor of excluding from the armed forces all persons discovered to have mental or personality handicap of any material degree.[16]

---

[13] In all the War Department directives, the term "physical" was used to include psychiatric or psychological aspects.

[14] Hill, Joel Milam, "Nailbiting Incidence, Allied Personality Traits and Military Significance," *Am. J. Psychiat.*, 103:185-187, Sept., 1946. The author concluded:

"1. In military combat, nail biters generally are less useful than non-nail biters.

"2. However some nail biters undergo combat without hospitalization for nervousness; and many nail biters experience prolonged combat prior to hospitalization for nervous conditions.

"3. Nail biters least useful for military combat purposes are characterized by:
   (1) Unhappy child-parent relationship.
   (2) Multiple early neurotic traits.
   (3) Very irritable, explosive temper.
   (4) Usual reaction of weeping and trembling when angry.
   (5) Infrequency or absence of fist fights in early life.
   (6) Emotionally disturbed response to combat killing."

[15] William Rottersman, in "The Selectee and His Complaints," *Am. J. Psychiat.*, 103:79-86, July, 1946, stated that in July, 1944, over 90 per cent of those with history of fingernail biting, past and present, were accepted for military service. He was referring to the induction station in which he served.

[16] Letter of transmittal from the Director of Selective Service System to the State Directors. May 19, 1941.

To fully understand the cautious attitude of psychiatrists in accepting draftees at induction centers and the tendency to reject every potential neuropsychiatric casualty, one should take into consideration the constant pressure from the War Department to keep such individuals out of its ranks. The attitude prevailed generally that man power was plentiful. This led to the adoption of the easiest policy, both at the induction center and in the field: elimination.

The neurotic or the psychopathic personality was indeed a problem in the basic-training camps and became a tremendous handicap overseas. Commanding officers quite justifiably developed resentment toward the War Department for sending them noneffective personnel. A sufficient number had been misassigned by early 1943 to provoke forceful protests against sending such men out of the country. The War Department then exerted further pressure toward the elimination of potential psychiatric casualties. The Adjutant General sent a memorandum to all Service Command commanders in March, 1943, which specifically stated that too many men mentally unsuited for ordinary military duties were arriving overseas [17]—a message reminiscent of the famous Pershing telegram of World War I. In April he issued a second memorandum on the same subject in which the statement was made, "There is no classification for duty of military personnel with such mental diagnoses as psychoneuroses. . . ." [18] Three months later, in July, still another memorandum on the same subject stressed the same facts and requested that special care should be used in screening men going overseas.[19] Therefore, it is not surprising that, with this constant pressure and a widespread trend to discharge all neurotic men, induction-station psychiatrists rejected those whom they believed might become psychiatric casualties.[20]

Many civilian psychiatrists serving as examiners or consultants on local examining boards tried very hard to eliminate such men. Reading the many

---

[17] Adjutant General's Memorandum W600-30-43 on Mental Condition of Men Ordered Overseas, 25 March 1943.

[18] Adjutant General's Memorandum W600-39-43—Revision of Memorandum No. 30, 26 April 1943.

[19] Adjutant General's Memorandum W600-62-43 on Mental Condition of Men Ordered Overseas, 29 July 1943.

[20] Typical of these attitudes, Col. Patrick Madigan, the psychiatrist in the Surgeon General's Office prior to the choice of a civilian wrote: "One of the most important duties of the Advisory Board or Induction Board psychiatrists is the elimination before enlistment or induction into the Army of those who manifest *any of the earmarks of mental, emotional or nervous instability.*" Madigan, P. S., "Military Psychiatry," *Psychiatry,* 4:225-229, May, 1941. One of our hospital psychiatrists, early in the war, expressed the same thought: "The psychoneurotic is mentally and constitutionally unsuitable for Army life." Michael, N., "The Psychoneurotic in the Armed Forces," *Am. J. Psychiat.,* 99:651-653, Mar., 1943.

professional papers that appeared in 1940, 1941, and 1942, one suspects that in their zeal psychiatrists promised more than they could deliver. They did so, however, on the premises that they would be provided with social history data from the home community and could have 15 minutes for each examination. They further assumed that a good psychiatrist knew enough about military life, and could, on the basis of his clinical experience, do an adequate job of evaluating the ability of a personality to withstand the stresses of that life. However, their presupposed conditions of examination were never realized and their basic assumption of their ability to estimate combat pressure proved to be faulty. In only occasional instances was a social case history provided from the home community. The average examination was nearer 3 than 15 minutes. The induction examiners (except those who had served in the last war) could not really anticipate the stresses of a soldier-in-wartime's life without personal experience; nor could they foretell the type of leadership or the toughness of assignment of any selectee. Moreover, there was no way in which they could check the accuracy of their prognostic selections by knowing which of the selectees proved to be "good" soldiers.

Many psychiatrists sincerely believed that very careful screening would result in many fewer psychiatric casualties in the field. Thus, Sullivan hoped that the future incidence of disability could be reduced "by a little more than 50 per cent." [21] Bowman [22] concluded that since, in the last war, 2 per cent of the candidates were excluded from military service because of nervous or mental diseases or defects and 3 per cent more were later discharged because of similar disability, the job of psychiatry was to pick out and exclude that 5 per cent.

However, others questioned the ability of a psychiatrist to judge the capabilities of an individual draftee. In a comment column in the *American Journal of Psychiatry*, there appeared the statement that,

There may be enthusiasts who would carry psychiatric scrutiny of recruits to extremes, or who would sell to the government infeasible mental hygiene schemes. Such promotions sometimes emanate from non-medical sources. They tend to discredit the real service which the psychiatrist can render. That all unsuitable cases should be discovered at the beginning, no one could expect or require, nor would it be advocated that all potentially neurotic or border cases should be indiscriminately rejected. All material which can be fitted into the military organization should be utilized. [23]

---

[21] "A Seminar of Practical Psychiatric Diagnoses," *Psychiatry,* 4:265-283, May, 1941.
[22] Bowman, Karl M., "Psychiatric Examination in the Armed Forces," *War. Med.,* 1:213-218, Mar., 1941.
[23] Comment column on psychiatry in the war, *Am. J. Psychiat.,* 97:975-976, Jan., 1941.

A similar point of view was expressed by Kardiner, who, on the basis of his extensive experience, wrote, ". . . though I have seen many hundreds of the chronic forms of these neuroses and have studied the psychopathologic picture, course, treatment and previous personality in many cases, I should hesitate to offer any criteria that can be used to predict that a given candidate will have a chronic neurosis." [24]

Lauren Smith expressed similar conservatism: "From a practical standpoint, it must be stated that just because a man may show a few or many signs of vasomotor instability, emotional tension and chronic transitory or organic dysfunction, it would not necessarily follow that he would be unable to adjust to camp or Army life. These findings only show us that such a man should be carefully studied." [25]

The Neuropsychiatry Consultants Division of the Office of the Surgeon General opposed the luxurious attitude of rejecting so many men on questionable grounds. It published a tactfully worded protest in December, 1943: "The possibility must be considered . . . that neuropsychiatric criteria for service are now being interpreted too strictly and that men are being separated from the service who could be of value were they retained." [26] This was the official word to the field. In 1944, Farrell and Appel sent an appeal to civilian psychiatrists: ". . . this means that screening can and must reject obvious psychiatric noneffectives. It must not be so ambitious in attempting to detect potential psychiatric casualties." [27]

As the war went on and there was an opportunity to see the results of selection, there was little doubt that, except for grossly abnormal personalities, an examining physician could not accurately determine who would be successful and who would fail as a combat soldier. Later experience proved the induction-center elimination of men with minor symptoms of instability to be overcautious and wasteful of man power.

The lack of separation of the function of selection from that of examination confused the selective process. Physicians, even with psychiatric training, are not specialists in selection; they really know little about it. The majority did not consider it their responsibility (and rightly so). They were qualified to make a medical examination. Examination and selection are not synonymous, though often assumed to be so. Furthermore, no one, except the chief

24 Kardiner, A., "The Neuroses of War," War Med., 1:219-226, Mar., 1941.
25 Smith, Lauren H., "Selective Service Seminar for Medical Advisory Board and Army Induction Board Psychiatry," Psychiatry, 4:241-249, May, 1941.
26 Surgeon General's Office Circular Letter 194, 3 December 1943. "Disposition of Individuals with Neuropsychiatric Disorders."
27 Farrell, M. J., and Appel, J. W., "Current Trends in Military Neuropsychiatry," Am. J. Psychiat., 101:12-19, July, 1944.

examiner who looked over the completed record, viewed the draftee "as a whole." Each physician in the "conveyor-belt" examining line looked at one small segment of each "specimen" as he was hurried onward.

The entire selective process as far as it concerned the psychiatric evaluation of personnel was one of trial and error. Experience dictated its revisions. Whatever the "official" statement, any standard was interpreted according to the training and experience of the examiner or his chief. Many psychiatrists had not had sufficient experience with the minor psychiatric deviations from the normal to know their real significance as criteria in selection for the Army.

The initial standards (in Mobilization Regulations 1-9, revised 1940) for the psychiatric induction examination were not specific.[28] Not until a 1942 revision was there a special section devoted to neurological disorders. At that time a new section was added: "Psychoses, Psychoneuroses and Personality Disorders." In early 1944, the public and Congress exerted great pressure toward lowering physical standards for acceptance. The President appointed a board, made up of the Surgeons General of both the Army and Navy and some prominent civilian physicians, to study the matter. Doctor Edward A. Strecker was the psychiatrist in the group. Their recommendations were included in the rewrite of MR 1-9, April 19, 1944; very minor changes were made in the psychiatric standards. To make this document more clear and to bring it into harmony with the new nomenclature, the psychiatric section was rewritten [29] entirely in 1946.

As a result of the many criticisms of the psychiatric standards and rejection rates by some individuals in Selective Service, the President of the United States appointed a committee of prominent civilian psychiatrists [30] to visit induction centers all over the country. This committee again recommended that the psychiatrist examine not more than 50 inductees per day. Also they believed that the psychological examination should accompany the inductee to the psychiatrist (which often was not done); that privacy and quiet should be provided for the psychiatric examination; that the provision for 3 days of observation in doubtful cases should be used more often; that the social-history plan should be put into general use promptly; and made other commendable recommendations. These were referred to the Service Command surgeons,[31]

---

[28] These even permitted the acceptance for limited service of individuals with conversion symptoms.

[29] Change 4, 26 August 1946.

[30] Doctors Edward A. Strecker, Winfred Overholser, Arthur H. Ruggles, Frederick W. Parsons, Karl M. Bowman, Raymond W. Waggoner, Titus H. Harris.

[31] Letters from Executive Officer, Office of the Surgeon General, Subject: Recommendation of Special Committee for the Study of Neuropsychiatric Induction Procedure, 4 October 1943.

but it is not known to what extent they ever reached the field. I know they were not distributed in the Fourth Service Command.

Two special efforts were made to change the practice at induction centers of routine elimination of men with only minor symptoms of instability. One was the preparation of a War Department technical bulletin,[32] written by the Neuropsychiatry Consultants Division. This stressed the importance of excluding men only on a longitudinal life study of the personality and not on a momentary cross section as seen at the induction center. The second was the issuance of a directive [33] devoted almost exclusively to a revision of the psychiatric examination. The changes made were in the wording rather than in the standards, in order to place the emphasis on accepting some of the questionable cases instead of excluding all of them.

The physical examination standards included a category for "limited service." This permitted the acceptance of men with mild physical and psychological defects. However, through much of 1944 and 1945, no men were accepted under this classification because no limited-service jobs were available—they were filled by soldiers already in the Army. Such men were therefore deferred as "4F."[34] In February, 1946, with a decrease in volunteers and a continuation of major commitments overseas, the Army became short of man power. It was necessary again to accept men in this "limited service" category. There was much newspaper publicity at the time to the effect that the physical standards had been lowered. Actually, there was no change in these standards as written, but there was a change in policy to permit the acceptance of men previously deferred. This seemed justifiable because at that time no inductees would be going into combat.

---

[32] "Induction Station Neuropsychiatric Examination," *War Department Technical Bulletin, Medical 33,* 21 April 1944.

[33] Change 3 of Mobilization Regulations 1-9, 4 June 1945, made minor and in some instances major changes in the wording of every section of the physical examination standards dealing with the psychiatric examination. For comparison, paragraph 94 D in Change 3 follows:
"Despite the handicap of time limitations, the neuropsychiatrist will carefully avoid unscientific methods which give inadequate and inaccurate data. Thus, a neuropsychiatric examination consisting of I. Q. reading and suggestive questions, such as 'Do you worry?' 'Are you nervous?' or 'Do you have headaches or stomach trouble?' is inadequate, and positive answers to such questions are not in themselves justifiable cause for rejection. Isolated signs, such as nail biting, slight tremor, or vasal motor symptoms, are not disqualifying."
The same section 94 in Mobilization Regulations 1-9, 19 April 1944, contained no such instructions.

[34] On 26 May 1945, the standards had been revised to defer certain conditions (AGPR-I, 327.31, Induction of Certain Selective Service Registrants under 26 years of age). These revisions were canceled by an order on 15 February 1946 and thus men with those minor defects were again acceptable. (AGSE-P 327.31, same title as last, 15 February 1946.) It is of more than passing interest that approximately 25 per cent of the psychiatric patients being evacuated to the United States from the Army of Occupation in Europe were former 4Fs, inducted following cessation of hostilities. Wessel, M. A. "Neuropsychiatry in an Army Hospital with the Army of Occupation," *Am. J. Nursing,* 47:1-5, Mar., 1947.

THE PSYCHIATRIC EXAMINATION

In all of the 108 [35] armed forces induction stations, the actual procedure of examination was very similar. A given number of men would arrive at the station to be processed in 8 to 10 hours. The psychologist gave group tests to the inductees. After giving the preliminary data for information and identification, the nude men started down the examining line of a varying number of doctors, 8 or 10 (as many as 160 doctors were required in a large station which moved the selectees in several lines). Each doctor examined a part of each man, such as lungs or heart, motor system, or eyes. Each individual carried his own examination papers. The process was so timed as to prevent any slowing of the flow.

The psychiatrist was usually the last physician in the examining line. When a man came into his cubbyhole, he sat down to be questioned. The previous examination findings (marked on his papers) often gave no information which was helpful to the psychiatrist unless to indicate that the man had already been rejected by some previous examiner in the line. In that case, the psychiatrist presumably examined him anyway, so that the records would be complete. If there was a neurological examination, the psychiatrist also made it.

The length of time that a psychiatrist spent in examining an inductee depended on the amount of time available. This varied with the number of men to be examined and the number of psychiatrists. Most of the medical examiners could check on their special interest in the inductee in a few seconds so that the line progressed rather rapidly. If there were many men to be examined, the line deteriorated into a "log jam" at the neuropsychiatric examination station unless there were several examiners there. Psychiatrists varied in their techniques: one might spend 10 seconds and another, 5 minutes with each man. Questionable cases always required extra time. In very well-staffed stations the probable rejectees might be seen for 15 to 20 minutes. From my observation of many centers, I would estimate an average examination of 1 to 3 minutes: in "normals" and previously rejected cases it might be less, in borderline cases, more.

The most common questions the psychiatrist asked concerned either mental or physical health or attitudes: "How are you?" "Have you any complaints?" "Have you visited a doctor often—and for what?" "Do you have

[35] This figure supplied by Col. Arden Freer, Office of the Surgeon General. Lieutenant Colonel F. E. Hall gave me the following figures on the average number of Armed Forces induction stations in operation: 1941—58; 1942—81; 1943—69; 1944—73; 1945—63; 1946 to May—59. Physical Standards Division, Surgeon General's Office, 9 May 1946.

any worries?" "Have you ever had a nervous breakdown?" "How do you feel about the war?" "About coming into the Army?" Many examiners, if not most, developed a regular set of such questions, which varied only when a draftee gave specific leads about himself. The experienced examining psychiatrist addressed the inductee by name; used the vernacular in questioning men about such facts as enuresis or sex habits; put the tense, apprehensive man at ease; explained to a rejectee, if time permitted, the basis of his rejection.

The original plans for a psychiatrist to have as much as 15 minutes with each inductee and a maximum of 50 patients a day were probably realized at comparatively few induction centers. In some centers which were located in large cities, it was possible to enlist the part-time help of civilian psychiatrists. However, many of the induction centers were located on Army posts, long distances from any large city. For instance, in the 11 induction centers in the Fourth Service Command (the seven southeastern states) only one had any civilian assistance. In that case, it was given by one elderly physician who had retired from practice. It was common experience for the psychiatrist to "examine" from 100 to 200 cases a day, and there were several instances where he had to go through the motions of examining as many as 500 inductees in one day.

All induction centers located on posts or in camps were the responsibility and under the jurisdiction of the commanding officer of the hospital. He had to staff both installations. If his load in the hospital became unusually heavy or he was short of personnel, he might have to steal a psychiatrist for the hospital from the induction-center staff, where he was also needed very much. Obviously any psychiatric examination made under circumstances of such extreme shortage of examining personnel was a farce, with extremely unfortunate results. It put psychiatry in a ridiculous light; it failed almost completely in its purpose; some of the psychiatrists involved tried to play the role of a god with omniscient clairvoyance.

The personnel shortage was helped somewhat in January, 1943. When the Navy failed to get sufficient volunteers and began drawing men from the induction centers, it supplied some 60 psychiatrists to assist in the examination of inductees.

An attempt was made to keep under observation for 24 to 72 hours those men who claimed to have epilepsy or enuresis. In many induction centers this was done only occasionally; in some it was routine. In others claims of enuresis or epilepsy were verified, where possible, by affidavits secured through local draft boards from local physicians or responsible witnesses. This system was undoubtedly subject to some abuses but on the whole worked satisfactorily.

Many physicians devised ways and means of improving their examination. In several stations each rejectee was seen individually by three psychiatrists. In others, tabulations were kept of the percentage of men rejected by each psychiatrist.[36] A questionnaire was used in some centers. It was given to each inductee prior to his interview with the psychiatrist; for those who were illiterate, it was filled out by an enlisted man. There were various types of such questionnaires; in general, they were lists of from 10 to 30 questions to be answered "Yes" or "No." From the answers the psychiatrist could discover what further information was particularly pertinent in each individual case.[37] The examination of several men as a group was another short cut. Thus at Fort Benning, Maj. Leo Orenstein examined five candidates simultaneously. Major Leo Alexander used a similar method at Fort Bragg. In another induction center men were first questioned in groups of 30, after which those who gave answers indicating some psychiatric difficulty were given individual examinations.[38]

One of the screening questionnaires (never officially used in the Army) which received wide publicity was the Cornell Selectee Index.[39] It initially contained some 64 questions and was later elaborated to assay the presence of psychosomatic disturbances. In the development of this test the results were checked against the findings in the psychiatric interviews. However, it was not validated on soldiers in the field, and so it is probably less accurate than a test simultaneously developed in the War Department.[40]

The Neuropsychiatry Consultants Division, in conjunction with the Research Branch of the Information and Education Division, developed a questionnaire known as the Neuropsychiatric Screening Adjunct. Its purpose was to provide a means of rapidly selecting those registrants with indications of psychoneurotic tendencies who should, therefore, have an individual, clinical psychiatric examination. At the same time it provided a means of selecting those with no conspicuous evidence of personality disorders who could be accepted for military service without further neuropsychiatric examination, if that was necessary.

---

[36] Bloomberg, W., and Hyde, R. W., "A Survey of Neuropsychiatric Work at the Boston Induction Station," *Am. J. Psychiat.,* 99:23-28, July, 1942.

[37] Such a questionnaire method was described by H. H. Goldstein and W. Rottersman, in "Induction Psychiatry," *Am. J. Psychiat.,* 101:210-215, Sept., 1944. See also a tabulation of complaints registered by W. Rottersman, "The Selectee and His Complaints," *Am. J. Psychiat.,* 103:79-86, July, 1946.

[38] See Chap. 7 for methods of psychiatric screening in the WAC.

[39] Weider, A.; Mittelmann, B.; Wechsler, D.; and Wolff, H. G., "The Cornell Selectee Index," *J.A.M.A.,* 124:224-228, Jan. 22, 1944; also *War Med.,* 7:209-213, Apr., 1945.

[40] Leavitt compared the two in 768 inductees and found they were equally effective as checked by psychiatric evaluation. He found defects in both; the NSA had several advantages. The true test is the soldier's adjustment in the field which Leavitt did not check. Leavitt, H. C., "A Comparison between the Neuropsychiatric Screening Adjunct (NSA) and the Cornell Selectee Index (Form N)," *Am. J. Psychiat.,* 103:353-357, Nov., 1946.

This test was made up of a series of 23 questions, 15 of which dealt with a history of personality problems and symptoms.[41] Eight additional questions concerned such subjects as alcoholism, drug addiction, hospitalization for mental illness, convulsions, and other serious evidence of psychiatric predisposition. Positive answers to these "stop" questions indicated those men who should have a psychiatric examination. These tests required only a few minutes and could be administered to 100 men simultaneously. The validity of the test was extensively checked not only with psychiatric interview findings but also against performance in the field.

Every man answering any of the "stop" questions affirmatively and those who made below a specified score on the total test were seen by a psychiatrist. After October 1, 1944, all inductees were given this test,[42] which pointed out with remarkable accuracy the more maladjusted individuals. In most induction centers, as previously, the psychiatrist continued seeing all inductees, but the results of the test gave him a lead as to those individuals who needed special study.

It was the consensus of opinion that this questionnaire was eminently worth while. There were some objections: It was claimed that such a questionnaire suggested complaints to the individual being examined (which to most of us did not seem valid); it was misused in some induction centers as a basis of rejection rather than to indicate the need of examination. Some very schizoid intelligent individuals gave very high scores on the test and, if not seen individually, would have been accepted.

THE MEDICAL SURVEY PROGRAM

From the beginning of the draft the local board was expected to forward to the induction station certain data about each draftee, including information about any previous mental illness or epilepsy. Often this datum was not received; rarely was it satisfactory. An initial recommendation of the civilian psychiatrists stressed the importance of information relative to the past history of the inductee.

The Medical Survey Program,[43] instituted largely through the efforts of Dr. Raymond Waggoner,[44] the Psychiatric Advisor for Selective Service, was

---

[41] War Department, AGO, Form PRT-204; Directions for Administering, Scoring and Interpreting Neuropsychiatric Screening Adjunct, WD AGO PRT-205.

[42] Adjutant General's Memorandum 40-44, 19 September 1944—Psychological Examination for Neuropsychiatric Tendencies. A forthcoming volume of the NSA, written by Dr. Sam Stauffer and the research group in the Information and Education Division, will record in detail the development and validation of this test.

[43] Program was set forth in Selective Service System Circular 4, 18 October 1943.

[44] Appointed July 2, 1943. Doctor Waggoner felt that the program would never have been put into effect had it not been for the fact that Gen. Hershey was strongly for it.

created to provide a means of procuring more adequate data. Under the plan the Selective Service System was expected to furnish the armed-forces induction station with adequate medical, social, and educational history on each registrant on four data sheets. These were supposed to be filled out by social workers who were to collect this information from all available local sources: home, school, employer, court, hospitals, etc. The principle and the aims of this effort were highly commendable, but actually it was never organized in any really effective fashion on a national basis. In some large cities it was reasonably efficient. Previously, a few states, notably Massachusetts, had developed a somewhat similar program. One or two states never made any effort whatever to implement the Medical Survey Program. Wherever it was put to work and was even 10 per cent effective, it saved its cost manifold.

There were serious handicaps to the effective use of the survey. Some individuals in the Selective Service Headquarters had reservations about it, and some state directors of Selective Service were never sympathetic. Volunteer social workers collected the data, and much of the credit for its success in larger cities and smaller states goes to them. But there were never nearly enough social workers, either volunteer or professional, in the nation at large to collect the necessary material. In many states there was no centralized file of state hospital commitments and thus no means of obtaining the information requested. At least two and perhaps three of the four forms were so rarely filled out that they were of practically no value. Yet, since they were confidential, blank or not, they were kept in sealed envelopes. Without an efficient system of opening these envelopes and sorting out the comparatively small number which contained pertinent information, the too-busy psychiatrists became weary and discouraged with the preponderance of blank forms and negative reports. A liberal estimate would indicate that in some states 20 per cent of the forms had helpful information; the national average was probably nearer 2 to 5 per cent.

Where the Medical Survey Program made information available to the psychiatrist, it was very helpful, but it fell far short of the hoped-for results. However, it did yield several by-products. In certain states it led to the development of a "central registry"—a list of all individuals with state-hospital commitment and court records. Through the program many people became aware, for the first time, of the importance of social history in evaluating personalities. It stimulated many local groups toward more effective social work.

THE NUMBER OF MEN REJECTED

Between January, 1942, and June, 1945, of approximately 15,000,000 examinations, there were 2,309,000 rejections for neuropsychiatric causes. Because of repeated examinations of the same individual, there were actually only 1,875,000 men who were rejected because of neuropsychiatric disability.

Neuropsychiatric Rejection [45]

	1942	1943	1944	1945	Average
For every 100 men examined the per cent rejected for NP was	9.7%	15.5%	16.0%	16.4%	12%
For every 100 rejections for all causes, NP causes amounted to:	28.4%	42.7%	45.8%	39.2%	39.1%

For several reasons, rejection statistics do not give an accurate picture of the true incidence of disabling neuropsychiatric conditions. While mobilization regulations called for a specific diagnosis if a man was rejected, there were many instances in which it was not possible to give an accurate, specific diagnosis at the induction station. This was due not only to the limited time for examination and the lack of any previous information or history but also because the condition of some men did not justify it. The requirement was retained, however, until 1944. The examiners were then instructed merely to list the inductee as "not suitable for military service, due to severe anti-social tendencies, due to severe neurotic symptoms, due to severe emotional instability, due to severe schizoid tendencies, due to mental deficiency" [46] or as due to epilepsy, sexual psychopathology, enuresis, or other specific, clear-cut entities when present.

Compilation of statistics was complicated by the variable meaning of the required diagnoses. In the initial Selective Service Circular No. 1 mentioned above, the causes for rejection for neuropsychiatric reasons were listed under eight categories: mental defect or deficiency, psychopathic personality, major abnormalities of mood, pre- and postpsychotic personalities, chronic inebriety, syphilis of the central nervous system, and organic disease of the brain, spinal cord, or peripheral nerves.

---

[45] Figures given by Medical Statistics Division, Office of the Surgeon General. In the figures supplied by Selective Service of registrants aged 18 to 37, up to January 1, 1945, there was a total of 4,493,000 men rejected, of which 801,700 or 17.8 per cent were for mental illness and personality disorders, not including mental and educational deficiency. These latter constituted 19.6 per cent of all rejections in white men, and 10.7 per cent of all rejections in Negroes. The rejection rate for this type of disorder increased from 22.3 per 1,000 examined in peacetime to 12.2 per 1,000 examined in 1944. Among 18-year-olds more than one-fifth of the rejections for mental and personality disorders were due to emotional immaturity. Of those gainfully employed, the psychoneurosis rejection rate was highest for professional and managerial workers and lowest for farm laborers, while the rate for other mental and personality disorders was lowest for the former and highest for the latter. Rowntree, L. G.; McGill, K. H.; and Hellman, L. P., "Mental and Personality Disorders in Selective Service Registrants," *J.A.M.A.*, **128**:1084-1087, Aug. 11, 1945.
[46] In *War Department Technical Bulletin, Medical 33*, 21 April 1944.

Consequently, any attempt to classify accurately the causes for rejections would be futile. For what significance they may have, based on 1,850,000 rejections, they were as follows:

	Total Neuropsychiatric Rejections
Psychoneurosis	25%
Psychosis	1%
Psychopathic personality	17%
Mental deficiency	37%
Other psychiatric	5%
Neurological disease (excluding epilepsy and neurosyphilis)	12%
Epilepsy	3%
Total neuropsychiatric disorders	100%

In his report, Lt. Col. John W. Appel followed similar figures with the pertinent observation: "During the greater part of the war, fitness for service meant fitness for full combat duty in the front lines; a significant proportion of the men rejected for psychoneurosis would have been capable of rendering service in non-combat jobs had such jobs been available; a certain proportion of the rejections were for psychiatric conditions which would not be disabling in civil life." [47, 48]

Furthermore, in studying the statistics of the rejections for psychiatric causes, one needs to know of the special method used in their compilation. On November 4, 1943, the Adjutant General [49] sent a letter of instruction to the induction centers concerning cases of multiple causes for rejection. It stated that if a psychiatric disability were present, the case should be classified as rejected for this cause. Thus, if a man had high blood pressure and a mild neurotic condition, he would be classified in the statistics as having been rejected for psychiatric causes. This system of tabulation was later changed, but over many months the percentage of apparent psychiatric rejections, while indicating the incidence, implied a disproportionate number of individuals rejected for psychiatric reasons.[50]

---

[47] Appel, J. W., "Incidence of Neuropsychiatric Disorders in the United States Army in World War II," *Am. J. Psychiat.*, 102:433-437, Jan., 1946.

[48] The value of a study of the men who were rejected is suggested in the elaborate and detailed investigations of Hadley on the age factor, social status, and economic levels of 58,000 men examined from the Washington, D.C. area. Other than Hadley's series, no other such observations have been recorded. Hadley, E. E., "Military Psychiatry: An Experiment in Military Selection," *Psychiatry*, 5:371-402, Aug., 1942; "A Note on the Factor of Age," *Psychiatry*, 5:543-550, Nov., 1942; "A Note on Social Status," *Psychiatry*, 6:203-213, May, 1943; "An Ecological Note," *Psychiatry*, 7:379-407, Nov., 1944.

[49] Letter from AGO, 20115 (30 October 1943) RR-1, dated 4 November 1943.

[50] See Appendix D for chart of incidence of NP rejections and the regulations and events which influenced it.

THE REJECTEE

One very important psychiatric feature of the draft was the 4F or "reject," particularly, the 1,875,000 [51] who were 4F for neuropsychiatric reasons (8 per cent of men of draft age). A total of 4,828,000 men were rejected who approximated 26 per cent of our man power in 18-to-35 age groups.

What happened to these men as a result of their rejection? Those who had not wanted to go into the Army were glad. The severely neurotic who had fears of the Army was reassured and hoped the standards would not change.[52] Others were keenly disappointed. But probably most, if not all of them, were sensitive about the reason for their rejection. They were the brunt of jokes; they were looked upon with suspicion as being either cowards or slackers; they were called upon for repeated explanations. They were stigmatized and knew it,[53] and often had a most difficult time on their return to the community. Undoubtedly, many went into defense jobs more to compensate for this feeling than for the possible monetary gain.

Many rejectees first learned of their disability at the induction center. This was specially true of men turned down for psychiatric reasons. Often, they, as others, had given up their jobs. This was particularly true in 1941 and 1942, when men passed by their local Selective Service medical board were turned down by the Army Induction Board 2 weeks later. Too often we received reports of employers who would not permit men rejected for this cause to return to their previous jobs. In one survey [54] of 84 per cent of 3,500 rejected men (for all causes) who had been employed prior to their examination, only 72 per cent regained their same employment following rejection.

Many of the psychiatric rejectees became upset or alarmed. For many, rejection was the first news of their condition either to themselves or their families. To others, what had previously been regarded as not serious suddenly appeared important because of the rejection. Very real problems were the dread of the stigma popularly given to individuals with psychiatric illness and the fear that they might suffer special vocational handicaps. Many men invented physical causes for their 4F category to satisfy the curiosity of rela-

---

[51] These are based on the number of persons in Class 4F (rejections for physical causes) in August, 1945.

[52] Rennie, T. A. C., "Psychiatric Rehabilitation Therapy," *Am. J. Psychiat.,* 101:476-485, Jan., 1945. Riemer found that it stimulated such individuals to overcome their illness. Riemer, M. D., "Effects of 4F Classification on Psychoneurotics under Treatment," *Ment. Hyg.,* 30:451-455, July, 1946.

[53] Overholser, W., "Contributions of Psychiatry to National Defense," *Am. J. Orthopsychiat.,* 11:634-637, Oct., 1941. At this early date attention was called to this problem.

[54] Orr, D. W., "The Rejected Registrant in the Community," *Bull. Menninger Clinic,* 5:184-187, Sept., 1941.

tives or friends. Undoubtedly, many sought medical help. Rich [55] reported on 44 such men who were seen in a clinic, a fourth of whom came because of worry over the cause of their rejection.

What most people failed to grasp, including the rejected registrants, was that military standards differed from civilian requirements. Lack of qualifications prevented many men from becoming good soldiers, but it did not follow that these men could not qualify for other work. This is excellently pointed out and discussed by Dumas and Keen [56] in their *Psychiatric Primer for the Veteran's Family and Friends*. A man may be disappointed if he does not make the first team, but he should not regard it as a disgrace. If an individual had managed satisfactorily before his induction examination, certainly the examination itself had not changed him, and he could function just as well afterward. Use of the term "rejectee" was unfortunate, since the average American resents and is offended by any form of rejection.

Part of the problem arose with the local boards. They had the dual responsibility of representing the government in selecting men for military service and also of maintaining the home front. Too often the latter responsibility was ignored. Occasionally these boards were even sadistic, returning the same man for several examinations because they wanted to force him into the Army—good or bad! Too infrequently did they realize that many men could function in civilian life and be an asset to the community who could not possibly be effective in the Army. The real misfits were those put into the Army by the local or induction-center boards who could not or would not adjust. Many soldiers who were discharged shortly after their induction represented such mistakes in selection.

Particularly traumatic to the psychiatric rejectees was the failure on the part of the induction-board examiners to explain, simply and helpfully, the cause for rejection. Too often the men returned home uncertain of the reason for their turndown and concerned about themselves as a result. No rationalization of lack of time can justify this mistake which was of sufficient concern to the War Department for it to issue a special bulletin to the field regarding the use of tact in rejection.[57]

The stigmatization of the 4F during the war was one of the grossly unfair aspects of our draft system, which is badly in need of revision. In a subsequent emergency certainly very serious consideration should be given to the drafting of all man power for assignment to industry, agriculture, and else-

[55] Rich, G. J., "Problems of the Rejected Man," *Dis. Nerv. System,* **6**:115-118, Apr., 1945.
[56] Dumas, A. G., and Keen, G., *A Psychiatric Primer for the Veteran's Family and Friends,* University of Minnesota Press, Minneapolis, 1945, p. 130.
[57] Adjutant General's Memorandum W600-22-43, on Rejection or Discharge for Psychiatric Reasons, 5 March 1943.

where as well as to the military forces. This method was used in Canada and Great Britain.

OVERSEAS PHYSICAL STANDARDS

Before a military unit went overseas, effort was made to prevent a man from going out of the country who was likely to have physical or mental difficulties. Consequently, all men to be shipped out were rechecked. The specific instructions regarding psychiatric defects requiring removal from alerted units included:

Chronic psychoses, or an authenticated history thereof; marked degrees of psychopathic personality, marked mental deficiency, and chronic disabling psychoneurotic disorders. Transient psychoses, psychopathic personality and psychoneuroses of mild and moderate severity, or a definite history of such, while not in themselves disqualifying, placed such individuals in a borderline group. The decision in such cases will be made on the basis of consideration of the following features: a. the severity or duration of symptoms; b. the type and degree of external stress precipitating the symptoms (imminence of departure for overseas, domestic difficulties, recent debilitating physical disorders, serious job misassignment); c. individual's basic personality strength and nature of previous adjustment and performance; d. actual residual impairment of the individual's functional capacity.[58]

For the direct redeployment of troops to other theaters following VE-day, May 2, 1945, the War Department made plans for a complete physical examination of each man, with psychiatric requirements [59] for overseas movement essentially as given above.

PHYSICAL PROFILE SERIAL

At the meeting of the American Association of Military Surgeons in Philadelphia in the fall of 1943, Brigs. G. Brock Chisholm and Jonathan Meakins [60] of the Canadian Army had a large display to explain their system of evaluating soldiers for specific jobs. A numerical series indicated the physical and mental capabilities of the individual. They called the system

---

[58] These were first published in War Department Circular 196, "Utilization of Manpower (all military personnel) Based on Physical Capacity," dated 30 June 1945. The circular was revised, although the psychiatric section was not changed, in War Department Circular 17 on the "Utilization of Man Power," dated 17 January 1946.

[59] Preparation for Inter-Theater Movements, Inclosure No. 1, War Department, 1 April 1945; Inclosure No. 1 to Annex B, Redeployment Movements of AG letter 320.2 (15 February 1945) OB-S-E-M, 27 February 1945, Subject: Policies and Procedures Governing the Redeployment of the Army upon the Cessation of Hostilities in Europe, para. 6b.

[60] Meakins, J. C., " 'PULHEMS' System of Medical Grading," *Canadian Med. Assoc. J.,* 49:349-354, Nov., 1943.

the PULHEMS: P stood for the physical capacity or stamina, U for the upper extremities, L for the lower extremities, H for hearing defects, E for eyes, M for mentality and intelligence, and S for emotional stability. The score was derived from the numbers which were substituted for the letters. The number (1-4) rated the function of the part of the body for whose letter it was substituted.

In December, 1943, Lt. Col. Malcolm J. Farrell and I went to Canada to visit some of their military installations. We were very much impressed with the effectiveness of this system. Not only was the individual scored, but we found that the personnel division of the Canadian army had graded every job in terms of the minimum PULHEMS requirements necessary to carry it out. If a man was defective in hearing or lower extremities or eyesight, it was comparatively easy to find a job, rated by experts as to physical requirements, into which he could fit. On our return to Washington we outlined this system in some detail and recommended it in our report.

The probability is that our recommendation received little if any attention by higher authority. Probably from other sources, however, some individuals in Personnel became interested in the Canadian plan. After many months of investigation and discussion our Army adopted a part of it with the purpose of improving the processes of screening and assignment of personnel.

The American system was known as the PULHES. Despite the strong recommendation of the Neuropsychiatry Consultants Division, the "M," intellectual status, was dropped. Since the record of the American soldier gave his score in the Army General Classification Test (the AGCT, which was a rough index of his intelligence), higher authority ruled that any numerical score of mental status was not necessary. Otherwise the letters represented the same body parts as in the Canadian PULHEMS.

Each of these letters had four potential grades: 1, was the highest and indicated perfect or ideal examination findings; 4, was the lowest grade and in every instance was nonacceptable. Most profiles when written out as numerical scores would read 111111. The minor deviations were acceptable. A man who had some slight defect in the upper extremity (like a missing finger on the left hand) and slightly defective eyesight would be graded 121121.

The psychiatric standards (S) were graded as follows: [61] profile serial 1 indicated that no psychiatric disorder was present; profile serial 2 stood for individuals with mild, transient, psychoneurotic reactions, mild psychopathic personality, or borderline mental deficiency (when the profile system was

---

[61] Supplement to Mobilization Regulations 1-9, Physical Profile Serial, dated 22 May 1944, revised 30 June 1945. The first instructions were sent out by the Adjutant General on 3 March 1944 [Letter ref.: SPX 220.01 (3 March 1944) OC-H-WDGAP] and followed by a War Department Memorandum W40-44, on 18 May 1944 on "Physical Profile Plan."

first inaugurated, there was no number 2 grade for the psychiatric evaluation, but so many men were eliminated who could have potential value for service that it was subsequently included as given); profile serial 3 represented individuals with mild but chronic psychoneuroses, moderate transient psychoneurotic reactions, or mental deficiency in mild degree; profile serial 4 denoted individuals with psychoses or with authenticated history of such, moderate to severe chronic psychoneuroses, severe transient psychoneuroses, marked degrees of psychopathic personality, or marked mental deficiency.

Following the adoption of the system, each soldier was profiled at the reception center when he came into the Army, and his assignment from there was to some degree based upon his profile. A low score on L, for instance, prevented him from being put into the Infantry. At or near the completion of basic training, each enlisted man received a physical inspection by one or more medical officers, and his profile was verified or revised upward or downward as the findings warranted. If and when he was hospitalized, his profile was revised in accordance with his condition at the time of his recovery or transfer. When he returned from overseas he was given an examination at the redistribution center, and again his profile might be changed.

While far less effective in the American than in the Canadian Army, the profile system did aid in the assignment of men to types of jobs. It was particularly helpful when there were transfers of large numbers of troops from one corps to another, since it was possible to check PULHES serial numbers quickly in order to determine who was physically capable of serving in the new unit. For instance, when large numbers of Air Corps personnel were to be transferred to the Infantry, those without sufficient physical stamina to be infantrymen were easily screened out. The profile also prevented, at least to some degree, the unloading by one unit onto another of men with some physical or mental defect.

EVALUATION OF RESULTS

The weight of evidence in our experience in selection indicates that a personality evaluation by a psychiatrist should be included in the induction examination. There is no doubt that the method by which this was made in this war had many flaws. Men were rejected who could have given good service, while others were accepted who should have been rejected. This is strongly suggested in a very small survey of 304 men inducted in 1941 who, at the time, were classified into two equal groups, one of good prospects and one of passable but questionable prospects. Aita [62] made a study of these men 5 years

62 Aita, J. A., "Efficacy of the Brief Clinical Interview Method in Predicting Adjustment." (To be published in *Arch. Neurol. & Psychiat.*)

after his examination of the entire group at their induction into the Army. He found that 4.7 per cent of the good prospects failed, whereas 50 per cent of the poor prospects turned out to be average soldiers, and 30 per cent of this same group turned out to be better than average. Undoubtedly the most common error of psychiatrists in evaluation occurred in borderline cases, many of whom were excluded during that long era of ultraconservatism and inexperience. The psychiatrists received the blame for both the mistakes in acceptance and rejection, without a fair consideration of the prevailing attitudes, the directives, the methods, and inexperience of the Army as a whole.

These figures from Aita's study re-enforce the point made repeatedly on previous pages. Psychiatric casualties resulted from poor leadership, faulty or no motivation to do a job, lack of identification with a unit, and severe external stress, in addition to whatever the subject's personality was at the time of selection. Ideal selection could—and we believe did—reduce the total number of casualties, but it was only one factor in the psychiatric casualty rate.

Our experience with combat taught us that no selection methods could have picked out the men who would fail. In other words, if a man succeeded in maintaining his mental equilibrium through the training period, shipment overseas, and training on foreign soil, there was no means by which unsuccessful combat service could have been forecasted.

From the point of view of man power, we must frankly face the fact that although they were poor risks, many unstable individuals could and did make excellent records. Many men who were rejected as questionable prospects might have been good soldiers under favorable circumstances. This problem is vividly related by one of the Infantry division psychiatrists, Plesset:

For these reasons and others, there were remaining in my division after the gang plank was raised, 138 men who during training had presented sufficient adjustment difficulty to necessitate psychiatric attention. Most were the chronic complainers who were referred by their unit surgeons. . . . I anticipated seeing most of the group of 138 in the first few days of combat or perhaps even earlier. . . . At the end of 30 days of combat, only one of the entire group had been evacuated for "exhaustion." No other had been evacuated for any reason—137 were on duty. "Duty" is not a particularly descriptive term for combat in winter, for living and fighting in snow and mud, for cold food and often little sleep, for constant proximity to death or injury, for loneliness and fear—but "duty" is the only available word. . . . After 60 days of combat, 3 had been admitted to the division clearing station for "exhaustion"—134 remained on "duty." In the subsequent three months of combat there were no other admissions from this group for "exhaustion" . . . . At the termination of the war, there were 120 remaining on duty (14 had been transferred, killed or evacuated for other reasons). Nine had received a Purple Heart for wounds, 8 had received a Bronze Star Medal for heroic or meritorious service.[63]

63 Plesset, M. R., "Psychoneurotics in Combat," *Am. J. Psychiat.*, 103:87-90, July, 1946.

Some of us in psychiatry in the Army were aware of such experiences as reported by Plesset. On the other hand, some others of our confreres seemed naïve in assuming that psychiatrists could adequately judge the degree of resistance a soldier could marshal against all the general and specific stresses which were to affect him in the Army. Too many of us did not appreciate the strength of the emotional supports which were provided by social forces operating in the Army. Nor was there any way to measure the capacity of the soldier to identify with his unit and to obtain strength from such a psychological process. The resiliency of the American soldier to regain his equilibrium under stress could not be anticipated.

Blame upon the inadequacy of wartime psychiatric selection techniques should be tempered with a wider recognition of the fact that the psychiatrist in the induction center had no possible way of evaluating the four most important factors of influence upon the adjustment of a soldier: the nature of the leadership that would be provided for him; the degree of motivation that he had to do his job or that could be instilled into him; the type of job to which he might be assigned; and the degree of stress that might confront him. If any or all of these were sources of sufficient psychological stress, even a well-integrated person might be unable to adjust.

CONCLUSION

As a result of our experience, we arrived at certain conclusions regarding psychiatric screening of recruits:

(1) A consistent policy as to whether we were to have a quantity or a quality Army would allow more consistent psychiatric selection. We started this war with an attempt to build a quality Army. Pressure for man power made us change to a quantity Army. The changing point of view and standards of examination, with so many examiners concerned, created difficulties.

(2) Everyone—line, medical, psychiatric officers—concerned with the program should fully appreciate that no type of psychiatric examination can eliminate all psychiatric casualties. At best, one can only expect to eliminate gross disorders, the psychotic and severe neurotic, the markedly feeble-minded, and those heavily predisposed to break down. There is no magic trick which will forecast those men who are going to break down as a result of terrific stresses or poor leadership.

(3) If psychiatry is to function in the selection of men, provision must be made for adequate personnel to do the job. A psychiatrist cannot be a crystal-ball gazer who, after 30 seconds with his subject, can determine his effectiveness for any job, certainly not for war. Had we been able to follow the original plan of 15 minutes, if necessary, for each candidate, with no more

than 50 examinations per psychiatrist a day, the job could have been done much more effectively. Even then, the psychiatrist could not pick out all those who might break in combat.

(4) A plan for better utilization of man power should be evolved so that the psychiatrist could accept a man of limited capacity and have some definite authority for recommending him to a certain type of work. On this score, we could learn much from the British who used their man power far more effectively than we did in the American Army.

(5) A social history is essential to effective psychiatric examinations. This does not need to be as complicated as the plan initiated in the Medical Survey Program. One short form should provide the pertinent facts, stated either negatively or positively, without being cluttered up with hearsay or opinion.

(6) In addition to what can be done at the induction-center level, the most effective method of screening would be a system similar to the one developed by the Navy. If the recruit faltered or failed during his first 6 or 8 weeks in training, it should be possible to discharge him from the service by a very simple administrative procedure. Such a system would provide a trial period to determine adjustability. This would permit the military force to save large sums of money and effort as well as to save the man, or excuse him before he develops severe maladjustment for which the nation would pay indefinitely.

This discussion of selection would not be complete without comment on the selection process in universal training—should it become a reality. (Many of us, who thoroughly disapprove of the principle of universal military training, accept as a necessity the recommendations of the President's Advisory Commission on Universal Training,[64] and this includes as one item in the national defense, the program of universal training. To this the author strongly subscribes.) An organized group of psychiatrists, many of whom saw active service during the last war, has expressed its consensus of opinion regarding the principles of selection *if* universal military training were adopted. These recommendations, bluntly, make good psychiatric sense.

The following resolution was adopted with two negative votes by the Group for the Advancement of Psychiatry at their meeting in Asbury Park, N. J., on Armistice Day 1947:

If universal military training is adopted, the Group for the Advancement of Psychiatry believes that certain lessons which developed out of the experience of psychiatrists who served the military and civilian forces during the recent war must be given urgent consideration.

---

[64] *A Program for National Security.* May 29, 1947. Report of the President's Advisory Commission on Universal Training. (Karl T. Compton, Chairman). U.S. Government Printing Office, Washington, D.C., 1947.

Information which could have led to the improvement of selection techniques, of morale, of motivation, and of treatment was ignored after World War I. The added experience of psychiatrists in World War II has demonstrated that medical facilities and personnel are wasted by prolonged and unprofitable hospitalization, and that selection and assignment of personnel under criteria appearing to the public to be arbitrary and unreasonable have done unnecessary damage to the morale and motivation of both the military and the civilian. The nation learned the need for the conservation of man power and the lesson must not be forgotten.

There was a strong recommendation in the Compton report that psychiatric advice be sought and followed in the planning for mobilization and training. There has now been almost two years of work on the program, but there is little evidence that psychiatric counsel has been fully used in developing the mobilization plans and operations. As a result of this failure to follow the Compton report recommendations, the most important factor in conservation of man power is again being ignored.

The Group for the Advancement of Psychiatry believes that changes in the policies and techniques of selection, induction, training, classification, proper job assignment, treatment, and discharge are urgently needed if full utilization of the nation's man power and motivation is to be achieved. These changes should include:

I. *Selection.* Mobilization for training should be universal in the broadest possible sense. Only those individuals obviously disqualified by disabling disease from rendering any service, should be exempted. All others within the eligible age group, without exception, should be called upon to serve.

II. *Training.* Diversification of training to take account of variations in individual capacity, based on differing psychological aptitudes, as well as on physical limitations, must be accomplished.

III. *Classification and Reclassification.* Classification and reclassification must be a fluid and constant process. It should always be both an adjunctive and controlling factor in the assignment and training program. Again, the classification and reclassification program must consider emotional and intellectual, as well as physical capacity.

IV. *Discharge.* Individuals should be discharged only when the most complete utilization of the training and classification programs has demonstrated the individual's unfitness for use in any capacity. (Those individuals disabled for civilian activity by intercurrent disorders should be medically discharged, but all other ineffectives should be disposed of through administrative channels.)

V. *Mental Hygiene.* The meaning of the steps in the mobilization program should be made clear to all mobilized personnel and to the public. Every means of raising the levels of morale, incentive, and motivation should be utilized by both the military and civilian agencies to the fullest possible extent.

VI. *Treatment.* It is essential that there be provided an adequate treatment program based upon the knowledge derived from experiences of World War II. This treatment program should envelop all aspects of the total psychiatric problem.

The Group for the Advancement of Psychiatry in no way implies endorsement or disapproval of universal military training. It believes that the above approach is essential in any universal military training program to obtain and maintain military and civilian morale and motivation, and the maximum utilization of the nation's man power.

20

THE TREATMENT OF PSYCHIATRIC PATIENTS

"MY BOY was brought home last week from the hospital at Camp ——. They told me he was all right, but he doesn't seem to know what he is doing."

"Why did the Army doctors send my boy home? Why didn't they do something for him? We kept him with us for ten days and then we had to take him to the state hospital. The Army caused this. He was all right before he joined up. Why doesn't the Army keep him till he gets well?"

These excerpts were typical of many letters I received—or at least that were referred to me—to answer in my official Army job. Following an article, "Psychiatry and the War," which I wrote for the *Atlantic Monthly* in November, 1945, a keen veteran discharged for psychiatric reasons wrote a sharp retort for the correspondence column in a subsequent issue of the magazine. He was critical of the fact that he had received no treatment.

These incensed relatives and the justifiably critical veteran were unaware of the strenuousness of our struggle to initiate psychiatric treatment in the Army. They did not know about the many, many obstacles to it, in addition to a previously established Army policy. They did know, what we also knew, that psychiatric patients received minimal or no treatment in the early years of the war.

The fact was that until the spring of 1944, the official point of view of the Army toward psychiatric illnesses was a mixture of fatalism and disinterest; treatment was discouraged. The psychiatric treatment program had to be evolved during the war. In its evaluation the opinion of the individual patient will vary, depending on the geographical location of hospitalization, his particular psychiatric problem, and on the date of his treatment.

During more than half of the war the official policy was: "Individuals permanently unfit for Army service because of neuropsychiatric disturbances will not be retained for definitive treatment but will be discharged and arrangements will be made for further care by the Veterans Administration if such is indicated." [1]

---

[1] *Army Regulations* 615-360. Sec. II, 25 May 1944. This had been unchanged from preceding issues of these regulations. By a very liberal interpretation one could treat "conditions incurred incident to the service who . . . may within a reasonable period be returned to duty." Change 16, *Army Regulations* 615-360, 15 December 1943.

As a result, the function of psychiatrists was merely to diagnose and dispose of patients according to existing regulations.[2] Usually the more prompt they were in the "disposition" of soldiers on their wards, the better was their standing with their commanding officer. In spite of specific instructions to the contrary and the conspicuous absence of official encouragement, psychiatrists did attempt to treat as many patients as they could with what time and facilities were available.[3] However, they were continuously under pressure by hospital commanders to get rid of all psychiatric patients. They were given little or no help in obtaining personnel or equipment to provide even minimal treatment.

During the time patients awaited their disposition, those with neurotic reactions almost invariably became worse. Most of them wanted a discharge; many of them openly said so. With nothing else to do they "suffered" with their symptoms, which they believed they had to maintain in order to get out of the Army.

Acute psychotic patients were given emergency treatment in some hospitals with sedation and, in a few instances, wet-sheet packs. In 1942, prolonged-immersion tubs were approved, but few were actually obtained. Not until April, 1943, was shock therapy authorized.[4]

The Surgeon General brought an additional psychiatrist into the Neuropsychiatry Consultants Division, Lt. Col. Walter Barton, to develop a program of occupational therapy for psychiatric cases, but he was shortly thereafter transferred to the Reconditioning Division. In August, 1943, occupational therapy departments were authorized for general hospitals in the zone of interior, but not until almost the end of the war were there anywhere nearly enough occupational therapists to man these departments. In the meantime, the American Red Cross recreational workers were of an inestimable help in their diversion program. In many installations they assisted the psychiatrist directly on the psychiatric wards.

Despite local efforts, no major change of attitude was voiced by the War Department until 1944.[5] At that time a set of suggestions was published in a technical medical bulletin. Although the instructions in a bulletin were not

---

[2] This point of view was accepted by psychiatrists through necessity as expressed by Rosenberg: "The primary functions of military psychiatry are essentially those of diagnosis and disposition." Rosenberg, S. J., "The Psychiatric Service of an Army Station Hospital," *Am. J. Psychiat.*, 99:864-868, May, 1943.

[3] Porter, W. C.; Novak, J. G.; and Lemkau, P. V., "Therapeutic Considerations for Army Psychiatrists," *Mil. Surgeon*, 92:372, Apr., 1943.

[4] Surgeon General's Letter 88, 23 April 1943.

[5] *War Department Technical Bulletin, Medical 28,* 1 April 1944. Revised and issued as *Bulletin 84,* 10 August 1944, and again on 20 February 1947, "Treatment Program for Psychiatric Patients in Station and General Hospitals."

official orders, nevertheless they carried sufficient authority to facilitate the development of a treatment program. Technically, treatment was not officially approved until a directive of March, 1945,[6] which ordered the retention of patients with psychoneuroses sufficiently severe to require hospital treatment. It was also ordered that other psychiatric cases would receive appropriate treatment while awaiting disposition. The directive was further elucidated in June [7] with the statement that individuals with psychoneuroses resulting from overseas service were not to be discharged until they had reached a point of maximum improvement in a convalescent hospital.

When the program of physical reconditioning [8] was introduced, its aim was to assist the soldier with a physical illness or injury to recover his full strength before returning to his unit. When started in September, 1943,[9] it did not specifically include psychiatric patients. A subsequent letter sent from the Surgeon General, December 10, 1943, indicated to commanding officers of hospitals that the psychiatric patients should be handled separately and at specific centers or on separate wards in such a way that they would not be mixed with other patients preparing for return to duty. This letter implied but did not state that the psychiatric patients were to have their own "reconditioning program." The principle of separation from medical and surgical patients was subscribed to by the Neuropsychiatry Consultants Division because many of the needs for the reconditioning of men with emotional disorders were not satisfied by the physical reconditioning program. Psychiatric patients needed special activities.[10]

These historical details demonstrate the entire reversal of policy and practice from no treatment to "maximum benefit of hospitalization" (treatment) for psychiatric patients.[11] They also mutely testify to the slowness of the battle to bring about this change. As the point of view changed, many steps were

---

[6] *Army Regulations 615-361,* Change 2, 1 March 1945.

[7] War Department Circular 162, 2 June 1945.

[8] The program has been described in the following: Thorndike, A., "The Reconditioning of Patients in Army Service Force Hospitals," Convalescence and Rehabilitation Conference, *New York Academy of Med.,* Apr. 25, 1944, pp. 51-55; Rusk, H. A., "The Convalescent Training Program in the Army Air Forces," *ibid.,* pp. 81-89; Barton, W. E., "The Reconditioning and Rehabilitating Program in Army Hospitals," *Am J. Psychiat.,* 101:607-613, Mar., 1945; Bingham, W. V., " 'Start Climbing, Soldier!' The Army Program for Rehabilitating Casualties," *Ann. Am. Acad. Polit. and Soc. Sc.,* 239:60-65, May, 1945.

[9] Surgeon General's Letter 168, 21 September 1943.

[10] *War Department Technical Bulletin, Medical 80,* 3 August 1944; an Army Service Forces Circular 175, 10 June 1944, had authorized reconditioning for psychiatric patients in general hospitals. See the discussion of W. E. Barton, "Convalescent Reconditioning Program for Neuropsychiatric Casualties in the U.S. Army," Chap. XXV, in *Military Neuropsychiatry,* The Williams & Wilkins Company, Baltimore, 1946, pp. 271-284.

[11] An excellent description of the total therapeutic efforts in psychiatry in the Army are given by L. H. Smith, in "Treatment Activities in War Psychiatry," *Am. J. Psychiat.,* 101:303-309, Nov., 1944.

necessary in order to implement the new program and to aid the psychiatrists.[12]

A recitation of these historical developments would be incomplete without reference to the very important boost given the treatment program by President Roosevelt. A letter from him left no doubt as to his desire to include treatment for the psychiatric casualties in the Army's medical services. As might be expected, this carried great weight toward giving the problem detailed attention.

December 4, 1944

My dear Mr. Secretary:

I am deeply concerned over the physical and emotional condition of disabled men returning from the war. I feel, as I know you do, that the ultimate ought to be done for them to return them as useful citizens—useful not only to themselves but to the community.

I wish you would issue instructions to the effect that it should be the responsibility of the military authorities to insure that no overseas casualty is discharged from the armed forces until he has received the maximum benefits of hospitalization and convalescent facilities which must include physical and psychological rehabilitation, vocational guidance, prevocational training, and resocialization.

Very sincerely yours,

FRANKLIN DELANO ROOSEVELT

Because the Secretary of War was aware of the special interest of the President in the neuropsychiatric problem, he sent the President a letter on February 28, 1945, which described the progress that had been made in dealing with this group of patients.

Feb 28 1945

The President
The White House

My dear Mr. President:

In your letter of December 4, 1944, you expressed concern over the physical and emotional condition of disabled men returning from the war and emphasized that no overseas casualty be discharged from the armed service until he had received the maximum benefits of hospitalization and convalescent facilities.

In addition to the Army program I outlined in my reply of the 20th, comprehensive studies have been made on the subject of psychoneurosis during the past few months both insofar as it affects the soldiers returned from overseas as well as those who have not yet had such service. These studies were conducted by War Department personnel, aided by five of the nation's outstanding civilian psychiatrists.

---

12 There were handicaps in the war construction; the atrocious W-8 wards, conceived after World War I, had to be remodeled and a new type devised. There were no facilities for activities treatment for closed-ward patients, so that in September, 1944, a request for a "Social Therapy" building for each psychiatric center was made and approved. Most of the 29 psychiatric centers became so equipped at an approximate cost of $60,000 per building, providing an OT shop and theater, in addition to treatment offices.

Specifically, the field of psychoneurosis insofar as the Army is concerned may be divided into two broad groups. First, those men who entered the Army as normal well integrated individuals whose type of psychoneurosis or maladjustment is a result of military service. The majority of such cases have developed as a result of the severe strains of actual combat. Second, those men who brought with them from civilian life inherent weaknesses such as emotional instability or inadequate personality traits. The majority of these cases appear among the maladjusted, inadaptable and inapt soldiers who cannot qualify physically for overseas service. Both groups include cases ranging from mild to severe, from cases correctible within the means available to a field commander to those requiring hospitalization and the most expert medical treatment.

The soldier who is emotionally sick will, as in the past, receive maximum hospital benefit and treatment. To this end facilities have been enlarged and training provided to increase the medical and other personnel required. In general, the treatment principles are based on well founded experiences gained in this war and in the last, and on sound medical judgment. Every effort is made to treat the combat case early, when treatment is most effective—even within the sound of the guns. As a result a majority of these cases recover and return to full combat duty. Another significant proportion can be salvaged for continued duty in rear areas. Cases that cannot be restored to duty in this manner are returned to the United States where they are treated by special psychiatric techniques which have been found to be both practical and effective. Cases developing in this country are also treated in this manner. No soldier who is emotionally sick will be discharged until every effort has been made toward maximum improvement. When discharge is required it will be through medical channels.

Too often in the past the soldier who is inapt or inadaptable has been classed as a psychoneurotic. Usually this group adjusted fairly well in civil life in spite of their deficiencies, but due to certain mild psychoneurotic tendencies or to an inadequate personality are unable to adapt to military life. Every effort is made through treatment, leadership, education, orientation, motivation and training to enable them to perform satisfactorily in the military service. Should this not be successful and there is no medical reason for a disability discharge, these men will be released through administrative channels without mention of psychoneurosis.

A related problem is created by those soldiers returned from overseas who find it difficult to readjust to life in the United States. These men are not acutely ill nor do they require hospitalization in the usual sense but their problems are no less real. Here readjustment is a matter of psychiatric treatment, leadership, education, proper motivation, and placement in a job where their ability and training may be constructively utilized. Proper jobs will be provided by shipping overseas all qualified soldiers who have not had such service. In the education and proper motivation phase all resources will be utilized. By following this procedure we will be able to better prepare these soldiers for their ultimate return to a gainful civil life. Those who are unable to readjust to Army life in the United States will be returned to civil life without the label of psychoneurosis.

It is significant that the general term psychoneurosis will be discontinued in medical records and a more definitive diagnosis used such as anxiety reaction or other accepted terms. It is believed the use of such terms will alleviate much of the disadvantage resulting from the overworked term psychoneurosis.

Extensive studies on the subject of psychoneurosis have been made and are continuing in the European Area. Specialists in this field will conduct additional studies in the Pacific Area. These studies are primarily concerned with the preventive phase of the problem.

Knowing your intense interest in the matter, I am forwarding to you this information, as I am confident that the above policies will be of benefit to the soldiers and are in furtherance of your desires.

Respectfully yours,
HENRY L. STIMSON
Secretary of War

The answer of the President to the Secretary of War is reproduced on the following page.

Treatment methods in psychiatry. These differ from those of medicine and surgery. It is not possible here to give an extensive review of psychiatric treatment methods. The techniques to investigate the psychological life of a patient (interviews, observation, contacts with relatives and friends, interviews under sedation, hypnosis, psychoanalysis) may be simultaneously forms of treatment. Sometimes treatment entails modifying or even changing the environment. More often it requires changes within the person which result from increasing his understanding of himself and his situation.

The most important general method is "psychotherapy." In his examination the psychiatrist investigates the background and emotional life of his patient. He not only makes notes for his own guidance but very often can show the patient some aspects of the illness which he, the patient, does not see. The psychiatrist may also make suggestions or recommendations to the patient about his method of living or his relationships. This type of treatment is called "psychotherapy."

All psychotherapy can be classified into the two types suggested above: one in which the psychiatrist attempts to uncover the conflicts in the life of the patient and another in which he tries to capitalize on the assets of the patient by making suggestions as to substituting new interests or recommending changes in the environment. The first type is called "expressive psychotherapy" [13] and the latter "supportive." Depending on the patient's needs, the physician offers understanding, reassurance, encouragement, considerate

---

[13] One of the more thorough-going expressive types of psychotherapy is psychoanalysis. In the Army, it could not be used except in so far as those physicians who had used this therapy in civilian life could apply its principles to more general treatment methods. The psychoanalytic influence was manifest in the courses presented to the students at the School of Military Neuropsychiatry; its principles were extensively presented in the lecture outlines for medical officers ("Lecture Outlines for Officers on Personnel Adjustment Problems," *War Department Technical Bulletin, Medical 12,* 22 February 1944); its theory was the basis for much of the nomenclature adopted ("Nomenclature and Method of Recording Diagnosis," *War Department Technical Bulletin, Medical 203,* 19 October 1945). However, no extended form of individual psychotherapy was possible because of the shortage of time and man power.

THE WHITE HOUSE
WASHINGTON

NOTED BY
SECRETARY OF WAR

RECEIVED
WAR DEPARTMENT
SECRETARY'S OFFICE

1945 MAR 25 PM 12:24

March 24, 1945

My dear Mr. Secretary:

Thank you for your letter of February 28, 1945, in which you further outline the scope of the psychiatric problem in the Army.

I fully appreciate the magnitude of the task of caring for the soldier who is emotionally sick as a result of combat, as well as the man whose service maladjustment is but a reflection of a long existant inadequacy.

It would seem that your program provides equally well for both groups and should be a material aid in their ultimate civilian adjustment.

Sincerely yours,

Franklin D Roosevelt

The Honorable
Henry L. Stimson
Secretary of War
Washington, D. C.

FIGURE 1

attention, suggestions, recommendations, or whatever may be indicated to improve or relieve the emotional conflict.

In addition to his recommendations for changes in the environment or attitudes, the psychiatrist may utilize many aids or "medicines" in the form of hospital treatment with occupational, recreational, educational, and physical therapies. All of these means of helping patients readjust, which have been well known and utilized in civilian psychiatry, were also used in the Army. Temporary job placement and vocational training also served as a type of therapy. Special treatments were electroshock, insulin, fever, sedation, drugs.

Obstacles in treatment. The obstacles to effective implementation of the treatment program were great. Many of them were situational. Man power and time were extremely limited. There were, however, three psychological factors that influenced all psychiatric treatment in the Army.

The first of these was the fact, which every soldier recognized, that there were often real advantages in being sick. This, of course, led to the widely prevalent attitude of a lack of desire to get well. As mentioned previously, many battle casualties referred to their wounds as being worth $1,000,000. The corollary to the recognition that sickness prevented a man from doing any type of duty was that, if he got well, he had to go back to duty. Not only the psychiatrist, but every physician, was confronted with this major obstacle— the resistance of many soldiers toward getting well.

A second obstacle, peculiar to the Army, was the fact that the doctor was an officer and the patient usually an enlisted man. Much to the credit of our doctors, a reasonably successful patient-physician relationship was usually established, but rarely did it have the ease or freedom of the civilian situation. This was not a problem with the disturbed or disoriented patient. On the other hand, it was a special problem with the neurotic or the mildly psychotic patient.[14]

The breach between the officer-doctor and his enlisted-man patient was more significant in psychotherapy than in surgical or medical treatment. The doctor was at one and the same time the commanding officer, the judge, the authority, the law, the benefactor, and the physician. He held the power of life and death over his patient in the sense, at least, that it was his responsibility to order the soldier back into combat if he believed the man could go on duty. The hospital was a part of the Army; the officer and the soldier were in the Army.

One could not do away with discipline because the soldier was sick. Yet because of that discipline some patients regarded the medical officer as a repre-

---

[14] Serota described the behavior of the medical officer toward depressed patients as contributing either toward alleviating the sense of guilt or indefinitely prolonging it. Serota, H. M., "A Note on the Treatment of Depressive Psychoses in Soldiers," *Bull. Menninger Clinic,* 10:10-17, Jan., 1946.

sentative of the Army he hated rather than as his doctor. However, in those cases where it was too relaxed, the soldier invariably tended to the free and easy civilian relationship, with consequent difficulty in resuming his soldier role when he went back to his company. On the other hand, there was no question that an antitherapeutic situation was created when a ward master would go into a psychiatric ward and call "Attention!" as preparation for the medical officer to make his rounds. In spite of the fact that maintenance of discipline was always a reminder to the soldier of the authority of the officer and a handicap to a beneficial rapport with the officer-doctor, it was essential in the Army.

The third obstacle in the treatment of all patients, but particularly in that of psychiatric patients, lay in the specific Army orientation of the doctor. In many situations, most vividly in combat, the aim of medical treatment was to return the soldier to duty which was often not synonymous with his return to complete health. Treatment, therefore, was aimed at improving a man sufficiently to function, not seeking perfection of his health. As Hanson described it, "This meant that discomfort is not synonymous with disability, and thus the individual who still retains minor complaints and symptoms which are not progressive must be made to carry out his duties in spite of these minor discomforts. It is impossible to make the majority of the psychiatric and psychosomatic patients symptom-free under combat conditions, but it is quite possible to return the majority of them to effective combat duty." [15] Although for a different reason, this principle is regularly used in the treatment of psychiatric patients in civilian life. A neurotic individual—if his illness forced him to give up his job—is encouraged to return to work before he is entirely well. Often he is urged to do so at the earliest possible time.

Psychiatric hospital centers. A major development in the effort to improve the entire medical treatment program of the Army was the concentration of patients with various types of illnesses (neurosurgical, orthopedic, tropical disease, psychiatric, neurological, etc.) in specially designated general hospitals. Each hospital became a treatment center for several specialized types of cases. At the height of the patient load, 29 of the 65 general hospitals in the United States had psychiatric treatment services. These psychiatric centers were specially for psychotic patients, and all regional and station hospitals referred these patients to a designated center. Two general hospitals were devoted entirely to psychiatry (Mason and Darnall), primarily for the care of psychotic patients.[16] Patients from overseas, who had recovered from psychotic illnesses,

---

[15] Hanson, F. R., *Combat Psychiatry Among American Ground Forces in the Mediterranean Area,* introductory chapter. (To be published.)

[16] The Army Air Forces developed an excellent specialized psychiatric hospital for the treatment of neuroses, Don Cesar Hospital, St. Petersburg, Fla., under the professional direction of Lt. Col. (later Col.) Roy Grinker.

were sent to these installations to await their discharge. Also some patients with severe neurotic reactions were often admitted to these special hospitals for treatment. Mason General Hospital on Long Island at one time housed more than 3,000 patients. Darnall General Hospital in Kentucky provided for almost 1,000 patients.

At the time of the maximum load, there were 5,871 beds in closed (locked) wards and 7,238 beds in open wards authorized for psychiatry in all of the general and special hospitals. (In addition, there were 17,000 beds in convalescent hospitals and 6,000 in regional and station hospitals reserved for psychiatric use.) At our peak load of 37,000 psychiatric patients in the United States, there were 5,300 psychotic cases in our general hospitals; the balance were chiefly neurotic patients.

In each of these hospitals an elaborate program of education, occupation, and recreation was developed in addition to facilities for treatment far superior to those of the average state hospital. By the concentration of patients, it was possible to organize a much more active and thoroughgoing program of treatment [17] than could be developed previously in the more numerous psychiatric sections of widely separated hospitals.

A sample study of the disposition of patients from these psychiatric centers was made when they were carrying a peak case load (May 11 through September 7, 1945). Approximately half of a total of 16,651 patients were psychotic, and they were discharged from the Army. In 1942, at least 7 out of 10 cases of psychoses were transferred to veterans' or state hospitals. In 1945, with the policy changed to permit treatment, at least 7 out of 10 cases were well enough to be discharged home.

Convalescent hospitals. Convalescent hospitals were activated in the summer of 1944, probably the most progressive step in furthering psychiatric treatment. They were originally conceived as a means of getting neurotic patients out of the formal hospital atmosphere and at the same time providing a suitable treatment opportunity for the psychiatric casualties returned from overseas. Patients in these installations lived in barracks, wore the regular uniform, and looked after themselves. An essential part of the.regime was the elimination of the hospital atmosphere of seriously ill patients, nurses, beds, and a prevailing tone of invalidism. Twelve such convalescent hospitals were

17 Simon, B., "The Treatment of the Neuropsychiatric Patient in an Army Hospital," *Med. Clin. N. America,* Mar., 1946, pp. 459-472; Katz, E., "A Social Therapy Program for Neuropsychiatry in a General Hospital," *Psychological Bull.,* 42:782-788, Dec., 1945; Menninger, W. C., "Opportunities for Treatment of Neuropsychiatric Patients," *Bull. U.S. Army M. Dept.,* 74:90-98, Mar., 1944; Barbato, L., "Closed Ward Psychiatric Reconditioning," *Bull. U.S. Army M. Dept.,* 5:210-214, Feb., 1946; Read, H. S., "The Administration of a Small Psychiatry Center (Z.I.) in a General Hospital," *Mil. Surgeon,* 98:404-408, May, 1946. For a review of the origin of these centers, see Ginzberg, E., "Army Hospitalization, Retrospect and Prospect," *Bull. U.S. Army M. Dept.,* 8:38-47, Jan., 1948.

developed. Though their internal organization was changed several times, the psychiatric service remained the major section, often having more than 50 per cent of the patients. At the time of the peak patient load, there were 14,800 psychiatric patients in these 12 hospitals, and an additional 1,700 in similar Air Forces hospitals.

Treatment [18] in the convalescent hospitals included a greatly expanded program of activities and therapies including education, physical reconditioning, recreation, and handicrafts, as well as prevocational training. These installations became an interesting combination of educational institution, playground, and hospital.[19]

There are no statistics to indicate the results of treatment in these hospitals.[20] A wide variation in the percentage of patients returned to duty resulted almost entirely from command policy. The attitude in one installation was to return every man to duty who could function, whereas in another the prevailing practice was one of liberal use of discharges with little or no effort made to push the man back to duty.

Return to duty. The Neuropsychiatry Consultants Division consistently supported a policy of returning to duty all hospitalized psychiatric patients who were not disabled because of current sickness. The reasons for its stand were that this policy helped salvage man power, strengthened the soldier's (eventual if not immediate) self-respect, prevented weakening the morale of other soldiers, kept those men with faulty attitude problems from receiving medical discharges, and minimized invalidism and future claims.

However, this policy was combated on the basis that limited-assignment jobs were filled already; commanders did not want to be bothered with "second-rate" man power; most of these men could not be returned to combat. We

---

[18] Outlined in detail in *War Department Technical Bulletin, Medical 80*, 3 August 1944. Revised in War Department Memorandum 40-590-7, 17 December 1946. Also see Cotton, J. M., "The Psychiatric Treatment Program at Welch Convalescent Hospital," *Military Neuropsychiatry*, Proc. Assn. for Research in Nerv. and Ment. Dis., New York, 1944, The Williams & Wilkins Company, Baltimore, 1946, pp. 316-321; Senerchia, F. F., "The Neuropsychiatric Service of the Percy Jones Convalescent Hospital," *Proc. Neuropsychiatric Conference of the Sixth Service Command*, Chicago, 16-17 Nov., 1945, pp. 57-63.

[19] Freedman, H. L., "The Mental-Hygiene-Unit Approach to Reconditioning Neuropsychiatric Casualties," *Ment. Hyg.*, 29:269-302, Apr., 1945; Dunn, W. H., and Selinsky, H., "Army Neurosis Center," *Bull. U.S. Army M. Dept.*, 7:868-876, Oct., 1947. None of these ever developed as far as the British system at Northfield where the patients all became a part of a community, each with his own job. See the entire issue of the *Bull. Menninger Clinic* for May, 1946, which described the Northfield experiment.

[20] Some samplings of dispositions of psychiatric (psychoneurotic) patients returned from overseas are available from the 12 convalescent hospitals between May 11 and September 7, 1945. During this interval, 38,361 such patients were dismissed, 31,967 (83.3 per cent) with a discharge from the Army and 6,394 (16.6 per cent) returned to duty—this latter figure being smaller than the corresponding figure from general hospitals for originally much sicker patients (20.6 per cent). The percentage of return to duty from convalescent hospitals for any given week varied from 59 per cent in Welch and Butner to 3.7 per cent at Wakeman, and 1.7 per cent at Edwards. The patients were essentially the same types.

in psychiatry were faced with the fact that, in most instances, there was no place where these patients might be given a bit of help in getting re-established. Many were sent from the hospital directly to replacement or re-distribution centers to sit for days or weeks awaiting indiscriminate reassignment. We knew they were often "batted" around from one assignment to another, only too often again to enter the hospital on the new post. A survey based on 439 replies from the field [21] indicated that 26 per cent of such patients reassigned were rated as excellent, 42 per cent were satisfactory, and 32 per cent were poor. Even with this record of the salvage of 68 per cent, many commands insisted on the discharge of these patients after maximum benefit from hospitalization, regardless of their status at that time.

Overseas hospitals. The treatment program in overseas general hospitals was greatly handicapped by the short stay of patients and their frequent transfers to other hospitals further to the rear. The even more important handicap was inadequate personnel. There were never enough psychiatrists, nor were there enough supplemental workers. Clinical psychologists were assigned to many overseas hospitals, but the assignments came comparatively late in the war. It was a new job and not understood by many hospital commanders. There was no theater psychologist consultant. As a result, these men never had the support or supervision that was provided in the Service Commands in the United States. Because of their scarcity, social workers were never routinely assigned to overseas hospitals. In most of them, the Red Cross recreational workers were too few to give any substantial help in the development of an activities program on the psychiatric service or section.

In the European Theater one general hospital was devoted entirely to the treatment and evacuation of psychotic patients. Therapy was reasonably effective, but most patients were held only until a ship was available to return them to the States. The therapy, therefore, was of secondary importance. Two station hospitals [22] and one general hospital were devoted to the treatment of "combat exhaustion" and of those soldiers with this diagnosis who later developed definite neuroses. These hospitals did an interesting job, using sedation over a period of 2 to 6 days, giving tonic doses of insulin, utilizing group psychotherapy, obtaining emotional catharsis under a sedative when indicated, and finally providing a terminal 2-week period in a modified training company.

In the Pacific Theater there were five station hospitals [23] devoted to the

[21] *Health.* Monthly Progress Report. Army Service Forces. "Salvaging Neuropsychiatric Patients," June, 1944, p. 14; "The Limited Assignment of Psychoneurotics," July, 1944, pp. 14-15.

[22] An excellent description of treatment measures in the 51st Station Hospital was given by L. L. Tureen, "The Base Section Psychiatric Hospital," in *Combat Psychiatry Among American Ground Forces in the Mediterranean Area,* ed. by F. R. Hanson. (To be published.)

[23] Colonel Allan Challman has told me that there were five station hospitals (125th, 126th, and

treatment of minor psychiatric disorders. Three of these hospitals made the phenomenal record of returning approximately 80 per cent of their patients to duty, despite the fact that many of the patients had seen combat for weeks prior to their admission to the hospital. Shortly before VJ-day a general hospital was established in the Philippines for the intensive treatment of psychiatric patients.

Psychiatric treatment of combat casualties. The record of the results [24] of psychiatric treatment of combat casualties was exceptional. It is all the more so in view of the fact that, as mentioned before, there were neither prewar preparation as to how this treatment should be done, plans as to where it should be done, nor much thought about who would do it. World War I should have taught us that it should be carried out close to the front line; that division psychiatrists were necessary; that for every four men wounded we would have one psychiatric casualty. Instead, initially, psychiatrists were assigned only to evacuation and base hospitals. For nearly 2 years combat divisions lacked psychiatrists. On the other hand medical and surgical facilities were planned to the last detail. Early in the war, plans for auxiliary surgical teams were made and were greatly expanded as time wore on.

When the American forces first engaged in combat in North Africa, psychiatric patients were transported from the fighting area back to the base hospitals, sometimes 300 to 500 miles. Less than 10 per cent of these were able to return to duty. The closer evacuation hospitals [25] were far from ideal for psychiatric treatment for the reason that they had to treat every surge of wounded men. They did the best they could, but in intense fighting, with large numbers of surgical cases in need of emergency care, there were often no beds for the psychiatric casualties. If there were psychiatric patients in the hospital, they had to be evacuated, regardless of their potential salvability had it been possible for them to remain.[26]

18th with 250 beds each, the 146th and 148th with 50 beds each) functioning in the Pacific area, though not all were in operation at the same time. In addition, the 314th General was put into operation near Manila; the 316th was built but not operated.

[24] Details as to the methods of treatment varied, depending on the geographical location of the soldier, the nature and severity of his disorder, type of facilities available, etc. See Chap. 9.

[25] For a description of the sorting process, treatment, and types of cases seen in an evacuation hospital in the Italian campaign, see Collins, R. T., "Neuropsychiatry in an Overseas Evacuation Hospital," *Military Neuropsychiatry,* Proc. Assn. for Research in Nerv. and Ment. Dis., New York, 1944, The Williams & Wilkins Company, Baltimore, 1946, pp. 147-155.

[26] Despite handicaps, good neuropsychiatric work was done in evacuation hospitals as indicated by the following figures obtained in September and October, 1944, on a personal visit to the European Theater: The 77th Evacuation Hospital neuropsychiatrist John F. McGowan was using 90 former neuropsychiatric battle casualties as litter bearers and for doing odd jobs. In 6 weeks only three had a recurrence. At the 34th Evacuation Hospital at Verdun, neuropsychiatrist Maj. Webster B. Majors received 225 psychiatric casualties at one time. With an average of 8 days' treatment he was returning 30 per cent to full duty and 40 per cent to limited duty. In the 101st Evacuation Hospital, neuropsychiatrist Maj. H. F. English kept pa-

When this situation was fully appreciated, after some months the psychiatric consultant for the Mediterranean Theater, Col. Frederick Hanson,[27] with the help of Col. Perrin Long, Medical Consultant, and Brig. Gen. Frederick Blesse, the surgeon of that theater, developed a pattern of treatment which was subsequently adopted with slight variations in the First, Third, Seventh, Ninth, and Fifteenth Armies.

By their plan the battalion aid station surgeons were indoctrinated with "first-aid" psychiatry.[28] It was they who had to decide whether a man should be returned to duty, given a brief respite, or evacuated on to the clearing station. It was fully appreciated that many soldiers, if returned to the battalion kitchen area and permitted a night of sound sleep with the help of a mild sedative and some warm food, would be ready in 24 hours to return to combat. No record was ever kept of the number of men so handled, but it is known to be a sizable percentage of the men seen at the battalion aid station.

The seriously upset soldiers were sent 2 to 5 miles farther back to the division clearing station [29] where the division psychiatrist had his headquarters and treatment center. This sometimes was in a tent or in a commandeered building such as a schoolhouse, factory, or whatever might be available. The soldier arrived here from his foxhole within 1 to 3 hours. Each one was seen

tients 5 days and returned 37 per cent to full duty and 32 per cent to convalescent hospital; he evacuated 20 per cent to England. At the 104th Evacuation Hospital near Etaine, neuropsychiatrist Maj. H. A. Christensen had 240 patients in the previous 18 days of whom 50 per cent returned to duty, 30 per cent to Army convalescent hospital, and 20 per cent to general hospitals; 5 to 8 per cent were repeaters. The 110th Evacuation Hospital in Luxembourg, Capt. Otto Bendheim, psychiatrist, had had 83 patients, sent 33 back to duty, 13 to noncombat duty, and 15 to convalescent hospital; 19 were evacuated. In the 107th Evacuation Hospital at Bastogne, neuropsychiatrist Maj. Max Unger had had 350 psychiatric patients with 18 per cent returned to duty.

[27] A description of the plan of treatment used by the Fifth Army in Italy is given by H. S. Wright, in "Psychiatry in the Fifth Army Area," Bull. U.S. Army M. Dept., 5:73-79, Jan., 1946.

[28] See Chap. 3 regarding the training program.

[29] A sampling of figures from clearing stations visited in October, 1944 are of interest: Fourth Armored Division, Maj. Earl Mericle division psychiatrist, had had 284 cases between July 20 and September 17, sent 144 back to duty and evacuated 140. In the following week he had 249 patients and on the day of the visit had 60 admissions. Eightieth Division Clearing Station, Maj. Isidore Tuerk division psychiatrist, had had 450 patients, returned 80 per cent to duty with 4 per cent repeaters. The Thirty-fifth Division, Capt. Harry Schwartz psychiatrist, had only 3 patients at the time of the visit with Capt. Schwartz absent on a visit to his collecting station. Second Armored, Maj. Himon Miller psychiatrist, had seen 270 patients, of whom 40 per cent returned to duty. Thirtieth Division at Heerlen, Maj. V. F. Lowell psychiatrist, had had over 200 patients, with 38.6 per cent returning to duty, 2.7 per cent being returned a second time, and the balance evacuated to the exhaustion center. Twenty-ninth Division at Maastricht, Maj. D. I. Weintrob psychiatrist, in 6 weeks had seen 352 patients, only 40 of whom were evacuated and 312 sent to a retraining platoon under his medical supervision. Fourth Division, Maj. Meyer Maskin psychiatrist, had had 2,263 patients, returning 811 to duty, including 216 for the second time. Second Division, Maj. Gilbert B. Kelley psychiatrist, had seen 2,200 NP casualties and had returned from 17 to 36 per cent, depending on the nature of the fighting.

initially by the psychiatrist and interviewed briefly. If he were recognized to be too sick to benefit from brief rest and such psychotherapeutic help as could be given in a short time, he was immediately evacuated farther back. The largest percentage of the soldiers who came to the clearing station remained there for 48 hours. These men were given sufficient sedation to insure a good 12 to 24 hours of sleep, only interrupted when awakened for food. On the second day they had an opportunity to shave and bathe. Approximately 40 per cent could return to combat on the third day. Follow-up studies suggest that many of these men carried on indefinitely. Perhaps 25 per cent of this group had recurrences of symptoms and became repeaters.

The men not salvaged at the clearing station were sent on to what was termed the "exhaustion center," [30] usually 10 to 15 miles behind the lines. This was an improvised organization made from a medical unit known as a "clearing company, separate," which was initially staffed by 12 officers and 99 enlisted men. Its psychiatrists came from the evacuation hospitals in the surrounding area, in so far as they were available, and an equal number of medical officers from this clearing company were sent to the evacuation hospitals to replace them. The average exhaustion center would have from four to seven psychiatrists and a capacity of from 200 to 500 patients. Because there were no advanced plans for this specific mission, they never had really adequate equipment or personnel.

A soldier patient remained here from 5 to 8 days. He was usually sedated sufficiently to sleep for most of the first 2 days. Every case received psychotherapy, and many selected cases were given the special treatment of psychotherapy with the aid of pentathol narcosis. In so far as personnel and equipment would permit, the psychiatric casualties were given several days of rest, recreational activity and treatment.[31] In conjunction with the exhaustion center some divisions developed a retraining platoon, under line-officer direction, which provided an additional 2 to 5 days of military activities at a graded tempo to prepare the men for return to combat. Of the combat casualties, 20 per cent were returned to combat from these centers.

As has been pointed out, the figure, based on the four active armies in the European Theater, of an average of 60 per cent [32] of combat casualties re-

---

[30] The official diagnosis written on the evacuation tag was "exhaustion," hence this term for the center.

[31] A description of the treatment of one group of patients (hysteria) in an exhaustion center has been described in some detail. Wadsworth, G. L., and Rath, O., "Treatment of Hysteria in a Forward Echelon," *Bull. U.S. Army M. Dept.*, 5:193-195, Feb., 1946.

[32] The figure of 60 per cent is and always will be a moot point. Lloyd Thompson, our consultant in the European Theater, gave this figure (Thompson, L. J., "Neuropsychiatry in the European Theater of Operations," *New England J. Med.*, 235:7-11, July 4, 1946), and I personally spent hours with him computing figures on the basis of information supplied by Army psychiatrists. Perry Talkington, the Army psychiatrist with the Third Army, published the statistics

turned to duty as the result of treatment in the clearing stations and exhaustion centers, requires further explanation. Whatever per cent were returned to duty does not mean that these men were completely well. It was the Medical Corps' chief function to maintain the fighting strength, so that, if a physician considered a man able to perform further duty he was sent back to the line. Psychiatrists had the difficult assignment of returning men to the hell of battle, knowing full well that in many instances it would make their illness worse. On the other hand they evacuated 40 per cent to the rear, even though improved, because they were judged incapable of further combat duty.

The men evacuated to hospitals within the Army area or farther back into the communication zone were sent either to a specialized hospital for psychiatric patients or to the psychiatric section of a general hospital. In so far as possible, the neurotic patients were sent to the general hospitals. In the European Theater the 130th General Hospital in Belgium supporting the First and Ninth Armies, the 51st Station Hospital in France backing the Third and Seventh Armies, and the 312th Station Hospital in England offered special treatment regimes for this group of patients. Their results, combined with the efforts of the general hospitals, salvaged an additional 30 per cent of soldiers for noncombat duty in the zone of communications. Only 10 per cent of the initial group of combat casualties were then left to be evacuated to the United States.[33] A significant percentage of these were psychotic patients.

There was a similar system in operation during combat in the Pacific. It differed somewhat because the fighting was in relatively short drives; there was no extensive front or continuous combat; the great distances made tactics very different. For example, in the Okinawa campaign a field hospital was converted into a combination exhaustion center and special neuropsychiatric hospital. In other campaigns the division psychiatrist sent his patients to evacuation hospitals and from there to special psychiatric hospitals or to general hospitals often even thousands of miles from the front. Approval was given and plans were made for a treatment plan in the Pacific more like that of the European Theater, if the fighting were carried to Japan.

The outstanding results of this hastily designed system, developed against

---

by month for the Third Army from August, 1944, through May, 1945, with an average of 72.4 per cent of 19,622 psychiatric casualties returned to duty. (Talkington, P. C., "Combat Psychiatry. Third United States Army Experience," *Mil. Surgeon,* 98:401-404, May, 1946.) On the other hand, many of the figures cited in footnotes 26 and 29 indicate a lower per cent returned to duty. The very carefully analyzed study of Glass of 393 acute combat casualties revealed that only about a third were salvaged for effective combat duty. (Glass, A. J., "Effectiveness of Forward Neuropsychiatric Treatment," *Bull. U.S. Army M. Dept.,* 7:1034-1041, Dec., 1947.)
[33] For Air Forces personnel, some of the most effective treatment provided in the Army was at the highly staffed Don Cesar Hospital at St. Petersburg, Fla., and at Fort Logan, Colo.

great handicaps, were due first to treatment in a forward area. The chances of returning soldiers to combat duty were much greater if they were treated promptly near the front lines. Second, the psychiatrist learned the necessity of preventing indiscriminate evacuation in order to avoid needless waste of man power and an adverse effect on the morale of those who remained. This required careful psychiatric screening and prompt treatment. Third, experience proved that although their disorders represented genuine sickness and required professional care by specialized medical personnel, the great majority of psychiatric patients did not require typical hospital facilities. Actually, they might be harmed psychologically by a hospital atmosphere. Fourth, since the entire program was based on the assumption that the chief preventive efforts were a function of command,[34] active support of the line officers was required.

Psychotherapy under sedation. Improvement of the techniques of psychotherapy was speeded under the emergency of military psychiatry. Like some other therapeutic achievements, its development was related to the fact that there never were nearly enough psychiatrists. Patients could not be given the amount of individual attention, particularly psychotherapy, they should have received. Psychotherapy under sedation was a short cut, a time-saving device. It was not entirely new, but the circumstances of the war forced its extensive utilization and consequent refinement and further development.

Psychotherapy under sedation was used extensively by both American and British psychiatrists. It was particularly effective with battle casualties. With co-operative patients capable of responding, probably nothing more can be accomplished by the use of this procedure than by ordinary psychotherapeutic methods, provided sufficient time is available. In some patients, no method is successful. The development of a method which enables the psychiatrist, in a short period of time, to explore, and aerate in some degree, the man's unconscious mind is often of great value.

While under the influence of some type of sedative—sodium pentathol, sodium amytal, ether, nitrous oxide—the patient is given psychotherapy. The individual is allowed, by control of the amount of the drug administered, to reach a state halfway between full consciousness and sleep.

Then under skillful direction he is able to recall and discuss memories of experiences which in his conscious state evade him. Success in finding

[34] This was described by Maj. (later Lt. Col.) John W. Appel following a tour of duty in an exhaustion center in the Italian Campaign. His report subsequently was sent by the Chief of Staff to all theater commanders, and by them to lower echelons of commanders within the theater. "Preventive Psychiatry. An Epidemiologic Approach," *J.A.M.A.*, 131:1469-1475, Aug. 31, 1946. The same theme was presented at the American Psychiatric Association by one of the few psychiatrists, Maj. Spiegel, to be awarded the Purple Heart. See H. X. Spiegel, "Preventive Psychiatry with Combat Troops," *Am. J. Psychiat.*, 101:310-315, Nov., 1944.

and verbalizing such memories depends entirely upon the ability of the psychiatrist. Those who are not trained in psychotherapeutic techniques do not know how much probing to do, when to remain silent, or when to make further queries. Under an untrained therapist, undoubted harm can be done.

When a patient discusses emotionally painful experiences, whether under sedation or in a conscious psychotherapeutic session, he may display considerable emotional feeling. Such a display is termed "abreaction." [35] It is a necessary step in successful ventilation of repressed emotionally charged conflicts. When this takes place under sedation, the patient can regain consciousness with the memory clarified and the emotion dispelled; often he will be greatly improved. The role of sedation is merely one of enabling the psychiatrist to reach more quickly the repressed material. In some instances the resulting emotion is too great, and it is wiser to send the patient on to sleep so that he has no recollection of the re-experience when he awakens. Such a treatment hour would be regarded at best as questionably successful. Very deeply repressed material cannot be brought to the surface in some cases.

Sodium amytal was first used by Bleckwenn [36] in 1930 for prolonged narcosis and as a method of obtaining information from mute psychotic patients. Until the war it was not employed widely as a treatment method for neuroses or allied conditions. Special credit belongs to Roy Grinker [37] and his associates for developing this technique as "narcosynthesis"; under the influence of the narcotic a synthesis of the personality conflicts is attempted. A majority of the American psychiatrists preferred the use of sodium pentathol over any other drug. Sargant [38] used pentathol as a method of placing the patient in a suggestible state rather than as a ventilation technique. Another modification by British workers, Horsley [39] and Wilde, [40] was called "narcoanalysis." They also employed ether, [41] as did the psychiatrists in one

---

35 A good discussion of the therapeutic value of this phenomenon was given by H. Rosen and H. J. Myers, in "Abreaction in the Military Setting," *Arch. Neurol. & Psychiat.*, 57:161-172, Feb., 1947.

36 Bleckwenn, W. J., "Narcosis as Therapy in Neuropsychiatric Conditions," *J.A.M.A.*, 95:1168-1171, Oct. 18, 1940.

37 Colonel Grinker has described in some detail the methods used in the combat cases. Grinker, R. R., "Treatment of War Neuroses," *J.A.M.A.*, 126:142-145, Sept. 16, 1944; with John P. Spiegel, *War Neuroses*, The Blakiston Company, Philadelphia, 1945, pp. 75-114; with John P. Spiegel, *Men Under Stress*, The Blakiston Company, Philadelphia, 1945, pp. 368-426.

38 Sargant, William, and Slater, E., *An Introduction to Physical Methods of Treatment in Psychiatry*, E. & S. Livingston Ltd., Edinburgh, 1944, pp. 111-117.

39 Horsley, J. S., *Narcoanalysis*, Oxford Medical Publications, London, 1943.

40 Wilde, J. F., "Narcoanalysis in the Treatment of War Neuroses," *Brit. M. J.*, 2:4, July 4, 1942.

41 A Maj. Palmer, RAMC, at a conference of British military psychiatrists at York, England, October 8, 1944, indicated that the British in North Africa used ether exclusively and regarded it far superior to the barbiturates. He reported 100 per cent success with conversion symptoms and amnesia.

or two American hospitals.[42] A similar technique used nitrous oxide.[43]

Related to this approach has been the therapeutic use of hypnosis. The subject was reviewed in detail by Brenman and Gill.[44] Through the generosity of the Josiah Macy, Jr., Foundation, this review was sent to each psychiatrist in the Army. The most extensive users of this method in the Army were Kaufman, Beaton, Markey,[45] and others on Okinawa where a field hospital was converted into a psychiatric treatment center. It was also reported on specifically by Hadfield [46] under the term "hypno-analysis," by Fisher,[47] by Alpert, Carbone, and Brooks,[48] and by Kartchner and Korner.[49]

It is difficult to evaluate the relative merits of these various methods. Each has been found useful to some degree. There seems little doubt, however, that the success of the procedure depends on the psychotherapeutic skill and judgment of the operator. Hypnosis, while a relatively simple procedure, is not widely used by American psychiatrists. Its efficacy in war neuroses seems to have been well demonstrated in the last war by both American [50] and German [51] psychiatrists, and it is therefore surprising that more use of it was not made. The security and ease of the drug sedation and the widespread lack of experience with and medical acceptance of hypnosis seem to be the most logical explanations. Grinker and Spiegel [37] regarded hypnosis of no less value than "narcosynthesis" when performed to induce abreactions and to effect adequate synthesis. They did not subscribe to using it to force the disappearance of symptoms by strong suggestion.

Certainly the workers who used various types of therapy under sedation

---

[42] Brewster, H. H., "The Use of Ether in Narcoanalysis of Patients with War Neurosis," *New England J. Med.*, 235:357-359, Sept. 12, 1946.

[43] Rogerson, C. H., "Narco-analysis with Nitrous Oxide," *Brit. M. J.*, 1:811-812, June 17, 1944.

[44] Brenman, M., and Gill, M. M., *Hypnotherapy*, publication of the Josiah Macy, Jr., Foundation, Review Series, Vol. 11, Nov. 3, 1944; *Hypnotherapy, A Survey of the Literature*, International University Press, New York, 1947.

[45] Official Army report of Okinawa Campaign to Surgeon, POA, 16 May 1945, by Lt. Col. M. R. Kaufman. Also NP History of Okinawa Campaign, to Surgeon Tenth Army, 3 October 1945, by Lt. Col. O. B. Markey. See also Kaufman, M. R., and Beaton, L. E., "A Psychiatric Treatment Program in Combat," *Bull. Menninger Clinic*, 11:1-14, Jan., 1947.

[46] Hadfield, J. A., "Treatment by Suggestion and Hypno-analysis," in E. Miller, *Neurosis in War*, The Macmillan Company, New York, 1944, pp. 128-149.

[47] Fisher, C. E., "Hypnosis in the Treatment of Neurosis Due to War and Other Causes," *War Med.*, 4:565-576, Dec., 1943.

[48] Alpert, H. S., Carbone, H. A., and Brooks, J. T., "Hypnosis as a Therapeutic Technique in the War Neuroses," *Bull. U.S. Army M. Dept.*, 5:315-324, Mar., 1946.

[49] Kartchner, F. D., and Korner, I. N., "The Use of Hypnosis in the Treatment of Acute Combat Reactions," *Am. J. Psychiat.*, 103:630-636, Mar., 1947.

[50] Schwab, S. I., and Fenton, N., "War Neuroses as a Medico-Military Problem," in *Medical Department of the United States Army in the World War*, Vol. X, War Department, U.S. Government Printing Office, Washington, D.C., 1929, p. 401.

[51] Simmel, Ernst, *Kriegesneurosen and "Psychishes Trauma,"* Otto Nemnich, Munich, 1918; also in "War Neuroses" in *Psychoanalysis Today*, ed. by Sandor Lorand, International Universities Press, New York, 1945, pp. 227-248.

produced excellent results, as indicated in their reports. It should be pointed out, however, that figures of recovery percentages are no sure index of the lasting results of any method.

RETRAINING PROGRAM

Psychiatrists believed that, if psychoneurotic patients could be assigned to a special training unit that would provide both the necessary psychiatric guidance and a regime which incorporated discipline and a military atmosphere, many men could be retrained for new jobs.[52] Many soldiers who had failed in one job might be salvaged. Their training for a specific assignment could go on during psychiatric treatment. Otherwise, the usual hospitalization often intensified symptoms to such a degree that any attempt to send them back to duty failed.

Numerous conferences between the Neuropsychiatry Consultants Division and the ASF Training Division took place. Largely because of the unusual insight of Brig. Gen. Arthur Trudeau, arrangements finally were made and authority granted [53] to establish "Developmental Training Units" in three of the Army Service Forces' basic-training camps—Aberdeen, Lee, and Belvoir. These were regarded as entirely experimental. In each of these camps a special battalion served under line officers. The staff of the commanding officer was augmented with psychiatrists and trainers. Each of these battalions offered a wide range of training opportunities for positions as bakers, clerks, chauffeurs, mechanics, watch repairmen, truck drivers, squad leaders, supply officers, auditors, welders, painters, and other military occupations.

During the experiment, 1,253 men were assigned directly to the unit from hospitals,[54] after passing through a special screening center to aid in the determination of the type of training to which they should be assigned. A joint team of line officer, trainer, and psychiatrist interviewed each patient to ascertain his capabilities, his wishes, and the nature of his sickness. They assigned him accordingly. The men remained for a period varying from 4 to 14 weeks, the length of time depending on their progress. When a man reached the point where he could be reassigned, he was reported to the Office

---

[52] This was attempted for neurotic patients in one staging area, where they were reassigned to the hospital complement of enlisted men, and to certain work throughout the camp. About one-fourth were so saved for full duty, one-half for "limited duty," and one-fourth discharged. Tousey, T. G., "Conditioning of the Transitorily Maladjusted Soldiers," *Med. Clin. N. America, New York Number* 29:751-759, May, 1945; Goldbloom, A. A., and Schantz, B. A., "The Management of the Emotionally Maladjusted Soldier at a Staging Camp," *Psychiat. Quart.,* 20:452-469, July, 1946.

[53] ASF Circular 40, 5 February 1944.

[54] Senerchia, F. F., "An Experimental Unit for the Retraining of Psychoneurotic Soldiers," *Military Neuropsychiatry,* Proceedings Assn. Research in Nerv. and Ment. Dis., New York, 1944, The Williams & Wilkins Company, Baltimore, 1946, pp. 87-93.

of the Adjutant General which sent him wherever someone with his particular training was needed. Those who could not be assigned were discharged. However, they should very definitely have benefited by the program. Of the entire group, 880 (70 per cent) were made available for limited assignment within the United States.

There was a heavy attendance on sick call during the initial weeks of the experiment. Through individual and group psychotherapy this was quickly and markedly reduced. Group discussions were scheduled 4 hours a week. In addition to regular military duties special emphasis was laid on an activity program of discussion groups, entertainment, and craft work.

All concerned in the Office of the Surgeon General, in the Army Service Forces, and in the units [55] were very encouraged with the results of the experiment. However, the plan created other problems in the field. Limited-service jobs were so well filled that these men were reassigned with difficulty. Also, instructions to give the salvaged soldier special consideration until he got on his feet in a new job were not sent out to the field. The result too often was that he was batted around, transferred several times, and ended up in a hospital. Several requests were made by the Neuropsychiatry Consultants Division that the field should be notified of this special problem if we were to complete the job of salvage. Much too late a circular was published on the subject.[56] By this time most of the men salvaged had long since left the training center.

Despite the fact that there was difficulty in finding jobs for these men, the Office of the Surgeon General strongly recommended continuation of the experiment. At one time the project went so far as to be approved by the Chief of Staff of ASF, but it was opposed by some not only because of the difficulty in assignment but also because of the cost in trainer personnel. The subject was revived again in 1945 and again strongly recommended by Gen. Trudeau in the ASF Training Division, as well as by the Neuropsychiatry Consultants Division. It was, however, again turned down.

GROUP PSYCHOTHERAPY

The military psychiatrist never had sufficient time to give much individual psychotherapy. Group therapy was used as a substitute, to give treatment to a number of different people at the same time. It helped to stretch the psychiatric man-power shortage over the psychiatric patient surplus and so became one of the more important treatment methods used in the Army.

---

[55] Olinick, S. L., and Friend, M. R., "Indirect Group Therapy of Psychoneurotic Soldiers," *Psychiatry*, 8:147-153, May, 1945.
[56] ASF Circular 169, 5 June 1944.

Some sort of psychotherapy was necessary for each combat case. It was also necessary for the maladjusted trainee who came to the mental hygiene out-patient clinic. Valuable psychotherapy could be given to groups of patients with similar problems.

Certain experienced psychiatrists took the initiative in using this method as an expedient in general hospitals. The British reported group discussions among their military psychiatric patients.[57] These had also been developed for the treatment of the neuroses of merchant seamen.[58] Those of us responsible for policy formation obtained the inclusion in the War Department directive on treatment in hospitals [59] of a direction that group psychotherapy should be used wherever possible. This bulletin gave some impetus to the utilization of the method. Usage was further stimulated by the publication of a War Department technical medical bulletin [60] which set forth specific suggestions as to the methods and techniques of conducting group psychotherapy.

Techniques. There have been many arguments as to whether any form of lecture or discussion should be called "group psychotherapy" or merely "group therapy." This seems a relatively unimportant semantic differentiation, if the purpose is to help people aerate their feelings and mental content. By talking about them they come to a better understanding of their symptoms. During 1944 and 1945, many reports were published which discussed the use of this principle in Army, Navy, and Public Health hospitals,[61] in the Mental Hygiene Consultation Services,[62] and in correctional institutions.[63]

[57] Rees, J. R., *The Shaping of Psychiatry by War,* W. W. Norton & Company, Inc., New York, 1945, p. 109; Snowden, E. N., "Mass Psychotherapy," *Lancet,* 2:769-770, Dec. 21, 1940; Blair, D., "Group Psychotherapy for War Neuroses," *Lancet,* 1:204-205, Feb. 13, 1943.

[58] Sherman, S., "A System of Combined Individual and Group Therapy as Used in the Medical Program for Merchant Seamen," *Am. J. Psychiat.,* 100:127-130, July, 1943. An excellent plan was developed by Dr. Robt. G. Heath at the Merchant Marine Rest Center, Sands Point, N. Y.

[59] "Treatment Program for Psychiatric Patients in Station and General Hospitals." *War Department Technical Bulletin, Medical 28,* 1 April 1944; revised and issued as *War Department Technical Bulletin, Medical 84,* 10 August 1944.

[60] "Group Psychotherapy," *War Department Technical Bulletin, Medical 103,* 10 October 1944, written by Lt. Col. N. Q. Brill.

[61] Shaskan, D. A., and Jolesch, M., "War and Group Psychotherapy," *Am. J. Orthopsychiat.,* 14:571-577, Oct., 1944; Rome, H. P., "Group Psychotherapy," *Dis. Nerv. System,* 6:237-241, Aug., 1945 (Rome has written several excellent articles on this subject.); Rubenstein, V., and Novick, A., "A Case Work-Group Approach to the Treatment of War Neuroses (in a Convalescent hospital)," *Jewish Social Service Quart.,* 22:274-299, June, 1946; Paster, S., "Group Psychotherapy in an Army General Hospital," *Ment. Hyg.,* 28:529-536, Oct., 1944; "Group Psychotherapy for Combat Neuroses," *Am. J. Orthopsychiat.,* 15:472-482, July, 1945.

[62] Olinick, S. L., and Friend, M. R., "Indirect Group Therapy of Psychoneurotic Soldiers," *Psychiatry,* 8:147-153, May, 1945; Cohen, R. R., "Factors in Adjustment to Army Life. A Plan for Preventive Psychiatry by Mass Psychotherapy," *War Med.,* 5:83-91, Feb., 1944.

[63] Abrahams, J., and McCorkle, L. W., "Group Psychotherapy of Military Offenders," *Am. J. Sociology,* 51:455-464, Mar., 1946; "Group Psychotherapy at an Army Rehabilitation Center," *Dis. Nerv. System,* 7:50-62, Feb., 1947.

The methods varied widely. The personality of the group leader and his leadership qualities were nearly as important as his technical knowledge.[64] In many places this therapeutic procedure consisted of a series of lectures on mental hygiene topics, which were given by the psychiatrist; a question-and-answer period followed. In other places, in a discussion group, the leader attempted to get each man to present his problems, his opinions, and his own point of view about them. In group therapy at its best the leader submerged himself as a member of the group, speaking only when it was necessary to direct the discussion to the point at hand. In this type of session all of the group listened to the verbal catharsis of one of its members, analyzed it, and then under the skillful leader synthesized the findings into an understanding of constructive solutions. Obviously, with so many psychiatrists or clinical psychologists or psychiatric social workers carrying out this type of program, there were many variations, both good and not so good.

Sometimes there was a definitely planned series of subjects to be presented and discussed. These, usually, directly concerned the men's experience and centered around their symptoms or present situation. Discussion usually answered such questions as: "What is a personal adjustment and the factors influencing it?" "What is 'NP'?" "What is a neurosis?" "How do emotions affect one?" Later, as the opportunity presented, there was discussion of such daily problems as defective attitudes, return to duty, or return to civilian life. Free use was made of visual aids in some treatment centers. Several hospitals utilized a modified "psychodrama." A scene, such as the first visit at home, the wife's first visit to the hospital, applying for a furlough, was enacted with the soldier-patient-actors spontaneously portraying various roles.

Where group psychotherapy was used most effectively, it became probably the most important activity on the daily schedule of the patient. In many hospitals it was given 1 hour each day. Such was the case at the Fort Knox Rehabilitation Center where it was unusually well administered. In other places it was only given 3 times a week. Where the medical officers were less acquainted with or interested in it, it had only a nominal place of 1 hour a week. A "course" might last for 3 or 30 sessions. Groups varied widely both as to number and basis of membership. In general, the smaller the group, the longer it met together as a unit; the more homogeneous the composition as to the type of disability of its members, the better were the results. Several of the installations developed rather effective manuals for the use of

---

[64] Friend summarized the primary psychologic mechanisms operating within the group as (1) positive transference and identification with the leader; (2) need for group acceptance; (3) repression of basic conflicts; (4) possibility of release from the Army. Friend, M. R., "Group Psychotherapy in an Army Hospital Relating to Civilian Readjustment," *Proceedings of the Neuropsychiatric Conference of the Sixth Service Command,* Chicago, 16-17 November 1945, pp. 85-97.

their own leadership personnel. Such manuals grew out of the experiences at Welch Convalescent Hospital, at the Fort Meade Station Hospital, at the Fort Knox Rehabilitation Center, at the Aberdeen Proving Grounds Mental Hygiene Unit.

Results. There was no carefully controlled study of the results of group psychotherapy.[65] The techniques were so varied that, even if statistics were available, they would perhaps be impossible to interpret. Consequently, one can only estimate from subjective impressions. These were generally favorable.

There were certain advantages in group psychotherapy which were not obtainable in individual therapy. The social factor could be capitalized upon when selection considered distinctive types of behavior or symptomatology. A group, if effective, developed a unit morale, an identification of the membership with each other. Often a patient might be able to see symptomatic behavior similar to his own with more objectivity when it was presented by a fellow patient in a group discussion. The individuals, as a group, were forced to consider the legitimacy of a complaint and the wisdom of different ways of dealing with a problem. The opinion of the entire group often molded the point of view of its individual members toward that same problem in themselves. They could sometimes achieve greater understanding in this way than at the suggestion of a psychiatrist in a private interview. In the presence of other soldiers it was often possible for one individual to express his hostile, aggressive feelings toward the Army and toward officers more freely than he could have to a medical officer in a private interview. This was particularly significant because of the importance that resentment played in the maladjustment of so many soldiers. The man who saw his problem in the light of the problems of many others, upon comparison, was often able to recognize the relatively minor significance of what had seemed so important to him. By so doing, he could, and would, relieve his feeling of isolationism or his need to hide his feelings from others.

Fundamentally, psychotherapy gives relief because feelings and emotions are expressed openly instead of being forced to masquerade because denied. For many the only hope of gaining any insight into their difficulties was through this type of therapy. The fact that all the men in the group were in the Army and faced the same stresses tended to make many of their problems take common patterns. However, group therapy should never replace individual psychotherapy where that is available, for while it may relieve some

---

[65] There is a report of a small series of cases in which the score of the Minnesota Multiphasic Personality Inventory was reduced in "the factors of depression, hysteria, paranoia and psychasthenia." Rashkis, H. A., and Shaskan, D. A., "The Effects of Group Psychotherapy on Personality Inventory Scores," *Am. J. Orthopsychiat.*, 16:345-349, Apr., 1946.

acute symptoms, it is not likely that it will ever be a practical means of eliminating neurotic reactions.[66] Although not as effective as individual psychotherapy in relieving symptoms, it may, however, be more effective in modifying attitudes. It is of questionable value for antisocial personalities.

Effectiveness of psychiatric treatment. On the whole, just how effective was psychiatric treatment? [67] Certainly there were criticisms of it by military

---

[66] Weinberg, working with a group of 6 to 10 patients at Don Cesar Hospital, concluded that group therapy failed to meet long-term needs and was not time saving; nor did he regard it as "real psychotherapy." Weinberg, J., "Group Psychotherapy as Developed in a Military Setting. Its Application to Civilian Therapy," *Psychiat. Quart.,* 20:470-484, July, 1946. In contrast to Weinberg's method, many if not most group psychotherapy in the Army was carried on in groups of 20 or more men. Many psychiatrists did use the method primarily as a time saver. Another small group experiment with minimal beneficial results, using psychoanalytic principles, was reported by C. N. Sarlin and M. A. Berezin, "Group Psychotherapy on a Modified Analytic Basis," *J. Nerv. & Ment. Dis.,* 104:611-667, Dec., 1946.

[67] To date, there are only a few follow-up studies of psychiatric patients who were discharged from the Army. Brill, N. Q.; Tate, M.; and Menninger, W. C., "Enlisted Men Discharged from the Army Because of Psychoneuroses," *J.A.M.A.,* 128:633-637, June 30, 1945. Questionnaires of 5,397 were sent to men discharged prior to January 1, 1944. They received 4,178 (over 70 per cent) replies. This group were discharged at a time when treatment methods in the Army were relatively undeveloped. Of this group of psychoneurotic patients, 93.7 per cent were employed prior to induction and only 85.9 per cent since discharge. Of the latter group, 72 per cent were working full time and 28 per cent part time. In general, these men considered their health to have been adversely affected by their Army service, though they considered this impairment chiefly in terms of physical disease. There was little indication that they were discriminated against by prospective employers. Of the entire group 14.5 per cent were hospitalized at least once after leaving the Army and 75 per cent had consulted a physician one or more times, generally for the same medical condition for which they were discharged.

Dallas Pratt "Reemployment of the Psychoneurotic Exsoldier," *Psychiatry,* 8:3-8, Feb., 1945, reported sending a questionnaire to 256 former soldiers who had been discharged with a diagnosis of psychoneurosis, on an average of 5 months previous to the study. Replies were received from 55 per cent. This group too were discharged before the War Department policy for treatment had been changed. Of them, 90 per cent were employed; 79 per cent reported no difficulty in securing work, but 21 per cent replied that their diagnosis did interfere with securing work.

A. J. Lewis (an English psychiatrist), "Social Effects of Neurosis," *Lancet,* 1:167-170, Feb. 6, 1943, reported that 12 per cent of 120 discharged psychoneurotic British soldiers were unemployed at an average interval of 6 1/2 months after discharge.

An unpublished study from the Fort Story Convalescent Hospital, conducted by Col. H. Brewer, Calvin L. Baker, Edmont J. Biancarelli, Benjamin Ruskin, James A. Flaherty, and Nathaniel S. Apter, was based on a follow-up of a random sample of 500 patients discharged following the intensive-treatment program at that hospital. They found that 85 per cent of the patients were gainfully employed, 8.5 per cent attending school, and only 6.5 per cent unemployed. Only 2.4 per cent had sought further hospitalization at the veterans' facilities, and 0.6 per cent were hospitalized in civilian institutions. Of the 97 per cent who had not been hospitalized, only 10.6 per cent received any additional medical treatment on an outpatient basis. Of these 500 patients 94 per cent expressed belief that they had benefited from the treatment program while at the hospital.

A small follow-up, reported from the Canadian Army, of approximately 200 men discharged with psychoneuroses indicated that of the urban group 40 per cent were worse than upon enlistment; in 28 per cent the work adjustment was at a lower level; in 20 per cent the home adjustment was not as satisfactory; in 25 per cent the community adjustment was not as satisfactory. The rural cases were slightly better off than the urban. Griffin, J. D., and Henderson, M. F., "A Study on the Post-Discharge Adjustment of Psychoneurotic Soldiers," Canadian Nat. Research Council, Report C-6071, 1946. A report from the same source (C-6164)

personnel, laymen, and civilian psychiatrists. Probably the most severe critics were some of us within the Army. The psychiatrist, like any other officer or soldier in the Army, was never a free agent. The commanding officer of a hospital could (and some did) disregard the advice of even the most competent psychiatrist by enforcing policies which undid all his efforts. Some of us regarded with skepticism and concern the trend in certain hospitals to rely on a conveyor-belt program of chemical and mechanical treatment methods for psychiatric patients.[68] Too few psychiatrists were dynamically oriented and understood how to conduct effective psychotherapy. All of us in psychiatry were hamstrung, to varying degrees, by regulations, pressures, and orders which were deleterious to our patients. The most severe frustration and the most legitimate complaint of every good psychiatrist at all posts was that there was too little opportunity to give treatment.

In terms of individual psychotherapy, treatment hardly existed except in two Air Corps hospitals under Roy Grinker and John Murray, where ample staff was provided. At one time, when Army psychiatrists were under criticism on this point, it was computed that if every patient were to receive only 2 hours a week of individual psychotherapy (peak load of patients in hospitals in U.S., 37,640; worldwide, 49,315), it would require 1,700 psychiatrists who could devote full time to such work. At the maximum strength there were only 2,400 physicians assigned to neuropsychiatry, with an effective working strength of only 1,700 to 1,800 (others being in transit, at staging areas, in training, on leave, or sick). Also every psychiatrist had to spend half his time on more or less essential "paper work." In addition, he had to make examinations, care for admissions, discharges, boards, outpatients. He did well to spend 1 to 2 hours a day on individual psychotherapy.

Essentially, only emergency psychiatric treatment was permitted prior to 1944. In that year major steps were taken to reverse this policy—not only to permit but to require that treatment should be given to every patient who could benefit from it. But, as viewed from the standpoint of the need, facilities were relatively slow in being made available and placed in operation. However, in striking contrast to usual civilian progress in building huge hospitals, credit should go to the Army for the 12 convalescent hospitals. Each with a capacity of 2,000 to 5,000 patients and costing from $3,000,000 to $5,000,000 apiece, all were in full operation 6 to 12 months after their inception![69] Always there were the bugaboos of too few psychiatrists, social

of 560 cases of psychoneurosis, followed 3 months or more after discharge, showed similar findings.

[68] Needles, W., "The Regression of Psychiatry in the Army," *Psychiatry,* 9:167-185, Aug., 1946.

[69] Ginzberg, E., "Army Hospitalization, Retrospect and Prospect," *Bull. U.S. Army M. Dept.,* 8:38-47, Jan., 1948. "On VE-day, convalescent hospitals alone were caring for 50,000 patients."

workers, and psychologists. Many assigned as such had little or no experience.

No one intimately connected with the program had any idea that it was nearly as effective as would have been desirable. Nor was it even satisfactory in many features. On the other hand, it would be wrong to assume that neurotic or psychotic patients should be entirely well before being discharged. A psychiatric patient can only become fully adjusted *after* he has returned to his home and re-established himself with his family, friends, and job. Furthermore, no civilian hospital discharges its patients with a promise that the government will pay them as long as they are not completely well. Every psychiatrist knows that such an arrangement is a major handicap to the recovery of any psychiatric patient.

However, though we in the Army are the first to admit our deficiencies and faults, we are also proud of our psychiatric treatment record. Oh, that every psychiatric hospital, public and private, would make equally earnest and sincere efforts!

21

THE EVACUATION OF PSYCHIATRIC PATIENTS

BY STRETCHER through steaming jungle or over enemy bombarded country-side, perhaps through bitter, life-taking cold or heavy, breath-taking heat, many a combat casualty started his ofttimes long road back. Every conceivable means of transport was pressed into service for the evacuation of sick or injured men. Within the battle zone, stretcher-bearing, jeep-, ambulance-, or truck-driving corpsmen of the Medical Department took patients from where they were to where they were supposed to go—or tried to.

Back in the communication zone the Transportation Corps took over the task of conveying patients from one installation to the other, until they were ready for discharge. In every large medical headquarters there was a Transportation Corps officer whose representatives were at every port of embarkation and debarkation. In the Washington headquarters office of the Transportation Corps a medical officer served as a liaison with the Office of the Surgeon General. For many months the man who served in this capacity proved particularly understanding about all efforts to improve the lot of the psychiatric patient during his transportation from place to place. Not until I was leaving the Army did I discover that the helpful Col. John C. Fitzpatrick was classified as a psychiatrist, D3130!

Water transportation. Initially, overseas psychiatric patients returned to this country by Army transports. Such ships were not equipped for the care of sick people. They lacked facilities. Their personnel was not adequate either in numbers or in training to care for psychiatric, especially psychotic, patients. Quite by chance, in January, 1943, it came to the attention of the Neuropsychiatry Consultants Division that psychiatric patients were being returned in wire cages, measuring approximately 3 by 3 by 6 feet. Similar cages are infamous because of their use in mental institutions of 50 years ago. They have been museum pieces for at least 30 years. There is no suggestion in the history of World War I that they were ever used.[1] Discovery of their existence brought prompt and effective protest. The Office of the Chief of Transporta-

---

[1] Bailey, Pearce, "Provisions for Care of Mental and Nervous Cases," *Medical Department of the United States Army in the World War,* Vol. X, War Department, U.S. Government Printing Office, Washington, D.C., 1929, pp. 46-51.

tion ordered [2] immediate removal of all such cages and specified individual rooms and acceptable treatment for disturbed patients. Interestingly enough, this order was protested by certain port surgeons although heartily approved by a great majority.

The Transportation Corps devised and put into effect [3] a system of classification for all of the psychiatric patients. They were sorted by the amount of care and supervision they would need on shipboard. This was extremely important. If a psychotic patient jumped overboard, as occasionally happened, the captain could not take his ship out of the convoy to search for him. To do so would have jeopardized the lives of all on board. Yet necessary restrictive care was neither necessary nor desirable for *all* psychiatric patients. The system designated patients requiring locked ward care as Class A; psychotic patients in remission, about whom there was uncertainty as to behavior, as Class B; neurotic patients as Class C.

While this plan solved some difficulties, it gave rise to others. Certain port officials and ship captains abused the system by classifying the patients according to the space available. Such abuses were usually well concealed. A well-known news writer, Albert Deutsch, discovered some gross instances and brought the reports of them to us. He held up the news stories about them until we in the War Department could and did do something about the matter. There was a tendency to keep all psychiatric patients in locked wards under the excuse that there was inadequate personnel to supervise their behavior. There were instances when neurotic patients remained under lock throughout a 2- or 3-week trip. There were other times when a psychotic patient was heavily sedated, classified C (as a neurotic patient), and placed on shipboard. Then when he awoke after the ship was at sea there was no provision for his care. A further complication arose from the shipping tags of classification. When first issued, they had NP in large black letters. This marking distressed the patients very much, until it was finally changed upon the strong recommendation of the Neuropsychiatry Consultants Division.

Experience and reports of abuse resulted in various improvements. The selection of personnel was more careful. Personnel received training while in port. Any departure from approved policies on the part of ship commanders or transport surgeons was supposed to be reported by the port surgeon. A psychiatrist was assigned to each hospital ship which carried 75 or more psychiatric patients. On the personal initiative of the Surgeon General, shock machines were provided for those ships carrying any large number of psychotic patients. The psychiatrists and the platoons of enlisted men from

---

[2] Office of Chief of Transportation Circular 35, 1 March 1943.
[3] Put into effect 10 August 1944 by a directive from the Office of the Chief of Transportation.

ship complements received training in the use of electroshock at psychiatric hospitals near all ports in this country.

The total number of patients evacuated from all theaters of operation to the United States during the years 1942 through 1945 are shown in the accompanying table and graph.

*Number of Army Patients Evacuated from Overseas to
the Continental United States, 1942-1945* [4]

Period	Total	Psychiatric	Medical	Surgical
1942 Total	8,880	2,746 (30.9%)	4,943	1,191
Jan-Mar.	807	276	498	33
Apr-June	1,240	436	785	19
July-Sept.	1,606	561	1,010	35
Oct-Dec.	5,227	1,473	2,650	1,104
1943 Total	69,336	19,455 (28.0%)	36,208	13,673
Jan-Mar.	7,324	2,076	3,863	1,385
Apr-June	15,392	3,946	7,344	4,102
July-Sept.	22,583	6,525	12,144	3,914
Oct-Dec.	24,037	6,908	12,857	4,272
1944 Total	161,848	37,309 (23.0%)	60,362	64,177
Jan-Mar.	26,116	7,528	13,445	5,143
Apr-June	26,790	8,723	11,103	6,964
July-Sept.	42,740	9,203	15,189	18,348
Oct-Dec.	66,202	11,855	20,625	33,722
1945 Total	386,426	58,006 (15.0%)	140,098	188,322
Jan-Mar.	117,413	18,001	31,183	68,229
Apr-June	147,207	17,959	44,981	84,262
July-Sept.	84,091	14,796	42,184	27,111
Oct-Dec.	37,720	7,250	21,750	8,720
Total				
1942-45	626,490 [5]	117,516 [5] (18.7%)		
1946				
Jan-Mar.	11,994	2,704 (22.5%)	4,237	5,053

As can be noted, the neuropsychiatric evacuations [6] amounted to nearly 31 per cent of the total in 1942. Following combat, with the resultant heavy

---

[4] From the Office of the Surgeon General, Medical Statistics Division, 14 March 1946.

[5] Figures on evacuation were available from the Transportation Corps and also through the Medical Statistics Division of the Office of the Surgeon General. Figures obtained at one period were corrected at a later period. On December 11, 1946, the Medical Statistics Division reported the total evacuations from December 7, 1941, through July 26, 1946, as 636,000 and the neuropsychiatric as 142,000, or 22 per cent of the total.

[6] In the Canadian Army, wounds due to war were the cause of evacuation at a rate of 37.2 per 1,000 per year; nontraumatic disabilities 28 per 1,000 per year; functional nervous disorders 6.8 per 1,000 per year. Tutle, M. J., "Analysis of Medical Repatriations," *J. Canadian Med. Services,* 3:210-226, Mar., 1946.

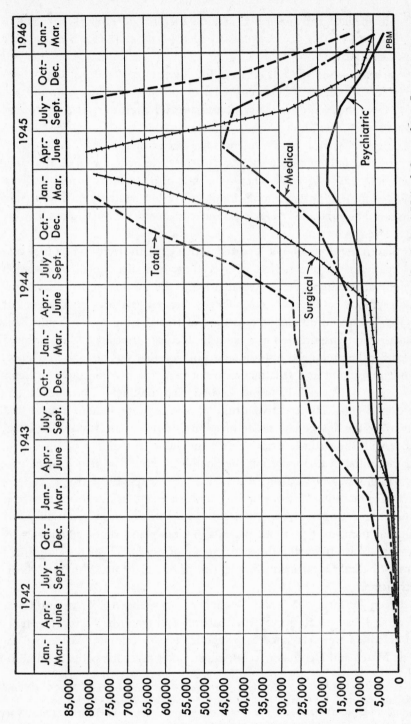

FIGURE 2. Evacuation. Number of army patients evacuated from overseas to the Continental United States from January 1942 to March 1946. Office of the Surgeon General, Medical Statistics Division, April 1946.

increase in medical and surgical casualties, they fell to only 15 per cent in 1945. The total of 117,516 psychiatric patients comprised 18 per cent of the 3-year evacuation load.

Air evacuation. In the fall of 1944 the long-accumulated backlog of psychotic patients in the Pacific area created a critical state of affairs. Two medical officers [7] from the Neuropsychiatry Consultants Division were sent out to find a solution.

Their report gave further evidence of a policy of too little for too long. Tents were the only available shelters for the disturbed as well as the other patients. Staff was insufficient. Therefore, little or no treatment could be given during the long wait, often in unbearably wet or hot weather, until some ship captain could be persuaded to take the patients aboard for the trip to adequate hospital care.

At that time (although not reported until 1945) the transportation of psychiatric patients was the subject of special study at the School of Aviation Medicine [8] at Randolph Field. Research led to the conclusion that air evacuation of psychotic patients was not only feasible but practical. Finally the Air Transport Command developed a method of transporting such patients. This provided rapid transportation to a point of adequate treatment which reduced the need for the prolonged restraint and isolation that was necessary on ships. Continuous restraint and sedation were not used for psychoneurotic patients who needed no special handling beyond that routinely available in air-evacuation flights. The sedative drugs of choice were sodium amytal and paraldehyde; the dosage and mode of administration were determined in accordance with the characteristics of each individual patient.

In the initial evacuation from the Southwest Pacific, a planeload of psychotic patients was flown from Australia to the States. But sedation and restraints were inadequate, with resulting confusion and serious threat to safety. This flight and further investigation led to the establishment of a policy [9] of limiting the number of psychotic patients to 5 per planeload of 28 patients. A medical technician trained in the management of psychotic patients augmented the usual Medical Department complement of one flight nurse and one medical technician.

Between January, 1944, and December, 1945, the Air Transport Command carried over 28,000 psychiatric patients (all from the Pacific Theater), 9,000 of whom were classified as psychotic. The evacuation was stepped up between March and December, 1945, when 5,094 psychotic patients, in addi-

---

[7] Lieutenant Colonel (later Col.) Malcolm J. Farrell and Maj. (later Lt. Col.) Ivan C. Berlien.
[8] Project No. 475. 27th AAF Base Unit, School of Aviation Medicine, 2 October 1945.
[9] Information furnished in a specially requested memo by Lt. Col. S. L. Gumport, Chief, Professional Division, Office of the Surgeon, ATC, 20 March 1946.

tion to 11,803 other psychiatric patients from the Pacific area, were brought to the States. This was accomplished without a loss or a fatality.[10] In the initial evacuations there were occasional complications due to dehydration or over-sedation. When experience yielded sufficient information, a "standard operating procedure" was formulated for the evacuation of psychotic patients. This was not completed until August, 1945. Due to the termination of the war shortly thereafter, it was never issued.[11]

In Europe, air evacuation was also used, chiefly within the theater. Instructions issued there included specific directions for the preparation of psychotic patients for flight. These specified a liquid diet for the preceding 12 hours, an enema given and completely expelled within a few hours prior to flight, the use of constipating drugs as indicated, with sedatives in sufficient quantity to insure orderly loading.[12] It is questionable whether the author of these instructions ever tried giving a psychotic patient an enema and then getting him to expel it! Nevertheless, special preparation and care contributed to the remarkable record of no serious accident due to the behavior of psychotic patients.

Air evacuation was actually a lifesaver for many patients. The hospitals overseas, particularly in the Pacific area, were often very inadequate for even housing psychotic patients. Rarely were there any facilities for treatment. The long return trip by boat (still with no definitive treatment provided), too often in the hold, through tropical weather for 2 to 4 weeks, resulted in terrific suffering for any confined patient. Evacuation by air was at first strongly resisted by some medical officers of high authority, presumably on the basis that surgical patients rated a higher priority. Only after ample evacuation was provided for these did the neglected psychiatric patients receive their due!

Rail evacuation. While air evacuation was used both within the European and Pacific Theaters and between them and this country, only rail transportation moved psychiatric patients within the United States. Certain hospitals became debarkation hospitals during the heavy load of evacuation from overseas. By a remarkably efficient system, medical personnel classified and sorted patients upon their arrival at a port of debarkation. Everyone was seen within the first 24 hours, interviewed, classified as to his diagnosis, and reported to a

---

[10] Corroboration of the effectiveness and the good condition of patients on arrival in this country was given in a personal communication from Brig. Gen. C. C. Hillman, Commanding General of Letterman General Hospital, San Francisco, where most of the patients from the Pacific were first received in the United States.

[11] This was written by Capt. A. F. Valenstein, MC., prepared at the Headquarters of the Pacific Division Provisional Medical Air Evacuation Unit, dated 20 August 1945. It outlined in detail the precautions to be taken prior to and in flight, the preference for paraldehyde as sedative, flexible wristlets and anklets when restraint was required, and special measures to prevent dehydration.

[12] Circular Letter 63, European Theater Headquarters, 18 August 1945.

central regulating office. In turn, the regulating office indicated where the patient was to be sent. In so far as possible, this was to a hospital in the Service Command in which he lived. When such a hospital lacked personnel in the specialty of needed treatment, the patient was directed elsewhere.

Psychotic patients were sent to the psychiatric centers located in the 20-odd general hospitals. The severe psychoneurotic patients needing hospital care were likewise dispatched to special centers. The open-ward, milder neurotic cases were sent directly to convalescent hospitals for their definitive psychiatric treatment.

Hospital trains made the trips between the ports and the Army medical installations which received overseas patients. Slight changes in hospital cars or standard Pullman equipment provided for adequate care and protection of psychotic patients. Such trains were, on the whole, well staffed, even though arranging this momentarily depleted the regular staff at some hospitals. In so far as psychiatric cases were concerned, there was a phenomenally low record of accidents and suicides en route.

The saga of evacuation of patients in World War II is filled with very human and heartwarming stories of bravery and lifesaving. It was a colossal job well done. The earlier evacuation of psychiatric patients contains some dark closets with skeletons. With pride we may now point to the aeration and lighting of these closets. The development of air evacuation was a miraculous achievement.[13] It was pioneering in the transportation of thousands of very sick soldiers, hundreds of thousands of miles by air, in order to provide better treatment more quickly.

---

[13] "News Note: Patients Evacuated by Aircraft," *Bull. U.S. Army M. Dept.*, 77:9, June, 1944.

22

PREVENTIVE PSYCHIATRY

WERE TREATMENT the only aim in psychiatry, we could never hope to catch up with the load. We could not train psychiatrists fast enough. The only hope of meeting the rapidly increasing need lies in greater knowledge of how to prevent mental illness, at least disabling mental illness. While treatment techniques in tuberculosis have been improved, the really great strides toward decreasing this curse have been taken in the wider use of preventive measures and earlier recognition and treatment. But preventive psychiatry—if we may call it by that term—is in its infancy. Nevertheless, its value was proved in the Army.

Not only is our experience in this field still very limited, but our knowledge is meager. The attempted reintegration of mentally ill personalities has given psychiatrists some clues as to how personality disintegration might be prevented. Human reactions are not governed by scientific rule of thumb. There are too many variables and unknowns in the algebra of personal relationships to establish formulae of behavior. However, bit by bit, demonstrable principles of cause and effect are evolving. Their application will be the means of preventing mental illness.

Preventive psychiatry is not truly a new field of endeavor. It has been one of the avowed interests of the National Committee for Mental Hygiene since its origin in 1909. Preventive efforts have been an important interest of the psychiatrists concerned with child guidance. Undoubtedly one of the greatest benefits of the child-guidance clinics established by the National Committee, with the financial help of the Commonwealth Fund, in 1920, was the secondary gain from the education of parents in preventive measures. Unfortunately, however, no widespread effort or concrete program has yet been developed. The demand for the services of psychiatrists has been so great in the field of diagnosis and treatment that psychiatry has lagged behind the general field of preventive medicine. Preventive psychiatry has not been taken seriously as yet by most state public health organizations and perhaps will not be until psychiatry has a more concrete program to offer.

In the Army the same factors of shortage of psychiatrists and a flood of patients prevailed. Nevertheless, it was of paramount importance to retain and salvage all man power possible. Pressure of circumstances led to the use of preventive measures that could contribute toward the maintenance and restoration of mental health in individuals and in units.

The influx of psychiatric patients to the hospitals brought about the establishment of the outpatient clinics and mental hygiene services. Many patients, who not only did not require hospitalization but would be made worse by it, could receive sufficient treatment in such clinics to prevent the development of more serious mental disorders. By enabling men to continue in service, the work in these clinics reduced man-power loss considerably.

The preventive medicine program of the Army did a marvelous job. But it, as well as that of most of our state public health divisions, did not include psychiatry. In an Army of 8,000,000 men the program of prevention of mental ill health had only one full-time expert.[1] Before early 1943 there was not even one. After his assignment, this officer developed a liaison with the Morale Services (which later became known as the Information and Education Division).

Many individuals and groups contributed to the total of the preventive effort. They did so, however, not as the result of plan or scientific direction but indirectly, by satisfying wishes and stimulating interests or providing advice, reassurance, and encouragement. When the soldier left his home supports to go into the Army, perhaps when he went overseas or to combat, he sought any available substitutes—the USO, the Red Cross, comrades in arms. Many found help through their chaplain. Just as in civilian life, the prevention of mental ill health is most frequently in the hands of the immediate available personnel—the corporal, instructor, military police, Red Cross. Without question these and many others did, to a greater or less degree, carry on meritorious work against the development of personality disorders.

There were two approaches toward maintaining good mental health. The first was to decrease the stresses of Army life, the second to increase the environmental supports. But the use of these approaches required an evaluation, through research and clinical observation, of what the stresses and the supports were. It also necessitated a constant running tabulation of statistics which would indicate the trend of the incidence of mental ill health. Consequently, psychiatrists in the field had to become statisticians. At headquarters their figures were consolidated to tell the story of which theaters and which divisions had the greatest number of neuropsychiatric casualties. Thus were ferreted out the causes of the high rate of mental illness in particular units or areas. Only by

---

[1] An officer was assigned to the Neuropsychiatry Consultants Division of the Office of the Surgeon General for the prime purpose of developing a program of preventive psychiatry.

tabulating such figures was it possible to discern the effects of the various practices of selection, rejection, treatment, discharge, command relationships, training procedures, etc., in various camps and posts. Such figures could not tell all the story, and alone they might even give an erroneous impression. Therefore, it was always necessary to supplement them with clinical observations and with the personal-inspection reports of the consultants in the field. With this information at hand two specific acts, equally important, included most of the preventive measures: manipulation of the environment, and education.

MANIPULATION OF THE ENVIRONMENT

Psychiatrists in the field. The first step taken in manipulating the environment was the placement of psychiatrists in the field with the troops. The two key positions were in basic-training camps and with the combat divisions. We must frankly admit that initially the purpose of their assignment was only indirectly preventive. The original conception of the role of the Mental Hygiene Consultation Services was to provide a psychiatrist to aid in the early recognition and the prompt rehabilitation of maladjusted soldiers.[2] The division psychiatrist was to screen the misfits out of a division before it left this country for combat service. Once in combat his main concern was with the treatment of psychiatric casualties. However, experience greatly expanded the work of both of these men to include responsibility for the morale and the mental health of the soldiers in their areas of influence.

Great credit must go to these particular psychiatrists, most of whom soon found ways by which to measure the need for preventive psychiatry. Study of the company and battalion leadership, the AWOL rate, the hospital admission rate, the company punishment rate, and many other records revealed the mental health or ill health status of a unit. The division psychiatrist was usually able to discover the reasons for any undesirable conditions. He then passed on pertinent information about them to the commanding general of the unit who took the steps that were necessary to improve the situation.

The assumption by the psychiatrists of the responsibility to advise with commanding officers on conditions affecting the mental health of their units depended entirely upon individual initiative until 1945. Many officers often welcomed the extremely helpful advice of the psychiatrists relative to personnel problems, factors that influenced the morale, mental health hazards in various training methods, disciplinary problems, and military offenders. Prevention of mental ill health depended essentially on the degree to which the

---

[2] Halloran, R. D., *Psychiatry and the War,* ed. by G. J. Sladen, Charles C. Thomas, Publisher, Springfield, Ill., 1943, p. 430.

psychiatrists could either manipulate the environment, or better, persuade the commanding officer to do so. A War Department circular [3] eventually gave specific Army-wide direction to both commanding officers and psychiatrists regarding their relations and responsibilities in this matter.

Tour of combat duty. One of the more important repercussions from the recommendations of the Army psychiatrists came from a study by the chief of the Mental Hygiene Branch of the Neuropsychiatry Consultants Division. Captain (later Lt. Col.) John Appel spent 2 months working in a division clearing company in the Italian campaign. On his return he wrote a report which the Surgeon General forwarded through channels. The Chief of Staff apparently was sufficiently impressed with it to send copies to all theater commanders. They, in turn, distributed it throughout their theaters, down to regimental commanders.

It is believed that infantrymen would be much more effective and would last longer in combat if they were provided with more incentive to do so. It is rudimentary knowledge that behavior is determined by motivation, but it is a fact which appears not to have been applied to the infantryman. Under present policy no man is removed from combat duty until he has become worthless as a fighting man. The infantryman considers this bitter injustice. He feels that he is expected to do ten or even one hundred times as much to win the war as anyone else, and that he can look forward only to death, mutilation or psychiatric breakdown. He feels that no one at home has the slightest conception of the danger his job entails or of the courage and guts it requires to do one hour of it. He feels that the command does not distinguish between him and the base area soldier, and is actually less concerned for his welfare. Base area troops occupy safe jobs and live in comfortable barracks, but they receive practically the same pay, rank, promotion, and priorities on furloughs to the States, and they are in a position to obtain a great deal more in the way of passes, entertainment, recreation, chocolate bars, cigarette lighters, and so on.

It would be convenient if the soldier were more concerned with winning the war. However, as I saw it on the Italian front, the command has failed to make the broader issues of the war meaningful for him. In itself, winning the war is unimportant for too many American soldiers. The realization has never dawned on them that there might be danger to them or to their families if they did not continue fighting. Winning the war is important only as the time when they can be relieved from combat, but that time to them is in some vague and distant future, too remote to have any real meaning. The Russians are fighting to avenge the death of their loved ones and to drive the enemy from their soil; the British fight for survival; and the French are fighting their way back to France. The doughboy fights because he has to. He fights for his buddies and because his self-respect will not let him quit. For a period this is a very strong incentive, but the time comes when it loses its effectiveness. After a man has been in combat for several months, and has fought well through several campaigns, he has proved to himself and others that

---

[3] *Non-effective Personnel,* War Department Circular 81, 31 March 1945.

he is neither a weakling nor a quitter. How he behaves after this point cannot disprove this. Moreover, after several months of combat he looks around to find that most of his buddies are gone. He is one of the "old" men. For whom can he fight now? What incentive has he to go on?

The doughboy is willing to do what he considers "his share," but after that he sees no reason to keep on. All he wants is to get out of combat duty. If he deliberately shirks his duty and runs away, of course he will be court-martialed. But if he becomes unable to fight further, then he gets out of combat on an honorable status. Thus a wound or an injury is regarded not as a misfortune but as a blessing. As one litter-bearer put it, "Something funny about the men you bring back wounded, they're always happy. . . . They're sure glad to be getting out of there." Under these circumstances it is easy for a man to become sincerely convinced that he is sick or unable to go on. This in turn leads to the premature development of genuine psychiatric disability and a needless loss of manpower. It also leads to self-inflicted wounds and to misbehavior before the enemy.

The first incentive is the one most strongly and desperately pleaded for by all combat men, namely a break. To be effective the goal must constitute something a man wants, and what a combat man wants above everything else except his self-respect is to get out of combat. Thus the most effective goal which can be supplied is the promise of an honorable release from combat duty at a definite time. The chief argument offered against such a policy is the claim that it would entail too great a loss of effective manpower. This argument can be met, however, by relieving individuals rather than entire units, and also by the fact that after 200 to 240 regimental combat days, the military value of the average man is negligible. He will soon break in any event. In rifle battalions in Italy the rate of attrition from all causes, with allowance for the return to duty, is such that only about 7% of the men ever attain 210 aggregate days.[4]

Unfortunately, supposedly because of the limited pool of trained man power near by, even though this report was highly praised and well received, a definite tour of combat was never established widely in the European Theater.[5] A compromise had been worked out in the event of prolonged land fighting in the Pacific. To Capt. Appel belongs special credit for having so clearly set forth the needs for this incentive.

The Army Air Corps, quite early in the war, instituted a tour of duty limited to a definite number of hours or combat missions. The operation of

4 This report was reproduced in the Monthly Progress Report of Health, Sec. 7, published by the Army Service Forces of the War Department, 31 August 1944. This was reported by J. W. Appel and G. W. Beebe, "Preventive Psychiatry," *J.A.M.A.*, 131:1469-1475, Aug. 31, 1946.
5 Some of the recommendations from Captain Appel's report were adopted in part. For example, according to an official report [Period Report, Jan.-June, 1945, Medical Department Activities, Hdq. Twelfth Army Group, Medical Section, APO 655, to the Surgeon General, Ref. No. 319.1 (Med.)], from the Headquarters of the Twelfth Army Group which included the bulk of the American combat divisions in Europe, combat infantrymen with an aggregate of 180 or more days of combat were given top priority for rotation to the United States for 30 days' rest and recuperation. They had an option on base area jobs when they came back to the theater. Corps or division rest centers were established so that personnel could be rotated through these centers. Also short term rotation was established in many small units ranging from 24 hours to 2 days to afford a rest for forward combat personnel.

this system was described in a personal communication [6] from Dr. Douglas D. Bond who served as the Psychiatric Consultant to the Eighth Air Force in England and later as the Neuropsychiatric Consultant in the Office of the Air Forces Surgeon in Washington.

I think the tour started in the RAF at the time of the Battle of Britain when it became evident to both administrative and medical officers that it was of the first importance. The RAF at the time had a slogan which ran, "Crackers or Coffins." As a consequence, they had a set number of missions, depending upon the depth of penetration and the type of ship flown. This was adhered to with the closest rigidity, and although men flew many such tours, for the most part they had a six months' break between. It was only on their own insistence that they skipped this. The Air Forces in Africa, England, France and Italy all attempted a modified replica of this.

The Eighth Air Force in the late fall of 1942, I believe, set the number of missions at twenty-five, but the chance of survival was low, approximately one in six. The length of the tour was based on the actual combat attrition and gradually was lengthened to thirty-five missions in 1945 when the chance of survival was very high. For the most part the length of the tour was maintained strictly, although some individuals who enjoyed combat went far beyond their mark. Fighter pilots were also given a tour by the number of hours in combat areas. At first it was three hundred hours, gradually diminished to two hundred.

As we saw it, the advantages, as one might expect, were in that it gave an immediate goal and allowed many men to push themselves over the hump who otherwise might have failed. It also was an enormous protection for those men who were on the verge of cracking up to be given a respite. Unfortunately, at first there was a rumor, confirmed by people in authority, that the end of the first tour was the end of the war for the person involved. This led to a great deal of hard feeling and difficulty when it turned out to be false.

The tour was never set in Washington but was the prerogative of the Air Force Commander, although the principle of the tour was accepted in Washington.

The flyers varied in their feelings about the tour. Those caught in the middle of their tour when the number of missions was changed were most bitter. None felt that it was not a good idea. One cannot generalize as to what part of the tour men felt most difficult. There were many who suffered most in the beginning or the middle or right at the end, the latter being perhaps the most frequent. It seemed to us that the man's anxiety depended upon circumstances obtaining in a certain part of his tour, such as heavy losses in his squadron or a bad mission which he himself

[6] August 19, 1946. Dr. Bond is now professor of psychiatry at Western Reserve University Medical School, Cleveland. Further information has been given to me by Col. W. H. Powell, Jr., Chief of the Professional Division of the Office of the Air Forces Surgeon. The tour varied not only between various Air Forces and theaters but was changed according to an evaluation of the hazard element. It varied with the types of planes and missions. In some theaters, it was based on the number of missions and in others on the total number of hours. It varied from as low as 25 missions (bomber) in the Eighth Air Force during its most hazardous operations to 1,000 hours for ferrying and transport pilots. In the Pacific area the combat tour of all types was based on hours in contrast to missions. In some instances, for certain types of flying, the tour was considered in total length of service, i.e., 4 months, regardless of hours or missions flown during the period.

had been on, rather than upon the time of the tour per se. In general I think the men in the Air Force were saved from the more serious disintegration by this procedure.[6]

Rest camps. As an alternative to limiting the tour of duty, the suggestion was made repeatedly that soldiers in combat should be given short periods of rest. In World War I, after a period of 10 days to 2 weeks, the men were taken out of the lines and a new group sent in. In this war this was rarely done.[7] Toward the end of the war certain divisions provided for a short rest period as a standard operating procedure. This was no great problem in the Pacific where rest was possible following the successful capture of an island.

According to a report of Dr. Hans Reese [8] who spent considerable time on a special mission interrogating German prisoners, the medical officer in the German Army could tell the commanding officer to take his men out of combat for a rest period. Such a procedure was never the policy in the American Army. In the first place, the medical officer did not have that much authority. In the second place, even if he had had, apparently in many situations there were no fresh or reserve troops for replacement.

Replacements. Throughout his hard-hitting book, Col. S. L. A. Marshall, a medical historian who lived in combat through the war, pointed out repeatedly the importance to a soldier of his companion soldier. "The heart of the matter is to relate the man to his fellow soldier as he will find him on the field of combat. . . . One of the simplest truths of war . . . the thing which enables an infantry soldier to keep going with his weapons is the near presence or the presumed presence of a comrade. . . . He particularly emphasized the uselessness of sending individual replacements into combat in a strange organization. . . . All other things being equal, the tactical unity of men working together in combat will be in the ratio of their knowledge and sympathetic understanding of each other." [9]

Initially replacements were sent in as single individuals who often did not have time to learn to know their officers before the ordeal of combat. In Capt. Appel's report he stated: "The stoutest force which keeps a man going in combat is his self-respect and pride. Its effect depends upon the bond between himself and his fellow soldiers. In this regard there is a marked disadvantage in going overseas and into combat as an individual. It is believed that combat infantry replacements would be more effective if they were requisitioned and assigned in small units of three to nine men who had been trained and kept together from the start of basic training." Toward the end

---

[7] Members of the military forces should refer to a line officers' study of "combat fatigue" for an enlightening review of this subject. See Report of the General Board, U.S. Forces, European Theater, "Combat Fatigue," Study No. 91, File R 704/1.

[8] Personal communications.

[9] Marshall, S. L. A., "Men Against Fire," *The Infantry Journal,* Washington, and William Morrow & Co., New York, 1947, pp. 38, 42, 150, 151.

of the war, this method of replacement was finally adopted, both as a policy for the Army Ground Forces and the theater.[10]

Other environmental manipulation. The psychiatrists in the field were frequently able to make recommendations in order to change the situation of a particular soldier. This could sometimes minimize the stress and increase the support for him. Reassignment to a different type of job, perhaps on limited service, was often desirable. Solutions to problems at home which were troubling the soldier could sometimes be arranged through the co-operation of the Red Cross social worker. A transfer to a different unit was occasionally possible. In many instances the training program was modified.

EDUCATIONAL EFFORTS

Army psychiatrists were impressed by the relationship of leadership to good mental health in a unit. Also they became convinced that many psychiatric cases could have been prevented. Our success in gaining consideration of these observations was varied. It was not possible to issue directions to the Army on these points. Recognition of them depended chiefly upon the psychiatrists in the field who could and did contact line officers and commanding officers. The War Department Circular 81, referred to above, was the culmination of a prolonged effort in that direction. In addition there were such media as Capt. Appel's report, which had widespread dissemination. The Army Service Forces report, *Health,* which all through the war included chiefly secret and confidential data, contained an article each month on psychiatry. This was circulated among high-ranking officers throughout the Army. The research surveys of the Information and Education Division often covered very significant facts about the mental health of troops.

Undoubtedly the most potent efforts toward the education of nonpsychiatrically oriented officers were the personal contacts made by the psychiatrists in the field and in the hospitals. In headquarters in Washington, the Neuropsychiatry Consultants Division worked continually with the Personnel, Intelligence, and Training Departments at War Department level as well as with the Army Ground Forces, Army Service Forces, and Army Air Forces in order to present the importance of the effect of certain policies on the mental health of the Army.

Education within the Medical Department. Every medical officer had many opportunities to prevent the development of emotional disorders. Unfortu-

---

10 Cable recommending this step, signed Stillwell, SF 1733, and approving cable to AGWAR for Stillwell, signed Eisenhower, 6 April 1945, E 297339. There was a letter order issued in the theater, 8 April 1945, file AG322, OPGC, to field force commanders directing the training and shipping of replacements in platoon and squad units or in groups of four men. See Chap. 5.

nately, many of them had a minimal understanding of or a resistance to a psychiatric approach to illness. Their training in the treatment of emotionally caused physical disorders had been insufficient to enable them to assume responsibility for their management in the Army setting. Since the doctors, nevertheless, held a vital key to the maintenance of maximum man power, the Neuropsychiatry Consultants Division accepted the responsibility of doing what it could to educate them about this problem.

One educational effort was the composition and publishing of a War Department bulletin, "Neuropsychiatry for the General Medical Officer." [11] This was supposed to be distributed to every physician in the Army. Its contents dealt with diagnostic and treatment techniques for handling the emotional factors in illness.

A second special effort, directed not only to medical but also to line officers, was the forceful circular of the War Department on the utilization of man power.[12] Many doctors were not aware of the difference between psychiatric illness and faulty attitudes. Since the Medical Department was one of the chief exits from the Army for all soldiers, the doctor was often forced to make the decision of whether to send a man back to duty or to recommend a discharge. It was the responsibility of the doctor not only to understand the criteria by which to choose one of these two dispositions but also, in the cases returned to duty, to help the soldier adjust to that decision.

The third educational (and in this instance organizational) effort on the part of the Neuropsychiatry Consultants Division was to work for a reorganization of the dispensaries in camps. The dispensaries, as they were operated in many places, caused neuropsychiatric difficulties. They did this because the physicians assigned to them were too often of lesser professional capability. Furthermore, these doctors were given only very limited authority in what they might do for a patient. Rarely did they have sufficient time to examine their patients. Some sick calls allowed only 1 minute to a patient. The result was that the patient who came with some physical symptom caused by emotional distress most often received a brush-off. The doctor had no time even to examine him carefully; therefore, the patient was often forced to intensify his complaints in order to try for relief a second time.

Following a study by Maj. (later Lt. Col.) John Appel a full agreement was reached by all the professional divisions in the Office of the Surgeon General to reorganize the dispensary system.[13] In the revision the dispensary

11 *War Department Technical Bulletin, Medical 94,* 21 September 1944. Parts of this are included and discussed in Chap. 29.
12 War Department Circular 81, 31 March 1945, on noneffective personnel.
13 "The Dispensary Organization and Function," War Department Circular 387, 29 December 1945.

was regarded as the front door to the hospital. Therefore it was staffed with better qualified men who rotated regularly into the hospital. Moreover, those whom these doctors could not diagnose and treat in a few minutes were referred to the hospital. The intent was to give proper consideration to each individual patient at the time of his initial interview.

Motivation of soldiers. While this subject has been discussed extensively elsewhere,[14] nevertheless it deserves a brief mention as related to preventive psychiatry. It was assumed that if the soldier were thoroughly informed about the necessity for his job and developed a conviction as to its importance, he would try harder to do it. The soldier who was motivated positively toward his job had a strong mainstay against mental illness. For this reason, throughout the war, the Neuropsychiatry Consultants Division maintained a close liaison with the Information and Education Division. As a part of this program, mental hygiene lectures [15] were prepared which were intended to help the enlisted men relate themselves to their task. Where effectively given, it is believed that they accomplished this purpose.[16] A series of lectures [17] was also prepared for all officers. These lectures would help them in their understanding of personality function.

WHAT WE FAILED TO DO

There were many vistas of preventive psychiatry that we saw, toward which we were not able to advance. When the war started we had few plans of any kind, and, except indirectly, they did not concern prevention. It must even be admitted that we had not appreciated adequately the need for or the possibilities of the use of preventive psychiatry. Although some thought had been given to the problem of morale by psychiatrists in civilian life, the field as a whole was not prepared to meet the challenge as we were confronted with it in the American Army. The number of obstacles met were legion. There were sufficient opportunities for 20 brilliant men to contribute their

---

[14] Chap. 6.

[15] *War Department Technical Bulletin, Medical 21,* 29 December 1945.

[16] Lieutenant Colonel Robt. R. Cohen, psychiatrist at Aberdeen Proving Ground (ordnance basic training) chose two companies of new trainees, formed at the same time and of essentially the same type of men as to age and social and economic background. To one group, he gave four lectures on resentment, regimentation, fear, and adjustment factors. A record was kept on all men through basic training. There were 3 times as many sick calls for neurotic symptoms among the control group as compared to the company receiving lectures; 10 to 18 times as many days lost in hospitalization; 20 times as much time lost by AWOL. See "Factors in Adjustment to Army Life: A Plan for Preventive Psychiatry by Mass Psychotherapy," *War Med.,* 5:83-91, Feb., 1944. See also Kraines, S. H., *Managing Men—Preventive Psychiatry,* A. B. Hirschfeld Press, Denver, 1946, Chap. V, pp. 28-37. This discusses four lectures, "Physical Life," "You Can Take It," "Training," "Taking Orders," designed to mold attitudes.

[17] *War Department Technical Bulletin, Medical 21,* 22 February 1944.

full time, yet the man-power situation was such that one man only was assigned to the job, aided and abetted by our representatives in the field.

There was neither time nor energy to make contacts with the Military Academy or with the Infantry Officers' Training Camp or to study psychiatric considerations in the classification and assignment of soldiers to jobs. No real progress was ever made toward the inclusion of a psychiatric evaluation of the personality in the selection of officers or noncommissioned officers. We cannot say that we really influenced the rotation policy, despite recommendations in this direction. Too many major personnel policies were adopted with little or no specific thought as to their influence on mental health. It is reasonable to believe that the War Department should have stimulated more home-front participation in order to increase the motivation of the civilian toward the wholehearted winning of the war. In turn this would have been reflected in the improved morale of the troops.

On the basis of our experience we feel strongly that a far greater effort should be devoted to the field of preventive psychiatry. The projects in which we invested time and effort could be developed and much expanded for peacetime application. The projects that we neglected or left after only a feeble beginning should be intensively pursued. Possibly new projects should be investigated.

The most important functions of military psychiatry are primarily preventive: to give counsel and advice regarding the attitude of military men toward their jobs; to minimize environmental stresses which tend to impair the efficiency of the personality; to increase environmental supports to the personality. The psychiatrist, with his training and experience in evaluating personality-environmental relationships, should learn how to point out the "why" and "how" of constructive, preventive effort.

23

PSYCHIATRY IN WORLD
WAR I AND WORLD WAR II

AN ATTEMPT to compare the psychiatric aspects of World Wars I and II is filled with pitfalls. Unless one had the opportunity for intimate contact with both, the comparison is likely to be distorted. The effort in this direction by Strecker and Appel [1] was creditably successful, except that it was presented nearly 2 years before this war ended and necessarily lacked many of the facts which are now beginning to stand out in some perspective. Therefore some of the comparisons, especially those relating to health, will undoubtedly change as time marches on.

Furthermore, the number of items which might be compared is so great that no comparison can ever be complete. The chief source of information about psychiatry in the last war is the remarkable "Volume X." [2]

THE NATURE OF WARFARE

Certain background facts of the two wars are of major significance for psychiatry. The differences in these facts account for most of the increase in psychiatric casualties in the second war.

World War I	*World War II*
Approximately 3,500,000-man Army. Number serving in Army, 4,451,000.[3]	Slightly over 8,000,000-man Army.[3] Number serving in Army, 11,367,989.[4]
Duration, Apr. 6, 1917 to Nov. 11, 1918. Approximately 18 months.	Duration, Dec. 7, 1941 to Sept. 2, 1945. Approximately 44 months.
Fighting limited to trench warfare in France.	Mobile and foxhole fighting, global in extent.

[1] Strecker, E. A., and Appel, K. E., *Psychiatry in Modern Warfare,* The Macmillan Company, New York, 1945.
[2] For convenience, where the material was taken from Vol. X of *The Medical Department of the United States Army in the World War* (War Department, U.S. Government Printing Office, Washington, D.C., 1929) the page is shown. Other sources are indicated in the footnotes.
[3] Figures from Medical Statistics Division, Office of the Surgeon General, May 1, 1946.
[4] Associated Press release of Apr. 10, 1947, gave this figure as the number of men and women serving in the Army between Nov. 1, 1940 and July 31, 1946.

Armament: Chiefly rifle and artillery. Relatively fixed positions.

Greatly increased variety of lethal weapons including rockets, bombs, liquid fire, atomic energy. Rapidly moving positions with proportionately greater speed, all types of fighting, communications, transports.

Minimal use of aviation.

Extensive use of aviation.

High enthusiasm and purpose, manifested on the home front and in the Army. "Save the world for democracy." Widely sung war songs.

Comparatively lower enthusiasm and home-front support. Much less obvious motivation on the part of soldiers. No mottoes, no great popularity of war songs.

Fought entirely in a temperate zone on land.

Fought in all climates, extensively in the air, on water, with numerous amphibious assaults.

Civilian population minimally threatened.

Civilian population greatly affected.

Nature of warfare provided certain areas of security and safety.

No places of security, with necessarily prolonged vigilance, alertness, tenseness, and fear.

CASUALTIES

Many of the facts and figures of World War II that would be of intense interest and importance to report are as yet not available. Figures given are only approximations.

World War I

Total strength of the Medical Corps:
  Medical officers, 30,591
  Army Nurse Corps, 21,480
  Enlisted Medical Department personnel, 264,181
  Medical Administrative Corps, 0

224,000 wounded in action (includes those dying of wounds).[3]

World War II

Total strength of the Medical Corps:
  Medical officers, 48,317
  Army Nurse Corps, 54,128 [5]
  Enlisted Medical Department personnel, 541,650
  Medical Administrative Corps, 19,-349

599,000 wounded in action.[3]

---

[5] This and other personnel figures supplied by Personnel Division, Adjutant General's Office. Colonel Florence Blanchfield, Chief Nurse, reported to me that on 1 August 1945 there were 57,286 nurses; between 1 July 1940, and August, 1945, there had been 67,371.

The figures of strength on VJ-day are given in "Developments in Military Medicine During the Administration of Surgeon General Norman T. Kirk." Prepared by the Historical Division, Army Medical Library, *Bull. U.S. Army M. Dept.*, 7:520-562, June, 1947.

51,000 battle deaths.

237,326 battle deaths.[6]

Neuropsychiatric admissions to hospitals totaled 97,577 individuals (p. 153). (Vol. XV, Part 2, p. 90 gives the figure of 105,869 NP admissions to hospitals.)

Approximately 1,000,000 neuropsychiatric admissions reported, representing about 850,000 individuals.[3]

ORGANIZATION OF NEUROPSYCHIATRY

World War I

Neurology and psychiatry were combined throughout the Army with a shortage of psychiatrists and a greater shortage of neurologists.

In 1918 neuropsychiatry was established as a Division in the Surgeon General's Office and in Nov., 1918, became a Section of Internal Medicine (p. 10).[2]

Clinical psychology began as a branch of neuropsychiatry and became an independent Division, Jan., 1918 (p. 10).

Neurologists were assigned to the Neurosurgical Service (p. 53).

All inspections of hospitals were made by the Division of Sanitation, Surgeon General's Office. Only special inspections were classed as "consultations" and made by professional personnel (p. 12).

Consultants to hospital centers in AEF (p. 291).

World War II

Neurology and psychiatry combined with acute shortage of both psychiatrists and neurologists.

Neuropsychiatry in the Office of the Surgeon General began as a Branch of Professional Service and became a Division in Jan., 1944.

Clinical psychology was established in the Adjutant General's Office, transferred to Neuropsychiatry Consultants Division, Surgeon General's Office on Sept. 1, 1945.

Neurologists were assigned as consultants to Neurosurgery Service but remained attached to the Neuropsychiatric Service.

Extensive consultant plan with neuropsychiatrists in each Service Command to carry on professional inspections.

Theater consultants and in some instances base-area consultants.

PERSONNEL

World War I

American Psychiatric Association membership 1920 was 892. Number in military service unknown.[7]

World War II

American Psychiatric Association membership 1946: 3,655; 900 in military service.[7]

---

[6] 175,407 killed in action; 26,706 died of wounds; 23,042 declared dead; 561 reported dead from missing in action; 11,607 died as prisoners from wounds and disease.

[7] American Psychiatric Association figures from Austin Davies, Executive Assistant, APA, January 29, 1946.

Total medical officers assigned to neuro-psychiatry, 673, with 430 in the United States, 263 overseas (p. 25).

Total medical officers assigned to neuro-psychiatry, 2,404.

The Division of Neuropsychiatry in the Surgeon General's Office had 5 officers (p. 25).

Neuropsychiatry Consultants Division had 8 medical officers, 2 clinical psychologists, and 1 psychiatric social worker.

The total rank held by neuropsychiatrists were 2 colonels, 2 lieutenant colonels, and 84 majors (p. 24).

Neuropsychiatrists included 1 brigadier general, 31 colonels,* 122 lieutenant colonels. Figures are not available for the number of majors.

Division Neuropsychiatrists, 41 (p. 26).

Division Psychiatrists, 91.

Three Army consultants who, however, were not appointed until Oct. 19, 1918 (p. 322).

All 10 Armies had consultants, the first being appointed Dec. 27, 1943. All others but one appointed in 1944.

Arrangements were made for the direct assignment of neuropsychiatric personnel including nurses and attendants directly from the draft.

No such arrangement and great difficulty in retaining trained nurses and attendants in neuropsychiatric work.

Clinical psychologists were widely used, 107 commissioned officers.

Clinical psychologists used in hospitals, mental hygiene clinics, induction centers, correctional institutions. Total approximately 450 commissioned.

"Psychiatric Aides" who were psychiatric social workers utilized. (Page 36 refers to there being 63 aides.)

711 military psychiatric social workers, approximately 100 of whom were trained in this field prior to the war but commissions never obtained for this group.

SCREENING

World War I

Neuropsychiatric examinations were made in preliminary examination of recruits upon arrival at camp and posts, and later others were screened through the survey of newly formed units (p. 61).

There were 69,394 rejections for psychiatric disorders in approximately 3,500,-000 examinations (p. 85).[8]

World War II

Screening was done at first by boards of local physicians, later at the induction centers; a second screening was given to men before shipment overseas.

There were 1,846,000 men rejected for neurospychiatric disorders among approximately 15,000,000.[8]

---

* Of these 11 were "terminal" promotions and 7 others were in administrative hospital positions.

[8] The following comment was furnished as of 1 May 1946 by Medical Statistics Division of the Office of the Surgeon General: "Information is available on only 2,511,000 men who were assigned during World War I. Of this number, 688,000 were rejected for any military

There was approximately 2% rejection rate (of all men examined).

Of all men examined, 12% were rejected because of neuropsychiatric difficulties, which amounted to 38% of all rejections.

The rejection recommendations of the neuropsychiatrists were sometimes overruled (p. 62).

Rejections by psychiatrists were occasionally overruled.

HOSPITALIZATION

World War I

World War II

Total hospital admissions Apr., 1917, to Dec., 1918, 2,500,000.[3]

Total hospital admissions, Jan., 1942, to Aug., 1945, 14,000,000.[3]

Total authorized hospital beds, 299,838.[9]

Total authorized beds (June, 1945) 763,000.[9]

Beds occupied (Nov. 21, 1918) 193,026.

Beds occupied 488,000 (June, 1945), 324,000 zone of the interior, 164,000 overseas.[9]

Neuropsychiatric patients admitted to base hospitals in this country up to the armistice, 28,000 (p. 42). The highest monthly admissions for neuropsychiatry in the AEF was 887 in Sept., 1918.

No comparable figures. There were approximately 1,000,000 admissions to hospitals for neuropsychiatric disorders, representing 6% of admissions for all causes; 40% were among troops overseas; 60% among troops on duty in the United States. In Apr., 1945, the peak load of neuropsychiatric patients in all army hospitals reached 49,315.

Neuropsychiatry was established in 7 general hospitals under the medical service (p. 43).

Neuropsychiatry established in 65 general hospitals in the United States and 217 general hospitals overseas. In 29 "psychiatric centers" it was supposed to be an independent service, though in some it remained under the Medical Service.

---

service. However, there were 867,000 defects recorded for the 688,000 men, of which 93,000 were neuropsychiatric. If it is assumed that each of the 93,000 men rejected who had some neuropsychiatric defects is to be considered as having been rejected for this cause, and additional men for some co-existing defect, then 93,000 of the 2,511,000 men for whom records are available could be said to have been rejected from NP reasons. By contrast, in World War II, there were 4,828,000 men rejected at induction, 1,600,000 for neuropsychiatric reasons, as based on the number of persons in Class 4-F in August 1945."
[9] From Resources Analysis Division, Office of the Surgeon General, 2 May 1946.

The advisability of separate neuropsychiatric hospitals was debated and 4 were established in the United States (p. 43).

Consideration was given to the establishment of 1 or more special camps. Not approved by the Neuropsychiatry Division. Two special neuropsychiatric hospitals for psychoses were established.

Nine special centers were created for epileptics and mental deficients, 11 for "insane," 1 for neurosis, and 1 for drug addiction and inebriates (p. 46).

No such specialized centers existed although psychotic patients were sent to the 29 psychiatric centers in general hospitals and neurological patients were sent to 18 neurological centers in general hospitals.

Three special "Neurological" hospitals established in AEF (p. 326).

Four special neuropsychiatric hospitals in European and five in Pacific area.

TYPES OF CASES

The only figures available are not statistically comparable because of different organization and classification of such cases. In World War I, all non-effectives with neuropsychiatric disorders were given medical discharges. In World War II, 388,600 neuropsychiatric cases were given certificates of disability (medical discharge), and an additional 163,000, including persons with mental deficiency, psychopathic personality, drug addiction, alcoholism, homosexuality, were all given administrative discharges. The following figures have other significant points. In Volume X (page 232) there is a statement relative to the psychoneuroses; "there is good ground for believing that they are often associated with disharmony or a defect in the function of the endocrine glands." Such a statement would never be found in the current literature. The discharges of neuropsychiatric cases in World War I included 6.9 per cent under the category "endocrinopathies." The majority of these cases were disturbances of the thyroid gland and, if occurring in World War II, would have been classified under the thyroid gland and not listed with the neuropsychiatric disorders. This represents both a change in point of view as well as progress in the two respective fields of psychiatry and endocrinology.

World War I

69,394 cases in the home forces divided as follows (p. 157):

31.5% mental deficiency

World War II

Based on 545,000 separations,[10] the following figures are available:

30% mental deficiency, including psychopathic personalities

[10] Appel, J. W., "Incidence of Neuropsychiatric Disorders in the United States Army in World War II," *Am. J. Psychiat.*, 102:433-436, Jan., 1946; also Med. Stat. Div. S.G.O.

8.9% constitutional psychopathic state

16.5% psychoneurosis

11.4% psychoses

10.0% neurological cases and injuries

9.2% epilepsy

6.9% endocrinopathies

2.9% drug addiction

2.7% alcoholism

No comparable figures.

No comparable figures.

No comparable figure

47% psychoneurosis

10% psychoses

6% neurological cases

3% epilepsy

No comparable figure

No comparable figure

No comparable figure

4% other psychiatric disorders

Of 1,000,000 hospital admissions for neuropsychiatric disorders:

63% psychoneurosis

6% psychosis

8% psychopathic personality

4% mental deficiency

10% neurologic diseases

9% other psychiatric diagnoses

Of 818 cases seen in Army Neurological Hospital No. 1, 36.3% were hysteria, 16.5% "hyperemotivity—state of anxiety (funk)," 13% traumatic neurosis.

"War Neuroses" included "concussion neurosis," "exhaustion neurosis," "traumatic neurosis," "gas neurosis," "anticipation neurosis," as well as standard forms (p. 337). There was also a diagnosis of "hyperemotivity, state of anxiety (funk)."

Of 1,654 neuroses in the Italian (Mtousa) campaign, July, 1945, 60% were anxiety states, 7.2% hysteria, 13.5% anxiety hysteria.[11]

"War Neuroses" included "combat exhaustion" of the Army, "operational fatigue" of the Air Forces, and "combat fatigue" of the Navy.

COMBAT

Lieutenant Colonel John W. Appel, with the help of Capt. G. W. Beebe and Maj. David W. Hilger [12] made an attempt to compare the incidence of neuropsychiatric disorders in World War I and World War II. Particular emphasis was laid upon possible comparisons of the combat situations. Because of the change in the nature of warfare and the number of supporting troops, it was not possible to contrast these accurately. Also neuropsychiatric conditions were reported less completely and in some instances, quite unreliably in World War I. Furthermore, the Army was much more alert to psy-

---

11 *Essential Technical Medical Data from Hdqts., MTO,* 19 August 1945.

12 ASF Monthly Progress Report, Section 7 of *Health,* Apr., 1945, "Comparative Incidence of Psychiatric Disorders in World War I and World War II." Also see Appel, J. W.; Beebe, G. W.; and Hilger, D. W.; same title, *Am. J. Psychiat.,* 103:196-199, Sept., 1946.

chiatric disorders in World War II. Even in this war, however, many clear-cut cases on medical or surgical wards were not recognized as psychiatric or at least not diagnosed or classified as such, and were labeled "gastrointestinal disorders," "low back pain," and the like. Admissions "to quarters" [13] were not recorded in World War I. Most of the following figures are taken from Appel and Beebe:

World War I	*World War II*
Combat treatment in front lines with rest and sedation (p. 313).	Beginning in 1943, there was treatment in the forward area similar to that in World War I.
Combat casualties for divisions in the line and in reserve were about 140 per 1,000 men per year.	For combat divisions on the European continent from June through Nov., 1944, the rate was 260 per 1,000 men per year.
With intensive combat, rates increased by about 150% for hospital admissions for psychiatric casualties.	The rates increased about 300% with intensive combat.
The rate for admissions for wounded ran about 163 per 1,000 per year in contrast to a neuropsychiatric rate of approximately 25 per 1,000 per year in the AEF.	For the total overseas forces in 1944 the admissions for wounded were approximately 86 per 1,000 men per year, and the neuropsychiatric rate 43 per 1,000 per year. This high ratio indicates that combat was not the only cause for high neuropsychiatric admission rates and that actually only one of the theaters (the European) reported a lower rate than that of the AEF in 1918. The Southwest Pacific area, with an intensity of combat less than half that of the Mediterranean Theater, reported a higher neuropsychiatric admission rate during 1944.
Of combat cases, 40 to 70% were returned to some type of duty in forward areas (pp. 317, 337).	Of neuropsychiatric casualties, 40 to 60% were returned to full combat and an additional 20 to 40% to noncombat duty in theaters.
There was a regular rotation and rest period for troops in combat.	There was no such rest period or rotation.
Each evacuation hospital initially had a psychiatrist who was taken out of it and reassigned (p. 291).	Evacuation hospitals each had a psychiatrist. Some were "loaned" to exhaustion centers (combat-exhaustion treatment).

---

[13] When not ill enough for hospitalization and not well enough for duty, a patient was "admitted to quarters."

TREATMENT

World War I	World War II
Neuroses were not treated in the United States (p. 95).	Neuroses not treated until change of policy in 1944.
In the one neurological center at Platts-burg, tentative plans for the treatment of neurosis in 1918 (p. 117).	Elaborate educational, occupational, and recreational program established for neu-roses in 13 convalescent hospitals.
Treatment of psychiatric cases was not emphasized. Good hospital care was pro-vided.	Treatment for psychiatric cases was not emphasized until change of policy in 1944.
Recovery rate in psychoses not known.	After intensive effort was instituted, 7 of 10 psychotic patients were well enough to send to their homes.
Group psychotherapy was used mini-mally.[1]	Group psychotherapy used extensively.
Hypnosis used in some places; no report of psychotherapy under sedation.	Hypnosis used extensively in some areas. Psychotherapy under sedation used very extensively.
Farradic electric current utilized in sug-gestion therapy in base hospitals in AEF (pp. 400-401).	Not used. (Used by German psychia-trists.)
No organized outpatient clinics in basic-training camps.	Extensive, intensive treatment provided 3 to 6% of all trainees in Mental Hy-giene Consultation Services in 36 basic-training camps.
Shock therapy unknown.	Used extensively for psychoses.
No mention of preventive psychiatry.	Extensive program of preventive psychi-atry.

DELINQUENCY

World War I	World War II
Psychiatrists stationed in disciplinary barracks (p. 131).	Psychiatrists, clinical psychologists, psy-chiatric social workers, stationed in all disciplinary barracks and rehabilitation centers.
From Apr. 6, 1917, to June 30, 1919, 25,057 general prisoners confined.[14]	From Dec., 1940, through Dec., 1945, slightly over 50,000 prisoners.[15]

[14] From Report of the Judge Advocate General, U.S. Army, to the Secretary of War, 1918 and 1919.
[15] From Correction Division, through Maj. Saul Steinberg, May, 1946.

Among 1,498 psychiatric cases of misconduct, there were the following categories (p. 165):

Mental deficiency	42.3%
Psychoses	27.0%
Constitutional psychopathic state	18.2%
Neuroses	4.4%
Epilepsy	3.5%
Alcoholism	1.6%

No comparable figures. Among 23,143 military offenders, 43% of whom were regarded as normal or without psychiatric diagnoses:[15]

Mental deficiency	6.8%
Psychoses	0.1%
Constitutional psychopathic state	24.4%
Neuroses	2.0%
Epilepsy	0.1%
Alcoholism	6.6%

DISPOSITIONS

World War I

All neuropsychiatric noneffectives were given a medical discharge.

Psychoneurosis discharge rate was 8 per 1,000 men per year.
Psychoses 2.5 per 1,000 men per year.[12]

Neurological cases 3 per 1,000 men per year.[12]

Among the recommendations of psychiatrists in regard to the dispositions recommended in 69,394 cases, 8.3% were recommended for limited duty, 0.8% to full duty, 3.6% for observation and treatment, and 87.2% for discharge (p. 175).

World War II

Psychopathic personalities, mental deficients, drug addicts, homosexuals, alcoholics were given an administrative discharge totaling 163,000 men.[16]

Psychoneurosis discharge rate was 18 per 1,000 men per year.
Psychoses 2.6 per 1,000 men per year.[12]

Neurological cases 1.5 per 1,000 men per year.[12]

Fluctuating discharge policy made figures meaningless. "Limited service" was abolished in 1943. In a sample study in mid-1945, of 16,651 patients dismissed from psychiatric centers (half of whom had been psychotic) 79.3% were discharged, 20.6% were returned to duty. In convalescent hospitals, of 38,361 patients dismissed, 83.3% were discharged from the Army, 16.6% were returned to duty.

Total number of Certificate of Disability discharge for neuropsychiatric conditions 387,000; 37% of CDD for all causes (1,049,000) between Dec. 7, 1941 and July 26, 1946.

---

[16] "Separations from the Army," *Health of the Army*, 1:20-21, 31 August 1946. Between 7 December 1941 and 26 July 1946, there were 168,000 men separated by Army Regulations 615-368 and 615-369.

Part II

IN PEACE

24

EVERYMAN: MAINTENANCE
OF HIS MENTAL HEALTH

OUR HUGE war machine was made up of Joe's and Mary's from Brooklyn and Kokomo—each an individual personality. Most of them were "normal" persons, and, although the war changed them, they remained "normal." Despite all of the stresses inherent in being in an army, going overseas, and being in combat, the great majority never had a severe enough personality problem to require medical attention. What were the factors that made them able to stay healthy? [1]

One might answer this question partially correctly by saying that the soldier knew that his was a temporary job and he could put up with it for the length of time that was required. Another answer could be that these individuals were not forced to extend themselves beyond their capacity. A third answer might be that a large segment of the Army was composed of simple, plain fellows whose Army career was far more secure, interesting, and promising than their previous civilian life. All of these factors were undoubtedly present. In any case, there were positive features which aided the soldier's adjustment. An analysis of these undoubtedly can give us pointers which are applicable to the life of Everyman in civilian life.

The adjustment process. The stresses and demands of Army life were greater than the average man in civilian life has to accept. For most of us, most of the time, life is a constant struggle in which we have to change continuously to meet a rapidly changing environment. We vary from hour to hour in our moods, our desires, our intentions, our information. Our environment changes radically from the job to the home; from the church service to a baseball game; from contact with little Johnny to phoning Jake Smithers, the iceman; from buying Christmas presents to paying bills. This constant necessity to adapt ourselves to the demands of our complex environment is sometimes referred to as the "personality-environmental struggle."

For the sake of popular understanding, personality [2] can be defined as

---

[1] See Chap. 6. In the present chapter it is the intention specifically to indicate the methods of application of certain of these supports to the civilian situation.
[2] See Chap. 4.

everything we are, have been, and hope to be; it includes our mind, our body, memories, habits, abilities, limitations, experience; it encompasses our red hair and our big feet. Environment is defined as everything outside ourselves, the things to which we have to adjust—our mates and our in-laws, the boss and the work, friends and enemies, bacteria and bullets, ease and hardship.

All of us are engaged in the personality-environmental conflict every minute of every day. In most cases, the struggle does not result in mental illness. Though we find it hard to recognize the symptoms of the conflict in ourselves, we see them very readily in others—moody spells, outbursts of temper, unreasonableness. Especially do we hear about the physical symptoms of our relatives, friends, and associates.

The struggle may be resolved on any level between complete success and complete failure. The outcome depends upon the strength and adjustability of the personality as well as upon the amount of stress the environment imposes. In other words, it is not just a matter of how tough our environment is at the moment, but how tough we are at the same moment—whether we are mature and stable enough and in good physical health.

The capacity to adjust, then, is the number-one factor in maintaining mental health. The soldier had to do it and many sought and found various compensations for doing it. He didn't have much chance to change the environment as the civilian often can and, therefore, he had to change himself, his behavior, his relationships. Letters from home, occasional good meals, a few hours on leave acquired very special value as compensations. Many a man demonstrated that, even with the odds against him, he could adjust. Even the unstable individual or the neurotic soldier could do so, if given sufficient compensatory support. We were repeatedly surprised at the number of men with a long-standing neurotic adjustment who carried on splendidly under "good" leadership when convinced of the importance of the job.

The lesson from this for Everyman is the necessity of recognizing the existence of the personality-environmental struggle. Sometimes he must make very major changes in the expression of wishes, desires, aims, or relationships. Often the environment must be altered, perhaps only a little, in order to make the struggle less difficult. Or he may have to change it radically. This can sometimes be done on the basis of his own judgment. It usually helps to counsel with the family or trusted friends. Occasionally, it is wise to seek professional advice.

A job with a purpose. The average *successful* soldier knew why he was in the Army, knew what his job was, and held the belief that it was important. In brief, he had a goal. The probability is that the stronger his convictions were as to the importance of that goal, the more successful a soldier he became. In the Army we referred to this consciousness of purpose as motivation,[3] and the Army went to great pains to provide and strengthen the motivation of the soldiers toward their task through lectures, discussion, and leadership.

All motivation is not necessarily healthy. Assuming, however, that the goal or the aim is worthy and at the same time within reach of the individual's capacity, it becomes a major factor in the maintenance of his mental health. In the personality-environmental struggle, only a strong inducement can overcome the obstacles, frustrations, conflicts, and disappointments. The moral, therefore, is that the mentally healthy individual must want to achieve specific goals. Motivation is usually multiple for most of us: we want to have a home and a family; we want to do our jobs well; we would like to achieve in a certain field; we want to enjoy ourselves in our recreation. In so far as one's judgment is good in the choice of those goals, the strength of one's personality can be judged by the persistence and forcefulness of determination.

Teamwork. The successful soldier, particularly if he saw combat, had a rare experience in life. His success depended partially upon the fact that he became a part of a unit which became a part of him. Its successes and failures were his successes and failures; its gripes and opinions were his, as were its laurels and its hardships. In the sacrifice of some of his individuality, he found the compensation of comradeship that rarely develops in civilian life. The resulting security and satisfaction were an important component of his mental health. In the experience he found a new kind of unselfishness. He discovered a rare unity in human relationships that erased differences in creed and color and in social, economic, and educational backgrounds. No one stopped to ask the color of the stretcher bearer; no one cared about the religion of the blood donors; if a buddy saved a life his prewar status did not matter. One of the rich rewards of the Army experience for many, many soldiers was the formation of not only new but very warm friendships. Both the identification with his unit and the close, even though new, friendships with his buddies were major factors in aiding him to maintain his mental health.

The emotional support derived from identification with a group and the value of friendship are recognized in civilian life. However, their importance in the maintenance of mental health and the living of a satisfying life have not been sufficiently stressed. The strength of the wish to belong, to be a part of some group, is certainly inadequately appreciated as a motivating force in life. In fact "doing as the Joneses" is a matter for joking.[4]

We are frequently impressed by the teamwork, self-confidence, and sense

---

3 Motivation is discussed at some length in Chap. 6.

4 Doctor Sylvia Allen described the wish to belong as one of the most frequently recurring themes appearing in neurotic patients in the course of their psychoanalytic treatment. "The Wish to Belong," *Bull. Menninger Clinic*, 4:74-81, May, 1940.

of satisfaction of members of a unit without quite understanding their source in the personality. On athletic teams, identification develops the spirit which counts for far more than the brawn. We are aware of it in the isolated instances of communities that have "spirit"; of employee enthusiasm and participation in some factories or offices; of a uniform devotion and faithfulness of purpose in some churches. There are some conspicuous examples in history, like the Alamo, of the determination and unity which permitted small numbers to accomplish "impossible" missions, because individuals identified themselves with a group.

Life in the Army illustrated clearly the basic principle that the man who made an identification with the unit benefited himself by his increased effectiveness and satisfaction because he benefited the unit of which he was a part. Unfortunately, too many individuals in civilian life do not expose themselves to the various opportunities for them to "belong" to even one group, and the situation often does not force them to do so. Their sense of insecurity or inadequacy prevents them from seeking the comradeship and shared experiences of a group. They may even avoid contacts and activities with other members of their families and coworkers on the job. Their shyness and uncertainty make them fearful of rejection. Deep in their personalities they have a feeling that they are unloved and unwanted. Such individuals can help themselves if they will accept or make the opportunity for participation in group experience. Sometimes a friend can help in making initial contacts. Many other people feel the same way. Someone must take the initiative, and for their own sakes, it must be they.

In this same connection, these timid individuals, along with all of the rest of us, are literally the gainers from contributions to community projects and activities. Initially we may think of ourselves as the givers; in the long run, we are the chief recipients. It is our responsibility to participate, to be a part of the community, to back up the constructive efforts of various types of community activity. How fortunate that satisfying the needs of others also benefits our own mental health!

Opportunities are legion. There is an acute shortage of recreational workers, Red Cross workers, Scoutmasters, Girl Scout leaders, Social Agency helpers in most communities. This means that many people, particularly young people, lack activity that could help them maintain their mental health. The psychiatrist can wholeheartedly recommend belonging to one or more groups in the community, participating in community activity, with a guaranteed return directly proportionate to the investment, for the timid and the bold and all those in between.

In addition to the value of identification with a group, every soldier can testify to the importance of the emotional support that he gained from close relationship with one or two friends. It was this comradeship that made him keep on fighting. This intimate bond of understanding was so deep that the death of his buddy sometimes precipitated him into a psychiatric illness.

A surprising number of individuals have few, if any, close friends. Again one must suspect that they fear rejection or that they fear disappointment. This attitude of withdrawal is a defective facet of the personality which can be corrected. Not only does it indicate a mentally unhealthy state, but by such activity an individual eliminates one of the strongest factors of support to mental health, namely, the rewards of friendship.

One might do well to evaluate his various friendships: What does he invest? What does he receive? This whole subject is far too complicated to discuss in detail here. Let it suffice to point out that some friendships which are superficially very pleasant, at the same time may be pathological. Some of us lean too much and receive far more than we give. Unknown to us, one of our friends may play a mother or a father role toward us; another may give us certain satisfactions we don't find in our own mate. Still others we may regard as our wards or as substitute children. Even though such friendships are pathological in some degree, they may be very valuable—perhaps even necessary for us. Ideally, however, the greatest value is achieved from those relationships in which there is a mutual investment and return.

Leadership. It was not a new fact but a vividly reviewed one that leadership was one of the chief factors contributing to mental health and ill health. In civilian life one has a chance to choose that leadership. Similarly, one has the obligation to give leadership whether in the family or the group or in an elected office.

One needs only to ask any thoughtful soldier or officer to learn of the importance of the role that his immediate commanding officer played in making or breaking his life in the Army. A leader made the soldier feel secure and inspired and enthusiastic or, on the other hand, he made the soldier miserable and unhappy.

As intimated above, there are two applications of this principle to civilian life: to the follower and to the leader. Most of us, sooner or later, have an opportunity to wear both shoes. As children we must learn to follow. The first leadership we know is that within the family. A large percentage of us are parents. It is the relationship of the parent to his offspring more than any other factor that colors the child's reaction to any authoritarian figure. Unfortunately, most of us are nearly, if not completely, blind to the role this factor has played in our lives and will play in the lives of our children. A harmonious relationship with parents during childhood can aid greatly in adjustment as adults.

As adults, our decisions depend upon relationships to authority as they were established in childhood. Should we work for ourselves and be entirely our own boss? Can we accept a demanding and exacting superior? As a woman, can we work for other women, under a woman's leadership? Do we require a lenient and charitable supervisor? Are we looking for a father or mother substitute in our mate? As parents, we will predetermine our children's answers to these same questions.

There are occasions when we can choose the leaders for our groups. In the final analysis, the success of our democratic system depends on our individual participation in the selection and election of government officials. Many of us harbor feelings of uncertainty about the highly praised power of the ballot because we are faced with so much evidence that our governmental structure is permeated by political "horse trading," lobbying by pressure groups, selfish interests fighting against selfish interests. We are reassured, and in some degree our mental health is improved, when we are in a position to gain personal knowledge of positive, vigorous, honest leadership, either through contacts back of the scene or through news stories. Despite our periodic feeling of helplessness we must remember that antidemocratic leadership is the result of discouraged apathy on the part of the electorate. Therefore, for good mental health we must concern ourselves about procuring and supporting wise leaders.

Each of us, in some degree, is by fate or intention something of a leader. Perhaps it is as a parent, and no greater responsibility comes to any citizen. We know some persons who, despite adversity, can make their families feel secure, and even if not economically secure, at least united. We know of employers who do not wait for any collective bargaining to improve the wages or the working conditions of their factory hands. We know executives who create an atmosphere in which no one thinks about punching the clock. Every father and mother, every supervisor, every employer, every executive, every teacher, every club or association president, and every public office holder can improve or impair the mental health of his group through the type of leadership he provides. As long as our society is organized biologically and socially in a structure which has authoritarian figures (parents, teachers, group leaders, public officials), these authoritarian figures have more to do in the maintenance of mental health or the production of mental ill health in its broadest sense in Everyman than any other one influence in our society.

Intellectual growth. Even though he may not have wanted to, every soldier learned much. Not only did he gain new ideas and discover new facts, but he had many new experiences. His continuously changing life, with new opportunities and new vistas, was an important factor in his adjustment. Granted that many times the soldier's life may have seemed routine and humdrum, in contrast to civilian life it was kaleidoscopic. The very experience of being in the Army provided that intangible quality that so many individuals seek for in civilian life—excitement. As the uncertainties and unknowns unraveled into daily experiences, they taught the soldier much. They stimulated intellectual growth which was, unknown to him, of major importance in the maintenance of his mental health.

For a limited number of persons in civilian life, study and reading, observation and learning are part of their daily existence. Unfortunately, too many people who would enjoy it fail to make any effort in these directions. They could, to their own great advantage, regularly brush their intellectual teeth through reading, music, art, drama, crafts, or in the pursuit of some specialized hobby that required study.

For the healthy personality, education must continue throughout life. When an individual assumes that he knows it all or if he becomes satisfied with his status quo, his personality vegetates. He exists but he doesn't grow. Either the blood vessels of his brain have become thickened or else he has some inherent fear that his security will be threatened by any change in his status or knowledge.

Promotion. The chance for advancement was closely related to the soldier's acquisition of new skills and information. Inherent within the Army organization, at least theoretically, was an opportunity to advance in rank and responsibility. For many men even joining the Army took them out of a rut, out of a situation in civilian life in which they had found minimal satisfaction. In addition, for every man there was the stimulus to improvement with the hope of being found worthy of promotion and its increased pay. Along with this stimulus for individual gain was also the challenge of improving the unit so that it might be cited for meritorious service.

In civilian life the individual who is in a situation that does not permit him to express his initiative and, therefore, look forward to advancement is, in all probability, in a mentally unhealthy state. If he is satisfied, one must assume he is dull or too insecure to seek a different status.

Good mental health requires the opportunity for the expression of initiative and a provision both for advancement and for its recognition. Not only does this apply to the individual; it is of equal importance to individuals united in a group. The group—the family, the neighborhood, the city, the state, the nation—must progress. Usually its success in improving is dependent upon the contributions of the individual members toward the common goal.

Not as remote as it appears is the dependence of the mental health of every citizen, particularly the veteran, upon the responsibility to actively advance the status of our nation and the world. There is an unhealthy state of mind that is apparent in too many of our veterans at the present time. Literally millions of men participated, and thousands of them died for the cause, in this war. Preservation of America and our way of life was, in the ultimate, the sole purpose of our fighting. Now that the soldier has returned to civilian life something has happened to his fighting spirit. He is aware of the fact that there are many inconsistencies in our community, in our state, and in our national government which are not in keeping with the principles for which he fought. Why is he not doing something about it? [5] Most tragic is the increasingly evident fact that the job is being left to those willing to work at it who often turn out to be advancing personal or anti-American aims.

In a few cases, the energetic, ambitious, and aggressive individual makes himself heard, but he is the rare exception. The great majority of our 14,000,-000 men returned from the military service to their former civilian ways of indifference toward national and international affairs. In social groups they gripe about the Congressional approval of foreign loans; they are still irritated and disgusted with the attitude that prevailed about the draft and the obvious political coloring that delayed and sabotaged it. But few did or will trouble to express to their Congressmen their thinking about how to improve our country's status. Fewer still will stimulate others to do so. These veterans thus represent another paradox in our midst: Men who fought at the risk of their lives to maintain certain principles have returned to a state of apathy or indifference toward the further maintenance of those principles. Many feel pessimistic about wielding any influence in changing things against the odds of rumored "strong lobbies," "business groups," and "labor pressure." They are too busy with their own problems, their own interests, to discover their own potency in changing the situation. Social ills which do not directly touch them are like the starving people in India—left outside the field of their concern.

This fundamental principle of mental health, self-improvement, family improvement, and community improvement can be applied only if each individual assumes his responsibility and takes some initiative. Too many of us devoted 3 or 4 or even 5 years of our lives to this war not to continue the battle for the advancement of peace. Too many others accepted upheavals, lonesomeness, and unhappiness to let it all be wasted because we fail to advance further on the road of national betterment and international understanding.

Recreation. The occasional opportunity to play was essential to the making of a good soldier. The contrast between recreation and work in the soldier's life was far more sharp than it is in the lives of most civilians. Some civilians work at something which to them is fun. The soldier in wartime did not play

---

[5] Julian H. Franklin described his frustrating experience in attempting to implement his war-born ideals. "Why I Broke with the Communists," *Harper's Magazine*, 194:412-418, May, 1947.

at his job. Therefore, he prized the more the occasional short intervals when he might do just what he wanted to do for fun.

Many soldiers did not have sufficient recreation. One of the great problems about the scattering of the American Army over the world was the provision of recreational facilities and personnel. In combat there was, of course, no time for play. A great deal of effort and money was spent in providing recreation and recreational equipment wherever it was possible to use it. The Army did not do this to please the soldier's folks at home nor because it wanted to appear to be humane. It did so because it paid dividends in the maintenance of the morale and mental health and was therefore essential for the soldier's welfare.

Psychologically, recreation is one of the best outlets for pent-up emotions, particularly hostile feelings. This is most obvious in competitive games in which there is running, hitting, throwing. It applies equally, however, to sedentary games like chess, bridge, poker.

It is an unfortunate fact that so many people do not recognize that some form of play is essential to the best mental health. Instead they stupidly brag that they do not know how to play or that they cannot take time to play. This may be bound up to the attitudes of one hundred years ago when play was forbidden; it was a waste of time and a sin. In highly organized business and industry the pursuit of a vocation allows no chance to express one's unrestrained creativeness or to release aggressions without punishment. Only in recreation and in hobbies can most men exercise free choice as to what they do, when they do it, and how they do it. "The fits and starts with which most of us carry on a hobby, the alternate enthusiasm and boredom, attention and neglect, are not permitted in our work. This element of freedom adds greatly to the attractiveness of a hobby; it deprives it of the irksomeness which attaches to any occupation which *must* be done, even though it be a task one loves." [6]

As psychiatrists we heartily endorse and strongly recommend that every individual develop a hobby or an organized program of play for himself. There is much less interest in hobbies and recreational activities among psychiatric patients prior to their illness than among well-adjusted persons. Hobbies do not necessarily prevent a mental illness, but their cultivation seems to tend to the development of a more stable personality by providing even a momentary diversion from stress.

As evidence of our strong belief in the importance of hobbies, our clinic in Topeka, some years ago, devoted a full issue of the *Bulletin* to the sub-

[6] Menninger, K. A., and Menninger, J. L., "Recreation for Morale: Some Tentative Conclusions," *Bull. Menninger Clinic,* 6:101, May, 1942.

jective accounts of the hobbies of some of the staff.[7] This issue was the personal testimony of a group of psychiatrists that interest in such activities is of great morale value. The civilian, as well as the soldier in the Army, can fortify himself against the frustrations, disappointments, and difficulties of his life by increasing his satisfaction in an activity chosen by himself. For the person who has a job in which he must follow orders or fight red tape or wrestle with monotony, making chessmen move at his will or the tennis ball respond to his wish or putting stamps [8] in their places can add much to his general contentment in life.[9]

Religious beliefs and convictions. One has difficulty in reconciling war with religion, at least with the Christian religion. Perhaps it is for this reason that one does not ordinarily think of the soldier as a religious person. The Army, however, was a civilian army and there were many individuals in it with strong religious beliefs and convictions. A very large percentage of soldiers and officers found help in prayer when they were in combat. Every chaplain could recite many instances in which the soldier's religious beliefs appeared to be a major factor in maintaining his adjustment.

Over the centuries, religion has always been one of the chief supports in adjustment for many people. It has been a source of comfort, reassurance, and hope, and probably always will be. Therefore, in seeking personal supports, in looking for opportunities for group identifications, in finding friends, in seeking outlets for constructive community activity, the church and religion stand available to meet these needs for many, many people.

Perhaps a word should be said regarding a widespread illusion that psychiatry is in some way or other antagonistic to religion. The subject is far too extensive to be argued here.[10] Many scientists, despite their life interest in material truths, are deeply religious. Many psychiatrists are religious men. Most of us feel that religion and psychiatry are in no way antagonistic; rather are

---

[7] "Recreation and Morale," a subjective symposium by various authors covering the subjects of horticulture, contract bridge, stamp collecting, classical music, chess, mask making, poetry, photography, and bird study. *Bull. Menninger Clinic,* 6:65-102, May, 1942. Some of the psychological values of hobbies are discussed in an article by the author, "Psychological Aspects of Hobbies," *Psychiatry,* 99:112-129, July, 1942.

[8] The author is biased as to the value of this activity because of his own philatelic interest. Nevertheless, it is impressive that President Roosevelt, throughout the period of great stress in the White House, "puttered" with his stamps for a period of relaxation nearly every night before going to bed. There was an album and some stamps at his side the day he died. See "The Great Philatelist," *The New Yorker,* Mar. 30, 1946, p. 48.

[9] An excellent discussion of the psychiatric aspects of play is given by K. A. Menninger, in *Love Against Hate,* Harcourt, Brace and Company, New York, 1942, pp. 167-188.

[10] Menninger, K. A., *The Human Mind,* 3rd ed., Alfred A. Knopf, New York, 1946, pp. 460-475. The discussion of the religious applications of psychiatry in this book is excellent, particularly with regard to its contribution to religion. See also the discussion of religion from the standpoint of psychiatrists in the chapter entitled "Faith," in Menninger, K. A., *Love Against Hate,* Harcourt, Brace and Company, New York, 1942, pp. 189-213.

they co-operative. Psychiatry can contribute much to the understanding of the personality. The fact that religion is frequently abused and distorted by sick personalities, even by ministers, is no more reason for its denial or rejection than is the condemnation of any other constructive force or movement because of crackpots who participate in it. Psychoanalysis has been accused of denying religion. One of the best refutations of such nonsense has been very well stated by Liebman, a rabbi, in *Peace of Mind,*[11] following his own analytical experience.

As an evidence of the psychiatrists' attitude toward religion, the following statement is of historical significance. It was approved unanimously by the Group for the Advancement of Psychiatry (approximately 100 psychiatrists) at their meeting in Minneapolis on July 2, 1947.

For centuries, religion and medicine have been closely related. Psychiatry as a branch of medicine has been so closely related to religion that at times the two were almost inseparable. As science developed, however, medicine and religion assumed distinctive roles in society, but they continue to share the common aim of human betterment. This also holds true for that method of psychiatry known as psychoanalysis.

We, as members of the Group for the Advancement of Psychiatry believe in the dignity and the integrity of the individual. We believe that a major goal of treatment is the progressive attainment of social responsibility. We recognize as of crucial significance, the influence of the home upon the individual and the importance of ethical training in the home. We also recognize the important role religion can play in bringing about an improved emotional and moral state.

The methods of psychiatry aim to help patients achieve health in their emotional lives so that they may live in harmony with society and with its standards. We believe that there is no conflict between psychiatry and religion. In the practice of his profession, the competent psychiatrist will therefore always be guided by this belief.

New awareness of emotional conflicts. There was not a soldier in the Army who was not familiar with and understood the significance of NP, the abbreviation for neuropsychiatric or neuropsychiatry. Along with slang usage of "psycho," it was the abbreviated label applied to men who had emotional difficulties sufficient to cause them to drop out of combat or to go to the mental hygiene clinic or to be sent to the psychiatric service or section of hospitals. Perhaps these casualties became such common knowledge because almost every soldier and officer in the Army was aware of the stress and the strain on his own personality. It was not hard for them to identify with and thus easily understand similar, though more acute distress, in a comrade.

---

[11] Liebman, J. L., *Peace of Mind,* Simon and Schuster, Inc., New York, 1946. Also see an excellent brief statement of the attitude of psychoanalysis toward religion which was given by Lawrence Kubie in the *New York Herald Tribune,* "Psychoanalysis—Costly Fad or Boon to Mankind," Apr. 20, 1947.

Tragic as it was that so many men became psychiatric casualties, there was an intangible benefit in the common knowledge about them. It forced the recognition of the fact that at different times the personality varies in its ability to resist stress, and that different personalities react differently to the same stress. Therefore the still-integrated person did not feel he was doomed to crack up and the disintegrated personality gained support from the fact that others had difficulty. Both could find courage to seek increased ability to resist stress.

A kind of "operational fatigue" occurs in civilian life just as it did in the Army. The mere recognition of its existence places us in a more intelligent position to deal with it. An orientation to the fact that it can and does occur in varying degrees in all of us at various times removes in large measure the stigma that for so long was attached to emotional illness. For the first time laymen have seemed to learn that the way men feel and think, love and hate, has an effect on their functional efficiency. For the first time we can hope for the co-operative understanding of millions of people in coming to grips with America's major health problem—mental illness.

What is mental health? By far the most comprehensive, accurate, yet simple definition that I know is that given in *The Human Mind:* "Mental health is the adjustment of human beings to the world and to each other with a maximum of effectiveness and happiness. Not just efficiency, or just content-ment—or the grace of obeying the rules of the game cheerfully. It is all of these together. It is the ability to maintain an even temper, an alert intelli-gence, socially considered behavior, and a happy disposition. This, I think, is a healthy mind." [12] Most of us do not reach that ideal. Our minds vary in their healthiness. The hope is that we will find the ways whereby to make our-selves more happy, more efficient, and more able to follow the rules of the game. It has been the purpose of this chapter to set forth some of the ways and means of achieving that end as we saw them operate in the lives of the soldiers. We know that they have equal validity and application to Everyman in civilian life.

---

[12] Menninger, K. A., *The Human Mind,* 3rd ed., Alfred A. Knopf, New York, 1946, p. 1.

25

SOCIAL REINTEGRATION OF THE VETERAN[1]

ON LAST Memorial Day I noted a very elderly, white-haired man dressed in a blue uniform, walking through the foyer of the Palmer House in Chicago. With the opportunity at hand, I stopped and talked to him. He was attending the day's ceremonies, wearing the uniform of the Grand Army of the Republic. I asked him if he, as a veteran, had had any difficulty with readjustment after the Civil War in '65. He had many incidents to tell of his struggle in settling down to civilian life. Despite his advanced age, those memories still seemed quite vivid.

Veterans of every war have more or less difficulty in readjustment, depending upon them and upon the environmental situation. The approximate 15,000,000 of us who have returned home from military service in World War II represent every community, every social group, every profession and trade. For that reason our concerns have been and will continue to be of such importance to the welfare of the country that for some time we will command the center of the spotlight in postwar planning of many sorts.

The year 1946 saw the return home of most of us.[2] How were we received? Many of us found housing conditions nearly impossible for comfortable living; if decent quarters were available their price was highly inflated. Those of us were lucky who had prewar civilian clothes which would fit; for a long time even veterans could not find shirts to buy. There was a great scarcity of new cars or used cars in good condition; if we had prewar models, until recently it was difficult to replace worn tires and parts. It often required months to obtain a phone in our homes. Good jobs were hard to find.

Public interest being feeble, the GI was frequently greeted with the sneering remark, "The war's over, soldier." General Bradley's answer to that was, "The shooting war may be over but the suffering isn't." [3] This is a truth that many people have forgotten. The soldier who did so much to make America

---

[1] Some of the ideas in this chapter had been expressed previously in an article, "Rehabilitation of the Veteran," which appeared in the *Ohio State M. J.* 43:504-510, May, 1947.

[2] As of June 30, 1947, it was estimated by the Veterans Administration that there would be 14,600,000 World War II Veterans!

[3] Bradley, Omar N., remarks over a nation-wide radio broadcast, Aug. 16, 1946.

secure returned to situations that made him and his family feel insecure. Laws and agencies were created to assist him. Without public support they can accomplish little. But now the public does not have to salve its conscience by treating the soldiers well. No longer does it feel guilty at not sharing their hardships, and so it has become more apathetic and indifferent to the needs of the veteran. However, those thoughtful Americans who are aware of the plight of many of our returned soldiers will continue to direct intensive thought, planning, and action toward helping them solve their problems. It will be dramatically tragic if such is not the predominant point of view and effort of our nation.

After months and years of being provided for and told what to do and when to do it, many veterans among us discovered that it took special effort to assume the initiative again. This was particularly true of the younger men who had not long been free of parental control before they were subject to Army direction. They had to learn or relearn independence of decision and action.

We have now been home long enough to be ready to take stock of ourselves, our emotional, social, economic, and political relationships. After a year or two of trying to catch up on all the things which we missed during our period of military servitude we can and should take the time to look about and realistically evaluate what we have, what we want, how we can get what we need and wish for, what our obligations are to others. This kind of thinking should be done in terms of family, community, national, and international affairs. Certain facts must become axiomatic in our minds.

We are now citizens first and veterans second.[4]

Enriched living is a combined responsibility of the individual and the community.

There is an important time element involved in civilian reintegration of an individual who has been in military service for 3 or 4 years. He did not become a soldier in a week and he may not become a civilian immediately.

The public is glad and willing to lend every assistance to its fighters BUT resents being imposed upon.

The civilians contributed to the winning of the war in so far as they were called upon or were able.

Some of the problems which many veterans face are similar to those resulting from civilian situations which cause long separation from home and a marked change in the character of one's life.

---

[4] This is the commendable motto of the American Veterans' Committee. The principle has been emphasized by G. Brock Chisholm and other psychiatrists since 1944 when the dischargees were fast returning to civilian life.

Just as rank has its privileges and therefore its responsibilities, the country has given veterans certain privileges and so it can expect they will assume certain responsibilities.

READJUSTMENT IN REVIEW

For purposes of discussion, veterans can be divided into two classifications, the "normal" and the handicapped. Probably 90 per cent of the men came back without any battle scars. They were "normal" in that they showed no physical or emotional disability at the time of discharge.[5] Then there was the smaller, although numerically large, group of men who returned to civilian life with some type of handicap—physical or emotional. Actually, some of the "normal" men also may have belatedly developed similar handicaps. Reactions sometimes do not show up until after discharge. Many of the veterans from World War I discovered a "service connected" [6] disability months or years after the armistice. Already veterans' hospitals are accepting post World War II admissions of this type.

Probably the great majority of the "average" veterans, those without physical or psychological disability, met with no serious emotional problems in the course of their return to civilian status. To be sure, some, for many possible reasons, such as not finding preferred employment or a proper place to live, reacted adversely. Nevertheless, while most veterans *were not* "problems" in themselves, it would be playing ostrich not to recognize that they *had* problems, both big and little ones. Men who had been away from home and job for several years, living under a military regime in an entirely different part of the world, were suddenly catapulted back into their former lives. Of course both effort and time were required for adjustment, especially when the home environment had also changed.[7] During this re-

---

[5] A certain number of "normal" men were found to have physical or emotional difficulties at discharge from the separation center. Every soldier who regarded himself as well or who was not disabled or ill was sent to the mass discharge centers where he was given a final physical examination. In a report of the psychiatric evaluation of 10,000 men in one separation center, 2.57 per cent had sufficient complaints to warrant a neuropsychiatric diagnosis; 0.51 per cent had a disorder sufficient in severity to cause them some degree of incapacity. Burton, I. F.; Eaton, M. T.; and McMahan, H. G., "Incidence of Neuropsychiatric Disease in the Demobilized Veteran," *Am. J. Psychiat.*, 103:165-171, Sept., 1946. On the other hand, another psychiatrist indicated that "the number of soldiers with relatively minor problems who may be aided much is indeed large and it is imperative that those who need additional help and guidance be given some information as to where such aid may be sought." Schneck, J. M., "Neuropsychiatry at a Separation Center," *Mil. Surgeon*, 100:232-233, Mar., 1947.

[6] Such disability could be considered "service connected" only by the liberal definition of Congress: Any neuropsychiatric disorder developing prior to 1925 was to be considered "service connected."

[7] This situation is not true merely of America and American veterans. Many articles on the subject have appeared in Britain. Typical is the excellent one by Lt. Col. T. F. Main, an Army

alignment of life many men were restless and ill at ease. Some had moments when they doubted the understanding of those about them.

When a veteran was confronted with unemployment, prolonged difficulties in finding a place to live, prejudices, or discrimination, both he and the community had trouble. Under such circumstances some veterans saw their problems as due only to failure on the part of others. They were unwilling to recognize their own inadequacy as well. Therefore these men assumed little or no responsibility themselves for the solution of the difficulties.

Insecurity was the basic cause of many problems. Men had to regain a sense of belonging. They had to relearn civilian ways. As Kupper [8] so excellently pointed out, they needed time to find an approved way in which to dissipate hatred, envies, and resentment. Increased drinking was the means some chose to evade or delay efforts toward the solution of their problems. Some sought an unhealthy retreat into a veterans' organization which promised, above all, personal support and understanding. [9]

When economically possible and sometimes when not, many veterans interrupted the shift from the routine and regimentation of military life to the routines and demands of civilian work, education, or social or family responsibility. They welcomed the interlude of self-direction on a full-time basis. It was a good time for reacquaintance with families and friends and interests of prewar years. It was also a good time to cast about as to just what they wanted to do to earn a living, a period for shopping as to choice of location for living and working after seeing a great deal of the country during military service. There were, of course, those who prolonged the interim simply because there was no pressure to end it—no one to tell them what or where or how to do, and "52-20 clubs" [10] flourished. Sometimes members of the family, friends, or counselors—religious or medical—had to step in and give that subtle extra push for them to make the fresh start in civilian life.

The popular claim that many veterans would be problem children or that they would continue to turn loose their overt aggressiveness into crime has been proved nonsense. An infinitesimal percentage of the veterans were criminals before and perhaps during the war. Similar behavior on their part

psychiatrist. "He Has Been Away from Home," one of a symposium, "Plan for Re-instatement," published by the Industrial Welfare Society, 14 Hobart Place, Westminster, S.W.1, London, April, 1945.

[8] Kupper, H. I., *Back to Life: The Emotional Adjustment of Our Veterans,* L. B. Fischer, New York, 1945, p. 125.

[9] Press release: Mackey, Joseph (North American Newspaper Alliance); "Veterans' Groups in New York Have a High 'Mortality' Rate," *Kansas City Times,* (Mo.), Nov. 8, 1946, p. 10.

[10] Twenty dollars a week unemployment "insurance" for 52 weeks! A GI Bill of Rights provision. As of January 31, 1947, there were 1,162,247 continued unemployment claims. Congressional Record—Appendix, p. A592, Feb. 17, 1947.

since that time cannot be justifiably attributed to war experience.[11] The actions and reactions of any man depend largely upon his own personality and his childhood experiences. Obviously these are modified by the environment in which he lives, but postwar pathological behavior in veterans has been seen most frequently in those who had a prewar warping of their personalities. In the majority of instances it was not the result of recent harrowing experiences or long isolation and separation from home: A distorted personality unfortunately tends to blame its inadequacies upon the world, while making few if any efforts to change itself. Some veterans in this class, who "got by" in military service, will "project" their difficulty onto their war experience.

Some of the dreams which made life possible for men enduring the hell of war were idealizations of people and situations whose real outlines were obscured by long separation. Extra patience and understanding were needed by veterans and their relatives and associates to weather the period of factual refocusing. Hopes were high in many hearts that the caustic burning of war experience on many lives would have destroyed some of the causes of the social ills which had seriously affected them and theirs. Such wishing and dreaming is necessary to inspire the hard work of making ideals materialize. In some veterans it was followed by souring disillusionment.[12]

---

[11] Inquiries to the correction division of six of the more progressive states revealed that no statistics are available regarding the number or percentage of veterans admitted. That the number of veterans will increase is to be expected. In the Municipal Court in Cleveland, they increased from 1,269 appearing between Nov. 20, 1944, and Dec. 31, 1945, to 2,318 for the first 9 months of 1946. Their charges: intoxication, 1,366; assault and battery, 102; traffic, 545; vice, 23; petty thievery, 33; miscellaneous, 249. Griffin, B. W., "Veterans Rate Special Handling," *Probation,* 25:65-69, Feb., 1947.

[12] The veteran, any and every veteran, can help himself by a periodic self-examination. This is facilitated by the reading of any of several books prepared for the veteran. Every one listed below discusses the common problem of all men discharged from the service. They are helpfully written and will aid a man in seeing himself more objectively.

(1) Baruch, Dorothy W. and Travis, Lee Edward, *You're Out of the Service Now—The Veteran's Guide to Civilian Life,* New York and London: D. Appleton-Century Company, Inc., New York, 1946.

An educator and psychologist combine to write one of the best books covering the gripes, the jitters, sex, the girl, children, family, school, job, where to find help, hobbies, the future.

(2) Bolte, Charles G., *The New Veteran,* Reynal & Hitchcock, Inc., New York, 1945.

The former leader of the American Veterans' Committee tells the story of his own experience and his orientation to the social issues confronting the nation and particularly the veterans.

(3) Droke, Maxwell, *Good-bye to G.I. How to Be a Successful Civilian,* Abingdon-Cokesbury Press, New York, 1945.

A merchandising counselor, a publisher, and a veteran writes in second person about the everyday problems of veterans—the family, the only girl, religion, education, the job, buying land, handicaps.

(4) Dumas, Alexander G., and Keen, Grace, *A Psychiatric Primer for the Veteran's Family and Friends,* University of Minnesota Press, Minneapolis, 1945.

A psychiatrist and a lay writer write about the uninjured veteran, the physically hurt,

In spite of the longing during military service to "live his own life," when civilian life looked difficult many a man looked back at his Army experience with nostalgia. He recalled: "We had the best damn outfit in the Army"; "We went places and did things"; "It was tough, but we did it"; "Old Blood and Guts was hard, but he knew how to lead." These thoughts unconsciously expressed his wishes for comradeship, unit identification, accomplishment with motivation, strong leadership. Discovery that these were not characteristic of many jobs in civilian life sometimes led to re-enlistment.

Disillusionment feeds rebellion of one sort or another. From 1919 to 1921, we can recall, there were fights about labor, about prohibition. During that era the Ku Klux Klan was re-created with enthusiasm, because it catered to unrecognized psychological cravings and satisfied unrecognized passive [13] longings of the former soldiers. It furnished an outlet for their hates and resentments; it provided them with a dictator leadership which they paradoxically disapproved and yet wanted.

Men in the Army and Navy submitted grudgingly to the almost complete dictatorship of military organizations because of the realization that it was essential to waging war. However, many former soldiers are very critical of our form of government in spite of the fact that it fosters the precious four freedoms. After a life which had been regimented for greater efficiency, veterans found upon their return to civilian life that they were annoyed with the inefficiency, the slowness, the indecisiveness, the bungling of our democratic system. Some of these men have been attracted to groups which hold forth promises of improved social relationships; some have withdrawn in

---

and the mentally hurt veteran. Although written for the relatives, it is helpful and very readable for the veteran.

(5) Kupper, Herbert I., *Back to Life: The Emotional Adjustment of Our Veterans*, L. B. Fischer, New York, 1945.

A psychiatrist in the Navy writes to all veterans on their place in the world, the fighting man, the return to the family, readjustment to civilian life. This book is for all veterans, not merely neuropsychiatric discharges.

(6) Pratt, George K., *Soldier to Civilian, Problems of Readjustment*, Whittlesey House, New York, 1944.

The psychiatrist writes on the equipment the soldier took with him, what the military service did to the former civilian, how the Army prevents strains of adjustment, soldiers with psychiatric disabilities, the first weeks at home, going back to work, getting reacquainted with the family.

(7) *Psychology for the Returning Serviceman*, prepared by a committee of the National Research Council, ed. by Irvin L. Child and Marjorie Van de Water, Infantry Journal Press, Washington, D.C., 1945.

With much help from various writers, this psychologist and science writer discuss choosing a job, learning new skills, getting married, returning to a wife, being a father, the veteran as a citizen, social conflict, POW, getting well, NP's, combat nerves, injury to sight or hearing, loss of limb.

(8) Waller, Willard, *The Veteran Comes Back*, Dryden Press, New York, 1944.

A discussion of both the individual and social aspects of the veteran's return.

13 Desire to be taken care of, looked after, provided for, told what to do.

disgust from other than essential participation in the community; some have started working hard to strengthen democratic processes and to support thinking, aggressive leadership.[14]

Family problems. The men who came back to long-established and satisfactory family relationships, to homes in cities or towns where they had lived previously, and to prewar jobs, slipped back into civilian life so easily that they wondered if they had really been away. Life seemed to go on from where it had left off when the draft notice with "Greetings from the President" arrived. Experiences—pleasant, interesting, or horrible—faded into memories which could be drawn upon during veteran "bull" sessions.

However, where the separation or isolation of war experience widened the gap between dreams about and the reality of family relationships, the readjustment was often very difficult. It was to the family with its illusions about him that the veteran first returned with his own dream images more clear than accurate. He also brought back the urge to run his own life and be his own boss. Wives and families were so glad to have him home that they happily gave way in making plans. As dreams were checked off against reality, sometimes painful adjustment took place. When various members of the family made an effort to understand the points of view of the other members of the family the process was simpler. However, certain attitudes complicated relationships.

There was the veteran who discovered a new negativism toward his father. He had learned to accept a life in which he was subservient and obedient to the orders of his commanding officer, while he simultaneously resented his authority. His father represented this same authority in circumstances which allowed him to dare an open revolt. Even when unspoken, such rebellion was obvious in disagreement with or resistance to parental advice or opinion. When the father could appreciate this problem and serve as a friend, as an equal, and not as an authoritarian object, the son had less difficulty in accepting him.

Many a mother was surprised to find that all her abundant maternal affection that she hoped to lavish on her returning boy was not particularly welcomed. He tolerated being fussed over a little, but only a little, unless he was seriously unadjusted. For better or for worse, although many parents had difficulty in accepting the fact, son had grown up. The boy who went off to war several years before had had experiences that had matured him perhaps far beyond his years. He came home a man. It was the happier family in which adjustment was easier for all concerned when the new maturity was

14 This point was forecast by R. R. Grinker, and J. P. Spiegel, *Men Under Stress*, The Blakiston Company, Philadelphia, 1945, p. 451.

recognized, accepted, and acted upon, even though it was not equaled in wisdom.

Readjustment to his wife. During the course of the war I had occasion to talk to many wives whose husbands were in the Army and overseas, and I learned a good deal from my own wife. It is my impression that they—our wives—were really "the forgotten" in the war. Nobody gave them any glamour and few gave them much support. Along with their soldiers, they had to "sweat it out" in insecurity and uncertainty. They tried to live from day to day, just waiting. They had suddenly to assume all the responsibilities of the household; they had to make the decisions, with little or no counsel and advice from their menfolk, especially when an interchange of letters often took weeks or months.

Because military service was so different and their sole contact with it was by mail, they often misunderstood and were hurt by what their husbands did or wrote. Some left the security of their own homes for a wandering life or a shared home. For financial or emotional reasons a good many made many new contacts in volunteer war work or business or industry. Often the new field of activity proved far more interesting than washing dishes and cleaning house, and it stimulated greater independence.[15]

With the development of new and unshared interests and contacts on the part of both the wife and the veteran, it is not difficult to understand that when the foundation of their married life was not very firm, many couples grew apart after long separation. The separation made their differences in personality and interests more apparent. Of necessity, each became much less dependent upon the other. Consequently their readjustment took time— time that was required to develop an understanding of the personal significance of the experiences and developments of each other and time to find a mutual aim whereby both could achieve emotional and economic security.

Certain kinds of distortions existed in this renewed relationship, at least at the start. Some wives had found too much satisfaction in their outside contacts to be willing to return to the drabness of domestic duties. Some others wanted to remain as the head of the house, forgetting that responsibilities and decision-making are best assumed as mutual tasks. Still others had grown so weary carrying the burdens of the house and family that they wanted to dump all of their load on the returned husband immediately.

The daydreaming of foxhole days may also have confused the wife and mother roles in the memories of the soldier, while the wartime experience of

---

15 An extremely interesting survey of service wives was made in Austin, Tex., by a community group, reported in a small booklet by H. E. and B. M. Moore, "Through Their Own Front Door," University of Texas, Sept., 1945.

his wife confounded reality further in increasing her independence of decision and action. At the same time her longing for the companionship and the affection of her mate may have led her to revise her concept of the real husband to match that of her imagining.

In those instances where the wife changed very little, her husband may have thought he had outgrown her. If she had changed a great deal, he may have felt strange and confused by the conflict between the now and then. Or sometimes it was the wife who felt unable to cope with the new in the personality of her husband. The differences may have been so obvious that the likenesses remained overshadowed until deliberately sought for, and the unshared experiences needed to be supplanted by shared activity and thinking.

Of special concern in some families was the sexual readjustment, since it is an important basis for a compatible, happy married life. There was a high rate of nonmarital or extramarital sexual activity among officers and soldiers. Undoubtedly, there were some lonesome wives who found momentary satisfaction with a substitute lover. Often the result in either case, when the reunion occurred, was an unvoiced sense of guilt, which was expressed by sexual uncertainty or disinterest. Because much of the extramarital sexual activity had personal pleasure as its sole aim, it was immature in the sense that there was no affection invested in another person. In the mature sexual relationship both partners must be satisfied, and it is probably more gratifying to give enjoyment than to receive it. Any marriage may go on the rocks without mature sexuality. The manner of handling such intimate and personal problems cannot be generalized, but the wise veteran or the wise wife will seek professional psychiatric help if they have continued to be sexually unadjusted.

Children. Many a veteran came home to a "new" child in the family. When he was overseas he may have been proud of the fact that he had a new baby. However, being a father did not cost him much, nor did it automatically make him capable of assuming his new role.[16] One has to live it in order to learn it. A father has to have time to learn how to love his child, both physically and emotionally, time also to gain the recognition and love of the child by sharing its care. A surprising number of men have an unconscious struggle when a child is born, particularly the first child, because no longer is the love of the wife all theirs. They are somewhat displaced and sometimes even consciously jealous. It was even more difficult for the veteran (and his

---

16 A helpful booklet, "Father Comes Home," was widely distributed by the Child Study Association of America, 221 W. 57th St., New York, 1945. A somewhat similar pamphlet, "When Your Man Comes Home," was issued by the Y.W.C.A., 600 Lexington Ave., New York, 1944.

wife and child) to walk into the picture at a late date. Because the child represented a part of her absent husband, in many cases the wife devoted extra time and energy to the infant. For financial or other reasons, including the dearth of "sitters," she may have been tied closely to her home. Trouble brewed for many couples from the annoyance and frustration inherent in the care of a child when father came home with anticipation of going places and doing things with his wife. The division of interest, the noise of crying, the lessened freedom were provocative stimuli or alibis for his irritability. Because the wife was forced to divide her interest and energy, she was also subject to emotional stress.

Both older children and the new child had to learn to accept the "strange man" as father. This was a challenge for him to "win" the child. It was unfortunate for both when he did not do so. The child usually did not want to share the mother as he had to do when father came home. Consequently, special efforts had to be made not only for all the family to become reacquainted, but also to re-establish for the children the normal parental relationships which would assure them of "belonging" to both father and mother and so to enable them to feel secure in a complete home.

The fiancée and bride. During the period of courtship in normal times, although the couple see each other only under more or less romantic circumstances, the ideal figure in the phantasies of future married life is checked frequently against the real person. When this relationship was affected by all the emotional and physical complications of wartime, the real personality became swallowed up in a symbolic one. Consequently, there were dramatic disillusionments for men who returned to prewar engagements. Apparently, also, many soldiers had to endure a brush-off before they ever got back; others did the brushing. In numerous war marriages,[17] life together did not begin until the husband's return from the war. Some of those hasty marriages have already ended. In those that have continued, success will depend on the maturity of the partners and their determination to make a go of it, starting from time of reunion.

---

[17] The unusual factors in many "war marriages" were excellently presented by Bossard: The hastening factors in the war situation; the cloak provided for sexual satisfaction; the girl's fear of being left unmarried; love-at-first-sight which sometimes faded but under the circumstances seemed the best bargain; the husband gone before essential marriage relationships were established. Mail was unsatisfactory because the writing was to the "last-time-I-saw-you" personality; some able to verbalize and others not; changes with time and an unreality or irrelevance entered correspondence. He returned changed and found she had changed. Bossard, J. H. S., *Family Problems in Wartime,* Pennsylvania University Carter Foundation, Philadelphia, 1944. See also Reinemann, J. O., "The War Veteran in the Domestic Relations Court," *Ment. Hyg.,* 3:409-425, July, 1947, whose study of 200 cases indicated that in any marriage, the war experience tended to intensify already existing marital difficulties rather than to create new ones.

Friends. There is nothing unusual about the drifting apart of friends who are separated for years. Yet many a man who went away from home for 3 to 5 years was surprised to come home and find many changes. He hoped to see many of his old friends. It was often difficult for him to accept the fact that in his absence everything had not remained as he remembered. Fortunately, the emotional attachments to friends were usually not so strong as those to the family, and consequently their loss did not cause quite so much distress.

His social relationships were and may also continue to be handicapped by his own ignorance and his own prejudices. There was a tendency to look down on the 4F as if he were some kind of weakling or slacker. Some veterans (as well as some civilians) stupidly continue to hold such an idea. Envy and resentment, sometimes not recognized as such, toward their friends who went into industry is evidenced in criticism of their assumed monetary profit. However, the interested veteran will find, if he has not already done so, that those big salaries he heard about were largely mythical. He may also be reminded that, in addition to his soldier pay, he received equipment, food, lodging, and travel. Furthermore he had no big income tax to take a sizable part of his pay. Regardless of the civilian employment situation from 1941 to 1945, the wise veteran recognized the large element of chance in who got what. Now that he is a civilian in a civilian world, for his own sake, he would best adopt wholeheartedly the motto that now we are all civilians, leaving bygones to the past.

Education and jobs. Partly through the generosity of the GI Bill of Rights and partly because of the ambition of many veterans, our colleges and universities have been stormed for admission. Even though the rush has been momentarily hard on the many institutions, it is a bright light for America that so many men and women have returned to the completion of their education. Study, often intensive, has been something these men and women have had to work to master after their very different lives of recent years. It is to be hoped that those who have set their eyes toward the goal of an education can find the stamina to reach it. It is to be hoped, also, that our communities, colleges, and universities can meet this, their "greatest opportunity and challenge," [18] without too great a dilution of inspiration and stimulation.

The question of finding a job has been even more complicated by the fact

---

[18] So defined by Francis Rosencrance, Professor of Education, Northwestern University, who, on the basis of a survey and his own experience, recommended that communities carry on the high-school courses; universities establish "consultation boards"; veterans' affairs be handled through student personnel; credit be allowed for military experience; establishment of "vestibule schools" and review courses, subcollege courses; re-evaluation of instruction methods. "Emotional Aspects of Educational Problems of the Returning Veteran. Readjusting with the Returning Serviceman," Illinois Soc. for Mental Hygiene, Chicago, 1945.

that the veteran, in many instances, did not know just what he wanted to do. He probably tried several different opportunities before he found his niche. Much shifting was obviated by the intelligent understanding on the part of personnel services. Many of the larger industrial organizations employ placement counselors; a few have full-time psychiatrists. A very helpful presentation in the form of a guide to employers, supervisors, interviewers, and foremen was written by Luther E. Woodward and Thomas A. C. Rennie.[19] It deals at length with special problems of veteran placement and employment. There are other very helpful pamphlets and booklets on the same subject.[20]

Community participation. The readjustment of the veteran is a *combined* responsibility of the man and of his community.[21] Both changed during the war; both probably had to change again as they collided, before they could again unite and co-operate. Each had to make allowances for the other and both had to "give and take." Aside from the emotional support which the family was able to provide the veteran after his return home was that which he could derive from his increasing identification with his home town or neighborhood. Either as a leader or a participant many a veteran has begun to gain satisfaction, a growing sense of belonging and real enjoyment, in a neighborhood card foursome, a church club, a community-center athletic team, a youth organization. Playing together with other people he enjoys has built a foundation so that group loyalty might supersede that of the military unit.

Many churches have done a very superior job in providing activities for veterans. An outstanding example of this is the Community Church in Columbus, Ohio, under the leadership of Roy A. Burkhardt, which developed a dozen different groups and methods to aid the veteran and his family in their reintegration into the community.[22]

Veterans' organizations. These have had and will continue to hold a special

19 Woodward, L. E., and Rennie, T. A. C., *Jobs and the Man,* Charles C. Thomas, Publisher, Springfield, Ill., 1945.
20 "Readjustment to Civilian Jobs," National Association of Manufacturers, 14 W. 49th St., New York 20, N.Y., 1945. See Bibliography of Mental Hygiene and Industry in Woodward and Rennie's *Jobs and the Man.*
21 This has been stressed by many individuals and groups. See Bleckwenn, W. J., "He Takes Off His Uniform. Readjusting with the Returning Servicemen," Illinois Soc. for Mental Hygiene, Chicago, 1945.
22 Burkhardt, R. A., *The Church and the Returning Soldier,* Harper & Brothers, New York, 1945. Another presentation of general problems of demobilization as they affect the church has been presented by J. J. Chamberlin, *The Church and Demobilization,* Abingdon-Cokesbury Press, New York, 1945. Extremely helpful surveys have appeared in the Bi-Monthly Demobilization Bulletin, published by the General Board of Education of the Methodist Church, 810 Broadway, Nashville 2, Tenn.

appeal.[23] With so many such groups it behooves the veteran to find out which of them represents his principles.[24] It is understandable that at times he will feel more comfortable with his former associates—those whom he thinks understand him better than civilians; those whose militant leadership dissipates his unrest or contributes to the satisfaction of his dependent needs. However, while the veterans' organization can and does serve a very important function, it may also retard the development of compatibility between its members and other civilians. The membership itself must correct this tendency, if and when present, in order to avoid the pitfalls of becoming a pressure group for veterans instead of Americans. If the former soldier lives too much in the past or has to cling to his veteran dependency, that in itself is an indication that he has not adjusted well. His first loyalties *must* shift from the Army or the Navy and his war experiences to his home, his community, his state, nation, and world.

Aside from the sociability such organizations provide, they can also give valuable group support for the veteran to:

(1) Become a civilian in heart and soul and get over wanting to remain a veteran in order to perpetuate certain rights and privileges.

(2) Recognize that he, as a veteran, does not have any special claim [25] on America over and above that of his wife or his father or the industrial worker or the 4F, who may have contributed just as much as he did, although in a different way.

(3) Expect no special privileges, no special acclaim, no special awards. Lots of civilians did a superior, difficult job too.

(4) Fight for America and for those special groups of Americans, be they civilians or veterans, who need help. The veteran group as a whole is a long way from being downtrodden, neglected, or forgotten.

Many veterans have had such advice, even from some of us who are veterans ourselves, but still they do not take it. They perhaps fool themselves into believing that since the country demanded their "all," now the government owes them "all" they wish or feel they need. They seem to forget that their "all" was threatened by Nazism and Fascism. Many feel they are due

---

[23] "Why Do Veterans Organize?" GI Roundtable Pamphlet EM 6, obtained through the U.S. Armed Forces Institute, Madison 3, Wisconsin.

[24] The *Washington* (D.C.) *Post* reprinted a series of articles by Sam Stavisky on "Choose your Veterans Organization," describing briefly the AVC, AMVETS, DAV, VFW, and the American Legion. Chas. G. Bolte gives some stimulating and provocative thoughts on veterans' organizations in *The New Veteran*, Reynal & Hitchcock, Inc., New York, 1945.

[25] Certainly the government has already been generous. An Associated Press story of August 10, 1946, quoted figures from Gen. Omar N. Bradley to the effect that Congress had provided $12,609,802,005 in cash or benefits for veterans, nearly $1,000 for every soldier discharged since VE-day. *Topeka Daily Capital*, Aug. 11, 1946.

reimbursement for the interruption of the normal tenor of their lives, forgetting also that they fought as a responsibility of their own citizenship.

Many fall for another illusion: A very large percentage of soldiers were never in any real danger during the war, and yet the public is encouraged to think of all of them as combat heroes. Many veterans even come to think of themselves in the same class as combat soldiers. Such men tend to demand more and more privileges and rights than an already generous Congress has given them. A minor but common example of this attitude is the number of veterans who go to a veterans' hospital and, regardless of their financial ability, sign a statement that they cannot afford to pay for hospitalization. In that case the government pays for it. No one raises any question about the way in which free medical care is taken for granted. Men who are economically secure seem quite willing to sign the statement that they cannot afford to pay for it. In fact, it is the very occasional veteran who pays for his treatment in a veterans' hospital.

THE HANDICAPPED VETERAN

The handicapped veteran may have experienced any or all of the difficulties of the "normal veteran," and in addition he has had a good many which are specifically the result of the type and degree of his handicap.

As of December 31, 1947, a total of 4,205,726 veterans had submitted claims for disability compensation which had been passed upon. Of this number 1,996,327 had been adjudicated and allowed. Comparable figures for all World War I veterans showed 897,499 claims filed; 888,156 passed upon; and 536,101 allowed. At that time it was anticipated that by 1949, 10 to 15 per cent of all the men (January 31, 1947, figure was 12 per cent) in military service during World War II will be drawing veterans' pensions for disability. In that year, the cost for medical care and pensions will be over $2,000,000,000!

Physically handicapped veterans. Before he was released from the hospital, the wounded or injured soldier was given the benefit, in so far as military medicine could provide, of a maximum of hospital treatment. The only exceptions to this rule were patients with tuberculosis or the chronic psychoses who were transferred directly from an Army hospital to a Veterans Administration hospital. Whatever treatment was given in the military hospital was provided in 98 per cent of the cases by a civilian doctor in a military uniform. Therefore, the quality of medical care given the soldier was equal and, in many cases, superior to any he would have received in civilian life.

Even so, there were nearly 1,000,000 men discharged from our Army hospitals, as of the first of January, 1946, with either a crippling disability or an illness which made further military service inadvisable.[26] Many of the medical cases had heart disorders, various types of arthritis, diabetes, peptic ulcers, nerve or spinal cord disease and/or injury, or tuberculosis.

There was also a large number of wounded men whose permanent incapacity varied from none to complete. It is estimated that approximately 15,000 men had to have a major amputation. Nearly 1,000 of this number lost two limbs; 9 lost three limbs.

It was estimated that there were 1,200 men who were almost or totally blind in both eyes. Evidence of the effectiveness of the rehabilitation efforts for this group by the Army is that as of June, 1946, only 6 of these were in veterans' hospitals, and all of those were there for disabilities not related to their blindness.[27] As of July 1, 1945, there were approximately 8,400 soldiers who had received special treatment for deafness. The very splendid reconditioning in deafness, along with the excellent mechanical aids which are now provided, make this defect much less of a handicap than formerly.

Probably the greatest physical disability occurs in those men who are totally and permanently paralyzed in both legs, as the result of spinal cord injuries. There were approximately 1,400 of these in the Army. The acceptance of such a handicap requires the greatest adaptive forces. Appreciating this the Army,[28] as well as the Veterans Administration, made and will continue to make a very special effort to help these veterans.

There is still another group of war casualties—those with head injuries in which the motor or the sensory areas of the brain that control speech were damaged [29] or injured. Men with this symptom, which is called aphasia, have also been the subject of very special efforts of the Army Medical Department.[30] Each large neurosurgical center (most of these patients required brain surgery) had an aphasia training program under the direction of a clinical psychologist who was usually assisted by speech teachers. Remarkable results were obtained in many cases through long and patient effort. Many of these cases will be referred to veterans' hospitals.

The emotionally handicapped veteran. The man with a spectacular handicap receives far more consideration than he who is equally incapacitated by a

---

[26] The American Red Cross issued an excellent booklet on "Helping Disabled Veterans," including many helpful and practical suggestions for relatives and friends on all types of disability. October, 1945.

[27] Rusk, Howard, "News of the Veteran," *New York Times,* June 9, 1946.

[28] *Rehabilitation of Paraplegic Patients,* Army Service Forces Circular 440, 10 December 1945.

[29] Irvin L. Child outlines these reactions and their management. "Personal Adjustment of the Disabled Veteran," *Ann. Am. Acad. Polit. and Soc. Sc.,* 239:135-143, May, 1945.

[30] See Aita, J. A., "Men With Brain Damage," *Am. J. Psychiat.,* 103:205-213, Sept., 1946; "Aphasic Language Disorders," *War Department Technical Bulletin, Medical 155,* April, 1945.

medical illness or emotional injury. In fact, this disproportionate, sometimes excessive attention, may add to his problem. Certain handicaps have invited more public attention than others. For example, there are 21 organizations of charitably minded persons who are concerned with the welfare of the blind, an admirable undertaking. On the other hand, there are only two whose chief mission is to help the emotionally handicapped.

In addition to the men who are handicapped by a serious psychiatric dis- ability, many of the men with physical disabilities have emotional handicaps also. When there is no sign to the outside world of inner damage, their inability to function seems harder to justify—to themselves and to others.

With an amputation or a facial scar, emotional difficulties caused by the evidence of the handicap are often added to the physical disability.[29] The men with amputations are of special interest psychologically. In the hospital, where they were living with men who suffered under the same handicap, their morale was good: there was comparatively little difficulty in their adjustment to their new status. In a survey by Hughes and White,[31] only 17 per cent showed any emotional problem in adjusting in the hospital. Only 20 per cent of a group studied by Randall and Ewalt [32] had trouble in the hospital. Superficially they appeared happy and content. On returning to their homes, many more emotional symptoms developed. In the Hughes-White study, a few months after they had left the hospital, 30 per cent were having serious difficulty, and it was estimated that this number would unquestionably increase when economic competition became keen. In the Randall-Ewalt study, nearly half the patients that could be followed on their return home were showing very real emotional distress.

A joint surgical and psychological study of 200 men with amputations was made by Wittkower [33] on British soldiers. He classified the emotional reactions following the early mood fluctuation into: depression, 15 per cent of patients; resentment and irritability, 21.5 per cent; anxiety, 5.5 per cent; defiance toward their handicap, 21.5 per cent; cheerfulness, 24 per cent; resignation, 8 per cent; indifference, 3 per cent; (not specified, 1.5 per cent). Prominent among the disabled soldier's problems were his attachment to and detachment from the Army, his reciprocal relations with women, and his present

[31] Hughes, Joseph, and White, W. L., "Emotional Reactions and Adjustment of Amputees to Their Injuries," *U.S. Naval M. Bull.,* Supplement on Rehabilitation, Mar., 1946, pp. 157-163.
[32] Randall, G. C., Ewalt, J. R., and Blair, H., "Psychiatric Reactions to Amputees." *J.A.M.A.,* 128:645-652, June 30, 1945. Randall, G. C., and Ewalt, J. R. "Psychiatric Reactions to Amputees—A Follow-up Study," presented Am. Psychiat. Assn. Meeting, Chicago, May 28, 1946.
[33] Wittkower, E., "Psychological Aspects of the Rehabilitation of the Limbless," mimeographed and distributed by the War Office, Division of Psychiatry, London, 1944.

and future employment. Wittkower dealt with these problems in detail in this study.

The men with blindness, like those with loss of a limb, often face their biggest personal problem in their emotional adjustment. We have no follow-up studies. However, in one of our blind centers, Dibble General Hospital, where nearly 150 newly blinded soldiers were thoroughly evaluated psychiatrically, 59 per cent were found to be well adjusted, 18 per cent definitely maladjusted, and 23 per cent showed mild or borderline symptoms. These symptoms included anxiety, moderate emotional disturbances, aggressive behavior, dependency, apathy, and unrealistic attitudes. Most of the symptoms were determined by pre-existing neurotic traits. A few were due to the blindness which occurred as a result of noncombat injury or disease, some resulted from a false forecast or an incomplete understanding by the patient of his disability.[34]

Wittkower and Davenport [35] made a somewhat similar study of a group of war-blinded persons in England. In many of these they discovered under the surface a depression or resentment or defiance. In a very practical paper they gave some helpful hints to the general public about blind men.

Address a blind person directly and not his escort.

Blind persons dislike pity, as well as admiration, therefore avoid such expressions as "Isn't it tragic?" or "Isn't he marvelous?"

Make one's presence known upon entering a room.

Indicate when someone is leaving a room.

Do not ignore, but disregard, the disability in conversation.

It is all right to use the word "see" literally such as "would you like to see this object?" "Did you see Mr. X. yesterday?"

Wait until assistance is wanted and then give it in a matter of fact way, perhaps even asking him how best to help.[36]

Certain comments should be made about the neuropsychiatric cases. There was always a shortage of personnel which handicapped the effectiveness of the treatment, yet on the whole it was good; in some places it was superior. Every man was not entirely well at the time of discharge. It was the exceptional soldier who would remain in the hospital passively once he began to feel reasonably well, even though further treatment might seem indicated. Very

[34] Diamond, B. L., and Ross, A., "Emotional Adjustment of Newly Blinded Soldiers," *Am. J. Psychiat.*, 102:367-371, Nov., 1945.

[35] Wittkower, E., and Davenport, E. C., "The War Blinded and Emotional, Social and Occupational Situation," Research Memorandum 4.24. Directorate of Army Psychiatry, War Office, London, Sept., 1945.

[36] In the training of hospital personnel with the U.S. Army, the Surgical Consultants Division of the Office of the Surgeon General published an illustrated guide "For Those Giving Rehabilitation Services to the Blind," printed by the Adjutant General, September, 1945. This sets forth in words and pictures, the "Do's" and the "Don'ts" for helping the blind.

often the gratification of his wish to go home would be a stimulus to his further rehabilitation. The neuropsychiatric patient, though not necessarily in the prime of condition when he left the hospital, could usually complete his readjustment and recovery only in his home and on his job and among his friends.

As of June 30, 1947, there was a total of over 475,397 [37] patients with neuropsychiatric disabilities from World War II and 61,707 from World War I [38] who were receiving pensions from the Veterans Administration amounting to approximately $20,000,000 monthly; these patients made up 26 per cent of all the disability cases on pension roles. Also as of December 31, 1946, 54 per cent of the patients in veterans' hospitals were neuropsychiatric. This large percentage included men who, though not discharged as psychiatric casualties, later needed psychiatric treatment, as many did after World War I.[39] Over a period of time the hospitalized cases [40] will make up only a small percentage of the total number of neuropsychiatrically ill veterans. Those who are able will live outside a hospital and be treated by the family doctor or local specialist—the gastroenterologist for their stomach troubles, the cardiologist for their hearts, the orthopedist for their back pains.

The emotionally handicapped veteran will, in many instances, have special difficulty in again becoming a civilian. In contrast to the scar or amputation, or even the heart disorder, a soldier's fear of his inability to sleep because of reliving battle scenes, or his excessive concern about his future, shaken

---

[37] Of this number, 286,000 are classed as having a "functional" illness, the balance as having organic nervous disorders.

[38] The peak load of neuropsychiatric patients from World War I was reached in 1941 with 68,906 patients.

[39] Twenty-eight per cent of 434 admissions of veterans to a state hospital for psychoses were men who had been separated on "points" and developed symptoms later. "It would appear that a period of sustained effort for a common purpose, as a member of a team, did not bring about mental symptoms. But the withdrawal of these factors plus the resumption of the complexities of civil life, did bring about mental symptoms or brought to light and aggravated symptoms otherwise latent." Campbell, J. A., "From VJ . . . Mental Disorder Following Service Discharge," Psychiat. Quart., 20:375-380, July, 1946.

[40] While the percentage is small, the actual number is staggering, the projected figures for the hospital load for veterans' hospitals is shown in the following table: GM & S refer to general medical and surgical patients; TB to tuberculosis; NP to neuropsychiatric. Figures supplied by Drs. John Baird and N. Q. Brill of Veterans Administration.

	GM and S	TB	NP	Total
Present capacity	28,332	6,804	50,662	85,798
Estimated load				
1950	60,500	14,150	70,200	144,850
1955	72,000	12,000	90,200	174,200
1960	86,500	9,800	109,000	205,300
1965	101,000	7,900	122,000	230,900
1970	117,000	6,900	121,400	245,300
1975	131,500	6,000	114,000	251,500

self-confidence, and many emotional symptoms are handicaps that only he knows. Because the illness is intangible, because its causes are multiple and often vague, the condition seems mysterious even to the patient. The victim feels people do not understand (and often they do not), and therefore an apology is necessary. Some of these men came into the Army already carrying the burden of mismanaged emotions, of emotional immaturity, or of an unseen psychologically heavy load that kept them in a precarious adjustment as civilians. Many others, however, were sufficiently "normal" for neither themselves nor their family or friends to be aware of any personality difficulties. With the greater stress and the inflexibility of living and working conditions of the Army they became mentally ill. When incapable of service they had to be discharged. The clinical pictures of these men did not vary greatly from those which the civilian physician sees, but the civilian patient is often able to prevent his symptoms from incapacitating him. He may take life a little easier, go on a vacation, or change jobs in order to adjust his activity or bosses to the limitations of his condition. This the soldier could not do. The neuropsychiatric veteran should have, without need for apology, the sympathy and support of family and friends. He and the public must learn about the structure and function of the personality in order to understand the psychiatric casualty. Many had been capable civilians before their military service and most of them will be again.

We do not know just what happened to the veterans who were discharged for psychiatric reasons. In one survey referred to previously [41] the findings indicate that 93.7 per cent of the men contacted had been employed before their induction as compared with 85.9 per cent employed after their Army service. The number of unemployed increased from 3.8 per cent prior to induction to 13.1 per cent following discharge. Their discharge occurred during a period of acute labor shortage which should have increased the potentiality of employment. There was no evidence that they were discriminated against by employers because they had received a medical discharge. (2.5 per cent of the men surveyed were students before induction and 1 per cent after discharge. The study was made before the G. I. Bill of Rights was enacted.)

Most of the men checked after discharge considered their health to have been adversely affected by Army service. They considered the impairment in terms of physical disease and failed to recognize the psychological aspects. The men who had had overseas service believed themselves sicker than those who had not been overseas; 75 per cent of them had consulted a physician one or more times since their discharge; nearly 15 per cent of them had been

41 Brill, N. Q.; Tate, M. C.; and Menninger, W. C., "Enlisted Men Discharged from the Army Because of Psychoneurosis," *J.A.M.A.*, 128:633-637, June 30, 1945; the overseas group were reported in *Ment. Hyg.*, 29:677-692, Oct., 1945.

hospitalized after they left the Army. This study indicated that there is a large war-induced or war-aggravated psychiatric problem. It also suggested that there was little if any spontaneous improvement in the psychoneurotic patient beyond his condition at discharge. This may have been the result of the need for a face-saving illness while the war continued, since the survey was made at that time.

Steps the handicapped veteran must take in his own behalf. The veteran, no matter what his handicap, must first face the reality of his own situation, with all its unpleasant attendants. It is to be hoped that he had the necessary medical help in the Army or Navy hospital from which he was discharged. If necessary, he must take the initiative to seek additional help, whether it comes from the Veterans Administration or his family doctor.

He must understand the nature of his problem within the limits of his intellectual capacity. This is especially true of those with emotional handicaps, particularly those discharged with a psychiatric diagnosis. It is not sufficient to know that there is nothing physically wrong or that he is "just nervous." He needs to have some rationale to explain himself to himself. It is likely that he will ponder many questions if they have not been answered for him: "Am I insane?" "Am I likely to become insane?" "I complained of stomach trouble, so why did they send me to see a psychiatrist?" "What are the different types of psychoneurosis?" "Will I get better as time goes on?" "How can I explain to my family?" "What do I say when prospective employers ask me why I was discharged?" "Who is going to know my diagnosis?" "Can I marry?"

A little booklet entitled "What's the Score in a Case Like Mine?" [42] was given to the veteran who was discharged because of psychoneurosis. Unfortunately it was not published until September, 1945, and many thousands of men were discharged before that. Much thought was put into the preparation of this booklet. It was written and rewritten many times, in order that the average individual could understand it. The answers to the question "What can I do to help myself?" were listed in a series of don'ts and do's. Because they may still be pertinent for some veterans, they are quoted here.

Don'ts.

(1) Don't shy away from your home or your friends because the reason you were separated from the service was psychoneurosis. Of course, if your plans for a job or school keep you away from them, that's different. But don't let your diagnosis have anything to do with it.

(2) Don't try to run away from your symptoms. If you still have them and feel

---

[42] This booklet is available to anyone through the Government Printing Office, Washington, D.C., War Department Pamphlet 21-35, price 10 cents. War Department Circular 205, 11 July 1946, authorized its continued distribution in Army hospitals in the United States.

that they are a real handicap, in spite of your best efforts, get help from a psychiatrist.

(3) It will be much better if you don't plan to "take it easy for a while" or "loaf for a month." Those periods have a nasty habit of stretching out into two months, or three. The longer you wait to settle down and get busy, the harder it will be. Besides, being busy on some useful activity is one of the best kinds of treatment.

(4) Don't let the folks at home shower you with too much attention and tender care. It will only irritate you, or keep you sick longer than necessary, or both. If you learn to like it too well and demand it, you're asking for trouble, because there is bound to be a letdown sooner or later. If it irritates you, it can spoil your homecoming. The best thing to do is to tell the folks to treat you like a man who has a job to do and who wants to get down to business right away.

(5) People at home can't possibly understand what you've been through because they have never been there. Don't make the mistake of expecting them to. Let them be helpful and friendly, but don't get mad because they can't understand.

(6) Don't be surprised if things irritate and upset you at times. You and the folks at home have been living in two different worlds. At first you'll feel a little strange as a civilian. Remember how strange you felt the first week you were in the Army? It is just about the same thing. The most important thing is to start building your life where you left off.

Do's.

(1) Tell people frankly that you have been nervous and may be hard to live with for a while. Let them make allowances, up to a certain point, but they shouldn't pamper you. Tell them that, too. You don't want that kind of treatment. If you really work hard to help yourself and still can't make the grade, get help from a psychiatrist.

(2) Get a job or go back to school. The longer you put it off the harder it is going to be. Get on your feet and be independent as soon as you can, even if it hurts.

(3) Get a hobby. If you're irritable, full of gripes, nervous, do something active. If you don't feel like taking part in competitive games, then saw wood, chop kindling, pound on a punching bag. Pick up new interests, photography, music, anything, just so it is constructive and interesting to you. Make plans for your spare time.

(4) Take regular exercise. Walk, swim, play golf. Set your own pace but be sure to do something which will take you out of doors. Push yourself if it is necessary, but don't overdo it.

(5) Find someone who understands your situation. The best person is another veteran who has been through the same thing you have. Talk to him about the things you don't like to discuss with others. You have to let off steam somewhere. If you bottle it up inside yourself it will take longer to get rid of your symptoms and it might make them worse. If you can't find another veteran, then find some good listener. A good listener is anyone who has sense enough to listen without gushing over you, or asking too many foolish questions. It might be your girl friend, your father, your preacher, or a good friend. Usually it's

better if you pick someone outside the family, because he won't be so closely tied into your life emotionally.

(6) Remember that a man's condition is his own problem, whether it is a pain in the belly or an ache in his soul. Try to whip it yourself. If you can't, don't hesitate to get help.

Additional treatment. Sometimes the question will arise about indications for further medical help. If the veteran has persistent physical symptoms or develops new symptoms, then certainly he should see a doctor. If he worries excessively, if he has difficulty in sleeping, has recurring dreams, is persistently jumpy or feels that he can't concentrate—any or all of these may be an indication that he needs medical help. This is more true if he has used all the ways he knows of helping himself. If any of these symptoms persist longer than a month, with no change for the better despite his efforts, he should betake himself to his doctor, who can refer him to a specialist if necessary.

The veteran must accept the fact that his readjustment and his satisfactory return to civilian status depend more upon his own determination to effect the change than upon any other help he may be able to obtain. Also he should appreciate that civilians have similar problems and tough adjustments, i.e., he is not unique.

He has to debunk himself of any illusions that he may harbor: that because he was discharged medically, he must continue life as an invalid; that because a pension is available, he should continue his symptoms indefinitely in order to obtain it. If he is a psychiatric casualty, it is better that he know that the pension may be one of the handicaps to getting well. He must accept the fact that just because he was a veteran who was discharged because of injury, he is not entitled to special consideration indefinitely.

As is pointed out in the brief "Do's and Don'ts," the veteran must take steps toward his reconversion to civilian activities and pursuits, even though there is no equivalent of a top sergeant to urge him on. With the obtaining of a new job should go a renewal, or in some instances the initiation, of civilian contacts and activities. There is every reason for him to avail himself of every type of assistance [43] that he may need to cultivate his civilian self.

What can the family do? When the family understands the significance of the attitudes of the former soldier, it will be better able to accept them without distress. We know from experience that a few of these former soldiers and sailors showed resentment in varying degrees against the Army or the Navy, against the government, the community, the family, and even against

---

[43] A helpful booklet entitled "Services to Veterans and Their Dependents" has been issued by the American National Red Cross.

themselves. The family may expect, in some instances, increased, perhaps greatly increased, self-interest, self-concern, and self-investment. It can expect, in other instances, a greatly increased dependency, passivity, or helplessness. The former soldier may be complaining or perhaps mildly depressed. Some veterans will manifest varying degrees of restlessness, being unhappy or perhaps dissatisfied in any situation and continuously wanting to change it, whether it is a job, a social stratum, or community life. Their attitude may be changeable, perhaps at times unreasonable, and certainly often inconsistent. Varying degrees of self-defeatism may show in passive acceptance of frustration, disappointment, or failure, with the result that very possibly there may be a reactivation or an intensification of some old symptoms. In a few instances one must anticipate the excessive use of alcohol or the retreat into a recluse or invalid state.

The former soldiers may not realize the reason for their feelings, but the family will be helped if it can recognize these feelings as symptoms; one does not argue with a symptom in any illness, so argument cannot help in this situation. The relatives will find that many of these symptoms will fade with the re-establishment of economic security in a job, of social security in old or new friends, of personal security through old or new interests or activities, and of emotional security within the family.[44]

Perhaps no better set of instructions has been compiled for families than those of Drs. Rennie and Woodward in their "talks to families of returning service men." Even though they are a little lengthy they seem of such practical significance that they are included here.

(1) Love him and welcome him. Show him how glad you are to have him back and if he has handicaps let him know that this makes no difference in your love and esteem. If you show real pleasure in his presence, he will know he is still loved and wanted and will quickly lose some of his fear and feel more comfortable. Welcome him in your own quiet way. Don't call a family reunion which would expose him to the curiosity of everyone. He will get around to Uncle Jim and Aunt Sue in due time and will take it much better that way.

(2) Listen well, that is, listen as understandingly as you know how, and don't pry into his personal experiences while in the service. To ask him about the new lands he has visited and the folk-ways of the people in these new lands is quite in order, but questioning him about his training and combat experience and the reason for his discharge are to be avoided. If he chooses to talk about these things, it will be helpful if you listen well.

(3) Face the reality of the disability. If he returns with one, whether it be a weak heart, impaired hearing, loss of a hand, or whatever, don't try to ignore it.

---

44 This subject has been excellently discussed by experts in family problems. Mowrer, E. R., and Mowrer, H. R., "The Disabled Veteran in the Family," *Ann. Am. Acad. Polit. and Soc. Sc.*, **239**:150-159, May, 1945.

As one columnist has put it, "I'd be as mad as a prodded wasp if I came home without an arm or a leg, and no one paid any attention to it and went on behaving nice and normal." But don't magnify it; focus on what is left, not on what is lost.

(4) Treat him as an essentially normal, upstanding, competent person, not as an invalid. More than anything else most men fear being oversympathized with, having too much done by their families. They do not consider themselves "washed up" and they don't want to be treated as though they were. If they are treated as well and competent, most of them will quickly prove that they are. Avoid doing too much for your returned service man. Rather seek his help with jobs that will help you or others.

(5) Commend his efforts and successes and ignore his slips. This is good policy with husbands, wives or children—in fact, with anybody at any time—but it is especially needed in dealing with men who come back feeling somewhat insecure. We are all so made that we try to do our best if our virtues and successes are acknowledged, but we are apt to repeat our faults if we are nagged about them.

(6) Expect him to be different in some ways. If he was very young when he went away, he is sure to have grown up a lot. He may have grown ten years in two. Because of nerve-racking experience in the Armed Forces and his worry about getting into the swing of civilian life, he may be more easily irritated and annoyed; he may tease you in a way he never did before, or he may appear quieter or more serious. You who have stayed home have changed also; in fact, one of the most common complaints made by returning servicemen is that the folks at home are different. Take time to get acquainted again and to find ways of getting along together. This is particularly true of younger men and their young wives or sweethearts.

(7) Allow him time and freedom in getting acquainted with the old places and in re-establishing his old contacts. When he comes back he may have an acute need to do this. No one can predict the order in which he will want to renew old acquaintances, but if he is like most men he will want to make such contacts one at a time, and not be drawn into family reunions and big parties.

(8) Create an atmosphere of expectancy: Encourage him to take up his favorite hobby or sport, to go back to work as soon as he is able and to lead a normal social life; but avoid pushing or regulating him, for top-sergeant methods won't work at home. Especially if he has some physical handicap or some mild nervous condition, he will tend to take on gradually the tone of the people he lives with. If you have a hopeful outlook, he is likely soon to share your view.

(9) Get professional help if it is needed. Don't just muddle through. The Medical Divisions of the Armed Forces gave excellent service in restoring as fully as possible the health of the men who were wounded, but the restoration may be incomplete when he returns in the case of nervousness, severe wounds, or some other ailments which are long drawn out. In fact, many men are discharged during convalescence so that they may have the invigorating benefits of home, friends, and a congenial job. Professional help should be obtained—problems should not be allowed to drag on. Most nervous ailments respond well to psychiatric treatment. Social workers can help with families and social adjustment. Vocational counselors can aid in the choice of training or employment.

(10) Let your own faith and beauty of spirit be your chief stock in trade. He needs chiefly an encouraging onlooker and a traveling companion. He has to make

his own way, but he will get on faster if he knows you are betting on him and if he sees that you enjoy even his small successes.[45]

WHAT THE COMMUNITY CAN DO

In considering the responsibility of the community for the returned veteran, we start on the basic assumption that the man belongs to that community, and therefore the community wants to claim him and wants to help him. Part of the responsibility of any progressive community is the development of the necessary machinery and facilities to help all of its citizens, including the veteran. It is a debatable point whether the community organization should not have a broader view than merely aiding returning veterans, and yet these men represent the immediate pressing need, and special plans must be made for the many handicapped veterans. "The nationwide planning should not be concerned so much with what we can give them in terms of bonuses and pensions, but what outlet we can furnish for their independent activities through which they may regain confidence in themselves." [46] This will be a continuing responsibility for a long time.

Different communities have developed varied methods of providing for the many types of assistance needed by veterans.[47] The development of some type of veterans' information center and a community committee for systematic counseling of the veteran have been established in most metropolitan cities and even in many small towns. Many of these need to be perfected: many agencies still do not participate; there is a tendency to pass the buck or give the veteran "the run-around" by referring him some place else. Too often the plan depends entirely on voluntary workers, and there still remain many organizational jealousies. The Bridgeport, Conn., and Peoria, Ill.,[48] plans have become well known as models, but many other communities have also pioneered and developed excellent veterans' centers. The Department of Labor issued a booklet on how to organize and operate a community advisory center.[49] A remarkable outline of plans, with charts and detailed instructions for

---

[45] Rennie, T. A. C., and Woodward, L. E., *When He Comes Back if He Comes Back Nervous,* National Committee for Mental Hygiene, Inc., New York, 1944.

[46] Grinker, R. R., "The Medical, Psychiatric and Social Problems of War Neuroses," *Cincinnati J. Med.,* 26:241-259, Aug., 1945.

[47] One of the first guides for communities was a joint effort of the member organizations in the National Social Work Council, titled "Community Services to Veterans," Sept., 1944. Available through the Council, 1790 Broadway, New York.

[48] Meyer, Agnes E., "Community Service. The Model Center at Bridgeport, Conn.," reprinted from *Washington* (D.C.) *Post,* Mar. 27, 28, 29, 30, 1945; Haberle, C. J., "The Peoria Plan," *Safety Training Digest on Industrial Rehabilitation,* 1945, New York University, 8 Fifth Ave., New York.

[49] "To Organize, To Operate Your Community Advisory Center for Veterans and Others," Retraining and Re-employment Administration, Department of Labor, Washington, D.C.

starting a community veterans' program, has been published under the title, "Making Home Town Plans Work." [50]

There are many governmental agencies to assist the veteran, but most of these prefer to work through the community. It is reasonable to assume that the ultimate success of the adjustment of any veteran will depend on the necessary assistance given as the result of personal contacts made in his own home town. The greater the handicap, the greater is the community responsibility.

The most pressing need in most communities still is for medium and low-rent housing facilities. This can only be met through community planning. While the need is so acute, it should be given the highest priority. Special attention should be given also to the provision of medical facilities.[51] These should include psychiatric services that are so organized as to be able to utilize the educational, recreational, vocational, and occupational activities in the community as means of therapy. This would enable men to rehabilitate themselves right at home.

Many community plans give consideration to placement in employment. It is essential that they should, for fundamental to the veteran's re-establishment is a job. To place men intelligently requires vocational counseling in many instances. This presumes a knowledge of possible openings for employment. It requires the personal interest of the employer members of the community in their jobless former-soldier citizens. Along with the employment placement, the community needs to plan for vocational guidance and training, either as a part of the state or the federal program. Additional counseling may be necessary to determine where the veteran can be placed effectively and without unlimited red tape in a vocational school, in an institution of higher education, in a night school, or in on-the-job opportunities for training.

An increasing problem in many communities is what to do about temporary financial assistance or economic rehabilitation of families of veterans. The backlog of bonds and other financial reserve of many veterans' families have been lost in the race against inflation. Too expensive housing, too expensive furniture, food, clothes, have edged higher and higher above income. Small high-interest loans, installment payments, and mortgages enable people to manage until an emergency. Then who is to help them out? A few months of

---

50 The *American Magazine, Colliers* and *Woman's Home Companion,* combined to sponsor three booklets called "Veterans Reports 1, 2 and 3," the last one: "Making Home Town Plans Work," Apr., 1946. Published by the Crowell-Collier Publishing Co., 250 Park Ave., New York.
51 Some of the best early pioneering in special clinics for veterans was sponsored by the Division of Rehabilitation of the National Committee for Mental Hygiene, Director T. A. C. Rennie and L. E. Woodward, Field Consultant, "Rehabilitation of the Psychiatric Casualty," *Ment. Hyg.,* 29:32-45, Jan., 1945.

help and advice on ways of retrenching could often get them back on their feet. But who shall give that help? Who will supplement disability pensions during temporary illness or unemployment when that pension, though below living cost of the family, is higher than public-welfare subsistence levels?

Perhaps the needs of veterans will stimulate many of our communities to give long-needed consideration to increasing recreational equipment, facilities, and program. Despite the fact that this is one of the most pressing mental health needs in every community, far too few have recognized it as an obligation. If they continue their blindness or lethargy in this direction, we should not be critical of the veterans, especially those who are handicapped, who try to eke out some fun in beer parlors or roadside taverns. The community should take the initiative to organize centers and develop a planned program which will include social outlets, entertainment, opportunities for the development of hobbies, music, dramatics, and athletics.

WHAT THE DOCTOR CAN DO

From our experience after World War I we know that many handicapped veterans will need medical help and supervision for years to come. It is to be hoped that the excellent progressive program of the Veterans Administration may be allowed to continue in its efforts to authorize private medical care for the veterans. Whether they do or not, many of these men will seek the advice and counsel of the family doctor. Regardless of what the veteran, the family, or the community may do, in the final analysis the readjustment of the severely handicapped veteran is likely to be an individual medical problem. Experience has taught us further that a great many veterans of the first war who were discharged without any apparent medical disability later developed such. This was specially true in the case of the neuropsychiatric veterans. Many of them first showed their emotional symptoms years after the war ended, but attributed them to their military experience. We can expect the same thing to happen again.

The physician with Army experience will have a better orientation to the veteran than the physician without such experience, not because of his professional ability, but because he can identify with the patient and the patient with him, as well as because he had many opportunities to treat symptoms of emotional origin. He saw the effect of the special stresses within the Army: isolation, discomfort, arduous training, and combat. He could not remain blind to the numerous instances of the retreat of the personality from stress into illness, a real but unwarranted benefit of illness. The medical officer with combat experience observed the unconscious, and even conscious, satisfaction of the soldier in a wound that excused him from the hell of battle.

However, the physician [52] who did not have Army experience is in no way less capable of caring for the needs of the veteran. As a matter of fact, his civilian status may make him somewhat more objective toward the veteran's difficulties than had he shared them. Furthermore, in his daily practice he sees similar emotional responses. In some instances, however, he may have to guard against being too sensitive to the problem of the veteran through some unconscious guilt reaction for not having been able to serve himself. In any event the ill veteran will get very real help from any alert, informed, intelligent physician. Service or nonservice status is of lesser significance.

How can the ill veteran be sure he has a good doctor? [53] This is a legitimate question, particularly since there are many who call themselves "doctors," who are not doctors of medicine. Consequently, the first requisite for the veteran who is seeking medical attention is to determine whether or not the "doctor" is an M.D.—a doctor of medicine. If it is not on his sign, ask him. But, just as in every field of human activity, there are good doctors and poor doctors, some who keep up to date and some who never make any pretense of doing so. In every county in America most qualified doctors are members of the County Medical Society (sometimes in sparsely settled areas two or more county groups combine). Each of these organizations has a president and a secretary, both doctors. It is quite proper to inquire from either of these men about the standing of any other particular physician. There are specialty societies (most of which are national, except in large metropolitan areas) from which one can learn of the standing of any "specialist." In most branches of medicine there are "specialty boards" which examine and "qualify" an individual specialist. The great majority of really qualified specialists (surgery, orthopedics, internal medicine, pediatrics, obstetrics, psychiatry, etc.) have been "certified" by the appropriate board. It is perfectly proper to ask an unknown physician, who claims to be a specialist, if he is "certified" in his specialty, or one may ask to see his diploma. Such questions may also be addressed to American Medical Association, 535 North Dearborn Street, Chicago, Ill.

The effect of pensions, particularly as they apply to neurotic illnesses, deserves the special understanding and attention of all physicians. Study of the neurotic process has revealed the disadvantage to psychoneurotic patients of a system of indefinite pensions. From such illness there are two gains: the primary gain of an escape from an insoluble problem, and the secondary gain of the advantages of being ill. Two of these advantages are the increased

---

[52] Some helpful, concrete suggestions for the handling of the veteran by the general practitioner were given by L. H. Smith and H. D. Wood, "The General Practitioner and the Returning Veteran," *J.A.M.A.*, 129:190-193, Sept. 15, 1945.

[53] Greer Williams dealt with this practical problem in a helpful way in the *Saturday Evening Post*, 219:17, 109-110, Dec. 21, 1946, in an article titled "Good Doctors Are Hard to Find."

attention and the unintentional but nonetheless effective club his illness holds over his family. Under our pension system we add to these a monetary value which in many cases amounts to paying the veteran to maintain his symptoms. Despite the chance of misinterpretation, this fact was pointed out in the hearings of a Senate committee on health.[54]

This was the subject of a recommendation by Mr. Baruch in his report on the Veterans Administration to General Bradley:

Examine the present pension system, both in administration and legislation, to eliminate or reduce deterrents to full recovery or incentives to malingering, while still retaining just compensation for disability. I am informed by many doctors that in certain cases benefits do the patient more harm than good, by encouraging so-called "pensionitis." No veteran should be deprived of any pension or benefit rightfully due him. But surely a system can be developed which will give the veteran his just allowance and still not hamper his physical recovery. Perhaps no aspect of veterans' medical reform is more important. Many so-called psychoneurotics could be left mental cripples for life, as if victims of botchy surgery, by an unwise pension and benefit system.[55]

Revision of the pension system was strongly urged by the President's Committee on Integration of the Medical Services of the Government.[56] Numerous physicians [57] have voiced their opinion similarly, most recommending either lump-sum settlement or specified number of payments.

Ideally, with any medically or surgically ill patient, the alert physician goes beyond the superficial complaint in order to determine how the man lives, feels, and thinks about the people and experiences in his daily life. With the veteran, he may find that his patient perhaps feels that he has made more than his share of sacrifice, that he has lost out, that he feels unappreciated. The physician—and it is hoped also the community—should understand that buried resentment can be expressed as symptoms or as protests against family or the social situation which permits unemployment, housing shortages, or interracial tensions.

Furthermore, the physician, where possible, should verify what the veteran tells about his social situation. In the small community the family physician

---

[54] Statement on Needs of Veterans Discharged for Neuropsychiatric Disabilities by W. C. Menninger. Hearings before a Subcommittee of the Committee on Education and Labor, S. Res. 74, Part 5, July 11, 1944, pp. 1689-1702.

[55] B. M. Baruch's report to General Omar N. Bradley, Director of the Veterans Administration 16 August 1945. This appears as Appendix A in *The New Veteran* by C. G. Bolte, Reynal & Hitchcock, Inc., New York, 1945, p. 196.

[56] White House Press release embodying the full committee report on June 17, 1946.

[57] Knight, R. P., "The Treatment of the Psychoneuroses of War," *Bull. Menninger Clinic,* 7:148-155, July, 1943; Lewy, E., "Compensation for War Neuroses," *War Med.,* 1:887-894, Nov., 1941; Menninger, K. A., "Civilian Morale in Time of War and Preparation for War," *Bull. Menninger Clinic,* 5:188-194, Sept., 1941; Kardiner, A., "Forensic Issues in the Neuroses of War," *Am. J. Psychiat.,* 99:654-661, Mar., 1943. Howard Rusk dealt vigorously with the subjects in an article for the layman in the *New York Times,* April 1, 1946.

may know the family problems, the employment situation, and the environmental conditions of a job. In the larger communities he may have available the help of a social worker. As a private practitioner he can gain such information through an organized social agency. All too often in the past the physician has failed to appreciate the diagnostic importance of the life situation of the patient and has not availed himself of the facilities at his command to amplify his information.

Of great importance is the doctor's role as an advisor. He has the opportunity of making suggestions as to how the man can alter his own behavior and how the problem can be alleviated or solved by changes in the environment. He can advise his patient about positive, constructive attitudes to develop and efforts to make. It is likely that, as a doctor, he may have to do some interpreting to the veteran of the meaning of the existing symptoms. The man cannot run away from his symptoms, and usually he is not helped by running away from his job and friends. As soon as he can understand these symptoms and their causes, and can accept and rationally explain them to himself and others, he can make an adjustment which will relieve the symptoms themselves. The physician can act as the interlocutor. He can reassure the man, if the family doesn't understand, and urge him not to make the mistake of expecting them to do so. At the same time, he, as a physician, may be able to give the family some understanding. He can help the veteran anticipate the possible recrudescence of symptoms and the significance of this return. He should encourage the veteran in finding substitute ways of expressing his emotions through new activities and interests.

In addition to whatever counsel and advice he may give, the physician has to assist the veteran and perhaps even take the initiative himself in making necessary changes in the patient's environment. As suggested above, this may mean the interpretation of the man's problem to his family or to his present or prospective employer. If the physician is going to help the veteran most effectively, he must be willing and ready, through personal contacts, to refer the man to the Veterans Administration representative, the community veterans' information center, the employment agency, the veteran's religious counselor, or to any other person or organization who can assist in the recommended modification of the veteran's environment.

If we meet the challenge and responsibility of molding ourselves and our lives and the life of the community to provide for our veterans, they will indirectly have done us another service. From our experience in so doing, we will have begun an approach to the solution of social and medical problems beyond a "welfare" level. A continued effort toward the improvement of community services will in the long run provide for the civilians as well as the veterans-turned-civilians.

26

MENTAL HEALTH IN THE HOME

WHAT DID the war do to the home? Many thoughtful people believed that family life in America was at a crisis before the war. Now we must face even more startling facts: one out of three American marriages ends in divorce; 47.1 per cent of our families have no children under 19 years of age and 21.6 per cent have only one; [1] juvenile delinquency is at an all-time high; parents are devoting much less of themselves to their children and their children respect them much less than in years gone by. Indeed, we must all admit that family life as we have known it is being changed.

The war gave the home a severe jolt. In many instances it caused a major upheaval, the reverberations of which will be felt for years to come. The departure of men for military service broke up many homes, for 2, 3, or even 4 years. Thousands of others were disrupted and moved *in toto* to follow the beckoning war industries. Approximately 6,000,000 women, many of whom were married and had dependent children, entered business or industry for the first time during the war years.[2] Irrationally high wartime salaries gave an increase in the scale of living, the loss of which is now being felt. Many thousands of service wives who were forced to become far more independent and worldly wise during those tense years must become more dependently co-operative. Children were born while their fathers were overseas; older children spent 3 or 4 years of the most important formative period of their lives without a father. Many young people with war-industrially employed parents had to shift for themselves. Few American homes escaped some sort of war-originated changes.

The family and the home are the essential foundation stones of our culture and our system of life. Every other factor in the development of mental health fades into relative insignificance in comparison to the importance of the home. The foundation for good or poor mental health is laid in child-

---

1 *A Program for National Security,* May 29, 1947. Report of the President's Advisory Commission on Universal Training, U. S. Government Printing Office, Washington, D. C., 1947, p. 170. See also a thought-provoking editorial, *Life,* Mar. 24, 1947.
2 The figure of 6,140,000 is given in "Woman in the Post-War," Women's Advisory Committee, War Manpower Commission, Washington, D.C., Apr., 1945.

hood, and therefore the effect of the failure to maintain healthy, happy home life is beyond calculation. The personalities of many of the men and women of tomorrow, and therefore the national health, will show war-caused scars for many years to come.[3] Those who were so fortunate as not to be involved directly will be affected by the increase in the social problems that will arise from such widespread mental ill health.

To be sure, many families benefited greatly from the war. Provincialism could not stand unaffected by life in various parts of the country or world. Individuals and familes, forced out of the deep grooves of daily routine, found stimulation in change. There were families to which the father returned with a new appreciation for them; with a willingness to share more equitably with his wife the responsibilities of the home and the children; with a determination to live more in the present with his family; with an increased tolerance of the whims and the foibles of relatives, friends, and associates. From some homes sons left as boys to return as men, having broken the ties of boyhood dependency by experience away from the home influence. Many men discovered a broader vision which resulted in a determination to live more usefully, constructively, and productively. Some came home resolved to help their offspring develop a fuller understanding of world affairs and the relationship of the individual American to, and his responsibilities for, those affairs. The hero worship of children for their fathers may serve to raise the aims and ideals of some of the younger generation.

However, any gains to the family were not in the province of the Army psychiatrist to observe. Instead, we saw the evidence of the previous war injury in the soldiers of this war. Men who came or were sent to us were children during World War I and soon thereafter. They were subjected to the same problems that confront us in family life today. The Army psychiatrists of World War II saw the scars upon manhood of the childhood experiences during wartime and the postwar adjustment. Regarding the major portion of the man power at its disposal, the Army of 1941-46 had to face problems which are traceable to the effect of the family life of 1916-20.

For better or for worse, the character traits and habits of an individual are formulated in the first 6 to 10 years of life. What he is at 8 is a fair indication of what we may expect him to be at 18 or 28.[4] The experiences

---

[3] Numerous articles appeared in sociological journals dealing with the family in wartime. Of the few in medical literature, one was by a social worker who canvassed the social agencies of New Orleans. Gentile, F. M., "The Effects of the War Upon the Family and Its Members," *Psychiatry*, 6:37-49, Feb., 1943. Sound advice on many home problems was given by Winfred Overholser, "Effects of the War on the Family," *Journal of Home Economics*, 35:393-396, Sept., 1943. See also Hymes, Jas. L., Jr., "The Teacher Can Prevent," *Child Study*, 24:41-42, Winter 1946-47.

[4] This does not minimize the importance of the second 10 years in the development of personality, nor should it indicate that all maladjusted children will be maladjusted adults. Many

of those first years wield a far more important influence upon personality development than does the original inheritance.

It is not appropriate here to attempt a presentation of all of the mistakes in parental attitudes and mismanagement of children. There were, however, certain observations which the Army psychiatrists could not escape making. The number of men rejected or discharged from the Army because of personality or character defects forced us to the realization that it is long past the time for making greater distribution of our knowledge about the ways in which we can prevent or correct such deficiencies. Scientists and students concerned with problems of social and human behavior have much yet to discover in this respect. However, certain conclusions can be drawn from the already accumulated data. Certain theories were particularly supported by the psychiatric experience in the social laboratory of the Army. Basically, the problem is, first, one of putting into the minds of parents an appreciation of the relationship between their job as a parent and the social-emotional failures in their children; second, parents need to have put into their hands the tools and into their hearts the desire to correct such failures in themselves and prevent them in their children; third, parents need society's help in supplementing and strengthening their efforts.

The family [5] is the institution that society has provided for the training, protection, and care of its dependent persons. But its main purpose and the reason for its survival through the ages has been to foster the development of independent individuals. Ideally, within its framework the child moves toward maturity by the steps which were discussed previously.[6]

His success in taking those steps should be the concern of his family. Intelligently planned observation, demonstration, testing, correction, and support on the part of the parents can prevent, compensate for, or correct defective development. Life within a family unit tests the capacity of the child to adjust his personality to the demands of the environment. Ideally, he learns to do so with minimal distress and maximum effectiveness for himself and his associates. It is under the aegis of the loved ones, the parents, that growth from complete dependence to almost complete independence of decision and action takes place least painfully. The more a child's development is stimulated, aided, guided, and tested within the home, the greater will be the ease with

---

solve their early problems if given help. Even adults can learn to modify their habitual reactions, though sometimes professional guidance is necessary for them to do so.

[5] The serious parent who wishes to read about the family can find a host of excellent books on the subject. Among the many to be recommended are: Folsom, J. K., *The Family and Democratic Society,* John Wiley & Sons, Inc., New York, 1943; Groves, E., *Family and Its Social Functions,* J. B. Lippincott Company, Philadelphia, 1940; Levy, J., and Monroe, R., *The Happy Family,* Alfred A. Knopf, New York, 1938; Foster, R. G., *Marriage and Family Relationships,* The Macmillan Company, New York, 1946.

[6] See Chap. 4.

which he will adjust to the outside world; the better his mental health will be. This then is the tremendously important role of the family. As life outside the home becomes more complicated and more fraught with emotional stress, this responsibility of the family increases.

Army experience highlighted certain factors which aided in the development and maintenance of good mental health. They are applicable within the home as they were within the Army. Specifically they are good leadership, motivation, and strong identification with the unit.

LEADERSHIP

The qualities of leadership necessary for an Army officer are essentially no different from those required for the leader of the home. The good leader creates a sense of security. He sets a good example. He aids the development of a sense of responsibility in everyone within his unit.

Security. The child, much more than the soldier, has strong dependent needs. He has to be fed, clothed, sheltered, and supplied with equipment for work and play. In addition to the provision for his physical needs each individual must feel that he is important to and respected by his leader. Further than that, to feel emotionally secure, he needs evidence of the leader's personal interest in him. Love is the strongest emotional force we know. Its variants are affection, interest, and approval. It is the basis of unit attraction, cohesion, and teamwork in any group—the Army or the family.

Every soldier wanted to feel a close relationship to his commanding officer, if he respected that officer. The wise commanding officer knew this and made special effort to learn to know each soldier as an individual. Theoretically, the enlisted man had the privilege of taking his problems to his commanding officer for help in their solution. Good leaders encouraged this practice.

So also does the child want a close emotional tie to his parents during the trial-and-error process of growing up. The wise parent will show his unvarying love for and interest in his child and that child's daily problems. He will aid and abet the child's natural desire to come to him for help by being a patient listener, avoiding condemnation, offering unsolicited approval when deserved, giving assistance on tough projects, presenting the other side of an argument or the other fellow's point of view. In such fashion does the parent encourage a child's sense of belonging to his family group. He feels secure.

Example. Leadership does literally entail leading. Stated another way this means that the leader is the example. The officer who did not expect of himself what he demanded of his men failed to lead them. No matter what he said, what he did was an example which was followed by his men, whether it was heroic valor in combat or blackmarketeering.

Within the family the example is even more powerful because of the long-continued and very close relationships. Scoldings, exhortations, or pleas are wasted effort in the teaching of grammar or manners, the management of money or habits of work, in the inculcation of ideals or the formation of opinions. Children have to be led, they cannot be shoved.

Of course children will not automatically adopt the practices of their parents. It would be fine if seeing the parent wash his hands before each meal would be a sufficient inspiration for the child to follow suit. "Come on, pal, time to get ready for dinner with *me*" expresses the spirit of leading by example. Perhaps shared participation could describe such behavior better than setting an example. Mom's fear of thunder, Dad's enthusiasm for a hobby, parental patterns of social activity, prejudices, finance, will be accepted almost unconsciously or rejected aggressively, depending upon the parental attitude toward his child. Leadership is not bossing or nagging or forcing.

Responsibility. Good leadership involves the delegation of responsibility to individuals in so far as they are capable of accepting and carrying it. Independence of action requires the assumption of responsibility, first, to decide on that action, and, second, to accept its consequences.

Part of the process of maturing psychologically is to incorporate within the personality a sense of responsibility for its behavior. The initial sense of security within the family must be replaced by a sense of security within oneself. Outward evidence of such a process is a gradually increasing self-confidence.

Unfortunately, in the Army we saw too many examples of the failure of the leadership in American homes to prepare its young people for unexpected responsibility. Men revolted against carrying their share of the load. Apparently no one at home had "led" them into developing a sense of obligation to do so. They had been "controlled" by nagging, dictating, "silver cords," or a policy of *laissez faire.*

Men lacked a willingness to see or carry their responsibility not because they were just perverse or were misbehaving. Nor was it because they were dependent. Certainly in most cases, it was not because of deficient intellectual capacity to understand. It was an evidence of immaturity related to home training. Such men never accept any real responsibility. Such men had grown up in homes in which they had not been expected to do things without being forced to. They never learned the teamwork necessary in group living. We saw it manifest especially in the gold bricker, i.e., the shirker. He tried to avoid an unpleasant duty by pretending to be sick when he was not or by any other excuse that would get him out of the job. He just did not know how to play as a member of a team.

There was convincing evidence that in some American homes the child had been subjected to a suffocating affection, initiative-smothering guidance, or solicitous overprotection. This had kept him emotionally dependent upon his parents even as an adult. It had not permitted a gradual increase in confidence in his own ability. This serious error seems to be made more commonly by the mother.[7] It is partly in the nature of things that she has a very close emotional relationship to the child, usually closer than that of the father. This tie to the child gives her much personal satisfaction which some mothers are unwilling to relinquish. It is particularly easy for mothers to err in that direction when fathers do not play their needed role in the family group. Strong dependence upon maternal control was particularly evident in those soldiers who were away from home for the first time. When they had not learned some emotional independence within the home, their immaturity made them unacceptable as soldiers. Such immaturity was seen more frequently after the drafting of 18- and 19-year-olds started. A considerable number of these immature youngsters were sent home from the draft examination to be recalled 6 months later.

Serious personality defects which stemmed from the opposite of overprotection showed up in the Army. In families which lacked direction, inspiration, and correction by their leadership, children grew into soldiers who were dishonest or guilty of disorderly conduct, and who went absent without leave. Upon them had been thrust too great a responsibility for their action, without proper guidance. There were many unreliable and undependable men in the Army whose personalities had been so warped by their early family experiences as to make them social liabilities. The leadership of their families had been defective in preparing them to assume personal responsibility for their behavior.

It is our best psychiatric judgment that the antisocial individual, the so-called "psychopath," is maladjusted as the result of mismanaged babyhood and childhood. Gross defects in character are expressions of pathological home life: erratic affection from parents whose attitudes alternate between overseverity and overindulgence; the lack of correction of or indifference to misbehavior; the loss of one or both parents by death or separation or divorce; the absence of a secure, continuous source of affection. The soldier who had

---

[7] This point was especially emphasized by R. R. Grinker and J. P. Spiegel, *Men Under Stress,* The Blakiston Company, Philadelphia, 1945, pp. 276, 456. It was specifically mentioned by J. R. Rees, "What War Taught Us About Human Nature," *New York Times Magazine,* Mar. 17, 1946. It was the subject of the Menas K. Gregory Lecture given in 1945 by Dr. Edward F. Strecker. He elaborated the theme further in *Their Mother's Sons,* J. B. Lippincott Company, Philadelphia, 1946.

not found satisfaction in loyalty to his parents and their standards of living was incapable of being loyal to any person or living up to an ideal. Thousands of such men received administrative discharges because of their faulty attitudes. Undoubtedly, many times that number were rejected at the induction center, for if they were recognized, they were automatically rejected.

In seeking parallels between the Army unit and the family, one should not presume that the roles of the commanding officer of the company and the leaders of the home are entirely equivalent. The most important difference is the fact that there are two leaders in the home—the mother and the father. They have a joint responsibility. They are a team. One source of much mental illness can be traced to disagreements between the parents: the father who shirks his responsibility, the mother who tries to compensate for her husband's neglect; divergence in their standards, ideals, and decisions. The poor example they set in their relationships is constantly within the plain view of the children. The younger generation absorbs such a parental pattern as easily as it would a more healthy one.

Character and behavior deficiencies which are encountered in so many soldiers in this war were not signs of a decadent younger generation. History records that homesickness was one of the chief illnesses in the Civil War. In that same war, certain companies were defeated because so many of their men were absent without leave to return home. It is questionable if there were any major differences in the incidence of these difficulties in World War I as compared to World War II. As life becomes subject to more tension-producing situations, these problems increase in incidence. Stronger leadership within the family fold would be potent antidote to the disintegration of the personality when under stress.

MOTIVATION

A man's attitude toward his job and his situation are expressions of his "motivation." [8] When a soldier had strong convictions as to his usefulness and the importance of his work, he tried harder to do what was expected of him. He adjusted better to dangers and discomforts; he was more effective and had better mental health than the man who thought he was being "wasted." One might profitably consider the role of motivation in the family. Just as in the Army, it would concern attitudes and convictions about ideals and goals, and permanent aims.

Fundamentally, motivation depends upon the sort of parental pattern the child incorporates, both consciously and unconsciously, in terms of ideals,

---

[8] See Chap. 6, where motivation is discussed in some detail.

standards, and methods of living together in the family. He will react to people and situations outside of his home just as he does to those inside. The child learns before the age of 10 to be honest or dishonest, tolerant or intolerant; to want to have or to lack self-control, to be sincere or insincere; to get along with people and be a participant in a group or to be a lone wolf. He learns to prefer to be considerate or otherwise; he develops a system of interpersonal relations that include or do not include good manners, generosity, courtesy, cleanliness. In other words, his pattern of motives is established by the behavior and attitudes of his parents.

The parent, therefore, has a grave responsibility, for he must help the child accept and then adopt a set of standards for lifetime use. Concepts of attitudes toward property, religion, social relationships, and law enforcement should protect, guide, and support both the child and the adult he will become. However, those attitudes may be antisocial instead of social. There are "normal criminals"—individuals who became so because they never knew any other standard of behavior.

After the acceptance of certain standards, the desire of the individual to live up to them must become a motivating force. That desire should be cultivated. Parental authority may use either wise or unwise incentives. The fear of punishment or the deep craving for the attention or the approval of someone in the immediate environment are all re-enforcing motives. The child may stay out of the cooky jar to avoid being spanked. Or, he may go to bed happily because Dad plays with him while he undresses. Frequently, some form of external discipline is essential to point out the consequences of behavior which runs counter to family standards.

In the Army, external authority was ever present. To many men it was too apparent. On the other hand, no well-adjusted soldier objected to an externally imposed discipline that was tempered with good judgment, with personal considerateness, with fairness. In civilian life we have the police and the law. Not even the rosiest of optimists assumes that we will ever be sufficiently mature as to make them unnecessary. Not enough of us can give up selfishness, inconsiderateness, and profiteering. We will always have moochers, poachers, robbers, and racketeers.

Sooner or later, however, the development of an internal authority—the conscience—is essential. To all intents and purposes the conscience is the means whereby the child can carry with him his father and mother as advisors about his behavior. The parental admonitions, advice, restrictions, approval, and disapproval, leave an indelible record on the impressionable conscience of the growing child. In the absence of the parents he can act without having to stop and think out all the pros and cons of this or that behavior. For example, the doughboy who risks his own life to go to the aid of a buddy probably grew up in a family whose members had confidence in each other and shared a pride in not letting each other down.

Discipline is far too often confused with punishment.[9] Punishment inflicted by authority because of its power or its strength rarely is effective, whether it is inflicted on a child or a soldier or a criminal. The only effective punishment is that which the individual inflicts upon himself as the result of his failure to play the game or to live up to the standards or to obey the rules. The child must learn that his failure to live up to expected behavior will result in a loss, exclusion, withholding, or directly resulting pain. It is the parental responsibility to help the child realize and anticipate the eventual result of negligence or defiance. The child must become his own disciplinarian. The result of lack of family training in this direction was glaringly apparent in the Army. The rebellious, unruly, and undisciplined personalities who had never learned to control or to adjust behavior to the demands of the situation could not be made into good soldiers. Nor could hard-boiled, big-stick authority change them.

Motivation that is not unconsciously automatic depends basically on understanding. So many things that soldiers and children have to do seem senseless or unreasonable to them. They resent having to do something because someone in a position of greater authority demands it. Occasionally, well-established confidence in that authority may be a substitute for understanding the why and the wherefore. But that develops only through mutual experience.

The adult forgets that the basic lessons of life have to be *learned* by the little child who is apt to be a reluctant pupil because society's precepts often run counter to nature's desires. Motivation for eating, getting attention, sleeping, exists in the baby's personality. But the desire to respect other people's property means substituting the socially approved technique of admiring the neighbor's tulips for the socially unapproved desire to take what looks pretty and is wanted. It is the fortunate child who has parental leadership in strengthening his desire to adopt socially approved family standards. Sometimes that means finding a way to make difficult tasks and dirty jobs tolerable, perhaps even enjoyable.[10]

---

[9] In an excellent article, Knight pointed out two common parental mistakes regarding discipline: the tendency to react to one's own rearing either by copying exactly the disciplinary methods used by one's own parents or else by swinging to the opposite extreme. In the latter case, the individuals hold unresolved resentments against their parents. They are likely to try to avoid their parents' mistakes by using indulgence where their parents were strict, liberality where their parents were niggardly, and so on. Knight, R. P., "Behavior Problems and Habit Disturbances in Pre-adolescent Children: Their Meaning and Management," *Bull. Menninger Clinic,* 8:188-199, Nov., 1944.

[10] Munro Leaf, in his pictorial books for children, has done all American parents a good turn. First he corroborated the parent's statement to the child that manners (and grammar and safety and health) are important. Then he described them in a language that the little child can understand. And third, he portrayed them attractively. Thus he developed a favorable attitude

IDENTIFICATION

In the Army we learned the tremendous morale and mental health value of helping the individual develop a strong identification with his group. When the crusty old soldier bragged that his was the "best damned outfit in the Army," he expressed in a few words his deep pride in belonging to it. This was evidence of good leadership. That unit had a cohesion which each member shared and which made possible an acceptance of assignment to disagreeable as well as to pleasurable tasks.

The same principles are applicable to the family. When there is good leadership, members of the family develop a mutual respect for the opinions of others, for their property and for their feelings. Then, also, do they feel that they have "the best family in town." From their identification with the family comes an identification with each other. The development of mutual respect, which is the basis of identification among siblings, is an extremely complex process in the face of many rivalries for parental favor. It is complicated further by intellectual and emotional differences in personalities and by physical or psychological handicaps. Fundamentally, sincere respect grows out of shared experiences which leads to confidence—parental confidence in the children, confidence of the children in the parents, confidence of the children in each other. That confidence breeds an interdependence and fosters affection. This is—or leads to—identification with each other and the group.

Mutual interests. Dramatic demonstrations of the tightening of emotional ties between men who shared interests and activities emerge from the talk of veterans. Living, hiking, fighting, eating, sleeping, and talking together for days and weeks on end bound fighting soldiers into effective teams. Individual responsibilities varied, but the consciousness of a common purpose gave validity to their separate efforts.

Wise parents recognize and accept the responsibility for encouraging the sharing of interests. Without parental stimulus and guidance, it is unusual for a child to develop any lasting or satisfying hobby. Some parents seem to pride themselves in not knowing anything about the particular project in which their child has become interested. Others give mere approval or only passing consideration. Ideally, the parents should manifest sincere, deep, and participating enthusiasm for those activities of the child which they wish to encourage and make a permanent part of him. The family is truly blessed when the group as a whole shares activities or hobbies or interests which give

---

toward acquiring good manners, etc. *Grammar Can Be Fun,* J. B. Lippincott Company, Philadelphia, 1934; *Manners Can Be Fun,* J. B. Lippincott Company, Philadelphia, 1936; *Safety Can Be Fun,* J. B. Lippincott Company, Philadelphia, 1938; *Health Can Be Fun,* J. B. Lippincott Company, Philadelphia, 1942.

genuine satisfaction to every member and can be carried out either individually and/or as a family. The sharing of fun and play makes acceptable the sharing of routine and drudgery, all of which leads to a willing acceptance of family standards.

Mutual sharing of problems. Along with the mutual aim or goal of the unit goes the mutual sharing of problems. The Army provided various ways in which the average soldier could procure counsel and advice about any aspects of his life, personal or military. However, most soldiers sought relief from concern by sharing their problems with their immediate associates. If things were not to their liking, they griped. It was legitimate release of tension for everyone to express vehement objections. If the gripes were serious, if they gained sufficient crescendo, they were carried to the noncommissioned officers, and, through them, to the commanding officers. The Army regulations permitted even the privates who wished it the privilege of seeing their commanding officer at any time. The smart commanding officer not only gave audience upon request but, in many of our training camps, held what were called "gripe sessions" at regular intervals. In other camps a definitely set time was established at least once a week, when any man could have access to the commanding officer's office to express himself and to be assured that his difficulties or complaints would receive consideration. Also, within the company, the battalion, the regiment, and the field Army there were many formal and informal counsels about plans and strategy, just as in every business there is a sharing of ideas in the development of plans.

It is a curious fact that few families have recognized the value of council meetings. Too often one or both parents make all decisions. In many families, the child or even the teen-ager has little opportunity to express his opinion, his differing point of view, or to ask questions about family affairs. He must either obey with submissive willingness and accept the situation without a chance for understanding, or he can pout or openly revolt. It would seem that the principle which has become so important in the management of groups of men could have a particular value in family life. Every decision submitted to the family council certainly would give to both young and old members an understanding of the problem at hand which would be commensurate with the maturity of the participating discussants. To be sure, there were some commanding officers who went through the motions of such conferences, who solicited suggestions or opinions, but who had already made the decisions. Similarly, in too many families a family council is a farce. The soldiers soon "had the number" of that type of leader. Like them, children will not be fooled indefinitely by mere gestures.

Tolerance. One of the supports which could be as valuable to the family as it was when encouraged in the Army was tolerance. There were, of course, many intolerant individuals and intolerant groups in the military organization. On the whole, it was impressive that in an Army made up of prejudiced civilians, differences in creed, religion, color, race, nationality were ignored even to the extent that they were.[11] Within a particular unit a man's name or his money counted for less than what he did or how he behaved. His eccentricities, even his stupidity, were tolerated if he "played the game" well. Individual differences seemed unimportant in comparison to the big problems for which the group had to find solutions.

Much of the difficulty in the family arises because of the intolerance of one member for another. One only has to read the details of a few divorce cases [12] to recognize the stupid, silly, and petty examples of the unwillingness or inability of one to understand the point of view of the other. The man and woman who are incompatible and fight and punish each other distort the emotional patterns of their children. A little more intelligence in the control and direction of emotion could often make marriage, home, and children more mutually satisfying.

Even so, the design for living will vary. In some homes the father is the head of the house. In others, even though it is not admitted, the mother is. In

---

[11] Unfortunately, there were too many instances of individual and of group intolerance, particularly as viewed subjectively by those concerned. It was opposed by our best leaders.

[12] A glance at the increasing divorce rates indicates not only the extent of intolerance (and probably many other factors) in our homes, but it also serves as a barometer of the seriousness of another major social problem confronting America.

Year	Divorce Rate per 1,000 Population	Marriage Rate per 1,000 Population
1910	0.9	10.3
1915	1.0	10.1
1916	1.1	10.7
1917	1.2	11.2
1918	1.1	9.65 World War I
1919	1.4	10.95
1920	1.6	11.96
1925	1.5	10.35
1930	1.6	9.15
1935	1.7	10.41
1940	2.0	12.1
1941	2.2	12.7
1942	2.4	13.2
1943	2.6	11.8 World War II
1944	2.9	11.0
1945	3.6	12.3

(Information from Bureau of Census through courtesy of J. C. Capt and B. L. Jenkinson, 1 July 1946.) Published in *Vital Statistics—Special Reports,* Vol. 23, No. 9, Sept. 10, 1946, "Marriage and Divorce in the United States: 1937 to 1945," by B. L. Jenkinson.

Obviously the marriage and divorce rate of any one year are not comparable. Stimulated by the war and the draft, the marriage rate hit a high in 1942. Perhaps the divorce rate is "catching up" with these. Regardless of the causes, the number of divorces is an indication of the unhealthy mental state of too many American homes.

still others, the children seem to be the only consideration. The making of allowances, however, on the part of each for the rest, is essential for the maintenance of a mentally healthy home.

Sometimes congenial families encourage intolerance by resistance to "outsiders." Those may be classed as "outsiders" who differ culturally, economically, socially, religiously, educationally, racially. Intolerance does not persist when there are an abundance of affection and understanding, a sense of responsibility, a confidence and pride in the outfit, and a sharing of interests and problems. In a sense tolerance is a very vital by-product of healthy family relationships. It is the application of habits of attitudes within the family to bigger groups of which the various members of the family are also a part: school, church, firm, city, state, nation, world.

The position and functions of the wife. These will undoubtedly be affected by the changed role of women in wartime. Some thoughts about it were expressed in the discussion of the remarkable record made by women in the Army.[13]

Before the war there were approximately 11,000,000 women working outside their homes. In February, 1945, of the 17,770,000 women at work outside the home, about 8,000,000 were single, about 7,000,000 were married, and 2,000,000 widowed or divorced. In June 1947, there were 18,500,000 women employed, or 28.8 per cent of the female population over 14 years of age. Even more important, 84 out of every 100 women do such work because they must support themselves or support themselves and dependents, either entirely or partially.[14]

The average discussion of this problem is colored by prejudices, preconceived notions, or the lack of even a faint recognition of the change in the woman's role, particularly in American culture, in the last 100 years.

Actually women have always worked. Until comparatively recently the work or supervision of the routine and drudgery of housekeeping kept women occupied at home. Smaller families, more labor-saving equipment, greater choice of activity have led women to seek away-from-home work in order to avoid the idleness which many individuals, particularly men, sometimes assume to be their proper though boring role. The move from pioneering to city life has gradually reduced the required activity in the daily schedule of the wife and mother. Formerly, she participated in church or club work in her occasional free time. Nowadays she seeks employment to replace her greater

---

[13] See Chap. 7.
[14] Information obtained from "Talk It Over. A Woman's Place Is—Where?" From Series G-107, 1946, published by the National Institute of Social Relations, Inc., Washington, D.C., and from "Women as Wage Earners," *New York Times,* Sept. 14, 1947, quoting figures from U.S. Dept. of Labor.

leisure. Nevertheless, the August, 1943, *Fortune* survey indicated that at least three-fourths of the women still want to be married and to have as their chief job, the running of a home.

Usually, several needs of the wife and mother—particularly in urban families—form the basis for involvement in activity outside of the home:

(1) All her life she has been in groups—school, club, at work, in a family. It is sometimes difficult for her to shift to a life of many hours a day alone or with young children. For some there are frequent lonely evenings added.

(2) So much household work is routine that some women crave a taste of something which seems important in the actual doing as well as in being necessary.

(3) After the planned schedule of school or office, some housewives drift into aimless days because there is no incentive to get through the daily chores at a particular time. Sometimes outside work or play is the dessert which encourages prompt eating of an uninteresting though nourishing meal of drudgery.

(4) In lives as separate in activity as those of husbands and wives, often little of the business can be shared with wives and household events seem dull reporting to the husband. The wife's outside activity can be her answer to a hunger for interest in the bigger world which she can share with her husband and family.

(5) By finding even part-time employment outside the home, wives can sometimes afford more help for the routine they dislike in the home. Or "her" income may be the "extra" on which the couple can do things that otherwise would be impossible financially.

(6) So many girls are trained and educated in particular fields that some of them want to continue working in them and so combine parent- and wifehood with work.

(7) Under emotional tension of one sort or another, an interest-compelling activity away from home may be a relief.

Because the traditional American pattern has been for a male wage earner and a female homemaker in the family team, definite prejudices have developed, particularly among men. Heated arguments raged between soldiers in lonely, isolated posts or in camp "bull sessions" when there was time for thinking during the war. In order to give a little more light and a little less heat, the question of "Do you want your wife to work after the war?" was made one of the subjects of discussion in the official GI Round Table Series.[15]

---

15 "Do You Want Your Wife to Work After the War?" War Department Educational Manual, EM-31, GI Round Table Series, 26 June 1944.

In the final analysis the answer to this question is an individual one, individual to the extent of being a matter to be decided upon by the two people concerned and plans made which are appropriate to their time, points of view, and circumstance. As long as they both have understanding and tolerance, as long as the decision is a mutual one, there will be happy and mentally healthy families in which the wife works. There will be many other happy and mentally healthy families in which the wife's chief occupation is that of homemaker and housekeeper. Under any circumstances some families won't be happy or mentally healthy. In any case, however, it is well to consider the requirements of work and home, the hours in the day, the energy, ability, and emotional needs of the couple, and above all, the needs of any children, both in terms of present care and the relation of that care to future personality patterns.

In the postwar home there will be problems of husband-wife relationships. Separate living interrupted the process of mutual adjustment. When such a separation followed many years of satisfying companionship, the readjustment was comparatively simple. If crowded housing, unemployment, or the unfamiliarity of new parenthood added to the difficulty inherent in reorientation to each other, it often created stress too great for the struggling personalities to bear. Any emotional conflict, no matter how hard parents try to conceal it, colors the emotional reaction of children in the family. In the chapter, Social Reintegration of the Veteran, certain problems of readjustment were noted. Here seems to be a good place to review the military wife's wartime problems. For they have left their mark on every other member of her family.

It seems indicative of a blind spot in the attitude of the public and the military leadership that service wives received so little recognition and help. Apparently, it was totally unexpected when some of them had the equivalent of combat fatigue. The enforced assumption of new and increased responsibilities and burdens came at a time when they had lost their chief emotional support for which there was no adequate substitute. There have been few medical papers on the subject,[16] but psychiatric clinics have been called upon frequently to render aid to the wives of servicemen.

Many were greatly distressed, not just because of their own home problems but because of the different behavior of their husbands and their changed attitudes. Without an opportunity for really sharing the new life they did not understand the requirements of service in the armed forces. When war took men far from home into new and sometimes terrible experiences, their

---

[16] Lawrence, B. G., "Psychiatric Problems of Service Men's Wives," *Delaware State M. J.,* 17:89-90, May, 1945; Patterson, R. M., "Neurotic Reactions in Wives of Service Men," *Dis. Nerv. System,* 6:50-52, Feb., 1945.

only chance of retaining their sanity and efficient performance lay in the superficial loosening of home ties. The letters which came from home were welcomed as a tightening of a deep-set anchor. But when a wife needed advice her soldier-husband felt too far away to make an intelligent decision only on the basis of the information she had put into her letters. Often the mail arrived so irregularly or prematurely or so late that it gave the latest developments of a problem or event before one knew the event. Consequently, it was difficult for the serviceman to really know just what the situation had been, was, or would be by the time his answer reached home, or the next letter came from home. In most cases his inability to help from long range was *not* indifference. That is a fact which wives often found very difficult to appreciate. It is also a fact that husbands did not appreciate the construction being put upon their inadequacy in family difficulties. Those who did give frequent pats on the back in words of appreciation and affection helped the wife a great deal.

Many realistic-thinking wives were often puzzled by the appearance of a change in a husband's attitudes. They wondered whether distance or tension made his mail seem different or whether his interest was slowly being weaned away. Other wives were startled by a husband's sudden announcement that their long-time, apparently mutually satisfying marriage was ended.

In seeking aid, many of these wives have written to the Surgeon General soliciting help. In the mail one day came the letter of a wife which started out, "While I was visiting in San Francisco about a month ago, I phoned my husband's family in Seattle, to find out if they had heard from him in Tokyo. I had had no letter for three months and I was worried about him. My husband answered the phone. He stated that he had been home for a month, and in an angry tone told me abruptly that all was over between us and had been for some time. This was the first time that he had informed me of such a situation and his letters had all been normal in tone."

The writers of syndicated columns for women in our daily press have received hundreds of such letters from service wives. These wives need help, and in many instances for a "service connected disability." They will seek it from the newspaper syndicate writers, from their friends, from their ministers, physicians, or lawyers. It is to be hoped that the trend toward the establishment of family counseling services with carefully trained consultants will continue. These agencies can provide guidance in many such instances. A certain number of these war-wife casualties will require professional psychiatric help, as will their children.

SUMMARY

It is an amazing paradox that our culture can develop such remarkable technological achievements as television and atomic energy and yet actually go backward in many ways in our social structure. America's future greatness is threatened unless life in many of her families is helped to become more healthy. Only in that way can she produce more stable and more mature adults. The situation could well call for a state of national emergency. Unlimited efforts should be spent on studies of the family to devise ways and means of strengthening it. The family should be the subject of continuing joint study by our most intelligent and sincere religious leaders, lawyers and lawmakers, social scientists, educators, industrial and business leaders, physicians, and any others who can contribute to it.[17]

This chapter was written not so much to point out the crisis of American family life as to report on observations that psychiatrists made during their service in the war which point out clues about ways to improve it. The intimate, detailed, individual studies of ill soldiers which investigated their childhood, home environment, and training showed a common denominator of mental ill health—mismanaged parental emotions. Because the Army units were pseudo families, they provided a testing ground to corroborate theories about personal relationships: affection and understanding between parents (leaders) and children are basic to mental health; the acceptance of responsibility and the sharing of activities lead to confidence and pride in the whole unit and in its individual members; the development of mutual interests and aims makes for easier acceptance of group standards and criteria; the development of tolerance of the opinions, eccentricities, and peculiar techniques of relatives makes living and working with strangers more pleasant and effective. The changing role of the wife will modify the way in which these basic needs will be met.

---

[17] There are several organized groups of social scientists and laymen which are concerned with the study of the family, such as the National Council on Family Relations. A National Conference on Family Life is to be held in Washington, D.C., May 6-8, 1948.

27

IMPLICATIONS FOR THE COMMUNITY

NATIONAL mental health, in a large degree, could be purchased if that were our aim.[1] Were we serious enough and unselfish enough to plan to organize and to contribute money, time, and effort, much of the unhappiness, inefficiency, waste, and ill health could be eliminated. It doesn't make sense to spend $7,700,000,000 a year on liquor and only $2,500,000,000 a year on primary and secondary education.[2] Nor does it make much sense to spend billions on handling delinquents and criminals and only a few millions on recreational facilities and programs. Destructive-constructive spending is totally out of balance when we are forced to expend $67,000,000,000 a year to fight a war and invest only $4,000,000,000 [3] a year on all the health services in our nation.

It is important to build new hospitals. Nevertheless it is somewhat paradoxical that we do nothing about the unhealthy conditions in underprivileged areas from which so many of the patients come. It is no cure to set up another dispensary in a crowded tenement district unless other improvements are made also. To decry the illiteracy rate is futile until we remove the obstacles to a good education for large numbers of our people.

Whether any of these paradoxes can be changed depends on the community. "Community" here connotes the hamlet as well as the metropolitan city, or its neighborhoods, the state, the national government, the United Nations. Apparently from the beginning of man's existence on earth, people have set up their shelters near those of other people. In community life they found social contact, shared responsibility, and gained greater protection. Experience has taught us that the congregation of people in groups provides opportunities to live richer, safer, and more satisfying lives than would be possible if every man tried to remain self-sufficient. In our democracy, by the voluntary pooling of abilities, interests, and skills, the members of a com-

---

[1] This is one of the chief points made by H. W. Brosin, in "The Army Has Learned These Lessons," *Modern Hosp.,* **64**:45-47, May, 1945.

[2] Walter Lippmann, "Federal Aid to Schools' Demands a Big Problem," *The Washington* (D.C.) *Post,* Apr. 27, 1947.

[3] *Free Medical Care,* compiled by C. A. Peters, Reference Shelf, Vol. 19, No. 3, The H. W. Wilson Company, New York, 1946, p. 154.

munity become parts of a big team whose responsibility is to serve its every citizen.

There are, however, many disadvantages to communal living. The group is only as protective of, helpful to, and profitable for its individual members as the average level of psychological maturity of that membership permits. In other words, upon the will of the individual citizens acting as one body depends the degree of collective exploitation of different sorts which is allowed.

Part of our American social-political heritage of freedom is freedom to choose the community in which we wish to live. The choice is fundamentally, and probably rightfully, a selfish one. "Here I want to live." "Here I can have a good job and this is a nice town in which to bring up our children." Rarely does one consider, unless it meets his own wishes, "Badger Town needs my skill. They don't pay as well as I was offered in Island City but I should go there to help them." Unfortunately, the disappointing corollary of the usual motivation is, "We want more paved streets in our area of the town." "We have to have a new school for our neighborhood." "I want lower taxes." "Why don't they give us more service in cleaning the place up?" Too infrequent is the question: "What can I do to help our city improve?" "Yes, I want my area better, but what does the whole city need most?"

In a country in which there is so much freedom in thought and action, many of our people are such individualists that they do not consider the effect of their freedom upon that of others. It is so easy to confuse freedom and license. Self-centeredness often closes our eyes to the needs of the village, the nation, and the world. It is too easy to find glaring examples of selfish, personal, or small-group interests which ignore other individuals, small-groups, and/or the ideals of the larger group. Because of this freedom we have political bosses, black markets, "white supremacy," strikes that threaten the nation, and hosts of different types of rackets.

Isolationism. The personal selfishness of considering only our own home or our own area of the city or our own part of the country is a phenomenon of special interest to the psychiatrist. By popular usage it has been called "isolationism." We know some families who stand aloof from the community, some communities that have no sense of relationship to the surrounding area, and some nations which have no interest in any other nation.

A classic example of isolationism [4] is seen in a severe type of psychiatric illness called schizophrenia, meaning "split mind" (formerly called dementia praecox). In this illness, the insecurity of the patient drives him to deny the real world and to build up his own world of phantasy. Psychologically, his

---

[4] Appel made an interesting comparison between isolationism and schizophrenic withdrawal and between sovereignty and illusions of power. Appel, K. E., "Nationalism and Sovereignty—A Psychiatric View," *J. Abnorm. & Soc. Psychol.,* 40:355-362, Oct., 1945.

behavior is interpreted as aggressive, hostile action toward those whom he thinks have deprived him of that which would have made him feel secure. By drawing into himself he can ignore the grim realities of life and live with his uninhibited hallucinations and phantasmic primitive thinking.

Because of some similar but less extreme sense of insecurity, too many people choose to act without regard to social realities, even though they hurt themselves and others in the process. Within our social structure a realistically oriented family cannot ignore the wishes or feelings of its various members or of its neighbors. The city which depends for its livelihood on a "trade area" cannot disregard the plight or the chaos, the lawlessness or poverty of neighboring communities. Only a few months before Pearl Harbor the narrow-minded "schizophreniclike" thinking of many people in America led them to believe that the difficulties of our neighbors overseas were none of our business. Unfortunately, such a point of view is being expressed again today. To many of us, the rehabilitation of Western Europe seems a necessity, not merely on the basis of generosity or humanitarianism, but for our own security and development. Nor is this conceivable without great individual cost—and sacrifice—to every American.

Lessons from the Army. What could we learn from the experience in the Army about living in groups? It, too, was formed into communities. Although their membership and location changed frequently, their organization and direction were regimented; each camp and post had to provide its own services of supply, sanitation, police, engineering, entertainment, and medical service. The Army had to blueprint the most feasible plans which could be followed quickly, wherever and whenever it created a new community. Its activities— education, practice, production, and total program had to be "standardized" so that everyone concerned, regardless of experience, could carry on toward a common goal. The purpose of every military unit of whatever type, in any and every location, was fundamentally the same. To win the war was its prime goal and reason for existence. Therefore, minimal diversion of energy was allowed for the establishment of these communities except where policy makers used poor judgment or misdirected effort. When time was vital, energy and money were used more recklessly, as the policy makers dictated. Even so the members had to do whatever would advance them toward the military goal.

The Army community was different from the civilian community. Its membership was, in most cases, not voluntary. Then too, all the activity of the entire community was directed toward a common purpose. The organization was determined and the leadership appointed by higher authority. Each and every person in the armed forces was responsible to some higher authority.

Experience in a military community, in spite of its advantages for its particular purpose, re-enforced the belief of most of us that we definitely do not want our civilian communities, our states, and our nation ever to be organized along dictatorial and compulsory lines. As protective units, the Army and Navy had to be so organized in order to act more quickly and more efficiently. Most veterans are more convinced than ever that the ideal social structure is a truly democratic state in which neither one man nor even a few men can control the economic, educational, social, or religious life of the nation. However, too many forget that the "Let George do it" philosophy of citizenship may produce just that situation in which the national economy can be disrupted by a small minority of vocal and energetic leaders.

Leadership. Granting that there are important differences between the Army and the civilian communities, nevertheless many experiences of the Army community can be of benefit to the civilian community. By all odds, the most important of these concerns leadership. I have already reiterated many times that the quality of leadership determined the mental health of the unit in the Army more than any other one factor. There were examples there, just as in civilian life, of good and bad leadership. Good leadership had a beneficial effect on the accomplishments, morale, and, particularly, on the mental health of the members of an Army community. The organization of the Army made it possible to observe this correlation.

In American civilian life our leaders who make the policies of the community are chosen in many different ways and for many different reasons, but their choice depends on us. Theoretically, the choice of the individual to serve his community is based upon that person's ability to perform an assigned task. Few of us are naïve enough to believe that this happens in most instances. Political office has not been made attractive as a career. Office holders are subject to abuse by displeased constituents; the meager salaries make bribery a temptation; a dearth of candidates from among men successful in other fields of endeavor leaves political office to less capable, more easily corruptible, immature seekers after power. Unless a candidate can afford to be philanthropic with his energy and time, our system of choosing leadership often does not even permit us to select the most capable individuals. The salary of a city commissioner of my city of nearly 100,000 people is $4,000 [5] a year. The legislators in my state are paid $3 a day for their service during the legislative term. Only recently our Congressmen in Washington had to vote themselves a supplemental income in order to maintain themselves. The better the pay the better the man who can be attracted to office.

Such a situation exists only because of the apathy of too many voters. That indifference, unfortunately, extends far beyond the salary we pay our public

---

[5] For years this was $3,000. It was increased by the 1947 legislature.

servants. There is a serious lack of interest in the qualifications and back-ground of who is elected and in what the officeholder does after his election. Only a vitally interested citizenry which elects strong, intelligent leadership can maintain a healthy social structure. The alert voter is the best insurance of executive, legislative, judicial, and social leadership which considers *group* welfare as more important than the wishes of one individual or a few obstruc-tionists. A political system such as ours needs a cornerstone of maturity of thought in both leader and led. Only then can it support the three pillars which are essential to the mental health of individuals or groups of people—security, satisfaction, and stability.

The responsibility of the citizen voter goes further. In a republic, freedom of decision must be based on a consideration of the reality of our local, na-tional, and international role. The ability of America to make wise future policies, even with its fine social ideals and democratic structures, is threatened unless we, the individual citizens, arouse to our responsibility to keep in-formed on local, state, national, and international developments and to main-tain a constant check upon our leadership.[6]

Motivation. The leaders, elected and appointed, provide the motivation for our communities. It is they who establish aims, standards and goals in line with the wishes of the citizens. Theirs too is the task of implementing the pro-gram they develop.

In the Army there were officers whose specific purpose was to educate the soldiers how to do the job. There were others who were responsible for ex-plaining why the doing of that job was important. There were still others who, through their leadership tactics, were responsible for inspiring the sol-dier to carry out his job and to provide the facilities whereby he could do it. The ordinary soldier was just one of our average citizens. Even at best, most of them could not have become leaders; they didn't have the native capacity. Without plans and directions they could not have executed their mission or the Army its mission. But with leadership, they won the war.

Similarly, in civilian life we must expect that some people never mature sufficiently emotionally to do a good job in raising a family. Some are able to participate only passively in the community. Some do not have the capacity to be vitally interested in the nation. There are others who perhaps do reach maturity but for many varied reasons return to a less demanding level of psy-chological development. Therefore, the minority, those who are truly adult psychologically, are subject to an excessive demand. They must plan for and

---

[6] One of our militant psychiatrists has expressed himself strongly as to the importance to men-tal health of the individual to participate in community activities and to take part in demo-cratic processes. Schreiber, J., "The Interdependence of Democracy and Mental Health," *Ment. Hyg.,* 29:606-621, Oct., 1945. This is the purpose of the League of Women Voters..

supply the needs of the total community, be it local, state, national, or inter-national.

We know too well that at present there is only a comparatively small num-ber of people in any community who are able and will give leadership and time and money to improve that community. Building an Army showed the appalling need of improvement in mental health. It is to be hoped that these persons in positions of community leadership will broaden their scope of interest in order to strengthen the pillars of community mental health—eco-nomic and emotional security, satisfaction, and emotional stability of the citi-zenry. America must strive toward the development of many more mature personalities in order to provide more and better leaders.

Family, school, church, club, government, business, industry, and other organizations and agencies can nurture or impede this development. It is through their programs that the capacity of their members can be expanded so that they may learn to give and take in social relationships. These leaders and these groups are presently the chief means of improving our national mental health.[7]

The leaders in our community must provide our motivation. They must determine the goal toward which the leadership must lead, toward what the civilian must be motivated. Furthermore, that goal must be chosen through democratic procedure.

Each institution, agency, and organization, from the family to the United Nations, must establish its own immediate and long-term goals. We are sur-rounded with immense social problems that are basically concerned with the happiness, security, freedom, i.e., the mental health of individuals. There-fore, it would seem very practical that every unit in our social structure might evaluate its programs in terms of the contribution to individual and group mental health. Such an evaluation, or survey, could be the basis of selection of the most important immediate, as well as future, goals of activity. The sum of what the various organizations believe their individual members want and need could become the total community program.

Certain questions which could be used in a survey of this sort might be: "What are the more serious community-caused sources of emotional stress?" "How can we effectively modify that stress by eliminating its source or in-

---

[7] One of our leading psychiatrist-psychoanalysts has expressed himself similarly. "My conclu-sion is that we are the victims of a cultural lag in as much as we still live emotionally in the past and have not caught up with the new conditions brought about by science and its technical achievements. . . . The remedy lies obviously in an emotional reorientation, restoring the dis-turbed relation between psychological attitudes and social structure. The achievement of this lies not primarily in the field of psychiatry or of mental hygiene. It is the function of the social institutions to which the shaping of the personality and of social attitudes are traditionally entrusted—first of all the family, then the church and the school." Alexander, F., "Mental Hygiene in the Atomic Age," *Ment. Hyg.*, **30**:529-544, Oct., 1946.

creasing the supports against it?" "What courses of action can be planned?"

After the goals are determined, motivation depends in part on education of the people in the community toward them. Support of leadership necessarily depends upon the distribution of information about the work to be done and the proposed plan of implementation. The "need" has to be shown; the solution must be common knowledge. Publicity and public relations committees are the civilian counterpart of the Army's Information and Education Service which endeavored and often succeeded in increasing the efficiency of a unit by an orientation of its men. Civilians need orientation to the importance of a project, to the value of the proposals of its leaders, and to the need for their participation in the program.

Open-minded discussions of the issues involved must include an acceptance of and respect for the leadership revealing them. As the acts of the leader check favorably with his platform, confidence in him increases. As confidence increases, so does the support of his program. When the program is achieved, everyone participating in its adoption shares the pride in the accomplishment.

Radio and news-projected personalities and propaganda can be used to clarify or to confuse basic issues. Therefore, any agency that is promoting action toward its goal should encourage the dissemination of factual, unbiased information and free discussion of it. In clubs and unions, churches and schools, in families and as individual readers and thinkers, an understanding of the situation furnishes a check against uncontrolled power and excessive waste of effort and money by the policy makers.

It is an encouraging sign that various agencies, both public and private, have been organized for the purpose of furnishing information and stimulating public discussion. An example of such a private group is the National Institute of Social Relations [8] which publishes the material, outlines the methods, and suggests the personnel necessary to organize discussion groups on the major social issues in communities. It does so on the basis that many of our social problems derive from the failure of our citizens to apply to their daily thinking the basic principles of our democratic credo. Psychological immaturity is not alone to blame. Lack of understanding of facts and ready source material for discussion of them are also to blame.

Another agency, the National Education Association, had similar aims when it held the first national conference on citizenship in Philadelphia, May 17 and 18, 1946. Its purpose was to "promote an active, alert, enlightened

---

[8] This group, now incorporated, is of special interest. Its dynamic director is a well-known psychiatrist, Dr. Julius Schreiber, who spent 2 of his 4 years in the Army developing the mental hygiene unit in Camp Callen, Calif., and there experimented with various devices for crystallizing the opinion and stimulating the positive motivation of soldiers. His last 2 years were spent in the Information and Education Division of the War Department.

conscientious and progressive citizenry, through the focusing of national attention on the value of American citizenship, together with its duties and responsibilities." Such discussion groups can and should lead to action and thus change a geographic community into a social community.

The community and the family. The community can only function as the family supports it, and at the same time the family has opportunities only as the community provides them. It is the primary function of the community to provide the family with a richer, more satisfying life. Yet only through the family's investment can this be attained. Therefore, the relationship of the family to the community is a mutual exchange. Through community leadership, the individual and the family must develop a sense of responsibility for the welfare of the community. Families and groups have to be helped to overcome their selfishness and provinciality so that they may recognize that they will profit in direct proportion to their contribution to the improvement of the entire community. This was a very fundamental lesson repeated again and again in our Army experience: to achieve a group goal the individual, at times, had to be secondary in importance to the group.

The individual and the family, if they are to be a part of the community life, must assume the responsibility of participation. This is an obligation of life in a democracy. Everyone has to be enough of a politician to act intelligently in the selection of leaders, in their election, in checking on their actions and accomplishments. Further than that, we must be members of social, educational, and economic groups in order to take part truly in community affairs. The community leadership, however, often must stimulate the formation of those groups in which we, the citizens, can function.

In the final analysis the success of any program will be determined by the extent to which individuals identify themselves as members of the family with the neighborhood, the neighborhood with the city, the city with the state, and so on. Similarly, there must be the opportunity for the individual to identify with the family, the family with the school, the church, the club, and other organizations within the community. The identification fosters a strong sense of belonging and approval and security.

SPECIFIC SOCIAL PROBLEMS

Social problems arise when either the environment is too tough or the personality too weak, or both. The community can and should make a greater effort to help maintain a balance between the environment and the personalities exposed to it. Unpleasant as it is to admit it, much of the mental sickness that we saw in the Army resulted from a failure of society to prevent it. This was partly due to defective leadership, partly due to traditional practices, partly due to the upheaval that the depression and the previous war had caused, partly due to immature personalities. In any event, there has not been enough concern directed toward the prevention of the ill effects of any of these.

If one could label as *most important* any one of the community responsibilities, it would be the necessity of giving its families greater support against environmental pressures and removal of the cause of the pressure when possible. Each local agency and organization really exists to supplement the family. Industry and business provide income for its maintenance; churches give spiritual support to its individuals and to the maintenance of its unity; government protects its property and rights; welfare agencies give it guidance and material aid.

Intelligent, thoughtful groups are already working on these problems, but more groups and more people should be thinking about all possible approaches to the reduction or removal of existing social stress. Psychiatric investigations and experience could help in problems of human relationships—the feeling and thinking of people. For example, housing committees could obtain helpful and powerful arguments from the psychiatrist which would present the effect of housing shortages on mental health. I wonder if, in the arbitration of strikes, thought has ever been given to the effect of decisions on the mental health or interpersonal relations of the workers and their families.

Unemployment. There are effects of unemployment which continue long after re-employment. It matters little that the unemployment is due to illness or injury, to depression or strike. The following excerpt was taken from a prepared statement for a hearing before a Senate Committee on the psychiatric aspect of the Full Employment Bill:

One can establish the basic premise that to be mentally healthy, one must have a purpose in life and society must be so organized as to furnish him the means of accomplishing that purpose. For the average man, as head of his family, this purpose is the building and maintenance of his home and the facility to be supplied by society is the work for which he shall receive the pay with which to achieve his goal.

The problem of unemployment affects not only the status of an individual, but much more important, the status of his family. The American culture is based on the family unit with its personal and group satisfactions, its participation in the community and ultimately in the nation's affairs. The father as the head of the family is the wage earner and so the active leader of this basic social unit. The mother is the custodian of the home and children. A family can be happy and successful and "normal" only if the parents are happy and successful in their roles and so are "normal." Unless the father has a job and assumes his responsibility towards that family, the children cannot be "normal." Consequently, unemployment becomes a problem concerning two generations—the adults and the children. Probably the most tragic result of unemployment from the mental health viewpoint is the effect on the children. Many opinions have been expressed regarding the causes of the high neuropsychiatric casualty rates of this war, and some have assumed that American youth was "degenerating." There is no evidence of this, although there is much evidence of a rather widespread social illness as manifested in a country which has recently had eight million men unemployed. The effect of this unemployment on the youth of these families is beyond calculation. We know that an individual's personality and character structure is very largely dependent on his early family environment. Not only are his codes of thought and behavior established at this period, but also his habits of personal relationships are developed. A healthy family relation is essential to the development of "normal" children. When that family is plagued with unemployment, it is impossible to conceive of the children maturing without some degree of warp in their personality structure and, consequently, subsequent difficulties in their relations to people and to the community—evidence of mental ill health.

There is fairly unanimous opinion among social scientists that unemployment is a problem of social organization and not one of individual personality. It represents a defect in our social structure. Most of the unemployed are not inferior, defective individuals who do not want to work. Recurrent business depressions, with as many as twenty-five percent of the able-bodied workers deprived of the means of livelihood, have shown the fallacy of the assumption that the laborer is at such times responsible for his plight. Despite the fact that these are the facts as judged by our best social scientists, there is a widespread tendency on the part of communities and individuals to regard the unemployed as "bums" or inferior specimens of humanity. By this self-deceptive attitude they adroitly fail in the acceptance of their individual and collective responsibility for our social organization.

Mental Health Problems With Unemployment: Many sociological and psychiatric studies have been made of unemployed persons. It is variously estimated that sixty to eighty percent of such individuals manifest definite signs of mental ill health. The great majority give conspicuous evidence of their economic insecurity in their thinking and in their relationships with other people. Many of them are definitely anxious in regard to their future; they maintain a lurking fear that there is no escape, no end to their predicament. In the majority of instances, the father [9] of the household appears to be a "failure"—a failure in the eyes of his wife, his children, his friends and the community, often even to himself. Without a job, he, to some degree, fails to be able to fulfill his purpose. Also, as a result of his loss of work, he loses some of the stabilizing factors in every working man's life—the association with fellow workers, the routine, the need to get up in the morning and to be at a particular place at a particular time, satisfaction in work done, receipt of remuneration for his effort.

Mental ill health is reflected in the wife. In many instances, in her effort to alleviate the situation, she shifts her role to being the wage earner of the family, and so its source of authority and leadership. There is inevitable marital friction

---

[9] This and many other mental health points on unemployment were discussed for social workers in an excellent little pamphlet by Dr. George K. Pratt at the time of the economic depression in 1933. *Morale. The Mental Hygiene of Unemployment,* National Committee for Mental Hygiene, New York, 1933.

resulting from this shift which is further aggravated by the presence of the husband in the home all day and the uncertain division of responsibility.

More tragic is the effect on the children—physically, educationally, emotionally. Again, one should stress the fact that unemployment becomes a mental health problem which always affects two generations. Studies have indicated the deleterious effect on the physical health of the children. In the majority of cases, their education is cut short. Emotionally, they become quite disoriented, not only because of the marital friction but because of the confused role of each parent in the. home. They are inclined to regard the father as a "failure" and so lose respect for him. Under our previously operated relief system, minor children gained little or no economic independence if they did work, because the amount of a large proportion of their meager income was automatically subtracted from the money provided the family from relief sources. Certainly, no part of the income of a child under sixteen should be deducted from the family relief funds.

Finally, a major symptom of mental ill health of the unemployed is displayed in their social insecurity. Because of what they believe their friends think of them, they tend to avoid them. Because of what their friends know, these friends tend to avoid them. The unemployed regard themselves as outcasts, disapproved of and looked down on by society. They often lose a fundamental necessity for good mental health—self respect.

Mental Health Problems From Threatened Unemployment: The threat of unemployment is of particular significance at this time to our veterans. They are the children of the last depression and they have not forgotten it. This concern of veterans in regard to their future is vividly described by Eli Ginzberg in his book *The Unemployed.* He pictures them as having fought all over the world, willing to make any sacrifice. They have had no doubt as to the outcome of the war, "but when they think of peace they are uneasy. These soldiers recall that the country fumbled badly in coming to grips with that scourge of peace—unemployment. They remember that pregnant women were dispossessed from their homes; that farmers were thrown off their land; that husky men became soft from idleness. They remember all this and more, and they wonder what will happen when they have won the victory on the battlefield. They wonder whether the country will also win the peace. They are uneasy but they are not pessimistic. They have seen much these last years. They have seen their country suffer the consequence of an unpreparedness, born of ignorance, and they have seen this failing remedied with speed and efficiency. They know there is nothing within reason that the United States cannot do, if it will." [10]

The same situation will be equally grave for the migratory war worker; in fact, his problem may be even more acute. With the tremendous turnover from war to peace industry, we must realistically face the uncertainty which prevails in the mind of the worker as to his chances and the chances of his family.

All that has been said above about the effect of unemployment on mental health applies to a greater extent to that group of individuals who have made a marginal adjustment to life—barely maintaining a delicate equilibrium between mental health and ill health. One of the lessons from this war has been to indicate the size of this group in our nation. In attempting to select fighting men for a fighting

---

[10] Ginzberg, E., and Associates, *The Unemployed,* Harper & Brothers, New York, 1943, p. 3.

Army, we found that thirty-eight percent of all men rejected at induction were suffering from some type of personality disorder—1,825,000 out of a total of 4,650,000 men. Most of these men were and are able to get along in their civilian jobs, but, in many instances, one can be sure that if confronted with unemployment, the balance of equilibrium would be definitely thrown toward mental ill health.

With demobilization of the Army and war industries, unemployment may confront us shortly, and not only will we have the inherent problems of unemployment, but these will directly contribute to making many of this group of veterans into confirmed invalids. If there were assurance of sustained employment opportunities for all, this possibility would be of less concern.

Our Army experience has revealed the immense scope of the problems to be found in a select age group. We must assume that these figures would be greatly increased if all age groups were included.

Again quoting Doctor Ginzberg's survey of an unemployed group, "It is a tragic paradox that these unemployed men found their salvation in America's entrance into World War II; that their return to work was made possible *only* because American industry was called upon to produce an ever-increasing volume of death-dealing instruments; that the unemployed man and his family were rescued from the community of outcasts *only* because of the holocaust which covered the earth.

"Yet there is meaning in this paradox and it has a moral, not only for war but also for peace. Once this country accepted the challenge and actively entered the war, we surprised ourselves and confounded our enemies. Goals were set which brought jeers from the Axis and questions from our Allies. But these goals were met and in many cases exceeded. Overnight, millions of men were mustered into an Army equipped with the most modern arms, and trained according to the latest doctrines. Planes rolled off the assembly lines and millions of tons of shipping were floated in the Atlantic and the Pacific. Clearly, there was no challenge too great for this country to meet. The people understood and they did not hesitate. Nothing frightened them.

"Money was needed—untold billions; it was found. Manufacturing plants had to be converted; it was done. Traditions had to be disregarded; no voices were raised in protest. Faith gave the country strength.

"So it was in war; so it must be in peace. The men who went forth to fight, and, if need be, to die, did so that the country might live, that their fathers, brothers, and sons could labor to build a more perfect union and a more perfect world. 'It is for us, the living, rather to be dedicated here to the unfinished work which they who fought here have thus far so nobly advanced.' " [11]

Recommendations Regarding Unemployment: From a psychiatric point of view, it is an established fact that unemployment produces a many-faceted mental ill health problem of serious proportions. Therefore, it would seem imperative for the government to establish an employment system which takes into account very specific consideration of:

(1) Methods of insuring the basic mental hygiene factors of security, gratification and self-respect for every individual.

---

[11] Ginzberg, E., and Associates, *op cit.*

(2) The fact that every home affected by unemployment involves two generations, with the children probably suffering more than the parents.

(3) The known facts regarding the incidence of personality disorders as we
have learned them from experience in the Army with special consideration given
to employment opportunities for all types of medically disabled veterans, including
neuropsychiatric dischargees.

(4) A revised and, if necessary, a greatly expanded relief program. A strenuous
and extensive educational campaign should be made to correct community attitudes
and individual attitudes towards the unemployed.

(5) The integration of relief and work referral on the assumption that if a job
is available for which a man is qualified, he will take it. If no job is available, the
relief system is so managed as to avoid gestapo technique whereby the unemployed
are hounded and depreciated to a point of severe mental ill health.[12]

Prejudice and discrimination. America's number-one social neurosis at the
moment is prejudice and its resultant discrimination. No intelligent individual
can be unaware of the social tensions between various racial, social, and religious groups. These have been superbly presented by the President's Committee on Civil Rights. This in turn has been strongly endorsed by a group of
psychiatrists.[13]

Prejudice is correctly regarded as a kind of neurosis, at least in so far
as it is based on the utilization of well-recognized neurotic mechanisms. The
subject was discussed at some length from a scientific point of view by two

---

[12] Unemployment and Mental Health. Prepared for Hearing before Senate Committee on Bank-
ing and Currency re the Full Employment Bill, 24 August 1945. In Hearings on S.380, pp.
433-445. Also in *Mental Health* (London), 6:5-8, Jan., 1946. These remarks are not made to
support one or another philosophy of how to prevent unemployment. They are one psychiatrist's
view of the problem of unemployment.

[13] *To Secure These Rights,* The Report of the President's Committee on Civil Rights, U. S.
Government Printing Office, Washington, D.C., 1947. The following resolution, formulated
by the Committee on Social Issues, was unanimously approved by the membership of the
Group for the Advancement of Psychiatry at their meeting in Asbury Park, N. J., on November 11, 1947:

The Group for the Advancement of Psychiatry welcomes the timely reaffirmation of the
basic rights and the dignity of man contained in the Report of the President's Committee on
Civil Rights.

As psychiatrists, we are convinced that the protection of civil rights is vital to the mental
health of our citizens. Experiences which result in frustration, insecurity, fear, and hate under-
mine the mental health of individuals and create unhealthy relations between persons and
groups of persons.

The social conditions necessary to insure mental health require the full protection for *all*
citizens of these basic rights as defined in the Report of the President's Committee:

The right to the safety and security of the person;
The right to citizenship and its privileges;
The right to freedom of conscience and expression;
The right to equality of opportunity.

Because these rights affect mental health, we strongly urge that the responsible governmental authorities promptly take action to secure them to our citizens. At no time in our history has this been more important. All means of communication should be used to inform the
public of the meaning of these rights and the recommendations of the President's Committee
intended to preserve them.

psychiatrists, one a white and one a Negro, at the American Psychiatric Association meeting in Chicago in 1946.[14] Both pointed out the well-accepted fact that the prejudice is produced by insecurity and ignorance which operate to warp the personalities of both the prejudiced people and their victims. McLean [15] clearly set forth the unconscious hostility of Negroes against white men which stimulated their anxiety and guilt because they need and are dependent on white men. On the other hand the white man claims an omnipotence and superiority he does not have. By claiming Negro inferiority, he projects his own weakness onto the Negro whom he uses as a whipping post for his own pent-up, frustrated hostility.

History records man's need to find a scapegoat, some devil onto which he may project his own doubts, fears, and inadequacies. Primitive tribes used animals and then killed the animals, hoping thereby to rid themselves of the evil. Throughout history people have used a series of such objects on which to project their insecurity: werewolves, incubi, witches, mental patients, Christians, Jews, Catholics, Negroes, and many other innocent victims. When another group seems threatening, the result is a sense of insecurity. This insecurity is a fear, usually a vague, ill-defined sense of threatening danger, of being conquered by this horde that is different in some way. Perhaps we think they threaten our jobs, our social standing, our families.

Undoubtedly, part of this neurosis has its very definite origin in childhood. The small baby refuses to accept a strange person immediately. Throughout life anyone different from ourselves is likely to be the object of suspicion and subject to our use of the psychological mechanism of projecting onto them our own feeling of inadequacy. By so doing we may also raise our own self-esteem, our own self-pride, our own power. Through any means of continuous humiliation, depreciation, and persecution of a threatening group, which keeps it harmless, helpless, dependent, subservient, we maintain our security.

The outstanding example of the psychopathic extent to which a nation may go in regard to racial intolerance was seen in the German persecution of the Jews. However, we in America cannot point our fingers at Hitler, if we are frank enough to evaluate our own hypocrisies and inconsistencies toward the minority groups in this country.

The Army [16] expended tremendous effort toward the solution of the Negro

---

[14] Stevens, R. B., Jr., "Racial Aspects of Emotional Problems of Negro Soldiers," *Am. J. Psychiat.*, **103**:493-498, Jan., 1947. Kaufman, S. H., "The Problem of Human Difference and Prejudice," *Am. J. Orthopsychiat.*, **17**:352-358, Apr., 1947.

[15] McLean, H. V., "Psychodynamic Factors in Racial Relations," *Ann. Am. Acad. Polit. and Soc. Sc.*, **244**:159-166, Mar., 1946.

[16] The Army published an exceptionally fine presentation on "Leadership and the Negro Soldier," as Army Service Forces Manual, M-5, Oct., 1944. They went to the further extent of

problem in its organization and, at least on two occasions, solicited a psychiatric opinion about certain phases of it. Our seven Negro psychiatrists were of great assistance to us in helping understand the inherent problems. We cannot ignore the fact, however, that the Army life reflected the widespread prejudices and discriminations of civilian life.

When the facts about Negro characteristics, ability, and desires are checked against those which are credited to them, there are many, many discrepancies. There is no basis from a scientific standpoint that the capacities or the abilities of a Negro differentiate his capabilities from those of any other race. He wants most to have an opportunity to get, hold, and advance on the job for which he is capable and for which he is paid the prevailing wage. He wants a decent place in which to live, good schools for his children. These desires are a far cry from those attributed to him.

Most conspicuous in this neurosis is the fact that many of our white citizenry make no effort to discover the real desires of the Negro. They have been vividly presented and portrayed by numerous American Negroes, particularly Richard Wright, in *Native Son* and *Black Boy;* or Spencer Logan in *A Negro's Faith in America.* Nor will many persons permit themselves to examine objectively the findings of neutral observers like Gunnar Myrdal in *The American Dilemma;* or Horace Cayton and St. Clair Drake in *Black Metropolis.* Equally to be decried are those individuals, many of whom are in political or economic power, who give a lip service to the more enlightened point of view, knowing full well that as long as theirs remains merely lip service, they are defeating such progressive measures as are indicated.

In Springfield, Mass.,[17] the combined efforts of school and community have fostered understanding between people. Several states have laws against discrimination in employment, using different means of enforcement. A survey of currently operating programs to reduce tensions among groups indicated that many of our efforts are as yet untested, as to either scientific validity or effectiveness, and that many research projects are needed in this area.[18]

Nor do we Americans have only the critical problem concerning the Negro relationships. Other racial and religious minorities are subject to discrimination. Our hypocrisy was obvious in the mismanagement of our citizen Jap-

---

making a penetrating investigation of "Utilization of the Negro Manpower in the Post-war Army," a document known as the "Gillem Report," which was released through the Bureau of Public Relations, 4 March 1946. From December 1, 1941 through December 1, 1946, approximately 970,000 Negroes served in the Army; peak strength was 703,000 on July 31, 1945.

[17] "How Your Town Can Build Real Democracy," series of articles on the Springfield plan printed as a public service by the *Bridgeport Sunday Herald,* distributed by The League for Fair Play, Inc., 11 West 42nd St., New York 18.

[18] Williams, R. M., Jr., *The Reduction of Inter-group Tension: A Survey of Research on Problems of Ethnic, Racial and Religious Group Relations,* Social Science Research Council, New York, 1947.

anese-Americans. Fathers, sons, and brothers served our country with outstanding valor in the war,[19] at the same time that many of their relatives were segregated into prison camps.[20] Neither can we afford to play ostrich regarding the strong anti-Semitic feelings [21] that exist, which were and are continually stimulated by Fascist groups.

Were it only the Fascist groups that are agitating intolerance, for the moment at least we should have little cause for concern. The fact remains that there are many intelligent individuals whose emotional attitudes on these problems preclude them from making an honest, intellectual, or scientific evaluation. It is a problem of and for all America, not merely of the South or the North, the East or the West. Few of us share the unprejudiced attitude of the British or the French. We in the North feel we are more liberal toward the Negro. Perhaps we do have less Jim Crowism, and there is a minimal amount of segregation in our high schools and colleges. However, in my own Middle Western city the Negro (or the Mexican) is not permitted to stay in the two first-class hotels or to sit on the ground floor of the main theaters.

We should be disturbed that prejudice and discrimination are present in every community in America. There are always some underdogs whose position is not based on economic status. In many areas, Negroes are given less pay than a white man for the same job. Some employers will not hire Jews. Catholics are definitely discriminated against in some areas. These same unreasonable practices apply to residential areas, clubs, fraternities, on no basis except race or religion. Certainly we should be admitting displaced persons from Europe into America, and, yet, some selfish people whose parents or grandparents came from Europe are afraid we are going to be surfeited with "foreigners," "refugees," "dirty Jews," "cheap labor." Such illogical nonsense!

I could cite numerous examples in which the implication was that in some way or other the psychology of the Negro or the Jew or the Jap was presumed to be so different from ours that they did not understand ours and we didn't understand theirs.

It is idealistic to hope that all America will realistically face the racial and religious minority problem. However, if we are going to divert disaster, we must face it. Perhaps we can start by recognizing that we can't talk glibly about our belief in the brotherhood of man and at the same time treat a minority in our own communities so shabbily. We have to recognize the farce that is made

---

[19] There were approximately 360 Japanese-American officers, 27,226 enlisted men, and 81 WAC's who served in the Army between July 1, 1940, and January 31, 1946.

[20] This subject is well presented under the title of "The Japanese-American Run-a-round," in the *Demobilization Bulletin,* Vol. 3, p. 5, Feb., 1946, published by the General Board of Education, Methodist Church, 810 Broadway, Nashville 2, Tenn. This particular issue also has an excellent résumé on the controversial problem about the Negro soldier.

[21] Any serious student of this problem should read *Anti-Semitism, A Social Disease,* ed. by Ernst Simmel, International Universities Press, New York, 1946.

of democracy when we talk about "white supremacy." We can't claim psychological maturity when millions of us prevent millions of others from having equal privileges and rights and opportunities to live because we use them as scapegoats. We can only hope that at least an increasing percentage of intelligent Americans will recognize that prejudice only exists on an emotional basis. It is America's number-one social neurosis, and it vitally affects the mental health of millions of individual Americans.

Housing. We are confronted with an enormous psychological problem that is directly related to the shortage of a physical necessity, namely, housing. We learn the amazing fact that we should have constructed approximately 3,200,000 new living units by the end of 1947 in order to have a home—"be it ever so humble"—for every American family. When it is recalled that even in the most productive house-building year in our history, 1925, we put up only 937,000 homes, it is clear that a prolonged and prodigious effort is called for.[22] Over 1,000,000 families living with other families in crowded quarters were augmented by 2,900,000 married veterans needing homes and 560,000 nonveterans establishing new families, by December, 1946. The various problems which arise in setting up a new family, the reunion of a separated one, or just the maintenance of long-established home life are exaggerated and intensified when more than one family is sheltered in one home. Lack of privacy, limited space, restriction in freedom of activity become cumulative strains on all concerned.

Community programs are needed which support building and remodeling expansion to provide for more dwelling units; which provide areas for recreation and relaxation that, in a sense, extend the family living space; which provide a counseling service that gives opportunity for help to those needing relief from emotional tensions.

A major consideration should be the further development of low rent housing projects and slum clearance. The potential improvement of mental health through this move—at least in its contribution to happiness and fuller life—is beyond calculation.

Delinquency. Still another social ill of major importance to America is the increase in delinquency rates. Accurate data are not available.[23] The juvenile-

---

[22] Taken from *"Talk It Over"*—*"Wanted a Home,"* Series G-103, 1946, published by the National Institute of Social Relations, Inc., 1029 17th Street, N.W., Washington 6, D.C. *Time* Magazine, Sept. 29, 1947, p. 28, gave the figure of 2,764,000 married couples living with other families.

[23] Mrs. Marjorie Bell, Assistant Director of the National Probation Association, wrote me on August 9, 1946 as follows:

"Delinquency statistics are not only scarce but undependable and not comparable. I think it is a safe statement that we really have no clear picture of the extent or variations of delinquency in the United States. The juvenile court statistics compiled by the Children's Bureau do suggest trends but even these are not very reliable for positive statements. The complications are

court statistics indicated an increase of 67 per cent [24] from 1938, through 1945, but these figures only include the cases of alleged delinquency disposed of by juvenile courts. They, therefore, do not indicate the total amount of delinquent behavior, nor even the total number of cases handled by the courts, social agencies, police, and schools. They do clearly reveal a trend, which in part may be due to better detection but undoubtedly shows a marked increase in incidence of such behavior.

In a mimeographed statement [25] issued by the Federal Bureau of Investigation, attention was called to an increase in 1942 over 1941 of 55.7 per cent in arrests for girls under 21; arrests for drunkenness increased 39.9 per cent, for disorderly conduct 69.6 per cent, for prostitution and commercialized vice 64.8 per cent, and for other sex offenses 104.7 per cent. Among arrests of minor youths, those for assault increased 17.1 per cent, for rape 10.6 per cent, for disorderly conduct 26.2 per cent, and for drunkenness 30.3 per cent. In 1942, people under 21 years of age accounted for 15 per cent of all arrests for murder, 34 per cent of all arrests for robbery and larceny, and 50 per cent of all arrests for burglary.

The significance of these problems was discussed with unusual understanding by Mr. Austin H. MacCormick.

It is only natural that, whenever I think of mental hygiene, I think of the field of delinquency and crime, where I have seen the need of it so clearly. Mental hygiene can be one of our most effective instruments of crime prevention and crime control. Never was acceptance of that fact more needed than now.

Although we have as yet no post-war crime statistics comprehensive enough or well enough analyzed to warrant definite conclusions, it is probable we have already had a considerable increase in crime over the war years' rate. It is reasonable to assume that we shall have a further increase and that we may conceivably reach an unprecedented high in crime as we get deeper into the post-war period.

We should face that possibility with our eyes wide open. We should do our best to prevent the increase but be prepared for it—mentally and emotionally, especially. If it comes, we should deal with it sensibly, not hysterically. We must avoid the old error of the last post-war period, when we tried to control crime by senseless and sadistic legislation, piling heavy mandatory penalty on penalty. This

---

many. The first difficulty is that we are not even agreed on a definition of delinquency. Many cases classed as delinquency in one community are classed as neglect in another. Sometimes a court changes its classification categories and this also confuses the statistics. Another important factor in the variability of the figures is that some juvenile courts end their jurisdiction at sixteen, some at seventeen, some at eighteen. This raises the question what is a child or a juvenile? A third complicating factor is the lack of any statistical understanding in a great many juvenile courts. Many of the statistics issued in annual reports are what I call 'inspirational.' I have seen probation officers guessing at totals and putting them into a report without any actual count as a basis. We are amazingly backward along the line when it comes to figures."

[24] U.S. Department of Labor, Children's Bureau. Preliminary Statement, Juvenile-Court Statistics, 1945. Division of Statistical Research, Mar. 8, 1946.

[25] Juvenile Delinquency. Sent through courtesy of Mr. J. E. Hoover, June 21, 1946.

archaic method, running contradictory to all penal history, was ineffectual, and deserved to be. This time we must utilize all we have learned about why people commit crimes and what will cause them to stop.

Whatever increase in crime we have so far is quite natural. Several million men have been released from the armed forces. They are in the age group that produces most of the crime in normal times. It is plain arithmetic that there would probably be an increase in crime now even if employment and other conditions were stable.

But social and economic conditions are not stable. Not only are the ex-servicemen restless and, in many cases, reckless and unstable, but the world to which they have returned is also restless, reckless and unstable. Their ranks, moreover, are swelled by former workers in war industries, whose jobs and high pay have suddenly stopped. They add to the uncertainty and instability, to the social and economic maladjustment.

It is my own opinion, however, that the present increase in crime can be attributed largely to younger offenders, the 16-21 age group. Very few of them are veterans or displaced workers from war industries. This age group has always been responsible for a very large percentage of the major crimes. Today they are truly "displaced persons." Some of them were anxiously waiting to get into the armed services; now they will be merely kid brothers who didn't make it. Many of them had real jobs and were paid more money than they ever dreamed of making, in many cases more than they were worth. They were the first to lose their jobs when the squeeze came. Now, with their distorted sense of values, they will soon be back on the dole: relying on their folks or on errand boy jobs for spending money.

I think we shall find more souvenir guns in the hands of teen-age stickup men than in the hands of veterans. But whether or not the veterans themselves and the former war workers begin to swell the crime total alarmingly, and to what heights they will send the crime rate, will depend in large part on how soon we have stable employment and living conditions. It is not merely the job and the home that they need, but the stability and security they bring. These men need and want stability and they are not likely to find it until they have a real job in the kind of world they are waiting to come back to.

Jobs and homes are not the only answer, of course. Many veterans and workers and their families are badly maladjusted. Roots were wrenched out of familiar and friendly soil. Some of them will never grow back in again—anywhere. There were hasty war marriages and men who are temporarily, at least, not ready for quiet domesticity are trying to get on with wives who are practically strangers and babies who are wholly so. With no civilian clothes in the stores, no homes for rent, and the employment situation chaotic, only the most stable young couples would find it easy to avoid demoralization and maladjustment. Veterans' and war workers' families are going to need guidance and help from mental hygiene specialists if they are to survive this period.

The statement one so often hears that crime and delinquency would be solved if the family would only accept its responsibility is far from the truth. It is true that many families are indifferent to their responsibilities, and that some are cruel. During the war children were found chained to the wheels of trailers while the parents were drinking down their wages in the bars and grills. But some families produce almost insuperable problems, not willfully but because there is conflict, maladjustment, unhappiness and insecurity in the home. The chief trouble is that so many families do not know how to deal with their problems. They are ignorant, bewildered, and confused rather than neglectful and indifferent. It is not enough to challenge them with their responsibility. We must try to teach them how to meet it and give them guidance and help as long as they need it.[26]

Constructive community forces. Despite the fact that its main mission was to fight and win the war, the Army tried hard to cope with its social problems. Any community seeking help from the war experience would find two basic assumptions which the Army used in handling these problems: those most important elements in the solution of social ills were competent leadership and planning, and individual participation and assumption of responsibility in carrying out the plan.

Of great value in interpreting men's motives to themselves and sometimes to their company mates or officers, were the Mental Hygiene Consultation Services which have been mentioned previously and described in Chapter 17. Surely the counterpart of this service in the community could reduce economic loss, individual unhappiness, and symptoms of social illness among civilians. Its resources and findings could be the means of locating and treating festering sores of community ill health by treating individuals most seriously affected by them.

The community can utilize other forces within its structure that were not available in the Army except in an attenuated form. Every community of any size has certain social agencies and civic clubs. Too often these are un-co-ordinated or their maximum efficiency is impaired with petty jealousy of donors or functions or domain. This unfortunate state of affairs was again brought to light in the attempts to develop community veteran centers. But such power could be harnessed and co-ordinated. The church is one of the pillars of every community, and more and more of its leaders are directing their efforts toward the satisfaction of social needs as well as in being spiritual guides. There are numerous character building agencies—the Y.M.C.A., Y.W.C.A., Boy Scouts, Girl Scouts, Campfire Girls, 4-H Clubs, and others—that have fortunately spread to many hamlets and villages. All of these could be far more effective in constructive efforts were they given the support and active participation of more citizens of the community.

Communities are beginning to think in terms of responsibility for solutions of social problems regarding the entire population rather than just the poor, the sick, the handicapped, or the unemployed. For this they need a

---

26 Remarks made at Annual Luncheon of the Child Study Association, Mar. 4, 1946, by Austin MacCormick, Executive Director of the Osborne Association and consultant to the Secretary of War on Military Justice. Mr. MacCormick had not written these remarks. At my request, he did write them. His extensive experience and knowledge carry great weight in the fields of delinquency and criminology.

clearing house of social information and a means of co-ordinating and pub-
licizing local programs of various types. A recruiting, training, and assignment service for volunteer workers would increase the man-power resources
for leadership in the community.

Recreation. In the years between the two world wars there was an increasing awareness of the need for and the means of providing recreative activities
for people of all ages. The shorter work week, the greater earning power, the
crowded housing of urban areas brought home the fact that too many people
do not know how to play. Play and creative experience give emotional release
and spiritual recharge for the psychological dynamo that must function
through a work week. Even those who know what sort of recreative experience they most enjoy are too often limited in their activity by shortage of
housing space, transportation, and lack of stimulation, which make such
recreation too difficult to procure.

The men in the military service were given the all-out efforts of the War
Department, the United Service Organization, the Red Cross, and of many
communities to make their free time pleasant in a wholesome way. It is too
bad that they came home to nothing more than taverns and beer halls. They
needed and still need the support of the knowledge that the community is
glad to help them supply their needs—not the least of which are the facilities
for satisfying and wholesome leisure-time activity.

The community should take the initiative in co-ordinating the recreational
activities within its area. It should supplement existing facilities and programs
to the extent necessary to supply unmet needs of its people. It should recruit
dynamic leadership and raise necessary funds. A growing number of cities
have established municipally financed programs with a small paid staff and
volunteer advisory boards and workers. In other places the organizations
which would be concerned in such a program set up co-ordinating committees, either through the Councils of Social Agencies or other community
councils.

The goal should encompass the interests of young and old, male and female, regardless of race, creed, color, or economic or educational status. The
strong emphasis should be on participation rather than observation, on introduction to new crafts, hobbies, and games as well as increasing skill in a
favorite pastime. Teachers and leaders will emerge from those who know
their chosen field well and who learn to feel comfortable in the role by first
demonstrating to a few. The program can be as varied as the interest of individuals willing and eager to participate. The budget can be small or large
depending upon the resources and demands of the community. Where dollars
are fewer, individual investment of effort will need to be greater which,

curiously, will result in increased satisfaction to the individuals concerned.

Where more money and effort is invested in community recreation, less will be needed for counteracting asocial behavior.[27] Some individuals will never lose their urge for delinquent behavior, but most will not find time or energy to get into trouble if there is something else to do that is more fun and brings them more social approval. The greater number of people who use the facilities will be happier and mentally more healthy by virtue of that experience. The National Recreation Association [28] will advise and aid a community in its efforts to expand or initiate a really adequate recreational program.

Medical care. The medical profession is one of the strong constructive forces in the community. Upon it depends the maintenance of mental as well as physical health. However, all is not too well with the methods of the practice of medicine. Much of the agitation at the moment, stimulated by the health bills before Congress, is an indication of the dissatisfaction on the part of both the doctors and the public.

The indisputable fact is that everyone does not receive adequate medical care: in too many instances one receives it only if he can pay for it. According to the findings of a Committee on the Cost of Medical Care,[29] in families with an income under $1,200, only 53 per cent of their members received medical care during the survey year; whereas, in families with an income of $10,000 or over, 86 per cent of the members received care.

The distribution of doctors is uneven: [30] 29 per cent of the population in cities of 100,000 and over are attended by 44 per cent of the physicians in the country, whose income consists of 54 per cent of that received by all physicians; 48 per cent of the population in communities under 5,000 have only 30 per cent of the physicians, and these doctors received only 18 per cent of the total income which is received by all doctors. In 1944, there were 81 counties in the United States without a single practicing physician. There was one physician to every 597 persons in New York State compared to one for every 1,784 people in Mississippi. Numerically, the distribution of psychiatrists is a little more even, though nearly one-fourth of all psychiatrists (962) are located in New York State. Another 500 are about equally divided be-

[27] Burgess, E. W., *Delinquency or Recreation. Delinquency and the Community in War Time,* National Probation Association, 1790 Broadway, New York 19, 1943, pp. 138-148.

[28] The National Recreation Association, 315 Fourth Avenue, New York, also has printed material available: "Fundamentals in Community Recreation"; "19 Recreation Principles"; "Publications on Play and Recreation."

[29] *Medical Care for the American People,* the final report of the Committee on the Cost of Medical Care, University of Chicago Press, Chicago, 1930, p. 9.

[30] Senate Committee Print No. 4. National Health Act of 1945. "Need for Medical Care Insurance," a memorandum prepared by Bureau of Research and Statistics, Social Security Board. Mar., 1946, p. 5.

tween Massachusetts and Pennsylvania. Because of the state-hospital system every state does have some psychiatrists, though there are many with less than 10.

Perhaps the spotty distribution of psychiatrists is not as serious, since the average physician is presumed to be able to take care of the minor emotional disorders. However, medical care for mental illness is inadequate, since most physicians have not had training in psychosomatic medicine.

Although there are state hospitals in every state, these are very inadequate. On the whole they are a disgrace to psychiatry, to medicine, and to America. The average cost of a patient in a general hospital is about $8.50 a day; in a state hospital it runs $1.22 a day.[31] In 1942, the cost of food in state hospitals averaged 22 cents per patient per day. In 1944, there was an average of only 1 physician to 305 patients and 1 graduate nurse for 158 patients. It was estimated [32] that in 1941, state hospitals had an over-all shortage of employees of 42 per cent. In physicians they were short 74 per cent of their needs; of graduate nurses, 78.8 per cent; of clinical psychologists, 91.9 per cent; of social workers, 70.8 per cent. These figures explain the lack of proper care in state hospitals, to say nothing about the absence of a treatment program.

The experience in the war indicated clearly that as a result of these gross inadequacies America isn't as healthy as it ought to be. The Federal Security Agency reported that about half of the 16,000,000 youths examined for the draft had physical or mental defects. This group "consisted of five million rejectees, a million and a half men with rejectable defects who were inducted into the Armed Forces and rehabilitated, and an additional million and a half who were inducted that had to be discharged for physical and mental defects not acquired in the Service." [30] Therefore, the problem of supplying sufficient medical care to our populace is a very vital and fundamental one.

The question of *how* to supply good medical care to the entire population is a moot question. Momentarily it is being given intensive consideration in many quarters. In November, 1945, President Truman asked Congress for legislation on national health. This was followed by submission to Congress of the Wagner-Murray-Dingell bill which proposed a national compulsory health insurance. In 1946, Senator Robert A. Taft introduced a substitute bill which would provide medical and dental care for "all families unable to pay for

---

31 Current Population Reports. Mental Institutions. Bureau of the Census. Series P-85, No. 17, Sept. 10, 1947.
32 Felix, R. H., "Mental Public Health: A Plan of National Scope," Annual Meeting, Mass. Soc. for Mental Hygiene, Jan. 24, 1946. Reports from 184 State Hospitals in 1945 showed 13 states to have no clinical psychologists; 5 have only one; 11 states reported no social workers and 10 had only one. See Report on Normal Capacity, Administrative Staff and Expenditure of State Hospitals for Mental Disease, 1945, Bureau of Census, Series MP, No. 13, Apr. 3, 1947.

such services." The organized medical profession through the American Medical Association has long argued for a voluntary insurance plan.

In an excellent résumé of the entire problem, Peters summarized the situation as follows:

To proposals to increase existing government aid for public services, including those for maternal and child health, there has been little opposition. The supporters of federal legislation, such as the Wagner-Murray-Dingell bill, however, go further in contending that compulsory insurance, provided for out of social security deductions or ear-marked income taxes, is the only means of spreading the risk and of extending medical care to the greatest part of the population. Justifiably or not, they feel that the government is obligated to protect the nation from ill health. The medical profession is equally adamant in its belief that "fee-for-service" private practice, supplemented by American Medical Association-approved, voluntary, non-profit, prepayment plans and government aid in public health services, is the only workable solution to the problem of extending medical care.[33]

In his compilation, Peters has collected much data on both sides of the question which is well worth careful study.

Many of us in medicine look with qualms on a system in which all doctors would become government employees.[34] On the other hand, many physicians have done little serious thinking about the problem, and too many have sought little or no information beyond that supplied through medical journals. Some

[33] *Free Medical Care,* compiled by C. A. Peters, Reference Shelf, Vol. 19, No. 3, reprinted by courtesy of The H. W. Wilson Company, New York, 1946, p. 4. See also *The Cost of Medical Care,* a study of costs in the families of the field employees of the Metropolitan Life Insurance Company, by D. B. Armstrong, L. I. Dublin, and E. J. Steele. Published by The Metropolitan Life Insurance Company, New York (no date given).

[34] One concern of the doctors regarding "state medicine" is, justifiably, their own salaries. Many persons do not know that the doctor's education costs about $15,000 after he graduates from an academic college, and requires a minimum of 10 years of training following high school. The average gross incomes of full specialists, by specialty * are as follows:

Type of practice	1935	1939	1943
All physicians	$ 6,139	$ 7,365	$14,341
Full specialists	8,446	10,057	18,367
Obstetrics-gynecology	8,158	9,273	22,219
Surgery	10,149	12,161	20,733
Roentgenology	12,128	13,534	20,358
Pediatrics	6,638	8,018	20,044
OALR	7,747	11,310	19,180
ALR	7,645	9,879	17,538
Urology	7,143	9,299	17,488
Dermatology	7,774	8,919	15,641
Ophthalmology	8,234	11,089	15,547
Internal Medicine	8,947	10,655	15,046
Neuropsychiatry	8,076	7,451	9,921

* "Average Gross Income of Full Specialists by 'Specialty.'" Reprinted from *Medical Economics,* by special permission. 23:57, Jan., 1946. Copyright by Medical Economics, Inc., Rutherford, N. J.

of us believe that, at least until recently, we physicians have been insufficiently constructive in our criticism of the various plans proposed. Most of us who served in the Army were delighted to return to civilian practice and our own "free enterprises," to be free of regimented government practice. Many psychiatrists have a healthy skepticism of government-controlled medicine because of first-hand knowledge of the sorry plight of the state hospitals.

Then, too, the government as yet, although participating in an extensive medical practice, has given evidence of too little concern about overlapping of effort. It runs the medical departments in the Army, the Navy, the Veterans Administration, and the Public Health Service. During the war there was some co-operation between the Army and the Navy, but much duplication in hospital facilities.[35] These four agencies have entirely separate medical organizations. Were it possible to combine them, or at least to unite certain common functions, there would be much saving of personnel, money, and facilities. Also there would undoubtedly be much more operational efficiency, better training facilities, and treatment. For example, in Washington, D. C., the Veterans Administration runs Mount Alto Hospital, the Army has Walter Reed, the Navy operates the Bethesda Medical Center, and Social Security supervises St. Elizabeth's. There is no functional relation between any of these or their downtown clinics or dispensaries. Could they be combined, exchanging patients and personnel, they could provide far better specialty treatment centers and much richer training programs and at the same time economize in personnel which is desperately needed elsewhere.

Whatever system of medical care may evolve, consideration of the broad aspects of mental health should be a primary concern. The feelings, motivation, and attitudes of the physicians can make or break a health program. If they cannot be shown the advantages and wholeheartedly accept it, any plan is damned. Of equal importance are the feelings, motivation, and attitudes of the patients. The only workable plan would provide a positive assurance to every person that he could obtain good medical attention, where and when he needed it. Probably few events in the life of an individual are so likely to produce anxiety as are illness, disease, and accidents. Therefore the type of national health program finally adopted is of prime significance to the morale of our people.

Psychiatric clinics. Adequate provision for psychiatric treatment is impossible at the present. Even before the war when there was far more prejudice against consulting a psychiatrist, there were too few private practitioners or clinics to meet the need. The growth in understanding of the help to be

---

[35] An excellent and clear presentation of this problem, with illustrative examples, was read into the *Congressional Record* by Senator E. Thomas, "Medicine and Hospitalization," Vol. 93, No. 49, Mar. 14, 1947.

gained from psychiatric consultation or treatment has greatly increased this need.

According to the annual report of the National Committee for Mental Hygiene, only 50,000 boys and girls could get help from child-guidance clinics, although between 250,000 and 400,000 teen-agers passed through our juvenile courts. Quoting from the report, "The fact is that instead of less than 400 child guidance clinics, most of them working part time, America needs at least 1400 full time community clinics."

Furthermore it is pointed out that many patients now in state hospitals could be given necessary treatment and supervision from an outpatient clinic. On the basis of a study in one state, it is estimated that, for the country as a whole, approximately 70,000 beds in state hospitals could be released if the clinics were available. "If each outpatient clinic prevented the commitment either of one veteran-with-a-service-connected-disability or five civilians a year, more than the estimated average cost of operating a clinic ($32,000 per year) would be saved."

Quoting further on this point from the National Committee report, "There should be at least one mental hygiene clinic for each 100,000 of the population, but this goal is not even on the horizon today on account of the shortage of psychiatrists. Even if we limit ourselves, as for the time being we must, to the goal of one clinic for each 500,000, we must work for the establishment of a hundred more clinics than there are today." [36]

While the National Committee for Mental Hygiene has long been an activator for community clinics, their development in a community is the responsibility of that community. The community leaders who have the vision of the need must aggressively plan for the establishment of such a clinic. Only when one of these can function with adequate staff can any area or group or community assume that they have provided the minimal service for the mental health needs of their constituency.

Welfare. Our communities suffer an unknown emotional expense in the toll paid to poverty, physical and mental handicaps, and other types of underprivilege. One of the great characteristics of the American community is its generosity—a powerful community force for richer life. In times past this has taken the form of charity, a doing for others, which often helps the self-esteem of the doer more than that of the done-for. More recently it has been translated into welfare activity that is governed by the needs of the individuals to be helped, regardless of the source of the assistance. Sometimes the aid is given in dollars, sometimes in an opportunity for training or employment, sometimes in treatment of psychological or physical ills. Moreover, so-called

---

[36] Annual Report, National Committee for Mental Hygiene, Inc., 1790 Broadway, New York 19, 1946, p. 16.

"welfare" services now are being made available not only to those who cannot afford to pay for them but to any who will benefit from them.

Short of a Utopia, there will always be individuals who are economically handicapped, whether permanently or because of an emergency. There will be others who will always be inadequate or incompetent. They will require the assistance of a public or private agency. Until we as a nation are far more emotionally mature, we will have a considerable number of "underprivileged" men, women, and children. They will need and should receive our thoughtful consideration and our generosity in order that they, too, may have at least a minimum of security and satisfaction and mental health.

Assistance for the physically and emotionally handicapped civilian, who has been called "the forgotten casualty," [37] is a great community responsibility. It has been estimated, on the basis of partial surveys, that there are approximately 10,000,000 physically disabled persons.[38] We can be sure that a great majority of these have emotional problems associated with their physical handicap. Dr. Howard Rusk developed a remarkable system of rehabilitation for the Air Forces Surgeon during the war. Since then, he has championed such a program for all types of casualties. He has pointed out that there were eight times as many amputations in civilians during the period of the war years as occurred in the Army. He challengingly asked, "What becomes of the three hundred and fifty thousand persons who are permanently disabled each year as a result of accidents alone? What opportunities are there for the two million Americans of working age whose physical impairments prevent them from working? The answer is there are few, very few." [37]

A major aspect of physical rehabilitation is the personality readjustment. When Doctor Rusk started the convalescent hospitals in the Air Forces, it was presumed that the chief job was a rehabilitation of a physical function. As time went on, in these hospitals as well as the Army Service Forces Hospitals, psychiatric aspects of the job assumed primary importance. Psychiatry came to play a leading role in every one of these hospitals. Why cannot the community develop similar opportunities on the basis of our experience, lessons, and techniques that were learned so expensively in wartime?

Summary. One can give of time or money to his community. He can be a leader or a worker. Social problems will decrease in proportion to the money and the effort invested in aiding the residents of any community to become more healthy and happy, better housed, and suitably employed. A policy of

37 Rusk, H. A., "The Forgotten Casualty: The Disabled Civilian," *New York Times Magazine,* May 12, 1946.
38 McFarland, R. A., "Physically Handicapped Workers: I. Experience in War Industries. II. Rehabilitation of Veterans," *Harvard Business Review,* 23: Part I, pp. 8-31, Oct., 1944. This subject has also been well covered by M. J. Shortley, "Rehabilitation of the Civilian Disabled," *Ann. Am. Acad. Polit. and Soc. Sc.,* 239:101-108, May, 1945.

isolationism avoids reality and is mentally unhealthy—whether in the form of aloofness to neighbors on the other side of the tracks, in the antagonism between the North and the South, or in the tendency of our nation to withdraw from the rest of the world. The whole can be only as mentally healthy as the parts. We have fought all of our wars for this principle. Should we not fight to clean up and make wholesome our own back yard?

28

DEFECTS REVEALED IN CIVILIAN MEDICINE

IN THE COURSE of the war, 47,000 doctors served in the Army—approximately one-third of the practicing physicians in the United States. They spent from 2 to 5 years in a special social situation, a military one, at times working under most difficult circumstances but always attempting to apply an old skill in a very new (to them) environment.

Excluding the scientific progress which has been well summarized by Perrin Long,[1] did they—did we—learn any lessons that we could apply to the civilian practice of medicine? The true answer to such a question could be arrived at only by canvasing the opinion of a large number of medical officers who had given the matter much thought. The ideas of any one individual are necessarily colored by his own experience and undoubtedly biased by his background and the specialty or job in which he practiced. However, it seems practical to point out some facts and factors about physicians and the practice of medicine that manifested themselves as weaknesses in the military setting, as seen from one psychiatrist's point of view.

Lack of integration.[2] There were three aspects of a lack of integration in relation to medicine: first, the separation of military and civilian medicine; second, the subservient position of the Medical Corps within the Army; and third, the aloofness of doctors from the community.

The first of these, the lack of integration of military and civilian medicine, was obvious too often. The doctors of America came into the Army as individuals. Regular Army officers of the Medical Corps and the line organization told them what to do and how and when to do it. Only as time passed was their own voice heard. Until the AUS physicians (the volunteers) from civilian life had articulate representatives in places of authority in

---

[1] Long, P., "Medical Progress and Medical Education During the War," *J.A.M.A.*, 130:983-990, Apr. 13, 1946.

[2] Doctor Edward Churchill, Professor of Surgery of Harvard and Chief Consultant in Surgery to the Mediterranean Theater made a suggestive remark in his lecture to the American College of Surgeons at Cleveland, December 16, 1946, describing the status of American medicine at the beginning of the war, "Poorly integrated but highly developed specialism in remedial medicine." Churchill, E. D., "The American Surgeon, A.U.S.," *Surg., Gynec., & Obst.*, 84:529-539, Apr. 15, 1947.

the Army, as consultants in the office of the Surgeon General and the Service Commands and the theaters, they were to some degree "kicked around," to use the Army jargon.

Whatever may be the causes, organized medicine had no plans and assumed no responsibility for military medicine prior to the war. Civilian medical organizations had never concerned themselves with the method or plan or practice of military medicine.[3] This may have been due to the fact that, for reasons unknown, the Medical Corps had never solicited civilian help or advice in an organized fashion.

The second lack of integration, between the Medical Corps and the Army as a whole, was apparent to many of us in the Army. The leaders within the Army Medical Corps had little voice in planning for the care of the casualties of a campaign.[4] It seemed to us that the physician in the Army did not receive authority commensurate with his responsibility.

Unfortunately, in many areas of the Army this attitude still persists. Doctor Churchill, who served as chairman of the Medical Advisory Committee to the Secretary of War, commented on a relatively recent document from one of the major forces. In discussing the status and function of the Surgeon General, it proposed a policy "whereby the technical services (*including the medical department*) will exist solely to serve the needs of combatant forces without the power or authority to dictate policy or to influence operations by imposing the will of the technical representatives upon the will of that combat commander." Doctor Churchill commented on this proposal in the following: "The profession harbors no ambition to 'impose its will' on a commander or to 'influence operations' that, in his judgment, are essential to the common defense. Disease, not the doctor, imposes its will on the commander; man's physiologic capacities limit and influence operations. These are the decimating forces that can dictate policy to the commander. It is both the concern and the responsibility of the Army Medical Department that this shall not happen." [5]

The third lack of integration, between doctors and the community, existed prior to, during, and since the war. The devotion of individual physicians to their work has made them, as Lord Dawson [6] pointed out, a somewhat cloistered class. They have left to the layman the making of policies, many of which create health problems and illness. They have also left to the

---

[3] Since the war, the American Medical Association has had a committee which is surveying, through questionnaires, the experience and suggestions of doctors both in and out of the military service. The first report of the questionnaires from physicians who remained in civilian life was published in "Physicians During World War II," *J.A.M.A.,* **134**:369-374, May 24, 1947.
[4] This is discussed at some length in Chap. 34.
[5] Churchill, E. D., *op. cit.*
[6] "Lord Dawson of Penn: Medicine and Statesmanship," *Atlantic Monthly,* **147**:206-210, Feb., 1931.

layman the correction of grossly unhealthy practices. In the local community, in the state and national governments, the particular knowledge of the physician should be contributed toward planning which affects the health of the people. The practice in the Army emphasized this point: The physician had to *learn* to take into account the sole and particular purpose of the entire military organization. He became very conscious of environmental and occupational factors in illness when he had to judge the degree of his patient's recovery in terms of how that patient could function in his job and contribute to the fulfillment of that mission.

Most physicians in civilian practice have not bothered themselves about social problems, even those wholly related to patient welfare. Fortunately, there is an awakening in this direction. In part this is due to social legislation which threatens the physicians themselves. For example, recently the president of my County Medical Society addressed himself as follows to the members of our society: "Doctors must join together and help the organization handle the many urgent problems at hand. In the zeal to increase individual acumen we have neglected the collateral aspects of the practice of medicine. Our society meetings have been altogether scientific, and important social and economic phases of medicine have been ignored. Now serious charges of malfeasance are made against us, some of which are true." [7]

Sir Alexander Hood,[8] the Director General of the Army Medical Services of the British Army, made an eloquent appeal for a broader point of view of physicians toward social issues. In his Harvey lecture on what he called "total medicine," he indicated that within the community the authentic voice of medicine must be audible and clearly heard above any political or other clamor. To do so, however, will necessitate that the community surrender certain freedom to the doctors, and that the doctors, on the other hand, must surrender certain freedom to the community. It is encouraging to know that a few far-seeing medical schools have organized chairs in social medicine. Psychiatrists, more than other medical specialists, became cognizant of the effect of personal relations and the environment of the soldier on the illness that he developed.

Medicine evidently needs to be better integrated in various ways. It needs articulate representation of a united front in the high councils of authority, both civilian and military, if it is to be able to make the most of the specific skills of its practitioners.

High specialization. American medicine, for better or for worse, has become highly specialized, although the general practitioners are still and should always be in the majority. Some specialization is necessary since the fund of

---

[7] Walker, W. J., *Bull. Shawnee County (Kansas) Med. Soc.,* 8:1-2, May 1, 1946.
[8] Hood, A., "Total Medicine; Harveian Lecture," *Lancet,* 1:711-715, June 9, 1945.

medical knowledge and the number of essential skills are far too great for any one man to accumulate and utilize.

The Army, however, prior to the war allowed only a very limited degree of specialization. As a consequence, when civilian doctors first began coming into the Army, there were many, many instances in which they were not used in their specialty role. Due to the insight and judgment of the Surgeon General and his advisors, the rapidly developing wartime Medical Corps went all out for specialization. In so far as possible, specialists were eventually assigned to practice in their own fields.

Among the disadvantages in the American system of specialization is the tendency of an individual in one specialty to be entirely unacquainted with those in other specialties. Perhaps we in psychiatry are especially sensitive to this fact. Many specialists have reached the place where, because of the number of medical societies, we rarely attend meetings of other than our own specialized organizations. We tend to take little or no interest in any other medical specialty or in the progress of medicine as a whole. Unfortunately, some physicians even appear to be proud of their ignorance of fields other than their own. This seemed to be especially true in the attitude of many physicians toward psychiatry. It was the more distressing because of the conviction of psychiatrists, as well as of some of our outstanding internists and surgeons, that every physician should understand the psychological as well as the chemical and the anatomical factors in illness.

The complete absorption of the physician's interest and energy by the practice of either general or specialized medicine has led to the elimination of other interests from his life.

Limitation to the practice of remedial medicine. The American physician's prewar interest was limited very largely to curative medicine. In the Army, of necessity, every practitioner of medicine not only had the job of treatment but was likely to be used in the selection process, in screening, planning, and administration. He had to be concerned with the prevention of ill health and the maintenance of good health. For almost everyone this included concern with regard to morale. For many of these responsibilities, our doctors were not prepared.

Particularly was this true for the prevention of ill health, both physical and mental. The average physician lacked experience and interest in this field. In most communities this responsibility is left almost entirely to the state or local health officers, only rarely being assumed by the average practitioner. Laymen usually have to persuade the doctors to participate in the establishment of a needed clinic. Civilian Defense Councils often had great trouble gaining medical support in emergency planning during the war. Physicians have not taken sufficient initiative in making their experience available to the community other than through their practices. In so far as psychiatry was concerned in the Army, prevention was the greatest need and the subject about which we knew least. The problem was not quite so acute in the field of general medicine because of the highly developed preventive medicine division whose civilian counterpart is the Public Health Service.

Unfortunately the War Department did not seem to realize the contribution that medical men could make in the planning, organizing, and administration of almost every phase of a field campaign. One of the most important aspects of this was the prevention of man-power loss through disease and personality disorders. The maintenance of good morale proved to be an especially potent preventive measure. Because the average physician's chief interest had been limited to curative medicine, there were only a few doctors who were competent to participate in this way. Unfortunately, not many were even asked to do so.

Selection of doctors. In the melting pot of the Army, where men of all backgrounds and vocations were forced into the same regimented organization, it was of special interest to see how the doctors fitted into that situation. Not only did the doctor enter as an individual, he entered as an individualist. He had always been his own boss. His life in the Army was difficult because not only was he prevented from practicing medicine in his own way but he usually had several bosses, some of them nonmedical men. Under military discipline, they could and did tell him "what" and "how" and "when." Having as his superior another doctor sometimes made life even more difficult, if that superior were of a differing school of medical thought.

It may be significant either of the inadequacy of the methods of selection for entrance into medical schools [9] or the philosophy of being a physician that doctors, taken as a group, are not too well adjusted. In our hospital in Topeka, for instance, with a maximum of 55 beds, we have repeatedly been impressed with the high percentage of patients who were either physicians or from the families of physicians. On two occasions, we have had six physicians at one time as hospital patients. Another most vivid evidence of this was the apparent fact that the discharge rate for neuropsychiatric disability was higher for officers in the Medical Corps than in any other corps in the Army.

A correlated observation of many of us was that there were far too many very mediocre physicians. Their knowledge, their attitude, their approach and understanding of patients were poor. Strong evidence that even strict medical-school entrance requirements have not insured excellency in performance!

---

[9] There is no available survey of methods of selection of medical students. A study recently reported from the University of Michigan described their system. Waggoner, R. W., and Zeigler, T. W., "Psychiatric Factors in Medical Students Who Fail," *Am. J. Psychiat.*, 103:369-376, Nov., 1946. An elaborate method of selection of graduate students for psychiatry and psychology is being used currently in the respective schools in the Menninger Foundation.

Attitudes of the doctor. Perhaps it is the role of magician which is attributed to them that distorts the approach of some physicians toward their patients. This has been encouraged by the great increase in technical knowledge which often produces dramatic effects. The doctor-patient relationship in the office or hospital is more conducive to this attitude than the intimate home relationships of days gone by. Before the days of specialization, the general practitioner was often a close friend of his patient. In many ways he was also a good psychiatrist. He did not know it and might not have admitted it, but he took the time and used the techniques of the psychiatrist when he acted as the family advisor. As we have become specialists, we have lost the art of listening to our patients, of learning their personal opinions and problems, and knowing about their families and businesses. Carl Binger pointed this out so clearly in his recent prize-winning book [10] that every physician would profit by its reading.

Too often in the Army we saw instances where the doctor, with an unconscious, smug complacency, falsely based on his highly specialized training and experience, was inclined to ignore what the patient said or thought. Some even brusquely stated that they were not interested in the patient's explanation; that they made a diagnosis solely on an examination. Unfortunately, the total examination of such a physician was limited to the physical findings about his patient, whereas we know now, with certainty, that even in an illness where physical symptoms are most obvious, they present only a part of the total clinical picture.

Goodpasture suggested that doctors have lost stature in the eyes of the public in another way.[11] In this industrial age the physician's authority is limited because of four major developments. First, public health doctors carry out many of the preventive measures—water purification, sanitation, food protection; second, industrial hazards are, in general, no longer the responsibility of the private practitioner; third, our increasing knowledge of chemistry, physics, physiology, pathology, bacteriology has made the physician very dependent on many other individuals to help him in what he decides about or does for his patient; and finally, the limitation of practice to hospital and office has greatly reduced his knowledge of the social aspects of disease.

Social medicine. For several years there has been increasing agitation over proposed legislation for socialized medicine, a system whereby medical service would be provided for everyone and regulated by the government. Most doctors strongly object to such a plan, and "organized" medicine has combated such legislation vigorously. But most thoughtful physicians know that, despite our convictions about the grave dangers inherent in state medi-

---

[10] Binger, Carl, *The Doctor's Job,* W. W. Norton & Company, Inc., New York, 1945.
[11] Goodpasture, E. W., "Research and Medical Practice," *Science,* 104:473-476, Nov. 22, 1946.

cine, our present system does not provide persons of all economic levels with the "best of medical care."

Medical men have watched the development of state medicine in other countries and seen its disadvantages. Many of us had some firsthand experience with it in the Army. Military medicine was a breed of socialized medicine. The average medical officer had from 2 to 5 years of regulated medical practice.

If he was objective, he could see some advantages. He was sure of his income, even if it was small. He found no competitive rivalries, nor need he fear that he was going to lose monetary gain if he lost his patient to another physician. He had the use of the best of diagnostic equipment and facilities. He never had to modify his diagnostic or treatment procedures because of their cost to his patient. Every soldier received equally excellent medical attention (except for the minority of inadequate doctors and unavoidable limitations on available facilities). There was no distinction in economic levels (except that officer patients usually received a little special consideration where it could be provided). Consultations were easily available in every specialty, and without extra cost to the patient, and were of great convenience to the physician in charge.

But with all of these advantages—assuming they *might* be present in government control of medicine—there were many disadvantages. Most of us felt these far outweighed the advantages. It was the rare doctor who did not look forward to his return to his "free enterprise" of civilian practice. Our greatest objection was the physician's lack of authority. Sometimes this was due to the necessary subservience to the line officers (laymen); often it was the unhappy result of having to serve under a stupid or incompetent medical officer. There was a rigidity which allowed little or no free choice of initial assignment or of change to another type of job even within the same unit. Always there was a sense of insecurity. We had bosses who rated us—made life pleasant and tolerable or unpleasant and intolerable, as they chose or were capable. We never knew when we might be transferred or reassigned, depending on theirs or others' wishes—at least not our own.

More serious was the handicap to the patient. Even with the best of facilities, he never had a choice of physician or treatment. He had to accept the doctor to whom he was assigned, even though he had no confidence in or liking for the physician. There were too many doctors who did not like their jobs and took it out on their patients, sometimes sadistically, sometimes by neglect, sometimes by poor medical practice. Individual attention very often was minimal. A surprising number of doctors fell quickly into the habit of arriving at 7:59 A.M. and leaving sharply at 4:30 P.M. Too many became clock punchers if their work permitted it. They were working for the government!

Their Army experience will not influence many doctors to be any more favorable to state-controlled medicine. But the thoughtful ones will recognize their greater responsibility to develop a system which does have the advantages of state medicine, but which they themselves will initiate and operate. One of the trends is likely to be toward group practice, which was one of the delightful aspects of Army medical practice.

PSYCHIATRY IN RELATION TO MEDICINE

"The greatest unpleasant surprise of the war for medical men was the importance of psychiatry and psychology. And yet so inconstant, evasive, or preoccupied are the majority of men that this greatest lesson can be disputed, evaded, and soon forgotten." [12] These words of Alan Gregg well introduce a point regarding the defects revealed in civilian medicine.

Although no specialist is in a position to be critical of the methods of other specialties, one does become aware of the blind spots in the relationships between those specialties and his own. The outstanding question to most Army (and many other) psychiatrists is, "When will practitioners in the field of general medicine accept the obvious role of the emotional factor in human illness?" This was the most important single cause of the heavy loss of military man power: 38 per cent of all rejections and 37 per cent [13] of all medical discharges occurred because of neuropsychiatric illness. We know this because in the Army we kept a record of the causes of ill health which could be reviewed and analyzed easily to learn the story they told. Because its organization was standardized, statistics were available that could never be obtained in civilian life.

What was true of military medicine is probably true about civilian medicine. It therefore seems difficult to understand why more physicians have not been sufficiently impressed with the significance of the role of the emotions in all disease.

By tradition in its practice and teaching, medicine has for too long emphasized the soma, the body, to the exclusion of consideration of the way the person in that body feels and thinks and behaves. Historically, the "person" within the body belonged to the realm of the church or philosophy. Medicine, proud of its knowledge of the soma, was all too willing to relegate the beliefs and feelings to other disciplines. As a consequence, the emphasis in training in medical schools has been on the anatomy, the physiology, the

---

[12] Gregg, A., "Lessons to Learn. Psychiatry in World War II," *Am. J. Psychiat.*, 104:217-220, Oct., 1947; see also *Bull. Menninger Clin.*, 12:26-30, Jan., 1948.
[13] Figures from Medical Statistics Division, Office of Surgeon General, Dec. 11, 1946.

chemistry, and the pathology of the body, with a minimal discussion of the psychological forces and their relation to the structure and functioning of the body organs. It is the exceptional medical school where the student even now is taught the relationship between body organs and their functions and the emotions, as seen in patients on the medical and surgical wards.

Medicine only recently has begun to accept the inclusion of emotional illnesses or character disorders in its domain. If, incidentally, there are emotional symptoms with a physical illness, as so often is the case, many doctors assume them to be a chemical or mechanical response and treat them with drugs, operations, or orthopedic supports. This comes about because they know little from their medical training as to how to understand or what to do about emotional difficulties. Some have learned from experience, but the great majority still know far more about the body organs (and are more interested in them) than they do about the personality.

There are some signs for encouragement; a few of our leading internists, particularly some of those who served in the Army, wholeheartedly subscribe to the importance of emotional factors in illness. However, beyond the acceptance of the validity of these factors and the common-sense handling of them, even they are somewhat at a loss as to what to do about them. One of these men told me that he was so steeped in organic medicine that he could think only in those terms. Another told me that the job of teaching internal medicine was already a tremendous one, with almost more factual information than the student could absorb; he felt unprepared to teach the psychological aspects. Still another one told me that he felt insecure in approaching the less tangible psychological aspects of his patients' illnesses. A very few internists outspokenly stress the importance of the psychological factors.

Some pediatricians have become aware of the contribution psychiatry can make to their field of interest. Many of the problems brought to them have nothing to do with feeding formulas or contagious disease. Special problems to them as well as to the mother are thumb-sucking, left-handedness, maternal solicitousness, and temper tantrums. However, punishment is still the most frequently prescribed treatment for behavior problems. Too many pediatricians do not take time to read even one of the excellent books on child development.

There are occasional surgeons who are impressed with the psychological forces in those patients who solicit operations, those who through multiple symptoms manage to have many operations, those in whom the necessity for an operation seems more psychological than physical. This behavior has appropriately been given the label of "polysurgical addiction." [14]

---

[14] Menninger, K. A., *Man Against Himself,* Harcourt, Brace and Company, New York, 1938, pp. 297-317.

Numerous orthopedists in the Army impressed me with their recognition of the power of the psyche. It was especially evident to them in the development of low back pain and "psychogenic" rheumatism.

Another encouraging sign is the growth in the *psychosomatic movement* (with an association and a journal),[15] but to date it has been too much dominated by psychiatrists. In 1946, for the first time, an internist was elected president of the association. An increasing number of general medical clinics include psychiatrists on the staff. In two of our leading university hospitals, residencies in psychosomatic training have been provided so that the internist may become oriented to the psychological and emotional factors in illness.

The real solution of the problem lies in the training of *all physicians* in a psychosomatic orientation, *not* only those who intend to be psychiatrists. At the present time, psychiatry has a maximum of only 4 to 5 per cent of the total hours in the teaching curricula of medical schools. This is an indication of the extent of the professional blind spot toward the importance of this field. Apparently too many physicians and medical educators are still thinking of psychiatry in terms of psychoses. Some class-A medical schools still limit the teaching of psychiatry to 30 or 40 hours, during the senior year, of demonstrations of patients in state hospitals. Discussing the "Lessons to Learn," Alan Gregg [12] stated, "Perhaps the most desperately and thoroughly proven of all [lessons] was that our medical schools had been giving grossly inadequate training in psychiatry. Their graduates as a rule misunderstood, ignored, and undervalued psychiatry . . . . There should be a major revision of medical education, for only a radical change will provide, in the education of the doctor, the opportunity for adequate training in the psychiatric care of human beings for a full and happy life as well as a symptom-free existence."

An increase in the number of hours allotted to psychiatry in the medical-school curriculum is not enough. Much more important is the permeation of the psychiatric point of view into the teaching of all medicine and surgery, so that the survey of a patient will not be complete without an evaluation of the psychological as well as the physical and chemical aspects of his illness; no treatment given will ignore the emotional factors.

Literally thousands of patients in the Army were referred to psychiatrists from other medical services. Too many doctors were unable to handle illness which was precipitated by the efforts of a soldier to adjust to the abnormal situation of war. The emotional factors in illness and in noneffectiveness were revealed in a vivid fashion. Keenly aware of the need and with the full co-operation of the Medical and Surgical Consultants Divisions in the Office of the Surgeon General, a War Department bulletin was published with the

[15] The American Society for Research in Psychosomatic Problems. The journal is called *Psychosomatic Medicine*.

title, *Neuropsychiatry for the General Medical Officer.*[16] Some of its contents may be helpful to the civilian physician.

THE PHYSICIAN'S ATTITUDES

The effective management of the emotional factors in any illness will be scientific in direct proportion to the physician's understanding of himself as well as his patient. If he has unrecognized personal conflicts, particularly as they represent neurotic tendencies in himself, he is likely to have a resentful attitude toward the psychiatric patient or a scotoma for the emotional factors in the illness. It is a recognized fact that many physicians are annoyed by neurotic patients. Their lack of understanding is demonstrated by various attitudes and practices used in their treatment of the emotionally ill person.

(1) Overhospitalization and overexamination of the patient from a physical point of view. This is usually due to the physician's confused search for a cause of the symptoms, which may be further expressed in his abuse of sedatives and placebos.

(2) The failure to recognize the medical nature of the problem and to pass off the patient with the platitude that there is "nothing the matter with him." This is an indication of the widespread failure on the part of medicine to acknowledge and accept emotional disorders, worries, and misbehavior as medical problems.

(3) Indifference on the part of the physician, usually because of a failure to appreciate the problem or lack of a sense of his responsibility regarding it, with the result of either ignoring or neglecting the patient or being apathetic toward him. This attitude is much more likely to occur in any socialized system of medicine such as the Army than in those cases where the physician knows that the patient is going to pay him for his services. The technique, however, in a disguised form used by the private physician, is equally poor medicine.

(4) Scolding or kidding the patient. In either case the physician belongs to the "buck up" category. In the rare case, this has a transient benefit because it represents reassurance. Encouragement of the patient is often indicated but cannot be provided in any scientific fashion by these methods.

(5) Annoyance on the part of the physician expressed in various ways. This attitude again varies depending on whether the patient was a soldier in the Army or a Park Avenue client in a private office. It is not very flattering to admit that this difference exists, and if only the scientific approach prevailed, it could not exist. In the Army we saw the medical officer with this type

---

[16] "Neuropsychiatry for the General Medical Officer," *War Department Technical Bulletin, Medical 94,* 21 September 1944. This was reprinted in *Ment. Hyg.,* 29:622-643, Oct., 1945.

of attitude express a vindictive response to the patient, even to derision in public. It might and often did progress to an expression of anger, accusing patients of cowardice or of evading duty.

CAUSES OF MISMANAGEMENT [17]

The causes for these erroneous attitudes as well as the practices to which they lead are numerous and should probably be mentioned even though they concern only the medical profession. The failure in medical education has been indicated above, particularly the failure to regard emotional symptoms as medical problems. An emotional bias against psychiatric study of medical problems frequently exists and owes its origin most often to a self-protecting device of the physician.

Psychiatric and psychological findings are as real and valid as those in any other field of medicine, even though relatively intangible. Unfortunately, because of their training, this fact is not accepted—or at least acted upon—by many physicians. The concrete nature of percussing a chest or examining a urine specimen makes these procedures *seem* more valid than investigating the emotions. To study the personality adequately, in addition to examining the body physically, requires more time. In organic cases, making a decision as to the use of a diagnostic or therapeutic procedure, be it a glucose tolerance curve or a gastrointestinal X-ray series, does not depend upon whether or not it is a time-consuming process (except in emergencies). In neurotic reactions, however, the time required to study the personality often acts as a deterrent.

Spectacular, immediate, and satisfactory results obtained in certain drug therapies and in surgery appeal to many physicians. Actually, these are no more spectacular than the results to be seen in cathartic psychotherapy under sedation, in hypnosis, or in electroshock therapy.

ERRORS TO BE OBSERVED AND AVOIDED [17]

Failure to assess the emotional factors. Frequently the physician fails adequately or correctly to assess the relative importance of the psychological and physical factors in the disease. Too many assume the "either/or" attitude— that the illness is either physical or mental. Instead, they should ask themselves, "How much of the picture is contributed by somatic pathology and how much by psychological pathology?" The net result of the failure to do so is a

---

[17] Modified from War Department Technical Bulletin, Medical 94.

diagnosis which is arrived at by exclusion; reached by a negative rather than a positive approach.

Failure to take an adequate history. If the doctor is to know the person as well as his disease, it is necessary to learn the background of the patient. It is far more important to know about his relationships to his parents than it is to note merely their age and state of their health. We need to know an individual's pattern of reaction to stress, his successes and failures in adjustment in relation to people, school, and jobs. Without such a history, the personality cannot be evaluated.

The establishment of rapport. Too often the physician, who does not appreciate the necessity for knowing the patient as well as his disease or his complaint, does not establish a rapport with the patient. The patient then does not feel his sincerity or his interest. It is often said that the patient does not know the cause of his difficulty, but he knows how he feels, while the physician may know the cause of the difficulty, but he does not know how the patient feels.

Overexamination. Many patients with neurotic complaints are given excessive laboratory and X-ray examinations as well as other types of tests, particularly by younger physicians. Too often this makes the patient feel that he has a serious and mysterious problem, or else that he has succeeded in misleading and thus making a fool out of the doctor.

Overhospitalization. When a patient's illness is difficult to diagnose, as so many times a neurotic reaction turns out to be, the patient is often kept in the hospital far too long. By such a procedure his symptoms become more fixed. When and if overemphasis through comment or overhospitalization is placed on a particular finding such as a slightly lowered blood pressure, a minor cardiac irregularity, or an indefinite shadow in the X-ray picture, this serves to convince the patient of the organic nature of his illness, even though such is not the intention of the physician. The physician *must* use the utmost care not to perpetuate a mistaken diagnosis or to give the patient an uncertain diagnosis.

Overemphasis on a physical treatment measure. To place a patient who has a neurotic reaction on a special diet is to infer it may have some magic quality. To direct special attention to his bowel movement, to apply a back brace, or to employ some other procedure or appliance, unless it has some real relationship to the nature of the man's illness, greatly reinforces the patient's conviction that his illness has some physical basis. While these procedures may have a valid psychotherapeutic value in some cases, in many more they will delay the patient's appreciation of the real basis of his illness. In the absence of organic disorder, special care should be used in the employment of any such procedures.

Mistaken diagnoses. Even though neurotic illnesses are often given an organic diagnosis, the opposite mistake also occurs. Occasionally a physician, including the psychiatrist, may label a patient with a brain tumor as having a psychoneurosis. The patient's difficulty "appears" to be without organic pathology, and the doctor "believes" it to be so. When treatment is based on such assumptions, sooner or later a tragedy will occur. Brain tumors are very often first evidenced in mental symptoms which are frequently psychoneurotic in character. The acute onset in a large percentage of pancreatic tumors is marked by mental symptoms.

Diagnosis. Every physician should recognize the fact that the labeling of a patient with a diagnosis which is unjustified, particularly in psychiatric cases, may be the first step toward making him a permanent invalid. To us a diagnosis is nothing more than a scientific label. To the patient, who rarely understands and often misinterprets it, it can be frightening. "Cerebral hemorrhage" is much more ominous in its sound than "stroke." "Psychoneurosis," so often misused as a diagnosis, is far more serious sounding than "nervousness." It is far more important to explain to a patient the nature of his illness than it is to give him the name of it. It is definitely harmful to do the latter without also doing the former.

Courage to face the issue. Many physicians feel too uncertain of their knowledge of psychiatry to feel secure in discussing emotional problems with their patients. The sincere doctor must have the courage of his convictions and give the patient his opinion. He need make no claim of being an expert; even more important, he need not feel apologetic either to himself or his patient that he is not. He should handle the case to the best of his ability, on the basis of the training he has had. When a patient requires more than he has to give, he can send his patient to someone more specifically qualified.

In summary, as a result of our experience in the Army, it is vividly apparent that psychiatry can and must play a much more important role in the solution of health problems of the civilian. This contribution must be made by the psychiatrists and, probably to an even greater extent, by every physician who will increase his psychiatric orientation.

If health *is* the concern of medicine, and if by mental health we mean satisfaction in life, efficiency, and social compatability, then the principles of psychiatry must apply not only to each of us as individuals but to our social relationships with each other. The field of medicine must be recognized as inseparably linked to the social sciences and concerned with the healthy adjustment of men, both individually and in groups. An increased emphasis must be placed equally on the preservation of mental health and the therapeusis of mental illness.

In conclusion, here are some immediate and concrete suggestions: [18]

Medical education. Every physician has his rationalized opinion about our medical education. I feel strongly that psychiatry should be a basic subject for all medical students in addition to elective courses for those who intend to become specialists in the field. The universality of emotions, of feelings, and their effect on the human body, makes it imperative that every individual practicing medicine be as firmly grounded in psychiatry as he is in physical anatomy, physical physiology, and physical pathology. Moreover, it should be taught from the first year through the hospital internship, in the medical, surgical, pediatric, obstetrical, and every other department.

Reorientation to the importance of the personality. The student in every medical school starts his professional training with hours, weeks, months spent in the dissection of the human body. Excellent courses in the physiology, pathology, and chemistry of this body follow. Nonetheless, our system of medical education suffers by so much emphasis on the study of the material body. The average medical student receives his diploma with only the vaguest conception that the most important part of his patient is the person who lives within the framework of the body. He leaves medical school with slight, if any, idea that it is our ambitions and our strivings, our loves and our hates, our successes and our failures, our aggressivity and our passivity that are probably the major determinants in the maintenance of health. From my psychiatric point of view, medical education must reorganize to present an adequate orientation to facts of the psyche.

Public health. If we physicians accept the premise that mental health is a medical responsibility, it must be included in every preventive-medicine program. Not only do I specifically refer to need for the prevention of serious and disabling mental illness. Much more important is the need for more extensive education about the principles of mental hygiene, just as we educate individuals in physical hygiene. There are more deaths from one expression of mental illness, namely, suicide, than there are from the five most communicable diseases! The paradox exists, however, that few of our public health agencies concern themselves in the least with the mental health of the commonwealth.

Medical assistants. As medicine becomes more of a social science, it requires the assistance of research workers, of lay assistants, of nurses and attendants, of social workers, clinical psychologists, and therapists of various skills. These individuals should have a much closer contact with medicine from an earlier period in their education than they do. In psychiatry, par-

---

[18] Modified from recommendations made to the Committee on Medical Care, New York Academy of Medicine. Menninger, W. C., "Perspectives of Psychiatry," *Ann. Int. Med.,* 22:170-181, Feb., 1945.

ticularly, is this important. No psychiatric team, whether it is in an outpatient clinic or in a hospital, can adequately function without their help. Their abilities could do much to lessen the load of the overworked doctor in general or specialized practice. It is to be hoped that sometime our medical schools can become universities which will provide training for these intimate associates and assistants of the physician.

Convalescence. The recovery of every individual from every type of illness is very possibly determined more by his psychological life than by any other factor. Through some sort of curious blind spot, the consideration of this factor has been conspicuously absent in most studies of the process of getting well. Because it happens reasonably regularly, we assume that the operation will heal, the pneumonia will resolve, the decompensated heart will readjust.

We have been aware vaguely of the fact that the speed in the recovery of a gastric ulcer has a direct and obvious relationship to the patient's emotional life. Yet, in general, we have ignored the emotional factor in the lives of general medical and surgical patients before, during, and after specific treatment. For pragmatic reasons 'in some cases, psychiatric study before emergency medical or surgical treatment is not so important as during and after such treatment. One lesson many doctors learned in the Army was the importance of conscious motivation. Unconscious motivation also made itself obvious to them. The existence of both should be considered in every convalescence. The physician who fails to do so is an offender against his patient —as well as against the best practice of medicine.

Reorientation to concepts of mental health. No field of medicine battles against such a welter of superstitions and misconceptions regarding its doctors, patients, and methods of treatment as does psychiatry. Unfortunately, the greatest lack of understanding, the most frequent source of misunderstanding, is the attitude of the medical profession itself. Perhaps it is due to the system of medical education or to the historical evolution of psychiatry from the period of werewolves and dungeons; it may have resulted from the use of the incomprehensible jargon of some psychiatrists. It may be related to the intangible nature of the subject in contrast to the tangible operative techniques, stethoscopes, Roentgen rays. Perhaps it arises from the presumed necessity of confirming the naïve belief of an individual that he is a "normal" personality.

Whatever the causes, the fact remains that the physician's bungling in the handling of psychological factors in illness keeps thousands of cults thriving. Because he is a physician and thus the authoritative source of opinions about health and ill health for the layman, his attitude and understanding of psychiatry can and do color the public attitude. Even though progress has been made, the public conception of psychiatric factors in illness is still a blurred picture of disgrace and fear, mysticism and self-exemption. Is it too much to hope that the medical profession might take a more forceful initiative to gain enlightenment and disseminate it?

29

LESSONS FOR CIVILIAN PSYCHIATRY [1]

THE DYNAMIC TITLE, *The Shaping of Psychiatry by War,* was the theme of the Salmon Lectures by Brig. J. R. Rees,[2] Consultant in Psychiatry to the British Army. The molding was chiefly toward a wider social application of psychiatric principles. Knowledge about human behavior and relationships, when used, played an important role in waging war. The biggest challenge confronting psychiatrists is how best to assist, to as great a degree, in waging peace.

Including the hospital admissions and contacts with outpatients, it is probable that Army psychiatrists were consulted professionally by approximately 5,000,000 patients. Our work also included responsibilities in selection, classification and assignment, personnel policy, education, prevention, discipline, and correctional efforts. We in the Army were aware of our deficiencies in plans, knowledge, relationships, and personnel. Of necessity we had to learn quickly how to correct them, or fail in our task. Many of these experiences may perhaps be prophetic of the future civilian need for psychiatric services; others indicate possibilities for the greater influence for psychiatry and are a challenge to its practitioners.[3]

Social issues. Our wartime experience and our greater knowledge should have value in meeting the social issues and problems in civilian life. Since many of the chief problems in social issues are not psychiatric, a psychiatrist has no right, perhaps, to more than an expression of his point of view. In the Army our opinions were requested on matters related to the social issues of the military organization. The psychiatrist was often able to give pertinent

---

[1] Some of the points mentioned in this chapter were presented in the Menas K. Gregory lecture at the Psychiatric Division of Bellevue Hospital in New York City, April 26, 1946, entitled "Lessons from Military Psychiatry For Civilian Psychiatry," published in *Ment. Hyg.,* 30:571-589, Oct., 1946. Others were included in a report to the Am. Psychiat. Assn. Meeting at Chicago, May 29, 1946, entitled "Psychiatric Experiences in the War, 1941–1946," *Am. J. Psychiat.,* 103:577-586, Mar., 1947.

[2] Rees, J. R., *The Shaping of Psychiatry by War,* W. W. Norton & Company, Inc., New York, 1945.

[3] Many of the points made in this chapter parallel the lessons learned by the British psychiatrists as given by G. W. B. James, "Psychiatric Lessons from Active Service," *Lancet,* 2:801-805, Dec. 22, 1945. They were verified in the American Navy as reported by F. J. Braceland, "Psychiatric Lessons from World War II," *Am. J. Psychiat.,* 103:587-593, Mar., 1947.

advice when special features of human relationships, methods of approach, or provision of better understanding were involved.

Often the effect of social factors as a cause of mental illness was so obvious in soldiers that not only the illness but the social situation which caused it needed treatment. In civilian life, also, social situations either can contribute to or prevent mental illness. The application of certain principles to public health, academic education, industry, criminology could strengthen their preventive role. Psychiatrists can help greatly, as will be noted in later chapters.

Beyond the social neuroses of our own American culture, there is another great area of responsibility for psychiatry, so broad and of such portent as to be frightening. That is the area of world democracy, international relations, and war. With the exception of the defunct International Mental Hygiene Organization and the International Psychoanalytic Association which exist only on paper, there are no world-wide psychiatric organizations. It may be presumptuous to even include international relationships in the purview of psychiatry. Nevertheless, the world has grown smaller; the peace and the mental health of all of us depend upon these relationships. We in psychiatry have so much work in our own back yard to which we must—or should—attend that we are not in a position to give much attention to world mental health, and yet we must! If we are capable of adding even a small contribution, it is our sacred responsibility.

Psychiatrists in 30 countries did draw up a statement about war in 1935— a statement signed by 339 psychiatrists.[4] Unfortunately it was a drop of water falling in a turbulent ocean. Nevertheless, there is no reason why we should not—and every obligation why we should—unite to make a great effort toward the development of a world mental health program. Our first opportunity will be at an International Mental Health Congress in London in 1948, from which there is the hope that a strong international organization will arise. Only through such an organization can psychiatry participate in any program of the World Health Organization.[5]

State hospitals. The status of our state hospitals [6] is a very special problem

---

[4] Recorded in the Comment Column as "Psychiatrists Warn Against Insanity of War," *Ment. Hyg.,* 20:167-169, Jan., 1936.

[5] This opportunity was challengingly presented by G. Brock Chisholm in a key address to the Am. Psychiat. Assn. meeting in New York, May 21, 1947. The tentative program for the International Congress was outlined by Dr. John R. Rees of London. *Am. J. Psychiat.,* 104:329-331, Nov. 1947.

[6] These remarks are expanded from a statement by the author, "What Is Wrong with Our Mental Hospitals?" in the *Woman's Home Companion,* Aug., 1946, pp. 34-35; an elaboration of the subject was given as "Our Mental Hospitals. What Can We Do to Improve Them?" A *Univ. of Chicago Radio Round Table Discussion* by Kenneth Appel, Walter Barton, Henry Brosin, and William Menninger, Sept. 21, 1947. No. 496.

confronting psychiatry. A few of those institutions are excellent in quality and sufficiency of staff, facilities, and treatment. A few more might be regarded as fair. Many are hospitals only in name. Essentially, these last are detention homes, where there is only a minimum of treatment if any. The only basis for calling them hospitals is the presence of some doctors on the staff.

Most of our state hospitals are overcrowded by from 10 to 30 per cent, so that it is the exception rather than the rule to have adequate housing or treatment facilities or personnel. Only a very small number of them maintain any semblance of training, teaching, or research programs, and many lack even the minimum requirements in personnel of an acceptable psychiatric institution. Some have no graduate nurses; many have no clinical psychologists or psychiatric social workers. The average attendant or hospital aide, so essential in mental hospitals, has no professional standing. He or she receives no training and is usually paid considerably less than $100 a month. Those who make up this classification of the mental-hospital personnel spend more time with patients than any other individuals on the staff. However, for the above reasons, they are often quite incompetent. In most state hospitals there is such a tremendous shortage of capable personnel that attitudes of hopelessness and discouragement over the impossibility of providing proper management and a sense of complete isolation prevail.

As Stevenson [7] has suggested, our whole system of state hospitals is probably wrong in the tendency to isolate them. Thus they are separated from the past and future of the patient and the community. Moreover, as long as they remain isolated, financially neglected custodial institutions, citizens will be too apathetic to force an improvement, and progressive young physicians will not be interested in such service.

Why do these conditions exist? Basically our state hospitals are neglected because of the widespread fear of mental illness and of those who are mentally ill. Remaining ignorant and uninformed on this social problem is a protective device against that fear. In the absence of factual information, misconceptions have grown up and continue to exist about both psychiatry and emotionally ill patients. For instance, most people are surprised when they learn that not more than 2 out of every 100 soldiers seen by the Army psychiatrists were in need of the type of care provided by state hospitals. Other misconceptions are even more erroneous. The prevailing attitude of the public is that patients in state hospitals are incurable and irrational, if not dangerous. Therefore, they never militantly demand that such patients should have pleasant living conditions and

---

[7] Stevenson, Geo. S., "The Crisis in the Psychiatric Functions of the State," foreword, Mar., 1946, issue of *Public Welfare,* official publication of the Wisconsin Department of Public Welfare.

kind attention, as well as the best of psychiatric treatment. The result of this apathy and indifference and the resultant misconceptions is a condition of abject poverty for most of our state hospitals. They are stepchildren of the state, and no one fights for the patients and their betterment except the superintendent. Too often, he is tired in the fighting of a losing battle or is persuaded, under political pressure, that economy is more important than good psychiatry.

Lay groups educate the public constantly about the need to support prevention, treatment, and research programs for cancer, tuberculosis, and infantile paralysis. There is no trouble in obtaining sympathy, consideration, and considerable sums of money under the pressure of publicity about the preventable loss these illnesses cause. So far no comparable program has attracted public attention to psychiatric patients who represent a far greater social, economic, and personal loss to the country. As long as the state hospital remains outside the realm of active public concern, it will continue to be a political football, maintained in a poverty-stricken condition. Fortunately, recently, there have been several courageous attempts to bring these problems into the limelight through the articles by Albert Deutsch [8] and Albert Q. Maisel [9] and the books by Mary Jane Ward and Harold Maine.[10]

What can be done about the situation? First and foremost, the public needs to know the facts as they presently exist; it needs to be informed as to what the conditions are and, more important, what the needs are in the various states.[11] Every public-minded citizen needs to be articulate to the public officials who can change the situation if they believe it is of vital concern to their constituents. Particularly needed are fighting laymen who, on the basis of expert guidance and advice, will work toward the enforcement of reforms, increased budgets, and facilities and personnel that will provide for mentally and emotionally sick persons the best scientific treatment available.

Probably no psychiatrist or group of psychiatrists could ever bring about these reforms. They would be accused of trying to promote themselves. On the other hand, they do have the responsibility, because of their knowledge

---

[8] Deutsch, Albert, "The Nation's Shame: Sick Minds on the Rack," and others in a series of articles in *PM*, Apr. 17, 1946, through June 9, 1946.

[9] Maisel, Albert Q., "Bedlam 1946; Most U.S. Mental Hospitals Are a Shame and a Disgrace," *Life*, May 6, 1946.

[10] Ward, M. J., *The Snake Pit*, Random House, New York, 1946; Maine, Harold, *If a Man Be Mad*, Doubleday and Company, Inc., New York, 1947.

[11] This point was urged by Dr. Frank Fremont-Smith: "New Opportunities for the Improvement of Mental Hospitals," an address delivered at the 48th Annual Convention of the American Hospital Association, Philadelphia, Oct. 2, 1946. *Ment. Hyg.* 31:354-362, July, 1947. See also the objective evaluation of Norman, J. P., "State-Hospital Psychiatry: An Evaluation," *Ment. Hyg.*, 31:436-448, July, 1947.

and their close contact with the problem, to stimulate the action of others. Eventually, the whole system must change so that the treatment of mental illness is a vital part of the community program, building bridges for the return from sickness to health through social work, family care, outpatient service, institutions, and trial visits.

PSYCHIATRIC PERSONNEL

Before we can do very much in the state hospitals or attack any social ills of our world psychiatrically, we have to increase the number of trained personnel—psychiatrists, clinical psychologists, psychiatric social workers, and psychiatric nurses. This need has a number-one priority for the further development and the effective utilization of psychiatry.

Recruiting. The average medical school has produced only one to three psychiatrists a year. Why? The answer is not simple. It may be a barometer of the attitude toward psychiatry on the part of most of the faculty members. It is surely suggestive that psychiatry has not been taught in an interesting and challenging way; the medical-school curriculum discourages rather than encourages men toward the study of psychiatry.[12] Current teaching in some medical schools tends to continue misconceptions about the practice of psychiatry rather than to clarify them. No doubt many medical students, and certainly most physicians, have thought of psychiatry as limited to the treatment of psychoses in a state hospital, isolated from the general medical field.

A serious defect has been the absence of a positive policy of recruiting. For too many years, for varied reasons, men have drifted into the field of psychiatry or have chosen it in the hope of solving personal-adjustment difficulties. Perhaps the Army's experience, when it was forced to find a way to increase the personnel in this specialty, can be of value to civilian medical groups.

The handwriting of an acute shortage of trained personnel was on the wall within a few months after the war began. It was apparent that we needed to enlist far more help than we could obtain from tugging at psychiatry's own bootstraps. Medical officers who wished the special training were carefully selected and given a short, intensive course in psychiatry. After this orientation they were assigned to positions under the supervision of more experienced psychiatrists. They did a very creditable job. Of 1,000 men who received the training, it is estimated that about half will continue in this specialty. This number represents a harvest of more potential psychiatrists than all of our medical schools combined produced in 10 years.

---

[12] Menninger, K. A., "Psychiatry in Medicine," *Interne,* 12:25-28, Jan., 1946.

It is interesting to note the type of training and positions these men desired on their return to civilian life. The National Committee for Mental Hygiene and the American Psychiatric Association jointly operated a placement service under the immediate supervision of Capt. Forrest Harrison (M.C.), U.S.N. Retired. Over 900 physicians registered with the placement service. Facts revealed from this experience have grave significance for state hospitals.

(1) Approximately three-fourths of the positions listed were in state hospitals.

(2) Only 188 of the physicians registered were seeking positions—the rest desired some form of training.

(3) Approximately 98 per cent who desired training stated that they wanted it in a medical school or in a teaching hospital connected with a medical school.

(4) Only 2 per cent of these indicated a willingness to accept a residency or any other type of training in a state hospital.

(5) There are more than 20 times as many jobs in state hospitals as there are candidates for them.[13] In an earlier news release by the National Committee, when 650 medical officers had applied for advice, there were 430 staff vacancies in state hospitals and only 19 men had indicated willingness to accept positions there.[14]

Psychiatric practice as experienced by medical officers in the Army was more attractive than supervising custodial care of patients with psychoses in a politically controlled state hospital. Military psychiatry was more concerned with treatment than that practiced in the average state institution.

The recruiting of men for psychiatry must occur during their medical-school experience. Current procedure has not encouraged this. Parallel with this failure, and probably even more important, has been the failure to teach the average medical student enough about the anatomy and the physiology of the personality to permit him to use psychiatric principles in all treatment. In competition for hours of instruction in medical schools, psychiatry is fortunate to get as much as 4 per cent [15] of the total hours in the

---

13 National Committee for Mental Hygiene, **Annual Report**, 1946, p. 27.

14 News release from the National Committee for Mental Hygiene: "Better Care is Seen for Civilian Mental Patients as Many Medical Officers Enter Psychiatric Field," May 2, 1946.

15 The 4-year medical curriculum contains 4,000 to 4,500 hours. Through the courtesy of professors of psychiatry in the following schools, the number of hours of psychiatry for all students is as follows: University of Texas, 307 hours; Harvard, 207 hours; University of Louisville, 185 hours; Iowa, 138 hours; Johns Hopkins, 136 hours; University of Pennsylvania, 134 hours; Cornell, 129 hours; New York University, 124 hours; California, 118 hours; Colorado, 115 hours; Stanford, 101 hours; Columbia, 101 hours. Many offer additional elective hours in the fourth year. Several schools have 50 hours or less. In contrast to these figures, instruction in medicine runs around 700 to 800 hours; surgery, 500 to 600 hours, in most medical schools.

curriculum, despite the fact, or in face of the fact, that a high percentage of patients who consult physicians in every field of medicine present primarily emotional disorders.

Graduate training needs. Even if all physicians were oriented to and capable of handling the minor emotional needs of their patients, we would still need great expansion of the personnel in the specialty of psychiatry.[16] The total need has been variously estimated to be between 10,000 [17] and 14,000 [18] psychiatrists as compared with the present number of 4,500. General Paul Hawley, as Chief Medical Director, stated that the Veterans Administration, to do its job in first-class fashion, would require the full-time services of every competent psychiatrist in the United States.[19] Instead, its Neuropsychiatric Division reported 592 psychiatrists on duty, with an immediate need for 1,875.[20]

Psychiatry is faced at this moment with a dilemma of far from sufficient opportunities [21] for formal graduate training, even for those who are already seeking it. For example, in the last year over 800 candidates inquired about training at one center.[22] The actual problem is far worse than the figures themselves indicate. Many of the "residencies" that appear on the approved list are certainly not adequate for good training. They provide little other than what the man can dig out for himself.

Good training must of necessity be on a broad base. In addition to the knowledge about the structure and function and pathology of the personality, this training ought to provide the young psychiatrist an experience with co-workers in allied fields so that he can learn how to use their contributions. It ought to provide some information about the relations of psychiatry to various facets of life in our world—religious, political, literary, artistic. Certainly it should introduce the student to psychiatric aspects of the social issues and problems of the day. The crying need for more training facilities should command the major attention of every qualified teaching psychiatrist we have.

Utilization and training of ancillary personnel. When we were so short of

---

16 A committee in New York carefully surveyed the needs for psychiatric help among a fair sample of rejectees and dischargees and found that three-fourths of the group were without psychiatric aid of any kind. Ginsburg, S. W., "The Need and Demand for Psychiatric Care Among Rejectees and Dischargees," Josiah Macy, Jr., Foundation, New York.

17 Rennie, T. A. C., "Needed: 10,000 Psychiatrists," *Ment. Hyg.,* 29:644-649, Oct., 1945.

18 Felix, R. H., "Mental Public Health: A Plan of National Scope," Annual Meeting Mass. Soc. for Ment. Hyg., Jan. 24, 1946.

19 Hawley, P. R., "Neuropsychiatric Problems of the Veterans Administration," *Mil. Surgeon,* 99:759-762, Dec., 1946.

20 Personal communication from Dr. Daniel Blain, December, 1946.

21 In 1940, the educational number of the *J.A.M.A.* listed 410 "approved" openings for residencies and fellowships for training in psychiatry in 111 hospitals (*J.A.M.A.,* 115:777-778, Aug. 31, 1940). Many of these, while "approved," could be considered only as mediocre. In 1947 there were 1,297 openings listed in 193 hospitals (*J.A.M.A.,* 134:1319, Aug. 16, 1947.

22 The Menninger Foundation School of Psychiatry.

trained psychiatrists in the Army, our only hope of adequately meeting the problem of treating so many patients was to utilize all of the additional help that we could obtain from any source. We developed harmonious, happy relationships with clinical psychologists and psychiatric social workers.[23]

There were many problems in the process, not only in helping the Army to recognize the need for these auxiliary workers but also in educating psychiatrists who had never worked on a team with members of these groups. Nor in many instances had the psychologists and psychiatric social workers had any experience as members of a clinical team. There were petty jealousies that, for the most part, were easily overcome. The final result was the development of a congenial and efficient relationship from which the patient profited, as did the workers in all three fields. Those of us most vitally concerned in this development were very proud of it.

Equally important, however, was the use of other ancillary workers, particularly occupational therapists, psychiatric nurses, educational and recreational therapists, and ward attendants. Psychiatrists multiplied their effectiveness many times by their use of trained people in each of these fields. A special word is due the ward attendant. Too often he has been looked down upon as some type of flunkey instead of being accepted as an individual with a professional job, which should entitle him to the respect and training and position that his intimate contact with patients deserves. We need to revamp our concept of what the ward attendant's job is and we must revise our training for and our attitude toward him.

More institutions are needed as training centers for these various workers; greater realization of their maximum contribution toward the recovery of the mentally ill would enable them to serve more effectively; for some of these the establishment of professional standards and organizations would add to their sense of satisfaction in their work. We have some estimates of the amazing number of these ancillary workers who are immediately needed. The Veterans Administration [24] has 155 clinical psychologists on duty but needs 546; it has 341 psychiatric social workers and needs 605; it has 2,200 psychiatric nurses but needs 4,285. Estimates of the total need are even higher. Senator Pepper,[25] in his summary of the National Mental Health Act, indicated that we need 1,700 clinical psychologists, 4,500 psychiatric social workers, 15,000 psychiatric nurses. Regardless of the number of psychiatrists we might have,

---

[23] The evaluation of our own experience has been presented by three of us in the three fields of clinical psychology, psychiatry, and psychiatric social work. Hutt, M. L.; Menninger, W. C.; and O'Keefe, D. E., "Neuropsychiatric Team in the United States Army," *Ment. Hyg.*, **31**:103-119, Jan., 1947.

[24] Personal communication from Dr. Daniel Blain.

[25] Pepper, Claude, National Mental Health Act, Report 1353, U.S. Government Printing Office, Washington, D.C., May 16, 1946.

many of us feel that the psychiatric job cannot possibly be done without these additional ancillary workers.

METHODS AND RELATIONSHIPS

The practice of military psychiatry brought about changes in certain of our methods and relationships. We carried a definite responsibility in a huge team that threw us into intimate contact with strong, influential forces that modified our work. Our limited personnel had to work against time. A major responsibility was a continued necessity to explain our problems to the laymen who controlled the policies. In contrast to our prewar experience as individuals in private practice or in isolated specialty hospitals, we were a part of the total medical team in every installation.[26] The experience made conspicuous the need for certain revisions in our practice: clarification of clinical concepts, modifications in our treatment methods, improved relationships with the other specialties in medicine, and the need for an articulate authority.

Clarification of concepts. Among the many lessons we learned in our Army experience was that psychiatrists are widely divergent in their concepts of different types of mental illnesses. The history of this problem, as we saw it and experienced it, and the composition of a revised nomenclature are given in detail in a previous chapter. Even though our revision is only one more evolutionary step toward further crystallization of our concepts, we hope it is a contribution and are gratified over its adoption by the Veterans Administration.[27]

Our military experience painted in bold relief the need for clarifying the concepts of the clinical psychiatric entities in order to be better understood, and also for the advantage of more uniform teaching of those to follow. This problem is intimately related to a needed increase in research efforts, which in psychiatry have been minimal so far. In spite of the fact that this medical field [28] affects more people than any other, a smaller economic outlay has been made than in some of those fields related to specific organic disorders. Overcoming the prejudices which have limited financial support to the neglect of a long-time research program is another of psychiatry's great needs.

Potential treatment modifications. Probably much of the pessimism about

---

[26] We had only two strictly psychiatric hospitals in the United States. There were three in the European Theater and four in the Pacific Theater.

[27] This revision was recommended for trial by the consultants in neuropsychiatry to the Veterans Administration on April 27, 1946; it was recommended for adoption on September 14, 1946. It was published, slightly revised, as Veterans Administration *Technical Bulletin* TO 10A-78, Oct. 1, 1947.

[28] An estimate of $350,000 annual expenditure in psychiatric research was given by L. S. Kubie, in Hearings in Science Legislation. S.1297 and Related Bills, Part 3, Oct. 22-26, 1945, p. 616. The Steelman report gave the figure of $110 million spent annually for all medical research. *The Nation's Medical Research,* a Report of the President's Scientific Research Board, Oct. 18, 1947. U.S. Government Printing Office, Washington, D.C.

and fear of mental illness, which is so widely held by the public, is related to the comparatively low recovery rate. Certainly it was the exceptional occasion, before the war, when a psychiatrist in civilian life was given the opportunity to treat an individual in the early stages of an emotional maladjustment. And, as recent publicity suggests, inadequate facilities and personnel currently prevent exhaustive treatment at any stage. The amazing result of early treatment in the Army, even though it was far from adequate, is one of the more significant implications for civilian psychiatry of any lesson from military psychiatry.

Psychiatry *must* be prepared to provide active early treatment; under many circumstances it may have to be abbreviated. Continued efforts must be directed toward finding the ways and means of making therapy effective through short cuts. Experience raises the question as to how much insight regarding his illness the patient needs to promote his readjustment. It may be more desirable, when we see the patient early, to give immediate corrective suggestions, re-enforcement, and support. Then we might trust the tendency of nature to regain equilibrium rather than attempt to expose contributory, deep-seated, emotional conflicts. This does not apply to long-standing incapacity as seen in the chronic neurotic adjustment. Such patients were in a minority in the Army, and probably are among potential civilian practice, but they do require long-time treatment. However, the great mass of average individuals who are momentarily or periodically thrown off their emotional balance could find relief in shorter psychiatric treatment. Our experience in the Army indicates positively that when psychiatry provides an abbreviated, intensive therapeutic program, its application and usefulness is increased manyfold.

In an expanded treatment program, we must make wider use of ancillary personnel. We must use group therapy more widely. It is probable that psychotherapy under sedation has some application in civilian life and has the great advantage of being a short cut. The extensive and often expensive provision for occupational, recreational, and educational therapy in Army hospitals showed that the initial expense of equipment and the increase in staff is compensated for by reducing the duration of an illness. Prolonged custody is costly. Shorter illness extends the capacity of an institution by permitting more patients to enter who do not have to remain so long. The principle involved could, and should, set a precedent which, if adopted in and necessarily adapted to every psychiatric hospital in the country, could go far toward revolutionizing the rate of recovery from psychiatric illness and reducing the cost per case.

In short, the use of ancillary personnel, short cuts in treatment, and reduction in paper work give the psychiatrist time for contact with more patients; all are very much indicated in any attempt to expand treatment programs. If we are correct as to the great need, then we need to seriously consider all possible means of extending the influence of each of the too few specialists in psychiatry.

Professional relationships. In addition to the need for clarification of our concepts and our needed improvement of treatment methods, psychiatry can well review its relationships to the total field of medicine. The working in close harmony of the internist, surgeon, and psychiatrist in the Army proved to be a stimulating experience for all concerned. It was one of the chief factors which helped psychiatry out of its isolationism. There was a continuous mutual indoctrination. This same source of rich dividends needs to be greatly developed in the practice of civilian medicine. Psychiatry is handicapped by the necessity of having specialized hospitals which tend to keep their physicians out of circulation with general medical groups. However, psychiatrists need the support and the intimate contact with the other medical specialists.[29] It is equally fair to state that the other branches of medicine need what psychiatry can contribute. Any community, including its doctors and their patients, would benefit from definite planning for the inclusion of psychiatrists on general hospital staffs, in outpatient clinics, in affiliations with medical and surgical groups, in general medical meetings. Other contributions could be the interchange of fellowships with internists and pediatricians, reciprocal arrangements between the American boards of these specialties, and the extensive development of short courses in psychiatry similar to the annual refresher courses arranged by the American College of Physicians.

Psychiatrists have failed to present short refresher courses for general practitioners, although there are many indications of the interest of this group of medical men in them. The preparation and conduct of such courses require experienced psychiatrists as faculty members; this is an expensive undertaking. Therefore, undoubtedly it should be a responsibility of organized psychiatry. Our own experience at the Clinic in Topeka in giving a "postgraduate" course each year from 1935 through 1939 [30] was eminently successful in presenting to general practitioners some basic concepts of psychiatry. Recently both faculty and students were enthusiastic about the two-week course sponsored by the Commonwealth Fund at the University of Minnesota and

[29] Psychiatry has a close working alliance with psychology and social work. But it needs a much closer alliance with other social sciences. Braceland, Chief of Psychiatry in the Navy during the war, indicated the point of view of many psychiatrists: "The psychiatry of the present age must ally itself with educational disciplines. Its meetings should be attended by other scientists, such as economists, sociologists, philosophers, and cultural anthropologists. Because of our isolation, we have become inbred and new ideas are looked upon with suspicion." Braceland, F. J., "Psychiatry and Atoms," *Ment. Hyg.*, 31:29-37, Jan., 1947.
[30] Brief outlines of the third, fourth, and fifth courses were given in the *Bull. Menninger Clinic*, 1:129-130, Apr., 1937; 2:63-64, Apr., 1938, 3:65-66, Mar., 1939.

reported upon by Smith [31] and Rennie.[32] An effort should be made to bring such instruction to many groups of physicians, and it is the responsibility of psychiatrists to see that such courses are given.

Articulate authority. As Dr. Alan Gregg pointed out 4 years ago,[33] one of psychiatry's great weaknesses was its inarticulateness. This has been inseparably combined with its isolationism. There were too few who could and would speak for it and present it in its most practical, helpful aspects. Perhaps because of this, in the early years of the war, there was an attitude of tolerant sufferance toward it on the part of Army personnel. The neuropsychiatric wards were placed in the far left corner of the hospital. It was usually a section of another service; its officers were often belatedly promoted; its patients were too often looked upon with skepticism and suspicion. Only after considerable effort on the part of informed people in the right places was some improvement made toward its greater acceptance by all concerned.

There is a very imperative need for psychiatry to present a better organized and articulate front to the public and simultaneously to come out of its isolation. It must become a part of the medical and civilian communities and function within those groups. It needs spokesmen who can present our best thoughts and best recommendations, who can press for the issues that are so important for our patients. Specifically, such persons could speak for the state-hospital superintendent who is harassed by politics and grieves because of the lack of understanding of members of his board and his legislature. Why should not organized psychiatry fight for him that he might have an opportunity to provide the best psychiatric treatment? Through official leaders, support can be given to the psychiatric programs in the military forces, in public health, in the Veterans Administration. Perhaps it was because of the silence of organized psychiatry that the military services ignored the psychiatric lessons of World War I. Leaders in the profession can best present to those who formulate medical-school curricula the needs for more courses in psychiatry in the medical school. As we became articulate in the Army, we gained in respect and standing. It is to be hoped that some of this gain can be carried over into civilian life. Unless psychiatrists make the necessary personal investment of time and money and effort, there seems little chance of consolidating our gains and making the advancement which is possible.

Summary. Organized psychiatry can learn much from our experiences in this field in the Army. Many of these experiences placed a new or different

31 Smith, G., *Psychotherapy in General Medicine,* Report of an Experimental Postgraduate Course, Commonwealth Fund, New York, 1946. The lectures are published in *Teaching Psychotherapeutic Medicine,* Commonwealth Fund, New York, 1947.
32 Rennie, T. A. C., "Psychotherapy for the General Practitioner: A Program for Training. Post-graduate Education," *Am. J. Psychiat.,* 103:653-660, Mar., 1947
33 Gregg, Alan, "A Critique of Psychiatry," *Am. J. Psychiat.,* 101:285-291, Nov., 1944.

emphasis on well-known or semiestablished practices. Similar findings resulted from World War I. Thomas Salmon [34] presented them and pled for their acceptance in the years immediately following that war, only to receive scant attention. The long list of psychiatric responsibilities above is only a partial one. Psychiatry is on the doorstep of greatly increased potential usefulness. Whether it will venture beyond depends most on those of us in the profession, upon our vision of its possibilities and our abilities to make these possibilities realities, accessible to all those who want and need them.

[34] Salmon, T. W., "War Neuroses and Their Lesson," *New York State J. Med.*, 109:993-994, June 7, 1919; "Future of Psychiatry in the Army," *Mil. Surgeon*, 47:200-207, Aug., 1920.

30

CONTRIBUTIONS OF PSYCHIATRY
TO PUBLIC HEALTH

OUR STATE public health programs have been and are concerned primarily with the prevention of physical ill health. They have devoted themselves largely to sanitation, epidemiology, venereal-disease control, and many important aspects of physical medicine. They have done an excellent job in pushing public education and practice as concerns vaccination, control of contagious disease, food inspection, water supply, sewage disposal, and many other health measures.

The public health services have not, in general, included mental hygiene. It is not easy to explain this blind spot for psychiatry. Such an excellent job has been done in the prevention of contagious diseases that we have reduced dramatically their incidence and mortality. But nothing is being done to reduce the number of suicides which account for more deaths than the five most common communicable diseases—mumps, measles, scarlet fever, diphtheria, and whooping-cough.

Some of the fault must rest with psychiatry. Its personnel have been short; they have been almost entirely identified with treatment and not prevention; and except for emphasizing the importance of state-hospital supervision and the establishment of outpatient clinics, until very recently, they have not presented any concrete program of prevention of mental ill health which could be offered to a state public health department.

Only Connecticut, Florida, Kansas, Maine, Mississippi, Wisconsin, and Washington [1] have a psychiatrist as a member of the public health division in the state. A few other states have a mental hygiene unit which is separate from the health department—California, Iowa, Maryland, Massachusetts, Michigan, New Jersey, New York, and Virginia. Psychiatrists function under the department of public welfare in Illinois, Ohio, Pennsylvania, Rhode Island, Utah, Vermont, and Wisconsin. Nine [2] states have one or more full-time psychiatrists supervising the state mental institutions. In only one school of public

---

[1] Oregon had a psychiatrist in the Department of Health until March, 1947. Economic factors resulted in his elimination.
[2] Indiana, Maryland, Massachusetts, Michigan, New Jersey, New York, Ohio, Pennsylvania, Wisconsin.

health, namely Johns Hopkins University, is there a full-time psychiatrist on the faculty.[3]

A very few states have near ideal laws authorizing their departments of mental health to carry on broad responsibilities. Thus, in Massachusetts, with probably the most progressive regulations of any state, the duties of the department were specified in 1922 as follows:

The department shall take cognizance of all matters affecting the mental health of the citizens of the commonwealth, and shall make investigations and inquiries relative to all causes and conditions that tend to jeopardize said health, and the causes of mental disease, feeblemindedness and epilepsy, and the effects of employment, conditions and circumstances on mental health, including the effect thereon of the use of drugs, liquors and stimulants. It shall collect and disseminate such information relating thereto as it considers proper for diffusion among the people, and shall define what physical ailments, habits and conditions surrounding employment are to be deemed dangerous to mental health.[4]

The Department of Mental Health in Massachusetts cannot begin to carry out all of these functions for lack of man power, facilities, and finances.

The United States Public Health Service, in contrast to the many states, has had a Mental Hygiene Division for years.[5] It was formerly under the

---

[3] This is an excellent course under Dr. Paul Lemkau. It is divided into three parts. Part I deals with mental hygiene in the community and contacts with social agencies. Field trips are made to nursery schools, special educational classes, social service exchanges, and other agencies. Part II consists of lectures on personality development and psychodynamics. Part III is devoted to statistics, and special studies in child psychiatry, industrial mental hygiene, publicity, educational methods, etc.

[4] *Handbook of the Department of Mental Health,* Commonwealth of Massachusetts, 1944, Section 3A, p. 16.

[5] A personal communication from Dr. R. H. Felix, March 24, 1947, sketches the development of psychiatry in the U.S. Public Health Service.

"The first psychiatrist in charge of the Mental Hygiene Division of the Public Health Service was Dr. Walter L. Treadway. He was assigned as Chief of the newly created Narcotics Division on January 23, 1929, which became the Mental Hygiene Division about a year later under the Act of June 14, 1930, which established the Bureau of Narcotics under the Treasury Department. He served in this capacity until June 30, 1938. Dr. Lawrence Kolb succeeded him as Chief on July 1, 1938 and served until November 1, 1944, when I succeeded Dr. Kolb.

"Dr. Parran became Surgeon General of the Public Health Service April 6, 1936.

"It is difficult to say who played the most responsible part in introducing psychiatry into the Public Health Service. The first contribution of the Public Health Service to mental health had its inception in 1875 when, by a decision of the Supreme Court, all State laws relating to foreign immigration were declared unconstitutional and the authority for the regulation of foreign immigration was vested in the Federal Government. The medical examination of arriving aliens has since 1898 been conducted by the Public Health Service, and since that time sincere efforts have been made to bring about greater perfection in the recognition and examination of mental defects and diseases among immigrants. I do not have any information as to who originated this work. For six years beginning in 1913 Dr. Kolb specialized in mental and nervous diseases of incoming aliens at Ellis Island. Between 1919 and 1923 he organized and conducted the U.S. Public Health Service Hospital for the treatment of nervous patients at Waukesha, Wisconsin. Then followed a five-year period of research at the National Institute of Health, Washington, D.C., into the prevalence and epidemiology of drug addiction and its relation to crime; personality, intelligence, and general characteristics of addicts; and methods

direction of Dr. Walter L. Treadway (1929-38), then Dr. Lawrence Kolb (1938-44), and since that time Dr. Robert H. Felix. Nearly half of some 60 psychiatrists in the U.S. Public Health Service are located in its two public health service hospitals (narcotic farms). Others are assigned to the Bureau of Prisons. The balance have shared the responsibilities of supervision of treatment of certain types of psychiatric patients in two federal hospitals, the psychiatric examination of alien emigrants, psychiatric services in federal prisons, advice to federal agencies, and the welfare and public health boards of many states.

Until comparatively recently the Public Health Service has given only minor consideration to the development of a national mental health program. Through the vision and initiative of the Surgeon General's Office and the current chief psychiatrist, the U.S. Public Health Service has established a broad program. It developed, initiated, and carried on to successful Congressional action, the National Mental Health Act.[6] This Act, as outlined and already put into effect, will encourage and foster, through financial grants, many research projects in psychiatry, psychology, and psychiatric social work, as well as training of personnel in all of these fields. In addition it will aid

---

of treatment. He spent the next three years in Europe traveling widely on the continent making studies on 3,000 cases, in six countries, of the intelligence of those who applied for visas for entry into the United States.

"Dr. Treadway engaged in similar work at Ellis Island for several years, beginning in 1913, and from 1915 to 1921 conducted field investigations devoted especially to the study of prevalence and needs of mentally defective and dependent children, of the relation of mental disorders to crime and of correctional institutions and systems throughout the country. From 1918 to 1925 he was assigned to various psychiatric activities for the service, among them being a research project at Boston, Massachusetts on mental hygiene and its relation to migrating people, and special studies with reference to the insane and chronic alcoholism. While on duty in Ireland and England during a period from 1925 to 1928, he carried on special studies at the National Hospital for Nervous Diseases and Epilepsy.

"The Act of Congress approved June 14, 1930 establishing a Bureau of Narcotics in the Treasury Department, authorized the Surgeon General of the Public Health Service 'to make such studies and investigations, as may be necessary * * * of the causes, prevalence and means for the prevention and treatment of mental and nervous diseases.' This was the culmination of interest aroused and fostered by the vision of Dr. Treadway.

"The present mental health program of the Division was originally visualized and stimulated by Dr. Kolb, and I have carried on since he left, bringing it to its present state."

6 This bill was known as S-1160, "The National Neuropsychiatric Institute Act" and HR-4512 "National Mental Health Act." In its completed form it was an amendment to the Public Health Service Act, Public Law 487, 79th Congress, to be cited as the "National Mental Health Act." The purpose as stated "is the improvement of the mental health of the people of the United States through the conducting of researches, investigations, experiments, and demonstrations relating to the cause, diagnosis, and treatment of psychiatric disorders; assisting and fostering such research activities by public and private agencies, and promoting the coordination of all such researches and activities and the useful application of their results; training personnel in matters relating to mental health; and developing and assisting states in the use of the most effective methods of prevention, diagnosis and treatment of psychiatric disorders." See Felix, R. H., "The National Mental Health Act. How It Can Operate to Meet a National Problem." Ment. Hyg., 31:363-374, July, 1947.

in the sponsorship of community programs and state health programs and will match state funds provided for any of these.[7]

State public health programs in mental hygiene. The United States Public Health Service has already collected much data on the national needs for a mental hygiene program. Felix outlined these as including the training of personnel, the provision of psychiatric service to those persons not requiring hospital care, improved services in mental hospitals, education of the public, and an augmented and co-ordinated program of research.[8] Furthermore, he has called attention to the fact that an adequate outpatient clinical service for a community would require 152 hours a month of operation for every 100,000 population, with a team of a psychiatrist, a psychologist, two psychiatric social workers, and clerical assistants. At a very liberal estimate, the present services available constitute only 19.6 per cent of the necessary clinics needed as a bare minimum.[9]

While these figures are helpful, and also alarming because they indicate such a gross shortage, they should not imply that the treatment program of outpatient clinics would constitute a total mental hygiene program in a state. Such clinics would provide for a primary need: the treatment of ambulatory patients with minor disorders whom we saw in large numbers in the outpatient clinics in our army basic-training camps. This same Army experience, however, left no doubt that while the psychiatrists in these clinics gave greatly needed treatment, they contributed even more importantly by concerning themselves with the maintenance of mental health in the troops in the field. Similarly, it would seem that the ideal mental hygiene program in the state

---

[7] The first year of operation of the Mental Health Act shows the following results: All states have designated for the first time a state mental health authority. 42 states and territories have submitted mental health plans, 21 of which had no mental health program prior to July, 1947. In general these plans include central administrative services, training, clinics, professional service, and preventive and educational activities; 36 states are initiating or expanding community health clinics; 34 are employing mental health personnel to serve in consultant, supervisory, or service capacities; 37 include plans for providing preventive and educational activities.

59 grants were awarded to universities, hospitals, clinics, and other teaching centers to improve training facilities. 212 stipends were awarded to graduate students in psychiatry, clinical psychology, psychiatric social work, and psychiatric nursing. 32 grants were made for research in some area of mental health. 21 fellowships have been awarded to advanced students to conduct research.

Congress appropriated $850,000 for the purchase of a site and the drawing of plans for the National Institute of Mental Health.

From Felix, R. H., "The National Mental Health Program, A Progress Report," presented at the State and Territorial Health Officers Meeting, Washington, D. C., Dec. 2, 1947, but corrected to January 1, 1948.

[8] Felix, R. H., "Psychiatric Plans of the United States Public Health Service," *Ment. Hyg.,* 30:381-389, July, 1946. Dr. Felix's predecessor, Dr. Lawrence Kolb, also appealed to State Public Health Departments to include mental hygiene in their programs. Kolb, L., "The Integration of Mental Health Programs," *Pennsylvania's Health,* 3:10-18, Mar., 1942.

[9] Felix, R. H., "Mental Public Health. A Plan of National Scope," *Bull. Massachusetts Soc. for Ment. Hyg.,* Mar., 1946.

should have maintenance of mental health and prevention of ill health as its chief function.

It might be wise to conduct a demonstration experiment which would begin with a survey of the mental health in a particular area. Certainly data should be collected on mental ill health statistics including facilities available for treatment and custody of patients, methods of care and management of patients, turnover of patients, effectiveness of treatment, training facilities for personnel, and outpatient clinic facilities. Statistics should include data of private and public services.

A determination of the extent of unhappiness and maladjustment would be more difficult. Without it, however, the real incidence of mental ill health could not even be estimated. Surveys of the extent of the so-called "social neuroses" would give a partial measure. Therefore, one should certainly investigate the presence of causes for and the incidence of crime, juvenile delinquency, truancy, venereal disease, divorce, illiteracy, illegitimacy, unemployment. It might be more difficult, but worth the effort, to discover the specific indications of racial tensions and the practices producing these, the degree and extent of unemployment, the housing shortage, absenteeism, and strikes.

A second step in such a program would be another survey, perhaps made simultaneously with the first, of all the facilities that were being used or could be used in an effective, preventive program. This would include the available medical, educational, vocational, and recreational facilities, their location and their use. The study should include an evaluation of other potential resources in the form of community groups, welfare agencies, religious bodies, social agencies, "character building" programs.

Finally, the checking of the needs against the resources would indicate the supplementary personnel, facilities, and program that would be necessary for the improvement of the mental health of the community. On the basis of this evaluation of the survey, plans could be made for the organization of a demonstration program. The needed increase in the specific types of facilities could be solicited from one or more sources—federal, state or local, public or private.

Just as the public health agencies currently assist in the solution of local health problems, whether they concern sanitation or epidemic, they could initiate and stimulate the expansion of community mental health measures. They could enlist the schools, churches, industry, civic groups, and private citizens, in a definite course of action: perhaps, to provide visiting teachers, expand recreational facilities, provide health and mental hygiene programs in industries and schools, increase vocational opportunities, establish community discussion groups, and direct welfare work or other types of constructive programs more specifically toward the improvement of mental health.

While such a program would momentarily make even more difficult the position in which psychiatrists currently find themselves, it is essential. The present clinical load for diagnosis and treatment is far beyond the capacity of the available personnel. It is questionable whether we will ever really catch up with the demand for psychiatrically trained people. Therefore, it seems all the more important to consider seriously the best way to reduce treatment demands by increasing preventive efforts.

The upheaval resulting from the war, and the long list of evidences of maladjustment make one wonder how we can expect good health when the social situation is so topsy-turvy.[10] Perhaps an intensive demonstration of how psychiatrists would contribute to the improvement of the mental health of the public might throw light on ways to reduce ill health.

Information and education. Any state mental health program would require much public education. The Information and Education Services in the Army were found to be essential in order to help the soldier understand the aims and purposes of the military organization and his responsibility toward them. A board of health should provide extensive public education about mental health so that the citizen might understand and know his responsibility for its maintenance.[11]

Such a program would depend upon the teaching and public speaking of specialists, including psychiatrists, psychologists, and social workers from medical schools, state hospitals, and private practice. The arrangements could be handled best by organized groups within the community, such as the local mental hygiene society. Such a society of laymen, constituted into active committees, with the stimulation aand leadership of health officials, could provide such a program of education.

Mental health hazards. As the war proceeded, experience dictated the decision to order Army psychiatrists to advise commanding officers on the hazards to the mental health of their units. The public health officials are concerned with physical health hazards as they occur in homes, in industry, on the farm. Similarly they should educate toward the eradication of hazards to mental health. As representatives of the public they could carry the brunt of developing methods for improving community morale; they could advise and counsel with industrial concerns relative to the mental health of their workers; they could assist educational and occupational groups, religious and civic organizations. Above all they should counsel and advise the "command" as represented by public officials, legislators, community leaders.

---

[10] Frank, L. K., "What is Ahead in Orthopsychiatry?" Round table, 1946, of the *Am. J. Orthopsychiat.,* **27**:5-8, Jan., 1947. Doctor Frank asked and discussed this question.

[11] This same point has been made by a former State Commissioner of Mental Health, F. F. Tallman, reported in *State Charities Aid Assn. News,* **37**:4-5, Dec., 1947.

State-hospital care. Not until top-level Army personnel could understand the importance of improved treatment procedures, were they made official. It is not likely that we will see a change in the state-hospital situation, with its lamentable lack of personnel and inadequate facilities for care and treatment, until we get an educated public which demands such needed reform. After all, the taxpayers, the voters, are the bosses of public administration. It is the public health departments of state government and of local communities which must undertake the development of a public mental health program which will educate the citizenry to these needs. This program should include not only the protests of a militant public against medieval situations, but it should develop an intelligent, long-range, legislative program. Legislation needs revision in regard to admissions to mental hospitals, to provide for the removal of state hospitals from the political system, for the mobilization and training of adequate personnel for these institutions.[12] A further step would be the development of a program of home placement for some types of cases of mental illness, as now provided for in a few states.

The status of our mental hygiene program in public health is not greatly dissimilar to the status of psychiatry in the Army at the beginning of the war. There were few definite programs or plans. No preventive measures were in effect; therefore 99 per cent of our psychiatrists were stationed in hospitals. There they were bound by insufficient supplementary personnel and facilities. Moreover the regulations (laws) either did not permit or were not conducive to intensive treatment. From experience we learned that we had to place psychiatrists "in the field" where soldiers lived and worked. Initially they limited their work to screening and providing treatment for maladjustment in an early stage. Both of these they did well. Further experience taught them, and us, that their most important function was to concern themselves with the maintenance of mental health and determination of steps to take in order to prevent mental ill health. This required organization, surveys, authority, and the implementation of plans by the *leaders* in command. We learned too that we had to set up outpatient clinics in connection with hospitals; that treatment had to be intensive and the facilities improved. We had to train psychiatrists and psychologists and psychiatric social workers. And gratifyingly, we demonstrated, at least with some success, that much preventive work and treatment could be done even in a complicated and urgent and unplanned-for situation. Perhaps this experience will give encouragement and serve in some degree as a guide to assist state and community public health leaders in meeting the pressing needs of our time.

---

12 A good summary of the problem of the state hospitals was given in "Our State Mental Hospitals. What Can We Do to Improve Them?" A radio discussion by Kenneth Appel, Walter Barton, Henry Brosin and William C. Menninger. The Univ. of Chicago Round Table, No. 496, Sept. 21, 1947.

31

ACADEMIC EDUCATION AND PSYCHIATRY

"WE CAN LOSE this total war on the battlefront as a direct result of losing it on the educational front. Education is the backbone of the Army." [1] So spoke Gen. Brehon Somervell, Commanding General of the Army Service Forces during the war. There were three aspects of that education: first, teaching men to live in the Army in all parts of the world; second, developing their skill in a particular, assigned job; and third, providing them with enough background and understanding as to the purpose of their service so that they might feel that their job was important.

Only the civilian soldier can fully appreciate the importance of learning how to live in the Army. Aside from explanations about military regulations and the articles of war, most of that learning was absorbed from the experience of being a soldier—through discipline, "courtesies," rules, language and "orders"; through uncertainties, frustrations, monotony, "sweating it out." The new recruit had to learn how to get along in the platoon or the kitchen-police detail or the reconnoitering squad; with the sergeant or the captain or the general. Most soldiers learned to do so—and quickly.

The effort of the Army to teach a man how to become a soldier and to do a specific job was labeled "training," of which there were many different types and systems. A program to give "pre-induction training" to 16- and 17-year-old youths while they were still in high schools in civilian life was planned by the Army. It was taught by the regular high-school teachers. The Army and the Navy joined in the development of "specialized training" [2] in selected colleges and universities in the fields of engineering, languages, science, mathematics, psychology, medicine, and other subjects. The Army developed an elaborate system for the education of illiterates.

Every inductee was assigned initially to "basic training," where for 17 weeks [3] he was taught the ABC's of being a soldier. Each soldier then received training for some specialized job, either for combat or for one of the

---

[1] Quoted by Witty, P. A., and Goldberg, S., "Evolution and Education Through Army Experience," *J. Educational Psychol.*, 35:338-346, Sept., 1944.
[2] Army Specialized Training Program, usually referred to as ASTP. In the Navy it was referred to as the V-9, V-12, and other programs.
[3] The length of time varied depending on the urgency for new troops.

technical Services such as Ordnance, Engineer, Medical Corps. This was "advanced training."

In the role of a soldier, many men "saw the world." The opportunity to go overseas which military service provided was a priceless educational lesson. It is impossible to calculate the significance to America of the world travels and the knowledge of people and places gained on the part of at least 5,000,-000 of our young men.

Finally, the Army assumed the responsibility, through the Information and Education Division of the War Department, of providing the soldier background information about why he was in the Army, why his job was important, and why he was fighting. This required an explanation of the war, the aims of the enemy and what they meant to America, and also an understanding of what our allies were doing. The various commanding officers carried an important part of this responsibility in convincingly relating the assignment of the particular unit to the total picture.

Educators contributed heavily to this variegated program. They [4] and others saw great value in some expedients that were used. For instance, it was discovered that a great many men could be educated quickly who had never had the chance for higher education in civil life—either because of poor educational selection, unequal opportunities, or poor school systems.

The Adjutant General's Office measured the ability of 10,000,000 men to learn, as well as their fund of information, through a test known as AGCT —the Army General Classification Test. By that test, 5.8 per cent of men examined were rated in the highest group, Grade 1; 26.2 per cent in Grade 2; 30.7 per cent in Grade 3; 28.5 per cent in Grade 4; 8.8 per cent in Grade 5.[5] When Dr. Walter Bingham [6] analyzed these figures he discovered that only one-fourth of the smartest group were college graduates. In Grade 2 there were only 184,000 college graduates; 1,666,000 had finished high school but not college; 858,000 finished the eighth grade but not high school, and 56 did not complete the eighth grade. His valid conclusion was that there are many of our population who could profit from more education and thus go much further in life if they had a chance.[7]

---

[4] The American Council on Education is sponsoring a commission on educational implications of the experience of the armed forces, under the immediate direction of Dr. Alonzo G. Grace. See a résumé of a questionnaire survey of the opinions of educator and student veterans by M. M. Chambers, *Opinions on Gains for American Education from Wartime Armed Services Training*, American Council on Education, Washington, D.C., 1946.

[5] See Chap. 14.

[6] Bingham, W., "Inequalities in Adult Capacity—from Military Data," *Science*, 104:147-152, Aug. 16, 1946.

[7] The extent of the acceptance (1,572,049 veterans on December 31, 1946) of the current GI education program in colleges and universities, even under difficulties, would seem to show that economic restrictions were the chief deterrent to advanced schooling. *Life*, Apr. 21, 1947, p. 105; Editorial Comment, *School Rev.*, 55:501-502, Nov., 1946; Bolte, C. G., "The Veterans

Substantiation of Bingham's conclusions are available from another source. Few if any intelligent individuals would disagree with the principle that the general education of an individual is an extremely important factor in his mental health. Its absence may be a direct cause of mental ill health. We may think that America is the land of opportunity, but educationally this is questioned in a very dramatic fashion by Norton and Lawler. They point out that it is not,

because

> 3,000,000 adults living in the United States have never attended any kind of school.

because

> 10,000,000 adult Americans have had so little schooling that they are virtual illiterates—they cannot read and write well enough to meet the demands of modern life.

because

> half of the brightest and most talented youth of the nation leave school prematurely—before they have had the kind and amount of schooling which would be justified by both their ability and the demands of our way of life.

because

> 2,000,000 children, aged six to fifteen, were not in any kind of school in 1940—and this number was substantially increased during the war.

because

> the schooling provided millions of American children who are in school is so inferior and brief that it leaves them unprepared to meet the demands made upon them as citizens and as individuals.[8]

In the evaluation of the total training program, psychologists specializing in this field have expressed the belief that no new principles or techniques were developed.[9] However, the Army served as an immense laboratory for the testing of "progressive" methods of teaching large numbers of men in a very short time. These methods included the emphasis on the value of realistic aims and goals for courses of study, of small-sized instructional groups, of diversified teaching methods, of applicatory exercises to fix and maintain desirable knowledge and skills, of appropriate visual and training aids, of tests for prediction, evaluation, and diagnosis.

As a psychiatrist, I cannot evaluate the effectiveness of the Army teaching

Seek Education," *Yale Rev.,* **35**:614-621, Summer, 1946; Events Column, *School and Society,* **65**:190, Mar. 15, 1947; "How Well Are Veterans Doing?" *ibid.,* **65**:210-212, Mar. 22, 1947; Toepelman, W. C., "The Veteran in College," *NEA Journal,* **35**:488-489, Nov., 1946; Stoddard, G. D., "Youth Storms the College Portals," *Nation's Business,* **34**:41-43, Sept., 1946.

[8] Norton, J. K., and Lawler, E. S., *Unfinished Business in American Education,* American Council on Education, Washington, D.C., 1946, p. 3.

[9] This attitude and the following principles of educational psychology have been elaborated by two educators associated with the Army, both with psychological training. Witty, P. A., and Goldberg, S., "Evolution and Education through Army Experience," *J. Educational Psychol.,* **35**:338-346, Sept., 1944.

program from a pedagogic point of view. On the other hand, there were certain very important mental hygiene values in the same practices and usages which the educators praised.

Learning was the chief job for most soldiers for at least the first 6 months. An important consideration in good mental health is effectiveness and success on the job. Anything which made the material to be learned more interesting and easier to understand was, therefore, an important aid to the maintenance of good mental health.

A realistic purpose in acquiring certain knowledge was an extremely important factor in speeding up the learning process. The rapid acquisition and improvement of a skill gave the soldier a sense of accomplishment, superiority, and security. Because much of the training was given in small groups, there was a much better chance for individual assistance. The visual aid program was certainly worth its great expense.[10] All of these made the job of learning easier and far more successful. They would have a similarly important value in so far as they could be applied to the civilian program of education.

The role of psychiatry. Even the most expansive psychiatrist in his greatest enthusiasm could claim no credit for influencing the educational program in the Army, even though we tried. On the other hand, we watched the effect of the training program on the mental health of the soldier. It was our task to try to repair the damage to personalities when it resulted from that program. Therefore, we could not help but have some opinions about the methods, which sometimes did precipitate neurotic reactions in individuals with borderline adjustment. Those who could not keep up with the established pace came to our clinics and to our sections in the hospitals. Relatively late in the war, in some basic-training camps, the psychiatrist became an adviser to the commanding officer and could point out the more obviously undesirable effects of particular methods on the soldier's mental health. Our military experience convinced us that certain common educational practices are unwise and certain others should be used more consistently and widely.

Motivation. The subject of motivation has been discussed extensively in a previous chapter.[11] In the Army the word was used to refer to the conscious attitude of the soldier toward his job. The aim of the commanding officer was to motivate his men toward doing what had to be done by convincing them

---

10 One of the moving-picture films (and the Army developed thousands) was entitled "Let There Be Light." It was made at the request of the Neuropsychiatry Consultants Division and under its supervision. It showed line officers and Medical Corps personnel the treatment methods for psychiatric combat casualties. It is a remarkable picture, but its 3,000 feet represented the best shots of 300,000 feet exposed, at an estimated cost of $150,000. An excellent review of the methods and applications of audio-visual aids has been prepared by J. R. Miles, and C. R. Spain, *Audio-visual Aids in the Armed Services,* American Council on Education, Washington, D.C., 1947.

11 See Chap. 6.

of the importance of their jobs and the specificity of those jobs for those soldiers. In so far as educational efforts were concerned, positive motivation meant that the soldier was ready and wanted to learn. Background material was prepared by the Information and Education Service for use in the stimulation of motivation. Success or failure in its use depended entirely on the leadership of each military unit.

Many soldiers initially were not interested in being in the Army; they did not want to fight. Therefore the first job of the Army educator was to overcome resistance toward learning how to fight by showing the new soldiers its necessity. Then came the task of making the learning of essential skills as rapid and easy as possible.

On the sidelines, the psychiatrist could observe the futility of the wrong type of motivation. For instance, when the fear of death or the threat of censure of the group were commonly employed, personality stress increased. The spirit of competition was used frequently in unwise fashion, particularly in trying to make the soldier qualify on the rifle range. On the other hand, superior leadership developed ingenious ways of motivating the soldier positively. Some instructors could make the most dull, routine information easily understandable. They made it vital and interesting. The good mental health of military units under such teachers was revealed by lower sick call and AWOL rates. The conclusion which seemed obvious to the psychiatrist was that, in the absence of favorable motivation, the material presented was not learned. Failure to learn was inevitably followed by emotional distress about it, or often a sense of inadequacy, and in many instances neurotic symptoms.

The question of motivation for the average teacher in our primary or secondary schools, our colleges and our universities, is undoubtedly one of his knottiest problems. Too much of what he must teach does not seem to the student to be of any immediate value.[12] Curriculum builders have too often been blind to evidence of which subject matter is valuable and which is only traditional. Consequently, it is difficult to harness a pupil's motivation to learning what educational systems have decreed he shall be taught. Sometimes both teacher and student are prejudiced against learning which is required rather than interesting. For example, civics and history have been "required" subjects for years, and yet in November, 1946, only 38 per cent of our people over 21 years of age voted.[13]

---

[12] A strong indictment of our educational programs for the lack of goal-directed purpose was given by one leading educator. "Present-day educational and training agencies are found utterly inadequate to meet the changing requirements for happy and successful living. A lack of coordination between educational institutions and the work-a-day world is apparent in nine out of ten of the schools and colleges investigated." *Readjustment or Revolution* by A. H. Edgerton, published by Whittlesey House, New York, copyright, 1946, by McGraw-Hill Book Company, p. 5.

[13] Gallup, G. H., "Why Don't More Americans Vote?" *Reader's Digest*, 50:76-78, Apr., 1947.

Considering motivation even at this superficial conscious level, one easily becomes involved in a discussion of the philosophy of education. Even a hasty review indicates a wide diversity of the current opinions and methods.

Regardless of what American education has been, certainly it must be modified by the needs of the troubled state of the world today. As Dean Gildersleeve, formerly of Barnard College, stated, "Never more sorely has the country needed an educated citizenry, educated not only in reading, writing and arithmetic, but in the right attitude of mind about the whole country and the world today." [14] Most assuredly there is great doubt as to whether we, as a people, have the intellectual capacity or the emotional maturity to handle the problem of atomic energy.[15] Brock Chisholm, a psychiatrist, raised the question as to whether or not we could learn with adequate speed to become sufficiently mature to prevent our own extinction.[16]

Quite beyond the conscious motivation, the educator must be concerned with unconscious motivation. In this area we must deal chiefly with emotions, not intellection. This implies that the teacher must know something about personality structure and development. He must be able to recognize the expressions of basic psychological needs of each individual—the need for love, for approved outlets for hostile feelings, for compensations. Then can the teacher understand the evidence of a feeling of insecurity, of inadequacy, of a desire to belong, of resistance to authority. Motivation in education, as everywhere else, resolves itself largely into a matter of interpersonal relationships between the teacher and the student.

It is an interesting corollary that in a recent survey of some 12,000 students the teacher's personality was evaluated as being far, far more important than was proficiency in teaching. The more important traits of a good teacher, listed according to the frequency of mention by the school children themselves, were: co-operative and democratic attitude, kindliness and consideration for the individual, patience, wide interests, pleasing personal appearance and manner, fairness and impartiality, sense of humor, good disposition and consistent behavior, interest in pupil's problems, flexibility, use of recognition and praise and, finally and last, unusual proficiency in teaching. It is significant that all of the first 11 traits fall within the definition of personality.[17]

---

[14] Gildersleeve, V. C., "Genius Can't Flower Because Our Schools Don't Give It Root," condensation of an address before the New York Academy of Public Education as reported in the *Washington* (D.C.) *Post,* Feb. 26, 1946.

[15] This crisis, in so far as it concerns education, was vividly described by R. M. Hutchins, "The Good News of Damnation," an address before the Publicity Club of Chicago, Jan. 8, 1947. It is also presented as a crisis to educators by H. M. Jones, *Education and World Tragedy,* Harvard University Press, Cambridge, Mass., 1946, pp. 78-79.

[16] Chisholm, G. B., "The Reestablishment of Peacetime Society. (1) The Responsibility of Psychiatry. (2) The Responsibility of Psychiatrists," *Psychiatry,* 9:3-20, Feb., 1946.

[17] Witty, Paul A., "The Teacher Who Has Helped Me Most," *National Parent Teacher,* 61:7-9, Feb., 1947.

Regardless of the subject matter taught, success in capitalizing on unconscious motivation will depend on whether the pupil is made to feel secure in a gradual maturing process; on whether he will find gratification in learning by approved methods; on whether he will gain satisfaction from his achievement and an increasing sense of self-confidence.

Individualized teaching. The psychiatrist who observed the serious loss of man power from psychiatric casualties caused by the inelastic educational program of the Army often believed it to be unnecessary. The Canadian Army graded its soldiers so that men of higher intellectual capacity progressed through courses at a faster rate. Presumably, this was never possible in the American Army because of the urgency of the situation. The training pace was the same for all, regardless of age, physical status, or mental capacity. Graded training would probably have been well worth its cost in extra planning, personnel, and time because of a lowered man-power loss.

The tendency of most school systems to cater to the "average" has resulted in a snobbery on the part of the intellectually superior students. When teaching is set on a dead center of "average" learning capacity, the quick thinker becomes lazy in the absence of necessity to make an effort, and the slow thinker becomes discouraged or indifferent to failure.

Child-guidance clinics and visiting-teacher programs discovered that in a surprising number of "problem students" emotional factors rather than innate ability prevented learning. However, as yet too few schools seriously concern themselves as to "why" a student does not learn. More and more, however, they are unable to escape the evidence that the presentation of basic knowledge is not "education." In some of the larger communities [18] there are trends toward the increased use of ungraded rooms, noncollege-preparatory courses, honor-student classes, custom-built courses of study, psychiatric evaluation of problem students.

Educators themselves will have to select the subject matter and develop the techniques of teaching. Psychiatrists can express the hope that they do not add to the stress of harassed personalities, and that their teaching effort is not wasted by not being used.

Understanding the personality. In addition to the points made above about the very great importance of the teacher's personality and unconscious motivation, the psychiatrist must add that it is not enough for the teacher to know the "laws of learning" and the "laws of habit formation." He must also understand the personality. The teacher along with the psychiatrist must know

---

[18] Few educational institutions place the individual student above regulations, standards, and administrative machinery, despite the urging in that direction by many leaders in education, particularly the American Council on Education. This point is especially stressed by H. E. and L. R. Hawkes, *Through a Dean's Open Door,* McGraw-Hill Book Company, Inc., New York, 1945.

the child's home background, which has formed that personality. Certainly of all the places in which organized courses [19] in personality structure and function should be included is first our teachers' colleges. For the teaching of the elementary grades, its basic principle should be that the teacher's understanding of child development is far more important than her knowledge of mathematics or geography.

The doctor cannot properly treat a patient by treating his symptoms without examination. Nor can the teacher handle the shy child, the bully, the overaffectionate, the failing pupil without some "case work." The social-worker–psychologist–psychiatrist team can often make the teacher's effort count for much more.

One of the special and important functions of the Mental Hygiene Consultation Services, located in each basic-training camp, was to give assistance to the individual soldier on his problems. Early help toward better adjustment, assistance in the solution of problems concerning his present status or his home, resulted in a great saving of man power. Its need was proved by the thousands of consultations referred to it.

A comparatively small number of our civilian educational institutions have learned this lesson. Too few provide mental hygiene counselors.[20] In some colleges psychiatrists are available to help the student who is having either scholastic or personal difficulty. On the basis of Army experience, however, it would seem advisable to extend this service. Not only in more of our colleges and high schools, but also in our grammar schools, the failing or the lonesome, the troubled, or the eccentric student needs particular help. When necessary for the mental health of the student, counseling should be made available to the parents.[21]

There is an increasing number of psychiatrists and educators who believe that the subject of mental hygiene can be profitably taught in school, from elementary grades through college. In the Army, when presented properly,

[19] Evidence of this awareness is seen in the increasing number of texts for teachers dealing with the field of mental hygiene. All of the following have excellent points worthy of the perusal of any teacher: Prescott, D. A., *Emotion and the Educative Process,* American Council on Education, Washington, D.C., 1938; Rivlin, H. N., *Education for Adjustment,* D. Appleton-Century Company, Inc., New York, 1936; Ryan, W. C., *Mental Health Through Education,* Commonwealth Fund, New York, 1938; Sherman, Mandell, *Mental Hygiene and Education,* Longmans, Green and Company, New York, 1936; Symonds, P. M., *Children's Behavior and Teachers' Attitudes,* Commonwealth Fund, New York, 1928; Witty, P. A., and Skinner, C. E., *Mental Hygiene in Modern Education,* Farrar & Rinehart, Inc., New York, 1939.

[20] Many of our colleges and universities have developed mental hygiene services, although few provide routine counseling facilities. Some of the metropolitan public-school systems have excellent psychiatric-psychological services. In many cities, a "visiting teacher" system is in effect which fundamentally is a type of parent-student counseling.

[21] Because many school systems advocate limitation of their role strictly to the educational process, they may limit their responsibility in the maintenance of mental health to identification of and referral to community clinics of those who need help.

the mental hygiene lectures for enlisted men and those for officers were found helpful.[22] Besides the tangible evidence that through them and the consultation service many men were saved for the Army was the greater satisfaction that the men themselves expressed when relieved of their psychological distress. Every psychiatrist received the gratitude and appreciation of many soldiers for the attempt to understand their problems and the suggestions made to them, which usually smoothed the path, if even only a little.

In civilian life an interesting and unusual experiment is being carried out under the direction of Mr. H. Edmund Bullis, Executive Director of the Delaware State Society of Mental Hygiene. Mr. Bullis has composed a series of presentations entitled "Human Relations in the Classroom," which are presented by the teachers of English and social studies to the students in public schools. As of January, 1947, 1,400 seventh- and eighth-grade pupils in 52 classes in 31 Delaware schools were having these weekly classes. Discussions in this course were concerned with psychological problems, leading the children to speak of their own fears, disappointments, and dissatisfactions.

In a very few of our colleges and universities there are organized courses in mental hygiene, but these are still very much more the exception than the rule. Since human relationships are basic, why should not all of our educational institutions provide a place in the curriculum for the study of the principles of mental as well as of physical hygiene? ·

Leadership. Undoubtedly the most important observation made by psychiatrists on the educational efforts in the Army had to do with leadership. In the final analysis it was the teacher-leader who improved the mental health or threatened it. He created the motivation, interest, confidence. It was he who took into consideration the individual's capacity. In its great urgency, the Army did not have time to carefully choose its teachers. Too often it assumed that because an individual was an expert in the field, therefore he was qualified to teach. Undoubtedly the leaders knew but often could not take into consideration the fact that the possession of technical information alone was not nearly so important as his personality characteristics, his capacity to stimulate, to inspire, to lead. Furthermore, as yet there is no very good technique of leader-teacher selection available for general use.

The matter of teacher selection, particularly for our primary and secondary grades, might well be reviewed from a psychiatric point of view. These teachers have a large role in the molding of a child's personality through the

---

[22] There was difficulty in referring to these as mental hygiene lectures. Consequently they went under pseudonyms: The six lecture outlines for officers were labeled "Personnel Adjustment Problems," and were outlined in *War Department Technical Bulletin, Medical 12,* dated 22 February 1944. The lecture outlines for enlisted men were labeled "Personal Adjustment Problems," outlined in *War Department Technical Bulletin, Medical 21,* issued initially 15 March 1944 and revised as of 29 December 1945.

most plastic years of life. The teacher in her 6 to 7 hours each day actually may spend more time in close contact with the child than do his parents. Unless the teacher is well adjusted and a mentally healthy individual, the effect on the child can be extremely damaging. Were we to select and employ only emotionally mature, intellectually superior teachers, our educational system would improve immeasurably.

The present dilemma of education is also that of psychiatry. There are not enough well-trained, well-qualified people in the field. Even more serious is the fact that the public is so inadequately educated that it does not create conditions amenable to the retention of many of those who start out as good teachers. A program of recruiting and selection and public education about how to improve teacher status in the community is essential. A "beloved" and a "good" teacher can teach anything so that pupils will remember it for years. A cranky, bitter, maladjusted teacher cannot teach so that the pupils will learn anything other than a dislike for the teacher and for learning in general. The teachers of America have a great responsibility in the making of the nation, and the world, of tomorrow.

The future. From direct observation, psychiatrists in the Army learned a great deal about the difficulties in the training program. From those who failed in it they learned much about human and methodological deficiencies.[23] Perhaps the psychiatric evaluation of student and teacher failures in the Army could supplement the growing appreciation of the value of such observations in civilian life. We saw the importance of realistic goals, of small classes with individual attention, of exercises in the practical application of the lessons learned. We recognized the importance of the motivating factors behind the program. We saw the necessity for individualizing the material to fit the person who was trying to learn it. We saw the advantages of presenting mental hygiene principles, both to teachers and students. We were convinced that leadership as provided by the teacher was the keystone in learning, which, when successful, fortified the mental health of the individual.

The direct application, however, of some of these lessons is not easy. Teachers are overworked now. Classes are too large. Many of our leading educators are warning us of the rut into which our American system has run. We don't begin to remunerate our teachers sufficiently. Their poor pay and

---

[23] At his request a special survey was made in the early part of 1944 for Mr. Harvey H. Bundy, then Special Assistant to the Secretary of War, on suggestions regarding psychiatric problems occurring in the basic-training camps, dated 7 June 1944. This was a survey of psychiatric opinion as to training methods and difficulties encountered in the educational program as seen in the basic-training camps. It outlined problems encountered in leadership, in the psychiatric understanding required by officers and cadre; problems concerning instructors, training methods; special comments on the infiltration course and rifle training; the relation of training, classification, and assignment to the development of psychoneurosis; the recommendation that labor battalions be formed; orientation problems; and other miscellaneous topics.

excessive restriction have become so unbearable that, for the first time in American history, a profession has resorted to a strike.

Even with all of these difficulties it is the psychiatrist's fervid hope that personality factors in the educational process rather than the subject matter can be given much greater consideration. Personality evaluation of the teacher would be helpful, both to himself and to his students. Above all, we need to learn to understand each other, to get along with each other. The child is going to learn this, for better or for worse, in his educational experience. This is the colossal responsibility that faces teachers—a far, far greater one than merely conveying information.

32

MENTAL HYGIENE[1] IN
INDUSTRY AND BUSINESS

THE ARMY functioned much as a huge industry does. In it psychiatry played a relatively prominent role. Why could psychiatry not also contribute to civilian industry and business? This specialty of medicine is concerned with the way people feel, think, and behave. Productiveness in industry and business depend upon efficient, satisfied workers. Great benefit therefore should come from a closer relationship between psychiatry and industry.

For 30 years psychiatrists have had some contact with industrial problems.[2] One of the early pioneers in this special field was Elmer Ernest Southard,[3] then Professor of Psychiatry at Harvard. He was impressed with the similarity of the psychiatric job in the Army during World War I and its potential application to industry. He set out to determine why employees were discharged. There were several forays of psychiatry into industry during the next 10 years. In the late 1920's, Dr. V. V. Anderson[4] established a model psychiatric setup in a large department store with 13,000 employees. His book, written in 1929, remains the only major treatise on this topic. Following this there was a decline in the mental hygiene efforts in industry until a new impetus was furnished by World War II.

There is no concrete evidence that the war particularly stimulated programs of industrial mental hygiene, except that interest increased in all psychiatric work. In addition to the indirect stimulus, employers were perplexed by the problem of the neuropsychiatric casualties returning to civilian

---

[1] The term mental hygiene is used to denote that aspect of psychiatry concerned with the prevention of mental ill health.

[2] In a recent historical review, Rennie, et al, cited the pioneering efforts of C. C. Burlingame in 1916 with the Cheney Silk Company, and referred to Jarrett, Mary C., "The Psychopathic Employee: A Problem of Industry," *Medicine and Surgery*, 1:727-741, Sept., 1917; Adler, H. M., "Unemployment and Personality—A Study of Psychopathic Cases," *Ment. Hyg.*, 1:16-24, Jan., 1917; Bailey, Pearce, "Applicability of Findings of Neuropsychiatric Examinations in the Army to Civil Problems," *Ment. Hyg.*, 4:301-311, Apr., 1920. See Rennie, T. A. C.; Swackhamer, G.; and Woodward, L. E., "Toward Industrial Mental Health. An Historical Review," *Ment. Hyg.*, 31:66-88, Jan., 1947.

[3] Southard, E. E., "The Movement for a Mental Hygiene of Industry," *Ment. Hyg.*, 4:43-64, Jan., 1920.

[4] Anderson, V. V., *Psychiatry in Industry*, Harper & Brothers, New York, 1929.

486

jobs. However, many experiences and lessons learned by Army psychiatrists could be applied with profit to industry.

Problems in applying psychiatry to industry. One might anticipate that one of the problems in introducing psychiatric principles into industry and business would be concerned with the psychiatrist himself. However, the job of an industrial psychiatrist is similar in many ways to that of an Army psychiatrist in the field. The descriptions of the job of the former, as given by Dershimer,[5] Himler,[6] and Brodman[7] show many parallels with the jobs of the psychiatrists in the Mental Hygiene Consultation Services and the combat divisions.

The psychiatrist who worked in the field had to know the Army and its mission; he had to be able to identify himself closely with the Army; he had to reorient from his interest in treating one person to the prevention of mental ill health in groups; he had to attempt to apply the best of his psychiatric knowledge to the social situation in which he worked.

To add more detail, the psychiatrist, like every other civilian, didn't become a good soldier just by putting on a uniform. His work specifically required him to know the structure of the Army and the methods that were used in the Army. He had to know the point of view of the men in the Army, what they were experiencing, what they were expected to do, how they felt about it, and the prevalent emotional stresses as well as the available emotional supports. Furthermore, he had to identify with the Army to the extent of believing in it, wanting to contribute constructively to it, and feeling a sense of pride in being a part of it.

The field psychiatrists, and even those within the military hospitals, served most effectively if they could change their civilian concept of only being therapists to one individual at a time. In the Army the primary concern was with the welfare of the military unit. This implied that the psychiatrist had to be interested in the factors that made the group function and those that interfered with its smooth-working relationships. Sometimes he had to transfer or hospitalize a particular individual for the benefit of the group. Other times he had to return to the group a man who was not in perfect health but was still able to give service. The psychiatrist was also expected to apply psychiatric principles to some types of activities in which he may have had no prewar professional experience: selection, training, advising, treatment, prevention. The lessons of wartime experiences of the Army psychiatrist in the field are equally applicable and essential to the psychiatrist working in industry.

---

[5] Dershimer, F. W., "Psychiatry in Industry," *Am. J. Psychiat.*, 103:145-148, Sept., 1946.
[6] Himler, L. E., "Current Trends in Industrial Psychiatry," *Am. J. Psychiat.*, 103:149-153, Sept., 1946.
[7] Brodman, K., "The Organization of a Mental Hygiene Unit in Industry," *Indust. Med.*, 15:259-262, Apr., 1946.

Another hurdle for the development of mental hygiene in industry is the shortage of personnel. This shortage exists in every type of psychiatric practice but is particularly pertinent as applied to industry. This is chiefly for the reason that there have been no opportunities for training the industrial psychiatrist. Except for the meager reports in the literature, until recently any psychiatrist going into this field had to learn as he went along. But a beginning, however small, has been made; in 1946, Wayne University [8] in Detroit initiated a course in occupational health, the first graduate training related to this field. A fellowship in industrial psychiatry was created in 1948 in the New York School of Industrial and Labor Relations at Cornell University under Dr. Alexander H. Leighton.

The inadequacy of our program for industrial mental hygiene is also related to the lack of opportunity for employment in this field. Nevertheless, a few industries have blazed a trail and programs are being developed. As yet they must be individualized to each particular industry or business in which they function.

Since there have been few definite programs of mental hygiene, it is not surprising that there is confusion about this field. What is it? Who runs it? What are its relationships to "personnel management," to "human relationships," to "industrial psychology," to "industrial psychiatry," to "industrial hygiene," and other currently active programs? These terms may or may not refer to the same types of activity.

Undoubtedly there will evolve a new alignment of the persons working in related activities. A mental hygiene program in industry, as we learned in the Army, must be headed by a psychiatrist. It is concerned with health, and it therefore lies in the field of medicine. But the psychiatrist needs the help of the clinical psychologist [9] who is the expert in personality testing. He needs the psychiatric social worker who is trained in "case study" and management. He could counsel with or, preferably, direct the "consulting" psychologists (who ordinarily do not give mental or psychological tests) who, although not physicians, are trained in counseling in regard to personal affairs, rights, privileges, and working conditions. There should be a definite working relationship between the mental hygiene program and the personnel division, which might involve advising, referrals, training, and research. Both military and civilian experience have shown that such teams can accomplish much more than when the various specialists work independently.

[8] Orientation course in occupational health and medicine, September 9 to December 21, 1946. This course included the general topics of administrative medicine in industry, preventive occupational medicine, occupational health, the surgery of trauma, and rehabilitation. A considerable emphasis was placed on the human relations in industry.

[9] In both his professional training and career, the clinical psychologist works with the psychiatrist for most effective results. Evans, C. E., "Consulting Psychologist in Industry," *Am. J. Orthopsychiat.*, 16:623-630, Oct., 1946.

There are numerous pitfalls in a lack of teamwork. If the psychiatrist is relegated to the limited role of giving treatment and handling problem cases (important as these are), his firm loses the benefit of much of his potential effectiveness. He must be concerned also with prevention. If the personnel division carries on selection without recourse to scientific knowledge about the personality, one can expect a higher turnover in personnel. Counseling given by incompletely trained people can result only in serious trouble for all concerned.[10]

An obstacle to the maximum contribution of psychiatry to industry and business is the variation in the labor market. At one time it is very difficult to obtain the right type of employee, and at other times it is very easy. In addition, there are the continuous pressures of labor on management and management on labor. These pressures rarely take into account the mental health of the individuals in either group. Bloomfield[11] pointed out that the interests of management are primarily economic, as are those of labor, which fights most often to obtain economic concessions rather than measures for increased employee health. Any really beneficial program must concern more than the field of compensation and insurance.

An ideal plan, suggested by Kubie,[12] is the placement of the psychiatrist and his findings in a neutral role rather than that of spokesman for either management or labor.[13] Management has not found any simple or effective way of gaining information about the way employees feel. Unfortunately, management often does not want to know; sometimes it does not recognize that it does not know.

This is paralleled by a conspicuous defect in the Army which resulted in the postwar furor of such magnitude about the officer–enlisted-man relationship. Any military advisor to a commanding general was, by rank and position, subservient to that officer. Most of us were aware of incompetence in high places, about which we could do nothing. Had there been a civilian attached to the command who was not dependent for his own status on that command, he could have been much more effective.

Similarly there was a real barrier between officers and enlisted men. The badge of military rank even when worn by our psychiatrists made a great

---

[10] This last point was emphasized by F. J. Gaudet of The Stevens Institute of Technology at a round table on "What Is Ahead in Orthopsychiatry?" *Am. J. Orthopsychiat.*, **17**:18-20, Jan., 1947.

[11] Bloomfield, J. J., "Labor-Management Relationships in Industrial Health Problems," *J.A.M.A.*, **128**:639-643, June 30, 1945.

[12] Kubie, L. S., "Psychiatry and Industry," *Ment. Hyg.*, **29**:201-204, Apr., 1945.

[13] Whitney, on the basis of his personal experience, indicated that the medical department and the physicians must maintain a neutral position. Whitney, L. H., "The Physician in Industry and Industrial Relations. The Physician's Viewpoint," Jan., 1946. A manuscript kindly sent by the author.

gulf between them and the enlisted man. The latter was often more impressed with the authority represented by the rank than he was with the friendly interest of the professional person. As a result enlisted men many, many times went to the Red Cross worker for advice about their psychological problems. With a civilian they felt immune to reprisal through the Army system and therefore had no fear of berating that system or the commanding officer.

The psychiatrist in industry is similarly handicapped if he represents only management, and management would be tempted to question his decisions if he represented only labor. Even beneficial personnel policy changes are sometimes unappreciated by the management. No better example could be given than the personal experience of Gaudet [14] with regard to labor turnover. It was his impression that industry was not aware of the cost. He cited an example of the executive who thought that his labor turnover cost was about $100,000 yearly. The author had been a consultant of the company and knew that it had cost approximately $2,500,000. His belief was that competition in the future will be largely a matter of which firms have more willing, efficient workers, who become long-time employees. As executives are made aware of the high cost of labor turnover, certainly the application of mental hygiene principles will be considered as more essential.

Leadership. To a psychiatrist it was distressing that so little attention was paid by the Army to teaching human relationships, personality structure and function, and factors in morale to men who were chosen to be leaders. Where the leader knew and practiced this knowledge, he was more successful.

There are too few industries in which there are established practices of leadership training and evaluation. In some the executives are graded by the employees and grade each other. Baldwin Locomotive Works conducted a school for its supervisory personnel in which the executives examined their own failures. A list of the complaints of enlisted men against officers would read the same as the list from Baldwin if we substituted "officer" for "boss": "Partiality by the boss; poor working conditions; failure to keep workers informed on subjects affecting their welfare or their work; poor planning; indecision on the part of the boss which keeps the workers in a state of uncertainty; the habit of passing the buck; nagging; public rebukes; incivility and unsociability; failure to listen to gripes or taking suggestions." [15]

Perhaps industry has been backward in teaching and developing leadership in human organization. Lewisohn in his stimulating book on human leadership stated, "The problem is largely that of securing a new emotional orientation towards the subject (human relations in industry) on the part of

---

[14] Gaudet, F. J., *op. cit.*
[15] An interesting report, "Boss is Willing to Learn, Too; Four Hundred to Go to School," appeared in the *Philadelphia Record*, Oct. 1, 1946, p. 25.

employers and executives. Along with pride in the size of their plants, the quantity of their output and the amount of their profits, they must find pleasure in boasting of the excellence of their methods of human organization." [16] Industry and business would do well to recognize the two major points regarding leadership as they applied to mental health in the Army: first, scientific selection of leaders; [17] and second, training in leadership, with particular reference to human relationships and personality management.

Education and training of supervisors. Every Army officer, both commissioned and noncommissioned, was given excellent training in the technical aspects of his responsibility. This was regarded as a necessity and therefore was carefully planned. On the other hand, one of the most important aspects of his job was how to manage people. For this there was no training plan.

From the psychiatrist's point of view successful leadership entails an understanding of the personality—its structure and function. This is not inherent knowledge, nor is it gained by osmosis. It must be taught. In the Army, psychiatrists participated in a small degree by presenting the 6-hour course of lectures on personal adjustment which was prescribed for all officers.[18] In relation to the need for the widespread dissemination of psychiatric principles, the effort was grossly inadequate. It was sufficient, however, to indicate one of the most important functions of the psychiatrist in a mental hygiene program. In industry, as in the Army, executives and supervisors need education in the same subject—personal adjustment.

A counseling system can be of great help, according to two experienced industrial psychiatrists.[19] The counselor need not be trained as a social worker or psychologist or psychiatrist. In fact, the outline of the counseling program of the CIO states very bluntly, "He [counselor] is not even going to be able to advise his fellow workers on their problems. He will only advise them where they can go for help on them." [20] One training center in the Army utilized platoon sergeants in a counseling system that was developed by Maj. Samuel Kraines and which yielded some beneficial results.[21]

Special problems arose in many industrial concerns because of the de-

[16] Lewisohn, S. A., *Human Leadership in Industry,* Harper & Brothers, New York, 1945, p. 41.
[17] Application of British method of officer selection to industry was suggested by S. A. Mac-Keith, in "Lasting Lessons of Overseas Military Psychiatry," *J. Ment. Sc.,* 92:542-550, July, 1946.
[18] War Department Circular 44, 1944, and renewed in Circular 43, 9 February 1946. Lecture outlines in *War Department Technical Bulletin, Medical 12,* Feb., 1944.
[19] Brody, M., "The Mental Hygiene of Industry and Reconversion," *Ment. Hyg.,* 29:371-384, July, 1945; Himler, L. E., "Current Trends in Industrial Psychiatry," *Am. J. Psychiat.,* 103:149-153, Sept., 1946.
[20] *Training Course Manual,* Union Counselling Program, National CIO Community Service Committee, 1776 Broadway, New York 19.
[21] Kraines, S. H., *Managing Men. Preventive Psychiatry,* A. B. Hirschfeld Press, Denver, 1946. Kraines' entire system is described in detail. Although written for the Army situation, it has features of value in civilian industry.

sirability of suitable placement and satisfactory integration of so many returned veterans. Several of the courses for supervisors, dealing with this
subject, have been published.[22] The most comprehensive guide for employers,
supervisors, interviewers, counselors and others in understanding and dealing
with workers was written by Woodward and Rennie, in which they discuss
the problem of veterans, their placement, treatment, techniques in interview-
ing, and the establishment of an employment program.[23] Many of the veteran-
employment problems have counterparts in former war-worker and new-em-
ployee difficulties.

Selection. The Army had the colossal job of examining approximately
16,000,000 men from whom to select those who seemed fitted to carry on the
job. Then came a further screening to find the niche for which they were
presumably best equipped. The experience of psychiatry in this process was
described in Chapter 19. Army psychologists under the Adjutant General
had the responsibility for classification and the initial assignment.[24]

There were many flaws in the Army selection program. One of the chief
handicaps was the "allotment system." A man with a specialized skill might
be held at a reception center for as long as 30 days, awaiting a requisition for
that skill; he then might be assigned wherever there was a need. Too often
there was a requisition for a large number of infantrymen and every available
man, regardless of skill, was used to fill it.

The attempt was made, however, with due recognition of its importance,
to give various tests and interviews in order to determine individual abilities
and aptitudes to facilitate the proper placing of a soldier.[25] The more technical the job, the more critical were the selective processes, so that the Army
would have the best possible chance of getting the right man for the
right job.

This idea has been used by some businesses and industries for some time.
In the Army experience, undoubtedly, of the many used, the most useful all-

22 "You and the Returning Veteran," guide for foremen prepared by Allis-Chalmers in collaboration with Esther and Ole DeWeerdt. Another type of booklet is "The Returning Veteran," a manual for employers prepared by the Veterans' Research Center, Milwaukee, Wis.
Still another is "The Adjustment of the Nervous Veteran in Industry," by Meyer Brown, prepared by the Industrial Welfare Department of the Zurich Insurance Co., 135 S. LaSalle St.,
Chicago 3.
23 Woodward, L. E., and Rennie, T. A. C., *Jobs and the Man,* Charles C. Thomas, Publisher,
Springfield, Ill., 1945.
24 *Personnel Classification Tests,* War Department Technical Manual TM 12-260, rev., U.S.
Government Printing Office, Washington, D.C., Apr., 1946.
25 The Army used a formula, for grading a soldier on the basis of his physical examination,
termed the "PULHES" (see Chap. 19). Himler reports one industrial plant developing a
"PHEWSO" system, referring to personality, health, education, work record, social factors,
and the interviewer's over-all impression of the applicant. Himler, L. E., "Psychiatric Rehabilitation in Industry," *Mil. Neuropsychiat.,* 25:297-303, The Williams & Wilkins Company,
Baltimore, 1946.

round test was the Army General Classification Test, developed within the Army. There were many others used. The significant point is that, no matter which ones are to be used, they must be appropriate and adapted to a particular organization.[26] Many of the mechanical and clerical tests were found to be far from standardized as measures of specific ability.[27] Personality tests were certainly very valuable, but they were by no means the entire answer to the placement problem.

Resistance to employment of handicapped persons. One of the important aspects of our present employment practice is the desirability of more intelligent selection and placement of workers. Personnel policy which has been to "take only the best qualified" might be modified to ask "Will this handicap interfere with his performance?" Physical or mental handicaps may or may not justify a refusal of employment. Each applicant must be investigated individually. Too often, however, blanket rejections are made. A year or so ago a Washington newspaper quoted an official, high in our government, as having stated that he would not want to employ a "psychoneurotic." Such nonsense is only a reflection of the official's ignorance. The adjustment of most veterans, including the psychoneurotic dischargee, is not really different from that involved in the placement of all other newcomers to a job. Those men who were in war industries also were displaced, and many had to start anew.[28]

A survey from the Office of the Surgeon General showed that 75 per cent of the individuals who returned to work after they had been discharged from the Army because of psychoneurosis had no difficulty in obtaining a job.[29] An even more interesting follow-up was reported by Rusk,[30] in a company employing thousands of men. The top management refused to allow the personnel department to hire men with a psychiatric disability. At the same time they were engaging men who had been turned down for the service

---

[26] This point is stressed by R. S. Schultz, "How to Use Personnel Tests," *Personnel J.*, **25**:94-99, Sept., 1946. M. S. Viteles makes the point with which, however, I think our Army experience would radically disagree, that the interview is no more reliable than certain paper-and-pencil tests. This, of course, depends on the type of interviewer and the interview. "Industrial Implications of War-time Developments in Psychology," *J. Consulting Psychol.*, **10**:85-92, Mar.-Apr., 1946.

[27] Bennett, G. K., and Fear, R. A., "Use the Right Selection and Testing Methods," *Factory, Management and Maintenance,* Aug., 1943; Crissey, O. L., "The Use of Tests in Improving Personnel Procedures," *Safety Training Digest,* Industrial Rehabilitation, American Museum of Safety and the Center for Safety Education, New York University, New York, 1945.

[28] A helpful booklet on this special subject is entitled "Readjustment to Civilian Jobs." This is a report on neuropsychiatric problems relating to unemployment in industry, prepared by a group of psychiatrists. National Association of Manufacturers, 14 W. 49th Street, New York, 1945.

[29] Brill, N. Q.; Tate, M.; and Menninger, W. C., "Enlisted Men Discharged from the Army Because of Psychoneuroses," *J.A.M.A.*, **128**:633-637, June 30, 1945.

[30] Rusk, H. A., in a special article on rehabilitation, *New York Times,* Mar. 17, 1946, p. 36.

because of neurotic tendencies. The industrial-relations director persuaded the management to change the policy. In the following 10 months the company employed 455 men with service-connected personality difficulties and 455 men who were regarded as being free of any such psychoneurotic tendencies or history. At the end of 18 months, 250 of the psychiatric group were still employed by the company, as against 245 of the nonpsychiatric personnel.

There is a very large number of Americans—more nonveterans than veterans—with physical impairment that prevents them from working in the ordinary type of job. They, too, need an income. In the interest of industry, these men must be placed in the appropriate position where they can feel worth while as contributing citizens yet not endanger themselves or other employees or equipment. From the Center for Safety Education at New York University, a review of the rehabilitation practices in 25 industries was made by Grimaldi. One of his findings was that "when the capacities of the disabled individual are properly matched with the job, the disability ceases to be a handicap." He further reported that "each company was definite, that the safety, reliability and productivity of the disabled were equal or superior to the able bodied." [31]

Dr. Howard Rusk has made a special appeal for the utilization of handicapped men in industry. He pointed out in a series of articles in the *New York Times* that in the selection and the placement of such men it is most important to focus on their qualifications rather than their handicaps. Several large factories, like the Ford Plant, International Business Machines, Allis-Chalmers, and Westinghouse have done extensive research in matching workers to the physical and environmental demands of their job. But there is still a great lack of openings for such persons.

The prejudice of many employers against hiring handicapped individuals is groundless.[32] The findings of two surveys indicated that there are more resignations, absenteeism, and accidents among normal workers than there are among handicapped workers. Productivity tends to be higher among handicapped workers.[33] In the Army it was apparent that where motivation could be created in the man, and an opportunity was available for him, the physically handicapped individual could often do a superior job. As evidence

---

[31] Grimaldi, J. B., *Safety Training Digest,* Industrial Rehabilitation, American Museum of Safety and the Center for Safety Education, New York University, New York. This excellent booklet also outlined the plans used by the Ford Motor, International Harvester, Bulova School, Consolidated Vultee, and American Legion for rehabilitation of veterans for jobs.

[32] Rusk, H. A., *New York Times, May* 12 and 19, 1946.

[33] Lynch, D. L., "Employment of the Physically Handicapped," *J.A.M.A.,* 116:1380-1383, Mar. 29, 1941; McFarland, R. A., "Physically Handicapped Workers: I. Experience in War Industries," *Harvard Business Rev.,* 23: Part I, pp. 1-31, Oct., 1944.

of the Army's point of view, the regulations [34] now permit a war veteran with any type of physical handicap to return to active duty in the service.

Motivation. Industry could well take a tear sheet from the Army's experience in attempting to stimulate and enthuse men about their jobs. The soldier needed to know the structure of the Army and his relative position in it. His attitudes toward the Army and his particular job in it were very important.[35] If he understood the military mission, knew what he was to do about it, and could be convinced that it was important, his job was much better done.

This same principle is used in varying degrees in some business concerns and industrial plants. Employees are given an initial orientation to the overall picture of the organization. This is usually followed by an orientation to his particular section and job. The importance of this procedure has been especially stressed as a factor in motivation by one of our few industrial psychiatrists.[36]

A very concrete example of its importance was reported in a special study by Stedman [37] who developed what he called an "Appreciation Index" of employees. He investigated 104 war plants and found that Servel Incorporated in Evansville, Indiana, ranked highest in the appreciation of the employees for the company. This resulted from a system, according to Stedman, which provided every employee with the facts about the firm. A highly developed method of communication, both from employee up and from the executive down, was a part of that system. A similar technique, called "briefing" in the Army, was extremely important for every unit and every individual; when it failed, morale—and mental health—invariably suffered. As Burlingame [38] stated, where it is possible to make the purpose of the industry the purpose of the worker, one can be assured of high motivation.

Minor maladjustments. One of the more important psychiatric developments in coping with the management of noneffectiveness in the Army was the establishment of the Mental Hygiene Consultation Services. In each basic-training camp one of these convenient, outpatient psychiatric clinics functioned to help the soldiers correct minor maladjustments. The psychiatrist in these clinics worked somewhat differently than in civilian life; he used

---

34 *Enlistment and Assignment of Partially Disabled Combat Wounded Veterans of World War II,* War Department Circular 6, 7 January 1947.

35 Cohen was outstandingly successful in the ordnance basic-training camp at Aberdeen Proving Ground. He developed a series of exhibits to educate the soldier to his job. He has suggested how this same method might be applied in industry. Cohen, R. R., "Application of Military Mental Hygiene to Industry," *Occup. Med.,* 1:333-344, Apr., 1946.

36 Himler, L. E., "The Counseling Interview," *The Bureau of Industrial Relations Bulletin 16,* University of Michigan, Ann Arbor, 1945, pp. 63-72.

37 Stedman, G. E., "An Appreciation Index," *Personnel J.,* 24:64-72, June, 1945.

38 Burlingame, C. C., "You Can Drive a Horse to Water . . . ," *Ment. Hyg.,* 29:208-216, Apr., 1945.

short treatment procedures, tried to relieve or help the soldier handle situational stresses, treated the individual in his relationship to group missions, and advised about the manipulation of environment.[39] This service enabled many men to remain on duty who otherwise would have lost much time, perhaps falling out of the unit entirely.

In a very limited fashion this has been used in industry under various guises. Lott [40] and Whitney [41] described it as an "emotional first aid station." Giberson [42] used the same phraseology but suggested that perhaps the responsibility might be best carried out through the health service in the organization. According to our Army experience a psychiatrist is the only one who could have done this job.[43] But it is important to recognize that he did have associated with him both the clinical psychologist and psychiatric social worker, often several of the latter. This function is very different from the counseling systems used much more extensively in industry. These latter undoubtedly have a very definite place, as evidenced, if by no other experiment, by that carried out at the Western Electric Plant.[44] There it was shown, without question, that if an opportunity was provided for the employee to have a sympathetic listener who was neither censorious, critical, nor even advisory, the efficiency of the worker increased noticeably. Care was taken in this particular experiment that the counselor made no pretense of being a therapist nor an arbiter of personnel problems.

The desirability of the emotional first-aid station need not be based only on the Army experience; it may also be apparent from the surveys in industry made by Southard,[3] Brewer,[45] and Anderson.[46] Their lists of behavior leading to referral were essentially the same as any Army psychiatrist

---

[39] Leggo, et al, pointed out similar differences from civilian psychiatry in their experience at the atomic bomb community of Oak Ridge. Leggo, C.; Law, S. G.; and Clarke, E. K., "Industrial Psychiatry in the Community of Oak Ridge," Indust. Med., 15:243-254, Apr., 1946.

[40] Lott, G. M., "Emotional First Aid Stations in Industry," Indust. Med., 15:419-422, July, 1946.

[41] Whitney, L. H., "Emotional First Aid Stations in Industry on the Job," Indust. Med., 15:336-338, May, 1946.

[42] Giberson, L. G., "The Role of Psychiatry in Industry," Dis. Nerv. System, 7:304-309, Oct., 1946.

[43] Credit is also certainly due a host of "counselors" who were of great help and comfort to the soldier about personal problems—the Red Cross workers, chaplain, personal-affairs officer.

[44] For a discussion of the Hawthorne technique, see Mayo, E., The Human Problems of an Industrial Civilization, The Macmillan Company, New York, 1933; Roethlisberger, J. F., Management and Morale, Harvard University Press, Cambridge, Mass., 1941; Roethlisberger, J. F., and Dickson, W. J., Management and the Worker, Harvard University Press, Cambridge, Mass., 1943. The most recent report of the Hawthorne plan, still in operation, was given by the chief of the Personnel Counselling Division, W. J. Dickson, "The Hawthorne Plan of Personnel Counselling," Am. J. Orthopsychiat., 15:343-347, Apr., 1945.

[45] Brewer, John M., "Causes for Discharge," Personnel J., 6:171-172, Oct. 1, 1927.

[46] Anderson, V. V., "The Contribution of Mental Hygiene to Industry." See Readings in Mental Hygiene, ed. by E. R. Groves and P. Blanchard, Henry Holt and Company, Inc., New York, 1936, pp. 357-366.

in an outpatient clinic would have made. In Brewer's study of over 4,000 cases, 62 per cent were discharged because of social incompetence rather than technical incompetence. He listed referrals for: insubordination, general unreliability, absenteeism, laziness, troublemaking, drinking, violation of rules, carelessness, fighting, misconduct, dishonesty, loafing or sleeping, dissatisfaction, habitual lateness. In Anderson's experience, 20 per cent of all employees were "problem workers." They were referred for varied reasons: "bad attitudes," "upsets morale of department," "poor production," "nervousness," "chronic illness complex," "attendance record," "constant disciplinary problem," "stupid," "error maker," "large shorts in cashiering," "indifferent," "resents authority," "daydreamer," "wastes time," "damages goods." These were essentially the same problems that we saw and had to deal with in the Army.

Psychological factors in illness and injury. On the basis of Army experience one of the psychiatrist's functions in industry should be to anticipate and trace the emotional complications associated with injury. Certainly one of the big causes for loss of man power is sickness. In industry, as in the Army, one can be sure that much of that sickness is emotionally colored or caused. It would be the psychiatrist's responsibility to spot these potential patients early and to attempt treatment if it were indicated. It would be his responsibility to diagnose the maladjustment and make recommendations in regard to it.[47]

Another aspect of the psychiatrist's interest in physical sickness is the rehabilitation of the injured worker. Rehabilitation is very largely a psychological process. The rehabilitation of many physically handicapped veterans must occur after these soldiers return to civilian life. Although the number of physically injured in the Army was large, it represents only a small percentage of the total number of civilians who are permanently disabled as a result of accidents each year.

One aspect of injuries, the phenomenon of accident proneness, was discussed in Chapter 12. It is of special importance in industry, as also is sick proneness. In both cases there is much evidence to indicate that the chief factor is a psychological one. In some instances the individual is beyond help; in many others he is quite responsive to psychological assistance. On the basis of our Army experience in the consultation services, it seems probable that

---

[47] An interesting questionnaire was devised for the detection of those physical complaints on an emotional basis among industrial personnel and it was tried out extensively in one industry. It was presented in a psychiatric interview during which pertinent questions about the past life were asked. With considerable effectiveness it revealed the frequency and incidence of this type of disorder among individuals who at the time were not complaining. Mittelmann, B.; Weider, A.; Vonachen, H. A.; Kronenberg, M.; Weider, N.; Brodman, K., and Wolff, H. G., "Detection and Management of Personality and Psychosomatic Disorders among Industrial Personnel," *Psychosom. Med.,* 7:359-367, Nov., 1945.

if psychiatric treatment facilities were available, many of the sickness-prone and accident-prone persons could be spotted, and many of them could be helped.[48]

A word about the neurotic individual. The important facts are that everyone is somewhat neurotic; many extremely neurotic individuals are excellent producers; many have superior intelligence. A great majority of our veterans discharged from the Army for this reason should have no more difficulty in business or industry than anyone else. For those who do, patience and reassurance for a while will help most of them make the grade.[49]

Personal difficulties. Morale most often becomes a matter of concern in wartime, but it is equally important to the attitudes and feelings of any group of workers in an industrial or business organization. The Army psychiatrist became acutely sensitive to the factors that influenced it. The incidence of mental ill health made him aware of the inadequacy of leadership. He saw the effect on morale of leadership which had an appreciation of the personal factors that make life rich or lean (to be discussed briefly but specifically below). Failure of leadership was related most often to this lack of recognition of and concern about the individual.

Everyone wants to feel he is important; that he *is* "someone"; that he "rates" individual consideration. Regardless of his capacity to invest interest and affection in others, no one entirely outgrows his infantile desire [50] to be the sole subject and object of interest. Some persons retain more of this need in adult life and thus demand much more attention than others. This characteristic is referred to psychologically as "self-love," or technically as "narcissism."

There were numerous minor matters that influenced his mental health about which the soldier "griped." These chiefly were concerned with his pride. Anything that occurred to devaluate him was a kind of a narcissistic insult. They were minor stresses compared to those inherent in joining the Army, leaving home, being separated from his loved ones for years, or facing combat. Even though they were less severe, they were factors which produced great dissatisfaction, often cumulative. They usually were evidenced first as complaints, as conscious attitudes. In many instances these later were augmented by unconscious needs. If uncorrected they often resulted in the development of neuroses. Every one of these stresses has comparable analogues in civilian life, particularly in industry.

---

48 See also Granniss, E. R., "Mental Hygiene as Applied to Industrial Accident Prevention," *Ment. Hyg.,* 19:399-404, July, 1935.
49 The Caterpillar Tractor Co., under the medical director, H. A. Vonachen, has developed a special program to aid the adjustment of the neurotic veteran where this was necessary. It is reported in a special series, Bulletin 4, "Putting the Disabled Veteran Back to Work," III, published by Industrial Hygiene Foundation, 4400 Fifth Avenue, Pittsburgh, Pa.
50 See Chap. 4.

Because rank had an inordinate value in the Army, it became apparent that *failure to receive promotion* was one of the keenest disappointments for any man. Morale was always better when advancement occurred. In the European Theater there were more corporals than privates, if one omits the privates first class. There were nearly twice as many privates first class as there were privates, because the Army knew the morale value of giving out chevrons (and pay increases).[51]

In every organization, the "normal" individual wants to know that he can advance. One might say that it is an evidence of maladjustment if an American has no interest in improving his lot. The Army met this problem by having very definite regulations with regard to advancement of officers. Unfortunately, there were many cases of earned but unreceived rank (as well as received but unearned rank). On the basis of those regulations every officer hoped that after a specific length of time, if he had done his job reasonably well, he would be promoted. The whole system of promotion and awards was of such positive morale value that it might well be adopted, in appropriate form, in many types of organizations.

Misassignment as to the type of job was a source of very great emotional stress. Men often developed, and rightly so, the feeling that they were not appreciated because their talents were not being used. In civilian life this is not such a problem, since a man may quit his job if such feelings become sufficiently strong. On the other hand, many industries have come to appreciate the importance of a personnel service which can provide an individual evaluation of each worker. Such a process has a double advantage. It utilizes the abilities of the individual most effectively for the company. At the same time it makes the individual feel that he is appreciated; that his superiors and employers are interested in making the most of his talents. It was such a conspicuous factor in the tone of morale in the Army that one questions whether its importance is fully appreciated by all employers in civilian life.

Personal consideration for his men, while elementary and fundamental, is probably the most obvious and important difference between a good leader and a poor leader. Where a man is made to feel that his individuality counts, that he is a personality and not merely a cog in the wheel, the chances of his being satisfied and well adjusted are infinitely greater. In so impersonal and rapidly changing a scene as the Army provided, this was a special challenge to those leaders who were broad enough to see and accept it. It was nearly always dependent upon the initiative of the commanding officer. Personal consideration by the leader of each individual within his group was so im-

---

[51] Distribution of enlisted personnel assigned to the European Theater as of 30 April 1945: master and first sergeant, 41,246; technical sergeant 69,094; staff sergeant 219,257; sergeant 410,069; corporal 638,382; private first class 958,596; private 484,738; total 2,821,382. Information from Chief of Manpower Control Group, GSC, 10 May 1946.

portant in reducing the incidence of mental illness that one is justified in stressing its importance in every civilian situation. The principle could well be applied to the factory, the office, or wherever people live and work in groups.

Inactivity was a curse in the Army. One of the hardest jobs a soldier had was waiting, and he did lots of it. It was the wise leader who found substitute forms of activity during such periods, even though they had no direct bearing on the eventual mission. It was during these lulls of activity that dissatisfaction and griping throve in fertile soil. This same problem exists in countless civilian situations, in the home and office, in school and factory. If inactivity follows overactivity, and rest is really needed, then the person or persons should be given free time (which could not be done in the Army). But often a lull develops in the ordinary course of events, and it is the smart supervisor or executive or manager who has some reserve jobs that need to be done but which in ordinary times are neglected or postponed. Another of the problems in the Army was to help the soldier feel that these were really important fill-in activities. The same would apply in the civilian situation. Neither a stenographer in an office nor a convalescent patient is normally satisfied or fooled when given busy work or boondoggling.

Unequal privileges between superiors and lower grades were a sore spot in the thinking of the soldier. This moot question will be discussed at some length in Chapter 34. In industry or business it is not so much of a problem, because of the free choice of an individual to change his job or his associates if and when he wishes. Nevertheless, ill feeling and dissatisfaction result when the superior, be he supervisor or executive, exploits his greater authority and abuses his privilege of power by making a conspicuous show of it. He should not expand by making others shrink. Morale was always threatened, and, in fact grossly damaged, when the officer did not lead; when he expected his subordinates to go ahead without him; when he ducked the dirty work or played safe. No executive or supervisor has any right to assume that he is doing an adequate job of leadership if his subordinates have to work longer or harder than he does. No one's narcissism will permit him to be exploited or made the "goat" unless his personality is already unhealthy.

It is certain that psychiatry has much to offer industry and business. In a small way, this is already a demonstrated fact. The lessons from Army experience in selection, motivation, treatment of men for maladjustments, utilization of the handicapped, and many other aspects of personnel management would seem directly applicable to industry.

Mental hygiene program in industry. On the assumption that preventive psychiatry in industry would be very similar to preventive psychiatry in the

Army, the Army psychiatrist would draw up the following tentative program on the basis of his tested experience:

(1) The first task of the psychiatrist should be to become well oriented to the organization—its function and its needs. Ideally, he would have a neutral relationship to any and all groups within the organization, i.e., management and labor, employer and employee. He would be identified with the medical service in the organization. To do his job most effectively he needs his teammates, the clinical psychologist and psychiatric social worker. He should have an advisory relationship to the personnel service.

(2) He should serve as an advisor about the processes of selection, placement, and promotion of personnel.

(3) He should have direction of training courses in the structure, function, and disorders of the personality to be given to all those in leadership positions from top management through the lowest supervisors. He should have an advisory role to those individuals who establish policies, particularly as they affect personnel.

(4) He should have a close advisory relationship with that section of the organization that is concerned with education and orientation of employees. His interest here is primarily in motivation.

(5) He should conduct an emotional first-aid station providing psychiatric advice and treatment for minor maladjustments, and should make recommendations regarding serious maladjustments.

(6) The state of morale should be a primary concern. This would entail the development of a research program into the causes and remedies of personality problems, the diagnosis of industrial trouble spots, and ineffective leadership.

At present there are not enough psychiatrists. Their introduction into industry and business in any large numbers is certainly not imminent. Consequently, the principles outlined in the above discussion may have their chief value in highlighting the need of psychiatric orientation for administrative and personnel workers. Only by such knowledge can these workers understand the all-important preventive aspects of a mental hygiene program in industry.

33

PSYCHIATRY IN CRIMINOLOGY AND PENOLOGY

CRIME COSTS America between $10,000,000,000 and $18,000,000,000 a year.[1] Our penitentiaries, reformatories, and jails cost us $100,000,000 dollars a year to operate.[2] If we want some money to apply on our national debt, the reduction of crime would be a fruitful place to start. Last spring J. Edgar Hoover, Director of the Federal Bureau of Investigation, reported [3] that the number of crimes in 1946 broke all records for the past decade, with a total of 1,685,203 during the year. This was an increase of 119,622 over 1945. The real tragedy is the admitted fact that while our penitentiaries, reformatories, and jails are momentarily protecting society, many of them are simultaneously converting amateurs into professionals! [4] The extent of preventive work is pathetically meager, so the increase in crime will probably continue.

COURT PROCEDURES FOR HANDLING OFFENDERS AGAINST SOCIETY

Court procedures are antiquated. This fact is attested to by many of our outstanding criminal lawyers. This is not the fault of the lawyers; legal and penal systems remain medieval because of public attitudes and indifference. People want the criminal "punished," regardless of the fact that thoughtful persons with experience know that mere incarceration in jails or reformatories or penitentiaries does not serve as a deterrent to crime. In most instances the "punishment" chosen is prescribed by "the law" for a particular offense,

---

[1] Morris, Albert, *Criminology,* Longmans, Green and Company, New York, 1938, p. 20. This author collected estimates from various sources.

[2] In a personal communication, J. V. Bennett, Director of Bureau of Prisons (Federal), indicated that the 27 institutions housing 18,698 prisoners cost $16,175,700 in 1946. But he had no figures on the cost of "an average of about 118,000 prisoners in State penal institutions for adults, perhaps 25,000 to 30,000 youngsters in state and local institutions for juvenile delinquents, and probably an average of some 110,000 sentenced and unsentenced prisoners in local jails and work houses." Letter dated Mar. 20, 1947.

[3] Press Release Mar. 20, 1947.

[4] And in *many* kangaroo courts still operate; the warden or jailor is paid "per head"; there is *no* attempt at rehabilitation; such small salaries are paid that only incapable help can be employed.

regardless of motives, circumstances, or consideration of what would be the most effective disposition either for the offender or for society.[5]

Although judges must deal out punishment prescribed by the law, there is no longer a minimum time to be served except in homicide cases. The only sensible plan is an indeterminate sentence so that a man is released when the penologist, psychiatrist, and sociologist agree that he is no longer a risk from the community's point of view. But such a system is rarely used. In most courts the judge, who may know almost nothing about the criminal, arbitrarily decides on the number of years of the sentence. This gives a sadistic judge a rare opportunity to assert himself. In one large city where there are three criminal courts, it is well known that one judge is twice as severe in his sentences as the judges in the other two courts.

Reformatories and penitentiaries fail even to protect society—one of their avowed functions—when they must turn loose a hardened criminal just because his "sentence" has been completed.[6] Not even after having experienced society's punishment does the fear of more of it deter a criminal from committing his offense, a fact attested to by many experienced penologists. It only makes him take precautions against being caught again![7]

Psychiatry has been articulate on this subject; its point of view has been well expressed:

It seems certain that an entire shift of attitude will be necessary rather than the various maneuverings of criminal procedure that are sometimes advocated. One immediate practical step in the right direction could be taken with a minimum of legislation and administrative readjustment; before paroles are issued, prisoners should be examined by a psychiatrist, and if evidence of mental disorder or defect

---

[5] Barnes, E. B., and Teeters, N. K., *New Horizons in Criminology. The American Crime Problem,* Prentice-Hall, Inc., New York, 1943, p. 12. "The reform program is frustrated by the fact that our criminal law is still based upon imposing a fitting punishment for a given crime and by the theory that prisons exist to punish men rather than reform them. Much lip service is given to the ideal of reformation, but repressive prison discipline fatally obstructs both the spirit and the methods which are needed to bring about reformation on a wide scale."

[6] Every warden, every medicolegal psychiatrist, and every intelligent citizen knows that our jails, reformatories, and penitentiaries fail to protect the public. One could cite many instances where the sentence is finished, and, regardless of the man's condition, he is discharged. National attention was called to this problem recently. In Malden, Mass., the parents of an alleged perpetrator of a sex murder had protested against the release of their son from a training school only 3 weeks previously and wrote a public letter to the governor to urge such legislative action as necessary to prevent this type of occurrence. (Associated Press story, "Parents in Grim Plea," *Kansas City Star,* Mar. 5, 1946, p. 6.) In "My Day," dated from Chicago, Mar. 3, 1946, Mrs. Eleanor Roosevelt describes a mother's plea for an institution in which she could place her child that the child might be helped and at the same time that society might be protected.

[7] According to Paul L. Schroeder, ". . . there is ample proof that they will continue in crime. In fact, there are indications that they have grown in criminality and in the ability to escape detection." *Psychiatry and the Criminal Law,* a symposium to be published by J. B. Lippincott Company, Philadelphia.

likely to cause a recurrence of misconduct is found, parole should be denied. Those who refuse the scientific point of view with a maudlin sentimentality may see from this that the period of treatment for many offenders would doubtless much exceed the terms of punishment "fixed by the law."

Ultimately there will be no important administrative distinctions between "asylums" and "jails." Both will have lost those atrocious names. Both will be institutions under state jurisdiction and under expert medical direction for the care of individuals committed to them by the state because of behavior ineptitudes, failures, and incapacity.

A "sentence" will be as unthinkable for a murderer as it now is for a melancholiac. Unkindness will be as taboo for a felon as it now is for a woman in delirium. Release before complete recovery will be as irregular and improper for a thief or a rapist as it now is for a paretic or a leper.[8]

Twenty years ago the American Psychiatric Association adopted a report on the improvement of court procedures of criminals. In August, 1929, the criminal law section of the American Bar Association approved a very progressive set of procedures in conference with the committee from the American Psychiatric Association.

Little has come of these efforts.[9] It is at least encouraging that here and there is an improvement. The famous Briggs Law in Massachusetts (1921) required a psychiatric examination as a compulsory routine procedure of persons indicted for capital offense, for persons indicted for felony who previously had been convicted of a felony, and for persons who have been indicted for any offense more than once. The recent enactment in California of the Youth Authority Act [10] and similar laws in Wisconsin and Minnesota represent very progressive steps forward. Treatment is the primary intent of

---

[8] Dr. Karl A. Menninger was chairman of the Medical-Legal committee of the American Psychiatric Association from 1924 to 1929 and was largely instrumental in formulating the recommendations mentioned in the following paragraph. He tells the story in detail in *The Human Mind,* 3rd ed., Alfred A. Knopf, New York, 1945, pp. 451-456.

[9] Barnes, E. B., and Teeters, N. K., *New Horizons in Criminology. The American Crime Problem,* Prentice-Hall, Inc., New York, 1943, p. 775. The authors review the extensive survey of Dr. Winfred Overholser in 1928 (*Ment. Hyg.,* 12:801-838, Oct., 1928; 13:800-808, Oct., 1929) of the psychiatric services in penal institutions and courts. They continue, ". . . in 1929, the American Bar Association passed a resolution calling for psychiatric service in all juvenile courts, criminal courts and every penal and correctional institution. This resolution was approved by the American Medical Association and the American Psychiatric Association. Little has been done in the various states to carry out this recommendation, but it indicates the newer and more enlightened trend in medical and legal circles."

[10] This was somewhat jeopardized by the changes in the juvenile court law in 1945. Adler, S., "California Juvenile Court Law—A War Casualty," *Probation,* 25:86-89, Feb., 1947. Wisconsin passed a law which took effect July 1, 1947 (Chapter 546, Laws of 1947) which sets up a new and separate division under the supervision of the State Department of Public Welfare. Its purposes are "to serve all the youth of this state more effectively and to reduce and prevent delinquency." The Minnesota "Youth Conservation Act" (Chapter 595—S.F. No. 337, Minn. Statutes 1945, Section 260.13) passed in 1947 is very similar to the California act, providing for a commission and divisions of prevention, research, diagnosis, and treatment.

these acts, not punishment. The offender is not regarded as a hardened criminal.

Although there is reason for discouragement in the slowness of progress made in changing court procedure, there is some room for encouragement in the increasing utilization of psychiatry in examining offenders. In 1914 [11] the Municipal Court in Chicago began using psychiatric advice and findings. The establishment of more clinics for such study followed in: the Recorder's Court of the City of Detroit in 1919, the Medical Department of the Supreme Bench in Baltimore in 1925, the New York City Court of General Sessions in 1931. Many others started, although at present there are only about 10 adult criminal courts utilizing psychiatrists.[12] About 20 juvenile courts have psychiatric clinics attached, and many others avail themselves of a psychiatric service for the study of some offenders.[13] Literature [14] on the psychiatric study of offenders is extensive, but the sum total of its influence on the study and management of such individuals has been minimal.

Nor was there much progress in this direction in the Army.[15] There were always too few well-qualified psychiatrists to permit taking the time for consideration of the ways and means whereby we might have influenced the Army procedure. Certainly the courts-martial system in the Army was no model of legal perfection. Many times psychiatrists were aware of its blundering.

Therefore it was the more refreshing when Secretary of War Patterson announced [16] some recommendations regarding that system in February, 1947 that were passed by the House of Representatives in January, 1948.

---

[11] See *A Dynamic Era of Court Psychiatry. 1914 to 1944,* ed. by Agnes A. Sharp, Psychiatric Institute of the Municipal Court of Chicago, Chicago, 1944.

[12] Personal communication from Dr. Manfred Guttmacher, psychiatrist to the Supreme Bench of Baltimore.

[13] A very small percentage of the 122,851 cases under 21 years of age in 374 courts in 1945 could possibly have had psychiatric study. Juvenile-Court statistics for 1945 from *Social Statistics,* Federal Security Agency, Social Security Administration, U.S. Children's Bureau.

[14] There have been many scientific investigations of criminals; one of the earliest was William Healy's *The Individual Delinquent,* Little, Brown & Company, Boston, 1915. An interesting follow-up study on the effect of so-called "present treatment" of criminals was given by Shelden and Eleanor Glueck in *Five Hundred Criminal Careers,* Alfred A. Knopf, New York, 1930, and in *Five Hundred Delinquent Women,* Alfred A. Knopf, New York, 1934. The psychoanalytic interpretation of behavior of criminals was set forth by William Healy and Augusta F. Bronner in *New Light On Delinquency and Its Treatment,* Yale University Press, New Haven, 1936, and also by Franz Alexander and Hugo Staub in *The Criminal, The Judge and The Public,* The Macmillan Company, New York, 1930. Two of the outstanding studies of the adolescent are those of S. W. Hartwell in *Fifty-Five Bad Boys,* Alfred A. Knopf, New York, 1931, and August Aichhorn's *Wayward Youth,* The Viking Press, New York, 1936.

[15] Maybe the Navy did better than we in the Army. Captain Francis Braceland stated, "From a psychiatric standpoint, disciplinary cases are being handled in a more enlightened manner in the Navy than they are in many of our civilian courts." Quoted by Albert Deutsch in *One Hundred Years of American Psychiatry,* Columbia University Press, New York, 1944, p. 439.

[16] Associated Press news release, "Moves to Permit G.I.'s to Sit on Court-Martial," in *Topeka (Kansas) Daily Capital,* Feb. 21, 1947; Associated Press news release, "Army Court Bill O.K." Jan. 15, 1948.

The main changes to be made in the present army trial system will be:

1 Provide for appointment of enlisted men to courts-martial if requested by an accused enlisted man. Only officers may serve on courts now.

2 Extend the jurisdiction of special courts to officers. They now may be tried only by general courts.

3 Give an accused the right to request representation by a lawyer at pre-trial examinations.

4 Authorize a lesser punishment than death or life imprisonment for murder or rape.

5 Set up a separate Judge Advocate General's Corps (the army's legal department) with its own promotion list and special professional qualifications. This would remove army lawyers from the jurisdiction of troop commanders.

In certain of the Service Commands a psychiatric examination was prescribed for each offender to be tried at a general court-martial. Serious consideration was given to making this procedure a uniform rule throughout the Army. This was not done, chiefly for lack of psychiatric personnel to carry it out. Moreover, many of our younger "psychiatrists" had had only 3 months of training in psychiatry. Had we succeeded in requiring a psychiatric investigation of all serious offenders, these doctors would have been used often. We did not regard them capable of making wise psychiatric judgments for presentation as testimony before such a tribunal.

One of our chief accomplishments was the writing of a War Department bulletin on psychiatric testimony before courts-martial.[17] This was due to the joint efforts of Col. A. E. Lipscomb, an attorney from civilian life working in the Judge Advocate's Department, and Lt. Col. Manfred Guttmacher, a psychiatrist, who in civilian life had been the psychiatrist for the Supreme Bench of Baltimore for many years.

One of the progressive steps reinforced by this bulletin was the legal standard of mental accountability. In most states there is a traditional concept known as the "right and wrong test." If the individual can be shown to be able to distinguish between right and wrong, regardless of the circumstances, he can be adjudged as accountable, as "sane." In the Army situation we were able to include the much more liberal concept involved in the so-called "irresistible impulse test."[18] According to this, the court had to decide the all-important

---

17 "Psychiatric Testimony Before Courts-Martial," *War Department Technical Bulletin, Medical 201,* 1 October 1945.
18 Only 17 states recognize the "irresistible impulse" as a legitimate plea. "Moral rather than scientific sensibilities are responsible for the prevalence of the right and wrong test—the test to which [Isaac] Ray objected in 1838, and which Sir James Stephen forty-five years later considered among the 'antiquarian curiosities' of the law." Zilboorg, G., "Legal Aspects of Psychiatry", in *One Hundred Years of American Psychiatry,* Columbia University Press, New York, 1944, p. 565. See also an older but highly documented review: Meagher, J. F. W.,

question of whether the accused was, at the time of the alleged offense, "so far free from mental defect, disease, or derangement as to be able concerning the particular act charged to adhere to the right." If the answer was negative the accused had to be found not guilty by reason of "mental defect, disease or derangement" (i.e., potentially subject to an "irresistible impulse"). Needless to say, it was a difficult battle to have this latter principle accepted as the guide for courts-martial procedure in the Army. If "not guilty," the man became a patient instead of being confined to a disciplinary barrack.

We failed in winning acceptance by the Army of the concept of misbehavior in keeping with the psychiatric view outlined above by my brother. In this same technical bulletin, however, we did make very clear that punishment was ineffective as a deterrent, and that in many instances misbehavior was the result of poor leadership.

PSYCHIATRIC PROGRAM IN CORRECTIONAL INSTITUTIONS

In the course of its care of over 50,000 men in its penal institutions, the Army blazed a new trail in setting the standards of management of such installations.[19] This came about primarily because the rehabilitation centers and the disciplinary barracks were of very special interest to Judge Robert P. Patterson as Undersecretary of War. He placed Col. Marion Rushton, a prominent lawyer of Montgomery, Ala., in charge of the system, and, throughout the war, he had the services of one of the best experts in this field as his chief advisor, Mr. Austin H. MacCormick, the director of the Osborne Foundation.

The program was established with uniform, high standards of management, which included psychiatry in an important role in every center.[20] Throughout the war there was a close liaison between the headquarters of the Army's Correction Division in Washington and the Neuropsychiatry Consultants Division of the Office of the Surgeon General. For several months there was a full-time psychiatrist assigned to the Correction Division. Because

"Crime and Insanity. The Legal as Opposed to the Medical View, and the Most Commonly Accepted Pleas," *J. Crim. Law and Criminol.*, 14:46-61, May, 1923.

[19] See Chap. 13.

[20] Due credit for the use of psychiatry should be given to the existing federal systems, particularly as developed at the U.S. Industrial Reformatory at Chillicothe, Ill., under J. W. Sanford. See Sanford, J. W., "The Administrator's Viewpoint of Psychiatric Services in a Correctional Institution," *Pub. Health Rep.* 50:79-83, Jan. 18, 1935; Bixby, F. L., "The Place of Psychiatry in a Coordinated Correctional Program," *Pub. Health Rep.*, 50:98-101, Jan. 25, 1935. (Colonel Bixby was one of Col. Rushton's chief advisors in the Correction Division in the Army.) Doctor M. R. King, Medical Director for the Prison Service, wrote in a personal communication, "Our psychiatric service in Federal Penal Institutions is rather limited and in a worse position than before the war. This is not due to lack of administrative support but rather to difficulties in recruiting experienced men in this field."

of these facts, psychiatry had a very special opportunity to work in the correction program of the Army. Like many other Army projects it was established and managed under optimum conditions of control, with the extensive resources of the Army behind it.

Rehabilitation or imprisonment? The correction program in the Army was established with the chief aim of rehabilitation. Offenders were held temporarily in post and camp stockades.[21] Once convicted and sentenced, they were sent to a rehabilitation center if regarded salvable, or to the disciplinary barracks if regarded less likely for salvage. The general program of management was the same in each, but the security measures were much greater in the disciplinary barracks.

The leaders in this program [22] certainly appreciated that punishment was no deterrent to committing offenses, that it was an expensive procedure, and that in a majority of instances it did not improve the man. The Army needed man power, and the more men who could be rehabilitated to give further service, the better for the Army. For these various reasons the prison system in the Army was directed toward the rehabilitation of the man for the benefit of himself, the Army, and society.

For emotional (and not intellectual) reasons, the public desires punishment for offenders against society. Where that is the purpose (which is unfortunately widespread) of the penal system, then no one should be deluded into the idea that the system will bring about extensive or successful rehabilitation. Psychiatrists have sometimes been misunderstood in their point of view of this problem, with the implication that they want to "coddle" prisoners. However, a psychiatric approach in no sense implies coddling, but it likewise is totally incompatible with sadistic punition. Fundamental principles of human behavior make it perfectly clear that hate does not turn into love, animosity into good will, destructiveness into constructiveness. It is a foregone conclusion that to beat a child does not make it love one; to make one's wife a slave does not build up affection; to make punishment the primary aim in handling prisoners does not increase their self-confidence

---

[21] Like our jails, these installations were not as uniformly progressive as the correctional system. They were under local supervision of the post. But by comparison, they were far superior to our jails which represent one of the worst features of our penal system in the United States. Of 3,154 jails inspected by the U.S. Bureau of Prisons up to June 30, 1945, 2,547 were rated under 50 per cent, only 5 had a rating of 80 per cent, and none were as high as 90 per cent. The Bureau, at the end of the war, carried 443 jails on its approved list, listed 350 others which it will use only in an emergency, and had condemned 2,349 as unfit for use. *Manual of Suggested Standards for a State Correctional System,* prepared by American Prison Association, Committee of the Model State Plan, Oct., 1946, p. 82.

[22] Certainly many Army officers did believe that punishment was a deterrent, perhaps not so much to the individual as to the group. There were the much-to-be regretted examples. See O'Connell, J. M., "Justice, Litchfield Style," in *The Purple Testament,* Doubleday, Doran & Company, Inc., New York, 1947, p. 258.

nor their respect for the superintendent, the state, or the nation. Fortunately, the leaders in the Army plan knew this, believed this, and, in so far as the limitations [23] permitted, put it into effect.

The role of the psychiatrist. In each of the Army correctional institutions there were one or more psychiatrists, a clinical psychologist, and one or more psychiatric social workers. The first job of the psychiatrist was to evaluate each prisoner, to determine first his salvability and second, as one member of an advisory council, to plan the program of rehabilitation.[24]

Despite the fact that selective screening in the Army eliminated a considerable number of misfits, many others were admitted by mistake. They continued to be misfits in the Army just as they had been in civilian life. Many men were released from penitentiaries to go into military services; [25] many did very well, but others could not adjust to the discipline. Then there was a large number of other men who could not accept or fit into the Army regimentation and discipline. Many were discharged, either through administrative or medical channels. Those who failed so flagrantly as to go counter to the regulations too often ended in the Army correctional system.

In this entire group, there were men with varying degrees of salvability; many men could again make good soldiers; others were borderline; some were hopeless. The Army went on the assumption that to mix these groups of men heterogeneously was somewhat like mixing patients with bronchitis and patients with tuberculosis: the same management does not apply, time and energy are needlessly wasted, and one is certain to contaminate the other and insure failure in the treatment of both.[26] Those offenders beyond salvage

---

[23] There were many limitations: untrained and inadequate personnel; insufficient personnel; very frequent changes of personnel; inadequate facilities.

[24] In the *Manual of Suggested Standards for a State Correctional System,* prepared by the Committee of the Model State Plan under the auspices of the American Prison Association, Oct., 1946, the function of the psychiatric service is given as follows (p. 25): "Psychiatric services are needed for more than the task of identifying the occasional insane prisoner who requires transfer to a state hospital. Psychiatrists are specialists in human behavior and the correctional institution's function is to influence human behavior in the direction of better adjustment to life in a free society. The institution psychiatrist can render invaluable service not only in the diagnosis and treatment of insanity and pre-psychotic states, the psychoneuroses with which the experience in the armed forces has made the public so familiar, psychopathic states, homosexuality, alcoholism, etc., but also in planning programs of training and treatment for the so-called 'ordinary prisoner,' whose conduct does not appear to have complex psychiatric implications.

"The psychiatrist can be one of the most useful members of the classification board, and of equal value as a member of or adviser to the disciplinary board. Full acceptance of the necessity for psychiatric services in correctional institutions will not come until it is realized that the psychiatrist has a contribution to make to the whole program and the entire institution population, not merely to the mentally ill or emotionally maladjusted prisoner."

[25] Not infrequently, criminals were given their choice at trials in criminal courts as to whether they wanted a penal sentence or service in the Army.

[26] Our Federal penitentiaries segregate prisoners into (a) admission, (b) medical, (c) punitive, and (d) administrative groups. King, M. R., *Segregation of Federal Prisoners,* Medical Corrective Association, New York, Nov. 22, 1943.

who continue to be a menace to society should be locked up indefinitely. In the Army the more dangerous offenders were sent to disciplinary barracks and the best prospects for salvability to the rehabilitation centers.

The evaluating study of a man might better have been accomplished prior to his being sentenced. Had this been possible, undoubtedly the sentence often would have been modified or altered. It is for this reason that psychiatrists are being utilized more and more extensively by civilian courts before and during trial. However, the trio of psychiatrist, clinical psychologist, and psychiatric social worker did survey each military prisoner as he was admitted to one of the correctional installations. They carried out physical and mental examinations, made all indicated laboratory studies,[27] and where possible obtained civilian records.

Unfortunately, very few of our state penitentiaries [28] make any type of psychiatric evaluation of inmates, although it is just as much indicated, if not more so, than in the Army setting. There was no difference in the type of personalities that became involved in military offenses from those involved in civilian offenses.

There was, however, a difference in the type of offense. For example, there is no civilian counterpart to absence without leave. Studies indicated that in many instances the offender who was absent without leave was too dull to appreciate the significance of his act. By comparison, a very small per cent of civilian crimes can be laid to stupidity. Furthermore, the dullard, only vaguely comprehending the meaning and consequences of AWOL, could see little difference between his lot in garrison life and his lot in the guardhouse, a fundamental question which concerned motivation also. Other military

---

[27] This plan of careful evaluation as carried out in one rehabilitation center was described in detail by Snow. He made the basis for the initial screening of soldiers "non-restorable" and "potentially restorable" categories. On the findings of examination, their subsequent rehabilitation was planned. Snow, H. B., "Psychiatric Procedure in the Rehabilitation Center, Second Service Command," *Mil. Neuropsychiat.*, **25**:258-270, The Williams & Wilkins Company, Baltimore, 1946.

[28] All the Federal penitentiaries do include a psychiatric service, a plan instituted through the initial efforts of James V. Bennett. He reviewed its origin in *Psychiatry in the Federal Correction System*, read before the Am. Psychiat. Assn. Meeting, Cincinnati, May 20, 1940. In the Classification Directory of State and National Penal and Correctional Institutions, prepared by the American Prison Association in September, 1942 (based on a questionnaire survey), in 28 states there was one or more institutions who had a psychiatrist or "psychiatric consultation" or "psychiatrist on call." There was a total of 76 such institutions that included such comment. (This directory was furnished through the kindness of E. R. Cass, General Secretary of the American Prison Association.) Surveys based on questionnaires are not reliable. These figures regarding the use of psychiatry in correctional institutions certainly give a far more favorable picture than exists in the actual situation. Freedman, who surveyed psychiatric services in prisons, indicated a dark picture. "Adequately trained penal psychiatrists are so few as to be totally incapable of meeting even the minimum needs of a modern program." Freedman, H. L., "The Psychiatrist Looks to the New Penology," *J. Criminal Psychopathol.*, 3:430-440, Jan., 1942.

offenses, such as being asleep on guard, and insubordination, are without similar counterpart in civilian life.

When recommending psychiatric evaluation, the psychiatrist has often been accused of trying to make it appear that mental illness is the cause of crime. Much breath has been wasted on this assumption. No one with a clear comprehension of misbehavior believes that labeling the individual with a psychiatric diagnosis satisfactorily explains or helps the situation. Many criminals are "normal" so far as psychiatric classification is concerned. But their behavior is also not adequately explained on the basis of "normality" any more than it is on the basis of "neurosis" or "perversity" or "sin." The psychiatrist is far more interested in understanding the "why" of the behavior and the factors in its development. In the light of the individual's personality structure, what can be done to change him? In a very small percentage of cases, perhaps 2 per cent, the criminal is psychotic; in perhaps 15 to 20 per cent he could be given some other psychiatric diagnosis; but in 100 per cent of cases he is out of step with society.

Personality studies reveal environmental influence during the childhood developmental period and consequently throw light on the pattern of relationships formed in those years. For instance, the individual who refuses to obey or is disrespectful to his superior officer is the type in which the personality study will nearly always show disturbed relations with the original authority—the father. Unless helped (sometimes one is beyond change) such individuals go through life with resentment toward any authority, defying it, fighting it, subtly or openly sabotaging it.[29]

Similarly, the personality study will cast light on the origin of other emotionally determined attitudes and behavior patterns, such as the capacity for loyalty, relations to associates, attitudes toward women, the degree of passivity and aggressiveness, vocational and avocational habits and capacity. Such a survey should determine the importance of the precipitating situation. How much weight in a specific situation did various factors carry—faulty home environment, poor associates, lack of supervision, unemployment, economic needs, personal-affairs problems, relations with others in the immediate environment.

It was on the basis of such studies that the Army psychiatrist made recommendations about each individual offender as to his degree of salvability. Those needing indefinite retention for the protection of the social situation were placed in installations which provided sufficient security. Such men were segregated from those for whom there was a strong hope for rehabilitation.

---

29 Jerome Frank, in *Law and the Modern Mind,* Brentano's, New York, 1930, developed the concept that the adjustment of the individual to the first important disciplinary authority became the pattern of his future adjustment to law and order. He gave case histories to illustrate his thesis.

Those who were unsalvable because of sickness similarly required special disposition. These included men with psychoses, the high-grade mental defectives, and in some instances the passive, inadequate, antisocial personalities.

Rehabilitation. The Army, having determined on the aim of rehabilitation, set about to establish such a program. This is the stated purpose of many of our civilian penal institutions, although in fact it is a very small number of them that effectively implement it. This is largely the fault of the public. There is a vocal group of our populace whose need for vicarious punishment on the principle of "an eye for an eye" loudly protests any rehabilitation program. Such people class all offenders in the same category and demand "punishment." What happens as the result of this punishment or following it does not concern them. Their protests are in line with other prescientific and unenlightened procedures, which prescribe specific punishment for specified offenses, regardless of personality and environmental factors in a particular case. An even larger group of good citizens remains silent. They are apathetic and indifferent. They do not know the facts and give no thought to the problem. At their feet must be laid much of the blame for the lamentable state of our prison systems. One wishes for more nation-wide educational programs along the line of the very superior program by the Columbia Broadcasting System on "The Eagle's Brood," a documentary on juvenile crime.[30]

If a penal program is to be aimed toward rehabilitation and character training, it must not be sabotaged by useless, nonconstructive activity. Unfortunately, this occurred sometimes in some of the Army installations because of inadequate leadership. One does not rehabilitate a man by marching him 8 hours a day with a wooden gun. A program cannot be effective if it exhausts a man physically during the day and allots time for classes or orientation or group psychotherapy only in the evening hours when he is too weary to profit from them. Arbitrary and ruthless sadism on the part of those in charge—the digging of ditches just to be filled in, the breaking of rock just to break rock,[31] the standing of inspection interminably just to prove the authority of the individual in charge—damns a rehabilitation program beyond hope. Such procedures destroy the confidence of any man and his respect for the program. More important, they engender a resentment which nullifies any re-

---

[30] Described and highly commended in *Time,* Mar. 17, 1947, p. 92.
[31] In the very excellent report of the American Prison Association on the "Model State Plan," in the chapter on discipline, there are many refreshing statements regarding punishment. "Rock piles have no place in adult reformatories. . . . They are symbols of an era in penology that has now gone. . . . It is justifiable to assign some prisoners to especially hard and disagreeable work but it should never be 'made work' and it should have definite production value." *Manual of Suggested Standards for a State Correctional System,* written by Austin H. MacCormick, published by The American Prison Association, 135 E. 15th St., New York, E. R. Cass, General Secretary, Oct., 1946, p. 70.

habilitation effort. For that reason, all of those institutions which have punishment as their aim are making men more criminally motivated than they were on their admission by increasing their resentment against certain persons or society as a whole.

Any successful program—and at least, this was the aim in the Army—must be constructive and filled with purposeful and interesting activities. It needs to be sufficiently flexible to allow for enough variation to meet the needs of the different types of personalities of the offenders. A major emphasis must be placed on the reorientation of the offender to himself, to his civilian situation, to the community, and to the privilege and responsibility of citizenship. Educational opportunities are essential for any adequate rehabilitation program. Rehabilitation *is* education, and plans must include courses in those subjects that are of value and related to the aim of the total program. Recreation [32] should be a planned and a mandatory part of the program, not merely an incidental or spontaneous, voluntary privilege.

Offenders, be they military or civilian, are regarded by psychiatrists as maladjusted individuals. They are socially sick. If they are going to be rehabilitated it means that they must gain a better understanding of the causes of their difficulties, just as any mentally sick patient must understand the factors that made him sick. This understanding of one's self, the psychiatrist calls "insight." Our patient as well as our offender first must recognize that he is maladjusted; second, he must understand the nature and causes of his maladjustment, in so far as this is possible; and, third, he must understand what his own contribution to the readjustment must be.

In the clinical practice of psychiatry, this is largely accomplished through individual interviews with the patient, and is called "psychotherapy." Unfortunately, time and man power prevent this from being possible in any penal institution, desirable as it might be. Psychiatrists have developed an expedient substitute—group psychotherapy—for use in the correctional institutions as well as in hospitals. It had a particular value in dealing with antisocial behavior. There are many individuals of this type who will not accept the attention or advice or criticism from religious leaders, judges, even doctors, on the assumption that these advisors are idealistic bigwigs who do not know the facts of life. On the other hand, they accept the judgments—and criticisms—of their fellows much more readily.

---

[32] Broad programs of education (of all types and at all levels), library service, and recreation are outlined in the American Prison Association's "Model State Plan." It is recommended that much of the recreation should be carried out by the education department. "Because of its general value and particularly its effect on morale and discipline, experienced administrators would not attempt to operate a correctional institution without recreation." *Manual of Suggested Standards for a State Correctional System,* written by Ausin H. MacCormick, published by the American Prison Association, 135 E. 15th St., New York, E. R. Cass, General Secretary, Oct., 1946, p. 57.

Group psychotherapy is not to be confused with a group "gripe session," which, while possibly very valuable for releasing irritations and opinions, does not necessarily provide understanding. The provision of psychotherapy [33] in groups was adjudged by some of the commanding officers, nonmedical individuals, as being one of the most potent factors in the entire rehabilitation process. There is every reason to assume that it could be and should be widely used in civilian penal institutions.

Trained personnel. Another feature of the Army correctional program was the training of the personnel who worked in these installations.[34] The job of salvaging the offender is a technical one. Nevertheless, too often our penal institutions are managed and directed more by brawn than by brain; too often sadistic, punitive attitudes prevail. In an attempt to salvage maladjusted men, it is of paramount importance to have a staff which is specially trained in techniques of education, in psychiatric orientation, and in recreation. Each member of the staff as well as every member of the guard needs, particularly, to have an understanding of mental hygiene which should include knowledge of personality structure and function.[35] Only to the degree that each individual understands the principles in this field can he apply them.

The Army believed sufficiently in this plan to establish a training school. To my regret, we in the Neuropsychiatry Consultants Division were never able to furnish a full-time psychiatrist as an instructor.[36] Fortunately, Col.

---

[33] The methods and results of group psychotherapy in the Army disciplinary barracks and rehabilitation centers were described in Chap. 20. L. W. McCorkle (see Chap. 20, footnote 63) carried on the group psychotherapy at Ft. Knox Rehabilitation Center and is currently organizing group therapy in the New Jersey prison system.

[34] Training of prison personnel has been an established practice in a few states and in the federal prison system. Among the better courses have been those in California, New Jersey, New York (especially the Wallkill State Prison program written by Dr. Walter M. Wallack), and Michigan. The extent of mental hygiene coverage in these courses has varied. It has been a definite part of the *Federal Prison Service Study Course* of the Department of Justice. In the "First Series, revised edition, 1939,"/there are presentations of "The Psychic Factor in Complaints of Illness," "Symptoms of Mental Illness and How to Meet Them," "The Psychiatric Factor vs. Malingering," and "Physical and Mental Disorders in Relation to Recreation and Employment." An excellent training manual has been prepared by Helen D. Pigeon and others, "Principles and Methods in Dealing with Offenders," State College, Penn., Penn. Municipal Publ. Services, 1944, for use in in-service training of correction employees.

[35] Mr. James V. Bennett, Director of the Federal Bureau of Prisons, explained in a personal communication that basic sanitary principles are pretty well known and observed by the majority of prison supervisors and employees. "On the other hand we do not have a comparable code of mental hygiene principles which are available to the average run of prison supervisory officials or workers. It would appear to be ideal if psychiatrists could eventually formulate principles of mental hygiene which in a measure at least, would be as applicable as those of ordinary sanitation." Mar. 17, 1947.

[36] Psychiatrists qualified to do penal work are very few. There are many openings for them in our federal and state systems. Through the efforts of Dr. Philip Q. Roche, an effort was made to provide a training course for penal psychiatry under a grant from the Commonwealth Fund. The course was established as a joint effort of the Eastern State Penitentiary (Pennsylvania) and the University of Pennsylvania Medical School. The war interrupted the program. Roche, P. Q., "Modern Training in Penal Psychiatry," *Pennsylvania Bar Assn. Quart.*, 12:161-168, Apr., 1941.

Paul Schroeder, one of our outstanding psychiatrists in the field of criminology and penology, was the consultant in the Service Command in which the training school was located. He devoted considerable time to it. We were able to furnish five clinical psychologists to this school as instructors. There is no question that the training program paid great dividends.

In summary, the Army established a correctional program with its chief aim as rehabilitation. The broad vision of the leaders included a prominent and important role for psychiatry. It was the psychiatrist's function to evaluate each offender and make his recommendations about the disposition. He had a part in a program that, at its best, was characterized by appropriate discipline, education, orientation, recreation, occupation, and psychotherapy. The degree of success achieved was in no small part due to a training program for all workers in these institutions. Would that our federal and state legislators could see the enormous dividends that such a program would pay, and that they would take this total model program as developed by the Army and install it in every state penitentiary, reformatory, and industrial school.

34

NEEDED CHANGES IN THE ARMY

REGARDLESS OF how smoothly or efficiently any Army might operate, there would certainly be psychiatric casualties. Their number would be greatly increased if and when that Army was to be made up in part or largely from civilians who were in it temporarily, through necessity and not choice. Their number would go higher when that Army engaged in combat. It is not likely that anyone will claim that our Army operated smoothly in this last war. Everyone knows there was much inefficiency. When one combines this state of affairs with a prevailing ignorance of and prejudice against psychiatry, it is not surprising that there was a staggering number of psychiatric casualties.

The points in this discussion obviously do not represent the view of a Regular Army officer, although several have read the following paragraphs with no essential disagreement. They are based on a little (noncombat) experience in World War I as a private and a second lieutenant and on nearly 4 years' service (also noncombat) in World War II. As a psychiatrist's evaluation, I believe from my many contacts, they would have the concurrence of most other psychiatrists who were in the Army.

In seeking the many causes of psychiatric disability in order to correct them, we must put first the absence of prewar planning to prevent and to treat them. This blunder was made by the War Department and the technical service of the Medical Department, and was ignored by the profession of psychiatry. Furthermore, any contribution of psychiatry in the Army was greatly handicapped by the lack of knowledge about it on the part of the general medical and line officers and their resistance to its acceptance. Certain factors within the Army—its organization and system—further added to the difficulty for psychiatry. Each of these contributed directly to the production of psychiatric casualties. All of them *could* be changed so that they would be much less of a menace to mental health.

The following "criticisms" are not made in any spirit of "now the story can be told." They are meant to be constructive. Most of them are well recognized by military leaders. Some are the object of energetic consideration and change. Certainly many changes are needed and *can* be made.

516

Most of us who served in the Army are a bit disillusioned about how many changes *will* be made. Perhaps it is a matter of lack of faith or confidence after our frustrating experiences with red tape. There is no lack of faith in the present Secretary of Defense or the present Chief of Staff. But there is the knowledge that some very superior officers are hamstrung in varying degrees by regulations or tradition; there is the knowledge of the presence of weak, limited-visioned advisers in influential positions; there is the memory of that experience when some major or captain in a low echelon threw a monkey wrench in the machinery by counterpersuasion of his chief to convince a higher chief, and so on. Some Army practices definitely contribute to mental ill health. They ought to be recorded with the hope that they might receive consideration.

The Surgeon General of the Army. A thorough critique of any segment of a technical division would be lengthy. Just before I left the Army, and as a part of my job, I attempted to formulate the organization, function, and relationships of psychiatry in the Army, to pass on to General Kirk, the Surgeon General at that time.[1] Perhaps a few of the criticisms of the medical department,[2] in headline form, are of general interest.

Most of us physicians felt very strongly that the Surgeon General of the Army should be on the General Staff rather than heading a technical service as a subdivision of one of the three major forces, the Army Service Forces. We held this opinion not because we thought medicine ought to be particularly honored. If the Surgeon General is to be responsible really for the health of the entire Army, he should advise directly with those who are directing and planning for that Army. He could not, and never will be able to exert the proper influence or authority that is desirable without being in such a position.

The Surgeon General had the theoretical responsibility of the health of the Army but in many ways lacked authority to assume it. There were thousands of doctors in the Army over whom he had no control. He could not change their assignment even though they might be surplus in one place and needed desperately some place else. The Surgeon General or his representatives did not have authority to go into certain areas occupied by field armies. In one famous incident the Surgeon General himself could not obtain permission even for his own visit. His professional consultants, because they belonged to the Army Service Forces, in many instances had no authority or jurisdiction in medical matters in the Air Forces or the Ground Forces.

Even more serious was the ignoring of medical authority in the planning

---

[1] A condensed version of this was published. Menninger, William C., "The Future Role of Psychiatry in the Army," *Mil. Surgeon*, 100:108-113, Feb., 1947.
[2] See also Chap. 17 for others.

of some of the major campaigns. Since the medical care of casualties was important in every campaign, theoretically the theater surgeon [3] was supposed to sit in on the planning. More than once the medical opinion was discarded and the invasion was carried out with inadequate provision for medical equipment and treatment. It is understandable that the commander of an invasion wanted all the men, ammunition, guns, and tanks that he could take. When, begrudgingly, he spared only insufficient shipping space for medical personnel and equipment, the Surgeon General had *no* authority in such a situation. Furthermore, even though he might know that an area needed medical personnel or supplies, unless the commanding general of that area requested such, the Surgeon General had no authority for sending it.

Medical officer relationships. One of the most widespread criticisms by doctors of their medical experience was the fact that they were subjected in most instances to the authority of line rather than medical officers. Line officers controlled their assignments, their promotions, their transfers. Because of this situation, hundreds of them, perhaps thousands, did no medical work for long periods at a time. They felt that they were wasted—and they were. The Medical Department had no authority to change this situation.

Many of the criticisms applying to the entire Army were, from my experience, equally applicable to the Medical Corps. We had our share of difficulties in selecting officers. We had our quota of incompetent officers. Many of us were aware of the resistance of Regular Army medicos to change, their tendency toward isolationism.

Traditions and practices in the Army. These have tended to remain static even while the civilian social organization has changed. At the same time the Army organization has grown beyond the status of merely a professional fighting force to one which has an increasing responsibility in the molding of world affairs. It has become a diplomatic representative of America; it must maintain order in various parts of the world; it must be ready to meet emergencies here at home. Even war has changed greatly in its nature.[4] But to some old-line officers, traditional procedures and privileges of authority are more important than efficiency, true representation of democracy, or maintenance of good morale.

It is understandable that the structure of any organization is based upon traditions, and these constitute some of the finest features of the Army. However, when these become distorted and applied to methods of functioning

---

[3] Representative of the Surgeon General in the theater of operations.
[4] The Osborne Report is a study made by Maj. Gen. F. H. Osborne, Director of Information and Education Division, entitled, "Observations on Army Policy and on the Training of Civilian Reserves," directed to the Chief of Staff, 16 November 1945. "War is no longer a game to be played by a guild of professional soldiers, but a business which involves mobilization of all the resources, human and otherwise, of the nation."

and to regulations, the organization is likely to become outmoded. One of the major handicapping features in the recent war effort was an all too prevalent attitude that the Army did or did not "function that way," the "regulations did not permit that," or "you don't understand the Army method." There was a standing joke about the first sergeant who was teaching some recruits about a gun, and he asked this intelligent group of young men why the stock was made out of hickory wood. One recruit promptly answered that it was because the wood was more durable; the second answered that it was lighter than certain other of the hard woods; another answered that it was because of its easy availability. The sergeant's reply was, "You are all wrong—it's made out of hickory because the regulations say so."

Some psychiatric casualties were directly related to the rigid enforcement of some traditional Army practices. Very great effort on the part of the Army and the individual officer and soldier had to be expended to overcome civilian resistance to entering military service. Then more effort was necessary to submit willingly to regimentation and all that military life entailed. Some men couldn't make that effort and became psychiatric rejectees; others made it at the cost of their precarious personality integration and were psychiatric dischargees. Many, many, many such casualties could have been prevented by a different relationship between the prewar Army and civilian life.

Along with the rigidity of some handicapping traditions, one wondered why certain other worth-while traditions had not been developed. In view of his importance, why has the infantry soldier not been more glorified? Why are not more medals awarded to enlisted men and far fewer to officers? Why has our Army never seen fit to establish permanent units with permanent names, the members of which are recruited from the same area, which have proven so valuable in the British and Canadian armies?

Attitude of civilians toward the regular Army. The civilian population in prewar days had a minimal interest in the Army. With a national policy of isolationism and pacifism, an Army did not seem a very great necessity. Perhaps because of the American "rugged individualism" but chiefly because they knew few individuals in the Army, civilians looked askance upon the professional Army officer for submitting voluntarily to a regimented life.

Civilians were prone to assume that enlisted men were the ne'er-do-wells who lacked ability and initiative to get along in civilian life or, very possibly, were roustabouts.[5] Apparently such an assumption was correct according to the Doolittle Report. "In this peacetime pre-war Army there was, in addition to the official gap between commissioned and enlisted men, a breach based

---

[5] Actually, a few men joined the Army as enlisted men in order to get a chance to take the West Point examinations. In all corps there were a small number of highly trained (and often well-educated) enlisted technicians.

upon the general caliber of the men. The official gap, established by law, regulations, customs and tradition, was accepted without question by the vast majority of those men then in the Army. The differential, due to the caliber of most of the enlisted as compared to that of the commissioned personnel, permitted the development of habits dealing with men in the ranks which later were to cause difficulties." [6]

Another set of recommendations of the Doolittle Board obviously implied the necessity for obtaining a higher caliber enlisted man. To do this it is going to be necessary to take "steps to provide all military personnel with a sense of security, substantial compensation for duty and responsibility from bottom to top, equitable distribution of allowances, and assurance of a chance for advancement."

The modern Army is primarily an educational organization for every individual in it. Consideration might well be given to the possibility of making the peacetime Army into a gigantic vocational educational system, thus making it far more attractive to the average civilian. This might best be done through relating it to our educational institutions along the lines of the Army Specialized Training Program. Our two military schools at West Point and Annapolis long have held a special attraction for many of our brighter young men, not always because they wanted to go into military service, but because of the high educational standards maintained in these two institutions where attendance was at government expense.

General Osborne suggested that the Army might develop a system to help men discover the work for which they are best fitted in civilian life, advance many of them through training which would be directly useful to them in civilian life, and make available reports on their qualifications to employers and educational institutions. Several other extremely important suggestions along this line were made by General Osborne. "The Army, employing the best classification tests which can be devised and making use of personnel fully qualified to administer and interpret these tests, should be able in the first three months of training to discover a great deal about the aptitudes, interests, and possibilities of each man entering the Army." At another point in the report, "The Army's information about the men who engaged in specialized work with direct civilian counterparts—radar, photography, communications, motor maintenance, clerical service, and the like—would be the most nearly complete from the standpoint of interested civilian agencies. If records were kept and properly handled, they could be widely used by educators, in industry, for the award of scholarships and for the recruitment of

---

[6] A War Department, Bureau of Public Relations, Press Dispatch on the report of the Secretary of War's Board of Officer-Enlisted Man Relationships, to the Honorable Robert P. Patterson, Secretary of War, 27 May 1946.

personnel, not only for specialized industries, but also for the more generalized vocational opportunities."

By such a plan the Army [7] could carry out the thought of many educators as expressed by Dean Gildersleeve,[8] that many of our best brains, because of their geographical location and economic status, did not have an opportunity to develop because of lack of education. The Osborne Report stressed this point:

For the first time the hidden talent of the country, coming from the poorer farms and the lower income groups, would have an opportunity to find expression in fair competition with men from better environments. The great mass of younger men would, for the first time, have an opportunity to consider and train in fields appropriate to their particular qualifications and interest prior to making a final decision as to their work and place in civilian life. The result for the country would be an assessment and utilization of our national talents, which has never before been done or even attempted. To the Army, it would mean an increase in voluntary enlistments, or ungrudging acceptance of compulsory training, because the Army would then come to be, in the minds of the young men of the country, an agency through which ambition and capacity could be capitalized in terms of career.

Whatever the methods, the Army must cultivate the respect of civilians for all its membership.

The prewar attitude of civilians toward the Army was in part (and I think chiefly) the fault of the Army. But the postwar attitude can be very different through an effort on the part of the civilians. If we, at least 10,000,-000 of us who served in it, want to drop it completely from our interest and horizon, it will be partly our fault if it doesn't change for the better. We griped enough when we were in it and should now accept some of the responsibility for improving it. We ought to do some effective objecting to the right persons in peacetime. Even though optimists, we can hardly assume man's aggressive nature is going to change in the next generation sufficiently to outlaw force—and war.[9] The city with a good police force is less threatened by lawlessness.

Officer—enlisted-man Relationships. Perhaps no subject of vital concern to the War Department has received more attention than this one with the re-

---

[7] The Army is directed in its functions by Congress, and such a plan would of necessity have to be authorized by legislation. It would therefore be a responsibility of the public and Congress if we want the Army to carry out such a mission.

[8] Gildersleeve, V. C., "Genius Can't Flower Because Our Schools Don't Give It Root," address reported in *Washington* (D.C.) *Post,* Feb. 26, 1946.

[9] The physicians who served as "consultants" in neuropsychiatry to the Service Commands, theaters, and armies during the war, have acted on this principle. They decided their job was not completed just because the shooting was over. As civilians, they have organized to review and formulate the mistakes and recommendations concerning psychiatry on the basis of their experience in this war. What could and should be done in the case of another emergency? They expect to give their specific recommendations to the Surgeon General and the War Department.

sultant appointment of the Doolittle Board to study the entire problem and make its recommendations. Throughout the war this relationship was of vital significance from the point of view of morale and thus of mental health. There were many abuses of officer privileges, and these have been aired widely in the press. A particularly capable and unemotional report was given by Robert Neville,[10] in which various of these abuses were specifically detailed. Anyone who experienced these, or even the civilian reader of Neville's story, can appreciate the effect of such practices on the mental health of the enlisted man.

The fact remains that where we had officers who were good leaders, there was relatively little or no complaint from their enlisted men. No well-informed GI would assume that the Army could be run without discipline. No one who understands human nature can ignore the psychological fact that it is very questionable whether officers and enlisted men can intermingle socially in mass groups and still maintain effective discipline.[11] Even when discipline is not involved, social organization is stratified by commonly shared interests. If the corporation board of directors' party included the banker, barber, and baker stockholders, their wide differences of interest would spoil the fun.

The great majority of the abuses can be laid at the feet of two groups of officers, some of the older, high-ranking individuals and the younger, inexperienced men. In both cases the most likely explanation for their behavior lay in emotional immaturity. It is not difficult to understand that under the pressure to develop a huge army, many if not most of the regular Army officers were placed in positions of considerable authority. No one probably appreciates any better than the Army itself that some of these men were incapable, emotionally and intellectually, of succeeding as high-ranking officers. A number of regular Army officers with one or more stars could not have possibly held a similar position of authority and responsibility in an industrial concern; they were not "big men." They were, however, in a strategic position to be promoted; then authority fell their way. In popular language their tremendously increased power "went to their heads." As the Army grew rapidly, more men had to be put in command. Thus, young men were given leadership before they could mature to its responsibilities.

In this same connection, consideration might be given to changing the frequently recurring phrase in Army Regulations of "superior officer" to "senior officer." This phrase "superior officer" is commonly used in the Army. The significant and unhealthy aspect is the assumption that rank makes a man superior, instead of indicating that he is more experienced in the Army program

---

[10] "What's Wrong with Our Army," *Life,* 20:105-114, Feb. 25, 1946.
[11] According to the Gallup poll of May 4, 1946, 72 per cent of the public and 78 per cent of the veterans favored the idea of officers and enlisted men having the same food, clubs, and social privileges. Officers were reported as about evenly divided on the question.

and methods. In our culture any system which designates that some man is superior to another one creates mentally unhealthy attitudes and consequent practices. It places far too much emphasis on rank, which in turn may tend to lead to its abuse. The term itself leads to the assumption, on the part of a few officers, that the "superior" in rank should have the superior quarters, the superior food,[12] and other special privileges. It may be the basis for referring, in the usual Army parlance, to "officers' ladies" and "enlisted men's wives."

When men of inferior ability fell into superior rank, they often tried to cover up their inexperience by tough, profane, hard, crusty behavior; they exerted their leadership through blunt, unexplained dicta. Such unconscious devices to feign great masculinity and ability are well recognized psychologically. Rarely if ever are such men aware of the true meaning of their actions. Unfortunately, there is no very easy way in which to bring it to their attention.

The Doolittle Board dealt courageously with many of these problems; their recommendations were certainly not couched in psychiatric terms, and it is questionable if they were aware in more than a general way of the psychiatric implications. They nonetheless pointed out fundamental psychiatric tenets that have been emphasized in many places in the previous chapters concerning better selection of officers, more adequate orientation and indoctrination, training which stressed personnel management and human relations, assignment on the basis of ability and training, promotion and/or demotion on the basis of merit, the employment of a rigorous method of screening and weeding out incompetents and undesirables and, probably the most important, a more effective internal policing system to prevent abuses of privileges other than those which enable an officer to do his job more effectively.

Similarly they dealt directly and extremely commendably with the problem of inequality that was existing between officers and enlisted men for misbehavior and military offenses. They made a sound recommendation relative to the inequality of the awards. They recommended what we learned in basic-training camps as extremely helpful in maintaining mental health, namely a system permitting the expression of complaints.[13]

Regular Army attitudes toward civilian Army. As was mentioned above, the Doolittle Report in more than one place referred to the necessity of changing certain traditions. This, like any attempt to alter human nature,

---

12 At least according to regulations, the field mess of an officer is exactly the same as of the enlisted man, unless paid for by the officer himself and purchased on the open market. The enlisted mess on a post is often superior to any other.

13 The Inspector General's department always has had the responsibility to "hear" complaints from anyone.

is difficult; only prolonged persistent education can eventually lead to insight which will permit modification of current practice. One of the important changes needed is in the attitude that prevails on the part of some West Point graduates toward non-West Point Regular Army officers, and some Regulars toward the Reserves and the AUS officers.[14] There is the tendency for some older officers to feel that their training and experience of many years, plus the tradition as to a particular method of doing something, has proved their way of doing things as the best.

There was often a smug, know-it-all, somewhat condescending attitude on the part of some Regular officers, as they labored to explain to the AUS officer why the regulation could not be changed or why the innovation would not work in the Army. This was most obvious when the Regular officer was the senior. This attitude gradually changed somewhat as the war progressed, partly through situational and mechanical changes demanded, and partly because of increased respect for the non-Regular Army officer and his ideas.

This attitude was present in every army and corps. It was always conspicuous to us in the practice of psychiatry, itself a relatively new field in the Army. For instance, in spite of the unswerving support of the Surgeon General, the nonmedical section of a major force refused for some time to consider changes in Section 8 (AR 615-360) because "it had worked satisfactorily for 15 years." [15] This might seem to be an adequate reason, except that the practice concerned was outmoded in a wartime civilian Army and was not in keeping with up-to-date knowledge about psychiatry.

Proved civilian practices were slow to be adopted in the Army because of this freezing to the past. Since the last war, clinical psychologists and psychiatric social workers have become extremely important to the psychiatrist in doing his job, a relationship somewhat similar to that of the X-ray technician and the surgeon. There were no such individuals in the prewar Regular Army, and only after many obstacles were met was it finally permitted to assign these personnel. Our best civilian psychiatric institutions gave up the use of walls and high fences to corral their patients years ago, but in the recent war the Army not only followed an earlier construction plan of making the closed wards look like jails but maintained the fences, often embellishing them with barbed wire.

Method of assignment of officers. The Osborne Report called attention to an Army tradition "deliberately overstated for the purpose of emphasis, that

---

[14] This was a matter of the personal equation of the individual; the system contributed somewhat: AUS often got higher commissions than Reserves; the "regulars looked after the regulars" but in some instances were more critical and exacting of their number; some "regulars" assigned to some National Guard units had a "rough" time.

[15] The question concerned the removal of enuresis and mental deficiency, then in Sec. 8, to a separate and newly created section, thus separating them from the antisocial-personality group. This was finally accomplished.

all Army officers are interchangeable units, each of whom can be given on-the-job training within the Army which will fit him for any staff or command function." Further on in the report: "The theory that a good artilleryman or a regimental commander will, with proper seasoning, make an equally good G-1 or G-3, runs counter to the policy and practice of other large scale enterprises whose success can be and is measured by their ability to operate at a profit. Adjustment to modern conditions of war requires that the Army recognize the specialized nature of the work to be performed by many of its top staff officers and offer thorough training in universities and in industry to the men slated to fill these positions."

There has been the common practice of expecting that a military officer should function efficiently on any job assigned to him (within rather wide limits) regardless of his background, training, or experience. One of the outstanding examples of this fallacy in this war was the appointment of information and education officers. In many instances it was just another job that had to be assigned; it was given to someone who had extra time, too often to someone who had no training or natural aptitude for it.

The Army was called upon to furnish Military Government personnel; many were given short training in this field, but some of the most important jobs were filled with infantry officers, artillery officers, and others who had had no special training. One night as I sat in my billet in Seoul, an officer came to pay his respects. He turned out to be an old college friend who had remained in the Army following the last war. He had made a remarkable combat record in the infantry in this war. When I asked him his present job in Korea, he announced that he was chief of police of Korea! When I chided him about his lack of knowledge of police methods he expressed his own surprise and amazement that he had been given such an assignment.

A more stupid appointment as viewed by the outside observer was the frequency of filling the important posts such as those of provost marshal, personnel, chief of training, intelligence, supply, and others, in large military units, with officers who had had no specific training in the field for which they were responsible. It is inconceivable that a large business corporation would use such methods, merely to preserve its older personnel or to give them safe berths.

A prewar practice within various corps, of which the medical serves as an example, was to make an officer Jack-of-all-trades. He might serve as a dispensary physician, a surgeon, the camp sanitary inspector, an administrative officer, a battalion surgeon, or he might prescribe for and treat patients in any medical specialty. Prior to the war it was the exceptional medical officer who had training in a specialized field other than his Army experience. Very few were permitted to remain long in the practice of a specialty in the Army.

The Osborne Report very clearly pointed out that "the apparent belief that rotation in itself makes experts out of amateurs is an obviously false one and should be abandoned. One practical possibility would be to select top staff officers two years in advance of their actual assignment to the War Department and permit them to use those years in training outside the Army, both practical and academic." This progressive step has already been instituted by the War Department in many of its fields, at least in so far as providing the officer with special training in civilian installations.[16] The Medical Department for some time before the war had sent medical officers to civilian institutions for training, but was handicapped for lack of sufficient personnel to supply both the needs in the Army and at the same time carry on with the educational program.

The practice of using an officer in many different jobs has a serious psychological effect on the officer. In one instance he may feel (with some justification) that he knows all the jobs but may little appreciate that he is not an expert in any of them, nor has he contributed to the improvement of methods in any. On the other hand, and far more serious, he is never given the opportunity to become an expert and thus become identified with the leaders and associates in the field, in both civilian and military life. An embarrassingly small number of G-1 personnel were identified with the numerous business and management personnel organizations in this country. Somehow it was recognized that a man must have training to be a radar operator, but apparently it was assumed that the chief of personnel of a division or in a staff assignment needed no training in personnel management, methods, or classification!

Few medical officers are identified with either the American College of Surgeons or the American College of Physicians or any of the other specialist societies. As long as a system prevails which permits, and even requires, a man to be a Jack-of-all-trades and master of none, the efficiency will suffer. The mental health of the individual and that of those serving under him will be directly and proportionately affected.

Disposition of noneffective officers. Unfortunately, with war aims to be pressed and with only extremely cumbersome red tape whereby to rid itself of incapable officers, some of these men were assigned to positions of too much power. The Doolittle Board specifically dealt with the inadequate Army machinery for removing such individuals. Similarly it dealt with the associated problem of the disposition of an officer who tried to "get away" with many

---

16 An Associated Press story released from the War Department on October 10, 1946, reported that 125 "carefully selected officers" would be sent to top colleges and universities to take intensive 1-year courses in handling personnel. More officers would follow this group into schools until the Army has enough instructors among its own people to teach the handling of personnel to other officers.

acts which would have brought court-martial to an enlisted man. It recommended the development of personnel machinery to rid the Army of all incompetent officers.

In this recent war, if an officer failed in some degree, he was tried out in another job. There he might—and often did—fail again and usually was shifted to still another job.[17] There were too many instances where an officer who failed flagrantly on one assignment was given another job (sometimes in the same echelon) with equal or even more responsibility. Most of us in administrative jobs knew numerous examples of this. An officer made a total failure of running a hospital; he was "relieved" of that post and put in charge of another hospital! It happened most often in much less important posts, but it happened also when generals were involved. On one of my overseas trips, I learned of a general officer who had behaved so reprehensibly that the commanding general of the theater is said to have "relieved" him. He was promptly reassigned to the same type of job in another theater!

This practice undoubtedly was related to the almost impossible system for the reclassification of officers. It was notoriously difficult to demote or relieve an officer from duty.[18] Short of very serious charges, this procedure was rarely used, and even then it required a long period of time (often months) and a book of certificates and documents.[19] Efficiency cannot possibly be maintained when there is no adequate system by which an incompetent officer can be removed. The lack of efficiency of an officer is of secondary importance in this presentation; of primary concern is his effect on the mental health of his soldiers. An incompetent officer is in a position to make many individuals under him suffer—the more so, the higher his rank and responsibility.

Officer selection. The method of selection of officers [20] and noncommissioned officers left much to be desired. Recent innovations of an interview system, biographical sketch, and examination make the process superior to wartime methods. However, they, too, are as yet inadequately validated, are based upon past performance and not future possibilities, and they include no

---

[17] There were even difficulties in this procedure for the commanding officer of a unit; he could get rid of such an officer by declaring him "surplus" to his unit's needs, but if he did so he was not permitted to request a replacement to do the job.

[18] Between September 16, 1940 and April 15, 1946, only 327 officers were demoted, 4,123 separated, 2,250 reassigned, and an additional 1,887 reassigned without appearing before the Reclassification Board. This is only a total of 8,570 officers in a total of over 950,000 officers.

[19] In fairness to the Army, it is no easy task to rid any public agency of an incompetent individual. Everyone is a "constituent" of some Congressman, and the number and types of levers for Congressional pressure is legion. One senator apparently assumed the Surgeon General's Office was totally incompetent and gained much publicity through his unfair criticism of the slow speed with which physicians were returned to civilian life following VJ-day.

[20] During the early years of the war, continuous pressure was placed on the officer-procurement group to secure officers as fast as possible. The War Department put on pressure for rapid expansion of each technical service (Medical, Chemical Warfare, Ordnance, Engineers, etc.).

tests to evaluate the unconscious factors in a personality structure. The personal interview, while as well standardized as a set of instructions on paper can be, will depend largely upon the board giving the interview.

Again will the Army ignore the experience of business in assigning trained men to do selection? From personal observations, the methods developed by the British Army [21] during the war are far superior to the plan tentatively outlined for the United States Army. Much more scientific care was utilized in the selection methods of the Office of Strategic Services personnel than is incorporated in the current Army plan.

The importance of officer selection was stressed in the Doolittle Report. The Osborne Report devoted an entire section to the necessity that "the Army can and should improve its procedures for the selection of officers and for giving them continuous training in ways and methods of leadership."

The average enlisted man has far more contact with noncommissioned than with commissioned officers. It would seem highly desirable, therefore, to give consideration to the development of a better system of appointment and special leadership training of this group. If the Army career were sufficiently attractive to highly capable, educated men, the rank and file of enlisted men should be the chief source of commissioned officers, as suggested in the Doolittle Report. They cannot with efficiency be started in that direction by a system which depends on favoritism. At present whether or not a man is a "good fellow" and the length of his service are the chief criteria for the selection of noncommissioned officers. As the Osborne Report indicated, the type chosen was more like that of the "labor foreman rather than the teacher or instructor with leadership qualifications."

Promotion. Another aspect of the problem relating to officers is the promotion system which would seem to be planned on the basis that all men are equal in capacity and potentiality, that they all run the course at the same speed, and that the plan must cover the whole gamut of men so that the average and mediocre are protected. An officer must serve as a lieutenant so many years, a captain so many years, and so on.[22] No allowance is made for any more rapid promotion of the very superior man or recognition of special training or achievement. The able and incapable both advance at the same speed as the years pass. Psychologically, every normal man needs a goal and,

---

[21] This plan is well described by J. R. Rees, *Shaping of Psychiatry by War*, W. W. Norton & Company, Inc., New York, 1945, pp. 67-77. The writer spent 2 days in a War Office selection-board installation in which the line officer, the psychologist, and the psychiatrist, along with an experienced trainer, required every candidate to go through a series of tests over a period of 3 days to determine his personality traits, his leadership potentialities, and his intellectual ability. See also Gillman, S. W., "Methods of Officer Selection in the Army," *J. Ment. Sc.,* 93:101-111, Jan., 1947.

[22] This older system is being changed, making it, at least theoretically, possible for an officer to be advanced much faster. It will not depend merely on years of service.

even more important, a recognition of accomplishment, but this recognition should not be based only on the length of service.

The writer is most familiar with the situation in the Medical Department but believes that it is very similar in other corps in the Army. Rank and prestige give personal satisfaction to the average scientist far in excess of the monetary reward, though this usually goes hand in hand with the prestige. When universities choose (as they have in three known instances within the last few months) men under 35 years of age to become full professors of a subject in the medical school, they are prepared to recognize ability. When the Army creates a system which is so rigid that it can give that same man only a captaincy, and perhaps some other man 2 or 3 years older but far less competent, a majority, it forces itself to lose most capable men.

Furthermore, to the outside observer (and to many of us who were on the inside) the medical officer is much underpaid, compared to the medical profession in civilian life, even including the increase of $100 a month granted by Congress in 1947. This is not important during wartime but is of life-and-death importance to the Medical Corps in peacetime. The medical officer's education was his own expense (and this is conservatively $15,000), and yet he has been paid at the same rate as the line officer who was educated at the government's expense at West Point. This gross discrepancy could be corrected. It is to be hoped that legislation [23] will reward, economically, the qualified specialist in medicine. Recognition of ability and achievement can be expressed both through monetary awards and promotion. This is particularly true of men in the scientific professions who can choose between Army and civilian work.

The answer to this dilemma is not easy.[24] In the case of the medical officer, the factors utilized by the university in the case of selecting medical faculty might well be weighed by the Medical Department of the Army—training, experience, recognition by boards, memberships in societies, and, most important, scientific accomplishments (research papers, contributions, etc.).

Isolationism. Of all the prewar practices which were self-destructive to the Regular Army, one of the worst was the tendency to isolationism from civilian contact and the social situation as it existed in communities near military posts. Related to this was the important failure to utilize near-by civilian

---

23 The Medical Department of the Veterans Administration has granted a 25 per cent pay increase to physicians certified by their American Specialty Board. It is hoped that medical officers in the Army will be so recognized. But inconsistencies in government agencies are conspicuous: The Veterans Administration pays a senior consultant $50 a day; the Army recently increased the free from $25 to $40; the Public Health pays $25!

24 It would be most important to protect the system against politicians, smooth-talking artists, and a group only describable in slang as "apple polishers" and "bootlickers."

facilities and experience and research. As the Osborne Report stated, one of
the traditions of the Army ("deliberately over-stated for purposes of emphasis,") was that "in time of peace, Army officers ought to maintain an
almost monastic seclusion lest they open themselves and the Army to the
charge of attempting to influence public opinion or 'militarize' the nation,"
and "that the Army is a unique institution with a unique set of problems."
The report goes on to state, "The mobilization of all the resources of a nation
cannot be engineered by men whose range of experience and association has
been deliberately limited in peace time to other men with similar training,
similar interests and similar prejudices; and public fear of military dictatorship
tends to be enhanced, rather than reduced, by the isolation of Army personnel from the main stream of American life."

This same general thought was expressed by Maj. Gen. W. S. Paul before
a civilian group of advisers, urging that the personnel system in the Army
become scientific.

The present system has been largely chance—it had to grow—so it grew.
At the beginning of the war little thought had been given to the procuring,
classification, assignment, utilization and accounting for an Army of a million
men, and *none* had been given to the same procedures for an Army of twelve
to fifteen million men and women. As the Army grew necessity forced piecemeal
procedures, instruments, policies, methods and plans into existence, so that we had
a hodgepodge, interlaced with the good and the bad. Scientific research and its
accomplishments, together with the spirit of a great nation, won the war. Let those
who are responsible for the Army's personnel problems consider this seriously, so
that they in the years to come, utilize to its fullest this same research . . . the
Army must likewise utilize the experience and sagacity of industry and the professions in addition to its own best men and experience in order to develop scientific
personnel procedures.[25]

The Osborne Report made a special point of the necessity that the Army
can and should "know and use the best civilian experience resulting from
research and experiment on problems of selection, personnel management,
training and leadership." It recommended that the Army pick the ablest
civilians and bring them in on a temporary basis to work with the Army.
"Such an arrangement would have the further advantage of keeping the Army
up-to-date on new developments in the social sciences and in personnel management under the constant training of officers in contacts with civilians."

This isolation perhaps was in a small part due to the fact that most of
military personnel lived on an Army post, often separated some distance
from a community. Even when they lived in a town or city it was unusual for
them to participate in the social life or in the solving of the problems of the

---

[25] From a presentation from Maj. Gen. W. S. Paul to the conference on Personnel and Administrative Division of the War Department General Staff, 6 June 1946.

civilian community. Much more damaging to the Army was the fact that the community (the civilian public) never learned to know them. This was in part due to the temporary nature of their assignment, usually for a 3-year period.

No doubt, there were many exceptions, but compared to the total strength of the Army they were rare. Again the writer is most familiar with the Medical Department, which probably had many more contacts with civilian life than some of the other corps. Nonetheless the lack of contact was conspicuous.

Probably one of the more important progressive steps initiated in this war by the Surgeon General was the creation of a consultant system. Civilian specialists supervised the professional standards of treatment throughout the Army. In order to do the job effectively, he chose those professional clinicians who were recognized as outstanding in their respective fields. With all due respect to the Regular Army Medical Corps, there were very few officers in the corps who would have been able to qualify for such jobs. There were—and are—many good clinicians in the Regular corps; unfortunately, most of them had to be used in administrative positions. On the other hand, very few (the wartime Surgeon General being an outstanding exception) were closely identified with or were outstanding in the countless medical organizations in the country.[26] It is no alibi to say that they were too busy; or that they were not "joiners." The leaders of American medicine *are* identified by their participation in professional organizations, by their research, their teaching ability, their "contributions" to medical science. It has been difficult for an Army medical officer even to attend a medical convention. When he did so, he had to go on detached service and pay his own expenses. For the younger officer this was financially impossible. What may be true for the Medical Department is very possibly true of other corps, where perhaps even a greater degree of isolation has been the practice.

Many medical officers have had short training periods in civilian institutions, but why should not officers—physicians—from the Medical Department be among the leaders in clinical medicine in America? Why should they not be associated with medical schools, at least as visiting professors? Why should they not be serving on the governing boards in the American College of

---

[26] Kubie analyzed the memberships and the diplomates of specialty boards in the Regular Army and Navy Medical Officers in detail. Kubie, L. S., "The Problem of Specialization in the Medical Services of the Regular Army and Navy Prior to the Present Emergency," *Bull. New York Acad. Med.,* 20:495-511, Sept., 1944. The shortage of qualified specialists in the Army was well known. As of May 1, 1946, there were 4 diplomates of the American Board of Neurology and Psychiatry, 1 in orthopedics, 1 in general surgery, 1 in obstetrics and gynecology, and 23 in internal medicine. As the result of the progressive efforts of the Surgeon General, Maj. Gen. Raymond W. Bliss, as of November 1947, there were 99 members of the corps certified by one or another of the specialty boards "and 205 are on their way to certification." See Bliss, R. W., "The Army Medical Department Faces the Future," *Bull. U.S. Army Med. Dept.,* 8:31-37, Jan., 1948.

Physicians and the American College of Surgeons, the councils of the radiographic, orthopedic, dermatological, tuberculosis, psychiatric, and neurological societies of America? Why should not every medical officer doing professional work be able to go to an outstanding civilian center for special training and become identified with it? He would bring back to the Army his increased knowledge and experience. The civilian institution would also benefit. To my personal knowledge, this is the hope of the present Surgeon General.[27]

If the Surgeon General would receive sufficient support, he could achieve his aims in this direction. The Doolittle Report has a recommendation on this point also, that "close contact and association with civilians be encouraged and maintained." It pointed out that a citizens' army must require the combined interest, effort, and contribution of both military and the public, and that a mutual exchange of information will enhance the military organization. Much more important than the recommendation on this point in the Doolittle Report were the positive instructions from the Chief of Staff, Gen. Eisenhower, to his directors and chiefs of divisions. "Officers of all arms and services must become fully aware of the advantages which the Army can derive from the close integration of civilian talent with military plans and developments. This cannot be achieved merely by sending officers to universities for professional training." [28] If these instructions are effectively implemented, the prewar isolationism of the Army from civilian life will disappear.

Changes in personnel policies. These were and are vital determinants of the feelings and attitudes of the soldier. Such important policies as those governing selection, assignment, transfer, rotation, leaves, tour of duty, and discharge have major repercussions on mental health. It would be an extremely progressive act for the Surgeon General to assign a highly qualified psychiatrist to the office of G-1. Even if he did nothing but study the proposed policies from a psychiatric point of view, his services could be invaluable. Actually, this occurred for a short time early in 1946, when without consultation with the Surgeon General, Lt. Col. (later Col.) Frederick Hanson was taken from the Mediterranean Theater to the office of G-1. Even though the method of his assignment was inconsiderate, those of us in psychiatry were delighted with his appointment.

As the section of the Army responsible for the maintenance of man power, G-1 was involved in policy making for all sections of the Army. In one instance during the war, it made a strictly medical problem a very important

---

[27] On a trip with Maj. Gen. Bliss and Dr. Eli Ginzberg to China and Japan in late 1945, 18 months before Gen. Bliss became the Surgeon General, we spent many hours discussing this and other hopes for the Medical department.

[28] Memorandum for Directors and Chiefs of War Department General and Special Staff Divisions and Bureaus and the Commanding Generals of Major Commands. Subject: Scientific and Technological Resources as Military Assets, 30 April 1946.

part of its business, namely psychoneuroses, and with the help of the Inspector General spent some nine months doing so. A high ranking medical officer became annoyed over a magazine article, "Repairing War-Cracked Minds," that appeared in *Collier's* magazine, September 23, 1944. He directed an inquiry to G-1 expressing his irritation. The result was an investigation "concerning the handling and diagnosis of psychoneurotics within the Army." [29] This was a major educational effort for G-1 and through the excellent management of Col. W. B. Boyce, it was of great benefit to the Army and to the application of psychiatry in it.[30] The findings and conclusions could be re-studied profitably; the recommendations [31] still apply in principle.

Among the personnel policies in vital need of change is the method of induction. The Navy seemed much more elastic and adopted far more satisfactory methods of dealing with personality disorders in a recruit. They accepted their men on trial and gave those who were unadaptable an administrative discharge within the first 6 weeks.

The Army also needs a plan, similar perhaps to the British Pioneers,

---

[29] A letter from the office of the Chief of Staff was directed to G-1, asking that G-1 investigate and submit appropriate recommendations on this subject. Memo: WDCSA 710 (28 Sept. 1944), memorandum for A.C. of S., G-1; Subject: Psychoneurotics, 28 Sept. 1944.

[30] This investigation required many hundreds of hours on the part of the Neuropsychiatry Consultants Division in preparing data, reports, recommendations, comments, and in conferences. The Inspector General, who was charged with the responsibility of making the investigation, worked for months. Major General Howard McC. Snyder made several inspection trips, enlisting the help of several civilian psychiatrists—Drs. Frank Fremont-Smith, C. C. Burlingame. E. A. Strecker, Harry Solomon, Karl Bowman. Lieutenant Colonel Norman Q. Brill went with an Inspector General's delegation to the Pacific Theater and Lt. Col. William H. Everts with another delegation to the European Theater. Both of the officers were from the Neuropsychiatry Consultants Division. Other parts of the inspection were carried on without medical advice and were reported by Brig. Gen. E. T. Cooke, *All But Me and Thee. Psychiatry at the Foxhole Level,* Infantry Journal Press, Washington, D. C., 1946.

[31] Although the investigation continued on into late summer 1945, the recommendations from G-1 went back to the Office of the Chief of Staff, dated Feb. 16, 1945 (WDGAP 710, 11-Oct. 1944, Subject: Psychoneurotics, from G-1/Col. Boyce/3026). The very helpful recommendations were:

  a. That a War Department circular substantially as the attached draft (Tab. G) be published. (The War Department Circular 81 was issued 31 March, 1945.)

  b. That instructions be reissued to Armed Forces Induction Stations to ensure that only those registrants whose social history and/or psychiatric examination definitely indicate inadaptability to military service will be rejected.

  c. That the recommendations of The Inspector General that combat-induced cases of psychoneurosis be released to the Enlisted Reserve Corps and be integrated with the present study on "Utilization of the returnee."

  d. That the recommendation for additional separate special treatment centers for psychoneurotics not be approved. (This was in accordance with our wishes.)

  e. That to the extent practicable the number of medical officers undergoing training in psychiatric schools be increased; and that psychiatrists, clinical psychologists, and psychiatric social workers be trained and assigned only in their specialized field. It is recommended that psychiatrists not be used on profile boards at reception centers.

  f. That full publicity of the psychiatric problem should be given in a factual manner. (In their conclusions, it was recommended that a full-time man be assigned this responsibility, but this recommendation was never implemented.)

whereby it can use more adequately that portion of its personnel with marginal intellectual endowment.

The British also had a far superior plan of assignment whereby the soldier was studied jointly by the trainer, a psychologist, and the psychiatrist through his first weeks of basic training. His further assignment was determined by their findings.

In the case of an emergency which would require large masses of troops, morale would be immensely benefited were it possible to determine and adhere to a firm policy of rotation of troops on active duty. Again, the Navy seemed to do this much better than the Army, particularly in the Pacific area.

For combat troops there was no more needed change than a limited tour of combat duty. As it was, they slogged off through the mud in the cold or heat indefinitely, with no goal in sight except the possibility of distant victory, of being killed, wounded, deserting, or becoming a psychiatric casualty.

Changes are needed in the discharge system, whereby a man who has recovered from a psychiatric illness (or any other illness or injury from which he is no longer incapacitated) will not be given a certificate of disability discharge. If possible, he should be salvaged for further Army service and not discharged as an invalid to receive a pension indefinitely.

Psychiatry's role in the Army. Every recommendation in this chapter has been made from a psychiatric point of view toward the mental health of the Army. Much of the discussion of the subjects covered in the first part of the book implied or specifically called attention to changes that were made or need to be made in regard to the functioning of psychiatrists in the Army. In many instances emphasis was placed on our responsibility to recognize more clearly the stresses and strains on the soldier and more adequately to provide support for him. We must avoid a repetition of our errors in selection, our mismanagement of psychiatric patients in many categories, our mistakes in evacuation methods. Probably most important were the lessons we learned in preventive psychiatry and the much greater role it must play in the Army, in peacetime and, more importantly, in wartime.[32]

---

[32] A most important postwar document has been released by the British Army. A special committee of experts, including the Director-General of the Army Medical Services (Lt. Gen. Sir A. Hood), made a survey of the work of the psychologists and psychiatrists in the British Army. Their recommendations regarding psychiatry, dated January 31, 1945, were summarized in *The Work of Psychologists and Psychiatrists in the Service*, page 24, (by permission of the Controller of H.M. Stationery Office) and consist of the following 10 points:

   1. To prevent undue wastage, psychiatrists should make their contribution to the appropriate aspects of selection, classification, training, mental hygiene and morale in the Services.
   2. In all this work, psychiatrists should collaborate as closely as possible with Service psychologists.
   3. More satisfactory procedures, in which psychiatrists should take part, should be de-

It is an enigma that despite the terrific loss from psychiatric causes which we suffered in World War I, the Army was essentially unaware of psychiatry at the beginning of World War II. Most Medical Department personnel, because mental ill health became one of its major problems, not only became acquainted with but wholeheartedly accepted psychiatric advice. This was conspicuously true of the wartime Surgeon General, Norman T. Kirk, and his successor, Raymond W. Bliss. But for much of the rest of the "official" Army, one must have qualms as to whether they have learned any of the psychiatric lessons of this war. To my personal knowledge there are still too many officials of high rank who ignorantly chatter about "shell shock being an excuse for not fighting" or how the "psychiatrists decimated the ranks of fighting divisions." Fortunately they do not so patently pretend to be experts in surgery and orthopedics, even if they do believe that their World War I experience qualified them as medical experts in psychiatry.

There were a few notable exceptions of high officials who did understand: the wartime Secretary of War was cognizant of its importance, and specially so was his assistant, Harvey Bundy. The wartime Chief of Staff personally composed an excellent five-page news release on the psychoneuroses which because of changing circumstances was advisedly not released. General Omar Bradley's deep interest in the psychiatric program of the Veterans Administration has become well-known. Major General F. H. Osborne was highly intelli-

---

veloped for keeping out of the Forces men and women who are incapable of rendering efficient service on account of psychiatric disability.

4. Recruiting officers and other non-medical officers concerned should be instructed on the criteria for judging a candidate's suitability for the Services. Better "psychiatric" training is needed for those who have the task of referring candidates to psychiatrists.

5. A screening procedure should be adopted whereby suitably trained medical or executive officers or instructors should refer to psychiatrists individuals of doubtful mental stability, since it is impracticable, and perhaps unnecessary, to carry out a psychiatric examination of each candidate.

6. More instruction than at present should be given to medical officers of units on the handling of psychiatric problems, and to officers of units, especially combatant, in the psychiatric aspects of man-management and the maintenance of morale.

7. More psychiatrists than are at present available in the Services are required to meet current needs and, if they cannot be provided, arrangements should be made to train suitable medical officers for the purpose.

8. Steps should be taken to ensure that the medical branches of the Services should include after the war regular officers who are closely familiar with the psychiatric procedures that have been developed in selection and other military application since 1939.

9. There should be some recognised meeting-ground at which the senior Service psychiatrists could discuss common problems and make available to one another the procedures developed in each Service. To the same end, close contact should be maintained between field psychiatrists in the three Services.

10. A central co-ordinating and statistical section should be established for bringing the civilian Neurosis Centres of the Emergency Medical Services into closer contact with one another so far as Service patients are concerned, and with the corresponding Service departments.

Report of an Expert Committee on The Work of Psychologists and Psychiatrists in the Services, His Majesty's Stationery Office, London, 1947, par. 60, p. 24.

gent in regard to psychiatry. There were probably a number of other high-ranking Regular Army officers who wholeheartedly endorsed and accepted psychiatric advice. From personal contacts, I know of the special interest of Lt. Gen. Al Wedemeyer, Commander of the China Theater; Lt. Gen. L. T. Gerow, Commandant of the Command and Staff College, Brig. Gen. Art Trudeau, Deputy Director of ASF Training; Brig. Gen. C. T. Lanham, Director of Troop Information and Education Service; two wartime division commanders, Maj. Gens. W. S. Paul and Louis A. Craig. We hope sincerely that many others profited from the psychiatric lessons of World War II.

In setting forth these needed changes in the Army I have not lost sight of the fact that they cannot be made easily. Throughout the war, momentous changes in policy and practice were made every day. There were thousands of us, each trying to effect these changes, but we were dealing with a huge and complicated machine. Certainly many of us who tried desperately to accomplish some small job were periodically very discouraged with what often appeared to be blundering, stupidity, and excessive red tape. Most of us would confess that we often wondered how America could possibly win the war. Now, as we look back, some of us at least can appreciate the sincerity of purpose of the leadership, and the wholehearted support of the public and Congress in providing the Army with unlimited wherewithal.

If the War Department is able to implement a major portion of the Doolittle and Osborne reports, it undoubtedly will go far toward the elimination of many of the mental health hazards that existed in our Army in World War II.

In peacetime, changes may not be so easy to make. Many of them will cost heavily. Not only must we overcome the prewar attitudes within the Army, but such changes will need the full support of the public—and Congress. We have had a long history of forgetting our Army in peacetime. Its greatest enemy is our apathy and our short memory of its necessity in times of crisis.

As a psychiatrist, I am sure love is a more powerful force than hate. But we can hardly assume that the world is soon to be flooded with brotherly love. We forget so quickly our unpreparedness, the treachery of other people, the terrific cost of war. We must recognize that an ounce of prevention is worth a pound of cure, and this means the preservation of a defense unit till world love and statesmanship become far more abundant than they are now. The Army is fighting to maintain the peace. But to return to our main theme, it needs many internal changes.

35

RESEARCH IN PSYCHIATRY

PSYCHIATRY WAS on trial in the Army. It is standing before the judgment bar in civilian life right now. One of my prepublication readers commented, when looking over the previous pages, "You have stuck your neck out a long way in promising so much from psychiatry." He was trying to tell me, I think, in a polite way that I was overselling psychiatry. *My* neck is not particularly important, but I have a strong belief that the wider understanding of the potential contributions of psychiatry *is* important. There has been no intention to make exaggerated claims as to what psychiatry has done or can do. Rather, the statements expressed represent my convictions about how psychiatric knowledge and skill can be used. In every instance they have been re-enforced by my experience gained during the war.

Moreover, in my opinion one cannot oversell a clearer and wider understanding of psychiatry. There is some risk, however, that one can lead people to expect more than the present limited personnel can deliver. At this time there are not nearly sufficient hewers of wood and carriers of water in the field of psychiatry to do the jobs that need to be done. It is readily understandable that persons who seek help and cannot obtain it from trained professional persons may become discouraged. They may turn to less experienced workers, to substitutes, to pretenders, and the job will be poorly done. The result may be their disillusionment with all psychiatry.

Consequently, it is essential that every interested person recognize that psychiatry has been and still is woefully deficient in three important respects: first, it needs more trained, experienced personnel who are able to deliver the fund of knowledge and experience now available to the people who need and want it; second, it needs a wider public understanding and acceptance of its potential contributions and limitations; and third, it needs to increase greatly its general fund of knowledge.

Need for psychiatrists. Before and during the war, as well as at the present time, psychiatry lacked a sufficient number of trained, experienced men in the field who could put its scientific knowledge to work. In addition to the shortage of personnel needed for the treatment of patients in clinics and hospitals, there are equally challenging opportunities for psychiatrists in the field of academic education, industry and business, and in legal and penological fields. There is also a great need for psychiatrists in preventive work. Associated workers—clinical psychologists, psychiatric social workers, and psychiatric nurses—are also far too few in number.

There is encouragement and hope for an increased number of psychiatrists soon. Thorugh the broad vision of the leaders in the Veterans Administration Medical Department, training programs have been established in connection with many of our medical schools and psychiatric institutions. Through the impetus of the National Mental Health Act there are funds, and we hope guidance, available for the further expansion of training centers for psychiatrists.

The greater use of psychiatry during the war has led most medical educators to an awareness of the need for a better psychiatric orientation of the medical-school curriculum. This was clearly demonstrated by the response from the majority of the presidents of the universities in the country in which there are medical schools to a letter that was sent to them by the civilian consultants in neuropsychiatry to the Secretary of War. Not only are they aware of the need for more specialists in psychiatry, but also they appreciate the importance of giving all physicians a better understanding of emotional disorders. It is believed that they are directing very special efforts to satisfy this need.

Public understanding. No one should assume that psychiatrists alone are the answer to the problem. All of medicine must take a major hand in the solution, if the mental health of America is to be improved. For this the interest and understanding of the public, too, is fundamental. As I have said previously:

We in *psychiatry* covet the growth of this popular knowledge of *psychiatry*. We hope it will eventually dispel the clouds of mystery and the irrational stigmatization of those afflicted with emotional illness and bring about a public demand for the application of psychiatric principles to our legal, our educational, our political and our medical practices. Some of us, at least, recognize that if psychiatry is to grow in effectiveness, it must be through the sympathy, the understanding and the demand of the layman. At no time in our history has it been so important that the layman have some grasp of its principles.[1]

This statement, made during the war, has even more significance as we try to establish our peace. Only as the individual is educated to the problem, to the most expedient ways of handling it, can he intelligently find an answer. Only as the layman becomes acquainted with the principles of mental health as they apply to himself, his family, his business, and the nation can he use them. Therefore, much of the progress, if progress is to be made, will come as

---

[1] "Psychiatry in the War," the Laity Lecture in the New York Academy of Medicine Series, January 11, 1945; in *Modern Attitudes in Psychiatry. The March of Medicine, 1945,* Columbia University Press, New York, 1946, pp. 90-115.

the result of an enlightened public, which not only understands the present needs for psychiatry but also accepts the responsibility of seeing that these needs are met.

Research. The third great need in psychiatry is for research, which is dependent upon adequate personnel and public understanding and support. Psychiatric research must be far broader than any concept involving merely laboratory study, important as this is. A comprehensive program must include psychiatrically oriented social, cultural, educational, economic, and statistical research, as well as investigations that are strictly psychological.

For this the leaders in psychiatry must look ahead and plan. They must enlist the aid and association of allied scientific fields interested in and already making contributions to the understanding and betterment of human behavior and relations. Like any widespread utilization of psychiatry and its techniques, ideal research in the field requires far more than the activities of a group of well-trained psychiatrists, even though they may be capable of research. Because it touches on every type of human behavior, it must include the scientists from many other fields, both the "pure" scientists and the "social" scientists. It requires the combined effort of the psychologists, social workers, sociologists, anthropologists, as well as members of many branches of medicine —internists, pediatricians, surgeons, and the help of the basic scientists in chemistry, physiology, anatomy, and pathology.

More study must be made of the psychiatric problems involved in the maintenance of mental health. Some thought has been given to this matter, and some plans have been made. Doctor Robert Felix,[2] Chief of the Mental Hygiene Division of the Public Health Service, has outlined five points of attack in a national plan: first, research; second, training of personnel; third, additional outpatient clinical facilities for prophylactic and early therapeutic work; fourth, better care of the hospitalized patient; and fifth, education of the public for better care of convalescent patients and of themselves. Note that his number-one point is research.

Another leader of American Psychiatry in a strategic position, Dr. Daniel Blain, chief of psychiatry in the Veterans Administration, also has expressed himself regarding national mental health planning. He asked some pertinent and provocative questions requiring answers (research) as a groundwork to national planning: "What is the real nature and extent of the psychiatric problem of this country?" "What are the available assets [to meet it]?" "What are the functions of each of us and of various professional groups in solving the problem?" "Where does psychiatry belong in the field of medi-

2 Felix, Robert H., "Mental Public Health: A Plan of National Scope," address before Ohio State Society for Mental Hygiene, January 17, 1946; see also, *Ment. Hyg.*, 30:381-389, July, 1946.

cine?" "What is the importance of the teaching program and where can we find the people to do the work?" "What will keep 19 1/2 million veterans, men and women, well?" "What is the relation of mental health to education?" [3]

Few people appreciate the minimal amount of research that has been done in this field. Senator Pepper summarized the findings on research needs for his committee on Education and Labor after they had heard testimony from many sources on the National Mental Health Act.

Research in the field of mental illness has up to the present time been utterly inadequate in view of the magnitude of the problem and its serious consquences to our society.

The history of public health shows that more substantial sums for preventive work must be expended and greater proportion of the greater expenditures for a particular disease must be allocated to research work if we are to make any real progress in this field. All public and private government agencies together are spending not more than 25c per year for research for each estimated case of mental illness and only $1 for each known case of total disability because of mental ill health, as compared, for example, with $100 per case of poliomyelitis, a disease which is far less widespread. The proponents of this legislation . . . have emphasized that Federal funds . . . should be devoted primarily to the further development of existing and new techniques of preventive and treatment methods as well as of training of much needed personnel. Significant advances in psychiatric research, at least in diagnosis and treatment, were made in recent years, particularly from the war effort, despite the meager resources available.[4]

It is difficult to obtain even an estimate of the amount of money that actually is being invested currently in psychiatric research. In the testimony of Dr. Lawrence Kubie in the hearings on the National Neuropsychiatric Institute Act, he made the statement that "for every dollar that we spend for psychiatric research in this country, we spend $2,500 in industrial research; for every dollar that we put into psychiatric research, we spend $65 in other medical research." [5]

Doctor George Stevenson of the National Committee for Mental Hygiene has indicated [6] that it is impossible for him, despite his extensive survey of research in psychiatry, to estimate even roughly the amount of money that presently is being invested. However, as was pointed out in the introduction,

---

[3] Blain, D., "Some Essentials in National Mental Health Planning," address before the National Conference of Social Work, Buffalo, N. Y., May 21, 1946; see *Social Service Review,* 20:374-384, Sept., 1946.

[4] Senator Claude Pepper, a report to accompany HR 4512, 79th Congress Senate Calendar No. 1378, Report No. 1353, dated May 16, 1946.

[5] National Neuropsychiatric Institute Act hearing before a Subcommittee on Education and Labor, United States Senate, S 1160, March 6, 7, 8, 1946, page 79.

[6] Personal communication.

the estimate in 1944, for the expenditure for research in all fields of medicine amounted to only $54,650,000.[7] A more recent estimate is $110 million annually for scientific research and development in medical and allied fields, one-tenth the amount spent for all other forms of scientific inquiry. Despite the generosity of many of our foundations,[8] the amount spent in psychiatry was a very small fraction of this total.

Furthermore, research has not been well organized. Two extensive surveys were made by the National Committee for Mental Hygiene.[9] Both of these were thoroughgoing studies which indicated that of some 613 nongovernmental institutions, only 37 professed to be doing any research and 17 of these presented small, informal projects with no evidence of an established research program. Of the 66 medical schools, 26 reported research activities. Many of the private foundations, notably the Rockefeller, the Josiah Macy, Jr., and the Commonwealth, have sponsored research projects.[10] The research carried on throughout the country has covered many phases of psychiatry, without any co-ordination or clearinghouse of information except through professional journals. There have been isolated projects which were co-ordinated, such as the set of studies sponsored by the Supreme Council of 33rd Degree

---

[7] An estimated minimum expenditure for medical research given by Dr. Lewis H. Weed of the National Research Council. For the following estimate see *The Nation's Medical Research,* Report of the President's Scientific Research Board, U. S. Government Printing Office, Washington, D. C., Oct. 18, 1947, p. 3.

[8] Doctor Alan Gregg, as director of the medical sciences of the Rockefeller Foundation, in his annual report for 1945, said: "It is surprising that it has taken so long to recognize that the structure of man's personality is no more indestructible than his obviously fragile body. Now that this recognition has made possible a really scientific approach to the problem of human relations, it seems more than ever wise to continue support for psychiatry." Total appropriations of the Foundation during 1945 were $11,330,689; for the medical sciences, $1,751,850; for psychiatry, $323,750; distributed to University of Edinburgh, $20,750; Harvard University, $112,000; University of Tennessee, $15,000; Vanderbilt University, $15,000; University of Illinois, $115,000; American Psychiatric Association for nursing, $32,000; Columbia University, $24,000. These grants run for periods of 1 to 4 1/2 years. *Am. J. Psychiat.,* 103:425-426, Nov., 1946.

[9] Research in Mental Hospitals, studies Nos. 1 & 2. The first was a survey and tentative appraisal of research activities, facilities, and possibilities in state hospitals and other government-supported institutions for the mentally ill and defective in the United States, published in 1938. The second was a survey of psychiatric research activities, facilities, and interests and interrelationships as they exist under nongovernmental auspices in the United States, in 1942.

[10] One of the most promising hopes for research into many problems in medicine has developed in the possibility of extensive and long-range follow-up studies of military cases. Combining forces of the Army, Navy, Public Health, Veterans Administration, and a group of civilian physicians, it was proposed to follow the course of many types of illnesses and injuries on patients initially examined and treated in the service. We in the Surgeon General's office in Neuropsychiatry suggested as illustrative studies a 20-year follow-up on combat-induced psychoneuroses, short-lived psychotic episodes, normal men exposed to great external stress, the personality study of heroes, men discharged dishonorably, the personality adjustment of maimed and disfigured men, and head-injury cases. A tentative program of these and problems in medicine and surgery was outlined by Drs. M. E. DeBakey and G. W. Beebe with the National Research Council, and accepted for sponsorship by the Veterans Administration. The program is being implemented by a Committee on Veterans' Problems and many subcommittees in the various specialties of medicine under the National Research Council.

Scottish Rite Masons and under the immediate supervision of Nolan D. C. Lewis,[11] to investigate schizophrenia.

Perhaps even with the same money invested, greater value might be obtained if there were a central clearinghouse which did not control or dictate, but which did survey and offer co-ordination to efforts. Such a clearinghouse could maintain a record of different types of research in progress, relay information, advise regarding projects.

Lack of money and co-ordination have been and are among the chief obstacles to scientific research, but there are others. Many of us believe that the prevalent attitude or philosophy about research work is incorrect. For some years technological bias has prevailed. The perfection of an established knowledge or procedure or material has become the chief job of research. The research worker or institution asks for, or is assigned, a limited and specific "project" toward which they must devote their entire effort. If the initiative arises with the investigator, he knows that his only hope in obtaining funds is to outline such a project and submit the outline to his hoped-for sponsor as a basis of his appeal for financial help. Unfortunately he can not forsake the project as described after a grant-in-aid has been given. Even if he discovers much more promising leads to new ideas early in his work, he can not follow them, his "hunches," as they were so labeled by Cannon.[12] He must save these for a later project and an additional financial request.

Many of us believe that, ideally, a capable research worker should be given the freedom to follow his own plans, change his course as he wishes, forsake one project for another at any time.[13] Such a method is expensive, but, as Goodpasture stated, "True emphasis of science requires investigations that involve a great risk, and if ultimate progress is to be expected in the application of scientific knowledge to human needs, the cost of the waste of original research must be made." [14] This was the approach of Edison, Steinmetz, and many others.

At present, universities do not have sufficient money to subsidize research workers on this basis. They are interested in and desirous of sponsoring more "ideal" investigations, but they, too, are hard-pressed by the present status of research. Industry, which finances much of the research in universities, wants assistance in working out the techniques of applications of facts and principles already discovered. According to President Carmichael of the Carnegie Foundation for the Advancement of Teaching, so widespread has the practice

---

[11] Published in the "Allocation of the Sovereign Grand Commander," Melvin M. Johnson 33°, delivered at the annual meeting of the Scottish Rite, Boston, September 25, 1946.

[12] Cannon, W. B., *The Way of An Investigator, A Scientist's Experience in Medical Research,* W. W. Norton & Company, Inc., New York, 1945.

[13] My associate, Dr. David Rapaport, has discussed these and other problems in "The Future of Research in Clinical Psychology and Psychiatry," *Am. Psychologist,* 2:167-172, May, 1947.

[14] Goodpasture, E. W., "Research and Medical Practice," *Science,* 104:473-476, Nov. 22, 1946.

become that university leaders have been alarmed lest the energies of the professors be absorbed in applied research to such an extent that basic investigation would be largely neglected.

He laments also the fact that the Science Foundation, proposed in legislation by the last Congress, eliminates the social sciences. From his experience, basic investigation of the factors that make for peace and stability is society's greatest need. The entrance of research into this field is essential to prevent chaos if the discrepancy between our knowledge of the physical world and the problems of social adjustment becomes any wider.[15]

Foundations do not often feel justified in making unspecified grants. However, recently the Nutrition Foundation, instead of asking for help in solving the practical problems of applying facts and principles, has encouraged and supported basic research in the field of nutrition. Unless many sponsors of research follow this plan we cannot have the ideal program where workers can be really free. Now they are limited to the service of the present social order or are trying to meet the specific demands of society.

Further, man power has been and is an obstacle to research. Some men are gifted in the field of teaching far beyond their education and experiences; some are gifted as leaders; fewer are gifted as research workers. Because a man has had scientific training in chemistry or biology or medicine does not make him capable of research. From his broad experience, Cannon points out some of the difficulties in the path of the research worker: "As an investigator he may, for example, be rich in suggestive ideas and yet be indolent and, therefore, sterile; he may be a hard worker but secretive about his results and suspicious of his fellow workers, so that he is despised by them; he may be an earnest experimenter but inconsiderate of his helpers, and therefore he may find that help is begrudged him; or he may be prone to display an attitude of superiority and consequently be subjected to derision, expressed or silent."[16] He listed the more important qualities of the investigator— imaginative insight, keen powers of observation, patience, critical judgment, thorough honesty, a retentive memory, good health, generosity.

Not only are such men rare, but, among those who are so endowed, the economic insecurity of full-time research in contrast to that gained through the utilization of their abilities otherwise has deterred many of them from becoming research workers. In the great majority of instances, research work has had to be a side issue, to be done when and if there was time. Consequently, we will be short of man power for research until medicine is able to give its workers an economic security proportional to practice or even teaching.

---

15 Carmichael, O. C., "Science and Social Progress," *Think*, Dec., 1946, pp. 11-12.
16 Reprinted from *The Way of an Investigator* by Walter B. Cannon, by permission of W. W. Norton & Company, Inc. Copyright 1945 by the publishers. P. 31.

The thoughtful layman may—and should be—interested in the areas within psychiatry that need investigation. An oversimplified list of the major groups of research problems in psychiatry follows:

(1) The study of the "normal." This would include the structure and the physiology of the personality as well as the psychopathology of everyday life; the reactions to stress and the emotional supports, i.e., the methods of maintaining mental health; cultural variations. All of these factors were extremely important to us in the Army.

(2) The psychological evaluation of the personality. One of the most promising fields of research is in clinical psychology which is developing and perfecting the present and additional tests for determining the structure of personality, for measuring the changes that take place in it after various experiences as, for instance, treatment; for discovering aptitudes or the correct vocational choice. All of these factors were extremely important in the Army. It would have been helpful if we had had more adequate tests to aid in classification and assignment of personnel.

(3) Child psychology and psychiatry. We need to know far more about the developmental factors that determine the personality, their contribution to the formation of character. We have needed very much to have organized information for parents to use in the guidance of a child. We lack any well-accepted understanding or even classification of behavior disorders in children.

(4) Psychodynamics. Through Freud's initial contributions and stimulus we learned much about the dynamics of personality function. However, we are still only scratching the surface in our knowledge of the functions of the conscious ego as well as the functions of the unconscious and the factors in its development and its relationship to other parts of the personality.

We need a much more comprehensive understanding of how psychological energy is converted into symptom formation and how it can be channeled into sublimation.

(5) Diagnostic entities. Many of the psychiatric clinical pictures are inadequately understood. This applies specially to the characterological defects and the schizophrenic reactions. These and many other mental illnesses bear investigation as to causes, pathology, and cure.

(6) The emotional factors in disease. This general field, called "psychosomatic medicine," has received a great impetus in the last 10 years, but again our knowledge is quite limited. We still do not know why an individual picks a certain physical system to express his emotions, how these emotions are expressed, the best methods of handling them.

(7) Anatomic, physiological, and chemical research are greatly needed in such fields as brain metabolism, electrical potentials, autonomic relationships with emotion and cerebration. These, perhaps, have received more

attention than many of the psychological forces and emotional components, but we are still in a relatively unknown sea. There is an understandable clamor for this type of research because of the preference of many persons to deal with the tangible or material rather than the psychic. It is to be hoped that they do receive attention, but that this may be proportionate to the many other necessary fields of research and psychiatry.

(8) Treatment must be divided into both preventive and therapeutic methods. There is not a single existing method that would not warrant much research—psychotherapy, occupation, education, recreation, chemical methods, surgical methods, mechanical methods, shortened analysis.

(9) Social issues. Research into man's sociology in relation to his personality structure is fundamental in understanding many of our most pressing social needs. This should include the study of group forces and pressures, the influence of cultural backgrounds and characteristics, the psychologic and psychiatric aspects of leadership, racial feeling, and aggressive and destructive as well as constructive forces.

(10) In view of the needs for personnel in psychiatry, we are justified in making special research studies of how best to select men and then to teach them. This is one small aspect of the total need for research in educational methods in general.

Any detailed discussion of research possibilities in psychiatry would take many pages. It was the intention here merely to outline a few broad fields and some of the specific possibilities. In so doing, it might appear that we know little in psychiatry. By comparison to what we should know, that is so. We have some well-established beacons, and it is from these that we can map the course of our research needs.

So where is psychiatry going? The answer lies in the unseeable future. We can be sure it will depend on the vision and the energy and the integrity of the workers in that field. It will depend on its acceptance and the adoption of its principles by the whole field of medicine. Perhaps it will depend most on how practical and helpful it can be to a public which is rapidly increasing its understanding and utilization of its principles.

APPENDIX A

PUBLICATIONS AND CIRCULARS

ANY PROGRAM or any individual could function in the Army only within the limits permitted by orders or directives published by some headquarters. At the beginning of the war there were no directives as to how psychiatry was to operate, except a few on the disposition of the "insane." Therefore it was vital that policies and practice be established, published, and disseminated to the field so that the commanding officers and the neuropsychiatrists themselves would be informed of the standards and methods, and have the authority to carry out the mission of neuropsychiatry. Unfortunately the establishment of a policy and having it published was often a very slow process— even requiring months. This fact, coupled with the relatively late inclusion of a psychiatrist in the Office of the Surgeon General, delayed the appearance of many of the important directives and bulletins until comparatively late in the war.

The more permanent media for directives and guides were the field manuals, technical manuals, and Army regulations. Because of the many necessary changes that occurred during the war, temporary media for instructions were widely used. For the Medical Department this included the Surgeon General's letters, Adjutant General's memoranda, Army Service Forces circulars, War Department circulars, and technical medical bulletins. In addition, there were the circulars from the Air Forces Surgeon. Each theater issued circulars. These latter two did not come under the jurisdiction of the Office of the Surgeon General but did have to conform to War Department policies. The Surgeon General's letters, Adjutant General's memoranda, and the Army Service Forces circulars applied only to the Medical Department under the Army Service Forces, the general, regional, and station hospitals, and all other Army Service Forces units, like Service Forces basic-training camps. On the other hand, the War Department circulars and the technical medical bulletins were circulated to all forces, Service, Ground, and Air.

Many, if not most, of these directives required a colossal amount of effort and salesmanship and persuasion. They represent the end result of a major portion of the work of the Neuropsychiatry Consultants Division.

THE ARMY REGULATIONS

These are, in a sense, the bible of the Army. They cover every activity. Those which have a pertinent reference to neuropsychiatry are as follows and it should be noted that every one of these listed was modified or changed during the course of the war:

35-1440, 17 November 1944. Loss of Pay During Absence Due to Diseases Resulting from Misconduct.

40-10, 7 March 1946. Change 3. Duties of the Division Psychiatrist.

40-1025, 12 December 1944. Line of Duty, Par. 63 (5) dealing with psychiatric cases. Paragraph 65 gives list of standard terms for diagnoses, superseded by TB Med. 203.

350-1010, 11 February 1946. Military Education. Professional Graduate Education for Medical Corps Officers. Includes neuropsychiatry.

600-375, 28 June 1944. Change 4. Prisoners General Provisions. Lists serious mental and neurological cases to be confined in disciplinary barracks.

600-395, 10 August 1942. Division of psychiatry and sociology to be maintained in disciplinary barracks, and duties of the psychiatrist.

600-500, 4 February 1946. Disposition of the psychotic patient. Totally revises the old AR as well as rescinding 600-505.

600-505, Rescinded in February, 1945, by AR 600-500.

600-550, 23 December 1944. Suicide. (As written, this is a poor exposition of modern psychiatric principles. We never got around to rewriting it.)

605-230, 6 September 1945. Reclassification of Commissioned Officers.

615-25, 31 July 1942. Initial classification of enlisted men. Change 4, 28 November 1942, rescinded "mentally limited enlisted men (Class C)."

615-28, 1 September 1942. Change 1. Reclassification of EM by a board of three medical officers "one of whom will be a psychiatrist, if available."

615-28, 28 May 1942. 15b re Special Training Unit, "use will be made of psychiatrist or neuropsychiatrists who may be assigned to the replacement training center."

615-361, 1 March 1945. Medical Discharge. Change 2. Authorized treatment for psychiatric illnesses except chronic psychoses and degenerative neurological diseases. "A diagnosis of psychoneurosis will not in itself constitute adequate cause for discharge."

615-361, 11 January 1946. Medical Discharge. Change 3, 27 September 1946, included most of WD Cir 81, 1945 on noneffective personnel.

615-368, 7 March 1945. Discharge for undesirable habits or traits of character or psychopathic personality manifested by antisocial or amoral trends, criminalism, drug addiction, pathological lying, or sexual misconduct in the service and cannot be rehabilitated to render useful service.

615-369, 20 July 1944. Discharge for inaptness, lack of required degree of adaptability, or enuresis.

THE SURGEON GENERAL'S LETTERS

These were issued as the necessity arose, during the first years of the war, through 1943. At that time they were replaced by other media which had been cleared and co-ordinated through a higher authority (Adjutant General's Office). On reorganization of the War Department in 1946, circulars from the Office of the Surgeon General were instituted. The most important of these letters and circulars dealing with psychiatry included:

SGO Letters 1941. Four letters were issued in 1941 which affected neuropsychiatry: Letter 12 on 19 February, Letter 19 on 12 March, Letter 64 on 24 June, Letter 106 on 21 October. Only Letter 19 is of more than passing interest. In this the various types of psychiatric and neurological syndromes are outlined for the examiners of selectees for induction.

SGO Letter 77, 29 July 1942. Interpreted WD Cir 270 of 1941, regarding the use of discretion and the middle road in the discharge of enlisted men on the basis of "disability, inaptness, or undesirable traits of character."

SGO Letter 99, 4 September 1942. Urged rapid disposition of mental cases in Army hospitals, in which it was pointed out that there was an accumulation of mental cases that had become a major problem, and hospital commanders were urged to speed up the dispositions.

SGO Letter 103, 9 September 1942. Prescribed the method of hospitalization of mental cases in the WAAC.

SGO Letter 88, 23 April 1943. Authorized shock therapy.

SGO Letter 110, 2 June 1943. Concerned with the disposition of the insane and instructions for the delivery of psychotic patients to the custody of relatives.

SGO Letter 149, 12 August 1943. Authorized occupational therapy for the general hospitals. (There were not nearly sufficient occupational therapists for even this group of hospitals so that they were not authorized for the smaller hospitals or the overseas hospitals.)

SGO Letter 168, 21 September 1943. Established convalescent reconditioning in general hospitals, but no mention of the psychiatric patients.

SGO Letter 176, 20 October 1943. Described the organization and treatment of NP conditions in the combat zone. This was the first comprehensive presentation of psychiatric treatment in the Army, but it was limited to combat casualties.

SGO Letter 194, 3 December 1943. Prescribed the disposition of individuals with neuropsychiatric disorders. "A man will not be separated from the Service merely because he has or has had a psychoneurosis or similar psychiatric disorder. . . . 'Physical standards' include nervous and mental conditions."

SGO Letter 200, 9 December 1943. Outlined the physical and mental qualifications of applicants for parachute duty. Warns against psychopaths.

A memorandum dated 10 December 1943 (memoranda were occasionally used to expedite action) dealing with convalescent reconditioning in hospitals, in which it was stated that "NP cases are not included (in this program) and should be handled in specific centers or wards."

SGO Letter 202, 9 December 1943. Discussed the mental responsibility of neuropsychiatric patients on discharge. Provided escort to patient's home in questionable cases.

SGO Cir 30, 19 June 1946. Outlined the postwar convalescent program in Army hospitals. This replaced ASF Cirs 419 and 440, 1945, describing the convalescent annex.

SGO Cir 44, 17 July 1946. Described the special training in neuropsychiatry. Outlined the residency training program and included a bibliography, which was amended by an enlarged reference list in SGO Cir 61, 4 September 1946.

THE ADJUTANT GENERAL'S MEMORANDA

These were used extensively in 1943. Subsequently they were used only for statements of policy and had a very limited distribution.

W615-4-43, 10 January 1943. Outlined the announced War Department policy of court-martial for sodomists.

W600-22-43, 5 March 1943. Discussed the rejection or discharge for psychiatric reasons in which it was pointed out that tact should be used, and, in some cases, had not been used, in the rejection or discharge of psychiatric patients.

W600-30-43, 25 March 1943. Warned officers regarding the mental condition of men ordered overseas. This indicated that too many men who were mentally unsuited for ordinary military duties were arriving overseas. This is reminiscent of the famous Pershing telegram of World War I, dispatched 15 July 1918, pointing out that too many noneffective soldiers were being received in the AEF.[1]

W600-39-43, 26 April 1943. This was a revision of Memorandum 30, in

---

[1] Bailey, Pearce, *The Medical Department of the United States Army in the World War,* Vol. X, U.S. Government Printing Office, Washington, D.C., 1929, p. 58.

which it states that "there is no classification for duty of military personnel with such mental diagnoses as psychoneuroses. . . ."

W615-53-43, 18 June 1943. This was an outline of a report form for the Section VIII cases, including mental deficiency, constitutional psychopathic states, and alcoholism.

W600-62-43, 29 July 1943. Further discussion of the mental condition of men ordered overseas. This, the third memorandum on the same subject, again stressed the fact that there was no classification for duty of those individuals with a diagnosis of psychoneurosis.

ARMY SERVICE FORCES CIRCULARS

The Medical Department was made a subdivision of the Army Service Forces in the reorganization of the Army in 1942. Consequently, ASF circulars only applied to the Army Service Forces and not to the Air Forces or the Ground Forces. While the Ground Forces maintained no hospitals (except evacuation, field, and Army convalescent in combat areas) the Army Air Forces did maintain hospitals in the United States. These circulars did not apply to psychiatry in the Air Forces hospitals.

ASF Cir 40, 5 February 1944. Established the developmental training units for psychoneurotic patients in three basic-training camps.

ASF Cir 169, 5 June 1944. Prescribed the method of utilization of recovered psychoneurotic patients. This dealt with the assignment of men from these special retraining units, established under Cir 40.

ASF Cir 175, 10 June 1944. Established reconditioning for neuropsychiatric cases in general hospitals.

ASF Cir 208, 6 July 1944. Established additional consultation services in all ASF basic-training camps.

ASF Cir 310, 16 September 1944. Provided a special designation for ward attendants, using the military occupational specialty number 409 for medical technicians and adding the letters "NP" after it.

ASF Cir 313, 19 September 1944. This was an amendment to 310 which exempted those individuals (ward attendants) with an MOS of 409NP from assignment to theater-of-operation units, excepting certain situations.

ASF Cir 355, 28 October 1944. Instructions to convert the locked wards, where necessary, into open wards by removing bars and window gratings.

ASF Cir 419, 22 December 1944. Revised the program of convalescent hospital including the "neuropsychiatric reconditioning section."

ASF Cir 36, 3 January 1945. Provided reconditioning and recreation on hospital ships and other ships carrying medical patients, including neuropsychiatric patients.

ASF Cir 74, 28 February 1945. Provided instructions that psychoneurotic patients were not to be retained on locked wards.

ASF Cir 96, 17 March 1945. Provided for the hospitalization of insane general prisoners.

ASF Cir 189, 26 May 1945. Gave instructions to commanding officers to help meet the shortage of psychiatrists by temporarily assigning general medical officers to assist on the NP service and sections of hospitals.

ASF Cir 281, 24 July 1945. Established the authority for the utilization of the Neuropsychiatric Screening Adjunct Test at induction centers, and collecting test results.

ASF Cir 310, 15 August 1945. Discharge of ineffectual enlisted personnel.

ASF Cir 354, 19 September 1945. WD Pamphlet 21-35, *What's the Score,* to be given each discharged psychoneurotic patient.

ASF Cir 440, 10 December 1945. The program for the rehabilitation of paraplegic patients, which was jointly worked out with the Reconditioning Division and the Neuropsychiatry Consultants Division, is outlined.

ASF Cir 445, 14 December 1945. Outlined a revision of the convalescent hospital, dividing the patients into medical, surgical, and neuropsychiatric battalions.

The above circulars refer only to those with major significance to psychiatry. During the years of 1944 through 1945 there were a total of 46 that were of specific interest to psychiatry.

WAR DEPARTMENT CIRCULARS

These circulars had an Army-wide jurisdiction, applying to all forces in the United States and abroad and all divisions—Service Forces, Ground Forces, and Air Forces. In 1941 there were only four (7, 66, 82, 243) that in any way referred to neuropsychiatry. There were four in 1942 (104, 112, 180, 243) that touched the field of psychiatry prior to 395. By this date, psychiatry had begun to function.

WD Cir 395, 5 December 1942. Directed the discharge of limited-service enlisted men, referring specifically to illiterates.

WD Cir 34, 1 February 1943. Urged the proper utilization of nurses with psychiatric training.

WD Cir 103, 15 April 1943. Provided instruction for the hospitalization of psychiatric cases by the Veterans Administration.

WD Cir 161, 14 July 1943. Did away with the designation of "limited service" and instructed commanding generals to discharge such men who could not be classified for full-duty service. This resulted in a wholesale discharge of psychiatric patients, and was done against the advice of the Surgeon General's Office.

WD Cir 290, 9 November 1943. Created the assignment and authorized the appointment of the division psychiatrist and outlined his duties.

WD Cir 48, 3 February 1944. Directed that training in basic medical subjects should be given all troops, including mental hygiene for enlisted men and officers.

WD Cir 270, 1 July 1944. Authorizing the procurement and utilization of psychologists. Rescinded by WD Cir 71, 1945.

WD Cir 295, 13 July 1944. Officially established psychiatric social work and indicated the method of the assignment of this personnel.

WD Cir 298, 14 July 1944. Gave a model letter for discharge of a psychotic patient to family care. Rescinded by WD Cir 386, 1945.

WD Cir 347, 25 August 1944. Established neurological centers in designated hospitals. Amended by WD Cir 323, 1945.

WD Cir 392, 2 October 1944. Provided the authority to commission enlisted men, who were qualified as clinical psychologists, in the grade of second lieutenants. Rescinded by WD Cir 235, 1945.

WD Cir 81, 31 March 1945. Defined and directed disposition of noneffective personnel. This was probably the most important single psychiatric message to the field during the war. It covered the abuse of medical channels in the disposition of noneffective personnel, eliminated the term "psychoneurosis" on clinical records, and outlined the responsibilities of the psychiatrist to advise command.

WD Cir 162, 2 June 1945. Concerned with the disposition of psychiatric cases. This authorized that individuals with psychoneurosis returned from overseas were not to be discharged until they had reached a point of maximum improvement in a convalescent hospital.

WD Cir 179, 16 June 1945. Outlined in detail the method of recording the diagnosis of various types of psychoneuroses.

WD Cir 196, 30 June 1945. Discussed the utilization of man power (all military personnel) based on physical capacity. Outlined the physical and psychiatric standards for dispatch of personnel overseas. Amended by WD Cir 17, 1946.

WD Cir 235, 3 August 1945. Directed the appointment of warrant officers and enlisted personnel as clinical psychologists in the grade of second lieutenants.

WD Cir 264, 1 September 1945. Authorized the transfer of the clinical psychologists from the Adjutant General's Department to the Medical Administrative Corps.

WD Cir 298, 29 September 1945. Outlined the War Department attitude on malingering.

WD Cir 359, 1 December 1945. Provided instructions regarding the minimal mental capacity for induction or enlistment.

WD Cir 385, 28 December 1945. This circular dealt with the management of homosexuals who had carried out homosexual offenses. Amended by WD Cir 85, 1946.

WD Cir 387, 29 December 1945. Prescribed the dispensary organization and its function. This circular was stimulated by an initial investigation of Maj. (later Lt. Col.) John Appel, who, with the collaboration of various divisions of the Surgeon General's Office, wrote the circular.

WD Cir 391, 21 December 1945. Disposition Policy. This enumerated the War Department policy of return to duty, from hospitals, of all patients including psychiatric, who could deliver some effective duty. It indicated that patients noneffective because of attitudes could be returned to duty for administrative discharge.

WD Cir 392, 29 December 1945. Specified the appointment of officers to the Regular Army which included [under Par. 14-k(4)] the clinical psychologist and the psychiatric social worker.

WD Cir 17, 17 January 1946. Discussed the utilization of man power. Devoted a section to the neuropsychiatric standards for dispatch of soldiers overseas.

WD Cir 43, 9 February 1946. Renewed the direction for training in basic medical subjects, including six lectures in mental hygiene for officers and three for enlisted men, which were originally directed by WD Cir 48, 3 February 1944.

WD Cir 73, 13 March 1946. Rescinded WD Cir 290, 1943, pertaining to the duties of the division neuropsychiatrists in view of the fact that these were published under AR 40-10.

WD Cir 85, 23 March 1946. Amended WD Cir 385, 1945, on the discharge of homosexuals, indicating that those who had not committed any sexual offense while in the service would be discharged under the provisions of AR 615-369, provided record of service otherwise justified honorable discharge.

WD Cir 101, 4 April 1946. Definitely established the professional consultants in the Office of the Surgeon General, in Service Commands, and in Army hospitals, outlining their duties.

WD Cir 103, 6 April 1946. Described a report on which to base a study of the effectiveness of men inducted for limited service. This primarily was a plan to determine the effectiveness of men being taken into the Army by the draft who previously had been under the 4F category because of personality disorders.

WD Cir 205, 11 July 1946. This replaced ASF Cir 354, 19 September

1945, continuing the WD Pamphlet 21-35, *What's the Score,* in hospitals in the United States.

WD Cir 209, 13 July 1946. Established the military occupational specialty of neuropsychiatric technician (ward attendant). SSN 1409.

WD Cir 240, 10 August 1946. Insured the continuance of the use of the Neuropsychiatric Screening Adjunct at induction centers, replacing ASF Cir 281, 24 July 1945.

WD Cir 241, 10 August 1946. Set forth policies pertaining to AR 615-369, indicating that the administrative discharge for noneffective personnel would "be more generally applied."

WD Cir 250, 17 August 1946. Continued the consultation services in training centers, outlining their organization and the psychiatrist's duties.

The above circulars include only those which were of major significance to psychiatry. During the years of 1943 through 1946, there were a total of 40 that were of specific interest to psychiatry.

WAR DEPARTMENT TECHNICAL BULLETINS, MEDICAL

These were issued by the Medical Department and began in January, 1944. While these were not directives, e.g., orders, they were regarded as guides and were often referred to as the established authority for modification in the functions and duties of individuals and in the treatment of patients.

TB Med 12, 22 February 1944. Suggested outlines of six lectures for officers on "personnel adjustment" (mental hygiene) problems. This bulletin and the next were utilized as the basis for the lectures on mental hygiene which had been directed in the WD Cir 48 dated 3 February 1944.

TB Med 21, 15 March 1944. Presented outlines for three lectures for enlisted men on "personal adjustment" problems. This series of lecture outlines, initially written by Maj. (later Lt. Col.) John Appel, was revised and reprinted as TB Med 21, dated 29 December 1945. This revision was necessitated by the cessation of hostilities, and troops had to be oriented for peacetime and occupation Army needs rather than combat. The continued utilization of TB Meds 12 and 21 was authorized in WD Cir 43, 9 February 1946.

TB Med 28, 1 April 1944. Prescribed and outlined the treatment program for psychiatric patients in station and general hospitals. This was the first Army-wide guide in the treatment of psychiatric patients which was actually not implemented until the publication of Change 2 in AR 615-361, dated 1 March 1945, which authorized the retention of psychiatric patients in hospitals for treatment. TB Med 28 was revised and reissued as TB Med 84, 10 August 1944, with the same title.

TB Med 33, 21 April 1944. The Induction Station NP Examination. This dealt with a change in policy, eliminating the necessity for making a specific diagnosis and substituting the clause "not suited for military service." It also indicated a change in policy from the original AG Memorandum 600-39-43, 26 April 1943, in which caution had been urged to prevent "all individuals predisposed . . . to psychoneuroses from entering the service."

TB Med 48, 31 May 1944. Management of neurosyphilis which outlined the treatment methods for this disease and was prepared by the Venereal Disease Section with the co-operation of the Neuropsychiatry Consultants Division.

TB Med 74, 27 July 1944. Electroencephalography—Operative Techniques and Interpretation. This and the following technical medical bulletin were primarily the work of Lt. Col. William H. Everts, Chief of the Neurological Branch in the Neuropsychiatry Consultants Division.

TB Med 76, 28 July 1944. Neurological Diagnostic Techniques. This bulletin covered the subjects of lumbar puncture, spinal manometry, pneumoencephalography, and cutaneous resistance testing.

TB Med 80, 3 August 1944. This bulletin outlined in detail the suggested program and schedule for NP reconditioning, along with the administration of the program, the records, and the disposition of patients. It was largely the work of Lt. Col. Norman Q. Brill.

TB Med 94, 21 September 1944. Neuropsychiatry for the General Medical Officer. This was prepared with the assistance of the Medical and the Surgical Consultants Divisions. It was reprinted in Mental Hygiene, 29:622-643, October, 1945.

TB Med 100, 4 October 1944. WAC Recruiting Station Neuropsychiatric Examination. Because the system of enlistment provided very different problems from the draft, special psychiatric instructions had to be issued to cover the Women's Army Corps.

TB Med 103, 10 October 1944. Group Psychotherapy. This bulletin outlined the suggested methods of group psychotherapy on the basis of extensive experience up to that time. It was prepared by Maj. (later Lt. Col.) Norman Q. Brill.

TB Med 115, 14 November 1944. Clinical Psychological Service in Army Hospitals. This bulletin was prepared by Lt. Col. (later Col.) Morton Seidenfeld, and covered the counseling, the preparation of clinical records, and the classification and tests of the clinical psychologists in the hospitals. Revised and reissued 21 November 1946.

TB Med 154, June 1945. Psychiatric Social Work. This bulletin established the standards of psychiatric social work and outlined the duties of this personnel. It was prepared chiefly by Maj. (later Lt. Col.) Manfred Guttmacher, with the assistance of Mrs. Elizabeth Ross. A minor correction, Change 1, was issued 19 June 1945. Revised and reissued 4 December 1946.

TB Med 155, April 1945. Aphasic Language Disorders. This was prepared for the guidance of neurologists and speech teachers in the field and was jointly prepared by the Neurological and Psychiatric Branches of the Neuropsychiatry Consultants Division.

TB Med 156, June 1945. Consultation Services. This was the first official outline of the duties and organization of the consultation service program which was in operation in 37 basic-training camps. It was prepared by Maj. (later Lt. Col.) Manfred Guttmacher. Revised and reissued 4 December 1946.

TB Med 170, June 1945. Medical Problem of Redeployment. Between the cessation of hostilities in Europe and the prospective redeployment of troops to the Pacific, major psychiatric problems were anticipated. These were covered, with emphasis on preventive psychiatry, in this bulletin, prepared jointly by Maj. (later Lt. Col.) Manfred Guttmacher and Maj. (later Lt. Col.) John Appel.

TB Med 187, 26 July 1945. Music in Reconditioning in ASF Convalescent and General Hospitals. This bulletin was prepared by the Reconditioning Division of the Surgeon General's Office and largely written by Capt. Guy V. Marriner. In view of the importance of the subject for neuropsychiatric patients, it was modified in several important details by the Neuropsychiatry Consultants Division.

TB Med 201, 1 October 1945. Psychiatric Testimony before Courts-Martial. This was a joint effort on the part of the Judge Advocate General Officer Review Board, as represented by Col. A. E. Lipscomb and the Neuropsychiatry Consultants Division. The psychiatric section was chiefly written by Maj. (later Lt. Col.) Manfred Guttmacher.

TB Med 203, 19 October 1945. Nomenclature and method of recording diagnoses, including a major section on psychiatric disorders and reactions, with definitions and the manner of recording such diagnoses. This section represented an extensive study by the Neuropsychiatry Consultants Division.

APPENDIX B

NOMENCLATURE[1]

THE NATURE of psychiatric practice in the Army required modification of the so-called "standard nomenclature" of psychiatric diagnoses. Over a period of approximately 18 months of study and with the help of nearly 100 leading psychiatrists, in and out of the Army, a new nomenclature was developed. This process required the circularization of approximately 15 drafts before the final one was evolved.

The final draft was published in WD TB Med 203, dated 19 October 1945, Subject: Nomenclature and Method of Recording Diagnoses. The portion of this bulletin devoted to the psychiatric disorders and reactions is extracted as follows:

PSYCHIATRIC DISORDERS AND REACTIONS: DEFINITIONS AND MANNER OF RECORDING.

I. *Definitions.*

    A. *General.* In setting up the definitions of psychiatric conditions, the term "disorder" has been used for the designation of the generic group of the specific reactions, while the specific reaction types have been termed "reactions." In classifying psychoneuroses, the dynamics of the psychopathology was chosen as the basis. Of necessity, a few terms remained descriptive (symptomatic). In general, an attempt has been made to retain only such formerly used terms as could be fitted into this general plan and omit categories which are "catch-alls," such as "Simple adult maladjustment," "Constitutional psychopathic state," etc.

    In recording a psychiatric condition, the particular type of condition ("reaction") will be specified, and not its generic term ("disorder"). Whenever a reaction is subclassified, only the subcategory will be recorded as the diagnosis.

    B. *Transient personality reactions to acute or special stress.*

        1. *General.* A normal personality may utilize, under conditions of great or unusual stress, established patterns of reaction to express overwhelming fear or flight reaction. The clinical picture of such reactions differs from that of neuroses or psychoses chiefly in points of direct relationship to external precipitation and reversability. In a great majority of such reactions, there is an essentially negative historical background.

---

[1] See Chap. 18.

This general classification should be restricted to conditions which are usually transient in character, though they may be acute and severe, and conditions which cannot be given a more definitive diagnosis either because of their fluid state or because of limitation in time permitted for their study.

None of the conditions included in the disorder group, transient personality reactions to acute or special stress, is acceptable as the cause of separation from the service for disability.

2. *Combat exhaustion.* Combat reaction is often transient in character. When promptly and adequately treated, the condition may either clear rapidly or it may progress into one of the established neurotic reactions. The term is to be regarded, therefore, as a temporary diagnosis and should be used only until a more definitive diagnosis can be established. It will ordinarily be used only in the "Army level," and should never be used back of the communications zone.

This diagnosis is justified only in situations in which the individual has been exposed either to severe physical demands or to extreme emotional stress, such as seen in combat soldiers within the combat area, or to both. In some instances, this diagnosis applies to more or less "normal" persons. The stress in such cases is intolerable. The patient may display a marked psychological disorganization akin to certain psychoses.

3. *Acute situational maladjustment.* This transient personality reaction is manifested by anxiety, alcoholism, asthenia, poor efficiency, low morale, unconventional behavior, etc. The clinical picture of this reaction is primarily one of a superficial maladjustment to newly experienced environmental factors or to especially trying and difficult situations, but exhibiting no evidence of any serious long standing or underlying personality defects or chronic neurotic patterns. If untreated or not relieved, such reactions may progress in some instances into a typical psychoneurotic or psychopathic reaction.

The term may be applied to reactions caused by cultural deficiencies and deprivations, when such show no definite neurotic type of reaction. It will also include some cases formerly classified as "Simple adult maladjustment."

C. *Psychoneurotic disorders.*

1. *General.* This generic term refers to psychiatric disorders resulting from the exclusion from the consciousness (i.e. repression) of powerful emotional charges, usually attached to certain infantile and childhood developmental experiences. Such repressed emotional charges, which may not be apparent without an extensive and deep investigation of the personality, may or may not be adequately controlled in the absence of external stress. Longitudinal (lifelong) studies of individuals with such disorders usually present evidence of periodic or constant maladjustment of varying degree. Special stress may make the symptomatic expressions of such disorders acute.

The chief characteristic of these disorders is anxiety, which may be either "free floating" and unbound ("anxiety reaction"), and directly felt and expressed, or it may be unconsciously and automatically controlled by the utilization of various psychological defense mechanisms (repression, conversion, displacement, etc.). In contrast to psychotics, patients with such disorders do not exhibit gross distortion or falsification of the external reality (delusions, hallucinations, illusions), and there is no gross disorganization of the personality.

Anxiety in psychoneurotic disorders is a danger signal felt and perceived by the conscious portion of the personality (ego). Its origin may be a threat from within the personality—expressed by the supercharged repressed emotions, including particularly such aggressive impulses as hostility and resentment—with or without stimulation from the external situation, as loss of love or of prestige, or threat of injury. The various ways in which the patient may attempt to handle this anxiety result in the various types of reactions.

Diagnoses of psychoneurotic disorders will be recorded as one of the following types of reaction. The term will not be prefaced by any broad group designation such as "psychoneurotic disorder." The term "traumatic neurosis (or reaction)" will not be used; instead the particular reaction will be recorded. The term "mixed reaction" will not be used; instead the predominant type of reaction will be recorded qualified by references to other types as part of the symptomatology.

2. *Anxiety reaction.* In this type of reaction the anxiety is diffuse and not restricted to definite situations or objects, as in the case of the phobias. Furthermore, it is neither "bound" nor controlled by any psychological defense mechanism, as in the other psychoneurotic disorders. In such reactions, both the psychological and physiological aspects of the anxiety are felt by the patient, but only the physiological aspects are observable by the physician.

This reaction should be distinguished from normal apprehensiveness or fear. This term is synonymous with the former term "anxiety state."

3. *Dissociative reaction.* This psychoneurotic disorder represents a type of personality disorganization which proves to be in the majority of instances a neurotic disturbance. (It should be differentiated, however, from a pre-psychotic disturbance.) The diffuse dissociation trends, seen in acute combat exhaustion, may occasionally appear psychotic, but nearly always the reaction becomes neurotic.

In acute cases of such reaction, the personality (ego) disorganization appears to permit the anxiety to overwhelm and momentarily govern the total individual, resulting in aimless running or "freezing." This may occur in well-integrated personalities. But even in less acute cases, or in less well-integrated personalities, the repressed impulse, giving rise to the anxiety, may be either discharged or deflected into various symptomatic expressions such as fugue, amnesia, etc. Often this may occur with little or no participation on the part of the conscious personality.

These reactions should be differentiated from schizoid personality, schizophrenic reactions, and from analogous symptoms in some other type of neurotic reaction. This reaction has been formerly often classified as a type of "conversion hysteria."

The diagnosis should specify the symptomatic manifestations of the reaction, such as depersonalization, dissociated personality, stupor, fugue, amnesia, dream state, somnambulism.

4. *Phobic reaction.* By an automatic mental mechanism, the anxiety in these cases becomes detached from some specific idea or situation in the daily life behavior and is displaced to some symbolic object or situation in the form of a specific neurotic fear. In civilian life, the commonly observed forms of phobic reactions include fear of syphilis, dirt, closed places, high places, open places, some animals, etc.; in military life, other specific neurotic fears have been observed, such as fear of specific weapons, combat noise, planes, etc. The patient can control his anxiety if he avoids the phobic object or situation.

In this group of reactions are included the sensitized residual states of combat exhaustion observed after the other acute manifestations have subsided. This term also includes some cases formerly called "anxiety hysteria." In recording such cases, the symptomatic manifestations will be indicated.

5. *Conversion reaction.* This term is synonymous with "conversion hysteria." Instead of being experienced consciously (either diffusely, or displaced, as in phobias), the impulse causing the anxiety in conversion reaction is "converted" into functional symptoms in organs or parts of the body, mainly under voluntary control.

In recording such reactions, the symptomatic manifestations will be specified, as pain (cephalalgia, myalgia, arthralgia, etc.), anesthesia (anosmia, blindness, deafness), paralysis (paresis, aphonia, mono- or hemiplegia), dyskinesis (tic, tremor, postures, catalepsy). However, if the manifestations do not fit the conversion pattern of immediate need and when they do not represent the result of chronic emotional tension states, the reactions will be properly classified under somatization reactions.

6. *Somatization reactions.*

a. *General.* This term is used in preference to "psychosomatic reactions," since the latter term refers to a point of view on the discipline of medicine as a whole rather than to certain specified conditions.

The anxiety is relieved in such reactions by channeling the originating impulses through the autonomic nervous system into visceral organ symptoms and complaints. These reactions represent the visceral expression of the anxiety which is thereby largely prevented from being conscious. The symptom is due to a chronic and exaggerated state of the normal physiology of the emotion, with the feeling or subjective part repressed. Long continued visceral dysfunction may eventuate in structural changes.

This group includes the so-called organ neuroses. It also includes certain of the cases formerly classified under a wide variety of diagnostic terms such as "conversion hysteria," "anxiety state," "cardiac neurosis," "gastric neurosis," etc.

It may become necessary to add certain other subgroups of psychogenic reactions. It is not intended that the six listed be interpreted as necessarily including all possible reactions of this sort. If additional subcategories are recorded as diagnoses, they should be clearly identified as psychogenic reactions and should specify the system involved and the particular symptomatic expressions.

Each type of this reaction should be amplified with the specific symptomatic expression, as anorexia, loss of weight, dysmenorrhea, hypertension, etc.

b. *Psychogenic gastrointestinal reaction.* This subcategory may include some instances of such specified types of gastrointestinal disorders as peptic ulcer-like reaction, chronic gastritis, mucous colitis, constipation, "heart burn," hyperacidity, pylorospasm, "irritable colon," etc.

c. *Psychogenic cardiovascular reaction.* This subcategory includes most cases of such established types of cardiovascular disorders as paroxysmal tachycardia, pseudo-angina pectoris, and some types of hypertension.

Neurocirculatory asthenia has been classically defined as an "anxiety reaction;" similar clinical pictures, without subjective anxiety, will be classified as psychogenic cardiovascular reaction.

d. *Psychogenic genitourinary reaction.* This subcategory includes some types of menstrual disturbances, impotence, frigidity, dysuria, etc.

e. *Psychogenic allergic reaction.* Occasional instances of apparent allergic responses, including some cases of hives and angioneurotic edema, have a major emotional element in their production. Such cases should be recorded as psychogenic allergic reactions.

    f. *Psychogenic skin reaction.* This subcategory includes the so-called neurodermatoses, dermographia, and other related disorders, when involving major emotional factors.

    g. *Psychogenic asthenic reaction.* General fatigue is the predominating complaint of such reactions. It may be associated with visceral complaints, but it may also include "mixed" visceral organ symptoms and complaints. Present weakness and fatigue may indicate a physiological neuro-endocrine residue of a previous anxiety and not necessarily an active psychological conflict. The term includes cases previously termed "neurasthenia."

    7. *Obsessive-compulsive reaction.* In this reaction the anxiety may be observable in connection with obsessional fear of uncontrollable impulses. On the other hand, the anxiety may be under apparent control, through a mental mechanism (isolation), by which the emotional charge becomes automatically separated from the main stream of consciousness and manifests itself in a displaced form through useless or excessive, and often repetitive activity. In the latter instance, the patient is utilizing the mental mechanisms of "undoing"—a symbolic act which temporarily protects the patient against a threat—and "displacement." The patient himself may regard his ideas and behavior unreasonable and even silly, but nevertheless is compelled to carry out his rituals.

    The diagnosis should specify the symptomatic expressions of such reactions, including touching, counting, ceremonials, handwashing, recurring thoughts, accompanied often by compulsion to repetitive action. This category includes many cases formerly classified as "psychasthenia."

    8. *Hypochondriacal reaction.* This particular psychoneurotic disorder is characterized by obsessive concern of the individual about his state of health or the condition of his organs. It is often accompanied by a multiplicity of complaints about different organs or body systems. Some of such reactions may become excessively and persistently obsessional and develop associated compulsions. Such cases may be classified more accurately as "Obsessive-compulsive reaction."

    In general, this type of reaction should be carefully differentiated from depression, obsessive-compulsive reaction, symptoms of pre-psychotic reactions, and various specific somatization syndromes. This term is synonymous with "hypochondriasis."

    9. *Neurotic depressive reaction.* The anxiety in this reaction is allayed and hence partially relieved by self-depreciation through mental mechanism of introjection. The reaction is often associated with the feeling of guilt for past failures or deeds. This reaction is a non-psychotic response precipitated by a current situation—frequently some loss sustained by the patient—although dynamically the depression is usually related to a repressed (unconscious) aggression. The degree of the reaction in such cases is dependent upon the intensity of the patient's ambivalent feeling towards his loss (love, possessions, etc.), as well as upon the realistic circumstances of the loss.

    The term is synonymous with "Reactive depression." This reaction must be differentiated from the corresponding psychotic response (see par. I F1d (2)).

    D. *Character and behavior disorders.*

    1. *General.* Such disorders are characterized by developmental defects or pathological trends in the personality structure, with minimal subjective anxiety, and

little or no sense of distress. In most instances, the disorder is manifested by a life-long pattern of action or behavior ("acting out"), rather than by mental or emotional symptoms.

None of the conditions included in this disorder group (character and behavior disorders) is acceptable as the cause of separation from the service for disability.

2. *Pathological personality types.*

a. *General.* The maladjustment of many individuals is evidenced in lifelong behavior patterns. Such individuals are frequently described as personality types. In the evolution of psychoneuroses or psychoses, these types may be likened to abortive stages. They do not usually progress to the stage of a psychosis, nor do they justify a diagnosis of any type of neurosis or psychosis, although they may show some of the characteristics of both. They represent borderline adjustment states. The following types of pathological personality types will be differentiated.

b. *Schizoid personality.* Such individuals react with unsociability, seclusiveness, seriousmindedness, nomadism, and often with eccentricity.

c. *Paranoid personality.* Such individuals are characterized by many traits of the schizoid personality, coupled with a conspicuous trend to utilize a projection mechanism, expressed by suspiciousness, envy, extreme jealousy, and stubbornness.

d. *Cyclothymic personality.* Such individuals are characterized by frequently alternating moods of elation and sadness, stimulated apparently by internal factors rather than by external events. The patient may occasionally be either persistently euphoric or depressed, without falsification or distortion of reality. The diagnosis should specify, if possible, whether hypomanic, depressed, or alternating.

e. *Inadequate personality.* Such individuals are characterized by inadequate response to intellectual, emotional, social, and physical demands. They are neither physically nor mentally grossly deficient on examination, but they do show inadaptability, ineptness, poor judgment, and social incompatibility.

f. *Anti-social personality.* This term refers to chronically anti-social individuals who, despite a normal moral background, are always in trouble, profiting neither from experience nor punishment, and maintaining no real loyalties to any person, group, or code. Ordinarily an individual of this type is not the calculating criminal, but one who is on the verge of criminal conduct and may eventually become involved in such conduct.

This term includes most cases formerly classed as "constitutional psychopathic state" and "psychopathic personality," but, as defined here, the term is more limited as well as more specific in its application.

g. *Asocial personality.* This term applies to individuals who manifest their disregard for social codes and often come in conflict with them, by becoming gangsters, vagabonds, racketeers, prostitutes, and generally environmental ("normal") criminals. Many such individuals are to be regarded as the normal product of a lifelong abnormal environment. This term includes most cases formerly designated as "Psychopathic personality, with asocial and amoral trends."

h. *Sexual deviate.* These conditions are often a symptom complex, seen in more extensive syndromes as schizophrenic and obsessional reactions. The term includes most of the cases formerly classed as "Psychopathic personality, with pathologic sexuality."

The diagnosis will state whether overt or latent, and specify the specific type of the pathologic behavior, such as homosexuality, transvestism, pedophilia, fetishism, and sexual sadism (including rape, sexual assault, mutilation).

3. *Addiction.* This diagnosis usually implies anti-social behavior, while the individual is under the influence of alcohol or drug, such as pugnaciousness, deception, stealing, sexual assault, etc. It represents a much deeper character disturbance than cases where the usage of alcohol or drug represents a symptom of some more extensive psychiatric illness. This term should not include excessive symptomatic utilization of alcohol, which is a symptom of depression or psychoneurosis; nor should it include acute alcoholic intoxication, which should be listed under the intoxications.

The term includes cases formerly classed merely as "Drug addiction" and also some cases which were formerly classified as "Constitutional psychopathic state."

The diagnosis should specify whether the addiction is to alcohol or drug.

4. *Immaturity reactions.*

a. *General.* This category applies to physically adult individuals, who are unable to maintain their emotional equilibrium and independence under minor or major stress, because of deficiencies in emotional development. Some individuals are classed in this group because their behavior disturbance is based on fixation of certain character patterns; others, because their behavior is a regressive reaction due to severe stress.

The classification will be applied only to such character and behavior disorders in which the neurotic features (such as anxiety, conversion, phobia, etc.) are not prominent and only the basic personality development, and not anxiety, is the crucial distinguishing factor. Evidence of physical immaturity may or may not be present.

The diagnosis should report the specific immaturity reaction as defined below.

b. *Emotional instability reaction.* In this reaction the individual reacts with excitability and ineffectiveness when confronted with minor stress. His judgment may be undependable under stress, and his relationship to other people is continuously fraught with fluctuating emotional attitudes, because of strong and poorly controlled hostility, guilt, and anxiety which require quick mobilization of defense, usually explosive in nature, for the protection of the ego.

This term is synonymous with the former diagnosis of "Psychopathic personality, with emotional instability."

c. *Passive-dependency reaction.* This reaction is characterized by helplessness, indecisiveness, and a tendency to cling to others. The clinical picture in such cases is often associated with an anxiety reaction which is typically psychoneurotic, but it may be also a type of emotionally immature personality development. There is a predominant child-parent relationship in such reactions.

d. *Passive-aggressive reaction.* The aggressiveness is expressed in such reactions by passive measures, such as pouting, stubbornness, procrastination, inefficiency, and passive obstructionism.

e. *Aggressive reaction.* A persistent reaction to frustration with irritability, temper tantrums, and destructive behavior, is the dominant factor in such cases. A specific variety of this reaction is a morbid or pathological resentment. Below the surface, there is usually evident in such cases a deep dependency, with "reaction formation." The term does not apply to cases more accurately described by the term "Anti-social personality."

f. *Immaturity with symptomatic "habit" reaction.* This category is useful in occasional situations where a specific symptom is the single outstanding expression of the psychopathology. These terms should not be used as diagnoses, however, when the symptoms are associated with or are secondary to organic illnesses and defects or to other psychiatric disorders or reactions. Thus, for example, the diagnosis "Immaturity with symptomatic habit reaction; speech disorder" would be used for certain disturbances in speech, often developing in childhood, in which there are insufficient other symptoms to justify any other definite diagnosis. It would not be used for a speech impairment that was a temporary symptom of conversion hysteria or that was the result of any organic disease or defect.

The diagnosis should specify the particular "habit" reaction, as, for instance, enuresis, speech disorder, etc.

E. *Disorders of intelligence.*

1. *Mental deficiency.*

a. *General.* Mental deterioration associated with chronic psychoses and blocking of intellectual function by emotional conflicts should not be included in this category. In recording mental deficiency, distinction will be made between primary and secondary types of the disorder, as defined below.

None of the conditions included in the group, "Disorders of intelligence," is acceptable as the cause of separation from the service for disability.

b. *Mental deficiency, primary.* The term will be applied to cases in which the mental retardation has been present since birth or infancy, without known organic brain disease. It includes clearly hereditary cases. In recording such disorder, the mental age should be indicated, along with the psychometric test by which it was determined.

c. *Mental deficiency, secondary.* The term will be applied to cases of mental retardation which have resulted from an organic disease of the brain, whether congenital or acquired. Frequently, therefore, when the organic disease is also present, the mental deficiency will be recorded only as a manifestation of the originating organic disease, as for instance, with cerebral agenesis, developmental defects of the central nervous system, microcephaly, hydrocephalus, cretinism, etc. In other instances, such as when secondary to encephalitis or birth injury, the originating condition may not be recorded as a diagnosis, because it is not then present. The diagnosis of mental deficiency in such cases will be qualified as secondary to the specific originating condition.

In all cases, the condition should be recorded as mental deficiency, secondary, and the mental age of the individual should be specified, along with the psychological test by which it was determined.

2. *Specific learning defects.* The diagnosis should specify whether the defect is reading, mathematics, strephosymbolia, etc. If known, the type of encephalopathy will be stated. This diagnosis is not acceptable as the cause of separation from the service for disability.

F. *Psychotic disorders.*

1. *Psychoses without known organic etiology.*

a. *General.* These disorders are characterized by a varying degree of personality disintegration and failure to test and evaluate correctly external reality in various spheres. In addition, individuals with such disorders fail in their ability to relate themselves effectively or happily to other people or to their own work.

b. *Schizophrenic disorders.*

(1) *General.* This term represents a group of psychotic disorders characterized by fundamental disturbances in reality-relationships and concept formations, with consequent affective and intellectual disturbances in varying degrees and mixtures. The disorders are marked by strong tendency to retreat from reality, by emotional disharmony, unpredictable disturbances in stream of thought, and by a tendency to "battening-out" the emotional and libidinal struggle which gives the appearance of "deterioration"—not necessarily fulfilled—that may progress to childishness ("dementia").

It is not essential to forcibly classify such patients into a Kraepelinian type. The predominant symptomatology will be the determining factor in classifying such patients.

(2) *Schizophrenic reaction, latent.* Certain individuals are found on examination to present definite schizophrenic ideation and behavior (e.g., mannerisms, unpredictable acts), beyond that of the schizoid personality, but not of an advanced stage as in acute or chronic schizophrenic reactions. These individuals may be incipient schizophrenics, and they may maintain their borderline adjustment over long periods. Among their friends, these individuals are regarded merely as queer or eccentric; under close examination, however, they show evidence of psychotic symptoms. They represent essentially borderline psychoses.

Important diagnostic evidence of such reactions consists of disordered conceptual (categorical) thinking as manifested in special tests, such as the Rorschach test, the Vigotsky (Hanfman-Kasanin) category tests, the sorting tests (Goldstein-Sheerer, Rapaport, and Halstead), proverbs and problems (J. Benjamin, N. Cameron), and the Murray Thematic Apperception Test. Hospitalization of such cases is rarely necessary.

(3) *Schizophrenic reaction, simple type.* This type of reaction is characterized chiefly by reduction in external attachments and interests and impoverishment of human relationships. It often involves adjustment on a lower psychobiologic level of functioning, usually accompanied by apathy and indifference but rarely by conspicuous delusions or hallucinations. In contrast to the long history —without any, or slight, change in symptomatology—of the schizoid personality, there is characteristically a change in the personality in the simple type of schizophrenic reaction.

(4) *Schizophrenic reaction, hebephrenic type.* Such reactions are characterized by shallow inappropriate effect, unpredictable giggling, silly behavior and mannerisms, delusions often of a somatic nature, and hallucinations.

(5) *Schizophrenic reaction, catatonic type.* The reaction is characterized chiefly by conspicuous motor behavior, exhibiting either marked generalized inhibition resulting in stupor, mutism, negativism and waxy flexibility, or excessive motor activity and excitement. The individual may regress to a state of vegetation.

(6) *Schizophrenic reaction, paranoid type.* This type of reaction is characterized by schizophrenic (dereistic and autistic) thinking and unpredictable behavior, with mental content composed chiefly of delusions of persecution, occasionally of grandeur, hallucinations, a fairly constant attitude of hostility and aggression, and ideas of reference. Excessive religiosity may be present and, rarely, there may be no delusions of persecution, but instead an expansive and productive delusional system of omnipotence, genius, or special ability. The systematized para-

noid hypochondriacal states are included in this group. It will be borne in mind that some patients manifest their paranoid ideas only when they are depressed, and others only when they are manic.

(7) *Schizophrenic reaction, unclassified.* There are two large groups (acute and chronic) of schizophrenic reactions which cannot be appropriately classified under the four Kraepelinian types.

The acute group of this reaction includes a wide variety of schizophrenic symptomatology, such as confusion of thinking and turmoil of emotion, accompanied by secondary elaboration manifested by perplexity, ideas of reference, fear and dream states, and dissociative phenomena. These symptoms appear precipitously, often without apparent precipitating stress, but exhibiting historical evidence of prodromal symptoms. Very often it is accompanied by a pronounced affective coloring of either excitement or depression. The symptoms often clear in a matter of weeks, although there is a tendency for them to recur.

The chronic schizophrenias exhibit a mixed symptomatology, and when the reaction cannot be classed in any of the four Kraepelinian types, it should be placed in this group.

c. *Paranoid disorders.*

(1) *Paranoia.* This type of psychotic disorder is extremely rare. It is characterized by an intricate, complex, and slowly developing paranoid system with the individual usually regarding himself as particularly singled out. The patient often endows himself with superior or unique ability, and even considers himself appointed for a Messianic mission. The paranoid system is particularly isolated from much of the normal stream of consciousness, without hallucinations and with relative intactness and preservation of the remainder of the personality.

(2) *Paranoid state.* This type of paranoid disorder is characterized by transient paranoid delusions. It lacks the logical nature of systematization seen in paranoia; yet it does not manifest the bizarre fragmentation and deterioration of the schizophrenic. It occurs most frequently in individuals between 35 and 55 years of age, and it is ordinarily of a relatively short duration, though it may be persistent and chronic.

d. *Affective disorders.*

(1) *Manic-depressive reaction.* This reaction will be further qualified by the appropriate one of the following terms: manic, depressive, stuporous, circular, agitated, with schizophrenic coloring, and mixed.

(2) *Psychotic depressive reaction.* This differs from the neurotic depressive reaction chiefly in degree. If the patient manifests evidence of gross misinterpretation of external reality (e.g., in matters of guilt and unworthiness), it technically becomes a psychosis and should be classified as "Psychotic depressive reaction."

(3) *Involution melancholia.* This reaction is characterized most commonly by depression, with or without agitation, without previous history of either manic or depressive illnesses. It occurs in the individual's middle life and in his later years. It tends to have a prolonged course and may be manifested by worry, guilt, anxiety, agitation, paranoid and other delusional ideas, and somatic concerns. Some cases are characterized chiefly by depression and others chiefly by paranoid ideas. Often there are gastro-intestinal or other somatic concerns to a delusional degree.

2. *Psychoses with demonstrable etiology or associated structural changes in the brain, or both.* The mental reactions with a system infection and with brain infection, neoplasm, trauma, degenerative disease, or vascular disease, are to be regarded as symptoms of the physical (non-psychiatric) condition with which they are associated. When the psychotic reaction does not constitute any of the clinical pictures defined above, it will be reported as "Psychotic reaction" and amplified by one or more of the following descriptive terms as types: schizoid, paranoid, depressed, manic, euphoric, deteriorated, confused, anxious, agitated, panic, excited, delirious, apathetic, stuporous, specific behavior disorder.

Included in this category are the psychoses associated with infections (general paresis, meningo-vascular syphilis, epidemic encephalitis, etc.), the psychoses associated with exogenous poisonings, and other associated psychoses such as ones accompanying pellagra, cerebral embolism, Huntington's chorea, etc.

II. *Manner of recording.*

A. *Individual medical records.*

1. *General.* The reactions, or specific types of psychiatric conditions (anxiety reaction; emotional instability reaction; schizophrenic reaction, simple type; etc.), are sufficiently well defined to justify their use apart from any generic terms indicating the broad disorder groups (psychoneurotic disorders; character and behavior disorders, immaturity reactions; psychoses without known organic etiology, schizophrenic disorders; etc.). In recording psychiatric conditions, only the lowest subclassification of the disorder will be specified, without being prefaced by any term such as psychoneurosis or psychosis.

In each case, the severity of the reaction will be recorded as "mild," "moderate," or "severe" and the reaction will be qualified as acute or chronic. The severity of a particular reaction should not be determined solely by the degree of ineffectiveness, since other factors, such as underlying defective attitude, other psychiatric or physical condition, etc., may contribute to the total ineffectiveness.

Outstanding or conspicuous symptomatology may be added to any of the psychiatric diagnoses: manifestations must be reported for those reactions indicated in the list of terms as requiring such reporting.

2. *Multiple diagnoses: psychiatric reactions with physical disorders.*

a. *General.* The general principle governing recording of all diagnoses will likewise apply to the selection of the first diagnosis in cases which involve psychiatric conditions. The immediate condition which was principally responsible for the initial admisson is to be considered as the primary cause of admission and recorded as the first diagnosis. In applying this general principle to cases involving psychiatric conditions, the following combinations may be considered.

b. *Unrelated diagnoses.* Physical and mental disorders may coexist, but be causally unrelated. In such instances the two or more conditions will be listed as separate diagnoses with the primary diagnosis being selected on the usual basis. *Example:* Diabetes mellitus; Mental deficiency, primary, etc.

c. *Related diagnoses.* Physical and mental disorders may coexist and be causally related. Whether the two conditions are recorded as separate diagnoses or as only one depends on the nature of the conditions.

(1) *Combinations requiring only one diagnosis.* In some instances, the mental reaction, though related, is not sufficiently developed as a clinical psychiatric entity to make a formal psychiatric diagnosis either necessary or indicated.

For example, a patient with pneumonia may be apprehensive and tense; the mental status should be described in the clinical history or physical examination along with any other symptom or sign. Minor non-psychotic mental reactions need be reported only thus: the individual medical record will carry only the non-psychiatric diagnosis.

Definite pathological mental reactions, other than well defined clinical syndromes, may often be symptoms of organic disease of the brain, including trauma or intoxication. These include such instances as delirium or febrile reaction, intoxication with uremia, mental reactions with any systemic infection and with brain infection, neoplasm, trauma, degenerative disease or vascular disease. As such, these conditions are to be regarded as symptoms of the physical condition.

Whenever such a mental reaction which does not constitute any of the well defined clinical pictures is sufficiently pronounced to justify mention in the diagnosis, it will be recorded as a manifestation of the primary diagnosis. Since it does not constitute a well defined clinical type, it will be specified as a non-psychotic or psychotic reaction and amplified by one or more of the following descriptive terms as types: schizoid, paranoid, depressed, manic, euphoric, deteriorated, confused, anxious, agitated, panic, excited, delirious, apathetic, stuporous, specific behavior disorder. The degree of stress, predisposition, and incapacity will not be listed.

Examples: 1) Syphilitic meningo-encephalitis, "old," etc., manifested by psychotic reaction, confused; 2) Epidemic encephalitis, acute, etc., manifested by non-psychotic reaction, behavior disorder.

There are other instances where physical and mental disorders coexist, and where the physical disorder is a manifestation of the psychiatric condition rather than a separate condition. Where this is true, only the psychiatric condition should be listed as a diagnosis, and the physical condition should be shown as a manifestation thereof. *Example:* Psychogenic gastro-intestinal reaction, chronic, severe, manifested by mucous colitis and hyperacidity.

(2) *Combinations requiring separate diagnoses.* Physical and mental disorders may coexist and be causally related, with both conditions being sufficiently marked and well defined to justify separate diagnosis. In such cases, the causal relationship of the diagnoses should be indicated. The selection of the order of the diagnoses will depend upon which condition was first in the chain of etiology; the one which caused or directly led to the other will be selected as first diagnosis. This order of diagnoses will be followed despite the fact that in most, if not all, cases the psychiatric symptomatology is related to personality factors existing prior to the physical disease or trauma. *Example:* (a) Fracture of skull, simple, depressed, left occipital area, etc.; (b) Paranoid state, precipitated by skull fractures, etc.

(3) *Multiple psychiatric diagnoses.* If and when two separate psychiatric conditions exist, such as anti-social personality and a psychosis, both shall be recorded. If a diagnostic entity (which, if encountered as an isolated personality disturbance, would be recorded as the only diagnosis) is a part of a more extensive process or secondary to it, the primary diagnosis will be given, with the less important condition given as a manifestation of that diagnosis. *Example:* Anxiety reaction manifested by somnambulism; Passive-aggressive reaction, manifested by enuresis (list other manifestations); Asocial reaction type with sexual sadism.

Some psychiatric conditions, if established as the primary diagnosis are incompatible with certain other psychiatric diagnoses and will not be recorded as existing together. *Examples:* Psychoneurotic and psychotic reactions; acute situational maladjustment with psychoneurotic or psychotic reactions; combat exhaustion with psychoneurotic or psychotic reactions. Many of these conditions may progress from one to another, but are not simultaneously present. Similarly, only one type of psychoneurotic or psychotic reaction will be used as a diagnosis, even in the presence of symptoms of another type. The diagnosis in such cases will be based on the predominant type, with a statement of manifestations including symptoms of other types of reaction thus: "Anxiety reaction, with minor conversion symptoms, etc."

B. *Clinical records.*

1. *General.* For certain conditions, the diagnosis of merely the type of reaction does not furnish sufficient information to determine disposition. Thus, for example, the term "anxiety reaction" does not convey whether the illness occurred in a previously normal or neurotic personality; it does not indicate the degree and nature of the external stress, nor does it reveal the extremely important information as to the degree to which the patient's functional capacity has been impaired. Therefore, for certain conditions as specified below, a complete diagnostic evaluation will be entered in the clinical records, including this information in addition to all of the requirements provided in IIA1 above for recording diagnoses on the Individual Medical Records. Each case so diagnosed will be evaluated from the following standpoints:

Type and severity of symptoms (diagnostic term, recorded on Individual Medical Records).

External precipitating stress.

Premorbid personality and predisposition.

Degree of resultant incapacity (psychiatric disability).

The complete diagnostic evaluation for such cases will be recorded in the clinical records and dated in those situations and installations in which the medical officer has sufficient opportunity to evaluate the various points. When he does not have sufficient opportunity or information, he should so indicate with the term "unknown" or "not determined." It is extremely important that those medical officers in the field, such as the flight surgeon, the division psychiatrist, and the mental hygiene consultation psychiatrist, should indicate the external stress, even though they may not have the opportunity to determine predisposition.

In the utilization of this method of recording a diagnosis it is essential to recognize that the time element is all-important; the diagnostic formulation on any particular date may (and in many cases, should) be changed at a subsequent date. A soldier may show marked incapacity upon admission to a hospital but a few days later can return to duty with minor or no impairment. The disorder diagnosis of any particular type will in no way determine disposition without consideration of the stress, predisposition, and the functional incapacity, in cases where these are to be reported. Heretofore, the disorder diagnosis was all-important. Under the present system, it becomes only one of the four factors to be considered in determining disposition.

2. *Conditions requiring complete diagnostic evaluation.* The four points listed above will apply to the following diagnostic categories: the transient personality reactions to acute or special stress (combat exhaustion and acute situational maladjustment), all types of psychoneurotic disorders, the immaturity reactions, and the various types of schizophrenic, affective and paranoid disorders. The stress, predisposition and degree of incapacity will not be outlined for the character and be-

havior disorders, except for immaturity reactions, mental deficiency, and psychotic reactions with organic etiology.

3. Requirements of complete diagnostic evaluation.

a. *Type and severity of symptoms* (*the diagnostic term*). The provisions of paragraph IIB1 above govern the recording of this first part of the four-part complete diagnostic evaluation. The diagnostic terms to be used are defined in paragraphs IA-F. The severity of reaction will be described by the appropriate word "mild," "moderate," "severe," and qualified as either "acute" or "chronic." Outstanding or conspicuous symptomatology may be listed. *Example:* "Anxiety reaction, mild, chronic, manifested by loss of appetite and insomnia." Obscure, ill-defined, and rarely used technical terms are to be avoided. If a reaction was severe and acute upon admission to a medical installation but improvement or recovery was effected with treatment, it will be recorded as "(type of reaction), acute, severe, improved, or recovered."

b. *Stress.* Under this heading the external stress is to be evaluated as to type, degree, and duration. The stress will generally refer to the environmental situation, Army or otherwise, which is the direct cause of the reaction manifest in the patient. Unconscious internal conflicts will not be considered external stresses. The evaluation of the unconscious internal conflicts is important both in the understanding of the nature of the clinical picture and in determining a basis for treatment and for estimating prognosis. It is omitted here only because of the difficulty in its uniform formulation and the varying degrees of understanding of psychodynamics by medical officers practicing psychiatry in the Army.

The judgment of the military stress can be made most accurately by the medical officer in the patient's own unit, since living in the same environment qualifies him to judge the stress. The opinion of the individual's commanding officer may be of value. It may be more difficult for a hospital psychiatrist to evaluate the stress to which the individual has been subjected, and when the stress cannot be determined, it should be recorded as "unknown."

The degree of stress, whether that of combat, regimentation, training, isolation, or other type, must be evaluated in terms of its effect on the "average man" of the group, rather than on the patient. It should not be presumed that a particular environmental stress is severe because one or even several individuals react poorly to it, since these individuals may have had poor resistance to this stress. Stress will be classified as "severe," "moderate," and "minimal." Severe stress is such that the average man could be expected to develop disabling psychiatric symptoms when exposed to it. Minimal stress is such that the average man could be exposed to it without developing psychiatric symptoms. Examples of recording stress:

"Severe stress of 60 days' continuous combat as a rifleman," "Severe stress of 30 hazardous combat missions," "Moderate stress of serious chronic domestic problems," "Stress unknown or not determined."

c. *Predisposition.* The description of the predisposition will consist of a brief statement of the outstanding personality traits or weaknesses which have resulted from inheritance and development and an evaluation of the degree of predisposition based on past history and personality traits, recorded as "no predisposition evident"; "mild"; "moderate"; and "severe."

(1) *No predisposition evident.* This description will be used when there is no evidence of previous personality traits or make-up which appear to be related to the patient's present illness, and when there is no positive history of psychoneurotic or other mental illness in his immediate family.

(2) *Mild predisposition.* This description will be used when the patient's history reveals mild transient psychological (emotional) upsets and abnormal personality traits, or defect of intelligence which, however, did not significantly incapacitate the patient or did not require medical care. It will also be used when there is a past history of mental illness in the patient's family.

(3) *Moderate predisposition.* This description will be used when the patient has a personal history of partially incapacitating psychological (emotional) upsets or abnormal personality traits or defects in intelligence which resulted in his social maladjustment.

(4) *Severe predisposition.* This description will be used in the presence of the patient's definite history of previous overt emotional or mental illness or disorder.

d. *Degree of incapacity (psychiatric disability).* The psychiatric disability represents the degree to which the individual's total functional capacity has been impaired by the psychiatric condition. This is not necessarily the same as ineffectiveness and therefore the degree of incapacity reported should not be determined solely by the degree of ineffectiveness. Effectiveness in any particular job is a resultant of the individual's emotional stability, intellect, physical condition, attitude, training, etc., as well as the degree and type of his psychiatric disability. Depending upon other circumstances, a man with a moderate psychiatric disability may be more effective than another man with a minimal disability. Degree of incapacity as used here refers only to ineffectiveness resulting from the current psychiatric disability.

The degree of disability at the time of original consultation or admission to the hospital will often vary from the degree of impairment after treatment. Disability at the termination of treatment represents the residual or persistent impairment. It will be recorded as "none," "minimal," "moderate," and "marked." The individual's capacity to perform military service will be used as the base-line in estimating the degree of impairment.

(1) *No impairment.* This term will be used, when, in the opinion of the medical officer, there are not medical reasons for changing the patient's current assignment or duty. An individual may have certain symptoms and yet have no medical reason for not performing full duty. For instance, symptoms of an anxiety state are present in the majority of troops engaged in combat; a returnee with mild symptoms may fail to function because of his attitude and not because of the severity of his illness.

(2) *Minimal impairment.* This term will be used to indicate a slight residual degree of impairment in the patient's ability to carry on in his current assignment or duty.

(3) *Moderate impairment.* This term will be used to indicate a residual degree of incapacity which seriously, but not totally, interferes with the patient's ability to carry on in his current assignment or duty.

(4) *Marked impairment.* This term will be used to indicate a residual degree of incapacity which totally prevents the patient from satisfactorily functioning in his current assignment. As in all cases of incapacity, the impairment may be temporary; in some cases it may be permanent.

APPENDIX C

THE CHARACTERISTICS AND ATTITUDES
OF THE SOLDIER IN WORLD WAR II

JUST WHO WAS the American soldier? [1] What were his characteristics, his habits, his attitudes? What was the pattern of his personality structure? What were his predispositions with respect to great psychological tensions? What were the changes that took place within the personality of the average soldier as the result of his entrance into the Army and his participation in the war?

WHO IS THE AMERICAN SOLDIER?

The fact that approximately 11,000,000 men were processed by the Army in the course of the war should lead us to expect certain general conclusions. In 1945, at its peak strength, the Army was constituted of 8,000,000 men. One cannot assume that this large segment of Americans is wholly representative of its age group because the Army chose only those who met its physical and educational standards. During much of the period of the draft, individuals who could not read and write were not accepted for military service. Nevertheless, within these limitations, the data of the Army processing and follow-up records do give us some idea regarding the outstanding characteristics of the membership of this age group. The age, marital status, and educational background of the inductees varied with changes in the standards of admission. This variation very definitely affected the attitudes of men in different units and should have indicated the type of training which presumably would have been most effective.

Age distribution. The age distribution of the Army varied considerably at different times during the War. For instance, the percentage of men inducted

---

[1] See also Chapter 7. Most of the material summarized in this chapter came from the army publication *What the Soldier Thinks,* published by the Information and Education Division. Permission was obtained for the utilization of this material from Brig. Gen. C. T. Lanham, the successor to Maj. Gen. F. H. Osborne. This Division is now known as the Troop Information and Education Division of the Special Staff, which, although greatly reduced in personnel, has continued to carry on an extremely important service. Much of it has a vital significance to Army psychiatry.

in a given month who were 30 years of age or over increased from 0.4 per cent in September, 1941, to 35 per cent in the fall of 1942, and then dropped to 12 per cent in February, 1943, when the induction of 18- and 19-year-old men began.

Age Distribution of Enlisted Men [2]

	Mar. 31, 1943	June 30, 1944
18-19 years	4%	9.3%
20-24 "	42%	39.9%
25-29 "	29%	27.4%
30-34 "	14%	14.7%
35-37 "	5%	5.6%
38 years and over	6%	2.9%

This variation in age grouping is also shown in a comparison of two divisions which were formed early in the course of the war and two divisions which were formed late in the course of the war.

Age Comparison in Two Groups of Divisions [2]

	Two Divisions Formed Early in War	Two Divisions Formed Later in War
19 years or less	2%	43%
20 "	3%	23%
21-24 years	39%	12%
25-29 "	38%	11%
30-34 "	13%	6%
35 years and over	5%	5%

Educational levels. The Army in World War II was a much better educated one than that of World War I.

Educational Background of Enlisted Men

	World War I [3]	World War II [4]
College training	5%	11.2%
High-school graduates	4%	27.6%
High-school nongraduates	11%	32.6%
Grade school	80%	28.6%

There were advantages and disadvantages to this phenomenal increase in the educational background of the Army. Undoubtedly the advantages far out-

---

[2] These and many of the figures that follow were obtained on tabulations of a 5 per cent sample of the cards of all enlisted men in the Army as of March 31, 1943, made by the Machine Records Branch AGO and recorded in *What the Soldier Thinks,* No. 2, Report 58, Aug., 1943, pp. 107, 108. Figures for 1944 from Manpower Control Group, 3 Sept. 1946.
[3] *What the Soldier Thinks,* No. 3, 25 February 1944, pp. 7-8.
[4] Information from Personnel Division, G-1, 3 September 1946.

weighed the disadvantages in that we had a group of men far more capable in their ability to do a job, to learn a new job, to serve well on jobs calling for intelligence and initiative.

It was discovered that high-school graduates and college men were more likely than less educated men to believe they could serve their country better as soldiers than as war workers and to want service with a combat outfit overseas. Fewer educated men went AWOL. More of them were self-confident. They were better informed on current war events, had a greater interest in keeping up with the news, were less confused and more internationalistic in their ideas about the postwar world; they were less vindictive toward enemy people. On the other hand, they were more apt to be critical of Army rules and practices; they condemned the lack of spirit in the early war effort of the nation; they were cynical about Army news releases.

The more highly educated man presented a greater problem in assignment. The white-collar work of civilian life had its counterpart in the Army, but the need for such personnel was definitely limited as compared to the greater need for combat and mechanically skilled man power. As a result many individuals had to be placed where they believed themselves to be misassigned because their previous training or experience was not being used.

Education was of advantage to the soldier as indicated by the statistics on promotions.

Promotions of Men Who Entered as Privates

	College Men		High-school Graduates		High-school Nongraduates		Grade-school Men	
	1/1/42	4/1/43	1/1/42	4/1/43	1/1/42	4/1/43	1/1/42	4/1/43
Became officers	2%	15%	1%	6%	0%	1%	0%	0%
Became noncommissioned officers	22%	31%	22%	32%	20%	27%	13%	18%
Remained privates	76%	54%	77%	62%	80%	72%	87%	82%

As the Army expanded, over 200,000 enlisted men, mostly high-school and college graduates, were commissioned from the ranks. In the spring of 1943, 55 per cent of the high-school graduate and college men surveyed said, "The Army is giving me a chance to show what I can do," in contrast to only 24 per cent of the men studied a little more than a year previously.[5]

Another comparison of the education levels of enlisted men and male officers (as of June 30, 1944) reflects the advantage of education.[6]

[5] *What the Soldier Thinks,* No. 2, Report 58, Aug., 1943, pp. 28, 29.
[6] Information from the Chief of the Manpower Control, War Department General Staff, 3 September 1946. These figures differ slightly for the average for the ten million men tested: I, 5.8; II, 26.2; III, 30.7; IV, 28.5; V, 8.8. Bingham, W. V., *Science* 104:147-152, Aug. 16, 1946.

	Enlisted Men	*Male Officers*
Grade school or less	28.6%	1.5%
1, 2, 3 years high school	32.6%	12.0%
High-school graduate	27.6%	22.2%
1, 2, 3 years college	8.2%	26.2%
College graduate	2.1%	21.7%
Postgraduate	.9%	16.4%
	100 %	100 %

AGCT score. The Army General Classification Test was given to all enlisted men and women at the time they joined the Army. It was not an intelligence test, but it did serve as a general guide to the individual's fund of knowledge and his ability to use certain information. As a result, it became regarded as an index of the individual's intellectual capacity. The results are tabulated in such a way as to be divided into five general groups beginning with the highest scores in Grade I and the lowest in Grade V. The distribution of the enlisted Army personnel at different periods on the basis of these scores was as follows: [6]

	Mar. 31, 1944	*Mar. 31, 1945*	*Mar. 31, 1946*
Grade I	6.34%	6.00%	5.42%
Grade II	31.00%	31.00%	28.73%
Grade III	30.68%	31.00%	32.60%
Grade IV	25.12%	27.00%	28.73%
Grade V	6.86%	5.00%	4.52%

The race distribution. Nine out of ten American soldiers were of the white race (90 per cent); 8 per cent were Negro, the majority of whom came from the South; 2 per cent were not classified as either white or Negro race and were chiefly Indians, Japanese, and Chinese. From December 1, 1941, through December 1, 1946, approximately 970,000 Negroes served in the Army with peak strength of 703,000, on July 31, 1945. Of this number there were 4,728 male officers, 697 warrant and flight officers, 121 WAC officers, 247 nurses, 2 physiotherapists, 3,645 enlisted WAC's, and 692,229 enlisted men. There were approximately 360 Japanese-American officers, 27,226 enlisted men, and 81 WAC's who served in the Army between July 1, 1940, and January 31, 1946.[7] Excluding new regular Army enlistments following August, 1945, there were 111,217 noncitizen (foreign born) entrants and 200,656 citizens of foreign birth as enlisted men and 4,392 foreign born citizens among enlisted women.[8]

Localities from which enlisted men came. The geographic area of origin

---

[7] Figures obtained from ASF, Division of Statistics, May, 1946.
[8] Figures supplied by Chief, Manpower Control Group, War Department General Staff, 3 September 1946.

corresponded exactly with the distribution of the male population aged 18 to 44 as reported by the census, with 61 per cent of the Army from the North, 29 per cent from the South, and 10 per cent from the West. Statistics applying only to white soldiers showed 40 per cent from rural areas, 30 per cent from cities of 2500 to 100,000, and 30 per cent from cities over 100,000.

Of the 11,367,989 men and women who served in the Army between November 1, 1940, and July 31, 1946, New York State contributed 1,157,000 men and 24,741 women to lead all states. Nevada had the smallest number, 11,000 men and 317 women.[9]

The marital status.

Marital Status of White Enlisted Men [10] Mar. 31, 1943

Married	
before induction	21%
after induction	9%
Divorced, widowed, separated	3%
Single	67%

This marital status influenced morale greatly. In answer to, "Are you ever worried or upset?" 75 per cent of the married men questioned replied that they were "often" or "sometimes" in contrast to about 50 to 60 per cent of the unmarried men.[11] The same survey indicated that about one-sixth of the married enlisted men in the continental United States in December, 1943, were expectant fathers and were even more inclined to worry than married men who were not expecting children. Their worries centered chiefly around financial problems and personal anxieties about the family. Married soldiers were twice as likely to go AWOL as unmarried soldiers.

ATTITUDES OF SOLDIERS

Through the Research Branch of the Special Services Division, particularly the work of Lt. Col. Charles Dollard, Dr. Samuel Stauffer, Dr. Carl Hovland, Dr. Leonard S. Cottrell, and their associates, many remarkable surveys of the attitudes and opinions of soldiers were made. These covered subjects of personal concern to the soldier and points of special importance to various technical services and to leaders in the Army.[12]

---

[9] Associated Press news release from Washington, Apr. 10, 1947.
[10] *What the Soldier Thinks,* No. 2, Report 58, Aug., 1943, p. 110.
[11] *What the Soldier Thinks,* Vol. I, No. 1, Dec., 1943, p. 11.
[12] All of the following statistics on attitudes are given from surveys made and reported by the Research Branch of the Special Service Division of the Army Service Forces, as reported in the publication, *What the Soldier Thinks.* Number 1 was published in December, 1942 and Number 2 in August, 1943. Beginning in December, 1943, the periodical, *What the Soldier Thinks,* was issued monthly until December 25, 1944.

The soldier's attitude toward the soldier's role. When this particular survey was made in the summer of 1943, less than half of the enlisted men believed that they could serve better as soldiers than at some war job. This same survey indicated that the average soldier who rated his role as less useful than that of a civilian in a war job was more likely than other men to be apathetic about the war, was distrustful of our allies, was not desirous of going overseas, was not very proud of his company, battery, or squadron, and was not desirous of a fighting job if he did go overseas.

Attitude of Enlisted Men [13]

	In Conti-nental U.S.	Fighter Bomber Groups in Middle East	Service Troops in Middle East
Felt they could do the best job in war as soldier	39%	48%	37%
As a war worker	49%	28%	44%
Were undecided	12%	24%	19%

In the spring of 1943 one-fourth of the enlisted men were 30 and over. Only 28 per cent of those older men who were single and 27 per cent of those who were married before joining the Army thought they could do more for the country as soldiers than as workers on war jobs.

The figures just cited relative to the preference for the soldier role were not necessarily indicative of the number of men who wanted or who did not want to be in the Army. They did not represent a cross section of the attitudes of draftees toward their entrance into the Army. They did indicate without question, however, that many of the men who were drawn from civilian life, when skills were in demand and wartime wages high, felt that they were making a sacrifice in accepting Army discipline, pay, and dangers without commensurate benefit to the country. Consequently, the men who said that they were less useful as soldiers than as war workers were expressing a fact without necessarily implying a lack of zeal for the war. However, such men were probably no less a problem in motivation for the Army than the soldiers who lacked enthusiasm.

Satisfaction with the job. A man's satisfaction and his attitude in the Army depended very largely on the type of work that he obtained or was given. In general, men liked their Army jobs if they could get those for which they asked. Assignments were usually requested on the basis of civilian training and experience. A spot survey of the Air Forces in 1942 showed that about 3 1/2 of every 10 men possessed critical skills that were not used. In April, 1943, it was shown that among soldiers who obtained their preferred job assignment

---

[13] *What the Soldier Thinks*, No. 2, Report 58, Aug., 1943, p. 11.

74 per cent had a high satisfaction, in contrast to 19 per cent of those with high satisfaction in their jobs who did not get assignments asked for, or had no chance to ask. Research studies among troops in various overseas theaters as well as at home indicate that satisfaction with job assignment is perhaps the single most important specific factor of morale. Where a reassignment was impossible, if a soldier was given the reason for it and "sold" on the value of his present assignment, he was more satisfied.

An important factor, however, in the degree of satisfaction with the job was respect for the leader. Those men with the greatest respect for their leaders invariably felt the greatest satisfaction with their job assignment. Another factor concerned the amount of work: Among soldiers who said that they had enough to do and who also regarded their duties as important, 71 per cent were satisfied with their job assignment in contrast to only 38 per cent of soldiers who said that they did not have enough to do; among soldiers who said they had enough or more than enough to do but did not regard their duties as important, only 44 per cent were satisfied.

	Men in Each Branch Getting Job Assignment Asked for	Men in Each Branch with Highest Job Satisfaction Scores [14]
Air Corps	54%	53%
Ordnance	39%	44%
Signal Corps	38%	44%
Medical	32%	41%
Engineers	32%	33%
Field Artillery	26%	41%
Quartermaster	25%	40%
Coast Artillery	25%	34%
Armored Force	24%	33%
Chemical Warfare	23%	33%
Military Police	19%	33%
Infantry	11%	17%

Attitude toward the branch of the service. The Air Corps had the highest proportion of men who were given the job they wanted. It also contained the largest proportion of men who were satisfied in their work. In another survey [14] 25 per cent of the soldiers in the Infantry liked service in the Infantry the least of any of the branches within the Ground Forces (Medical, Engineers, Signal Corps, Quartermaster, Ordnance, etc.). On the average, only 3 per cent of the men in other branches of the Ground Forces liked their own branch least. It was suggested that the factors depreciating the Infantry were the misconceptions of the place of the Infantry in the teamwork of modern

[14] *What the Soldier Thinks,* No. 2. Aug. 1943, p. 51; *What the Soldier Thinks,* Report 46, Dec., 1942, p. 23.

war, the reactions against marching and close-order drill, the misconceptions about the failure of the Infantry to teach something useful for postwar civilian life. There was also a widespread feeling both in and out of the Army that infantrymen were cannon fodder.

In 1945, inductees at six reception centers tended to have a much healthier attitude toward the Infantry in some respects than did the infantrymen themselves in 1944. They were less likely to think that the "Infantry gets more than its share of men who aren't good for anything else." A greater percentage of the 1945 men than of the 1944 men believed that "soldiers in other branches of the Army have plenty of respect for men in the Infantry." [15]

Attitude toward combat duty. A survey made in 1942, before any actual combat had taken place, showed that among the soldiers in the United States, 49 per cent expressed preference for combat or at least wanted to go overseas; 31 per cent expressed preference for noncombat duty or wanted to remain in the United States; 20 per cent were mixed in their choice. Those who wished to stay at home tended, more than others, to be less educated, married, over 30 years of age, isolationists rather than internationally minded, and optimistic that the war would soon end; of the single men 53 per cent preferred duty in a combat outfit overseas; this was in contrast to 35 per cent of the married men.

The soldier's worries. The types of worries of a group of combat veteran officers and men in a division in the Pacific were studied in order to inform the officers of such units. Each man was given a list of items and asked to check two that had worried or bothered him most during the previous two months, with the results shown in the accompanying table.

Officers and Men Checking Each Item

	Officers	Enlisted Men
Financial matters	0%	3%
My health	18%	34%
Physical danger I might be faced with before the war is over	12%	16%
The progress of the war	6%	5%
What is going to happen to me after the war	31%	18%
Being a long way from home	20%	21%
Matters concerning my family or friends back home	23%	21%
The way I am getting along in the Army	11%	3%
News about national events in United States	13%	1%
Not knowing what is going to happen next	11%	15%
What will happen in United States after the war	14%	6%
Whether we will get what we are fighting for	7%	10%
Purely personal matters not included in above	22%	12%

---

[15] *What the Soldier Thinks,* No. 13, 20 April 1945, p. 11.

The items are listed in the order in which they appeared on the original questionnaire, and the percentages do not add up to 100, as some officers and men failed to check two items. While reading these figures it must be remembered that these were combat-experienced men. Therefore their concern with health and danger was much stronger than it would have been among non-combat troops stationed in an inactive theater overseas.[16]

Attitude toward training. In three divisions of the Army Ground Forces it was found in May, 1942, that 3 men out of 10 thought that too much time was wasted during the training period; 6 out of 10 did not. The more zealous a man for combat, the more he complained about his training, because it was not more warlike. Also the greater his education and the higher his rank, the more he criticized the training program.

A survey of the opinion of combat veterans about Army training, made in early 1944, revealed that 7 per cent viewed it as being "too tough," 51 per cent "about right," 30 per cent "not tough enough"; 12 per cent were undecided or gave no answer. There was the high agreement of 81 per cent who thought going through "tough" realistic battle conditions on maneuvers was very important. Only 38 per cent of these veterans regarded hiking 25 miles over rough country with full field equipment as being very important. Two combat veterans out of three indicated they had had too much close-order drill.

Attitudes toward provisions and equipment. The kind of food, clothing, medical and dental care, and fighting equipment were factors that determined in some degree how a soldier felt toward the Army and toward his job. The improvement and distribution of all of these were subject to much study and research by many experts. They were also the object of special opinion surveys in order to determine the attitudes of the soldiers toward them.

Food was a basic source of satisfaction or dissatisfaction. Generally speaking, while in camp in the United States, men liked Army food and thought they had enough. However, despite the most careful scientific thought regarding caloric and vitamin content of K and C rations, as a steady diet they soon became monotonous and unpalatable. To combat veterans, a particular canned meat became one of the most unpopular foods. In one installation I visited, the lemon crystals, which were supposed to be used for lemonade, turned out to be the best floor wax obtainable.

In general, the soldiers said the food was good, but the preparation was poor. There were excellent cooks who could even prepare dried eggs so that they were delicious, but there were more cooks whose preparation turned them out looking and tasting like sawdust. In one inactive overseas area, two-thirds of the soldiers thought that their food was of good quality; but three-fifths of them felt that it was poorly prepared.[17] When several installations were sur-

---

[16] *What the Soldier Thinks,* No. 5, 25 April 1944, pp. 10-11.
[17] *What the Soldier Thinks,* No. 9, 25 September 1944, p. 1.

veyed, opinion about the preparation of the food varied widely. Consequently, while every soldier griped, this variation probably reflected some real basis for complaint.

Early in the war, attitudes toward the clothing of the enlisted man were investigated. The majority (60 per cent) of those contacted [18] felt that they needed more clothing, and many (39 per cent) said that the clothing issued did not fit well. The shortage was greater in khaki shirts and trousers. Fitting was more often necessary for trousers and shirts. If there was any alteration it was usually done at the expense of the individual. The study was partially responsible for special effort by the Quartermaster Corps to improve this situation. While there was no subsequent opinion survey, there was general agreement that the fitting of clothes was greatly improved. Postwar criticism has resulted in further improvement.

Medical and dental care in general received the soldier's approval. In a survey made in October, 1942, 80 per cent of enlisted men felt that good medical attention had been provided by the Army; 68 per cent felt that good dental care had been provided. Their complaints centered chiefly around the doctor's lack of personal interest in the patient and the red tape of delay in treatment and disposition.[19]

Hospitalized enlisted men overseas had some special attitudes, stemming from their desire to get home, which influenced their opinion of the Medical Department. In a survey made in overseas hospitals of a group of soldiers composed equally of combat casualties, surgical patients not hospitalized for combat wounds, and nonsurgical or medical cases, 95 per cent of them felt that the doctor in charge of their case was competent; 75 per cent felt that most of the doctors were really good doctors. Despite this fact, 56 per cent felt that they should be sent home, and 53 per cent believed that they would get better treatment in an Army hospital in the United States.[20]

Confidence in equipment, i.e., rifles, guns, planes, depended first on the relation of the soldier to his leader, second, on his own experience with that equipment, and third, upon comparison with enemy equipment. It was shown without doubt that among those men whose respect for their leaders was highest, the highest confidence in their equipment was found; the converse was equally true.[21] No surveys are available as to the effect of experience, perhaps because of the generally accepted fact that as a man became acquainted with and used his weapons his confidence in them increased.

The American soldier respected both the fighting ability and the equipment of the German soldiers. Their 88-millimeter gun was regarded as the

18 *What the Soldier Thinks*, Report 46, Dec., 1942, pp. 38, 39.
19 *What the Soldier Thinks*, Report 46, Dec., 1942, pp. 44-45.
20 *What the Soldier Thinks*, No. 13, 20 April 1945, pp. 12-14.
21 *What the Soldier Thinks*, Vol. I, No. 1, Dec., 1943, p. 5.

most deadly German weapon, and so was the most feared. In answer to the question as to how German fighting equipment measured up to their expectations, 62 per cent of Infantry soldiers rated it better than anticipated; also rating it similarly were 52 per cent of the Armored Forces, 31 per cent of Air Corps, and 54 per cent of other arms of service.[22]

Leisure-time activities. Leisure-time activities varied widely depending upon the soldier's location and the facilities available to him. It is interesting to compare what the soldier in different areas did in the minimal amount of time he had off duty.

Men Off Duty Saying They Took Part in Each Activity on a Typical Evening

	United States [23]	England [23]	New Guinea [24]
Write letters	62%	49%	74%
Listening to radio	47%	11%	28%
Reading a magazine	41%	21%	48%
Seeing a movie	31%	24%	46%
Drinking beer or liquor	23%	36%	—
Taking part in sports	15%	15%	16%
Reading a book	11%	10%	21%
Playing cards, checkers	11%	25%	37%
Dating a girl	9%	21%	0
Go dancing	6%	8%	0

The total of these columns is more than 100 per cent of the men surveyed, since many reported more than one activity. In New Guinea there were no towns and no women and comparatively little beer or liquor, so that letter writing, reading, and the movies all consumed a much higher percentage of the leisure time of soldiers stationed there.

What the soldier actually did off duty and what he preferred to do presented quite different pictures. Enlisted men in the United States stated their preferences for leisure-time activities as follows: [25]

Seeing a movie	25%
Taking part in sports or athletics	20%
Going dancing	14%
Listening to music	10%
Seeing a play	5%
Spending time on hobbies	5%
Other activities	6%
No preference	15%

22 "Fear of German Weapons. A Survey of Enlisted Men Recently Evacuated from North Africa," by J. W. Appel and Sam Stauffer, published as Report B-66, Research Branch, Special Service Division, Oct. 1, 1943.
23 *What the Soldier Thinks,* No. 2, Aug., 1943, p. 67.
24 *What the Soldier Thinks,* Vol. I, No. 1, Dec., 1943, p. 15.
25 *What the Soldier Thinks,* No. 2, Report 58, Aug., 1943, p. 69.

Of the sports preferred, another survey indicated baseball or softball as the favorite of 39 per cent of enlisted men, football of 18 per cent, basketball of 11 per cent, swimming of 6 per cent, and boxing of 4 per cent. Various other outdoor sports were preferred by 16 per cent, and other indoor sports by 6 per cent. In the same survey it was discovered that 4 enlisted men out of every 10 in the United States said that they were not given enough opportunity to take part in sports and athletics, 3 out of 10 said their outfits did not have enough athletic equipment, and 3 out of 10 indicated that the sports and the athletic programs in their outfits were poorly arranged.[26]

A high percentage of men spent their leisure time with magazines and books. It was shown that at least five out of six of our men in England read the enlisted man's weekly paper, *Yank,* a publication which was edited entirely by enlisted men. Only 1 man in 100 called it "poor." The daily newspaper, *Stars and Stripes* was read by a slightly larger proportion of the men in England, but it was not as well liked as *Yank.*

As to the choice of books, a large group of soldiers in England were asked the question: "If you were to spend an evening in camp reading, what type book would you prefer?" The answers revealed the following information: [27]

Recent novels of the best-seller type	26%
Mystery and detective novels	25%
Adventure and romance stories	14%
Historical novels	13%
Western novels	10%
Nonfiction	7%
Classics	5%

The libraries were widely used, but their use depended in considerable degree on their proximity to the reader. Approximately 51 per cent of the men did not use the libraries; of those who did, the frequency of use was influenced largely by educational background.[28]

	Used Library		Never Used Library
	Within 2 weeks	Not within 2 weeks	
Grade school	13%	24%	63%
High school	23%	33%	44%
College	47%	33%	20%

The soldier's attitude toward his postwar plans. Throughout the entire period of service most soldiers gave considerable thought to the future and their own particular postwar hopes. However engrossed a man was in the all-

26 *What the Soldier Thinks,* No. 2, Report 58, Aug., 1943, pp. 69-71.
27 *What the Soldier Thinks,* No. 2, Report 58, Aug., 1943, pp. 74-75.
28 *What the Soldier Thinks,* Report 46, Dec., 1942, p. 63.

important job of winning the war, in the back of his mind he was thinking of the time when he would resume his civilian career. A survey of cross sections of enlisted men in United States and various overseas theaters indicated that 75 per cent of the soldiers were thinking a great deal about their future after the war, 20 per cent had given some thought to it, and only 5 per cent indicated that they hardly thought about it.[29] They thought about the kind of a postwar situation they would find at home: 51 per cent wanted to have some orientation talks on plans that were being made for soldiers when they got out of the Army; 26 per cent wanted talks on what America's part would be in world affairs after the war; 23 per cent wanted talks on what things would be like in the United States after the war.

The soldier's attitude toward his Army experience. At the end of the war the survey group made an extensive investigation of cross sections of both white and Negro enlisted men, in continental United States and in four major overseas theaters, as to their attitudes toward their Army experience. The question was asked: "In general, do you feel you yourself have gotten a square deal from the Army?" The answers were: [30]

Yes, in most ways I have	33%
In some ways yes; in others no	53%
No, on the whole, I have not gotten a square deal	14%

About one-third of the enlisted men questioned made some comment in which they gave reasons why they felt they had or had not had a square deal from the Army. The overwhelming proportion of comments were unfavorable.

Complaints About	in Per Cent of All Comments
Job assignment	16%
Promotion policies	12%
Branch, outfit, force	10%
Rotation, furloughs, passes	9%
"Politics," favoritism, broken promises	9%
Officers, officers–enlisted-men relations	6%
Point discharge system	6%
Difficulty of getting discharged	5%
Training	3%
Medical care	2%
All other complaints	16%
Favorable or neutral comments	7%

In the category listed as "all other complaints," were included the following: "I should never have been drafted in the first place"; "racial discrimination";

---

29 *What the Soldier Thinks,* No. 13, 20 April 1945, p. 8; No. 9, 25 September 1944, p. 5.
30 *What the Soldier Thinks,* No. 16, 25 September 1945, pp. 2, 3.

"too much snafu in my own case"; "too many unnecessary restrictions"; "poor noncoms"; "unfair award policies."

Attitudes toward our allies. The war required the greatest international co-operation of our history. There is little doubt that the personal experiences of our soldiers and their opinions of our allies will influence postwar international relationships. Therefore, a spot survey [31] of the opinions of a large group of returnees should be of special interest.

Rating of the War Effort of Our Allies

Percentage of Men Who Said

	"Doing her share" or "More than her share"	"Undecided"	"Not doing her share"
Russia	90%	9%	1%
England	60%	16%	24%
China [32]	50%	33%	17%
France	45%	34%	21%

The attitudes toward the peoples in the countries of our allies may be even more significant of future relationships. Many men had personal contact with soldiers and civilians of the countries in which they were stationed. Most of them, however, based their opinions on what they heard or read. The large number who had "no opinion"—a majority in two instances—should be taken into consideration before drawing any conclusions.

Opinions about Allied People [33]

	Favorable	No Opinion	Unfavorable
Russians	42%	54%	4%
English	43%	25%	32%
French	32%	57%	11%

Critical comments about the British were varied and included disapproval of their colonial policy, "seem to think they are winning the war," "backwardness," class distinction. However another survey [34] of the opinion of GI's in Britain indicated that 78 per cent of men who had been in England a year or more liked the British; 15 per cent were "somewhat irritated by the British"; only 7 per cent expressed "dislike" for them. Resentment most commonly expressed toward the French people concerned their falling out of the war and then wanting reinstatement as a leading nation and their "greed for the American dollar."

[31] *What the Soldier Thinks,* No. 15, 25 July 1945, p. 11.
[32] In another survey of soldiers in China, 86 per cent regarded the Chinese as "doing as good a job as possible of fighting the war, considering everything." *What the Soldier Thinks,* No. 7, 25 July 1944, p. 11.
[33] *What the Soldier Thinks,* No. 15, 25 July 1945, p. 12.
[34] *What the Soldier Thinks,* No. 2, 25 January 1944, p. 15.

Opinions as to postwar co-operation showed varying shades of optimism and pessimism among returnees. Most of the men appeared to be realistic in their appraisal of our international future. They recognized that problems would inevitably crop up, but generally felt that a solution would be worked out without recourse to war.

Postwar International Relations [35]

Percentage who said U.S. will	With Russia	With England	With China	With France
Get along very well	14%	9%	34%	22%
Disagree about some things but manage to get along	24%	37%	26%	36%
Have some serious disagreements but won't fight each other	16%	27%	11%	16%
Very likely to fight each other sooner or later	19%	11%	3%	1%
No answer, undecided	27%	16%	26%	26%

In answer to the question, "Do you think there will be another war in the next 25 years or so?" 41 per cent of the men asserted that there would be, and an equal proportion were undecided. Only 13 per cent believed there would not be, and 4 per cent gave no answer. Among men who prophesied another conflict, the blame is most frequently laid at the door of England (38 per cent) or Russia (35 per cent).

Knowledge of these soldier attitudes could have been and often was extremely helpful to officers commanding troops and to technical services who provided care and equipment. The opinion surveys were as accurate as any such surveys could be. They provided interesting and helpful background for understanding the soldier. They were the only reliable information as to what the GI thought. Despite these advantages, they were regarded as nonsense by some intelligent officers. The research group was often accused of "putting ideas into the soldier's head." The surveys were stupidly forbidden by the theater commander in one large theater, possibly on the basis that the research workers were regarded as "snoopers."

Like all opinion surveys, the findings represented the soldier's orientation; they were limited by his information; they represented his passing opinion without explanation as to the why of the opinion. From a psychological point of view, they could only represent his conscious thought and motivation, not his unconscious and unrecognized feelings or attitudes. This last point was of special importance to the psychiatrist and was essential in the understanding of every psychiatric casualty.

---

[35] *What the Soldier Thinks,* No. 15, 25 July 1945, p. 13.

APPENDIX D

REFERENCE DATA

THIS APPENDIX includes graphs, charts,[1] tabulations of figures, and lists of names which make dull reading but have special value as reference material.

The Magnitude of the Neuropsychiatric problem, 1942-1945 (Fig. 3). This indicates by comparison the number of rejections for military service, the admissions to hospitals, and the separations from the service for neuropsychiatric disorder in each diagnostic category. The figure of 545,000 men separated from the service includes 163,000 men who were discharged administratively for "inaptness, lack of adaptability," etc. This latter group are included in the 30 per cent figure discharged for psychopathic personality and mental deficiency.[2]

Number and percentage distribution by cause of rejections at inductions and separations from the Army for disability (Fig. 4). This portrays a graphic comparison of the disability discharges and the rejections at induction for all diagnostic categories. One point of interpretation on this chart: The 228,600 men discharged for "musculo-skeletal" causes includes the majority of those receiving injuries in combat.

Data on the neuropsychiatric conditions in World War II. The following table summarizes the statistics in outline and headline form: [3]

I.   INDUCTION: November 1940 to 1 August 1945

    Total No. of Men Rejected for all Causes   4,828,000

    Total No. of Men Rejected for all NP Conditions   1,846,000

    Total No. of Men Rejected for all NP Conditions   1,153,900
       excluding Mental Deficiency

    % NP, including Mental Deficiency, of total Number 38%
       of Men Rejected for all Causes

    % NP, excluding Mental Deficiency, of total Number 24%
       of Men Rejected for all Causes

---

[1] Charts from the Office of the Surgeon General, Medical Statistics Division.

[2] Navy personnel increased from 403,390 on December 7, 1941, to 3,594,180 on VJ-day. From June 1, 1942 to July 1, 1945, there were 149,251 patients admitted to Navy hospitals for all types of neuropsychiatric disorders. There were 76,721 discharged or 32.4 per cent of all medical discharges. There were 91,565 men separated from naval training centers because of neuropsychiatric difficulties. Braceland, F. J., "Psychiatric Lessons from World War II," *Am. J. Psychiat.*, 103:587-593, Mar., 1947.

[3] Office of the Surgeon General, Medical Statistics Division, 11 December 1946.

II.   CONTINENTAL U.S. HOSPITAL ADMISSIONS:
      7 December 1941 to 26 July 1946

      Total No. of Admissions for all Causes...................... 9,868,000
      Total No. of Admissions for NP Conditions.................. 670,000
      % NP of total No. of Admissions for all Causes............. 7%

III. OVERSEAS HOSPITAL ADMISSIONS: 1944 to 26 July 1946

      Total No. of Admissions for all Causes...................... 4,445,000
      Total No. of Admissions for NP Conditions.................. 261,000
      % of Total No. of Admissions that were for NP.............. 6%

IV.   EVACUATIONS: 7 December 1941 to 26 July 1946

      Total No. of Evacuations to ZI............................. 636,000
      Total No. of Evacuations for NP Reasons.................... 142,000
      % NP of Total No. of Evacuations for all Causes............ 22%

V.   SEPARATIONS: 7 December 1941 to 26 July 1946

      Total No. of CDD's for all Causes......................... 1,049,000
      Total No. of CDD's for NP Conditions..................... 387,000
      % NP of CDD's for all Causes.............................. 37%
      Total No. of Separations by AR 615-368 and 369............. 168,000

Rejection rates. The following table indicates the rejection rate per 1,000 men examined for all neuropsychiatric reasons combined by month and year from 1942 through 1945. The rejection rates per month through January, 1944, are based on all examinations; rates for subsequent months are based on preinduction examinations only.

   It was well recognized that there was a very wide fluctuation in the rejection rates for neuropsychiatric causes at the induction center. In the following

Month	*Rejections for All Neuropsychiatric Reasons per 1,000 Men Examined* [4]			
	1942	*1943*	*1944*	*1945*
January	51.3	107.1	178.9	168.1
February	62.5	100.3	156.7	159.5
March	78.9	109.2	152.0	143.6
April	79.1	127.3	133.9	136.7
May	93.5	151.5	138.0	136.5
June	102.9	171.3	171.4	170.4
July	117.0	174.1	191.5	197.3
August	94.8	190.7	198.7	216.4
September	88.9	204.3	198.8	237.9
October	91.6	203.7	228.1	187.8
November	109.4	188.5	229.6	175.2
December	104.1	200.6	209.5	141.7
Total Year	93.6	155.1	160.7	165.2

[4] Office of the Surgeon General, Medical Statistics Division, 13 June 1946.

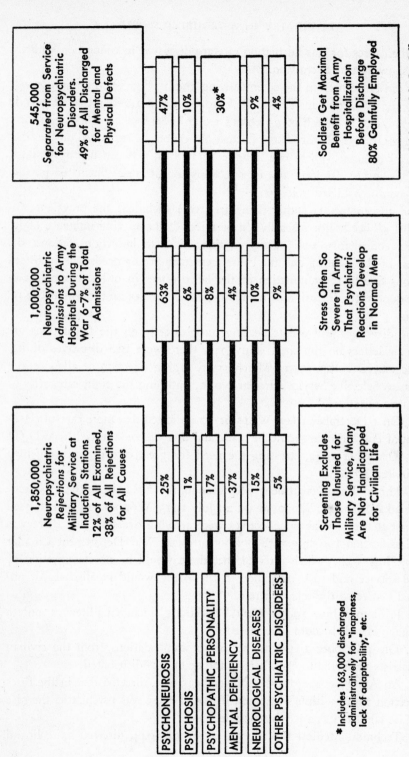

FIGURE 3. The magnitude of the neuropsychiatric problem, 1942-1945. (Through courtesy of Col. John M. Caldwell, M. C., Office of the Surgeon General. See p. 587.)

pages the causes for this fluctuation rate are discussed in connection with the graph showing this fluctuation.

As can be seen from the accompanying graph (Fig. 5), the rejection rate for neuropsychiatric causes fluctuated from 50 per 1,000 men per year in January, 1942, to a high of 237.9 per 1,000 in September, 1945, with three sharp rises, one each year. These fluctuations cannot be explained on the basis of directives alone. There is a definite parallelism between neuropsychiatric rejections and total rejections, i.e., rejections for all causes fluctuated parallel to the neuropsychiatric rejections.

The unseen factors (other than directives) included: the prevalent attitude that *all* borderline cases should be rejected; the varying influence of inspectors, consultants, audit teams on their visits to induction stations; the progress of the fighting and the consequent man-power needs; the increased rejections due to re-examination of the 4F draftees in order to meet man-power quotas; the inclusion of mental deficiency as a cause for psychiatric rejection.

The directives and events bearing most directly on the fluctuations are shown by letters on the chart. (In 1941, there were two directives of importance: SGO Letter 19, 12 March 1941, urging rejection of all questionable cases; Selective Service Circular No. 1, outlining the eight categories of psychiatric rejections.)

A. On 1 December 1942, W615-61-42 indicated that more careful classification of enlisted men should be made and this was re-enforced by WD Cir 395, 5 December 1942, stressing the need for great care in accepting men for "limited service."

B. Three War Department Memorandums (25 March 1943, W600-30-43; 26 April 1943, W600-39-43; 29 July 1943, W600-62-43) all stressed the point that too many noneffectives were arriving overseas, that there was "no classification for duty with psychoneurosis." War Department Circular 161, 14 July 1943, which directed that there would be no classification of limited service and such men then in the Army would be discharged, undoubtedly affected the rejection rate.

C. Prior to 1 June 1943, "mental rejections" included illiterates, only a percentage of which could be accepted.

D. On 4 October 1943, the set of recommendations from the civilian psychiatrists (referred to elsewhere in the text) was distributed.

E. An AGO Letter 20115, 4 November 1943, directed that in the cases of rejection with multiple diagnoses, if one of these was psychiatric, the case would be tabulated as a psychiatric rejection.

F. Technical Medical Bulletin 33, 21 April 1944, directed more liberal

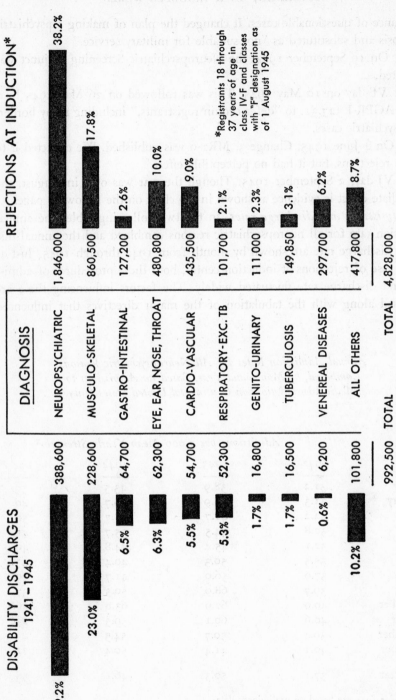

FIGURE 4. Number and percentage distribution, by cause: rejections at induction, separation from the Army for disability. (Through courtesy of Col. John M. Caldwell, M. C., Office of the Surgeon General. See p. 587.)

acceptance of questionable cases. It changed the plan of making a psychiatric diagnosis and substituted as "not suitable for military service."

G. On 19 September 1944, the Neuropsychiatric Screening Adjunct was instituted.

H. VE-day on 10 May 1945. This was followed on 26 May 1945 by a letter, AGPR-I 327.31, to "defer certain registrants," including many border-line psychiatric cases.

I. On 4 June 1945, Change 3, MR1-9 was published. We expected it to reduce rejections, but it had no perceptible effect.

J. VJ-day, 2 September 1945. Though the war was over in August, the immediate effect is evidence as shown in the chart on the following page.

Admissions and discharge rates. In the two following tables the annual admission rate for all neuropsychiatric reasons combined and the annual disability discharge rate are shown by month from 1942 through 1945. Just as in the case of rejections at induction center, both these procedures of admission and discharge rate fluctuated widely. The factors influencing these are discussed along with the tabulation of the major directives that influenced them.

Annual Admission Rates for All Neuropsychiatric Reasons Combined, by Month and Year, Based on Admissions to Medical Installations in Continental United States Only

Month	Admissions per 1,000 Mean Yearly Strength [5]			
	1942	1943	1944	1945*
January	31.2	38.9	43.5	50.
February	31.3	38.9	38.7	49.
March	32.2	41.7	38.7	50.
April	32.8	44.5	35.7	45.
May	32.1	45.4	44.8	49.
June	35.5	50.3	40.4	43.
July	37.9	56.0	41.7	39.
August	39.7	68.9	50.3	37.
September	40.9	62.9	63.8	26.
October	40.6	60.1	59.5	23.
November	39.4	50.7	54.3	23.
December	40.1	41.4	50.4	21.
Total year	37.1	50.3	46.1	38.

* Rates for 1945 are based on preliminary data.

[5] Office of the Surgeon General, Medical Statistics Division, 13 June 1946.

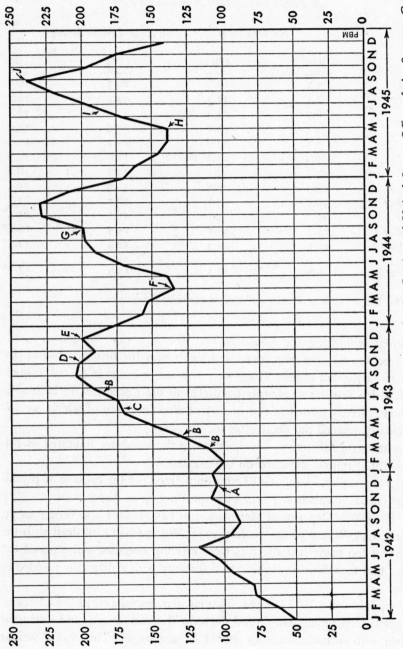

FIGURE 5. Neuropsychiatric rejections, per 1000 men per year, in the Continental United States. Office of the Surgeon General, Medical Statistics Division, June 13, 1946 (see page 590).

Annual Rates of Disability Discharges of Enlisted Men for All Neuropsychiatric Reasons Combined, by Month and Year [6]

Month	NP Discharges per 1,000 Annual Mean Strength			
	1942	*1943*	*1944*	*1945*
January	5.7	10.9	20.3	10.9
February	5.5	11.3	14.3	12.2
March	6.9	14.4	12.3	16.5
April	7.2	15.2	11.0	13.9
May	8.3	17.0	11.1	17.3
June	8.4	21.2	11.0	19.6
July	7.5	24.1	12.1	18.4
August	9.7	28.8	13.0	20.3
September	8.7	35.6	16.7	22.1
October	10.2	34.6	16.6	25.3
November	10.2	27.1	15.5	16.7*
December	11.3	21.7	12.9	12.3*
Total year	8.8	22.3	13.9	17.1*

* Rates for last two months of 1945 are based on preliminary figures.

Factors influencing the admission and discharge rate. As shown in the chart (see fig. 6), the admissions and discharges for neuropsychiatric disorders ran a parallel course. There were two major peaks in the admissions, one of which was not so sharply paralleled in the discharges. In both cases these were directly related to two important directives both of which, we felt in psychiatry, opened the flood gates for discharge.

The numerous directives which influence the trend are indicated as follows with the initials indicated on the graph:

A. 4 September, 1942, SGO Letter 99 pointed out the backlog of psychiatric patients in hospitals and urged the speeding up of dispositions.

B. Three War Department Memorandums (25 March 1943, W600-30-43; 26 April 1943, W600-39-43; 29 July 1943, W600-62-43) all dealt with the protest that too many noneffectives were arriving overseas, and stressed the directive that there was no classification for duty with a diagnosis of psychoneurosis.

C. 14 July 1943, WD Cir 161. This circular, issued against the advice of the Medical Department, eliminated the term "limited service" and instructed that men with such classification should be discharged. This was a serious error and the following four directives attempted to correct it.

---

[6] Office of the Surgeon General, Medical Statistics Division, 13 June 1946.

D. 31 July 1943, WD Cir 176. This indicated that a man who did not meet the physical standards for admission but was "physically qualified" to perform his job might be retained if his commanding officer should so desire.

E. 13 August 1943, W615-61-43. This indicated that if such exceptions were made as permitted by Cir 176, the physical disability should be noted on the man's personal record.

F. 26 August 1943, W615-64-43. This memorandum interpreted WD Cir 161 as indicating that *all* men not meeting physical standards would not require examination or discharge.

G. 11 November 1943, WD Cir 293. This circular rescinded 161 but not until after many thousands of men had been discharged.

H. 3 December 1943, SGO Letter 194. This circular letter from the Neuropsychiatry Division indicated that the criteria for discharge were interpreted too strictly and too many men were being separated.

I. 1 April 1944, TB Med 28. This outlined treatment procedures and instructed that they be provided in all hospitals for psychiatric patients.

J. 26 April 1944, WD Cir 164. This dealt with the use of man power based on physical capacity, and the trend was again to discharge men if they could not be used.

K. 29 May 1944, WD Cir 212. This again dealt with the man-power problem and rescinded a section in WD Cir 164. It stressed the fact that the discharge of men who could render effective service was prohibited by the same paragraph which indicated that it was wasteful to keep a man who could not render service. It was in this period that the biggest overseas shipments were being made, and as a result of this circular there were many men combed out who were regarded as unfit for overseas duty.

L. 12 September 1944, WD Cir 370. This was the second major opening of the discharge gates, and it was rumored that it came about in part because of the need for hospital beds in the United States for the large numbers of casualties being received from overseas. It was also rumored that this was motivated on the supposition that the war would be over in November.

M. 23 September 1944, ASF Cir 318. This was written by the Neuropsychiatry Division because of our concern over the number of noneffectives that were receiving certificates of disability. It urged that men be returned to duty.

N. 27 January 1945, WD Cir 32. This rescinded WD Cir 370; because of the Battle of the Bulge man power had become short.

O. 31 March 1945, WD Cir 81. This stressed particularly the utilization of man power instead of discharging noneffective individuals with a psychiatric diagnosis by way of a disability discharge.

P. 2 June 1945, WD Cir 162. This indicated that patients were to be retained in hospitals for maximum treatment, and it is perhaps of significance in maintaining the discharge rate, although there was a sharp drop in this period in the hospital admissions.

Q. 30 June 1945, WD Cir 196. This was also devoted to the utilization of man power, urging the effective placement of men not capable for full combat duty.

In August, 1945, at a conference of the commanding officers of convalescent hospitals, the Deputy Surgeon General gave verbal instructions that soldiers not capable of doing full field duty should be given a certificate of disability discharge.

R. 21 December 1945, WD Cir 394. This definitely instructed hospitals to return all men to duty who could deliver some effective work.

Treatment results in the psychoses. As was indicated in the text, in the early part of the war the Army directed that all psychotic patients—in fact, all neuropsychiatric patients—should be promptly disposed of out of the Army. Beginning in 1944, the Neuropsychiatry Consultants Division was able to have this policy changed so that such patients would receive treatment. In the table on page 598, the figures are shown from 1942 through 1946, in so far as they could be obtained from some of the general hospitals. They indicate the change from a large percentage of patients being sent to Veterans Administration or to state hospitals in the early years of the war, to discharge home or to relatives in the later years.

With the exception of the statistics from Valley Forge General Hospital, these figures all show a marked increase through the 3-year period in the percentage of patients discharged to their own care or to relatives. While these figures are correct, one must point out certain minor factors not apparent in them: Cases of temporary psychotic episodes, including alcoholic psychoses, are included in those sent home; when there was a rush of patients into some hospitals, the situation could only be eased by transferring some patients immediately, and in such instances there was an increased number who were sent to the veterans' hospitals who might have gone home had they been held for treatment; for any particular short period of time, the number of patients sent to veterans' hospitals might depend upon the rapidity with which authorization for transfer and acceptance might be obtained; among the patients sent to relatives, there are included a few cases who were placed in private hospitals after discharge.

Bed and patient data. The following memorandum from the director of the Resources Analysis Division of the Surgeon General's Office indicates some pertinent information relative to the authorized beds for neuropsychiatric patients in Army hospitals.

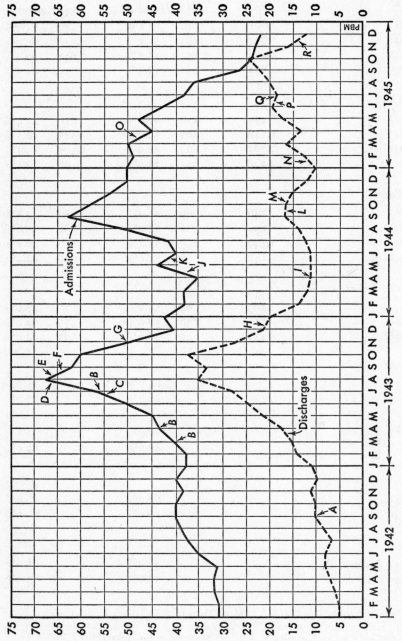

FIGURE 6. Admissions and discharges of neuropsychiatric patients, per 1000 men per year, in the Continental United States. Office of the Surgeon General, Medical Statistics Division, June 13, 1946 (see page 594).

Disposition of Psychotic Patients [7]

Mason *	Total Discharges	To VAH (State Hospital)		Home Alone or to Relatives	
1943	601	146	24.3%	455	75.7%
1944	2,832	983	31.1%	1,849	68.9%
1945	6,464	831	12.8%	5,633	87.2%
1946	851	132	15.5%	719	84.5%
Darnall †					
1942	494	278	56.6%	216	43.4%
1943	1,356	808	59.5%	548	40.5%
1944	2,701	1,106	40.9%	1,595	59.1%
1945	4,148	952	22.9%	3,196	77.1%
Valley Forge					
1943	146	66	45.2%	80	54.8%
1944	694	426	61.4%	268	38.6%
1945	1,347	799	53.2%	548	46.8%
1946	142	82	57.8%	60	42.2%
Newton D. Baker					
1944	163	85	52.0%	78	48.0%
1945	615	236	38.0%	379	62.0%
1946	111	40	36.0%	71	64.0%
Fitzsimons					
1943			85.0%		15.0%
1945			40.0%		60.0%
McClosky					
1945			40.0%		60.0%
Kennedy					
1943			60.0%		40.0%
1945			20.0%		80.0%
DeWitt					
1944 (4 months)			42.0%		68.0%
1945 (May-December)			14.8%		85.2%

---

[7] Mason figures furnished by Col. C. C. Odom; Darnall by Col. T. C. C. Fong; Valley Forge by Col. F. E. Weatherby; Newton D. Baker, by Maj. J. J. Michaels; Fitzsimons by Maj. L. Barbato; McClosky by Lt. Col. Guy C. Randall; Kennedy by Col. Sam Paster; DeWitt by Lt. Col. Dan Sullivan.

* These total figures include only 6,173 psychoses, the others being psychoneuroses, etc.

† Figures do not include transfers to other Army hospitals or to duty, and include about 12 per cent of psychoneuroses.

2 May 1946

MEMORANDUM FOR THE DIRECTOR, NEUROPSYCHIATRY CONSULT-
ANTS DIVISION.[8]

SUBJECT: Bed and Patient data, World War I and World War II.
1. In accordance with your request, the following data are submitted:
   a. *World War I.*
   The annual report of the Surgeon General—1919 contained the following
   information.
   (1) Hospital beds consisting of general, base, embarkation and debarkation
   under the SGO in the Zone of Interior as of 12 October 1918 totaled
   173,505. Beds occupied on this date totaled 131,213.
   (2) Hospital beds including convalescent for the American Expeditionary
   Forces as of 21 November 1918 totaled 299,838. Beds occupied totaled
   193,026.
   (3) The highest monthly admissions for NP's in the AEF totaled 887 in
   September 1918.
   b. *World War II.*
   (1) The peak number of authorized beds totaled 763,000 in June 1945. Patients remaining on this date totaled 488,000. A breakdown between
   overseas and Zone of Interior follows:

	Authorized Beds	*Patients Remaining*
Total	763,000	488,000
Z/I	346,000	324,000
Overseas	417,000	164,000

   (2) The number of NP beds for all hospitals is not available. However, NP
   patients remaining as of June 1945 totaled 38,000 in the Zone of Interior and 9,000 in overseas theaters making a total of 47,000.
   (3) The peak number of NP patients remaining was in April 1945 totaling
   approximately 50,000, of which 36,000 were in the Zone of Interior and
   14,000 in overseas theaters.

Medical personnel. Information obtained from the Personnel Division of
the Surgeon General's Office contrasts the total number of personnel in World
War I and World War II as follows:

	World War I	*World War II*
Total		
Medical Corps	30,591	48,317
Dental Corps	4,620	14,848
Veterinary Corps	2,002	2,056
Medical Administrative Corps	0	19,439
Army Nurse Corps	21,480	54,128
Enlisted Medical Department Personnel	264,181	541,650

---

[8] Information from Isaac Cogan, Assistant Director, Resources Analysis Division.

Distribution of neuropsychiatrists as to theater and major forces. The following memorandum supplied by the Personnel Division of the Surgeon General's Office indicates the distribution of neuropsychiatrists on VE-day and the status of those located in the zone of the interior.

1 May 1946

MEMORANDUM FOR FILE:

SUBJECT: Distribution of Neuropsychiatrists as of V-E Day, 2 May 1945.

European Theater	488
Mediterranean Theater	66
Southwest Pacific	98
Pacific Ocean Area	39
China, Burma, India	43
Other small theaters	28

Attached to War Department 125, which ordinarily includes about 90% of those assigned to the Veterans Administration.

Located in the Zone of Interior:

Army Service Forces	1,012
Army Ground Forces	42
Army Air Forces	200
Overseas Shipment	43
In numbered units in Z.I.	26
War Department Replacement Pool	129
Returned from overseas	29
Returned from overseas as patients	15
Patients in Z.I. hospitals	19
Total	1,515

In the above figures the theaters' figures represent the psychiatrists in the ASF, AGF, and AAF combined.

Clinical Psychologists. The following summary was provided, on request, by Lt. Max L. Hutt who served as the chief of the Clinical Psychology Branch during the latter months of the author's service in the Surgeon General's Office. It summarizes briefly the total utilization of clinical psychologists in the United States Army during the war.

SUBJECT: Utilization of Clinical Psychologists in the United States Army [9]

1. Due to the fact that this Branch no longer has current data on the utilization of clinical psychologists and to the fact that MPD (Military Personnel Division) is unable to furnish such data without exhaustive effort, this analysis of the utilization of clinical psychologists must be an approximate one.

---

[9] Max L. Hutt, Lieutenant, MAC, Chief, Clinical Psychology Branch, 25 February 1946.

2. At the maximum, there was a total of 380 clinical psychologists in the Army program.

a. 130 of these commissioned officers were transferred to the clinical psychological program, and had obtained their commissions through the Army Specialist Corps, or through attendance at OCS.

b. 244 officers received direct commissions as clinical psychologists, having previously been part of the enlisted ranks of the Army. Of this number, 5 were women and 1 was a Negro.

c. 6 psychologists received direct commissions from civilian life in the Sanitary Corps and were assigned to permanent general hospitals on an experimental basis prior to the inauguration of the clinical psychological program.

3. At the maximum, about 80 clinical psychologists were assigned to general hospitals overseas. At the present time, the number of psychologists thus assigned is probably below 35.

4. As of recent date (last month) the commissioned clinical psychologists were distributed in ZI installations, in the following manner:

General, Regional, and Station Hospitals	107
Convalescent Hospitals	55
*Disciplinary Barracks and Rehabilitation Centers	
(Correction Division)	29
Consultation Services	5
AG School (Instructors in Psychology)	4
OSS	3
Central Transit Processing	1
WD Personnel Center	2
Station Complements	1

* This is a relatively large number due to assignment of officers to cover current, special projects.

5. The total number of officers upon whom the figures in paragraph 4 are based is 207. These are the best data currently available. While they undoubtedly do not give a precise picture, they may be taken as representative.[9]

Division neuropsychiatrists. The following list of division neuropsychiatrists was obtained through the Personnel Division of the Surgeon General's Office. It includes not only those men who actually served during the war but in a few instances some psychiatrists in the divisions that were active after VJ-day. All of these physicians were under the direction of the Army Ground Forces and not under the jurisdiction of the Surgeon General. The list is not entirely accurate. It represents original assignments from the Army Service Forces to the Army Ground Forces and subsequent changes were made without notice to the Office of the Surgeon General. Many were promoted above the rank given here, but because of regulations, none above a majority. The list as furnished by the Personnel Division of the Surgeon General's Office was supplemented from the personal experience of the author.

Name	Unit
Maj. Gilbert B. Kelley	2nd Inf. Div.
Capt. Edward S. Holcomb	3rd Inf. Div.
Maj. Meyer H. Maskin, O-466205	4th Inf. Div.
Capt. Milton Berger, succeeded by	
Capt. Julian E. Rosenthal	7th Inf. Div.
Capt. Walter Musta, O-373141	8th Inf. Div.
Maj. Donald M. McIntosh, O-476741,	
succeeded by Maj. W. T. MacLaughlin	9th Inf. Div.
Maj. Lewis Thorne	10th Light Div.
Capt. Harry L. MacKinnon, p-1685958	11th A/B Div.
First Lt. Stanley B. Crosbie, O-438160	13th A/B Div.
First Lt. Arthur L. Hessin, O-493737	17th A/B Div.
First Lt. John G. Freeman	24th Inf. Div.
Capt. Hyman H. Goldstein, O-337032	26th Inf. Div.
Maj. D. I. Weintrob	29th Inf. Div.
Maj. Vivion F. Lowell, O-314238	30th Inf. Div.
Maj. James T. Ferguson, Jr., O-369799	31st Inf. Div.
Capt. Harry H. Schwartz, O-488319	35th Inf. Div.
Capt. Jules V. Coleman, O-486259	38th Inf. Div.
Capt. Jack L. Chumley, O-357740	42nd Inf. Div.
Capt. Theodore P. Suratt, O-483448	44th Inf. Div.
First Lt. Leon N. Goldensohn, O-503397	63rd Inf. Div.
First Lt. Norman J. Kelman, O-504307	65th Inf. Div.
Maj. Sidney L. Sands, O-381053	66th Inf. Div.
Maj. Josiah T. Showalter, O-309348	69th Inf. Div.
Capt. Howard McR. Burkett, O-373060	70th Inf. Div.
Maj. Edward R. Janjigian, O-346230	71st Light Div.
Capt. William Furst, O-357095	75th Inf. Div.
Capt. Benjamin Wiesel, O-344460	76th Inf. Div.
Capt. Blaney B. Blodgett, O-344611	77th Inf. Div.
Capt. Marvin R. Plesset, O-345107	78th Inf. Div.
Capt. Orrin R. Yost	79th Inf. Div.
Maj. Isadore Tuerk, O-323748	80th Inf. Div.
Maj. Heyman Smolev, O-250272	81st Inf. Div.
Maj. Allen W. Byrnes, O-318458	83rd Inf. Div.
Maj. Richard H. Parks, O-355549	84th Inf. Div.
Capt. Emanuel Messinger, O-291869	85th Inf. Div.
Maj. Arlen Cooper	86th Inf. Div.
Capt. Anthony B. Stabile, O-498838	87th Inf. Div.
Maj. Joseph L. Knapp, O-322952	89th Light Div.
Maj. Glen Q. Street	90th Inf. Div.
Capt. Abraham L. Kauffman, O-498866	91st Inf. Div.
Maj. Rafael Hernandez	92nd Inf. Div.
Capt. George W. Little	93rd Inf. Div.
Capt. Albert N. Mayers, O-358725	94th Inf. Div.
Capt. Frank Costa, O-474402	95th Inf. Div.
Maj. Eugene J. Alexander, O-342813	96th Inf. Div.

Name	Unit
First Lt. Daniel S. Jaffe, O-499886	97th Inf. Div.
Maj. Kenneth Rew, O-285959	98th Inf. Div.
Capt. William L. Sharp, O-468282	99th Inf. Div.
Capt. William H. McCullagh, O-496214	100th Inf. Div.
Maj. Edward S. Tauber, O-467362	102nd Inf. Div.
Capt. Roland E. Neiman, O-381190	103rd Inf. Div.
Capt. George M. Cowan, O-345634	104th Inf. Div.
Capt. Martin M. Fischbein	106th Inf. Div.
Maj. Himon Miller	2nd Armd. Div.
Maj. Earl W. Mericle, O-331995	4th Armd. Div.
Maj. Lazarus Secunda, O-347988	5th Armd. Div.
Capt. Albert J. Boner, O-505650	6th Armd. Div.
Capt. Benjamin F. Vogel, O-267994	7th Armd. Div.
Capt. Nathan N. Root, O-344393	8th Armd. Div.
Capt. Theodore J. Dulin, O-384268	9th Armd. Div.
Capt. Bertram H. Schaffner, O-414476	10th Armd. Div.
Capt. Jerome S. Beigler, O-518932	11th Armd. Div.
Capt. Mortimer T. Shapiro, O-469201	12th Armd. Div.
Capt. David R. Wall, O-309694	13th Armd. Div.
Capt. Walter Baer	14th Armd. Div.
Capt. Irving R. Berger, O-426533	16th Armd. Div.
Capt. Frank T. Rifargioto, O-381715	20th Armd. Div.
Lt. Laynard Holloman	2nd Cav. Div.
Maj. Robert E. Bowman	11th Armd. Div.
Maj. Claude H. Butler	20th Armd. Div.
Capt. Frederick A. Robinson, Jr.	12th Armd. Div.
Capt. Raymond G. Cannon	20th Armd. Div.

Chiefs of the neuropsychiatric services in general hospitals during the war. With the help of the Personnel Division of the Surgeon General's Office, the general hospitals active in the United States are listed with name of the chief of the neuropsychiatric service or section during the major portion of that hospital's existence in wartime. Many of these officers received advancement in rank above that given here.

Hospital	Chief
Bruns GH, Santa Fe, N.M.	Maj. Jacob H. Friedman
Ashford GH, White Sulphur Springs, W.Va.	Capt. Leo M. Traub
Baxter GH, Spokane, Wash.	Capt. J. Ray Van Meter
Billings GH, Ft. Benj. Harrison, Ind.	Capt. Sprague H. Gardiner
Brooke GH, Ft. Sam Houston, Tex.	Maj. Louis Shapiro
Crile GH, Cleveland, Ohio	Maj. John A. Holland
Cushing GH, Framingham, Mass.	Maj. Jackson M. Thomas
Darnall GH, Danville, Ky.	Lt. Col. Theodore C. C. Fong
Deshon GH, Butler, Pa.	Maj. Peter H. Knapp
Fitzsimons GH, Denver, Colo.	Maj. Louis Barbato

Hospital	*Chief*
Foster GH, Jackson, Miss.	Capt. Luis Perelman
Gardiner GH, Chicago, Ill.	Lt. Col. Willoughby P. Richardson
Halloran GH, Willowbrook, S.I., N.Y.	Maj. Joseph Weinreb
Hammond GH, Modesto, Calif.	Lt. Col. Mark Zeifert
Hoff GH, Santa Barbara, Calif.	Lt. Col. Andrew I. Rosenberger
Lawson GH, Atlanta, Ga.	Lt. Col. Joseph S. Skobba
Letterman GH, San Francisco, Calif.	Maj. Clarence H. Godard
Lovell GH, Lowell, Mass.	Lt. Col. Duncan Whitehead
Madigan GH, Tacoma, Wash.	Maj. Carl H. Jonas
Battey GH, Rome, Ga.	Lt. Col. Louis Pillersdorf
Birmingham GH, Van Nuys, Calif.	Maj. Garland H. Pace
Finney GH, Thomasville, Ga.	Capt. Bernard A. Kamm
Harmon GH, Longview, Tex.	Lt. Col. Arthur Colley
Kennedy GH, Memphis, Tenn.	Col. Samuel Paster
Oliver GH, Augusta, Ga.	Lt. Col. Geo. Frumkes
LaGarde GH, New Orleans, La.	Maj. Hanson H. Leet
Woodrow Wilson GH, Staunton, Va.	Maj. Edwin J. Palmer
McCaw GH, Walla Walla, Wash.	Maj. Samuel Cohen
Mason GH, Brentwood, L.I., N.Y.	Lt. Col. Benjamin Simon
Stark GH, Charleston, S.C.	Lt. Col. John E. Davis
Bushnell GH, Brigham City, Utah	Col. Olin B. Chamberlain
Dibble GH, Menlo Park, Calif.	Lt. Col. Hyman D. Shapiro
Mayo GH, Galesburg, Ill.	Maj. Edwin O. Niver
Northington GH, Tuscaloosa, Ala.	Lt. Col. Nicholas Michaels
Newton D. Baker GH, Martinsburg, W.Va.	Maj. Joseph J. Michaels
Fletcher GH, Cambridge, Ohio	Lt. Col. Charles E. Nixon
Schick GH, Clinton, Iowa	Maj. Franklin O. Meister
McCloskey GH, Temple, Tex.	Lt. Col. Guy C. Randall
McGuire GH, Richmond, Va.	Maj. John M. Mays
Moore GH, Swannanoa, N.C.	Maj. Marcus P. Rosenblum
Nichols GH, Louisville, Ky.	Capt. Samuel Silverman
O'Reilly GH, Springfield, Mo.	Lt. Col. John H. Greist
Percy Jones GH, Battle Creek, Mich.	Lt. Col. Paul A. Petree
Rhoads GH, Utica, N.Y.	Maj. Soloman M. Haimes
DeWitt GH, Auburn, Calif.	Maj. Daniel J. Sullivan
Thayer GH, Nashville, Tenn.	Lt. Col. Richard P. Stetson
T.M. England GH, Atlantic City, N.J.	Maj. Emile G. Stoloff
Walter Reed GH, Washington, D.C.	Lt. Col. Oswald A. Kilpatrick
Winter GH, Topeka, Kansas	Maj. Forrest N. Anderson
Tilton GH, Ft. Dix, N.J.	Maj. Earl Saxe
Torney GH, Palm Springs, Calif.	Capt. Donald A. Shaskan
Valley Forge GH, Phoenixville, Pa.	Lt. Col. James A. Gould
Vaughan GH, Hines, Ill.	Lt. Col. Stephen C. Sitter
Wakeman GH, Columbus, Ind.	Lt. Col. Herman Selinski
Wm. Beaumont GH, El Paso, Tex.	Lt. Col. Geo. T. McMahan
Barnes GH, Vancouver, Wash.	Maj. Fred J. Bradshaw, Jr.
Borden GH, Chickasha, Okla.	Maj. Geo. Sam Ingalls

Data from man-power control group. Through the courtesy of Brig. Gen. Arthur G. Trudeau, his office supplied the following information regarding the age distribution of men in the Army, foreign-born personnel, and Negro strength.[10]

1. Age Distribution of the Army:

Enlisted Men

| | 31 March 1946 | | 30 June 1944 | |
	Regular Army	*Other*	*Total*	
Strength	670,000	1,335,014	7,144,601	
A G E				
18	27.27%	12.02%	3.15%	
19	17.04	23.24	6.17	9.32
20	7.43	14.56	7.79	
21	4.66	7.31	7.99	
22	4.13	5.02	8.33	39.97
23	3.56	4.09	8.18	
24	3.69	3.92	7.68	
25	3.84	3.82	7.18	
26	3.48	3.57	6.25	
27	3.16	3.59	5.27	27.44
28	2.74	3.58	4.60	
29	2.65	3.70	4.14	
30	2.16	3.26	3.75	
31	1.69	1.99	3.29	
32	1.46	1.44	2.85	14.75
33	1.44	1.53	2.54	
34	1.27	1.23	2.32	
35	.88	.72	2.09	
36	.87	.51	1.88	5.63
37	.79	.38	1.66	
38	.85	.18	1.26	
39	.70	.08	.59	2.89
40 & over	4.24	.26	1.04	
	100.00%	100.00%	100.00%	

[10] Furnished by the Director of Personnel and Administration, Arthur G. Trudeau, Brigadier General, GSC, Chief, Manpower Control Group, 3 September 1946.

Officers

| | 31 March 1946 | | | 30 June 1944 | |
| | Male | | | Male | |
	Commissioned (Incl. WO & FO)	Female Medical	WAC	Commissioned (Incl. WO & FO)	Female Officers
Strength	376,265	23,237	2,789	729,244	47,736
A G E					
18	.05%	.00%	.00%	3.15%	.00%
19	.36	.00	.00	6.17	.00
20	1.20	.26	.00	7.79	.00
21	2.92	1.63	.05	7.99	1.72
22	4.38	11.23	.40	8.33	6.65
23	6.08	16.73	.63	8.18	9.93
24	7.27	13.04	4.53	7.68	9.86
25	7.57	6.88	6.91	7.18	9.16
26	7.13	6.64	7.09	6.25	8.51
27	7.44	5.12	7.65	5.27	7.68
28	6.43	4.74	6.86	4.60	6.56
29	5.52	4.69	6.77	4.14	5.58
30	4.59	3.22	6.09	3.75	4.71
31	4.08	3.79	5.73	3.29	3.90
32	3.62	3.35	5.11	2.85	3.41
33	3.41	2.59	5.15	2.54	3.16
34	2.80	2.15	3.92	2.32	2.73
35	2.55	1.81	4.02	2.09	2.35
36	2.24	1.59	3.79	1.88	2.17
37	2.07	1.43	4.01	1.66	2.10
38	2.36	1.38	3.56	1.26	1.90
39	2.18	.73	3.42	.59	1.73
40 & over	13.75	7.00	14.31	1.04	6.19
	100.00%	100.00%	100.00%	100.00%	100.00%

2. A report of Army enlisted accessions * by nativity indicates the following:
a. Foreign-born entrants: [10]

Enlisted Men

Non-citizens	111,217
Citizens	200,656

Enlisted Women

Non-citizens	0
Citizens	4,392

b. Born outside United States (possessions and departments) and United States at large and at sea:

Citizens male	92,230
Non-citizens male	4,740
Citizens female	443

(* Excludes new Regular Army enlistments August 1945-March 1946.)

3. From 1 December 1941 through 1 September 1945 approximately 853,000 *men* were appointed as commissioned or warrant and flight officers. Of these, approximately 650,000 were appointed from the ranks. There is no report available, indicating educational levels for this group.[10]

4. Approximately 970,000 Negroes served in the Army from 1 December 1941 through 1 January 1946: [10]

Negro Strength of the Army as of 30 June 1946

Male commissioned officers	1,874
Enlisted men (no grade breakdown available)	175,701
Warrant and Flight Officers	108
Female Medical Officers (Nurses)	100
WAC officers	15
WAC enlisted	658
Total	178,456

INDEX

Figures in *italics* refer to footnotes on page specified.

in education, 478-481
in family, 399-402
in industry, 495
lack of, 87, 125, 126, 130, 178, 577
relationship to mental health, 41, 89, 125
in WAC enlistment, 105-109
Movies, "Why We Fight" series, 87
Mowrer, Ernest R. and Harriet R., *385*
Mulinder, E. K., 169
Murphy, Miles, *243*
Murray, John M., *51, 236, 237, 253, 262,* 318
Musser, M. J., *240*
Myers, H. J., *310*
Myrdal, Gunnar, 424

Nail biting, rejection for, 271
Narcissism, 498
Narcissistic stage, psychosexual development, 222
Narcoanalysis, 310
Narcosis, resisted by malingerers, 214
Narcosynthesis, 310, 311
National Education Association, 416
National Guard, no psychiatric examination in, 268
officers from, *78*
National Institute of Social Relations, 416
National Mental Health Act, 462, 470, *471,* 538, 540
National Recreation Association, 431
National Research Council, 10, 263, 269, 541
National Safety Council, statistics from, 188
Navy, discharge method, 260, *262,* 533
disciplinary problems in, *505*
enuresis in, *182*
and nomenclature, 263
nurses, numbers of, 119
physicians, induction center, 278
psychiatric combat casualties, 148, 149, 262, *587*
psychoses in, 164, 174
Needles, William A., 137, *318*
Negro, discrimination against, 423-425
personnel in Army, 575, 607
Neurocirculatory asthenia, 158, 560
Neurological disease, enlisted personnel, 115
extent of, 344, 347, 589
rejection for, 283
WAC, 115
two World Wars, 340
Neurological examination at induction, 277
Neurologist, Civil War, 3
field of, *3,* 233
Office of Surgeon General, 233, 241

NP, 361
Neuropsychiatric disturbances, *13,* 589
Neuropsychiatric screening adjunct, 279, 554, 592
Neuropsychiatric service vs. section, 19
Neuropsychiatrist, attitudes toward, 3, 5, 18, 23
court, 505
credo for, xiv
distribution of, 6, 237, 431, 432, 600
graduate training, 461-465
inarticulate, 7, 23, 466
induction center, 29, 266-292
in industry, 487-490, 496
military, administrative responsibility, 14, 26, 27, 318
adviser to command, 31, 34, 84, 330, 552
assignment of, 26, *63,* 237-241
civilians, recruited, 14, 26
classification of, 238-240
in the field, 329
hospital ships, 321
mistakes of, 40-42
number of, 26, 240, 341
orientation to role, 22, 32, 35, 36, 49, 301
promotion and rank of, 20, 240
Regular Army, 14, 26, 532, 533
rehabilitation centers, 197-201
relation to commanding officers, 31, 34, 84, 329, 330, 489, 552
Surgeon General's Office, 3, 13, 241-243
training, 27, 28
work of, 5, 15, 16, 26, 27, 37, 42, 131, 220, 233, 239, 294, 328, 534
number of, 26, 340
prisons, 509-512
and psychologist, 5, 243-245. *See also* Psychologist, clinical
public health, 7, 468-474
schools, 482
shortage of, 4, 6, 25-29, 232-255, 461, 488, 537, 538
and social worker, 245-247. *See also* Social worker
Neuropsychiatry. *See* Psychiatry
field of, 3, 233
two World Wars, 338-350
consultants, 3, 13, 40, 163, 218, 241-243, 340
Neurosis. *See* Psychoneurosis
vs. social maladjustment, 36, 41, 219
with somatic complaints. *See* Psychosomatic disorders, somatization reactions